Component-Based Software Engineering

Component-Based Software Engineering

Putting the Pieces Together

George T. Heineman
William T. Councill

Boston • San Francisco • New York • Toronto • Montreal
London • Munich • Paris • Madrid
Capetown • Sidney • Tokyo • Singapore • Mexico City

The publisher offers discounts on this book when ordered in quantity for special sales. For more information, please contact:

Pearson Education Corporate Sales Division

One Lake Street

Upper Saddle River, NHJ 07458

(800) 382-3419

corpsales@pearsontechgroup.com

Visit AWL on the Web: www.awl.com/cseng/

Library of Congress Cataloging-in-Publication Date

Component-based software engineering: putting the pieces together/George T. Heineman, William T. Councill, editors

p. cm.

ISBN 0-201-70485-4

1. Software engineering. 2. Component software. I. Heineman, George T. II. Councill, William T.

QA76.758.C58 2001

005.1—dc21

2001022552

Cover art by: Philip Habib

Production services by: TIPS Technical Publishing

ISBN 0-768-68207-X

This product is printed digitally on demand.

1 2 3 4 5 6 7 8 9 10—CRW—0504030201

Second printing, Novermber 2007

As always, for Jen.

—GTH

To my loving wife, Carol,
with whose pure patience
I endured this endeavor with great joy.

—WTC

Contents

Foreword

The use of components to build software systems is not a new idea. We have always had software components of different sorts. More than thirty years ago I worked on a telecommunications software product constructed from components, which we called blocks. The product became the largest commercial success story in Sweden ever—very much thanks to those blocks.

At that time I had a dream. I dreamt that decomposing the whole system into blocks with clearly defined signal interfaces would be an accepted technology. I dreamt that modeling control flow using sequence diagrams and state diagrams would not be dismissed by computer scientists or software engineers. I dreamt that blocks would be used not just for telecommunications switching but for all kinds of applications.

In recent years the software world has developed the technology and initiated the standards that bring component-based software engineering from the dream stage to the level of practicality. Potential users don't need, as they once did, to develop their own home-brewed modeling language; we have a standard, the Unified Modeling Language. They don't need any more to develop a programming language that supports components; we can construct components using nearly all standard programming languages. They don't need to develop their own operating systems or computer platforms to support component management; we have standard environments from which they can choose. Soon PCs will support multiple operating systems constructed upon software components.

To the contrary, the time has come for the software world to take advantage of this base. Component-based software engineering (CBSE) is now the way to produce software fast, with less effort, of high quality—not just the first time a product is released but for its entire life. More and more it is being applied to industrial strength and mission-critical software. It is becoming the indispensable element in the mainstream of the software world.

Now, it is clear that the software world has come a long way. It is clear that the means exist to fulfill the dreams I have long been dreaming. But—and it is a big "but"—my dreams can become reality only through understanding how to make CBSE happen. The book you are now holding, *Component-Based Software Engineering: Putting the Pieces Together,* is the first handbook-like volume to present this state of the art.

That understanding—in depth—does not reside with any one author. Indeed, the editors, Bill Councill and George Heineman, had to bring together 45 specialists to bring you this depth. They realized, however, that a variety of authors would have a variety of terminologies and writing styles. This multiplicity in multi-authored compendiums often baffles the reader. As soon as he/she penetrates the language of one chapter, he/she encounters a different persona in the next chapter. These differences all too often find expression in definitions that are contentious, incomplete, often circular in reference, and less than rigorous.

To achieve book-length consistency, the editors devoted 18 months to harmonizing definitions. More than 20 authors worked with the editors, offering criticism and advice, to develop definitions that would be used by all the authors throughout the book.

The editors, however, were not unmindful of the need for diversity of opinion. They wanted to, and did, encourage the contributors in an area of research or practice to write for themselves, recounting their successes and reviewing their pitfalls. As the authors completed chapters, the editors made the writing seem as if it had been written by one guiding intelligence. But what an intelligence! It reflects the variety inherent in CBSE, but avoids the bewilderment normally accompanying multiple authorship. As a result, readers will not experience what I, somewhat diffidently, label "cognitive reorientation" when they begin a new chapter.

To help readers relate this great field to the more familiar world of common experience, the authors employ a construction metaphor. Just as construction creates original buildings out of common components, so too does CBSE create application systems out of large-scale software components. At the same time, while the authors place primary stress on component building and assembly, they are mindful of the effects that component-based development has on change and configuration management, version control, and project management itself. Looking to the still farther future, the book includes a chapter by Martin Griss on software agents and their relationships to components.

I still have another dream. I dream that we will get a component marketplace where different players can work. Some will play the role of selling components; others will buy components. Inspired by this book, all of us will have agreed upon standards for what a component is and what kind of artifacts or models players should expect to accompany a component. In my dream, a component is always accompanied by use cases, design models, and an implementation model. Components definitely are always associated with test cases, traceable to use cases. Successful component producers will voluntarily follow such standards because they are necessary to develop components for reuse and to develop solutions for customers as quickly and inexpensively as possible, while assuring high reliability and quality.

In the coming years, we will be able to revolutionize the production of software and then bring my final dream to fruition.... We will then have other dreams to fulfill!

—Ivar Jacobson

Introduction

Component-based software engineering (CBSE) is a subdiscipline of software engineering. CBSE shares some of the same strengths and weaknesses of the discipline of software engineering. However, software engineering is currently an unregulated discipline that has adopted a professional appellation. Even more confusing, it has adopted terms that lack meaning in other engineering disciplines and many of software engineering's leaders eschew licensure or required certification of engineers. While retaining the engineering label, far too many in software engineering promote an agenda that is only quasi-scientific and pseudo-engineering. Students often graduate from computer science and software engineering academic programs without a thorough grounding in the engineering sciences.

The editors and many of the authors of this book advocate a formal association between CBSE and the profession of engineering and its various disciplines. We unambiguously declare that software engineering, implemented as an engineering science, is required for the successful adoption, integration, and maintenance of complex, heterogeneous, and distributed software systems. As editors we recognized that many contributing authors wholeheartedly disagreed with our view. We accept and respect their opinions. Nevertheless, until a well-defined engineering approach is embraced by producers and consumers of component-based systems, CBSE will be more art than science and the engineering label will lose its lofty connotation and esteem.

We did not impose our views on our writers. Heaven knows that they are highly opinionated and have every right to be. Most have written software engineering articles and books for as long (or longer) than the editors have practiced and taught software engineering. Neither of us claims to be a software engineer as defined by the Texas Board of Professional Engineers. We have learned from some of our authors, however, that a basis in engineering sciences is required to plan, design, develop, test, integrate, and maintain such complex systems as are described in this book.

Therefore, it was our ambition to edit a book on software engineering that had the structure and content of an engineering text, a book unlike so many software engineering treatises. Definitions would be rigorously defined. Concepts would be presented in a clear and concise manner so that even the casual reader will understand the topic. The references for each group of chapters would lead readers to books and articles that provide much more detail about each topic. While we have adopted an engineering model for the book, you do not have to be an engineer of any sort to read and understand what CBSE is all about. Just as a hydraulics technician should be able to understand the complexities of cantilevered bridges by reading a bridge engineering handbook or standards manual, software component programmers and testers should be able to comprehend even the most difficult aspects of CBSE.

Without regulations and with minimal standards guiding the development of software, software vendors develop applications for a public that has unfortunately learned to accept the constant rebooting of operating systems and defects that cause the corruption, and often irretrievable or loss, of considerable personal and organizational time and effort. All the while, software engineers are building worldwide bridges of information and electronic commerce. Web and software component developers must inevitably ensure the stability of, and continuous access to, their applications, yet they routinely watch helplessly as their applications demonstrate critical defects and crash.

Brief Description of CBSE and Software Engineering

CBSE is primarily concerned with three functions.

- Developing software from preproduced parts
- The ability to reuse those parts in other applications
- Easily maintaining and customizing those parts to produce new functions and features

CBSE involves much more than structuring a comprehensive reuse program. It *should* provide both a methodology and process for developing components that work continuously, with the ability to return to a previous stable state when encountering an error without corrupting any components. CBSE aims to demonstrate accountability and sensitivity to the public's concerns for defect-free software. Therefore, CBSE is concerned less with building parts than providing users with constantly reliable parts that maintain continuously functioning software.

Nevertheless, consumers' demands are increasing for software that can be built more reliably and with less time between versions with new features (not just defect repairs). Software engineers have the unenviable job to develop methods to meet consumers' perceived needs. The editors of this book and many contributing authors advocate the development of software through reusable parts that are thoroughly certified for their intended purposes. Yet, software engineers have met great resistance in promoting software component development and reuse because so many software vendors and information technology organizations adhere to the "not invented here" concept. That is, the same types of applications—for example, order entry and order processing—are developed by countless organizations at the same time with insufficient human and economic resources because management and developers alike believe the application will not work correctly "unless it is invented here." We believe you will agree that quality generally suffers.

As one of the youngest disciplines in the field of engineering, software development has not yet matured as a profession and industry to the same level as other recognized engineering professions. The current leadership of the software engineering studies and debates whether software engineering *is* an engineering discipline. The subdiscipline of CBSE will be shown to require adherence to established engineering practices in order to produce the assembly and integration of software required by industry and the public. Because of software engineering's resistance to maturity, externally motivated development of nationally or internationally recognized engineering, manufacturing, and testing standards is emergent. Without recognized and accepted engineering practices, processes, guidelines, and standards, software component development will remain a mixture of competing and confusing processes, methodologies, and languages.

As an engineering discipline software engineering is arguably advancing more rapidly than other engineering disciplines, and continues to outpace development of the supporting standards. The advent of the Internet and World Wide Web-based technologies and business models has only accelerated this growth. Small wonder, then, that software engineers often look for quick solutions for their growing problems.

Small groups of engineers and technicians can produce reusable artifacts in building large-scale projects such as bridges, skyscrapers, and airplanes. These engineers or technicians are able to produce high quality (that is, "trusted") components precisely because of reliance upon, and adherence to, accepted national or international engineering, manufacturing, and testing standards. However, many practitioners of software engineering often do not even understand the similarities, much less the differences, between well established engineering professions (for example, mechanical engineering, electrical engineering, aerospace engineering, and civil engineering) and the disciplines of software development and software engineering.

History of the Automobile: An Analogy

Most people recognize that Henry Ford did not invent the automobile, but legend attributes the development of the moving assembly line to Ford. However, while he did not invent the assembly line process, Henry Ford devoted seventeen years to trying to increase the efficiency of automobile assembly. He accurately predicted that he would only achieve his lifetime's goal—that is, to produce cars that the masses could afford—if his employees could build cars faster.

Ford hired a team of efficiency experts who examined every aspect of automobile assembly and tested new methods to increase productivity. The boss himself claimed to have found the inspiration for the greatest breakthrough of all, the moving assembly line, on a trip to Chicago. "The idea came in a general way from the overhead trolley that the Chicago packers use in dressing beef," Ford said. At the stockyards butchers removed certain cuts as each carcass passed by until nothing remained. Ford reversed the process. He designed the automobile moving assembly line to such a degree of efficiency and production cost savings that even his workers (some of the highest paid in the industry at $5.00 per day in 1914) could purchase the cars they made.

Prior to Ford's implementation of the assembly line for automobiles, numerous wagon builders constructed cars. Automobiles were made one or a few at a time. Many parts were hand-hewn. If a running board or fender did not fit correctly, the manufacturer would chisel, sand, or otherwise force the part to fit. Automobile assembly was a slow, tedious process.

In 1914 Ford opened the world's first assembly line. He then saw the significant inefficiencies in building parts and visited Arthur O. Smith—the son of a Milwaukee blacksmith. At the time Smith produced 12 pressed steel frames a day and sold them to the Peerless Motor Company. Ford challenged Smith and ordered 10,000 frames for delivery in four months. The challenge was accepted and by 1921 the A. O. Smith Corporation was capable of producing Ford's first order in a single day (*www.autoshop-online.com/auto101/histtext.html*).

Component Production and Assembly

Software engineers specializing in component-based development intend to develop an analogous mechanism for developing software parts. Software developers now understand how to employ top-down design to subdivide a software system into modules and objects that can easily be implemented. Less well understood by producers and consumers of software is an efficient means for manufacturing software parts that can later be used to construct inexpensive component-based software systems. We believe that the majority of software development practitioners—business and systems analysts, designers, developers, and testers—are not fully aware of the benefits that component-based technology has for the future of software development.

The authors and editors of *Component-Based Software Engineering* (CBSE) have begun a journey similar to the work of Henry Ford and his efficiency experts. We observed that Henry Ford succeeded because the mass production of highly desirable, well-designed Model T automobiles satisfied the public demand of consumers. In like manner, a true component marketplace will only be achieved by the hard work of both component producers and consumers to construct inexpensive, as well as easy to use, applications developed from those parts. The first edition of this book endeavors to present a snapshot of the state-of-the-art of CBSE in the year 2000. We anticipate that subsequent editions will assist component-based developers and software engineers with a more effective, empirically-based approach to the assembly of reusable software parts.

The Promise of Software Components

In 1975 Fred Brooks, an IBM project manager, wrote *The Mythical Man-Month*. In this book of short essays that describe the difficulties involved in developing complex software, Brooks wrote an intriguing chapter entitled "No Silver Bullet," explaining that software systems are by nature complicated. He predicted there would be no technology—that is, no silver bullet—that would improve productivity by an order of magnitude. Brooks' chapter is often cited as a reason why the "software crisis" has, and will, continue to exist until a technology such as CBSE becomes more scientific and truly engineering-based. During the original NATO conference in 1968 the participants strongly debated the use of the term *software crisis*. Many preferred the unemotional term, *software gap*, to highlight the widening gap between the achievements of software engineering, as compared with its ambitions. As David and Fraser stated in 1968, "The gap is arising at a time when the consequences of software failure in all its aspects are becoming increasingly serious." This quote is just as relevant today.

The silver bullet for solving our software problems is elusive indeed. We were mindful of the unfulfilled promises of earlier computer science technologies as we collected the chapters for this book. Nevertheless, we believe that CBSE represents the "best practices" in software engineering produced during the last thirty years. Brooks himself presents two possible methods to avoid the complexities of software, namely "Buy before Build" and "Reuse before Buy." These concepts are central to CBSE and may dramatically reduce the costs associated with software engineering. CBSE offers powerful abstractions that will help developers organize their software systems to achieve lower maintenance costs and higher reusability.

As component-based software engineers we must learn to build exceptional parts that, based on requests for proposals or master and subproject designs, will *fit* with other components without force (redesign) in much the same way that Ford and Smith could agree to produce cars with trustworthy interconnections. Our challenge as consumers of software components is to build an industry where we can purchase and integrate components sold by producers with the assurance that they meet consumers' needs for users' satisfaction.

Scope

The once grating sound of two modems completing their "handshaking" has recently become music to users' ears. We merely tolerated the sound before. Now many of us have learned that this sound, followed by static, then finally with a period of silence, reveals that modems have established communication. That once insufferable noise is now the sound of success and reliability. In contrast, we consider software to be so defective that a day without a reboot is a novelty. Many of us perceive that two applications, an application and a component, or two components working together without daily errors are luxuries.

Diverse parties, perhaps with their own agendas, have described component technology as either mature or immature, two diametrically opposing viewpoints. Some parties argue that the term *component* has been correctly and effectively defined, while many other users and authors posit that components are inscrutable and therefore have not been clearly defined. We have devoted countless hours to rigorously defining the terms used in this book in the most generic but proficient manner possible. Likewise, we intend to present CBSE and CBD as it exists in the year 2000, as well as its assets and liabilities. As editors, we will both promote CBD and expose its weaknesses.

This book does not claim to address all the issues regarding software component-based technology. The editors do believe, and will demonstrate, that component-based software engineering in many ways now comports with, and in the near future shall conform to, criteria established for many of the recognized engineering disciplines.

The editors are an academician and an industrial software process consultant and lecturer. The first editor desires that his students learn the skills that will make them viable software developers and assemblers early in their work lives. The second editor must assure that all new industrial contributors to the software development process and more experienced business analysts, designers, developers, and testers understand and can implement component technology according to the tenets of "true" engineering practices. Both editors believe the path to CBSE requires that well-recognized authors contribute as quickly as possible to the aggregation and publication of that knowledge.

We selected authors based on their commitment to CBSE, not just because of their previous publications. The writings of the early CBSE adopters are equal to or even more important than the studies of consultants and academicians in providing real-world experiential evidence. We also solicited contributions from those who tried and failed to use component-based software engineering on their projects. You can learn as much from failure as from success. Only the software engineering industries' early collective documented experiences will provide sufficient evidence for the success or failure of the nascent field of component-based software engineering.

You may disagree with the authors' and editors' findings. Your point of view may be equally as compelling as those set forth in this text. Hopefully, we will stimulate you sufficiently to join the ranks of those who seek to improve the state-of-the-art of CBSE. Our simple goal for this first version in a line of edited texts is that readers will directly benefit from reading this book by learning how to produce, assemble, test, or manage trusted components more effectively than current solutions allow.

Methodology and Organization

Introduction

We found that writing this book was analogous to developing a software application. An edited text such as this can be as poorly written as a program developed by inexperienced programmers or as elegant and robust as an application constructed by an experienced, process-oriented, quality-driven team.

An edited text should provide more than the sum of its parts. A multi-author book ought to assemble a wide range of state-of-the-art topics to help you synthesize its knowledge and achieve insights beyond what even the editors and authors intended. We hope you will read the book and formulate inferences that will help you develop practices and component-based products that are even more successful than those described in the text.

Many of us have learned to initially survey a reference book for value, searching through chapters as though they were features to be explored. We select a chapter because of some anticipated promise or out of need and hope that it will provide some benefit. Then we buy the book. In too many cases edited texts are more like a repository of generic components from different producers; each chapter has its own texture and style. Such books, which include all too many handbooks, compile numerous chapters and previously published articles without sufficient consideration for related content, context, purpose, theme, and design.

A reference text may have dozens or even hundreds of contributions, all written and printed according to the same formula, yet there is no internal consistency. Such books appear like a spaghetti code of facts, ideas, opinions, formulae, and recommendations, but coherence is often lacking. These texts may include redundancies or even contradictions. They appear as poorly written programs where the programmers do not really understand that high cohesion and low coupling increase the usability and reusability of components.

Methodology

Our desire for efficiency and practicality at the beginning of this project led us to develop coherent parts and chapters and limit redundancies. To accomplish this challenge we followed a process comparable to software development. Thus, we implemented a comprehensive literary iterative and incremental component-based software life cycle (CSLC).

First we conducted an extensive feasibility study. Prior experience guided us during this developmental phase; we were exceptionally excited because there were no edited texts on component-based software engineering (CBSE) and well-published authors were willing to contribute. We had to determine whether we could actually complete the project and ensure a cohesive and interesting text. Additionally, we conducted a risk analysis to mitigate any problems we could anticipate.

Requirements for this book were elicited from prospective authors and our publisher and then entered, reviewed, and controlled in Caliber-RM, a requirements management application. The "IEEE Recommended Practice for Software Requirements Specifications" for software development guided the elicitation and refinement of requirements. Requirements kept us focused on the many facets of our complex task. Project schedules were developed, published, and managed. Milestones were established. Reviews of tasks occurred weekly, especially because falling behind on any part of the book would adversely affect the book's deadline and quality.

The theme of the book is as complicated as the design of a moderately complex application. The concept of the book, its constraints, and the interrelationships among the book's parts and chapters (as you will see later, the book's parts are analogous to software components), as well as additional text were mapped.

Design is a complicated task. In component-based development (CBD), as in object-oriented development, design is a phase of the iterative and incremental SDLC. The challenge for top-down design is to produce an initial design of a system that can be decomposed into independent subprojects to be carried out independently. Concurrent engineering enables independent projects to be pursued simultaneously so long as the risks of concurrent development are carefully managed. We discovered initially that many of the terms used to define software components and related vocabulary were used without scientifically rigorous definitions. Unfortunately, we could not afford the time to develop a consistent definition chapter for use by all authors. We pursued a riskier approach. We started to develop the definition chapter for the book early in its design. As editors we assumed the responsibility of ensuring that the chapters written by our authors would be consistent with our definition chapter.

Therefore, we developed the definitions during the construction of the book—and even afterwards—as our authors wrote and refined their chapters and as we researched the literature and reviewed our authors' chapters to enhance our definitions. We decided to use several chapters "as is" based on extensive literature reviews. We shared our definitions with our authors and then offered our continually refined definitions of software components and accompanying elements to a small group of software engineering specialists that helped us differentiate our terms from those that create confusion in software engineering and CBSE. Often we had to derive terms from engineering disciplines, such as civil and industrial engineering, because these fields have developed consistent terms; this common vocabulary ensures the public's safety and welfare.

Ultimately, we shared our definitions with our authors to assure that a consistent set of terms was used throughout the book. In most cases the authors were willing to comply with our new terminology. In other situations some authors disagreed with certain definitions and agreed to state their objections to the new definitions and clearly declare their reasons for retaining their own terminology. Nevertheless, this continual design of definitions required authors to rewrite their chapters or us to revise the authors' chapters with their permission. We mitigated the risk, but we were fortunate to have authors who were willing to accept definitions that were often different from terms they had used for years. The resulting book is more cohesive because we have ensured a degree of consistency throughout each chapter.

We anticipated that five well-respected component methodologists assigned the task of reaching agreement on a definition of the term *software component* would find common ground for a definition acceptable to each. We also emphasized that if, during a reasonable period, consensus was not reached, the editors would produce a final working definition from the ongoing discussion and debate. Despite considerable effort exhibited by the methodologists in a virtual workshop setting, consensus was not reached. Therefore, in consultation with the workshop participants and other authors, we developed the definitions for software component that guided all authors in this book.

We have presented other authors' contentious topics we also offered the various authors' views or solutions and, without imposing our own biases and prejudices, derived from their collective works the benefits and liabilities for implementing their ideas. Where authors did not, or would not agree, the editors attempted to resolve nonmutuality. As editors we expected to differ from various authors' perspectives. Our views are expressed as conclusions derived from our own research, experiences, and perspectives. Our mission was to instill a sense of consensus among the authors. When that was not possible we chose to resolve our own differences. When harmony was implausible we each presented our views and described how the authors influenced our separate opinions.

Construction occurred on two fronts. First we gave authors guidelines and templates to follow and set a relatively low page limit for each chapter. Therefore, all authors faced the challenging task of distilling the essence of their particular subject areas. For anyone who knows a subject well the assignment of writing a synopsis of the topic can be very difficult and can take considerably more time than writing chapter after chapter on the subject. We are reminded of the story of a keynote speaker who was told on short notice that he had to prepare a lecture. He replied "If I have an hour to speak, I can do that for you tomorrow; if I only have fifteen minutes, I'll need several weeks to prepare."

On the second front we reviewed and revised chapters written by some of the most prolific and well-respected writers in the fields of CBD and CBSE. We previewed chapters within the part prefaces and included the essence of the parts' chapters. Additionally, in the prefaces and summaries we described the authors' agreements and contrasts, yet tried to leave you with a feeling of completeness and a basic understanding of the salient principles.

Our authors are exceptionally well suited to writing a text to help you understand how to take advantage of CBSE. They will show you how to effectively apply CBSE and avoid the pitfalls that may occur.

You may consider these authors to be like your friend the auto mechanic, whom you call on to help you evaluate a used car. You may not know whether the car is worth the sale price or how much longer the car is expected to operate, but you trust your friend to inspect the engine, listen to the car as it runs, and ask relevant questions. You make the final decision, but the input from your friend is invaluable.

For authors to take many years' experiences and condense them into a brief chapter is a major challenge. Many, if not most, of the authors have written books on the subject matter of their chapters. Because of their penchant for the technological, we asked them to describe the essence of their work with software components. The concept of essence is important to this book. The *Oxford English Dictionary*'s definition of "real essence" appears as a highly cohesive object:

> [O]f a conceptual entity: The totality of the properties, constituent elements, etc., without which it would cease to be the same thing; the indispensable and necessary attributes of a thing as opposed to those which it may have or not.

Indeed, this book is based solely on the "indispensable and necessary attributes" of the topic of each chapter. No chapter provides a simple "how-to" operation. Nevertheless, the authors have sought, and the editors have attempted to assure, just enough information for a sufficient description of the essence of the subject matter. Each part contains a collected set of references of the chapters within that part, providing ample reading for those interested in pursuing topics further.

Finally, as the book grew we pursued a strategy of constant editing to ensure that each chapter conformed to our definition chapter and high standard for quality. Each chapter was reviewed by us on five or six occasions and most authors revised their chapters three times. We created a Microsoft Visual Source Safe project to manage the chapter revisions. To enable the editors to work collaboratively (one in Massachusetts and one in Texas) we employed SourceOffSite, from SourceGear Corporation to provide secure, remote access to the repository of chapters. We worked collaboratively with the authors to ensure that the book reflected the state-of-the-art of CBSE in 2000, as well as an edited text that reads as if it were written by a single author. Our goal is to assure that you find that this edited text is readable despite the large number of individual authors.

Organization

This book is constructed like a component-based application. Chapters are the equivalent of objects and parts (compilations of topical chapters) are analogous to components. Each chapter is focused on a specific topic and a few authors expanded on these topics to include additional subject matter. From inception we intended to produce a book of coherent, but minimally redundant, parts and chapters that actually achieves one of the profound aims of science and engineering. That is, we worked closely with each author to discover and present the highly refined essence of that particular topic of CBSE. We believe that our experience as software engineers has produced a reference text that succeeds where most "stapled together" edited texts fail.

Parts are the components of the book. As you will learn, software components have interfaces that describe their functionality and how to interact with them. Each part has two simple interfaces, a preface and summary. While the interfaces hide the details of the chapters contained within, they provide transitions from one part to another. Parts are like components; they are self-contained. That is, they do not require reading other parts to understand a specific topic. However, as the old saw goes, if you are a blind Indian, you have to handle more than the elephant's tail to identify the whole animal.

To assure that readers can easily select the part or parts of particular importance or need, the prefaces clearly identify the subject matter. Our aim was to clearly and concisely present the "flow" of the subject matter in the chapters that follow the preface of each part. In each preface we tried to present sufficiently relevant information to establish a context so you can understand, and even implement, knowledge gained from reading one or more of a part's chapters.

Prefaces were intentionally designed to further refine the essence of each chapter and to compare and contrast the various chapters. In no way did the editors seek authors with complementary views. In many parts we selected authors with contrasting perspectives.

The prefaces will help readers make decisions about component technology and software engineering in many ways. We recommend that you at least skim the prefaces of each part. You can then make decisions about how to read the book. We organized the book so you can

- Read the book from cover to cover
- Select two or more parts (or chapters) that most closely fit your needs
- Use the book as a reference book whenever questions concerning software components and reuse arise (the book has extensive references, a comprehensive glossary, and a detailed index)
- Combine the approaches of two or more chapters to develop your own success stories
- Read further into this book for additional alternative methods for component production or assembly, in other parts for reference materials cited by the chapters' authors in each part's references, or at this book's Web site, which is updated regularly

The summaries present our views about the assets and liabilities of each part's chapters, the successes inherent in implementing each chapter's concepts in actual practice, and research required to assure that ideas presented can be accomplished within a reasonable period. We make comparisons among the perspectives presented by the various authors and often try to resolve conflicts among their apparently irreconcilable views. Sometimes we highlight the disagreements to demonstrate multiple methods to achieve the same results or the need for more research to determine best practices.

The summaries also provide references for all chapters within the parts. Our authors have generally provided substantial references to support their perspectives on CBD and CBSE. Many of the references are to journals or magazines that can be viewed on Web sites. Therefore, URLs are offered.

While parts and chapters cannot, of course, be rewritten, your disagreements and corrections can be submitted to the Web site provided below so that the authors and editors can assure higher quality components in the future. Because readers can access all revisions to parts and chapters of this book through its site, reasonable and correct input may result in chapter changes that can be viewed within days to weeks of submission. Furthermore, chapters that address new or enhanced component-based topics will be added to the site after strict editorial review. This book's Web site is:

www.cbseng.com

This book will be one of an ever-growing number of books on component-based technology. We developed this book to focus on an engineering approach to CBSE. It is a unique book; it provides a review of the state-of-the-art of CBSE at the time of publication. We all know too well that fields such as CBD and CBSE are forever changing. Therefore, we hope to produce another version of this edited text in two years. That work will incorporate some chapters without change. Many chapters will necessarily be updated. New authors will contribute innovative or revised ideas and methods.

The Web site will provide the integration between the existing text and new ideas and processes. While the site cannot assure the same consistency of style and cohesion inherent in this book, the authors will continue to update the site with material from a variety of books and journals. The material may support and enhance the contentions of various chapters' authors or it may refute the current knowledge or vastly extend that which we know now. We will offer a discussion forum for various subjects described in this book on the site.

Science and engineering are constantly changing. As CBSE emerges as a viable engineering discipline and software engineering continues to search for its identity, many of the concepts presented herein will appear antiquated a few years from now. Nevertheless, in this book the editors and authors present the state-of-the-art of CBSE and what the future is anticipated to hold for adherents to, and implementers of, CBSE. As engineers we all are willing to be proved wrong, for in the process of the proof of error, CBSE will mature. That is our greatest quest: to derive the highly-refined essence of CBSE.

Preface

Introduction

This book is about the processes required to implement component-based development (CBD). Many software development organizations throughout the world have learned to recognize that component development is an engineering activity. Just as CBD is a revolutionary activity emerging well beyond the programming paradigms that preceded it, component-based software engineering (CBSE) is both a subset and a revolutionary extension of current software engineering practices. In the same way that civil engineers have established standardized, time-tested engineering principles to building bridges using reusable parts, component-based software engineers must define and describe processes to assure timely completion of high quality, complex software systems that are composed of a variety of pre-built software components.

In the infancy of software development programmers focused on structured techniques and procedural programming. Structured techniques defined a system through the information it received as input and the output produced. Software development advanced with the advent of data modeling, which mapped the flow of complex data and information within a system and presented a step towards "real world" modeling. Object-orientation showed developers how to design units of code based on the perceived metaphor of real world functionality. The latest advance in software development, CBD, promises the possibility of extending the real world approach to create well-specified parts and to incorporate legacy code "wrapped" as components.

Our approach in creating this book was to select well-respected authors and researchers in the field and throughout the world and collectively determine the state-of-the-art of CBSE. Our goals are to establish

- The first state-of-the-art text on CBSE
- The degree of empiricism that drives CBSE endeavors
- The number of domain areas that comprise CBSE
- The depth and breadth of knowledge of each domain area
- The content of the domain areas in capsule format supported by considerable references and a Web site that is continually updated with new material for chapters and new references
- A reference book that will be updated every two to three years and provide requested unpublished chapters about the state-of-the-art of CBSE with increasing emphasis on empiricism

The issues that CBSE faces are reflected in cohesive parts that encapsulate the most appropriate chapters. The issues are

Component Definition—Many definitions have been offered and cited repeatedly, yet no definition we encountered in an exhaustive literature review met our criteria for rigor as opposed to description. Most purported definitions were circular in reference.

The Case for Components—The transition from other forms of development, generally object-oriented design and development to CBD and CBSE, must consider a variety of risks and how to mitigate them. Cultural, budgetary, process, and numerous other factors must be considered before undertaking CBD and CBSE. Success and failure stories should be considered before implementing a pilot project.

Software Engineering Practices—What software engineering practices impact positively on CBSE? What software engineering processes affect CBSE negatively? What can we learn from the technical history of software development that applies to the design and implementation of components today? How can an engineering approach to software development reduce the number of software projects that are not completed, which currently stands at 31.1% (*standishgroup.com/visitor/chaos.htm*)? What can engineering teach us about developing software as complex as components? What can we learn from the European Union and Japan that would positively affect the design and assembly of components in the United States and elsewhere throughout the world?

The Design of Software Component Infrastructures—Numerous models are available for developing component infrastructures. The Unified Modeling Language (UML) is the prevalent model, or more appropriately, modeling language. Still, there are various methods for designing software component infrastructures, establishing metamodels to ensure tailorable component processes, and integrating component models.

From Software Component Infrastructures to Software Systems—While software component infrastructure is rigorously defined, the contributors to this part do not offer a rigorous definition of software architecture. Engineers recognize incremental and refined levels of design; software architects, who have had little impact outside academia, offer differing perspectives of their field, most of which is descriptive only.

The Management of Component-Based Software Systems—With 31% of software projects canceled before completion and 33% of the remaining projects affected by time and cost overruns and changes in scope, the technologically more complex CBD and CBSE will require more technically and engineering management trained managers. Will Frederick Taylor's "one best way" that influenced all disciplines of engineering and much of business have an impact on CBSE? That is, will the discipline accept that large problems can be broken into smaller problems, each with one and only one best solution?

Component Technologies—A limited number of component technologies exist. COM+, CORBA, EJB, Bonobo, and software agents all have a place depending on an organization's short and long-term needs. Which component technology or technologies will benefit the development of your component-based application? How should you evaluate the technologies to assure your organization meets its needs and does not make a long-term mistake?

Legal and Regulatory Issues—One of the most important parts in the book, this is not the dry legal drivel you might expect. The issues of licensure and organizational certification are explored. Voluntary business-to-business third-party certification is described. Commerce in software components is presented historically and currently. One of businesses' greatest concerns, methods of protection for

- Component producers
- Component consumers
- Purchasing end-users

are presented. Because 99% of all businesses in the U.S. are small (*www.sba.gov/advo/stats/facts99.pdfwww.sba.gov/ADVO/stats/profiles/98us.html*), many, if not most, component producers and consumers are small businesses. How do you protect your company when conducting commerce with larger businesses?

Because of the diversity of subjects that currently comprise CBSE, we asked the most knowledgeable participants in CBSE's various subdisciplines to write concise chapters describing the essence of their field or study. Therefore, this book is not a "how-to" book or a handbook. It is an edited text that clearly and concisely identifies the level of sophistication achieved by CBSE at the time of this book's publication.

Contributions

Many software engineers contributed to this book. A simple glance through the table of contents shows the wide-ranging content presented by many educators, practitioners, and others who are involved with component-based technology. To achieve consensus we sought authors with highly divergent and often conflicting views to present their perspectives on CBSE.

The authors' writing assignments, despite their uniformly remarkable knowledge of the particular subject matter, were exceptionally difficult. Authors were asked to distill vast knowledge about a topic into no more than ten book pages. Generally it is easier to write a comprehensive journal article or a book than to condense and refine a well-known subject to a few pages. Nevertheless, the authors contributed their chapters, presenting just enough information—that is, the essence of their work—for you to make well-informed decisions about CBSE.

Who Should Read This Book, And Why

Henry Petroski, in his *Engineering of Dreams* (Vantage Books, 1995), described the work of James Buchanan Eads, a pioneer in the engineering and construction of highly complex bridges. The following quote attributed to this nineteenth-century bridge builder to his company's board inspired us as editors.

> I have deemed it proper that everything of interest connected with my department should be placed in such form as to be clearly understood, not alone by your stockholders, but also by every person of ordinary intelligence in the community.

The book is divided into parts consisting of a preface, a few chapters, and the editors' summary. Each part is intended to be a model of conciseness and clarity for its particular CBSE-related subject. All parts of the book are relevant for those interested in CBSE. No part serves as a precursor for any other part. The parts are self-contained; they can be read independently and provide usable information without the need to read any other part. Some chapters within the parts are contentious and sometimes two or more authors present radically different views. Therefore, you may need to read multiple chapters to understand both sides of an argument. By comparing and contrasting the range of CBSE perspectives your options are increased, thus enabling you to make more effective decisions.

We expect that you will read a part or a chapter or two and then pick up the book later to learn and synthesize more. Similar to a handbook, it is not a text that most will read from cover to cover over a few days or weeks. Therefore, the path you take as you use the book is the one that will make the most sense for you or your organization at the particular time when you read it.

We strongly recommend that you first read Part I, a part that was developed by a consensus of experts who had previously used various definitions of *software component*. There are many definitions concerning the term software component. You might have your favorite, but this book uses one set of definitions throughout. Because this part served as the starting point for all authors, you will benefit by understanding the term as discussed and negotiated tirelessly by the authors, who struggled to achieve a consensus definition.

We have designed the book for the following audiences:

- *Chief executives, senior technology executives of independent software vendors, and chief information officers* have been sold new technologies repeatedly. Generally, few of the new methods, processes, or applications provided the functionality its sales force claimed. This book does not promote component-based technologies. We do not attempt to sell CBSE; rather we present a balanced picture of the technology's successes and pitfalls. While most authors and the coeditors believe that implementation of software components development is beneficial, you will discover the many "*ifs*" required to make software component-based development work for you and under what conditions it can successfully increase your ROI. Executives and managers will benefit most by first reading Parts II, "The Case for Components," and VI, "The Management of Component-Based Software Systems."
- *Software engineers and project managers* can gain broad knowledge of the complexities of the component-based software life cycle. This book is written especially for you. Because software engineering as a profession is not sufficiently mature to support a comprehensive handbook, this text serves as a precursor for the discipline because it explores only a segment of the field in an extensive state-of-the-art manner. We anticipate that you will use this book as a reference both before and repeatedly during the implementation of your first component-based project, and throughout your experience with CBD. Prior to this book you had to search out many books and numerous articles to learn about CBSE. We have collected all this expertise to enable you to learn what you need from one place.
- *Software developers* can learn the strengths and pitfalls of CBD and CBSE as well as how to make effective decisions about what component technologies to implement and when and how to influence management to adopt an appropriate component-based project plan. Both Part VI, "The Management of Component-Based Software Systems," and Part VII, "Component Technologies," will initially assist you as you consider implementing or revising a CBD project.
- *Business analysts and software designers* will learn how to make and support software component-based build versus buy decisions. Methods for diagramming and communicating rich semantics concerning components are provided. We believe that analysts and

designers are most likely to use the book most frequently. Therefore, this book was not developed as a how-to text for building software components. The text was designed to assist those involved throughout the life cycle to determine collectively when and whether CBD can be implemented reasonably and how to correctly and effectively communicate to managers and developers the most adept component structure that will meet users' needs. Part VI, "The Management of Component-Based Software Systems," is an excellent place to start your adventure in CBSE.

- *Software testers and quality assurance analysts* often have a limited set of concerns and this is covered in Part VI, "The Management of Component-Based Software Systems." We believe, however, that software testers should be involved in every phase of an iterative and incremental life cycle. Therefore, knowledge of all phases of the life cycle will enable you to become a more informed and competent tester of software components, as well as to know what issues will arise that present particular test-related problems.
- *Computer science and software engineering academicians* can use this book to teach current CBSE practices and develop directions for research on CBD or CBSE. Each part's summary describes areas required for research to enhance the state-of-the-art, as well as to enable the discipline of software engineering to advance as an engineering profession. Additionally, the editors will present opportunities for research that will lead to the successful implementation of CBSE by students and their future employers. This book can also be used as a supplementary text on CBSE. As educators your diverse interests will determine where you start to read and what you desire to acquire from your reading.

Our Goals

As editors we had two primary goals. The first was to inform you as clearly and concisely as possible about the state-of-the-art of CBSE. The second goal was considerably more difficult but just as important. Both of us agreed that the book should read as if it were written by one author. With 40 authors and 42 chapters, assuring a single style was a considerable task. We strongly believed, however, that you would be able to learn more about the field of CBSE if we ensured that consistent terms and a consistent writing style were used throughout.

We sincerely hope you enjoy the experience of this state-of-the-art book and its accompanying Web site. It may at first seem awkward to navigate a book that was not designed to be read from cover to cover. As you read the first recommended chapters and then a few chapters of significant interest, we believe you will refer to this book with increasing confidence. We expect you will pull it off your shelf to learn another aspect of CBSE or refresh your memory on a previously read topic. You may go to the part's references or the website to locate the latest references on a specific subject. Because of the unique broad range of topics available in this edited work, you will soon be on your way to mastering CBSE.

Acknowledgments

Aside from our authors, many people contributed to this book. Most were satisfied to work in the background to help us ensure that the book read, as we desired, as a one-author book. They participated in writing inspections by proxy; in other words, they were participants in meetings to improve various authors' work to make it the best it could be. These meetings are very much like Fagan code inspections, except that the editors served as substitutes for the contributing authors. These people deserve our heartfelt thanks and admiration. They were participants in the software reuse class for the Spring 2000 semester at the University of Texas at Dallas and students in the Worcester Polytechnic Institute graduate course on component-based software engineering.

We owe untold thanks to the five members of the virtual workgroup established to define the term software component. We selected the participants because of their reputations as CBSE methodologists and their willingness to participate in a three-week Web-based discussion forum. Little did they know how much work was involved when five very opinionated, yet diplomatic scholars devote three weeks to one task: defining one term anew. Each member initiated the virtual workshop with a five-page position paper. From those papers flowed many daily, vibrant, and sometimes contentious discussions. The participants were

- John Cheesman
- Janet Flynt
- Johannes Sametinger
- Clemens Szyperski
- John Williams

Because of their innovative and constructive conceptual work, we continued the next 19 months refining the definitions that form much of the basis of this book. Their position papers can be found on the book's Web site.

Many of the authors helped us conduct numerous peer reviews on the definition chapter and the technical chapters. Additionally, we to thank the Aonix team of Barry McGibbon, Hedley Apperly, and Steve Latchem and Davyd Norris of Rational Software Corporation for reviewing UML diagrams throughout the book. We thank Judy Stafford of the Software Engineering Institute for working closely with us on the glossary and the definition chapter. We also want to thank Martin Griss for his many recommendations when we most needed them. He opened doors that otherwise lie in wait behind shadows.

Additionally, our authors and the external reviewers devoted untold hours to assure a technically correct book. The text was placed on the book's Web site 40 days before the book was presented to Addison-Wesley. Numerous authors, unfortunately too many to name, participated in the technical review. Their purpose was to assure that this book was correct in its assertions about all technical statements. We are grateful for all their tireless help.

Also participating in the technical evaluation were reviewers selected by Addison-Wesley to assure that the book would meet the market's needs, and its requirements for technically accurate books. These reviewers—Scott Ambler, Dorothea Beringer, Wolfgang Emmerich, Gilda Pour, and Heinz Schmidt—helped assure that the book was technically correct. We would not have been successful without them. We thank them for reviewing a large, multi-author book in a short period. For all their dedicated work, we are forever appreciative.

We revised the book based upon many comments from the authors through a virtual discussion forum hosted from the book's Web site. We hope we have accurately captured a snapshot of CBSE from the perspectives of component consumers, component producers, software component implementation vendors, and software component model designers. Any responsibility for errors, however, must be shared by the editors and authors because we diligently worked together to ensure technical perfection—a difficult task, indeed, especially when the technology changes so rapidly.

Our greatest thanks are reserved for Peter Gordon, publishing partner at Addison-Wesley, and Asdis Thorsteinsson, assistant editor, who gave two unknown journal authors an opportunity to write Addison-Wesley's first edited text on CBSE. We told Peter that we would assemble the world's best-known and most knowledgeable CBD and CBSE experts. We expect that he was somewhat reticent to take on the project; nevertheless, the project soon took on a life of its own. Each expert who joined the project helped bring on the next. Soon there was a demand to participate in the project. Yet it started with Peter's confidence in us. Thank you, Peter. Asdis worked routinely with us to assure that our numerous needs were met and to maintain a collegial working environment with Addison-Wesley. Asdis, you were our lifeline and we were always appreciative of your efforts to help us.

Finally, we must thank our wives, Jen and Carol, who gave up the better part of their time with us so that we could devote ourselves to the book for close to two years. Their selflessness is rare and so meaningful. We can't thank them enough. They supported us in our work, provided useful feedback for our ideas, and helped make the book more readable.

Part I

Component Definition

Component-based software engineering (CBSE) derives from software engineering. As a subdiscipline, however, its roots are closer to civil and industrial engineering than to software engineering. One of CBSE's challenges is to establish a marketplace of software parts that can be used on multiple projects, similar to the way shock absorbers are designed for a variety of automobiles. CBSE must develop a means to assure that interoperable software components can be traded in the marketplace to the same extent as programmable components in safety-critical electrical appliances.

For seventeen years, Henry Ford had no industrial means to produce enough automobiles to lower the price of his cars—one of Mr. Ford's unwavering goals. Ford observed that "[I]f production is increased 500%, costs may be cut 50%, and this decrease in cost, with its accompanying decrease in selling price, will probably multiply by 10 the number of people who can conveniently buy the product" (Ford, 1926). Fortuitously, in a meat packing plant in Chicago he was inspired by the packaging process to develop the idea for the assembly line, which sped up automobile manufacturing by making the same auto parts completely interchangeable and mechanizing their assembly into a car. Assembly line processes are designed and implemented by mechanical engineers to assure that automotive parts are assembled en masse precisely within minimally acceptable tolerances.

CBSE is at a similar crossroads. Our approach to CBSE is engineering-based. Automotive design and construction started as an art and often focused on aesthetics; early car builders chiseled and then forced parts together. Similarly, in procedural and object-oriented programming, software developers often work hard to make things fit, even though simple patterns abound that will help objects to connect easily. In CBSE precision is exceptionally important; components must compose precisely through their interfaces, much as an automobile's transmission must join precisely with the differential gear that turns the controlling wheels. Trial and error has a place in software engineering, but nothing substitutes for an understanding of the basics of engineering sciences and years of increasingly detailed design and responsibility for larger and larger subproject teams.

The definition part starts where most good engineering books commence, with a chapter of empirically rigorous definitions. We devoted 18 months to define, as precisely as possible, the term *software component* and offer equally rigorous definitions of its elements. We use standards and accepted texts to explain the definition so that no reader should be confused about what a software component is and what it is not. All authors had access to the definitions throughout this project and many used the definitions in their practices long before this book was published. No author refused to accept the definitions—and this book is comprised of chapters written by 45 different authors.

We discovered that few tasks are more difficult than developing a concise, definite, and clear definition. We had to define the term software component, then define all the terms that support, or are associated with, its definition. Fortunately, we began with a Web-based discussion with five long-term component specialists to assist us with the basics of a definition. We finished the process of refining the definitions 18 months later with numerous authors reviewing, editing, and commenting on the definitions. We learned to appreciate, and sympathize with, semanticists (dictionary writers).

Complementing the definition chapter is Chapter 2, "The Component Industry Metaphor," which compares the engineering of a high-rise building to CBSE. The author, Hedley Apperly, is both a manufacturing and software engineer. He develops a persuasive metaphor for CBSE as high-rise building construction, which involves more than a building plan and a contractor. The processes are virtually identical but are referred to by different names. The design and construction phases may appear familiar as well. The similarity between cataloging both building parts and software components, and their replenishment when necessary, is a revelation. Configuration management and component libraries in software development plainly have precursors in builders' merchant yards and paper catalogs. Because CBSE is rooted in the engineering and construction traditions, it supports the use of interoperable parts.

In Chapter 3, "Component Models and Component Services: Concepts and Principles," Rainer Weinreich and Johannes Sametinger describe the concepts and principles that guide component-based software development (CBD). They first present an analogy comparing components and component infrastructures to applications and operating systems (OS). Using the OS analogy, the two experienced software component authors describe dissimilar forms of components and the differences between objects and components.

They then take our definitions, mere abstract foundations, and build upon them so that software engineers and project teams are prepared for later chapters, where they will learn to apply component-based analysis and design and implement a CBD process. They successfully make the definition of difficult terms, such as *component model*, apply to the work lives of CBSE engineers, component designers, developers, and testers.

Chapter 4, "An Example Specification for Implementing a Temperature Regulator Software Component," by Janet Flynt and Jason Mauldin of Underwriters Laboratories, contains a simple example of a programmable component that interfaces with a microelectronic device. The chapter clearly presents the types of documentation required for third-party certification of software components. As the author describes, end-users demand trusted software components, just as they demand trusted hardware components. The process of certifying software components is similar to the procedures for certifying hardware. This chapter provides a fitting end to the definition part.

The "examples" chapter presents, in text and diagrams, the requirements for documenting a trusted software component that may be developed by a component producer for licensing to a microelectronics vendor. The vendor would then sell the software and hardware components to a scientific hotplate vendor. Each producer or vendor must have implicit trust in the original producer. Otherwise, the final product could cause substantial bodily harm or death to the end-user. Because more functionality in electronic products is directly controlled by software, there must be an increased focus on safety critical issues. In the hot plate example, if the software fails to regulate the temperature, a fire may ensue, leading to potential fatal results.

This part prepares you to read the rest of the book. As each chapter demonstrates, the goal of CBD and CBSE is no different from automobile and construction development: the precise assembly of well-documented, quality, trusted components. Both the automotive and construction industries developed reliable parts because of standards, regulations, and laws. CBSE has no standards. Especially lacking are standards for the education of component-based software engineers. The authors of this part hope we have provided something the field so sorely needs: a consensus set of definitions and a statement of concepts and principles. Perhaps from here we can start to develop standards for CBSE so that we can fulfill the need for precise assembly of components for different component models as described in Chapter 2.

We hope you have fun learning the basics of CBSE. It is a broad discipline with opportunities for many jobs on the cutting edge of various new technologies. Everyone who contributed a chapter in this part is excited about CBSE and its potential for growth. We view it as having great promise, something that object-oriented technology, like so many of its predecessor technologies, did not deliver. The future of CBSE is as much in your hands as it is in ours. Through reading the chapters in this part, we hope you are inspired to become one of us: advocates for a true engineering method for the development of reusable components.

Chapter 1

Definition of a Software Component and Its Elements

Bill Councill
George T. Heineman

1.1 Introduction

The goal of this chapter is to rigorously define terms that describe the best practices of component-based software engineering (CBSE). We will develop and describe in detail the term *software component* and its constituent elements to provide clear, unambiguous, and rational meanings to the terms used to describe CBSE. You will find some terms used here for the first time. The reason for this is simple: many terms in software engineering emerged without precise definitions in publication and were subsequently used without reflection or scientific review. We avoid the use of any terms that, although popular, are not rigorously defined, are circularly referenced, or are simply descriptions of software engineering phenomena. When nonrigorous terms are used we rely on the engineering sciences, particularly industrial and civil engineering, which require precise definitions because of the demands for safety and public welfare inherent in their disciplines.

For too long a so-called engineering discipline has not trained its practitioners in engineering practices, not subjected its students to internships and then tested their knowledge and expertise, and not prevented untrained and undisciplined employees from taking jobs of authority. Meanwhile, project managers are not engineering-trained software engineers or managers with full knowledge of the complete life cycle. We are at a crossroads. Project managers must know the intricacies of design, development, testing, and component management to successfully manage the assembly of complex components and their even more complicated maintenance. These managers must also be aware of the need for second- and third-party certification and contractual relationships.

1.1.1 Background

We first define a set of basic terms required to explain the characteristics assigned to the definitions. *Software* is constructed to execute on a general-purpose von Neumann computing device (henceforth, a *machine*). A software element contains sequences of abstract program statements that describe computations to be performed by a machine. A software element is *machine-executable* if: (1) the machine directly executes the program statements or (2) a machine-executable *interpreter* directly understands the program statements and the machine directly executes the interpreter.

The *source code* for software is the set of *machine-readable* files containing program statements written in a programming language. These statements are either compiled into *machine-executable* statements using a compiler or executed by an interpreter.

1.2 Definition

A software component simply cannot be differentiated from other software elements by the programming language used to implement the component. The difference must be in how software components are used. Software comprises many abstract, *quality* features, that is, the degree to which a component or process meets specified requirement (IEEE Std 610.12-1990). For example, an efficient component will receive more use than a similar, inefficient component. It would be inappropriate, however, to define a software component as "an efficient unit of functionality." Elements that comprise the following definition of the term software component are described in the "Terms" sidebar.

> A *software component* is a software element that conforms to a component model and can be independently deployed and composed without modification according to a composition standard.
>
> A *component model* defines specific interaction and composition standards. A *component model implementation* is the dedicated set of executable software elements required to support the execution of components that conform to the model.
>
> A *software component infrastructure* is a set of interacting software components designed to ensure that a software system or subsystem constructed using those components and interfaces will satisfy clearly defined performance specifications.

These definitions demonstrate the important relationship between a software component infrastructure, software components, and a component model.

1.2.1 Interaction Standard

One underlying concept of a component is that it has clearly defined interfaces. We pattern our definition for the term *interface* after the object composition model for Reference Model of Open Distributed Processing (RM-ODP). A joint effort of international standards bodies, the RM-ODP describes a framework and supporting infrastructure that enables the integration of distribution, internetworking, interoperability, and portability of applications ([Raymond, 1995] [ISO/ITU Open Distributed Processing—Reference Model—Part 2: Foundations, 1995b]. An *interface standard* is the mandatory requirements employed and enforced to enable software elements to directly interact with other software elements. An interface standard declares what can comprise an interface.

Terms	
Standard	An object or quality or measure serving as a basis to which others should conform, or by which the accuracy or quality of others is judged (by present-day standards). This term includes proprietary vendor and producer standards as well as national and international standards produced by recognized standards bodies.
Software element	A sequence of abstract program statements that describe computations to be performed by a machine.
Interface	An abstraction of the behavior of a component that consists of a subset of the interactions of that component together with a set of constraints describing when they may occur. The interface describes the behavior of a component that is obtained by considering only the interactions of that interface and by hiding all other interactions.
Interaction	An action between two or more software elements.
Composition	The combination of two or more software components yielding a new component behavior at a different level of abstraction. The characteristics of the new component behavior are determined by the components being combined and by the way they are combined.

A component supports a *provided interface* if the component contains an implementation of all operations defined by that interface. The interface hides the component implementation. A component needs a *required interface* if the component requests an interaction defined in that interface and the component expects some other software element to support that interface. A component may be unable to provide an interface if one of its required interfaces is unfulfilled. A component should ideally deploy with descriptive information that completely specifies all provided and required interfaces.

Software elements interact with a component using the component's clearly defined and documented interfaces. An interaction standard defines the elements of an interface. If the component can perform its function only by interacting with other software elements, all explicit context dependencies should be clearly specified in the component's documentation. An interaction standard is actually a superset of the interface standard previously discussed. The interaction standard covers both direct and indirect interactions that may exist between components.

A component may have an *explicit context dependency* on the operating system, a software component, or some other software element. An *interaction standard* specifies the type of explicit context dependencies a component may have. Another form of explicit context dependency occurs when a component must execute on a computer with a specific clock speed to achieve its performance objective. If the component must interact with a hardware device the component uses application programming interfaces provided by the operating system or an interface provided by the component model implementation. In both cases the descriptive information for the component must clearly define the explicit context dependency. To enable reuse and interconnection of components, component producers and consumers often agree on a set of interfaces before the components are designed. These mutual agreements can lead to standardized interfaces.

1.2.2 Composition Standard

For independent deployment a component must be clearly separate from an operating system and other components. Thus, the component encapsulates the necessary data and algorithms to perform its tasks. The way in which a component is deployed is determined by the component model and typically involves three steps.

1. Installing the component in preparation for its use.

2. Configuring the component and perhaps the operating system where the component will be executed to make the component available.
3. Instantiating the component for use.

The source code for a software component is the full set of machine-readable software files (containing procedures and modules) and machine-executable files (containing run-time libraries and pre-compiled object code) required to package the software component into a machine-readable software element. A software component may be packaged in binary form to:

- Protect the proprietary intellectual property of the software component producer because it is nearly impossible to reverse-engineer the source code for a component from its binary packaged form
- Decrease installation and deployment costs
- Reduce explicit context dependencies (the consumer, for example, must have Gnu C++ compiler version 2.8.1)

The component producer will decide whether the source code should be deployed with the component. It is possible that a consumer or third-party certifier will require access to the source code.

A composition standard defines how components can be composed to create a larger structure and how a producer can substitute one component to replace another that already exists within the structure. We pattern our definition for the term *composition* in the **Terms** sidebar after RM-ODP.

In addition to an interface description, the component producer should provide sufficient descriptive documentation to enable a component consumer to assemble the component into a target application. Third-party certifiers will also use the documentation to verify the process used to develop the component and ensure that the final product fulfills the specifications. The component producer or the third-party certification organization will decide the most appropriate form for the documentation, that is, whether to store it with the component, in either source or binary format, or provide it separately. The forms of documentation generally deemed most advantageous to component consumers are

- Business rules
- Business processes
- Functional requirements
- Nonfunctional requirements
- Use case scenarios
- Design documentation using Unified Modeling Language diagrams and Object Constraint Language
  - Preconditions
  - Postconditions
  - Design contracts

1.2.3 Component Model

A component model operates on two levels. First, a component model defines how to construct an individual component. For example, Microsoft's Component Object Model (COM) requires each COM component to provide an `IUnknown` interface. Second, a component model can enforce global behavior on how a set of components in a component-based system will communicate and interact with each other. A component model enables composition by defining an interaction standard that promotes unambiguously specified interfaces. A component can be composed with another component or other software element (for example, legacy code) by creating assembled or integrated connections respectively.

The component model defines the permitted mechanisms for creating assembled or integrated connections. D'Souza and Wills (1999) observe that "plug-in compatibility" only succeeds if a component can accurately declare its expectations of the other component to which it is connected. The process of assembly may be as complicated as necessary to achieve the goal of precise specifications. We use the term *assembly* to include the many different forms in which components compose, such as wrapping, static and dynamic linking, and "plug-and-play."

The component model may define customization mechanisms that describe how components can be extended without modification. We treat customization as an advanced form of interaction. A component model may also define mandatory component properties, such as coding formats, documentation standards, or obligatory producer-independent interfaces.

1.2.4 Component Model Implementation

The component model implementation is the dedicated set of executable software elements necessary to support the execution of components within a component model. An operating system (OS) could embed the component model implementation but that would only further complicate the OS and might restrict the applicability of the component model. The component model implementation is typically a thin layer that executes on top of an OS. Multiple OSs can port this layer to ensure maximum applicability of the component model.

The interaction standard for a component model determines whether an interface must be registered with the component model implementation prior to use. Interfaces are typically defined by using an interface definition language (IDL) and registered with an interface repository associated with the component model implementation. The composition standard for a component model determines whether a component must be registered with the component model implementation prior to its use. The vendor of a component model implementation may provide tools such as an IDL compiler to support the development of components.

The component model implementation makes it possible to execute components that conform to the component model. The Object Management Group's (OMG's) Common Object Request Broker Architecture (CORBA), for example, functions in an open distributed processing system using Object Request Brokers, software applications that execute on OSs such as Microsoft Windows or UNIX. CORBA is an open standard, which means that the OMG promotes the standard but is not a component producer that provides the component model implementation. When the producer of a component model implementation is also the designer of the component model, the component model could be proprietary (that is, only one component model implementation is available).

1.2.5 Summary

Our definitions and descriptions of components, component models, component infrastructures, and component model implementations do not explain how software engineers should design and construct components. As software engineers we must only promote new technologies that provide state-of-the-art design and deployment methodologies for software systems to support immediate empiricism. Eventually Engineering scrutiny will eventually be applied to design and deployment methodologies.

One more definition must be added at this point to differentiate software development and the component life cycle. In a traditional software development life cycle developers are often analysts, designers, and developers. A project has a well-defined beginning, when requirements are elicited, and a well-defined ending, when the final software system is delivered. Component production is different. Considerably more time is devoted to business rules, business process modeling, analysis, and design. Much less time is spent in development while testing occurs throughout. Accordingly, we introduce the following definition

> The *component-based software life cycle* (CSLC) is the life cycle process for a software component with an emphasis on business rules, business process modeling, design, construction, continuous testing, deployment, evolution, and subsequent reuse and maintenance.

The analysis and design phases for a CSLC are significantly longer than during a traditional software development life cycle. At least one verification activity is conducted at the end of each CSLC phase. While recommended in various software engineering guides and standards, verification is an absolute necessity throughout the analysis and design to ensure a successful construction and unit testing phase. During development unit testing, using the "one best way," (see Chapter 37) is implemented and tested. Testing against each component will be performed separately. Software testers participate in integration and system testing cooperatively with all team members. Maintenance is designed into the component for evolution that may occur years away.

The component model implementation that supports interaction and composition must also enable engineers to create domain-specific software component infrastructures whose components interact to realize the functionality and behavior of a desired system during the CSLC. The next section describes our vision concerning how to successfully integrate component-based technology into existing software development processes.

1.3 The Master Software Development Plan

1.3.1 Background

Software engineering literature commonly defines the term software component by describing "software component framework" or "software architecture." Indeed, it is often difficult to describe the details of a smaller part without referring to the greater whole to which it ultimately belongs. After an exhaustive literature review we discovered that authors generally use the terms *architecture* and *framework* (often without definition) interchangeably and in a variety of dissimilar ways. Both terms, however, are used solely within the software engineering community and not in other engineering disciplines.

Software architecture and frameworks are essentially synonymous with the elicitation of the highest levels of design elements for software systems. Instead of creating more confusion by trying to differentiate these terms and their complementary theories, we describe a simpler concept, that of increasingly discrete and detailed design. We start with the concept of a master software development plan borrowed from the well-established practice within industrial engineering.

1.3.2 Definition

In any meaningful engineering endeavor a lead engineer or component-based software project manager (hereafter, engineer) establishes the scope of the project, generally according to an RFP, identifies the performance specifications of the finished product, and determines how to validate the success of the requested product. When establishing the product's scope the lead engineer divides the work into *subprojects*, self-contained processes of analysis and design that produce elements that will be incorporated into the final design. The elements from all subprojects are managed by subproject engineers and customized to implement an integrated design that will satisfy the performance specifications. In CBSE and software reuse we use the engineering term *performance specification* rather than requirements specification because the term foreshadows the need for decomposing a problem into subproblems to be solved, while requirements are often global in scope and can't be reused easily.

> A *performance specification* defines the functional requirements for a product, the environment in which it must operate, and any interface and interchangeability requirements. It provides criteria for verifying compliance, but it does not state methods for achieving results. (*www.dsp.dla.mil/documents/sd-15.html*).

In the field of software engineering the master software development plan created by the lead engineer ensures the success of the project and its subprojects.

> A *master software development plan* describes the methods adopted by the lead software engineer or manager for a system's composition and interaction. It is a conceptual plan that defines the boundaries of the system, its elements, interactions, and constraints on these elements and interactions. The master software development plan consists of a global design that identifies discrete and manageable subprojects.

1.3.3 Description

The lead engineer is responsible for ensuring the success of the project by adapting existing models to fit the needs of the software under development. Traditional professional engineering practices require that the processes necessary for each project are determined by the lead engineer based upon the performance specifications of the project. While nationally or internationally prescribed organizational processes are helpful—such as the Software Engineering Institute's Capability Maturity Modeling and the International Standards Organization (ISO) 9001—the lead engineer is responsible for the project and subprojects. Engineers are also responsible for compliance with laws and regulations as well as industry standards.

Realization of a comprehensive and frequently complex master software development plan results in the design of a software component infrastructure. The component infrastructure embodies the design decisions and trade-offs of the project. The lead engineer ensures that descriptive documentation is developed that precisely describes the interactions among components in the software component infrastructure. Through increasingly detailed design the component infrastructure is refined and a component model is selected. The final implemented components in the infrastructure will conform to this component model. The component model implementation enables the interaction and composition of the components in the software component infrastructure

The lead engineer may select an existing component model, design and implement a proprietary component model, or develop a component model implementation for an existing component model. The component model implementation will support the execution of the components in the software component infrastructure. Lead engineers do not work in isolation; they rely on the judgment of subproject engineers and the analysis and design team. Therefore, the choice is based on best practices, according to the professional assessment of the lead engineer—as influenced by engineering and design staff—to satisfy the original design goals of the desired system within existing budget and staffing constraints.

The lead engineer may choose to design a software component infrastructure that includes components that conform to different component models. In this case the lead engineer must ensure the interoperability of the respective component model implementations of these component models.

Because of the different types of performance specifications a system must satisfy (such as efficiency, use of resources, and integration with legacy data), software engineers, analysts, and designers benefit from "visualizing" any proposed software system from a variety of viewpoints. The software component infrastructure that supports the master software development plan can be analyzed from multiple viewpoints to evaluate global performance requirements. We derive our viewpoints from the RM-ODP standard (ISO/ITU Open Distributed Processing—Reference Model—Part 2: Foundations, 1995b). The RM-ODP framework is composed of five viewpoints that provide sets of concepts, structures, and rules. These viewpoints are used to specify ODP systems. They are also applicable to component-based systems:

- *Enterprise* (purpose, scope, and policies) - An enterprise specification contains policies determined by the organization rather than imposed on the organization by technology choices.
- *Information* (semantics of information and information processing) - The individual components must share a common understanding of the information they communicate when they interact.
- *Computational* (functional decomposition) - The computational specification describes how the overall functionality of an application is distributed between the components.
- *Engineering* (infrastructure support) - The engineering specification describes the design that enables communication between components.
- *Technology* (choices of technology for implementation) - The technology specification describes the implementation of the system and the information required for testing.

More information is available about each of the viewpoints in the ISO/IEC *Overview* document (ISO/ITU Reference Model of Open Distributed Processing - Part 1: Overview, 1995a).

We have been influenced by the RM-ODP definitions of composition, interfaces, and viewpoints because the reference model is an international standard developed jointly by ISO and ITU-T to support the distribution, internetworking, interoperability, and portability of ODP. Although developed to provide a "big picture" to organize pieces of an object-oriented ODP system into a coherent whole, the RM-ODP is designed as an abstract standard because it carefully avoids prescribing an implementation.

Many sets of viewpoints are available for decomposing, analyzing, and distributing systems' functions and components. Incorporating a set of concepts and rules for each of the viewpoints, the RM-ODP provides a method to specify systems from particularly important software engineering viewpoints. The RM-ODP is appealing because it offers languages for analyzing and resolving the requirements of businesses for software based on these viewpoints, although the languages are object-specific. We find that CBSE, in general, has similar needs, and this book provides many chapters to help you understand its complexities.

1.4 The Big Picture

Figure 1-1 graphically demonstrates the relationships among the master software development plan and software components, software component models, software component model implementations, and software component infrastructures. The lead engineer is responsible for selecting the component model that can best implement the logical design as described by the software component infrastructure created for the master software development plan. The design elements produced by the subprojects must interact effectively and efficiently to achieve the overall project goal and software engineers must determine how to map the logical elements into physical components. The RM-ODP viewpoints can help engineers make successful decisions for the producer or consumer. Therefore, actual implementation of the system becomes an engineering endeavor.

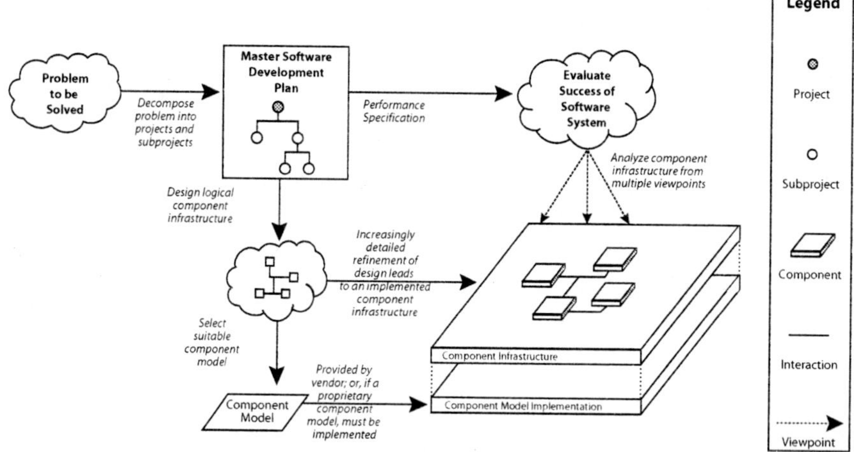

Figure 1-1: *The big picture.*

As a small example, consider a component producer that has won a competitive bid for designing and deploying a component-based general ledger system. The lead engineer first decomposes the project into its constituent subprojects, such as inventory, accounts receivable, and merchandise distribution. The business or contracting organization may already have a legacy inventory system. Therefore, a subproject engineer is assigned the task of designing a component that effectively wraps the legacy system and provides an interface that conforms to the component model used by the other system components. Then the lead engineer would probably schedule a design inspection with everyone involved in the initial design to verify that all components interact and integrate logically according to the master software development plan.

The component infrastructure in Figure 1-1 is the result of the design process followed by the project engineers and design team. Through increasingly detailed refinement the software component infrastructure is implemented and forms the basis for the desired software system.

1.5 Conclusion

One of our goals in creating this book was to develop a set of rigorous definitions that clarify many of the terms used in the CBSE literature. CBSE is a challenge even for experienced software project team members because of the lack of rigorous definitions, the use of confusing and circular definitions, and descriptions passing for definitions. We have ensured that all the chapters in this book conform to the definitions presented in this chapter. The term software component has the same meaning in this chapter as in every other chapter in this book. Achieving these definitions was more than an academic exercise_it was a necessary step in defining the emerging field of CBSE. We have devoted considerable energy in developing these definitions and we expect you will find them extremely useful as you develop your CBSE vocabulary and skills.

Chapter 2

The Component Industry Metaphor

Hedley Apperly

2.1 Introduction

In this chapter, I hope to communicate the experiences you will need to derive real business benefits from using software components. Previous design experience is invaluable, but CBSE is both a new perspective in software engineering and a tested solution in other engineering disciplines. Before I became involved in software engineering, I was an engineer in the physical world, using a real drawing board to design and build tangible, usable objects. Many industries have matured over a long period to a point where they now consistently use components, including the manufacturing, electronics, construction, and automotive industries (D'Souza and Wills, 1999). Prior engineering endeavors have taught me that businesses will have to clearly see a reasonable return-on-investment (ROI) before they will invest in the design, construction, and marketing of components. The same is surely true of component-based software engineering, the design, development, assembly, and marketing of intellectual components.

2.2 The Problem

Although CBSE is founded upon a solid background of experience within the software industry, as an engineering science it is immature. It is my experience that successful processes need to be shared and evolved into best practices if more organizations are to succeed with CBSE. The first problem is that software development organizations and information services (IS) departments are often in competition with closely guarded proprietary processes. For example, if an IS manager fails to deliver a software system, one option is to outsource the development wholesale. If you assume that the in-house and outsourced staff and development tools are equivalent, then the primary difference is the process used to develop the software system.

While few people have had experience with information services, in some form, the construction industry should be familiar to all readers. You live in a building, made changes to a building, or are involved in construction. I believe a *high-rise construction* scenario will therefore best describe the opportunities and problems inherent in component-based construction. To distinguish the construction scenario, I list the steps required for construction development within Table 2-1.

2.3 The Basics of Construction

Building a high-rise building can be decomposed into a set of very high-level steps. Table 2-1 shows a simplified life cycle. The general flow seems to be a standard waterfall development process (Bocij et al., 1999), but we should bear in mind that increments and iteration will occur. For example, you may choose (or be forced) to occupy the lower level floors of a building before all of the construction is completed, which maps to incremental development. Incremental development is a technique for identifying priorities and delivering high priority items first. When building a high-rise building you may be

Table 2-1: *Steps for Building a High-Rise*

Step	Construction Phase
1	Analyze Business/Owners' Processes
2	Define Business/Owners' Requirements
3	Design Building
4	Hire Construction Company
5	Lay Foundation
6	Construct Infrastructure
7	Build Façade
8	Decorate
9	Occupy

happy to move staff into the building while the roof garden is being completed near the end of construction. The same is true for software, as you need working input screens before monthly reports. Iteration can be mapped to walls, as you usually start with bricks and come back to add a plaster coating, followed by paint or paper. This technique is termed *additive*, where a basic infrastructure is built upon. The infrastructure maps to software development as early versions of software evolve over time.

We can continue this table to include building maintenance, as shown in Table 2-2.

Table 2-2: *Maintaining a High-Rise*

Step	Construction Phase
10	Remodel Foyer
11	Build Extension
12	Join Two Office Blocks Together

These typical construction steps can be easily mapped to a traditional software development life cycle. Before I move on to a comparison of software components with high-rise construction components, I will compare the processes for constructing both buildings and software in Table 2-3.

Table 2-3: *Building Software*

Step	Construction Phase	Software Development Life Cycle Phase
1	Analyze Business/Owners' Processes	Model Business Processes
2	Define Business/Owners' Requirements	Manage Requirements
3	Design Building	Model System Design
4	Hire Construction Company	Select Integrated Development Environment (IDE)
5	Lay Foundation	Build Database
6	Construct Infrastructure	Build Middleware
7	Build Façade	Build Client Software
8	Decorate	Test
9	Occupy	Roll-Out
10	Remodel Foyer	Maintenance
11	Build Extension	Extension
12	Join Two Office Blocks Together	Merge Systems

The mapping of construction to software component development phases is straightforward, and you can see how increments and iterations map to the construction and software processes.

2.3.1 Componentization

Over the years the construction industry realized that it is impractical to build everything from scratch every time. Doors, windows, and bricks are all built off-site, often by a different companies or teams. In most cases, standard construction components will fit the needs of the designer and builder. At other times, a new component will be specified and built to suit the needs of a single building. I assert that no industry can become componentized until it has successfully shown how to consume, supply, and manage components.

In Figure 2-1, a repository is at the center of solution development, component development, and management. All the terms will be described in this chapter at length, while the term repository or component library will be explained more effectively in Chapter 32. A component repository is similar to a place where construction goods are stored and can be instantly retrieved for use when needed. Many parts may be very similar, but the warehouseman can find the exact part in minutes. The component repository provides the same services for components, their associated interfaces, and documentation, distinguishing one version of a component from another easily.

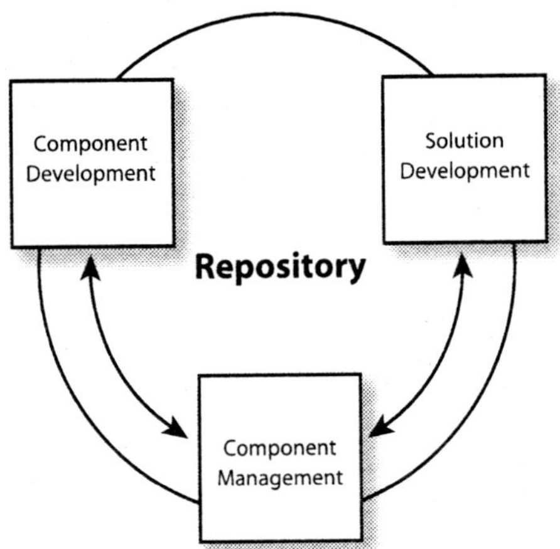

Figure 2-1: *Consume, supply, and manage.*

2.3.2 Consume

The basics of building a high-rise building map to the construction of a solution or application. The focus for this *solution building* process (Allen and Frost, 1998) is provided by the customer or the business (Eles and Sims, 1998). In the software engineering world this is usually achieved by modeling the required business processes (Jacobson, 1994). The contract between the customer and the designer can be achieved by documenting requirements or reviewing the designs as they progress. Once solution design starts, components begin to have an impact. The group responsible for building solutions is actually consuming components. This highlights a problem: not only is it important to stockpile components to prepare for the construction process, it is also important to design the solution using information about available components. One option for the design of interacting components is based on the UML and is proposed in Chapter 14. However, I believe the UML is better for designing the internals of black box components rather than designing static and dynamic relationships among components. The challenge for the solution builder is to assemble a large system from components. To do this successfully you will need information about the available software components, their required interfaces, and their services, operations, and methods.

The process of finding the right components is important to the component designer and is usually termed *gap fulfillment* (Bellows, 2000). The gap fulfillment process can have one of two outcomes: either an ideal (or similar) component is found and used or no relevant component exists. This introduces new issues to the stockpiling process because you may need to create a subproject to build a specific component. This means that the stockpiling process is not just about static holding areas for built components, but also an enabling process. The real productivity benefits of CBSE will only be realized by enabling parallel solution and component development, and this is achievable only through planning and design. For components that cannot be found, the stockpiling process must allow consumers to post a *wanted* notice for others to respond to.

Once you use a component, whether off-the-shelf or bespoke (a term used to describe unique, specially developed components), you need a process for configuration management. Because new versions of a component may be provided at any time, and the solution builder may want to take advantage of an upgrade, component consumers need a process to inform them when updated components are added to the stockpile. The solution builder must be able to easily replace an existing component with a newer version. This can be achieved, for example, if the solution builder registers to receive a notification when new component versions are stockpiled. Table 2-4 shows the application development life cycle with these additional component-based steps.

Table 2-4: *High-Rise and Software Life Cycle with CBSE*

Step	Construction Phase	Software Development Life Cycle Phase
1	Analyze Process	Model Business Processes
2	Define Specifications	Manage Requirements
3	Design Building	Model System Design (Components)
CBSE	Find Windows and Doors	Gap Fulfillment
CBSE	Sub-Contract Roof Joists	New Component Specification
CBSE	Design Windows	Component Use
CBSE	Get on Mailing List	Get on Mailing List
4	Hire Construction Company	Select Integrated Development Environment (IDE)
5	Lay Foundations	Build Database (Comp. Assembly)
6	Construct Framework	Build Middleware (Comp. Assembly)
7	Build Façade	Build Client Software (Comp. Assembly)
8	Decorate	Test
9	Move In	Roll-Out
CBSE	New Catalogue	Receive Notification, New Component
CBSE	Read Catalogue	Review New Component
CBSE	Update Design	Update Design
10	Remodel Foyer	Maintenance
11	Build Extension	Extension
12	Join Office Blocks Together	Merge Systems

This simplified table communicates the component considerations that improve the standard solution-building process. We can take this model one step further by considering the actual deployment of the components on the run-time environment. Typically, the computers on which the components run are called *nodes* (see UML 1.3), and mapping these nodes to the components allow system administrators to manage the deployment configuration. This is particularly important when components are widely distributed across an organization and updates occur. To handle this complexity the process is enhanced to include deployment recording during the application rollout stage. The distribution among appropriate nodes generally completes the steps in the solution development process or, as I call it, component consumption.

2.3.3 Supply

The component producer is responsible for building completed components, usually to predefined specifications. In the construction industry, for example, there are window supply companies whose sole source of revenue is window manufacturing. Windows generally come in standard sizes, though builders can request special sizes and materials described in a comprehensive specification. Roof joists, by contrast, are a good example of specified components that are often distinct to a particular building. As well as the customer's component specification, there may also be industry standards to apply. In the case of the high-rise building there will be safety, structural, emergency, and materials standards. These standards map to the concepts of quality, performance, error handling, and technology standards in software components.

Applying similar logic to the evolving discipline of CBSE, the component specification may come from the component producer's desire to provide a generic component or the solution builder's specific needs. The specification may also derive from an industry standard for component interaction or a component kit (D'Souza and Wills, 1999).

A component producer starts by identifying the discrete requirements of the component specification. An important step in the producer/consumer process, the component specification forms the contractual expectations of both parties to the component development process and final product, sometimes termed *design by contract* (Meyer, 1988). In the construction industry the specification is represented by a comprehensive design developed by a contractor for a subcontractor or a contractor's use of industry standards for components, such as bricks, windows and doors.

The component producer starts with this specification and perhaps some component-specific use cases and iteratively and comprehensively develops a design that satisfies the specification. Typically, the design and development of the internals of the component will be carried out using techniques such as the Unified Modeling Language (UML) and object-oriented (OO) languages, or even plugging together smaller components. Tools for design and code generation may also be used. Testing, debugging, and compilation generally are applied. The important result, for the subject of this chapter, is the completed component. Building upon the definition of a component provided in Chapter 1, I identify four levels of abstraction, as shown in Table 2-5.

Table 2-5: *Component Abstraction Levels*

1	Component Specification
2	Component Implementation
3	Component Executable
4	Component Deployment

The component specification or *façade* (Gamma et al., 1995) includes the technology independent definition of the component, but also information to facilitate gap fulfillment. The minimum requirements for a component specification are defined earlier and these form the binding contract between the supplier and consumer. Component management tools can help with this process, as well as ensuring that authority to proceed is granted. The component specification will be the primary reference resource used at design time. It has been my experience that component specifications change during the development life cycle; therefore, component producers will generally develop multiple versions of a particular component.

A component implementation occurs when you decide on the language to use to develop the component. This defines the *inside* (D'Souza and Wills, 1999) of the component, with its internal components and collaborations. The implementation source code is typically what will be stored in a configuration management or version control system. Because a component specification can be implemented using more than one language, there is a *one-to-many* relationship between a specification and an implementation; multiple versions of an implementation will occur during the course of the life cycle. The component executable is the real *pluggable* component used in the assembly of the solution. Each executable may result in more than one version and there may be more than one executable per implementation. Finally, the executable is deployed on a number of nodes. All nodes need to be inventoried and tracked so that updates are managed and a stable production environment is maintained.

The producer will need to publish accurate information about a component, such as its available interfaces and its services. Most important in publishing the component is communicating the specification of the component and its interfaces with a focus on making the physical component available. Updates to software will occur, so new component versions will need to be published in the same manner as the original. When you buy building materials from a builder's merchant, you are typically added to a mailing list. As a component consumer, you receive the latest catalogs, updates, and information about recalls.

The process of building and marketing software components is similar to the company that builds windows or doors for the construction industry. A window can be viewed as a black box component. The high-rise contractor will not need to know the size of each pane of glass or the size of nails used in the windows' construction. The contractor does not need to know the thickness (3 inches), and information about its functionality. The functionality information is required because the builder's component specification, acquired from the developer of the high-rise building, likely in consultation with an engineer, forms the contract among the developer, the contractor, and the subcontractor. Double or single-glazed, top or side-opening, and tinted windows are all examples of functions of a window that do not relate directly to the interface. In the case of a window, the interface is where it touches the brick, that is, the 3-foot by 4-foot hole in the wall.

We can see from this short discussion that you need more than just an interface specification to find and use a component. A degree of functionality and how it is achieved needs to be communicated as part of the component specification.

2.3.4 Manage

The third high-level role in general component-based engineering is component management. In this chapter, I have referred to a stockpile of components and that is exactly what a typical component library is.

A component library is similar to a builder yard or warehouse; both environments are where construction companies order and purchase their components. Component producers publish their components in both settings. Builder yards and warehouses are staging areas between producers and consumers. They serve as the middlemen for construction component businesses.

In the construction world there are various levels of interacting component stores. The top level is the warehouse of the component producer. Component producers that assemble windows will typically have a central store used to supply all of the builder's merchants. The builder's merchants will have their own warehouses that are closer to the construction company sites and will typically service many companies. Warehouse organization is important, as cataloguing helps to manage and locate components. The standard way to support multiple sites and interacting levels of warehouses is usually an integrated set of component repositories or catalogues. In this example, a third level would be the builder's yard for the construction company. The stock in the builder's yard will consist of newly acquired components and components left over from previous jobs. Therefore, construction companies develop an inventory from previous contract assignments and attempt to use existing stock before they purchase more, or before building the stock themselves. This technique is typically termed *reuse before you buy, and before you build.*

Component producers should not simply ship new components to the builder's yard. Effective yards will employ a *receivable goods clerk* who will assure that the products arriving at the warehouse are of acceptable quality. If the components do not meet quality standards, the shipment will be rejected. If the components comply with standards, the clerk will certify the components for consumers and end-users of the warehouse to purchase the stock.

New components are the other key factor for component librarians, as they may not always arrive fully documented or designed. Generally, with new components, extra information will need to be recorded if the components are to be easily retrieved and used. Especially with software components, required information, often referred to as meta data (see Chapter 3) can include technology type, features provided, where to get support, examples of use, help files, and installation procedures.

2.4 Conclusion

It was my intent to demonstrate that the development and maintenance of software components is similar to other engineering endeavors, especially the analysis, design, component warehousing, construction, and maintenance of high-rise buildings. Constructing from components is more complex than building from scratch. The transition from building the same sets of software products repeatedly to componentization demands new and existing roles. It can be seen as requiring a cultural shift, but this is not really the case.

Building systems from components is a natural evolution from existing methods and can always be related to other industries. Car manufacture, electronics, construction, and many other industries' engineering disciplines have adopted—because of economics, or otherwise adapted to—componentization, and matured into more productive and profitable industries.

CBSE techniques apply equally to one or two-person projects and large inter-enterprise CBSE endeavors. The chapters in this book enlarge on this underlying concept, with a specific focus on the engineering of software.

Chapter 3

Component Models and Component Services: Concepts and Principles

Rainer Weinreich
Johannes Sametinger

3.1 Introduction

In this chapter we describe, comment, and motivate discussions upon basic concepts and principles of component models and component services. We argue that component systems have been used at a coarse-grained level for decades. Discussions and disagreements concerning the term *component* have appeared because industry and academia have tried to develop technologies for smaller, fine-grained (refer to Chapter

16) components. In this chapter we extend the definitions from Chapter 1 to describe the essential elements of a component model.

3.1.1 Early Component Systems

Operating systems are among the first successful component systems (Szyperski, 1997). We expect readers to be familiar with at least one operating system, so we will use operating systems to illustrate the basic ideas behind component models and component model implementations. Operating systems provide an execution environment for software applications. In particular, operating systems present an abstraction of the underlying hardware to applications and regulate their shared access to various resources. They also provide basic services, such as memory management, file management, inter-process communication, process synchronization, and security. Without operating systems, each individual application would have to implement such general functionality. The availability of a wide range of services simplifies application development. Naturally, interfaces have to be defined to let applications use these services. These interfaces are called application programming interfaces (APIs).

To make an analogy, operating systems are component model implementations (see Chapter 1) for applications, which may be viewed as coarse-grained components (refer to Chapter 16). Once a component model implementation is developed and documented, multiple vendors can develop applications that use the low-level services provided by the component model implementation. At the granularity of an application there is a functioning component market. You can buy applications from different vendors and use them together on a single computer; the applications all adhere to the *standard* defined by an operating system. These standards are often part of a particular operating system implementation. Sometimes they are specified more explicitly and made available to the public, such as the UNIX 98 standard promoted by the Open Group (*www.opengroup.org*) and the Linux Standard Base (*www.linuxbase.org*).

3.1.2 Deficiencies of Early Component Systems

Continuing our analogy, we see several shortcomings. Components at the application level can be used, but they insufficiently enable widespread software reuse. The lack of reuse occurs because applications are too coarse-grained, they lack composition support, and operating systems lack domain-specific standards.

- *Lack of granularity*—Applications are too coarse-grained to improve software reuse. Application developers are often required to design and implement common functionality that any application may have. Component-based software engineering (CBSE) seeks to factor out these commonalties into either services provided by the component model implementation or components that could be purchased and integrated into a component infrastructure. A central concept of CBSE is to develop technologies for smaller, fine-grained components and enable a similar degree of reuse on the level of application parts as was possible at the application level.
- *Lack of composition support*—While applications have long been units of independent deployment, there has typically been no support for composition, including third-party composition (recall the definition of the term "software component" in Chapter 1). In fact, operating systems ensure that applications execute in complete isolation from each other. Mechanisms such as inter-process communication have been introduced to enable data exchange among applications, but application interfaces are often poorly specified and composition standards are missing. While applications deploy in the operating system and use its services, they are rarely units of composition.
- *Lack of domain-specific standards*—The services provided by an operating system are too general to support specific application domains. For example, a simulation system needs different services and APIs than a process control system or a telecommunication application.

The goal of CBSE is to develop software systems by composing reusable components at a finer level of granularity than applications. Naturally, these fine-grained components need standards for interaction and composition, as well as standardized infrastructures and services. The challenge of CBSE is to define component models with such standards and to provide associated component model implementations to enable components and component infrastructures to be designed, implemented, and deployed.

3.1.2.1 Components and Objects

CBSE is commonly considered the next step after object-oriented programming. It is not surprising that components are often related to objects and sometimes the term *component* is simply used as a synonym for object. However, the concepts of components and objects are independent, although most component models are based on object-oriented concepts. To avoid further confusion we will briefly characterize objects and components and outline their differences.

Objects are entities that encapsulate state and behavior and have a unique identity. The behavior and structure of objects are defined by classes. A class serves multiple purposes. First, it implements the concept of an abstract data type (ADT) and provides an abstract description of the behavior of its objects. Class names are often used as type names in strongly typed systems. Second, a class provides the implementation of object behavior. Third, a class is used for creating objects, that is, instances of the class.

Nearly all modern component models are based on the object-oriented programming paradigm. The basic premise of object-orientation is to construct programs from sets of interacting and collaborating objects. This does not change with component-based approaches. Components are similar to classes. Like classes, components define object behavior and create objects. Objects created by means of components are called component instances. Both components and classes make their implemented functionality available through abstract behavior descriptions called interfaces.

Unlike classes, the implementation of a component is generally completely hidden and sometimes only available in binary form. Internally, a component may be implemented by a single class, by multiple classes, or even by traditional procedures in a non-object-oriented programming language. Unlike classes, component names may not be used as type names. Instead, the concept of type (interface) and the concept of implementation are completely separated. Finally, the most important distinction is that software components conform to the standards defined by a component model.

3.2 Component Models

A component model defines a set of standards for component implementation, naming, interoperability, customization, composition, evolution, and deployment. A component model also defines standards for an associated component model implementation, the dedicated set of executable software entities required to support the execution of components that conform to the model.

There are numerous component models currently available. The main competing component models today are OMG's CORBA Component Model (CCM), Microsoft's (D)COM/COM+ family, and SUN Microsystems' JavaBeans and Enterprise JavaBeans. We need generally accepted component models to create a global component marketplace. It is not necessary to agree on one standard, but at the same time there should not be too many standards. The market share of a particular standard has to be large enough to make the development of compliant components worthwhile (Szyperski, 1997). In this chapter we comment on important elements constituting a component model.

3.2.1 Elements of a Component Model

In the global software component marketplace components are independently deployed and subject to third-party composition. This marketplace requires standards. Standards for communication and data exchange among components from different component producers are obvious. Such an interoperability standard—sometimes called a wiring or connection standard—is a central element in a component model. Other basic elements of a component model are standards for interfaces, naming, meta data, customization, composition, evolution, and deployment (see Table 3-1).

A component model can also have specialized standards for describing domain-specific features required for certain applications. For example, the composition of components in domains with concurrent activities requires appropriate standardized threading models and synchronization mechanisms. An open distributed processing system requires standards for remote method invocation and security. Three-tiered business applications need standardized transaction services and database APIs. Finally, a component model for compound

Table 3-1: *Basic Elements of a Component Model*

Standards for	Description
Interfaces	Specification of component behavior and properties; definition of Interface Description Languages (IDL)
Naming	Global unique names for interfaces and components
Meta data	Information about components, interfaces, and their relationships; APIs to services providing such information
Interoperability	Communication and data exchange among components from different vendors, implemented in different languages
Customization	Interfaces for customizing components. User-friendly customization tools will use these interfaces
Composition	Interfaces and rules for combining components to create larger structures and for substituting and adding components to existing structures
Evolution Support	Rules and services for replacing components or interfaces by newer versions
Packaging and Deployment	Packaging implementation and resources needed for installing and configuring a component

documents (like OLE) needs to specify part and container relationships and interfaces. Domain-specific component models offer such special functionality in the component model implementation.

3.2.2 Interfaces, Contracts, and Interface Definition Languages

The main purpose of software components is software reuse. The two main types of software reuse are white-box reuse and black-box reuse. *White-box reuse* means that the source of a software component is fully available and can be studied, reused, adapted, or modified. White-box reuse plays a major role in object-oriented frameworks that rely heavily on inheritance for reusing software implementations (Gamma et al., 1995). The problem with white-box reuse is that component consumers depend on the internals of a component and they will be affected adversely if the internals change.

Black-box reuse is based on the principle of information hiding (Parnas, 1972), which states that a component should reveal as little about its inner workings as possible. Users of a component may only rely on interfaces, which are descriptions or specifications of component behavior. By using interfaces, components may be changed internally so long as they continue to satisfy the responsibilities defined by their interfaces. Changes to interfaces are made explicit and tools, such as compilers, can statically verify compatibility with client components.

An interface is not a constituent part of a component, but serves as a *contract* between a component and its clients. An interface specifies the services a client may request from a component; the component must provide an implementation of these services. Additionally, an interface may include constraints on the usage of these services that must be considered by both the component and its clients.

Interface specifications are a central element in a component model. A component model defines how a component's behavior is described by means of interfaces, other (nonfunctional) specifications, and appropriate documentation. A component model defines the elements that may constitute an interface as well as the semantic meaning of these elements. Well-known elements of an interface are

- Names of semantically-related operations
- Their parameters
- Valid parameter types

Interfaces may also include exceptions that may be raised, preconditions and postconditions that have to be met when using individual operations, and partial specifications of the expected behavior of a component implementing the interface (Büchi and Weck, 1999). Many component models have an interface definition language (IDL) for describing interfaces and their elements using an implementation-independent notation.

The component model may define a set of specific interfaces that need to be implemented by components that conform to that model. In general, these interfaces will be used by the component model implementation to provide dedicated services expected by the components, such as transactions or security.

3.2.3 Naming

The global marketplace requires uniquely identifiable components and interfaces. Name clashes (when two different components are assigned the same name) have to be avoided or at least should be highly unlikely. Thus a standardized naming schema is a necessary part of a component model. The two main approaches to such a naming schema are unique identifiers and hierarchical namespaces.

- *Unique IDs*—Unique identifiers are generated by dedicated tools (for example, compilers) that use a combination of specific data to guarantee the uniqueness of each generated identifier. An example of unique IDs are Global Unique IDs (GUIDs), which are used by Microsoft's COM/DCOM/COM+ family. A GUID is a 128-bit number that combines a location identifier (for example, the address of an Ethernet card), the time of creation, and a randomly generated number. GUIDs were introduced by OSF/DCE, where they are called Universally Unique IDs (UUIDs)
- *Hierarchical name spaces*—Hierarchical namespaces are guaranteed to be unique if the top-level names are uniquely registered with a global naming authority. Most Java-based component models use hierarchical namespaces (although there is no global naming authority). SUN Microsystems advises manufacturers to adhere to a registered Internet domain name as the root name for their components (Gosling et al., 1996)

3.2.4 Meta Data

Meta data is information about interfaces, components, and their relationships. This information provides the basis for scripting and remote method invocation and is used by composition tools and reflective programs (see Maes, 1987 and Kiczales, 1991 for a good treatment of reflection). A component model must specify how meta data is described and how it can be obtained. Component model implementations must provide dedicated services allowing the meta data to be retrieved. There are many ways in which metadata can be provided, such as interface and implementation repositories of CORBA-based systems, type libraries in COM-based systems, and introspection in Java-based systems.

3.2.5 Interoperability

Software component composition is possible only if components from different vendors can be connected and are able to exchange data and share control through well-defined communication channels. Component interoperability or wiring standards are thus a central element of any component model.

An operating system executes applications in separate and isolated process address spaces, but communicating components may reside in the same space. If the component model allows the implementation of components in different programming languages, calling conventions must be standardized at the binary level to ensure interoperability of these components. Even if component implementations share the same language, the binary layout of interfaces and parameter types may still be different. Interoperability of components within a process address space is possible if the component model defines the binary interface structure and calling conventions.

A component model may also support communication of components across processes on the same computer or over the network. Remote interoperability is based on remote method calls (RMCs), an extension of the concept of remote procedure calls (RPCs) introduced by Birell and Nelson (1984). An RMC consists of a client invoking a method of a remote server. To the client an RMC appears similar to a local method invocation because the client actually invokes a method of a local proxy object that offers the same interface as the remote component. The proxy transforms the method invocation (including parameters) into a linearized network format (a process called *marshalling*) and sends the data to a corresponding *stub* object on the remote machine. The stub receives the data, reconstructs the invocation (unmarshalling), and forwards the invocation request locally to the component instance for which it was intended. Proxy and stub are called stub/skeleton in CORBA-based systems.

A component model supports distributed components by defining common data representations and invocation semantics. Often component models also standardize the network protocols used for communicating among different components based on the same component model. Examples for remote method specifications are the Simple Object Access Protocol (SOAP) for Windows, .NET platforms (*msdn.microsoft.com/soap*), Remote Method Invocation (RMI) for Java-based platforms (*java.sun.com/products/jdk/rmi*), and Internet Inter-Orb Protocol (IIOP) for CORBA-based systems (*www.omg.org*). SOAP, for example, uses the eXtensible Markup Language (XML) for data encoding and the HyperText Transfer Protocol (HTTP) as standard transport protocol. To increase programmer productivity, interactive development environments (IDEs) supporting a particular component model usually provide dedicated tools for automatically generating proxies and stubs for remote communication. More sophisticated component model implementations support on-the-fly proxy and stub generation (or generic proxies) based on metadata from component interfaces.

An interoperability problem of a different sort occurs when developers attempt to connect together different component models that support incompatible remote method specifications. A component model should explicitly define how to *bridge* communication among implementations of different component models. For example, the CORBA Specification (OMG, 1999) describes how to access Microsoft COM objects from CORBA environments and vice versa.

3.2.6 Customization

Interoperability standards and meta data about components and interfaces provide the basis for component customization and composition. We define component customization as the ability of a consumer to adapt a component prior to its installation or use. Since components are generally treated in black-box fashion, revealing as little as possible of their implementation, components can only be customized using clearly defined customization interfaces. A customization interface enables customization and deployment tools to modify simple properties, or even complex behavior, by providing instances of other components as parameters to customization functions. Customization tools may learn about the customization interfaces of components using meta data services.

3.2.7 Composition

Component composition or assembly is the combination of two or more software components that yields a new component behavior. A component composition standard supports the creation of a larger structure by connecting components and the insertion or substitution of components within an existing structure (see Chapter 1). Such a structure is a component infrastructure, sometimes called a component framework. The components within a component infrastructure interact with each other, typically, through method invocations. The two basic types of component interactions are *client/server* and *publish/subscribe*. Components may act as clients, requesting information from, or method invocations of, other components. A component may register itself with another component or a dedicated service and receive notifications of pre-defined events. The component model must define how to design interfaces to support such composition. Meta data about imported and exported interfaces of a component is required for composition tools and languages.

Various approaches to component composition at different levels of abstraction have been identified (Weinreich, 1997). Components may be connected using all-purpose programming languages, scripting or glue languages, visual programming or composition tools, or component infrastructures. Glue languages, such as VisualBasic, JavaScript, and TCL, support component composition at a higher level of abstraction than all-purpose programming languages, such as C++ and Java. Composition through visual programming raises the level of abstraction further, and there are drawbacks to visual approaches, such as the lack of density and structure of graphical representations and the extra effort needed for graphic editing and layout operations (Petre, 1995).

The disadvantage of composition languages and tools is that the glue code has to be written or graphically specified from inception. Maximum reuse is achieved with component infrastructures designed for a specific domain where the interaction among component instances is predefined. Composition with a component infrastructure is a matter of inserting and substituting components conforming to the interaction standards defined by the component infrastructure. Interaction standards specify which interfaces participating components must implement and rules governing component interaction.

Component infrastructures enable not only the reuse of individual components but of an entire design. For example, Weinreich (1997) describes a trader-based component infrastructure for graphic editors, Szyperski and Pfister (1999) describe a component infrastructure that supports compound documents, and Praehofer et al. (2001) describe a component infrastructure, based on JavaBeans, for simulation systems.

Only a well-designed component infrastructure enables the effective and efficient assembly of components.

3.2.8 Evolution Support

Component-based systems require support for system evolution. Components acting as a server for other components might have to be replaced by newer versions providing new or improved functionality. A new version may not only have a different implementation but may provide modified or new interfaces. Existing clients of such components should, ideally, not be affected or should be affected as little as possible. In addition, old and new versions of a component might need to co-exist in the same system. Rules and standards for component evolution and versioning are thus an exceptionally important part of a component model.

3.2.9 Packaging and Deployment

Widely accepted component model standards, as well as high-bandwidth Internet connections, will change the deployment of what is now called *shrink-wrapped* software. It will become superfluous to bundle big software systems and their documentation to sell off-the-shelf. In addition to well-defined component model implementations, only small components will be needed to construct applications. Fast Internet connections will allow component consumers to conveniently download packaged components with documentation to develop comprehensive software systems.

A component model must describe how components are packaged so they can be independently deployed. A component is deployed, that is, installed and configured, in a component infrastructure. The component must be packaged with anything that the component producer expects will not exist in the component infrastructure. This may include the program code, configuration data, other components, and additional resources. A deployment description provides information about the contents of a package (or of a number of related packages) and other information that is necessary for the deployment process. This description is analyzed by the target component infrastructure and used for installing and configuring a component properly.

The deployment standard specifies structure and semantics for deployment descriptions and it may define the format of packages. In addition, the component model may define processes for deployment, including component registration.

3.3 Component Model Implementations and Services

An important part of a component model is the standardization of the run-time environment to support the execution of components. This includes the specification of interfaces to both general and more domain-specific run-time services. General services to support object-based component systems include object creation, life-cycle management, object-persistence support, and licensing. Component models for distributed systems additionally have to define services for:

- Other forms of communication, such as message queues
- Remote event-based notification
- Locating remote services
- Security

Component models supporting the construction of multi-tiered information systems may specify data access APIs and services for transaction management and load balancing.

A component-based design will typically reflect the standardization process from general to more domain-specific services (see Figure 3-1). For example, a general component model for distributed systems may form the base on top of which additional, more domain-specific component infrastructures and services may be defined. Horizontal services and infrastructures provide additional functionality across multiple domains. Typical examples of such services include user interface management services, such as compound documents, and system management services. Vertical services and infrastructures support a particular domain. Examples are financial, healthcare and telecommunication services.

An example of such a family of standards that is built on a general component model is the object management architecture (OMA). The OMA is defined by the Object Management Group (OMG), a non-

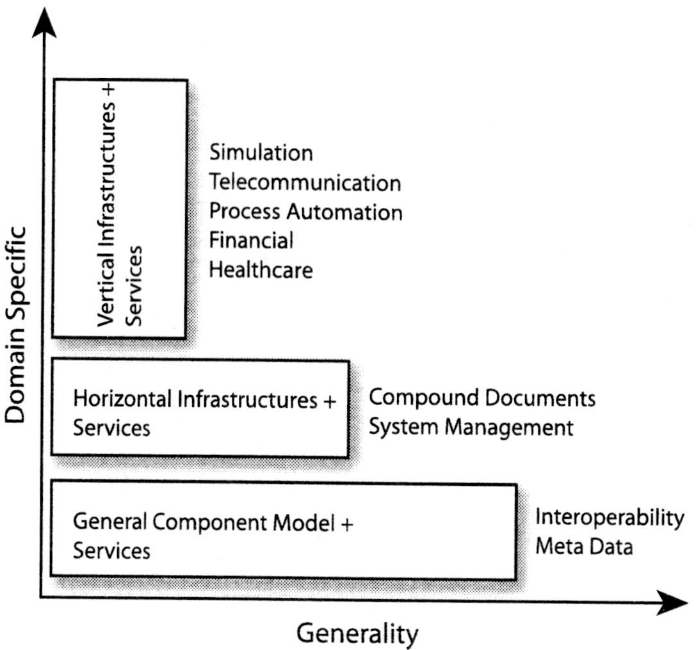

Figure 3-1: *From general to domain-specific standards.*

profit organization with about 800 industrial and academic members (*www.omg.org*). At the heart of this model is the Common Object Request Broker Architecture (CORBA), an interoperability standard for distributed object-based applications supporting various implementation languages. CORBAservices and CORBAfacilities are specifications built upon CORBA. CORBAservices are a standard for general services of distributed object-systems while CORBAfacilities standardizes horizontal services. The most specialized standards of the OMA are vertical services for various application domains.

Other well-known component models such as Microsoft's COM family and Sun's JavaBeans define similar services that are useful for systems in multiple domains. All major component model implementation vendors are also developing domain-specific interaction and composition standards.

3.4 Conclusion

We introduced the concept of component models using an analogy comparing operating systems with component model implementations. Operating systems provide the basic component model for applications through interfaces and services and provide integration and communication mechanisms. CBSE makes it possible to consider fine-grained components to enable more flexible component composition. CBSE will enhance the level of software reuse and provide necessary component models for establishing component marketplaces at this level. Standardized component models are necessary to realize this vision.

We have presented the basic concepts and principles of component models and component model implementations. Component models define standards for interfaces, naming, interoperability, customization, composition, evolution, packaging, and deployment. Additionally, specifications of run-time environments and services are needed to standardize component models. Typically, component model implementations exist on top of an operating system. However, some operating systems, such as Microsoft Windows, have already begun to incorporate component model implementations. Eventually, operating systems may directly serve as component model implementations for CBSE.

Operating Systems

Operating systems provide:
- an abstraction of the underlying hardware (infrastructure)
- an execution environment
- basic services for applications

Component Models

Component models define standards for naming, meta data, component behavior specification, component implementation, interoperability, customization, composition, and deployment.

Component Model Implementation

Component model implementations are based on a particular component model. They provide:

- a run-time environment
- basic services
- horizontal services that are useful across multiple domains
- vertical services providing functionality for a particular domain for software components

Chapter 4

An Example Specification for Implementing a Temperature Regulator Software Component

Janet Flynt
Jason Mauldin

4.1 Introduction

This example chapter illustrates a temperature regulation class implemented as a component. The example will be used to demonstrate software safety design, with consideration to potential software and hardware failures. This example will utilize the Unified Modeling Language (UML 1.3, 1999) as an aid in the analysis, design, and documentation of components and ANSI/UL 1998, *Software in Programmable Components*, to assist in developing safety-related components for embedded systems. This serves to provide readers with a real life example of what the design of an embedded (software and hardware) system looks like on paper. For those who have never designed a component-based system, let us make this perfectly clear: designing an infrastructure on paper is difficult enough; designing it while writing code is impossible. The necessity of all the diagrams and textual documents explains why CBSE software engineers and designers devote so much time to getting the design right. A mistake in design can cost many days or weeks in trying to find another way to recreate the infrastructure.

Robert Davidson prepared the previous version of the hot plate example, which he and Janet Flynt presented as part of the tutorial entitled *Developing the Link Between Product Safety Standards for Software* at the 1996 Annual Reliability and Maintainability Symposium.

> **Note**: This is the form that proposed certification documents would support, including a table of contents and information about previous versions of the document.

4.2 Purpose

This example is intended to illustrate the use of various techniques to implement a software component. The functionality of the software is a temperature regulation component. The software is intended for use in various devices and software products that require temperature control.

Table 4-1: *A Sample TOC*

Table of Contents

Note: This example is strictly hypothetical and intended solely to illustrate basic concepts. No inference should be made concerning the compliance or noncompliance of actual software, present or future, with the requirements of Underwriters Laboratories, Inc. based on this example.

This example also introduces the idea of a Technical File, which is a component-descriptive file recounting the behavior, assumptions, and structure of the component before, and at the time it was listed by UL.

The information contained herein is intended as an introduction to the component, how the component is designed, and how to interface with the component.

Much of the Technical File is developed using The Unified Modeling Language (UML) diagrams. The UML is designed for use during all phases of the component software life cycle (CSLC) process. It provides a standard and consistent layout that makes it simple to communicate a complex design to those with little experience involved in the project. Of course, they will need your help in becoming proficient with your design. You will find various diagrams specified by the UML. These diagrams contain information specific to your project and each be followed by a brief explanation. For more information on the UML, see *www.omg.org*.

The example will also consider safety requirements because the component will be used in applications that involve products that must meet safety standards.

> **Note**: The example is not intended to actually be implemented. It is an oversimplified view of software that controls temperature. In an actual implementation, the component would need to retain a recent history, eliminate erroneous data, and implement a device control feature more elaborate than the one illustrated here.

4.3 Technical File

The Technical File is used as an introduction to the software component. It includes overview information on the component that includes version number, a brief description, input/output variables, language that the component was implemented in, and other vital information.

The version number listed in the technical file of the component is the overall version. It can be used internally to reference the information relevant to this release of the component. Relevant information can include version numbers of the algorithm, the UML diagrams, the code implementation, and other information.

A brief description along with the data information should include enough information to allow a component consumer or purchasing end-user to determine if the component is relevant to what they are trying to accomplish and to determine if further investigation of the component is needed.

4.3.1 Sample Technical File

Name: Temperature Regulator
Version: v.rr (version number 0.9.1.2., release number 62)
Source Code Checksum: 0x2741
Brief Description: This software is used as a regulating function for products that need temperature regulation. The software is designed to read inputs and maintain a constant temperature. It also contains safety functionality for the monitoring of a device and self-checking so that it stays within set limits.
Language: C++
Input Variables:

- DeviceTemp: int = 0
- ProbeTemp: int = 0
- SetPointTemp: int = 0
- AlarmLower: int = 0
- AlarmUpper: int = 0

Output Variables:

- DeviceCtl: bool = False
- ShutdownCtl: bool = False

Certifications: (Standards Information)
Assumptions: The component was designed for use on a 16-bit or larger processor. It will not function correctly with an eight-bit processor. Operating ranges are [-100,500]. This component does not contain functionality for signal smoothing. This functionality may be added later.

4.4 Variable Definitions

The names of the input variables and their definitions and values are provided in Table 4-2.

4.4.2 Input Variables

Table 4-2: *Input Variables and Their Definitions*

Name	ProbeTemp
Description:	Temperature as measured by temperature probe
Units:	Temperature
Data Type:	Integer
Safety Related:	Yes
Values:	[-100,500]

Name	DeviceTemp
Description:	Device temperature as measured by the sensing thermocouple
Units:	Temperature
Data Type:	Integer
Values:	[-100,500]

Name	SetPointTemp
Description:	Desired temperature value
Units:	Temperature
Data Type:	Integer
Values:	[-100,500]

Name	AlarmUpper
Description:	Upper limit for notification of desired temperature value
Units:	Temperature
Data Type:	Integer
Values:	[-100,500]

Name	AlarmLower
Description:	Lower limit for notification of desired temperature value
Units:	Temperature
Data Type:	Integer
Values:	[-100,500]

4.4.3 Output Variables

The names of the output variables and their definitions and values are provided in Table 4-3.

Table 4-3: *Output Variables and Their Definitions*

Name	DeviceCtl
Description:	Signal from module for on/off control of a device
Units:	Binary
Data Type:	Boolean
Values:	1 (on, energized) 0 (off, de-energized)

Name	ShutdownCtl
Description:	Additional control to disable software/hardware in the event of an unsafe condition.
Units:	Binary
Data Type:	Boolean
Values:	1 (on, energized) 0 (off de-energized)

4.5 Safety Requirements

- If `DeviceTemp` or `ProbeTemp` is outside the range determined by `AlarmLower` and `AlarmUpper`, then `ShutdownCtl` shall be set to a value of 1.

4.6 FMEA for SafetyChk.

Input	Failure Mode	Output	Value	Safety Related
HeaterTemp (any value)	SafetyChk Not Executed	ShutdownCtl	De-Energized	Yes
SafetyLimit = 550	Used <= instead of >	ShutdownCtl	Energized	No
	Used De-Energized instead of Energized	ShutdownCtl	De-Energized	Yes

4.7 The UML Diagrams

Figures 4-1 to 4-5 are samples of implementing the UML specification in this component description.

The UML diagrams are produced to present multiple views of a software component. The diagrams provide a model of the software component so that who needs to find information will have a standardized method to assess the design and validate the completed product against the *requirements* and design. The included diagrams are only an introduction to the complete UML model. They are provided as a starting point in developing diagrams that may be useful to you.

Use Case Model Detail: Set Operational Parameters

Used by:

[Actors]

User Input, Displayer)

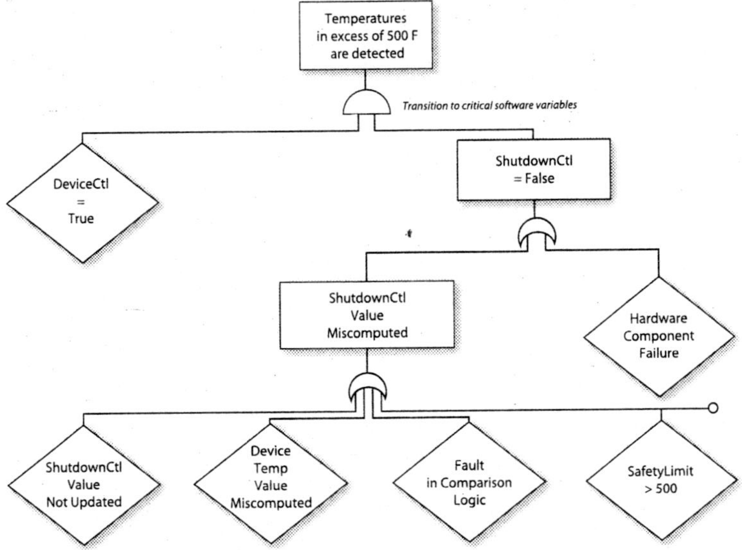

Figure 4-1: *Fault tree.*

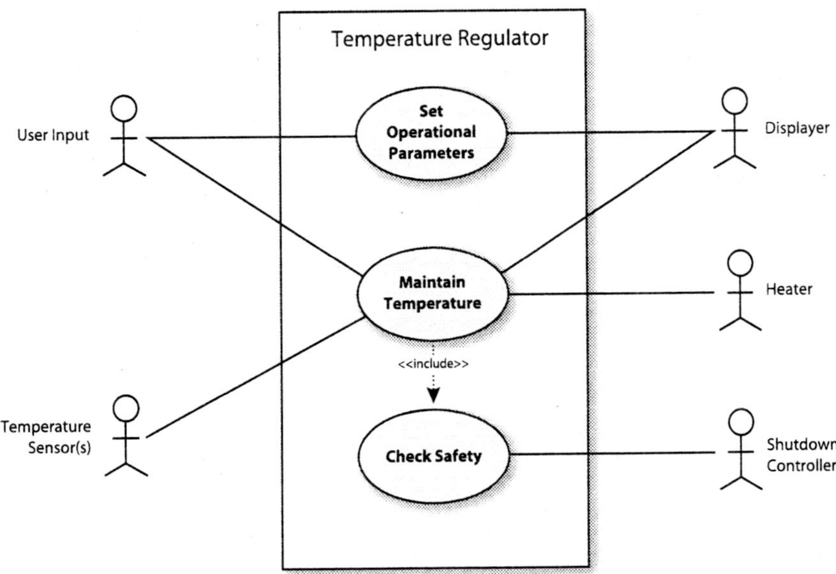

Figure 4-2: *Use case model.*

Intent:

To accept and validate operational values for the Regulator, for example, Alarm Upper Temperature

Description:

User supplies type and value of operational parameter
(types are: Set Point, Alarm Upper, Alarm Lower
Component validates value for range and consistency, for example, Alarm Upper greater than Lower
Component sets valid values
System returns results of validation

Pre Conditions:

None

Post Conditions:

Valid operational parameters stored

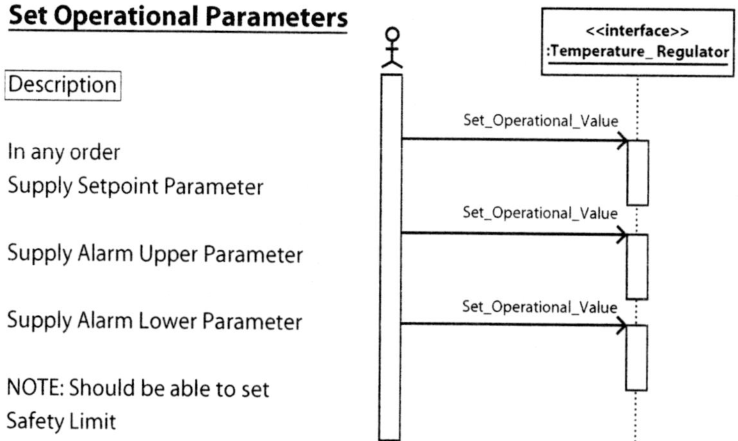

Figure 4-3: *Sequence diagram: set operational parameters.*

Use Case Model Detail: 'Maintain Temperature'

Used by:

[Actors]

Temperature Sensor(s), Displayer, Heater, User Input

[Used Use Cases]

Check Safety

Intent:

To ensure temperature remains constant and within safe operating limits

Description:

Temperature Sensors (device & probe) supply values
Perform Safety Check
IF safety check okay
  Component records sensor values
  Component checks for alarm conditions
  IF not in alarm condition
    Component compares sensor values...
    ...and adjusts Heater if necessary
  ELSE
    Component signals alarm
  END alarms
END safety check

Pre Conditions:

Component is active (ON) with valid parameters

Post Conditions:

Sensor values are stored

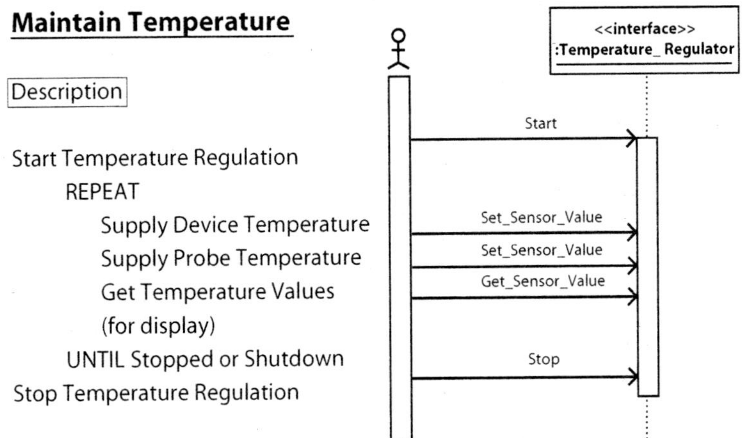

Figure 4-4: *Sequence diagram: maintain temperature.*

Use Case Model Detail: 'Check Safety'

Used by:

[Actors]

Shutdown Controller

[Used By Use Cases]
Maintain Temperature

Intent:
To ensure operation with safe conditions

Description:
Component compares value against preset safety limit (550)
If outside limit, Shutdown signal issued

Pre Conditions:
Safety limit set at 550

Post Conditions:
None

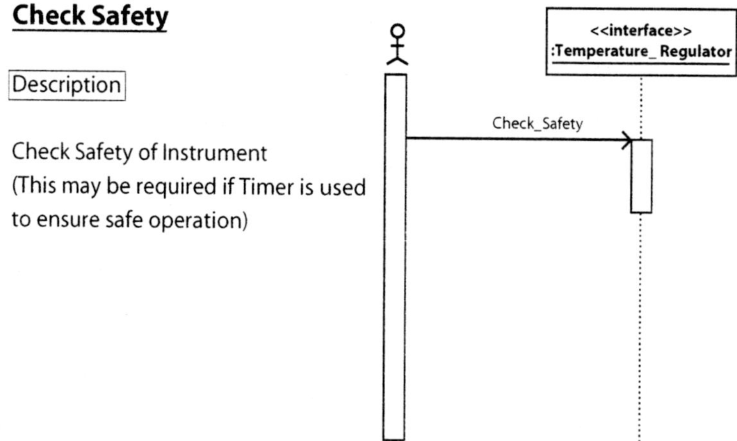

Figure 4-5: *Sequence diagram: check safety.*

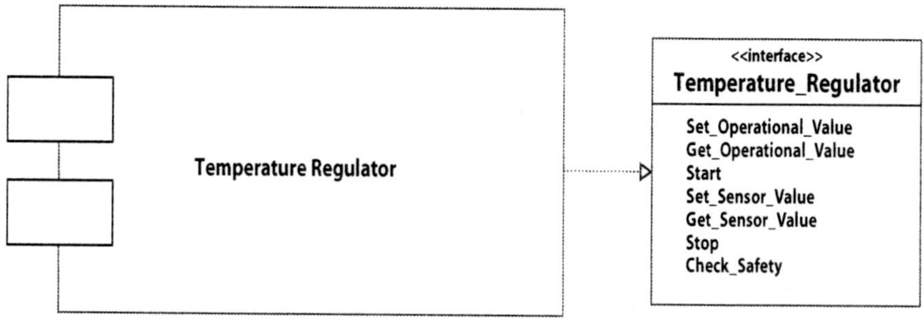

Figure 4-6: *Class model.*

4.8 Laboratory Hot Plate – Example

4.8.1 Product Description

This example product, using the Temperature Regulator Class, is a laboratory hot plate. A hot plate is typically intended to heat liquids. The electrical components consist of a power on and off switch, a resistance-type heating element, and a microprocessor-based programmable electronic system (PES). The components must have hardware and software designed to interface with the software component.

Laboratory Hot Plate Illustration

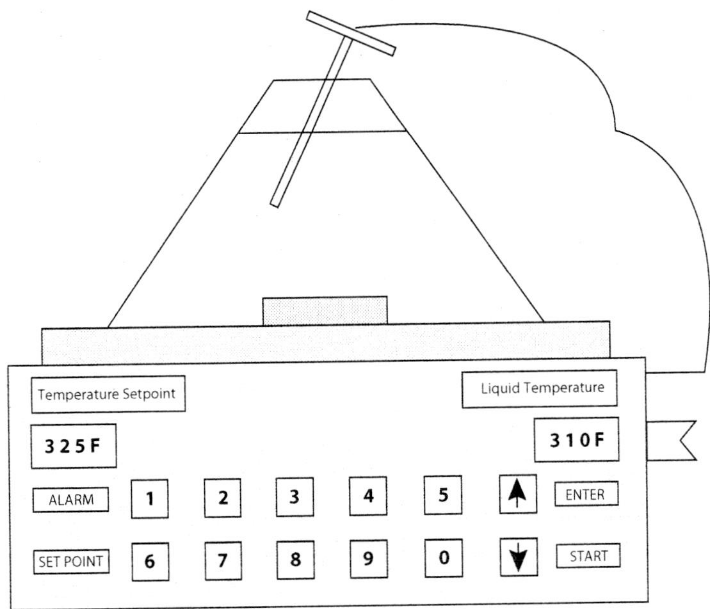

Figure 4-7: *Hot plate example.*

The temperature sensor in the hot plate is a thermocouple that generates a millivolt output proportional to the temperature of the plate. The desired operating temperature is selected by the user by means of a potentiometer coupled with a constant current source that generates a millivolt output proportional to the desired temperature selected. The thermocouple output and temperature select output are fed as inputs to the PES that includes the needed circuitry to convert the analog to digital inputs and to compare the desired temperature to the measured temperature. When the temperature measured by the sensor falls below the selected value the microprocessor causes the control relay to be energized. When the temperature exceeds the selected value voltage is removed from the relay coil.

Electrical Schematic

> **Note:** The heater temperature is not displayed. This feature could be a later enhancement.

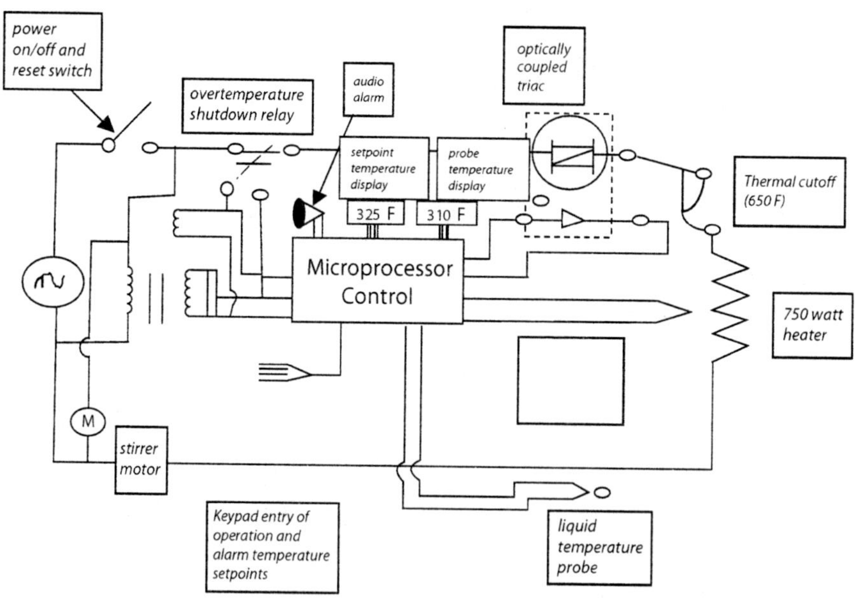

Figure 4-8: *Hot plate electrical schematic.*

The outputs of the PES include signals to operate digital displays of the selected and measured temperatures and to energize and de-energize a relay that controls current to the heater. In addition to the

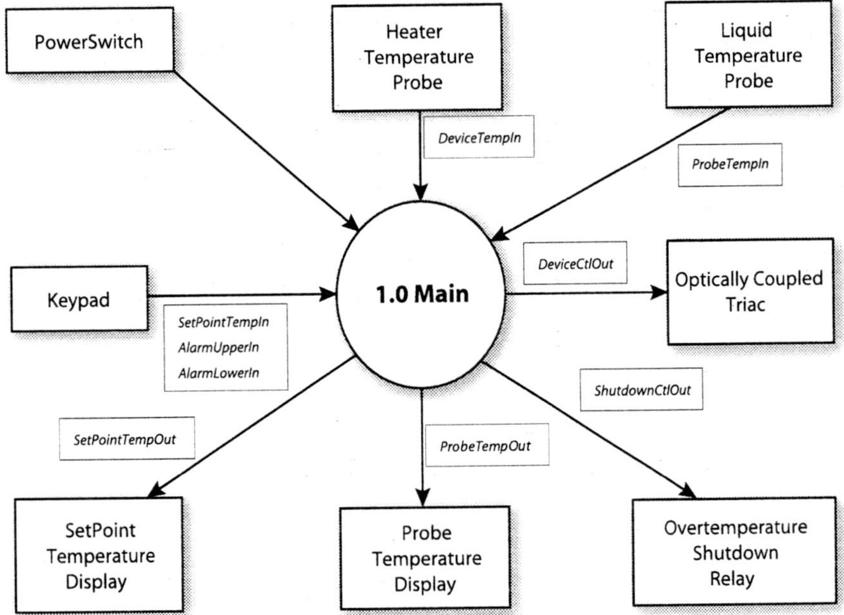

Figure 4-9: *Hot plate example hardware/software interface.*

thermocouple sensor built into the hot plate, the product can also be controlled by connection to an optional remote thermocouple probe that can be inserted into the heated substance. A temperature sensor select switch selects either the hot plate thermocouple or the remote sensor thermocouple as the value to be compared with the selected value. An independent connection from the hot plate thermocouple to the PES monitors the hot plate temperature at all times.

4.9 Conclusion

With this example, we hope that you have learned something about components. As described by the editors in Chapter 1, a component is more that its source code assembled in an encapsulated black box with interfaces to other software or hardware components. A software component must be thoroughly documented so that component consumers, purchasing end-users, testers, and maintainers of the software and hardware components can maintain and evolve the system through many versions of the software, defect patches to the software component, and enhancements to the hardware system.

Since this system is safety-critical programmable software operating in a programmable component, it is subject to third-party certification. For more of what a ten-employee organization can do to assure processes are sufficient to meet the requirements of the ANSI/UL 1998 standard that governs safety critical software component, refer to Chapter 41, written by colleagues at Underwriters Laboratories. If we can ensure safety-critical components, we can certainly help the software engineering community certify operating systems, applications, and software components.

Part I

Summary

The chapters in this part are the result of component-based software life cycle design and construction. Since the definitions and their real world explanations are the foundations of the book, the definition chapter itself went through over 30 increments, the concepts and principles chapter went through at least 15 (we stopped counting), and the "examples" chapter underwent innumerable UL design inspections, in addition to our reviews. That is the design process of component-based development as dictated by CBSE.

As the book title states, CBSE means putting the pieces together. We left out the concept of assembling the pieces together precisely. Could you imagine putting together a 1,000-piece puzzle where the pieces fit only slightly, haphazardly? We can't. Can you imagine the feeling you'd have after purchasing a $35,000 automobile and you discover when you arrive home that the doors don't close precisely. It happens, but ever so rarely.

You can imagine, however, buying software that does not install correctly and crashes your computer the first time it runs. You wait on the phone 45 minutes before you connect with a person who has never encountered your particular problem. He will call you back after a conference with more experienced technical representatives. The next day you get a call and an answer, but it does not work. After the second call from the technical representative, the application works effectively, but only for a while.

Unfortunately, this situation is reflective of the state of software today. This part is representative of the entire book because we offer a solution, not a panacea. The book, as we will continually remind you, is a state-of-the-art book; it is not a handbook. We strive to develop a CBSE practice, but we are currently a subdiscipline of software engineering, a community that appears to disdain certification and licensure. This book is an indication that the field of CBSE desires to develop beyond software engineering that has neither a state-of-the-art book nor a handbook. We aim to become an engineering science. The definitions necessitate that goal.

Where do we fall short? The definitions, developed over 19 months by a group of about 20 experts, are now available for widespread review. First, support for, and severe criticisms of, the definitions will follow. The definitions will grow because of both. Second, researchers in industrial organizations and academicians conducting small projects will produce empirical studies using our definitions. We welcome their studies. Empiricism will inform all involved of the assets and weaknesses of our definitions and permit other industrial researchers and academicians to take the basis of our work and make our fledgling definitions grow to full potential.

Likewise, as the definitions grow, so will the concept and principles of software components. In reality, the concepts and essence of components are more mature than the definitions. They have been tested in other forms, but not using the definitions provided by this book. Weinreich and Sametinger had significantly more courage than most to abandon

- Pseudo-definitions that are descriptions accepted by the field as definitions
- Circular references that confuse true definitions
- Definitions from others eras of software engineering carried forward to CBSE that masqueraded as component-based definitions, but had nothing to do with CBSE but to carry the authors' names to a new discipline

Weinreich and Sametinger demonstrate clearly how the definitions are applied by designers, developers, and testers to assure robust components, component models, and component model implementations.

Their descriptions of component models and component infrastructures are immediate classics. Yes, they will be argued, but the descriptions are clear and describe the essence of their concepts. We are envious when we state, "They took 15 months of work and made it real and readable, a worthy task of exceptionally knowledgeable scholars."

Hedley Apperly's chapter comparing high-rise building construction and CBSE is an unexpected masterpiece. Only an engineer with one foot in mechanical engineering and the other in software engineering would come up with such an example. To realize the metaphor involving the two forms of engineering virtually phase for phase is ingenious. Yet, engineering follows established patterns, as in the approach of Frederick Taylor, the creator of the scientific management system, which guides much of modern day engineering. Kanigel's (1997) biography of Taylor is entitled *The One Best Way*. It refers to Taylor's insistence that one method of solving an industrial engineering problem had to be the "best" method. For Taylor, the "best" solution for each provided discrete and simple steps—or components—that formed the basis for the engineer's fundamental problem-solving approach. That notion has so permeated society as a whole that almost every business setting, from industrial manufacturing to fast food preparation, still searches for "one best way" of conducting their processes. Most importantly for this discussion, Taylor's process for resolving efficiency problems involved breaking large problems into smaller ones and implementing solutions as discrete "components."

John Speed agrees with us that many software engineers and computer scientists are not trained in this scientific tradition. Apparently, Hedley Apperly has been educated in Taylorism because you can repeatedly determine in his chapter that he has previously searched for, or is now attempting to develop, the one best way. His tables comparing construction to CBSE are invaluable. There is a correspondence between construction engineering and CBSE on a one-to-one level at almost all phases of development. Notice, however, the many different phases of construction development and the corresponding phases of CBSE. We have to rethink the traditional five phases of software development and adopt a more engineering-based approach to CBSE. Also, notice the limited role that architects have in high-rise building design.

In real life they are relegated to residences and small buildings, whereas in CBSE most software systems are large domain-based systems. We agree with Hedley and the engineering community that software architecture, although well accepted in software engineering, is misplaced in both software engineering and CBSE. As one engineer told us, "In engineering, there's just increasingly refined levels of design. There's no such thing as architecture. We work with architects to appease our clients' needs for aesthetics, but the architects leave us alone when it comes to building sophisticated high-rise buildings."

Hedley's construction metaphor chapter and his Chapter 29 on "Configuration Management and Component Libraries" are outstanding examples of real-life needs for managing, finding, and delivering reusable components for later projects. We have a long way to go before CBSE can reuse parts as effectively as the construction industry. Hedley shows us the way, however, and provides an application to assist CBD librarians to help reuse committees and software engineers to accomplish the tasks of effective reuse.

Finally, the example in Chapter 4 presents the concept of documentation described in the definition chapter and demonstrates its importance. Can you imagine a black box component and its interfaces to the hardware unit and the OS describing only the interfaces? As editors, we would be really lost. Less experienced CBD designers and programmers would certainly find the interfaces indecipherable. Underwriters Laboratories presents the minimum documentation required for a software component designed for a programmable microelectronics device. In Chapter 38 Janet Flynt and Manoj Desai describe the benefits of certification. In our opinions, no third-party software components should compose with other third-party software components unless certification occurs on a voluntary basis. Yet, when we suggest voluntary certification, we also mean that the customer has the power, and the responsibility, to demand that the producers and the component consumer "voluntarily" submit to third-party certification to assure its end-users of a safety-critical product.

Certification applies not only to safety-critical components, but to any OS, application, or other software components that will affect the profits and well being of the company committed to the CBD project. As software engineers we have a fiduciary duty to our companies or contractors to comply with the state-of-the-art of CBSE. In this part, we began our presentation of the state-of-the-art of CBSE. Those who would aspire to be component-based software engineers must thoroughly understand this part before attempting the more complex parts and chapters that follow.

Part I

References

P. Allen and S. Frost, *Component-Based Development for Enterprise Systems: Applying the Select Perspective*, Cambridge University Press, Cambridge, UK, 1998.

J. Bellows, *Activity Diagrams and Operation Architecture, Part II*, CBD/e White Papers, *www.cbd-hq.com*, 2000.

A. Birell and B. Nelson, "Implementing Remote Procedure Calls," *ACM Transactions on Computer Systems*, Vol. 2, No. 1, Feb., 1984, pp. 39-59.

P. Bocij, D. Chaffey, A. Greasley, and S. Hickie, *Business Information Systems: Technology, Development and Management*, Financial Times—Prentice-Hall, Upper Saddle River, NJ, 1999.

M. Büchi and W. Weck, "The Greybox Approach: When Blackbox Specifications Hide Too Much," Technical Report Number 297, Turku Centre for Computer Science, Aug. 1999.

W. Councill, "Third-Party Testing and the Quality of Software Components," *IEEE Software*, Vol. 16, No. 4, July/Aug., 1999, pp. 55-57.

T. Demarco, *Why Does Software Cost So Much? And Other Puzzles of the Information Age*, Dorset House, New York, NY, 1995.

D. D'Souza and A. Wills, *Objects, Components, and Frameworks with UML: The Catalysis Approach*, Addison-Wesley, Reading, MA, 1999.

P. Eeles and O. Sims, *Building Business Objects*, John Wiley & Sons, New York, NY, 1998.

E. Gamma, R. Helm, R. Johnson, and J. Vlissides, *Design Patterns: Elements of Reusable Object-Oriented Software*, Addison-Wesley, Reading, MA, 1995.

J. Gosling, B. Joy, and G. Steele, *The Java Language Specification*, Addison-Wesley, Reading, MA, 1996.

ISO/IEC, ITU Recommendation X.902, Open Distributed Processing-Reference Model—Part 1: Overview, 1995a.

ISO/IEC, ITU Recommendation X.902, Open Distributed Processing-Reference Model—Part 2: Foundations, 1995b.

I. Jacobson, *The Object Advantage, Business Process Reengineering with Object Technology*, Addison-Wesley, Reading, MA, 1994.

R. Kanigel, *The One Best Way: Frederick Taylor and the Enigma of Efficiency*, Viking Penguin, New York, NY, 1997.

G. Kiczales, J. de Rivieres, and D. Bobrow, *The Art of the Metaobject Protocol*, MIT Press, Cambridge, MA, 1991.

P. Kruchten, *The Rational Unified Process, An Introduction*, Addison-Wesley, Reading, MA, 1999.

Linux Base, Standardizing the Penguin, *www.linuxbase.org*, 2000.

P. Maes, "Concepts and Experiments in Computational Reflection," Proceedings, 2nd International Object Oriented Programming Systems, Languages, and Applications (OOPSLA) Conference, Sigplan Notices, Vol. 22, No. 12, 1987, pp. 147-155.

B. Meyer, *Object-Oriented Software Construction*, 2nd Ed., Prentice Hall, Upper Saddle River, NJ, 2000.

Object Management Group, A Discussion of the Object Management Architecture, *www.omg.org*, Jan., 1997.

Object Management Group, The Common Object Request Broker: Architecture and Specification, Revision 2.3.1, *www.omg.org*, Oct., 1999.

D. Parnas, "A Technique for Software Module Specification with Examples," *Communications of the ACM*, Vol. 15, No. 5, May, 1972, pp. 330-336.

M. Petre, "Why Looking Isn't Always Seeing: Readership Skills and Graphical Programming," *Communications of the ACM*, Vol. 38, No. 6, June 1995, pp. 33-34.

H. Praehofer, J. Sametinger, and A. Stritzinger, "Concepts and Architecture of a Simulation Framework Based on the JavaBeans Component Model," *Journal of Future Generation Computer Systems*, Special Issue on Web-based Simulation, Elsevier Science, Vol. 16, No. 5, 2001, pp. 539-559.

K. Raymond, "Reference Model of Open Distributed Processing (RM-ODP): Introduction, CRC for Distributed Systems Technology," Centre for Information Technology Research, University of Queensland, Brisbane, Australia, *http://archive.dstc.edu.au/AU/research_news/odp/ref_model*, 1995.

C. Szyperski and C. Pfister, "Component-Oriented Programming: WCOP '96 Workshop Report," Special Issues in Object-Oriented Programming, 10th European Conference on Object-Oriented Programming (ECOOP) Workshop Reader, Linz, Austria, 1996, pp. 127-130.

C. Szyperski and C. Pfister, "BlackBox: A Component Framework for Compound User Interfaces," *Implementing Application Frameworks: Object-Oriented Application Frameworks at Work*, M. Fayad, D. Schmidt, and R. Johnson, eds., John Wiley & Sons, Inc., New York, NY, Sept., 1999.

C. Szyperski, *Component Software: Beyond Object-Oriented Programming*, Addison-Wesley, Reading, MA, 1997.

UL Standard for Safety for Software in Programmable Components, Underwriters Laboratories Inc., Northbrook, IL, May 1998.

Unified Modeling Language, 1.3, Object Management Group, *www.omg.org*.

Unified Modeling Language 1.3, Rational Software Corporation, *www.rational.com/uml/resources/documentation/index.jsp*, available in PDF or zipped PostScript.

R. Weinreich, "A Component Framework for Direct Manipulation Editors," Proceedings, The 25th International Conference on the Technology of Object-Oriented Languages and Systems (TOOLS), IEEE Computer Society Press, Melbourne, Australia, 1997, pp. 93-101.

Part II

The Case for Components

You should not assume that components are the only way to solve your problems. In fact, you should always beware of a salesman who tries to sell technology without understanding your needs. In Part I we presented our comprehensive definition of software components. Now we must convince you why you should consider using software component technology in your organization. It is important for us to do so, especially because of the well-documented, high-risk mistakes that occurred in the past decade as organizations struggled to develop state-of-the-art systems.

For component-based software engineering to be successful, we feel it is important to return to an engineering foundation. That is, instead of building software systems to include the most recent technology (the phrase "on the bleeding edge" comes to mind), software engineers should be using tried and tested processes and technologies that have proven themselves to be state-of-the-art.

Only managers and their integrated product teams (IPTs) can decide whether to use component technologies and on which projects. To help you make decisions we have brought together authors who provide their perspectives on the successes and failures in applying component-based software engineering. In some ways it is more important to learn about potential failures because you can identify whether your organization would be susceptible to the same failures.

There are many reasons why you should seriously consider component-based software engineering. First, CBSE embodies an engineering approach to solving complex systems that divides large projects into smaller subprojects. The earliest proponents of software engineering always envisioned this approach. Second, CBSE is language-independent and can easily be used with legacy systems. You can develop component-based solutions using C, C++, Visual Basic, and Java; you can also pursue CBSE with software written in FORTRAN and COBOL. CBSE has even been successfully applied to embedded software systems and other resource-constrained devices. Third, components are often the only answer for complex and mission-critical systems.

In this Part you will learn how to avoid the most common failures of component-based software engineering. In general, there are many organizational issues that must be resolved before successfully applying CBSE. We believe that migrating to a CBSE approach will help your organization better understand the roles played by all stakeholders in software systems. In particular, you should pursue an incremental strategy that incorporates CBSE technology in small pilot projects before launching major CBSE initiatives. We have assembled a group of chapters to help you begin to integrate CBSE.

To initiate your own CBSE efforts, you will probably have to present a convincing business case. Chapter 5, by John Williams, should provide you with all the supporting arguments you'll need. Will Tracz's Chapter 6 exposes many myths and other exaggerated claims about using COTS components in your organization while Chapter 8 highlights the mistakes likely to occur on enterprise-wide CBSE projects. Chapter 7 describes the numerous roles needed to successfully develop CBSE processes. In Chapter 9 you can learn from the successes of Hewlett-Packard in organizing their software assets into component infrastructures aligned with their hardware products.

John Williams starts with "The Business Case for Components," a lesson for CIOs, potential component development and reuse managers, development managers, software process managers, test managers, and quality assurance managers. The purchase and management of various forms of components have different requirements based on the components purchased, as well as the organization's readiness, infrastructure, and costs.

In Chapter 6 Will Tracz offers a concise presentation of the myths of purchasing and implementing COTS components and their corresponding realities. For naïve readers who have bought the "hype" of COTS components, Will provides a real-world view of components unavailable to even many of the later adopters of object-orientation, when salesmanship overwhelmed technology.

Paul Allen and Stuart Frost catalog the roles required to implement a highly functioning CBD and CBSE program in Chapter 7. As Paul and Stuart state, "The sheer diversity of required technical skills is also increasing, reflecting the wide range and deep complexity of today's technical issues." The costs of CBD and CBSE are higher at the commencement of a pilot project and decrease once the project produces reusable components. Still, be prepared to explain to your management the need for yet unforeseen but required roles.

In Chapter 8, "Common High-Risk Mistakes," Wojtek Kozaczynski takes a previous project and performs a public postmortem, a commendable gift in software engineering where we tend to sweep our pitfalls under the rug. People generally learn more from mistakes than successes, and Wojtek gives us a retrospective of a project where the managers experienced successes as well as mistakes. His chapter is useful because he explains the mistakes readers are likely to make.

Martin Griss is the most prolific author in this book, writing three chapters. In Chapter 9 Martin writes about the requirements for developing a successful product-line. A product-line is described as a "set of applications that share a common collection of requirements but also exhibit significant variability in requirements." Not only has he chosen to write about the development of a successful component-based project, but he also describes in detail the criteria for reusing components among various products that are similar enough to comprise a product-line.

This Part is intended for anyone interested in exploring the concept of implementing software components now or in the future. Just as the assembly line was bound to occur and revolutionized manufacturing, we believe CBD and CBSE will revolutionize software development. This Part, however, does not set false expectations. It provides stories of complex successes and mistakes, myths that must be challenged by realities, and roles that will change the resource structure of software development as we know it. Remember that Henry Ford's assembly line significantly decreased the cost of automobiles and eventually increased quality. Those were his unerring goals in automobile manufacturing, and in the world of software they are ours as authors and editors.

Chapter 5

The Business Case for Components

John Williams

5.1 Introduction

I recently heard of a doctor who sued his bank. It appears the bank kept bouncing his checks. It turns out he was overdrawn by $50,000. He complained that he went to medical school to become a doctor not an accountant. He was upset that he was expected to do more than practice medicine. The good doctor's attitude reminds me of many technical people I know. We work hard to understand technology and use it well. We often rankle at the thought of dealing with business cases, budgets, and schedules. These things are just not as neat and clean as technology. Just like the doctor, we find ourselves embroiled in tasks we would rather avoid.

However, you need a high-quality business case to successfully deploy component technology at the enterprise level. A business case provides both the rationale and plan for a project—in this case, deploying component technology. A well thought out business case identifies the benefits and risks in adopting a technology. It also calculates the costs and payback for using the technology. A good business case provides the foundation for technology success. Without it, you may never get the chance to deploy your technology.

As you move beyond simple GUI components, making a business case for component technology can be a complex task. No matter what approach you take to building a business case, you have to make assumptions about your technical environment, organization, infrastructure, and business drivers. Technology advocates often miss many factors while building their business case. This chapter should help you identify and understand the key issues you need to address in your business case. There are also critical problems for which you need to prepare.

Rather than promote a single approach, I will examine three different models for building your business case. The model you ultimately choose will depend on your goals and the level of component technology you are trying to introduce. These models are based on differing levels of technical sophistication, organizational preparedness, and commitment to the technology. No one model can meet all needs. However, you will see that, as shown in Figure 5-1, business models build on one another by identifying the incremental issues and costs you encounter as you move from one level of complexity to the next.

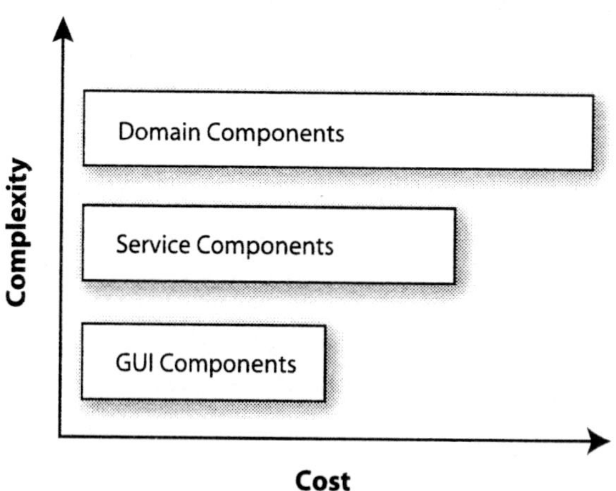

Figure 5-1: *Relationships between business models.*

5.2 Key Issues

There are important issues you need to consider in your business case. These include business goals for the technology, technical sophistication, organizational readiness, infrastructure support, and reuse. These issues are not isolated from one another, but interrelated. Overlooking any of them can lead to failure in deploying component technology at the enterprise level.

5.2.1 Business Goals

Business goals help you understand when you should or should not use component technology. You should not immediately assume that components are the only way to solve your problem. HTML and JavaScript can support a simple Web site. Perl is perfectly adequate for many CGI and scripting needs. If your application is simple or not mission-critical, non-component based tools may be quicker or cheaper to use.

When should you use component technology? Components are the right answer for complex and mission-critical systems. They are robust, scalable, and flexible. These are critical factors for mission-critical systems. Many find that component technology often trades simplicity for scalability and flexibility. Anyone who has deployed an n-tier application will acknowledge that this is more challenging than deploying a client/server or monolithic application. Simply managing the increased number of software assets and multiple platforms makes it a more challenging task. This trade-off with simplicity is not always the case, but it is usually true for most medium to complex applications.

One problem is that the potential payback for components may be too low for a given application. Suppose your company is new to component technology and doesn't have the infrastructure or skills needed to deploy a moderately complex component application. You may not be able to justify the startup costs for the technology with that single application. Many organizations address this by identifying ways to distribute the costs and benefits across the enterprise. Unfortunately, this is not always possible.

Component technology can show real benefits if your organization calculates the total cost of ownership (TCO) of an application. A TCO viewpoint makes it possible to demonstrate the development and maintenance savings component technology can bring to an organization. We also know that development costs can be reduced through reuse. A component infrastructure can also reduce maintenance costs through its use of encapsulation, well-designed interfaces, and reuse. The scalability of component infrastructures avoids the need for expensive redesign and implementation.

Increased software quality is another reason to use components. I know of one organization that reduced application defects through the reuse of known good software. The effects were so dramatic that it found unit testing to be of little value and dropped it. Many companies give lip service to quality, but those who take it seriously, such as the one mentioned above, will want to adopt component technology.

Recognizing that using components is a business decision, how do we go about building a business case for components? One technique is to partition the business case by the level of technical sophistication of the components you want to use. Each level of sophistication has corresponding specifications on infrastructure, organizational readiness, and cost. By dividing a business case in this fashion, you can create incremental business cases to guide your organization in its use of component technology. This particular approach is useful in large organizations where the cost of wholesale component adoption is viewed as prohibitive.

5.2.2 Technical Sophistication—Not All Components Are Equal

Not all components are created equal. Components differ in complexity, scope, and level of functionality. They differ in the skill sets needed to use them and in the infrastructure they require. *This differentiation among components makes it difficult to create a single business case for components.* However, it provides a way to create a useful set of business cases. To create this set of cases we can divide components into three categories.

- GUI components
- Service components
- Domain components

These categories let you divide the business case into models that differ based on complexity, cost, and organizational readiness. You will also find that each category has different productivity factors. Another benefit of this approach is that it lets you select the appropriate business case based on your company's environment and needs.

GUI components are the most prevalent type of component in the marketplace. GUI components encompass all the buttons, sliders, and other widgets used in building user interfaces for applications. Reusing such prebuilt components is fairly easy and has a quick payback. Building a robust GUI component requires a greater level of skill and commitment to component-based software engineering. I find it is rarely cost-effective to develop your own GUI components. In 1999 the market for GUI components was about $300 million. Most of these components were COM technology components, but the market for Java technology components is growing.

In the next category, service components provide access to common services needed by applications. These include database access, access to messaging and transaction services, and system integration services. One common characteristic of service components is that they all use additional infrastructure or systems to perform their functions. For example, you may wrap an existing system to create a service component that becomes a service to other applications. Service components also provide infrastructure support. Another common use of service components is to facilitate Enterprise Application Integration (EAI). You will find these components combined with other EAI tools such as message-oriented middleware (MOM), transaction servers, data transformation engines, and workflow systems. Since they don't provide the full functionality of these systems in themselves, these components are usually less complex than domain components but more sophisticated than GUI components.

Domain components are what most developers think of when they talk about business components. They may be reusable or not. Nonreusable domain components have an impact on an organization similar to service components, and you can use the same business case to justify them. In this chapter, however, I only consider domain components that are truly reusable. I call them domain components because truly reusable ones are often found only within a singular domain. For example, the domain components in an insurance application could include Bill, Policy, and Claim components. It is unlikely that they would find broad reuse outside of that domain. Reusable domain components are also difficult to design and build. They may have their own application context dependencies as part of an application infrastructure. They also require a high level of domain expertise to build and deploy. The business case for domain components builds on the technical sophistication required of both GUI and service components.

5.2.3 Organizational Readiness

One of the greatest challenges you will face in successfully using component technology is organizational readiness. Organizational readiness encompasses existing development processes, developer skill sets, and corporate culture. These areas are often overlooked in establishing business cases, yet it is here and not with technical issues that we spend much of our time. Consider the non-technical challenges you face in deploying a new technology. Who needs to say yes to your project? It isn't usually just the people funding it. How will you build a broad base of support for your project? Whom do you need to convince to adopt your technology? If you ignore these questions and focus only on technical issues, you will fail. One approach to answering these questions is to put together a communication and marketing plan that will help you sell the technology to those you want to adopt it. Refer also to Chapter 24, by Don Reifer, on reuse strategies.

Every organization believes it has a development process. I find, however, that most organizations' processes are less well-defined than they believe. You might be able to use GUI components in a haphazard fashion, but that approach won't work when using service and domain components. When building a component, an undisciplined process will cause you to fail. You can assess your organizational readiness most directly by evaluating the development process documented and followed by your organization. To gain the full benefits of component technology, you need a software engineering approach to development and deployment.

What kind of processes does your organization use? You don't need to use an excruciating and overblown process, but don't confuse "just enough" process with no process at all. By just enough process I mean you need a consistent and repeatable approach to engineering software. It doesn't have to be the most detailed process ever published. If you don't have a repeatable process, however, you don't have a process at all. Don't forget that the process must encompass everything from requirements elicitation and domain analysis to testing, configuration management, component management, and release engineering. All of these areas are affected by component technology.

A consulting organization generally helps companies new to component-based development (CBD) and CBSE to establish

- A software engineering process
- Measurement and metrics (to compare existing projects against a CBD project)
- A training program for the organization on components and reuse
- A training program for the software development organization on all aspects of component analysis, design, development, and testing, as well as detailed documentation
- A mentoring program for a pilot project team on a small, but relatively important, software component project
- A mentoring program for a larger project team on a longer, more complex software component project
- A training program for the project teams that will routinely design, develop, and test for reuse

It is unlikely that one organization can provide all these services. Many consulting organizations might offer to provide them all, but no handbook for CBSE exists. Many approaches to all services are available; it is incumbent upon you to select the various consultants that can provide the services your organization needs. Expert trainers and mentors will make a positive impact on your project team without disturbing their current working equilibrium.

Once developers begin to acquire new skills you will find that you can't propagate them fast enough. This delay in developing deeply honed skills affects an organization in two ways. First, it slows the adoption of a technology because there just aren't enough skilled people to do all the potential work. Proper organization can minimize the number of people who need extensive skills. At the same time, an effective organization can use a wide variety of development talents. Proper training can enable developers to focus on specialized skill sets that let them become productive more quickly. Second, the payback and benefits of the technology are delayed. This is one area that needs serious attention in any technology business case. You must be careful not to be overly optimistic when forecasting the payback in using component technology. There is often a strong negative impact in using a new technology when promised rewards do not materialize.

Over the past two years there has been much discussion about the best way to organize component-based development. One of the early suggestions was to divide people into component builders and component assemblers. This certainly has some merit. This division of labor allows your most skilled developers to focus on the more complex task of component creation. Less skilled developers can work on the simpler task of assembling the components. It appeared to be a good idea, but it was not the solution early component managers anticipated. Assembling components can be a complex task, depending on the application layer you are working in.

An alternative to simply dividing people into builders and assemblers is to organize their skills by design layers for component infrastructures (refer to Chapter 15). A component infrastructure will typically be divided into four layers: GUI, Workflow and Process Control, Business Services, and Data Services. For example, the GUI layer can use less skilled staff to assemble simple GUI components while your more skilled developers focus on developing Workflow and Business Service components (together often called the middleware layer).

The middleware layer needs skilled developers for both component development and assembly. These are not the same skills. Component development at this layer is focused on business logic and the developer must be a skilled domain expert. Assembly at this level requires developers skilled in using application servers and other middleware components. The developers also need to be adept at defining and implementing interfaces to other layers. These skills are often tool-specific.

The Data Services layer needs people knowledgeable about databases and skilled in the development tools that will access them. These tools often provide a database access layer and require tool-specific knowledge. To produce efficient Data Services components, developers must have a working knowledge of databases, including query optimization and table layout.

Once you've designed the most appropriate organizational structure, you can focus on staffing and training. Fortunately, not everyone needs to be an experienced generalist. Instead of trying to give everyone the same skills, you can focus training in three areas—by layer, by process, and by tool. The proper organization will minimize the amount you need to spend on training in these areas.

5.2.4 Infrastructure Support

Infrastructure support becomes an important issue when you move beyond using simple GUI components. Any time you start using components in middle or lower layers of an n-tiered architecture, you need to think about infrastructure support. In a business case this becomes an issue when organizations consider service or domain components. Any time a component needs to make use of middleware services such as application servers, you need to consider the cost of the new middleware. For example, Enterprise Java Beans (EJB) requires an application server to run. If you don't already have one in production, you need to consider what it will take to make it possible to deploy EJBs (refer to Chapter 33). You will need to set up development, testing, and production environments. You may need to acquire additional hardware servers, as well as multiple application servers. Then you must consider the costs and personnel support for the application server in production. You must also determine whether your existing technical support staff understands how to operate the application server, respond to its errors, or restart jobs with it. You will likely experience additional training costs or staffing needs just to manage middleware components. This isn't simply a matter of having the component development team support its work. Reusable components and component infrastructures may be used by many teams and require more central support.

5.2.5 Reuse

Reuse is something developers have talked about for years but have had great difficulty in achieving to a significant degree. Component technology strongly supports reuse and this can have a significant impact on your business case. Reuse also has costs associated with it. You need to consider both the savings and costs in your planning.

The productivity factors I use in my business cases are ultimately based on the productivity gained by reusing components. If we are developing complex systems we can gain an advantage simply by using a component-based approach, but we gain much more when we can reuse components. One reason for dividing the business case into three categories is because of the different reuse productivity factors experienced with each type. Companies that have implemented carefully planned reuse processes have seen millions of dollars in savings. Even the simple reuse of GUI components has positive payback. This wide range of values will be seen in the cost models.

Reuse programs can pay for themselves, but you cannot implement reuse without spending money to get it. You may purchase simple components or spend time and effort developing them. Their cost is relatively small and the payback is small. At the other extreme we have domain components that are serious business assets. Domain components usually have a high development or purchase cost. Developing domain components generally requires additional people, processes, and tools to initially manage the software component life cycle effectively. The cost is higher, but the payback can be substantial. Additionally, the initial component life cycle is longer than the traditional life cycle, but with reuse it decreases substantially. Either way, you must account for these costs in your business case.

5.3 Key Problems

It is one thing to develop a business case for components. It is another to actually obtain the value you hope to achieve. Because most business cases require that you identify areas of risk, it is worthwhile to review key problem areas. Knowing the problems to face will help you develop good business cases and understand which battles you need to fight and when. The key question organizations need to answer is: "What will keep us from obtaining the value we desire from using components?" Evidence suggests that there are three areas that can cause significant problems.

- Wrong culture
- Wrong goals
- Wrong purpose

5.3.1 Wrong Culture

The wrong culture is one that is not prepared to make good use of components. This is not simply a matter of being ready or not. Just as there are different levels of components, each of these levels requires a corresponding change to the development culture to take advantage of them.

Does the following describe your culture? There was a ditch digger who had the job of digging a particular ditch by 6:00 PM. It was a challenging task, but he figured if he worked hard all day, he just might get the job done. He had been working for about two hours when a fellow pulls up with a backhoe and asks the digger if he would like some help. The ditch digger tells the other man to go away and not bother him because "I've got to get the ditch dug by 6:00 PM."

Some cultures can be narrowly focused. Because of time or cost pressures they feel they can't take the time to consider alternatives to how they work. A narrow focus is understandable, but organizations often do themselves a disservice by not considering alternatives to current practices.

Developers usually approach this problem in one of two ways. They either wait for a brief respite to bring in new technology or they bring it in by stealth and declare victory when they've accomplished their goal. The latter approach carries great risk. If the effort fails it may damage the reputation of the technology. It may no longer be possible to bring in the technology by other means. Either way, moving to a new technology in this environment can be a real challenge.

Another organizational problem is the lack of infrastructure for the level of technology you want to use. This is most often seen when moving to more advanced levels of component usage. The organization may not be inclined to make the move because of the investment required. Even if you make the case for a good return on investment, budgetary constraints may derail the project. The business may have other high priority projects that consume all available resources and funding, leaving none for your component project. One approach to this problem is to deploy new technology on a small scale before deploying it across the enterprise. However, some pieces of hardware and software infrastructure are so expensive that a small-scale deployment makes little sense.

Reuse can deliver great value to an organization, but organizations often have to change both their processes and structure to take full advantage of it. Developing truly reusable components is hard work and requires a software engineering process to do it well. Furthermore, you often need to modify your development process to include reuse. *I find that most organizational processes fail to have any allowance for either creating or using reusable components.* You also need someone to support commonly reused components. That means establishing some type of reuse center. Corporate culture can also inhibit reuse. I know of a company that rewards its developers based on the amount of code they write. This company will never achieve significant reuse while it rewards the exact opposite behavior. People will work according to how they are measured and rewarded. You need to ensure that your performance measures and goals don't hinder the change you are trying to accomplish.

5.3.2 Wrong Goals

When you build reusable components you are building for the future. You try to envision not only today's needs, but also how your components may be used in the future. What if you get it wrong? This could happen in different ways. You simply may not anticipate some usage of a component. This is not unusual. Developers will often try to use components in ways their designers never imagined, and you may be unpleasantly surprised by the results. For example, you may have designed a component that is incredibly flexible and has a correspondingly reduced performance. What happens when someone wants to reuse it but needs high performance within narrow constraints? Your component may not be the right one to use even if the functionality is correct. A developer considers many factors when determining if a component is a good fit for a particular application.

Another area where goals can be wrong is when the component is well-designed but the business needs change. When you design a reusable component you make some assumptions about the nature of a domain and processes that will work in it. In today's economy it's not unusual to have your assumptions challenged and discarded. Businesses change processes and models to meet the changing demands of their customers. Some businesses even change the type of business they are in. This is one reason it is so difficult to build good domain components. You're betting that your assumptions about the future of a business are correct and that's not always a good bet. This is also the reason it's easier to gain value from service components. While your business may change, your need to access a database probably won't. In dynamic markets infrastructure services may remain more stable than the domains they serve.

5.3.3 Wrong Purpose

Closely related to the issue of wrong goals is the problem of wrong purpose. For example, service components and domain components are different from each other. They have a different scope and purpose. They have differing needs in terms of infrastructure support and developer skill sets. You cannot use the same component for both purposes. This happens when analysts have poorly abstracted their components and mixed types of functionality. Good analysis and design can overcome this problem.

5.4 Building the Business Case

The models we use in these business cases are necessarily broad and generic. Your particular situation may have unique issues or issues that need a different emphasis. The purpose of these models is to help you quickly build a business case without getting caught in the details. To use these models, there are three things you will need to do

1. Understand the concepts behind each model
2. Make sure you address the issues they raise
3. Modify the models for your situation

Each model builds on the previous model. It is useful to build a single spreadsheet for all the calculations. Be sure to include calculations for both buy and build scenarios. Once the spreadsheet is built, filling in a few values can quickly help you assess any component project.

5.4.1 GUI Components

The business case for using GUI components is the easiest to build. Many development environments come with free GUI components.

One caveat about using this type of component is the need for a developer with enough skill to use them. Fortunately, this is a fairly low skill level and should have negligible impact on your organization. You may have to allow for a few days of experimentation, but this is less costly than building a component from scratch. Can you justify purchasing more sophisticated controls? The business case here is almost as easy. Consider this example: there is a vendor who sells a developer license for either their ActiveX or JavaBean spreadsheet component for $399. You can't develop a fully functioning spreadsheet component for $399, so clearly it's cheaper to purchase the component.

Unfortunately, things become more complicated when you want to deploy an application using purchased GUI components. For components that come with a development environment, there is usually no extra cost to deploy them. This makes them the most cost-effective to reuse. With other components the cost of deployment changes with either the number of users (typically for client-side components) or the capabilities of the server hosting for the component. In your business case you should look at the value of a component in terms of its cost per user. The idea is that a reused component adds value to the business and the more it is reused, the lower its per-user cost. Many vendors have aggressive pricing for large-scale deployment. Using the component from our previous example, let's look at the deployment cost.

For a small deployment of less than 10 people, assume the per-user cost is $99 and a 10% discount is available when 10 or more licenses are purchased. To purchase a developer version and deploy this component for 10 people will cost $1299. Compare this to the cost of developing a GUI component. Let's assume a developer costs $50 per hour. At this rate, the cost of the purchased component is worth about 26 hours of a developer's time. Clearly no developer can create the equivalent component in 26 hours.

What happens when we expand the user base and the deployment costs go up? The purchased component may still be a bargain. Remember, each time you reuse a component you save on both development time and cost. The amount of savings will be based on some productivity factor. Reuse can pay for itself even for these small-scale components. Reuse of GUI components can typically lead to a 40% improvement in productivity. This is a nice payback for a low cost. I use this factor (0.4) in the application reuse savings equation in Figure 5-2.

If you choose to build your own reusable component you are responsible for its maintenance and support. Therefore, you need to account for more than development costs. Each reusable component you create will have ongoing support and maintenance costs. How much support and maintenance you need for a component depends on the complexity of the component and the skill level of those who will use it. A component such as a fully functional spreadsheet may require as much support as an equivalently sized stand-alone application.

Another issue for developing your own GUI components is the need for more skillful developers. A solid grounding in component-based software engineering and object-oriented methodology is needed to create reusable components. While GUI components lack the infrastructure issues of more complex components, you still need sound engineering practices to create good ones. If you already have skilled developers there is no additional cost. If your organization doesn't have this skill set you will either have to develop it internally or hire appropriately skilled developers. You need to add this cost to your development cost (see Figure 5-2).

Build Component cost = Cost to build + cost to maintain components you build
Purchase Component cost = Developer cost + End user cost + maintenance cost for components you buy
Buy a component if: Build component cost > Purchase component cost
Improvement in productivity factor for GUI components = .4
Your application reuse savings = (.4* Cost to build) * Number of applications > 1
Your cost per user = Component cost/sum of users across all applications (ignoring overlap in users)

Figure 5-2: *GUI component calculations.*

I summarize the business case for GUI components with the calculations in Figure 5-2. Using these calculations for both buy and build scenarios can help you determine at what point each scenario is most appropriate. For example, with GUI components, if end-user cost is relatively high, then building a component becomes more cost-effective for large-scale deployment.

5.4.2 Service Components

With service components the business case becomes more complex. You should extend the earlier basic calculations by accounting for additional factors. From our discussion of issues, these additional factors fall into three categories

- Technical sophistication
- Infrastructure support
- Organizational readiness

Let's examine how each of these affects the business case.

5.4.2.1 Technical Sophistication

Service components are more complex because they must integrate with other pieces of software to function. They are not as stand-alone as GUI components. Server components may wrap legacy systems or require additional middleware such as application servers, message brokers, transaction servers, or EAI tools to function. You can't simply deploy a service component. You must pay for and deploy the appropriate supporting software. This means a higher cost.

5.4.2.2 Infrastructure Support

Unfortunately, it's not enough to simply deploy the additional middleware—you need to support it. You may have to provide (or outsource) operational support 24 hours by seven days a week for the middleware, separate from application support. Another issue is that new middleware often requires new hardware to ensure promised performance and reliability. Both additional support and hardware can add often-unanticipated costs to service component deployment.

5.4.2.3 Organizational Readiness

Because using service components is more complex than using GUI components, you need developers with higher-level skills. This is true for both use and development. If your developers do not have those skills, you will either have to hire those who do or train programmers and give them a chance to develop the needed skills. Furthermore, you will need to use a software engineering process to develop and deploy these components. If your organization doesn't have the right processes, you will need to develop them. If you have none of these capabilities or resources, you really need to ask yourself if your culture is ready for service components. Expect resistance to the imposition of software or component development processes. To account for these new costs I will create a complexity cost to show their impact.

Implementing interfaces between systems can account for as much as 40% of the cost of deploying new systems. Accordingly, service components have a higher payback when they are reused. Service components, as in Figure 5-3, typically have a reuse productivity factor of 150% because they do so much to ease the pain of integrating systems.

Your new Complexity cost = Middleware cost + operational support cost + hardware + organizational readiness cost
Improvement in productivity factor for service components = 1.5
Your application reuse savings = ((1.5 *Cost to build) * Number of applications > 1) - Complexity cost
Your cost per user = (Component cost + Complexity cost) / sum of users across all applications (ignoring overlap in users)

Figure 5-3: *Service component calculations.*

We can summarize the business case for service components with the additional calculations shown in Figure 5-3. As with the GUI component business case, it is useful to build a spreadsheet with both build and buy scenarios. One thing you will notice is that it is more costly to deploy service components. This usually means you need a larger user base to spread the costs across. Still, their productivity factor can have a very important affect on your calculations.

5.4.3 Domain Components

The last business case is for what I define as domain components. Domain components are the most difficult to build as reusable components. If you construct or derive a class-level diagram of your system you will find that domain components are your key abstractions. They are among the most central and highly connected components in the system. They are not usually monolithic. For example, you don't have a monolithic component named Customer. The Customer component contains many others such as name, address, and demographics. This aggregated Customer component may require interaction with other key abstractions such as Order and Bill. These interactions are often constrained by business rules, thus it is often most effective to deploy domain components within a business component infrastructure. This component infrastructure requires a cast of supporting components. Building these key abstractions and their associated component infrastructures is very difficult. Most component infrastructures require four iterations before they are truly useful and reusable. Accordingly, deploying domain components will be the most costly use of component technology. They will also provide you with the highest payback. Domain components typically have a reuse productivity factor of 1000%.

My calculations need some modification to account for these new costs. We now need a domain cost, which is the sum of the costs for a domain component and its associated supporting components plus the cost of the component model within which the component infrastructure will work. We treat these two items separately because of the variations in component models. We can summarize the business case for service components with the additional calculations shown in Figure 5-4.

Your Domain cost = Sum of costs for the domain component(s) and its supporting components + application framework costs.
Improvement in productivity factor for domain components = 10.
Your Application reuse savings = ((10* Domain Build Cost)* Number of applications > 1) – Complexity cost.
Your Cost per user = (Domain cost + Complexity cost)/sum of users across all applications (ignoring overlap in users).

Figure 5-4: *Domain component calculations.*

These components are usually only cost-effective when their costs are spread across the entire enterprise. Purchased domain components and component models may be a real bargain due to the difficulty in creating them. However, purchased component models and domain components often need modifications to fit your particular business. You need to account for these modifications in your cost model.

5.5 Conclusion

Clearly, component technology can be a cost-effective way of constructing systems. Reuse of components can have a significant impact on your productivity, but you may encounter resistance as you put into place CBSE processes. Developing a business case may be the only way to convince skeptics in your organization. When generating a business case for component-based development and component-based software engineering, be sure to select the appropriate model based on your organizational readiness and business goals. Choosing the appropriate consulting organization can be unduly difficult. Once selected, ensure that the consultant does not sell you a package of component services developed solely by the consultant. The field is too immature to bet on any one approach to component development.

Using three levels of models provides you with an incremental approach to building your business case. Use the right business case to help you incrementally deploy component technology within your enterprise. Your success at simpler levels will lay the foundation for future success and justification.

Chapter 6

COTS Myths and Other Lessons Learned in Component-Based Software Development

Will Tracz, Ph.D.

"Having divided to conquer, we must reunite to rule."

—Michael Jackson (Jackson, 1990)

6.1 Introduction

By using commercial off-the-shelf (COTS) components, software project teams not only have increased opportunities to rapidly create new applications today, they are also confronted by increased challenges to configure, integrate, and sustain these applications in the future. The technical key to success arguably lies in the *software component infrastructure* that the system designers select to integrate the components into, as well as the middleware, or *glue*, that holds them together. Unfortunately, as proven by countless COTS-based project failures, project managers must consider certain nontechnical factors such as the volatility and flexibility of the requirements, the stability of component producers, and the respective components that producers are supplying.

This chapter describes some of the misconceptions that software developers and managers often have in planning for COTS-based systems (SEI, 2000). I first expose a series of myths disproved by lessons learned from real-world experience. These myths are followed by some rules of thumb for developing COTS-based systems.

6.2 COTS Components and the Terminology Tar Pit

The material in this chapter extends the definitions presented in the introductory chapters because the components addressed by these myths and lessons learned may be both "fine-grained," as in the case of JavaBeans (*java.sun.com/products/javabeans*), or "coarse-grained," as in the case for complete off-the-shelf applications (also called COTS software). A large-grained COTS system may include an Enterprise Resource Planning (ERP) component combined with a COTS Human Resource component, along with a Customer Relationship Management (CRM) component. The major difference between a small-grained component and a large-grained component is that the glue that holds the components together may be different. Similarly, while the material in this chapter addresses both COTS software and COTS component logistic issues, the lessons learned apply equally to COTS hardware. Again, the difference encompasses the kinds of solder used to connect components. All three kinds of components

- Have published interfaces
- Are commercially available
- Require integration

Finally, the term *software architecture* is used in this chapter to refer to the subset of the overall *system architecture* of the application being developed (Rechtin, 1991). In this context the software architecture encompasses all five viewpoints of the Reference Model of Open Distributed Processing (RM-ODP) framework. Most importantly, the viewpoints emphasizes the differences between the design, the allocation of the functionality to components and their connections to meet functional requirements, and the *architecture*, the overall definition of design and implementation strategies and policies to meet nonfunctional requirements.

6.2.1 Operational Model

The COTS-based system acquisition and development model used in this paper assumes the following roles for the three major stakeholders:

- *The customer*—pays for the application to be built. The customer also selects the consumers, producers, and system integrators, generally through competitive bid.
- *The component consumer*—builds the system out of COTS or legacy components. The consumer may not always be the one who selects the COTS components because the customer may have stipulated them as part of the system requirements.
- *The COTS producer*—supplies components to the consumer and customer along with support and upgrades.

The customer must account for the maintenance of the COTS-based system or total cost of ownership (TCO) (see Chapter 30) because system maintenance can be adversely affected if certain architectural or infrastructure and procurement factors—that is, licensing fees, security, and technology refresh—are not properly addressed early in the design of the system.

6.3 Myths

This section contains a collection of COTS component lessons learned and is organized into two parts. The first subsection focuses on infrastructure issues. The second focuses on management and procurement as well as nontechnical issues.

6.3.1 Infrastructure Issues

The following myths address issues that the developer needs to consider when conducting the initial trade-off analysis for a COTS-based system. The last two myths in this section apply to both the customer and the component producer.

Myth #1: *It's important to know what COTS components can do* for *you.*

Reality: *It's important to know what COTS components can do* to *you.*

Discussion: A system designer must always evaluate the "build, buy, or modify" trade-off when determining how to provide the functionality necessary to meet the customer's requirements. COTS components, in general, provide certain functional capabilities at an extremely attractive initial cost. Experience shows that the functionality may come with certain limitations and implications. As the designer considers integrating more COTS components, the dependencies and interactions among them become more complex and can lead to intractable problems or to difficult negotiations between different suppliers as to whose product is really at fault when things do go wrong. To complicate matters further, certain "nonfunctional" requirements such as security, fault tolerance, or error handling may not be uniformly supported by all components to the degree necessary to guarantee overall system performance. The sidebar on page 110 lists the commonly cited nonfunctional requirements. These potential "hot spots" typically form a list of risks that the architect must trade off in deciding the overall composition of the system under development.

Myth #2: *COTS-based systems can be designed "top-down."*

Reality: *COTS-based systems are built "bottom-up."*

Discussion: COTS components facilitate a spiral development model in the sense that functionality can be demonstrated quickly in most applications. Customers benefit from early verification of requirements and producers reduce risks by learning first hand about the capabilities, configuration, and integration difficulties associated with the components. Most designers understand this need to check out components and do not limit their choice of components by making design decisions too early. Designers recognize the need to remain flexible in trading off functionality across components until the components are fully proven and the integration mechanisms identified.

Myth #3: *An "Open System" architecture solves the COTS component interoperability problem.*

Reality: *There is no standard definition for "open system," and "plug-and-play" doesn't always work.*

Discussion: Customers and developers clearly recognize the advantages of having plug-compatible components. They not only like having a choice of components; they also like knowing that if one component supplier goes out of business, another source for compatible components is available. It is debatable as to how successful open system initiatives have been (such as the Defense Information Infrastructure Common Operating Environment (DII-COE) (IPSEO/DISA, 2001)). Most will agree that when it works, it's great, but the number of plug-compatible components has yet to reach critical mass.

Myth #4: *You don't need to test COTS components.*

Reality: *You need to test COTS components more thoroughly because you don't understand how they were built.*

Discussion: It would be nice if all COTS components worked as advertised, but there is often a gap between what is advertised and what is delivered. Producers know that it is economically and physically impossible to test all their components in combination with all other components under all operating conditions because subtle, and often abrupt, totally unexpected feature clashes can occur. Furthermore, when developers are trying to leverage emerging technology, marketing pressures force COTS producers to deliver products with reduced capabilities along with a promised increased in functionality in future versions. Because the system integrator is usually responsible for the overall performance of the system, the integrator should evaluate the behavior and interoperability of all components before they are selected for inclusion in the system.

Myth #5: *COTS product selections are based on extensive evaluation and analysis.*

Reality: *COTS product selections are often based on slick demos, Web searches, or reading trade journals.*

Discussion: Because component-based infrastructure development is a relatively new field, systems integrators, consumers, and customers are still struggling with methods to keep abreast of technology advances and ways to determine which product best suits their needs. In the rush to make a decision, the choice of COTS products is not based on a strong business case or on the total cost of ownership (TCO). Other ways of dealing with premature or poorly considered business decisions are trade studies, use of test labs, and verification and validation performed by independent product certification agencies (refer to Chapter 41), all of which can be discriminators used by the customer to reduce risks associated with acquiring a COTS-based system.

Myth #6: *COTS components come with adequate documentation.*

Reality: *Features sell COTS components, not documentation.*

Discussion: This myth can be thought of as a continuation of the previous two myths. The lack of documentation is a risk the system architect faces in determining the suitability of COTS components. Furthermore, in some instances the customer, upon being exposed to certain component features demonstrated in a certain (sometimes contrived) context, may place unnecessary or unrealistic constraints on the producer's implementation (without adequate justification or flexibility in negotiating for different and possibly "better" components).

Myth #7: *You can configure a COTS-based system to meet your requirements.*

Reality: *You can configure your process to meet the COTS component's capabilities.*

Discussion: The 80/20 rule applies to most COTS-based system efforts. The rule states that the customer can satisfy 80% of the desired business process for 20% of the cost of a custom system (in 20% of the time). Most difficulties occur when a customer or producer believes that the additional 20% is achievable at traditional software development costs. The cost of modifying COTS components or providing extra functionality is more difficult for software development organizations because they have little control or insight into how the COTS product was designed, documented, constructed, or tested. This information is usually proprietary. Furthermore, because of planned and emergent upgrades and new versions, maintaining compatibility becomes a challenge. Most successful system integrators: 1) never modify COTS components and 2) thoroughly understand the requirements, that is, they assume that all requirements are negotiable.

6.3.2 Managerial Issues

The following myths deal with issues customers consider when selecting a contractor to develop COTS-based systems. Some of these lessons learned also apply to customers, consumers, and producers.

Myth #8: *The processes COTS products utilize reflect our industry's best practices.*

Reality: *The processes COTS products utilize often only reflect the market schedule and domain experience of the producer.*

Discussion: As much as COTS producers would like customers to believe that "one process will fit all," this is simply not the case (See ROT #12). Market considerations drive product offerings and most COTS component producers have product rollout plans that include extended features and configuration parameters and hooks that allow tailoring and customization to support a "better" fit of users' processes to current industry best practices.

Myth #9: *You buy a COTS component.*

Reality: *You buy the right to use a version of a COTS component.*

Discussion: COTS components provide immediate solutions at a fixed cost, but most applications have a life cycle that spans several releases of those components, which means that it is unrealistic (except in the case of hardware components) to expect the follow-on costs to be zero. In addition to the acquisition cost of the components, the customer and developer need to explore the cost and level of support services as well as opportunities for commodity purchases.

Myth #10: *Vendors will fix problems in the current release of the software component.*

Reality: *Vendors may fix problems in the next version of the product.*

Discussion: (See ROT #6) As mentioned in the previous myth, the level of service one receives from the component supplier is negotiable. Therefore, unless the contract explicitly states it, the type of problem fixes one receives will be market-driven. The duration between versions, or even between patches, can be considerable, and the market is often not considered. Thus the component may not operate, or only operate intermittently, for short periods between failures (Councill, 1999).

Myth #11: *If you are a large enough customer you can influence COTS component suppliers.*

Reality: *The market influences COTS component suppliers.*

Discussion: (See ROT #6) A COTS component supplier will decide how to respond to feedback from its component users. This response will be based on the size of the current and future customer base.

Myth #12: *COTS-based systems are a panacea.*

Reality: *COTS components exacerbate inadequacies in the system development process by compressing the development schedule.*

Discussion: To some, COTS components may seem like a silver bullet (Brooks, 1995) because COTS components can provide faster, cheaper, and often better solutions for

- Relatively simple applications
- Immature problem domains
- Using a small number of mature, unmodified components
- Proven integration mechanisms

However, not all applications fall into this low-risk category. Because applications can be developed so quickly, it is possible that the wrong application will be developed, the wrong COTS components initially selected, and the perceived near-term success will pave the way to long-term disaster.

6.3.3 Additional Myths

The following myths are relatively clear and reflect some of the points made in the rules of thumb stated in previous myths or the next section.

Myth #13: *COTS components are free except for the purchase price.*

Reality: *COTS-based system sustainability issues overwhelm acquisition costs.*

Myth #14: *You can ignore producer upgrades.*

Reality: *You lose support of back systems if you ignore vendor upgrades. Additionally, producer upgrades are often required to repair previously defective versions. One must remember to test upgrades considerably because they are subject to Myth #10.*

Myth #15: *You can pay a vendor to modify COTS components to meet your requirements.*

Reality: *You can pay a subcontractor to modify COTS components to meet your requirements.*

6.4 Rules of Thumb (ROT)

ROT #1: *The cost of COTS software is 1/100th that of traditional single-use code.*

This ROT is attributable to Ed Feigenbaum of Stanford University, and formerly the Air Force's Chief Scientist. To apply this ROT take the cost of a shrink-wrapped component and multiply it by $100 to get a rough approximation of the development cost for a comparable function. Clearly, there are other factors, such as the size of the customer base, for determining the cost of most COTS products, so one needs to use this ROT judiciously. In addition, this cost estimate was observed in 1995, prior to the ubiquitous Internet and large-scale open source initiatives, so the estimate may be even more extreme today.

ROT #2: *The maximum shelf life of a COTS software component is two years.*

This ROT factors into the TCO of an application all COTS components that have been configured and integrated. COTS components will probably have to be replaced two years after each is first introduced into the marketplace (see Chapter 30). To complicate matters, each new version of a component might have additional dependencies and possibly introduce new conflicting functionality. Also, the updates may not be released at the same time or validated with the same versions of other components, thus complicating matters further.

ROT #3: *The half-life of COTS product expertise is six months.*

This ROT is attributable to Kurt Wallnau of the Software Engineering Institute, who observed that with the fast-paced introduction of new product versions, as well as competing products, there is an unprecedented obsolescence associated with "current" technology. The companion to this ROT is that every six months you need to plan to evaluate a new version of a COTS product.

ROT #4: *You need to evaluate COTS in an environment as close to the operational environment as possible.*

This lesson comes from many bad experiences that have been documented and described in conferences (for example, Software Technology Conference) and workshops (like the COTS Workshop on Continuing Collaborations for Successful COTS Development at the International Conference on Software Engineering). The most significant problems occur with components that have been initially selected and then incorporated into a design. Shortly afterwards, some components may be determined to have a pathological dependency that either completely precludes their incorporation or makes the integration process much more complex and costly.

ROT #5: *You can never make a 100% DMS-resistant (Diminishing Manufacturing Source) COTS-based solution.*

Any commercial source of technology is outside the direct control of the customer. Consequently, for certain critical applications, system integrators and the customer must work together to take precautionary measures to ensure the sustainability of the application.

These measures include paying a third party to store ongoing design documentation and evolving source codes of the components or negotiating for the establishment of an open application program interface (API) in hopes of stimulating plug-compatible competition (that is, a second source).

The following ROTs are self-explanatory. It is debatable which of the last two ROTs is more important, but it is clear that they determine the success of any development effort.

ROT #6: *The smaller the customer base, the higher the COTS cost and the better the service.*

ROT #7: *The largest problem with COTS is its short life span.*

ROT #8: *Stay away from innovative COTS products unless cutting-edge COTS components are the only way you can attain the performance you need.*

ROT #9: *By using COTS components you decrease development time and increase integration time.*

ROT #10: *The selection of COTS components either creates or mitigates risk.*

ROT #11: *A COTS-based system may not be the cheapest solution.*

ROT #12: *A COTS-based system will never completely satisfy a customer's needs.*

6.5 Conclusion

Who is at fault for most COTS-based system failures? Component producers are to blame for not using good engineering judgment in identifying risks and then mitigating them. Customers must share the blame for expecting COTS to be a panacea. Customers must be flexible and understand the short-term and long-term trade-offs with respect to certain COTS options. Current customer acquisition processes ask customers the wrong questions at the wrong times. Furthermore, in the case of government acquisitions, the customer generally does not have enough COTS-smart people nor has there been strong policy guidance.

Nonfunctional Specifications

One of the more subtle challenges of component-based system development is matching nonfunctional system specifications to nonfunctional component properties. While it is easy to select components based on their functional capabilities, most components do not readily reveal their nonfunctional properties.

Nonfunctional specifications (also called "extra-functional" requirements, a term coined by Mary Shaw at the Software Engineering Institute (SEI)) are commonly referred to as "ilities," (though not all properties end in "ilty"). The following taxonomy is based on the work done on software product lines at the SEI (Bass, Clements, and Kazman, 1998). It addresses nonfunctional requirements according to various phases in the software life cycle:

1. Planning
   - Robustness
     - Conceptual integrity
     - Completeness
     - Coherence
   - Affordability
     - Purchase price
     - Support cost
     - Integration cost
2. Design
   - Portability
   - Reusability
   - Testability
   - Extendibility
   - Configurability
   - Scalability
   - Interoperability
3. Run-time
   - Performance
     - Throughput
     - Response time
     - Resource consumption
   - Reliability
     - Availability
     - Security (vulnerability)
     - Safety
     - Fault Tolerance
   - Usability

The customer should not take all the blame. Customers and component consumers have been naïve in trusting producer vaporware claims and in underestimating the challenges of component configuration and interoperability. Fortunately, customers are becoming increasingly savvy in their testing and integration capabilities.

The ultimate solution, used by many of the leading system integrators, relies on setting up integrated product teams (IPTs) consisting of customers, end-users, consumers, and the COTS producers. Such a forum often provides a venue where all stakeholders can better understand the requirements, their priorities, and the TCO tradeoffs that are available with full insight on their short-term and long-term impact.

In conclusion, many COTS-based system development lessons have already been learned. Unfortunately, the near-term trend seems to indicate that these lessons will be relearned by many customers and consumers unless proper education, policy definition, and sharing of experiences occur. Finally, it should be clear that a COTS-based system might not always be the "best" solution available. When all the factors are considered, the business case laid out, and a TCO study done, a custom implementation may be more cost-effective over the life of the project.

Chapter 7

Planning Team Roles for CBD

Paul Allen[1]
Stuart Frost

7.1 Introduction

Good professionals know their roles. Ask an airline pilot or air steward and there's no question about what they have to do in flying the aircraft or keeping the passengers happy. In most industries the situation is pretty much the same. On a film set, you'll find a director, a gaffer, a make-up artist, and the various actors and actresses with clearly defined parts to play. In software the situation is not so clear-cut. Many of us have become generalists, epitomized in titles like analyst/designer that disguise a multitude of different roles. The larger the project, the more the lack of role definition starts to hamper the project. Migration to component-based development adds further

1. This paper is reprinted from *Component Strategies*, Aug. 1998.

dimensions of scale and complexity, which demand a clear definition of team roles. This article provides guidance for projects at various stages along the road to component-based development and builds on concepts outlined in our book (Allen and Frost, 1998).

7.2 CBSE Teams and Roles

7.2.1 Team Roles in Context

Component-based development does not "happen over night." It requires a migration plan, an important element of which is the question of teamwork. One approach is to continually remind ourselves that reuse is a long-term investment. To successfully institute a reuse regimen, you must fight the "Not Invented Here" syndrome, provide artificial incentives, and constantly preach the gospel of reuse. Our experience in the field suggests that it is not possible to create a separate reuse group responsible for ensuring that developers reuse components. This simply does not work. A much more realistic approach starts with a clearly defined process for different types of projects to follow. Team roles are defined as part of the process and used by the projects to focus attention on required skills (see sidebar).

A well-defined process encourages interplay between solution and component projects. This is very important in cross-fertilizing good practices across solution projects and in pollinating reuse from component projects as illustrated in Figure 7-1. Solution teams should ask key questions at the right points in the process as they seek to harvest reuse. For example, at the feasibility stage, "Have we solved this problem before?"; at the analysis stage, "Can existing models be used to solve the problem?"; and at the design and build stage, "Can existing software components be used to solve the problem?" This requires open discussion with the component team, who in turn will bring their own set of questions to the table in their mission to sow reuse.

7.2.2 How Team Roles Help

Team roles are useful because they help the project manager by providing a convenient catalog of the different skill sets that apply to dif-

Processes, Teams, and Roles: Basic Concepts

Process	A process provides the overall shape to the phasing of software development activity from inception to delivery. Each step in the process is defined by templates that include inputs, outputs, task catalogs, and team roles. Component-based development (CBD) uses a dual process aimed at the respective needs of solution assemblers and component builders. Sound component management enables developers to locate, publish, and catalog components. Solution assemblers bolt together components, with minimum additional coding, to provide software that is of immediate business benefit. Component builders provide the underlying software building bricks. They might code new components, but also they might modify existing components, wrap existing systems, or acquire components from an external source. The solution and component processes are ideals. Elements of both processes are commonly adapted to specific needs.
Project	A project is a set of activities that organizes and employs resources to create or maintain a product or part of a product. Projects can follow the solution or component processes, but will typically apply elements of both, customized to particular organizations' requirements.
Team	A team is a number of individuals working together in a coordinated fashion to meet a defined set of objectives.
Team Role	A team role is a related set of responsibilities and skills. Team roles bring objectivity to the process in that one person may fulfill more than one role and one role can be supplied by many individuals. Different roles, played by various individuals at appropriate times, are applied through the stages of a project.

ferent parts of a project, which is useful for planning and structuring a project. A project is like a bus that travels a route (the process) from a source (set of requirements) to a destination (the product). Team roles help guide the project manager in selecting different individuals with appropriate skills who need to come on to and off the bus at different points in the journey.

Another important feature of team roles is that they are organizationally neutral. Traditionally, team members have always worked in close proximity for the same employer within a common corporate culture. This situation is changing fast. We are increasingly seeing the emergence of teams whose members are not only geographically sepa-

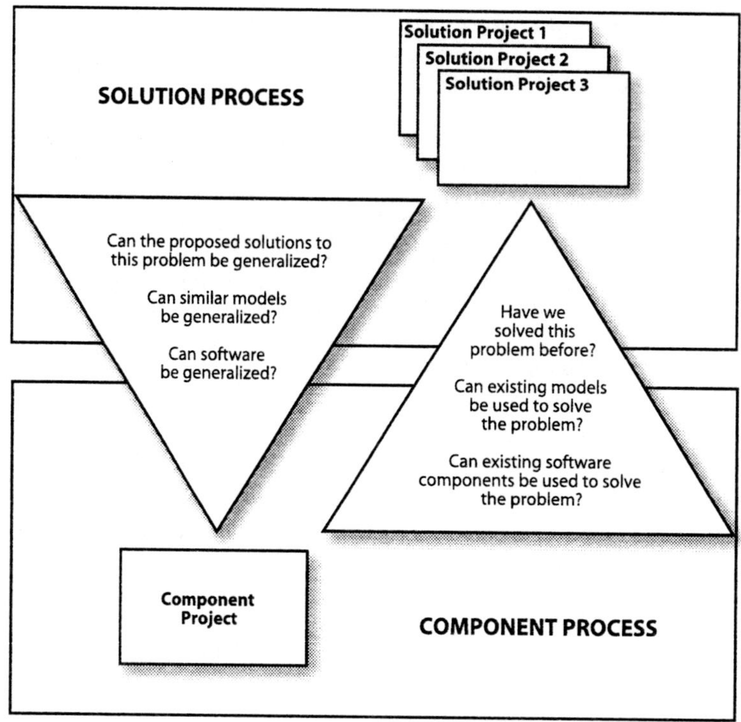

Figure 7-1: *Dynamics between solution and component projects.*

rated but also work for different employers (including self-employed contractors) with different cultures. Corporate loyalty and careers for life have become the exception rather than the norm. In an extreme case this results in virtual teams whose members communicate only by email and conference calls. The magic ingredient of team spirit can be hard to muster in such projects—team roles bring a sense of focus and help to convey a sense of responsibility.

The sheer diversity of required technical skills is also increasing, reflecting the wide range and deep complexity of today's technical issues. Increased participation of business people, fueled by a need to align IT much more effectively with business needs, calls for a clear definition of the roles that business people play on a project—the term "user" is no longer sufficient. Again, a catalog of team roles helps with planning the right resources at the right time.

7.2.3 Cataloging the Roles

The number and kinds of roles on a project are closely tied to the types of activities that have to be carried out to meet the project's goals and mitigate the project's risks. There are a large number of potential roles in addition to those discussed in this chapter. For example, the configuration manager where version control is complex and the production control manager where packaging and distribution of software is key. We present those roles that we have found to be particularly critical and cataloged them accordingly. However, there's nothing sacrosanct here. Treat the roles as a starter for cataloging your own role set!

7.2.4 Solution Development Roles

The roles, shown in Table 7-1, draw heavily on work done by the DSDM (Dynamic Systems Development Method) consortium (DSDM, 1997) and emphasize the business-driven development culture that is fast becoming characteristic of successful solutions development. A solution project may also involve component development roles, depending on the required level of software generality, and works using the iterative incremental delivery cycle discussed in Allen and Frost (1998).

Table 7-1: *Solution Development Roles*

Role	Responsibility
Executive Sponsor	Owns the solution and as is ultimately responsible for it. The role must hold a sufficiently high position to resolve business issues and make appropriate funds and resources available.
Visionary	Acts as the driving force behind the project and is responsible for ensuring the project delivers a solution that meets the original business objectives. The role is normally from the business community and contributes to key design decisions and resolves any conflicts arising from different business areas.

Table 7-1: *Solution Development Roles (Continued)*

Ambassador User	Drives the business requirements and provides a key focus for bringing in input from end-users, user management, and the business community in general. The role is normally from the business community and understands and communicates the business context of the project.
Adviser User	Brings practical knowledge of relevant business practices to the project. The role is often fulfilled by someone who will eventually use the solution to be developed and plays an important part in activities such as prototyping and usability testing.
Solution Developer/ Senior Developer	Models and interprets user requirements and uses a range of skills (for example, analysis, design, coding, and testing) to develop the models through to effective solutions. The role should be particularly skilled in the design of user service components and have appropriate programming language skills. The role increasingly encompasses human factors skills (human factors can be a separate role), such as graphic design skills for Web pages.
Project Manager	Coordinates projects involving several teams, ensures good team motivation, and reports to senior management. The role plans, estimates, and performs risk management. Has responsibility to ensure that the solution as a whole is delivered as agreed. The role may be staffed from either the business or IT communities.
Team Leader	Runs the team on a day-to-day basis and ensures the solution for which the team is responsible is delivered as agreed. The role is responsible for promoting team well being and motivation.

7.2.5 Component Development Roles

The roles summarized in Table 7-2 work in two ways. First, at the ongoing *strategic* level, to ensure overall architectural context for reuse and to continuously assess and promote reuse opportunities with respect to business plans. Second, at *delivery* level, to upgrade existing components or deliver new components in iterative incremental fashion. A component delivery project may also involve solution roles, particularly the user roles, depending on the degree to which users interact with the components. An iterative incremental delivery cycle is again used. Whether a separate component team physically exists and the numbers of individuals comprising the team depends on the size of the organization..

Table 7-2: *Component Development Roles*

Role	Responsibility
Reuse Sponsor	Authorizes resources for component projects and ensures that component projects are not just technical fads, that is, they address real business needs. The role should be from management ranks (the higher the better) and ensures that the corporate commitment needed for component-based development is not beyond the scope of influence of the reuse manager.
Reuse Manager	Plans and controls the overall activities of component projects and makes policy decisions concerning reuse. The role assesses and reports on the impact of software reuse on business needs, often in liaison with the metrics expert role.
Reuse Assessor	Identifies areas for reuse improvement and pollinates reuse across solution projects. The role has good awareness of existing systems, packages, databases, and available components. This knowledge is used to assess reuse opportunities and to evaluate reuse requirements. This is a very proactive role, calling for good interpersonal skills, in that it must help solution developers to grow reuse into their solutions where appropriate, as well as alert them of opportunities to reuse existing services.
Reuse Architect	Identifies and acquires components, carries out architectural modeling, ensures consistency of design across projects, and promotes the value of reuse via the reuse sponsor. The role must have good awareness of patterns and frameworks, keep good contacts with industry bodies, and have good overall vision.

Table 7-2: *Component Development Roles (Continued)*

Business Component Developer/ Senior Developer	Models and interprets generic business requirements and uses a range of skills (for example, analysis, design, coding, and testing) to develop the models through to effective business service components. The role should have a good knowledge of relevant business practices (or at least have access to appropriate sources), be particularly skilled in the design of business service components, and have appropriate programming language skills.
Data Component Developer/ Senior Developer	Models and interprets stored data requirements and uses a range of skills (for example, analysis, design, coding, and testing) to develop the models through to effective data service components. The role is particularly skilled in the appropriate database programming language.
Business Process Coordinator	Demonstrates the value of components[a] with respect to business processes. Also, coordinates the development of new or changed business processes in relation to component projects. This role is expert in business process modeling and understands the relevance of the components to business needs.

a. The business process coordinator role has greatest value in component projects where the effects of new, changed, or acquired components typically stretch across different business processes. However, the role is often applied on solution projects to ensure tight integration with a complex business process.

7.2.6 Support Roles

The purpose of support roles is to ensure that solution and component teams have the necessary technical infrastructure and knowledge base to meet their needs. Table 7-3 details support roles that are particularly important for migration to component-based development, but it is not an exhaustive list. It may or may not be that separate technical infrastructure and software expert center teams physically exist to meet these respective needs. Size and number of teams depends on the size of the organization. However, at the very least a single individual should be responsible for each of the technical infrastructure team roles.

7.2.7 Architecture and Team Roles

A sound software architecture provides an overall structure and set of rules for managing the scale and complexity inherent in enterprise software development. A component-based architecture uses separate service layers and is usefully modeled with UML package diagrams (Booch, Rumbaugh, and Jacobson, 1998) as illustrated in Figure 7-2. Not only does the architecture play an important part in helping to

Table 7-3: *Support Roles*

Role	Responsibility
Reuse Librarian	Controls the component repository, publicizes capabilities of components, checks components in and out of the repository, and controls configuration management of components. The role has a combination of administration and technical skills and is expert in using component management software. The role can include the role of *database administrator*.
Metrics Expert	Provides projects with guidance using estimation. Collects project metrics and maintains the metrics database. Measures and assigns cost-benefit data to projects (activity-based) and to components (asset-based). This is a key role in migration to component-based software economics based on assets.
Tester	Provides independent advice and assistance on testing strategy, planning, and practice. Component-based development presents the tester with the added challenge of whether the component's interfaces can be extended or specialized to support the kinds of contexts for which it was designed. With the incremental approach the role must encompass regression testing to ensure that previous increments, as well as the current increment, are up to scratch.
Certifier	Sets component specification standards and ensures compliance and consistency of components across different teams. This involves helping projects ensure that quality runs right through the process and is not "bolted on" as an afterthought. The role is responsible for quality metrics and should have a thorough knowledge of quality requirements and specification criteria.

Table 7-3: *Support Roles (Continued)*

Legacy Expert	Advises on the suitability of legacy assets for wrapping and on the impact of proposed new components. The role should be expert in renovation techniques to get legacy assets in a fit state for wrapping as well as maintaining the legacy asset to align with any changes to wrapper design and code. In a large organization the role may split into separate roles for legacy system code, legacy databases, and software packages.
Human Factors Expert	Advises on design and ergonomics of the user interface. The role may also provide specific expertise such as graphic design skills for Web pages. The role requires up to date knowledge of the very latest techniques for designing good user interfaces.
Technical Facilitator	Works with the solution and component projects to ensure that the technical architecture is correct and consistent with standards. As well as "soft" skills this involves a range of "hard" skills that may split into subroles, including Web expert, Network Expert, and Capacity and Performance Manager. Obviously, each role calls for appropriate skills. For example, the Web expert has a specific knowledge of Internet and Intranet software.

shape the software, as part of the component process it also plays an important part in shaping the projects and is particularly relevant to the subject of team roles. Project management is facilitated by allocating service packages to different teams, each service layer calling for different skill sets.

Business processes are integral to the architecture. To convince management of the value of components, it is important to link the concept of software reuse to strategic business planning. Business processes that are strategically important need to be understood and commonality identified across those business processes. The business process coordinator role identifies specific areas of commonality where reuse can have a positive impact on improving the organization's business processes.

The different development roles correspond to each of the user, business, and data layers of the architecture. Developer skill sets are perhaps most obvious in terms of proficiency in different types of programming language. For example, Visual Basic at the user layer, C++ at the business layer, and SQL at the data layer. However, analysis and design skills are also likely to exhibit some significant differences.

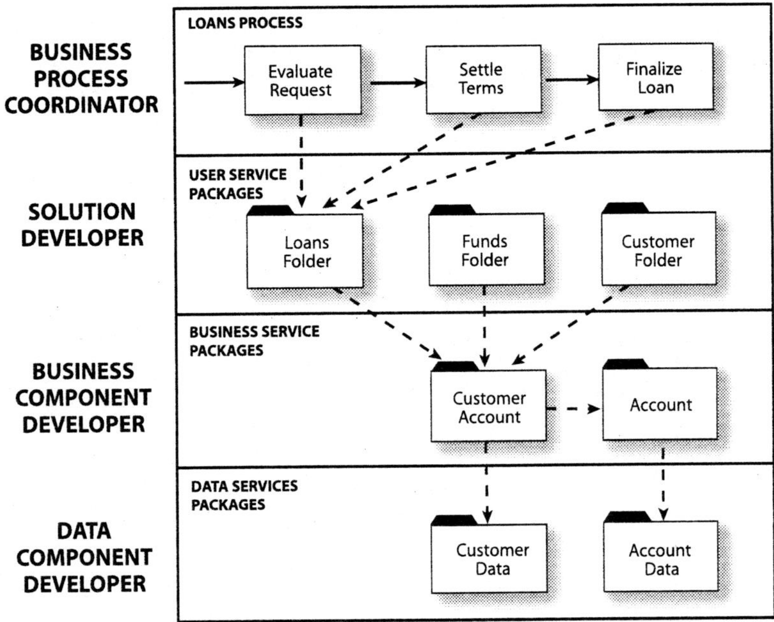

Figure 7-2: *Architecture and development roles*

7.2.8 Types of Teams

Let's look at some examples of how the roles are put to work. The following tables provide a number of example configurations for a six-person team. The tables include only core roles—roles that will play a more or less permanent role throughout the project. As the projects progress some roles will exit the projects and others will enter.

Table 7-4 describes three possible configurations for a six-person solution project team. Although they are not ongoing permanent roles, the roles of executive sponsor and visionary are critical to all of these projects in providing business commitment. Also, the reuse librarian plays a key role in providing component management assistance to the latter two projects. Let's look at each team in more detail.

- *Solution Delivery*—This team is tasked with developing a highly visible set of user interfaces to automate a front-office insurance data capture process to deliver maximum business benefit. The team is actually led by an ambassador user from the business community and includes a human factors expert to supply the necessary user interface skills and an adviser user with business process skills to ensure fit with an existing business process model. The main driver is understood to be early business benefit where reuse is not an issue.

Table 7-4: *Example Solution Team Configurations*

Solution Project Teams		
Solution Delivery	**Solution Harvesting**	**Solution Sowing**
Ambassador user and team leader	Business process coordinator and team leader	Senior solution developer and team leader
Adviser user	Ambassador user	Ambassador user
Adviser user and business process coordinator	Adviser user	Adviser user
Human factors expert	Senior solution developer	Solution developer
Senior solution developer	Solution developer	Business component developer
Solution developer	Reuse assessor	Reuse architect and tester

- *Solution Harvesting*—This team is tasked with assembling components from an insurance package to meet the needs of a policy sales business process. A member of the business community fulfills the ambassador user role with an adviser user providing detailed business input. The business process coordinator ensures the solution fits the business plan and also runs the project. A reuse assessor with good knowledge of the vendor product determines which components might be "plugged in."

- *Solution Sowing*—This team is tasked with building an agent commission system but has few available components to reuse. A member of the business community fulfills the ambassador user role with an adviser user providing detailed business input. Solution and business component developers are both included because, although the main aim is to deliver business value quickly, the solution needs to be sufficiently modular for long-term migration to component-based development. A reuse architect role is included because the reuse potential of the project is high. The individual playing the reuse architect role also acts as a tester. This helps independence of testing and also ensures the architect is accountable for the detailed consequences of his or her decisions by staying through the project.

Table 7-5 describes three possible configurations for a six-person component project team. Although the role of reuse sponsor is not included as a core role, this role is nevertheless vital for providing the required business authority. As on the first two projects, the reuse librarian plays a key role in providing component management assistance and the technical facilitator role provides direction concerning hardware and software infrastructures. Let's look at each team in more detail

- *Component Harvesting*—This team is required to wrap part of an existing COBOL system to make insurance premium calculations available to a number of new policy servicing systems. The ambassador user acts as a broker between the component team and the user community affected by the changes. An experienced solution developer sits on the team full-time to ensure the first solution to use the wrapper is as risk-free as possible. Two business component developers work with a legacy system expert to provide the core functionality. The reuse assessor ensures the wrappers are sufficiently generic for wider use and is also responsible for testing throughout the project.
- *Component Sowing*—This team produces a number of data services providing integrated client facilities based on existing relational databases and used in several different contexts. Because of the potentially far-reaching impact of the data services, the reuse manager runs the project. The services are "black box" sitting under existing user interfaces that remain unaffected. .Therefore, user

Table 7-5: *Example Component Team Configurations*

Component Project Teams		
Component Harvesting	**Component Sowing**	**Component Planning**
Senior business component developer and team leader	Reuse manager	Reuse manager
Ambassador user	Senior data component developer	Business process coordinator
Business component developer	Data component developer	Senior business component developer
Senior solution developer	Legacy database expert	Reuse architect
Legacy system expert	Reuse architect and tester	Reuse assessor
Reuse assessor and tester	Reuse assessor and certifier	Technical facilitator

involvement is minimal. Two data component developers work with a legacy database expert to provide the core functionality. The reuse architect ensures design consistency and also plays the tester role, ensuring that the existing functionality is preserved and that the underlying data integrity is kept intact. The reuse assessor works with the legacy expert to evaluate generality of data services and is responsible for certification of quality criteria.

- *Component Planning*—This team operates at a strategic level in producing a component-based architecture together with some prototypes that demonstrate technical feasibility. This involves the tasks of architectural scoping and assessment of the potential of legacy systems. The reuse architect and reuse assessor therefore play central roles. The business process coordinator helps align the architecture with strategic business requirements expressed in business process models. The senior business component developer creates the prototypes. The technical facilitator ensures that the architecture is consistent with the organization's hardware and software infrastructure plans.

7.2.9 Migration to Component-Based Development

To consider how the team roles help with migration to component-based development, let's consider the spectrum shown in Figure 7-3. Projects at the extreme left are characterized by a need to deliver software that provides quick business payoff. The core role involved is solution development (and support) only. Although reuse is not a driver of solution delivery projects, other quality requirements (particularly usability) certainly are. Projects at the extreme right are characterized by the need for effective architecture demanded by component-based development. The role involved is component development (and support) only. Such projects must be kept short (two to three weeks) to avoid analysis paralysis syndrome and aim to produce prototypes that demonstrate technical feasibility.

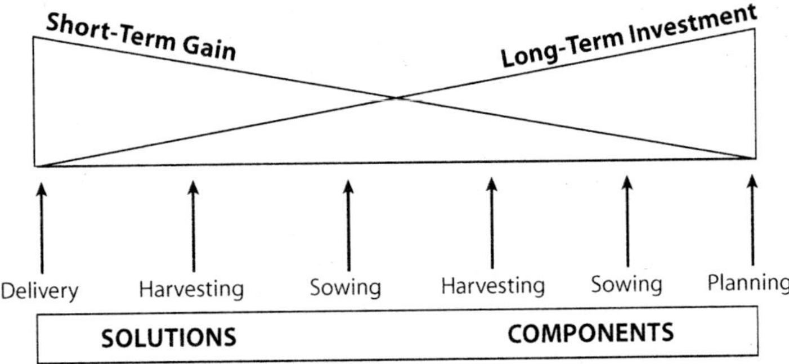

Figure 7-3: *The project type spectrum.*

Between the two extremes are various types of projects that mix and match roles from component and solution development. Left of the middle are projects whose primary goal is business impact but which have an impact on component-based development. These projects might assemble preexisting components with minimal modification and new code (solution harvesting) or look to create some reusable software as opportunist "spin-off" from the project (solution sowing). Right of the middle are projects that work to confer direct early-user value by capitalizing on existing software either by wrapping or acquiring from an external source (component harvesting). These projects are particularly important as they can provide early opportunities to demonstrate business cost justification for component-based development. Moving further right, a component project may work "under the covers" on preparing black-box software for longer-term use (component sowing). These projects are much less visible and therefore often difficult to cost-justify on business grounds.

Migration to component-based development does not work in a simple sequence throughout the spectrum. The long-term vision must be balanced against today's immediate needs and capabilities. In the real world planning and delivery must take place side by side. Only once there is an organizational vision and efficient delivery does it make sense to gradually "converge" on the harvesting and sowing types of projects.

7.2.10 Roles "In the Small"

As well as for application throughout a project, roles are also useful "in the small" to foster communication at team meetings, particularly using Joint Application Development (JAD). JAD is an approach for effective employment of workshop environments that can be used at certain points during a project in order to foster good communication among end-users and members of the CBD and CBSE teams to accelerate the development process.

JAD is applied at frequent points in both solution and component development, especially at baseline points. All project participants are assembled in one place at several different times to establish objectives, to agree what is needed and how it will look. Participants work toward an agreed objective and agenda in order to focus the session. Sessions are often time-boxed to further assist in keeping participants geared to tight objectives. Each participant performs a specified role within the JAD session. The team roles described above can all be applied depending on the purpose of the session. Also, there are two additional roles that apply specifically to JAD sessions.

Facilitator—The facilitator structures and prepares the sessions. He or she encourages the participation of all the attendees and ensures that the session move forwards (particularly if it is timeboxed). The facilitator should be a skilled moderator acting as an independent arbiter and working to stimulate an egoless environment.

Scribe–The scribe is responsible for the production and maintenance of all the documentation resulting from the session. It is important that this role should not be considered as being suitable for a clerical secretary, as the ability to capture business rules or technical information during or after the session is paramount.

We have in fact only touched on the subject of JAD here. For a practical step by step guide to the use of JAD the reader is referred to August (1991) and Wood and Silver (1995).

7.3 Conclusion

Migration to component-based development, driven by business needs, requires a good process that provides guidance on team roles as well as deliverables, techniques, and activities. The different types of processes have roles that can be mixed and matched to suit your needs.

There are different project types that can be characterized along the road to component-based development. In reality a team may well exhibit a mix of characteristics, as we saw in the examples. Team roles are useful in helping to achieve the right balance of skills and bring order and objectivity to the challenges of migration to component-based development.

Chapter 8

Common High-Risk Mistakes

Wojtek Kozaczynski

8.1 Introduction

In this chapter I summarize my personal experiences and observations about putting into place an industrial-scale component-based software development process and organization to build a very large business system. I hope that our pitfalls will help others avoid mistakes, and our successes will allow managers of component-based organizations achieve great successes.

Generally, it is easy to write success stories. If given the opportunity, most of us would just as soon forget our mistakes and failed projects. I believe, however, that software engineering can learn equally from successes and failures. Any judgment of the described experiences should occur only within the context of the specific, declared objectives and constraints of the particular project. I have decided not to reveal the name and particular business of my previous employer, as this information does not add any value to the story.

Large system development is a complex undertaking stretching over long periods and involving multiple stakeholders and concerns. It is hard to assess the risks of such development with respect to a specific aspect or facet. Hence, it is difficult to separate the risks introduced by component-based development from all other risks, such as poor personal skills, insufficient software development and other processes, and non-supportive organizations. Nevertheless, I hope you benefit from my subjective recollection of the key risks of building what my current organization calls a *Component Factory*. The scope of this chapter restricts the extent to which I can describe what the term Component Factory implies, so I will provide below only a summary of the key concepts. Although the thoughts articulated in the section are cast in the context of the described situation, in reality they are findings that matured over time and, in particular, during my work at Rational Software. As always, retrospection and reflection permits me to better see the nuances and pitfalls of my own actions and those of others.

8.2 The Context

My story starts when I was asked to participate in the redesign of a very large, widely deployed Enterprise Resource Planning (ERP) system that had been repeatedly extended and ported to different platforms during its long lifetime. What makes that effort relevant to the discussion of CBSE is that the following two decisions were made early in the rebuilding process:

1. Object and component technology and methods would be used for the development
2. The development process, resources, and the infrastructure were to be organized as a Component Factory

Because of the limited nature of the explanation, I refer all interested readers to a book written by my colleagues Peter Herzum and Oliver Sims, who have eloquently described the theoretical foundations and practical aspects of setting up a Component Factory (Herzum and Sims, 2000). Both Peter and Oliver were members of the project. Henceforth, when I refer to the project as ours, I am describing the contributions of Peter, Oliver, and others involved in the large-scale project.

A Component Factory is a process, organization, tools (the development infrastructure), and the run-time infrastructure that separates the following key concerns and responsibilities:

- Development of the component infrastructure
- Design, integration, and system testing of application components
- And development and unit testing of application components

In other words, you can think of three cooperating groups each responsible for one of the above aspects of development. The lead group is the Application Development Group. It designs application components, defines the specifications for the component infrastructure (that is, the horizontal mechanisms and services), subcontracts development of components to the Component Development Group, defines functional and nonfunctional exit criteria (such as, performance,) for that development, and then integrates and system-tests the components. A component infrastructure is a technology base to which the application components are plugged in to form a working system. The Infrastructure Group is responsible for developing a dedicated and focused architecture comprised of key mechanisms and services (start-up and shut-down, distributed communication, persistence, error handling, and transactions) and policies for using these services and mechanisms at the component level.

The last group is the Component Development Group (sometimes referred to as the *Component Factory*, although the context presented here assigns a broader meaning to that term). This group receives specifications for the application components together with exit criteria such as functional test scripts, size, and performance, and develops the components "to order." The relationships among the three groups are shown in Table 8-1.

In our context, a small organizational unit called the Architecture Group performed the role of the overall architect. The key responsibility of that group was to ensure predictable and repeatable component development on a stable, tested infrastructure.

Table 8-1: *Relationships Among the Three Major Development Groups*

	Application Development	**Component Development**	**Infrastructure**
Application Development		↑ Provides component designs and development exit criteria	↑ Provides requirements for the component infrastructure properties, mechanisms, and services
Component Development	↑ Develops components according to specifications		↑ Provides feedback on component development tools and the infrastructure
Infrastructure	↑ Delivers component infrastructure that meets the specific application requirements. Provides infrastructure tools and training	↑ Provides parts of the component infrastructure necessary for individual component development. Provides tools to be used with the framework	

The relationship between the Architecture Group and the three groups described above was multifaceted.

- The group was responsible for key design decisions about the run-time and development infrastructure
- The group coordinated and participated in development of early prototypes and exemplars of application components and then captured the experience for reuse
- The group facilitated the coordination of infrastructure and application development

In our case the groups were distributed. The Application Development Group and the Architecture Group were located in the United States while the Infrastructure Development and Component Development Groups were located in two different places in the UK.

8.3 The Pitfalls

In this context we executed four iterations similar, at a high level, to the Elaboration Phase of the Rational Unified Process described by Kruchten (1998). I list below my thoughts about the key risks of setting up and successfully executing a Component Factory approach to develop a large and complicated software product. There is no significance to the order in which the thoughts are presented.

8.3.1 The Lead Architect's Role

The very nature of the Component Factory approach is the separation of the responsibilities for the component infrastructure selection, component development, and application development. Not recognizing the potential danger in this separation may lead to serious problems. Because of the separation of responsibilities there will always be tension between the application architect (or lead application designer) and the component infrastructure lead designer. The separation of their design responsibilities is not always obvious. The error-handling mechanism could arguably belong to the application or the infrastructure or both. It is my experience that if the separation of responsibilities is strictly defined, the respective designers tend to push development of such mechanisms outside their scope of work.

A more subtle reason for the tension is that infrastructure and application designers perceive their work very differently. The application lead designer is usually a domain expert interested in decomposing the system into elegant, durable application components and considers the infrastructure as just supporting scaffolding. The infrastructure designer is usually a technologist interested in employing the "right technology," sometimes at the expense of recognizing the customer's needs for the application. This tension can be a propulsive force, but can also create personal conflict and, if left unchecked and unsupervised, may destroy the project. Hence, a large component-based development effort requires a lead architect role that is responsible for the overall design of the product including both the decomposition of the application into components and the component infrastructure. I have seen ineffective architectural "committees" and I have seen the application and the infrastructure teams pointing fingers at each other when trying to locate the cause of a defect. I would go so far as to say that the success of a large component-based development effort critically depends on:

- Clear separation of the application and component infrastructure development responsibilities
- The quality of, and the authority given to, the lead architect role
- And the quality of the working relationships of the lead architect with the lead application and infrastructure designers

8.3.2 Immature Component Infrastructure

A related pitfall is building an application on an immature component infrastructure. The required capabilities of the infrastructure (services and mechanisms) should be anticipated and developed at least one iteration ahead of the components that will use them. I have seen application components designed for "yet to be delivered" services that were "stubbed just for now" so the development could move forward.

The problem is that a mechanism, such as persistence or handling mega-data[1], is not just an interface, but may involve a complex programming model. Such a programming model defines how a mechanism must be used from within a component or how multiple components must interact to use it. Changes in a mechanism (nonfunctional requirements such as performance) may easily invalidate existing component designs.

An immature component infrastructure forces designers to make difficult decisions about the sequence in which components are developed. One of the key software development best practices is to first

---

1. The term *mega-data* refers to a mechanism that supports managing a large collection of data that has to be moved between the system presentation tier and the resource management tier. For example, a user asks an open-ended question that can result in a very large response set.

develop a small set of components implementing a few critical system use cases. The reason for this practice is to test critical mechanisms end-to-end while proving that the system will provide the expected functionality. An immature, patchy component infrastructure makes following the practice almost impossible. What usually occurs instead is that designers build components in isolation hoping that they will come together at a later time.

8.3.3 Size and Packaging of Subcontracted Components

In the component factory context, one group subcontracts component development to another group. Decisions about component size and how components should be packaged for single delivery impact the development process. Inter-group communication is required to assure that component size and packaging meet product specifications.

Specifying components for development by a different, remote team and then accepting the results without validation can be a costly process. The specifications should include the component design itself, but also all the assumptions about the context within which the component will have to operate. The specifications with assumptions are necessary to build and test components in isolation. Subcontracting a very large component or a large group of components forces the Application Development Group to make assumptions without the benefit of frequent feedback from the Component Development Group. The Application Group has described the subcontracting process as being similar to sending a space probe to Mars and waiting for months to see the results of the tests performed.

In contrast, subcontracting many small components to the component development team in short, rapid cycles has some undesirable side effects. It forces the Application Development Group to assume more testing and integration responsibility than it would have otherwise. It also turns the Component Development Group into a group of "code cutters" who do not have a good understanding of the overall systems structure and functionality. In my experience this issue, if not addressed, becomes a serious programmer retention problem.

The guideline for selecting components for single delivery is relatively straightforward. Specify and package the smallest group of components that delivers an observable end-user function or business concept. This minimal set is often called a *business component* and is defined as a collection of system components that collectively implementing a business concept or function (see Chapter 16). In practice a business component is a collection of elements from different systems tiers: presentation, session management (assets such as Web server and Web resource management), business logic, and resource management.

8.3.4 Distributed Development is Not Synonymous With CBD

Running a distributed development organization—a CBD and CBSE organization dispersed across a country or around the world—is always hard. I raise this point because Component Factory and distributed development are synonymous in the minds of many development managers. Unfortunately, distributed development and component factories are not alike. A component factory clearly defines the division of responsibilities and concerns. It also helps manage inter-team communication, but a Component Factory does not bring teams together.

In practice, the interaction between the application team and the component development team is not limited to sending component specifications and component code back and forth. The teams must share the process, the tools, the development, and testing environments. They should also share attitudes and cultures. The simplest way to achieve most of these characteristics is to think of the teams as virtual organizations. This means that individuals can move between teams or play roles shared between teams. The process support role is common to both teams and is usually assigned to one individual. It should also be common to move developers' and designers' responsibilities between teams. A designer profits greatly by actively participating in the development of his component. There is also no better way for developers to learn how to specify (and read the specifications of) components than to work with designers for a lengthy period.

These interactions are difficult to achieve in a distributed environment. In our case, we selected key people who physically moved among groups to increase the time when they were shared time together. This introduced extra costs and, in the early phases of the project, made certain employees spend extended periods of time away from their homes. Ultimately we discovered that, as we rigorously unified the training, perfected communication, and gained experience, the need to co-locate employees diminished. However, we incurred significant unforeseen costs before reaching a mature state of operations.

8.3.5 Achieving Unambiguous Communication

Unambiguous communication is essential for successful distributed development. All three teams (design, development, and infrastructure) should rigorously follow the same process and plan. Quality of communication between the design and component development teams is critical. Any ambiguities may result in faulty manufacturing and product delays. By far the most significant element of this communication is component specifications. Component specifications are very extensive and must include

- Services provided by the components
- All temporal dependencies among the services
- Interactions with other components to obtain required services
- Nonfunctional properties, such as footprint (size of the component at runtime) and response time

A component specification may also include a description of the behavior of related components or even stubs of these components. A specification of a performance-critical component may include stubs of the components with which it will interact. These stubs should realistically simulate the time behavior of their future implementations.

To have such quality communication the project must use a component specification standard and tools. By "standard" I don't mean an industry standard—it does not exist—but an agreed-upon and rigorously followed set of specification rules. Simply using an Interface Definition Language (IDL) is not enough. A complete specification may include UML models, forms, tables, and documents captured with a requirements management tool. In most cases a paper-based set of rules and guidelines is not enough. What is needed is a set of tools that are integrated well with the component infrastructure. Some commercial component infrastructures come with tools. IBM's WebSphere is tightly integrated with VisualAge and Object Builder. Object Builder is integrated with Rational Rose, a UML modeling tool, which is used for some aspects of component specifications.

If a component infrastructure is homegrown, the lead architect is responsible for defining component specification standards and the Infrastructure Group is responsible for integrating the infrastructure with tools. In our context we had a separate team responsible for tools integration and a dedicated person traveling between the Application and Component Development Groups with full time responsibility for teaching and mentoring the developers and designers on how to use the tools and how to write and interpret component specifications.

8.3.6 Large-Scale Legacy Integration Difficulties

I have learned not to underestimate the difficulties introduced by integrating new system components with legacy components. Since large systems cannot be redesigned and replaced at will, large systems evolve as a combination of the new and the old. Componentization of legacy systems is difficult, especially because there is rarely a clear sequence of steps that will achieve the desired result. For example, the heart of any ERP system is inventory and production planning. Any attempt to componentize only a single part of either inventory or production planning is often impossible because of their very high coupling. Componentization of both of them, however, ripples through the entire system. If we were to introduce a well-articulated inventory management component, every direct access to the inventory database would have to be replaced by an invocation of a service on this component or on some of its boundary objects. In some cases the cost of integrating the new component with the old code may be higher than the cost of developing the new component.

In addition, integrating with legacy systems always limits design freedom and can easily corrupt component design. Instead of developing new components the architect is forced to design around the existing software.

8.3.7 Collect Metrics Early

The last pitfall on my list has to do with reliably estimating the cost and time of component design, development, testing, and integration. There is a common belief that a Component Factory will greatly reduce system development costs. In reality, cost savings can be obtained only within a mature organization and they will not be dramatic. After all, the cost of software is most strongly related to its size and complexity. Creating a mature Component Factory is expensive and takes a long time, for the reasons discussed above.

What is different about Component Factories is that the development cost can be predicted better. This is mainly because of the contractual relationship between the application group and the component development group. Both groups have to be able to predictably estimate both the cost and time it will take to develop components. To coordinate their activities, both groups must collect metrics very early. If either group has insufficient data for a reasonable prediction of cost and time, conflicts will arise between these groups.

In our case the organizations collected the necessary metrics only after two full development iterations. Once we had these metrics, our time and cost estimates were reliable. An important side effect of having predictive metrics was that we could reliably size and cost the entire system.

8.4 What Would I Watch For?

The list of pitfalls above is certainly not exhaustive. Many readers will be able to add their own risks or further evidence for the ones described here. Creating a Component Factory and then building a complex component-based system using the approach described in this chapter are not easy tasks. What are the most important things to watch for? Well, if I get to do it again, I will implement the following:

- A proven commercial component infrastructure integrated with good modeling and code development tools
- A co-located organization (I would avoid distributed organizations)
- A mature organization that can follow complex development processes

If I have a proven commercial component infrastructure, I can concentrate on developing application components rather then on developing mechanisms and infrastructure services. If I have a group working in the same environment, I can rotate designers and developers between the application and component development groups. If I have a mature organization that understands the importance of software development processes, I can quickly put in place the process foundation for the Component Factory.

8.5 Conclusion

Component-based software development is a sound approach to building large, complex systems. It provides better control over the technology infrastructure. It naturally supports better architecture. It helps separate development concerns better. At the same time, component-based development does not remove or mitigate the typical challenges of large software projects such as the need for a sound process or communication between teams. In fact, it introduces challenges of its own as described in this chapter.

From my perspective, I cannot imagine building a system any way other than by breaking it up into clearly defined, autonomous components. This type of architectural thinking has become second nature. In my new role I often find myself reaching back for examples of what we did on the project described in this chapter. Every time I do that, I learn something new.

Chapter 9

CBSE Success Factors: Integrating Architecture, Process, and Organization

Martin L. Griss, Ph.D.

9.1 Introduction

A *product-line* is a set of applications that share a common collection of requirements but also exhibit significant variability in these requirements. Component-based software engineering (CBSE) can exploit this commonality and variability to reduce overall development costs and time (see Part V for more details on product-lines).

Important connections exist among product-line CBSE, systematic reuse, component infrastructure, and the processes and organizations that produce a product-line. Most organizations successfully adopt CBSE incrementally by carefully matching the new technology with a business need and organizational process maturity. To develop a product-line effectively, you need a coherent approach to architecting the system, to designing and structuring the components and component infrastructure, to organizing the workforce of architects, designers, and implementers, and to converting the development and business processes to CBSE-based methods.

A reuse-driven software engineering business (RSEB) is a software development organization that practices large-scale component-based product-line development and systematic reuse. Business engineering and model-driven techniques provide a comprehensive and systematic approach to orchestrate the large-scale investment and change needed to establish an effective component-based reuse program. In some cases, optimizations and the specific situation may allow or require that some steps be omitted or modified.

Business process engineering, Unified Modeling Language (UML) modeling, and the Software Engineering Institute (SEI) process maturity frameworks have shaped my approach. This chapter draws on my book, *Software Reuse: Architecture, Process and Organization for Business and Success* (Jacobson, Griss, and Jonsson, 1997), and recent articles (Griss, 1998 and 2000).

9.2 Obstacles to Effective Component Reuse

Many organizations engage in informal reuse through code sharing or design patterns. However, systematic reuse of software components across multiple applications and projects remains in its infancy. You will face many obstacles as you make the transition from traditional software development to component-based enterprise software development (Frakes and Isoda, 1994). To overcome these obstacles, a variety of issues must be addressed ([Jacobson et al., 1997] [Favaro et al., 1998] [Pour, 1998] [Bosch, 1999]).

- *Business*—How component development, support and training should be funded; lack of access to vendor-supplied components; lack of a convincing business case and economic model for long-term investment; and unclear definition of product-line
- *Process*—Low process maturity of the organization; ill-defined or unfamiliar reuse-oriented methods and processes; new coordination and management needs; and absence of well-tested and documented methods and models to relate features to component sets and variability
- *Organization*—Lack of a systematic practice for reuse activities and enterprise component development; lack of management expertise and support; and cultural and trust conflicts
- *Engineering*—Lack of adequate techniques and tools for identifying, designing, documenting, testing, packaging, and categorizing reusable software components; and too few and poorly understood standard patterns and architectures
- *Infrastructure*—Lack of widespread use of a standardized design notation such as the UML; lack of tools and components; too many different programming languages and environments; and lack of support for multi-group configuration management

Companies must make numerous decisions as they develop software-intensive products for rapidly moving markets, such as Web-enabled applications or e-commerce systems (Griss, 1997 and 1998). These involve

- *Time*—Rapid product development and market agility are critical when developing distributed software products. How should these time pressures affect processes, new architectures and component infrastructures, business measures, and organizational structures?
- *Process*—How do you adjust your process to move from a strictly feature-driven process to a reuse-driven process? Instead of planning releases based only on the features delivered, you increase the priority of those features that can be delivered by reusable elements. What standard processes and process maturity levels (such as the SEI Capability Maturity Model (CMM)) should be selected? How do you achieve widespread use in the most expeditious way? How do the various processes relate to reuse and CBSE?

- *Organization*—There may be cultural and organizational issues that impede effective ways of working with architected systems and components. Who owns standards, architectures, and component infrastructures? Who pays for component development? What discourages component sharing? What organizational, management, and measurement changes are needed to encourage change?
- *Coordination*—Coordination between new and ongoing technical and process improvement initiatives is needed to avoid redundant or conflicting efforts. What are the connections between new technologies and strategies for component development, improving process predictability, improving quality, and decreasing cycle time? What are the priorities? What standards are needed?
- *Technology*—Common architecture, patterns and component infrastructures, reusable components, and leverageable platforms are key to achieving decreased cycle time. What notations, standards, and technologies should be used? How should they be introduced? What about standard tools?

9.3 Critical Success Factors for Product-Line CBSE

You need a systematic approach to coordinate the management and development efforts and resources effectively. In my work at Hewlett-Packard (HP) and study of Ericsson, Rational, Intecs Sistemi, and several HP customers, I have found that a successful, large-scale component reuse effort must be coherent and holistic. Foremost, the component-based software reuse program must be aligned with, and driven by, a compelling business reason, such as the critical need to decrease time-to-market or to meet competitive market forces. Business needs and product-line development provide a context of organizational commitment in which CBSE can be justified economically, technically, and strategically. This will then enable process and technical change.

An effective product-line CBSE program has the critical success factors shown in Table 9-1. Because of the magnitude of the changes and the careful orchestration needed, I advocate a business engineering strategy to restructure a software engineering organization for large-scale reuse (Griss, 1995). The processes are built on Jacobson's use case driven methods (Jacobson, 1994) to produce the RSEB—an integrated, model-driven approach..

Table 9-1: *Critical Success Factors for Product-Line CBSE*

Business-driven Product Line	• The organization must have a visible, articulated, and compelling need for dramatic improvement in cycle time, cost, productivity, agility, and/or interoperability • The organization must produce software (applications, embedded systems, or key components) that forms an obvious product-line, application family, or coherent "domain"
Architected	• Applications, systems, and components must be purposefully designed and structured to ensure that they fit together and that they will cover the needs of the family or domain • A well defined, layered, modular structure and various design and implementation standards (such as the UML and patterns catalogs) will be of great help
Process-oriented	• Distinct software development and maintenance processes for architecture and component infrastructures, components, and applications must be defined and followed • These processes must explicitly incorporate reuse. They systematically identify and express commonality andn variability, and include standards for designing and packaging components for reuse
Organized	• Long-term management commitment is needed to ensure that the organization is structured, trained, and staffed to follow component reuse processes and conform to standards • Distinct subgroups are needed to create, reuse, and support reusable components. These teams must be trained to follow the specific processes • People must have well defined reuse-oriented jobs, with appropriate training, skills, and rewards for effective reuse performance

9.4 Integrating Architecture, Process, and Organization

An RSEB is run as a software engineering business. Software engineering goals are key to accomplishing the organization's business goals, and, as a consequence, the software organization itself must be operated with compatible customer and financial objectives. All processes and work products should be aligned to these business goals. For example, in several HP divisions a dominant and compelling business goal is to reduce product development times yet retain market agility across product families. Such families are conceived to meet different customer and country needs by combining reusable components. For example, a group of divisions at HP (now at Agilent) builds microwave instruments from common firmware components to create a family of compatible test systems that are configured to a variety of situations. One cross-divisional team was set up to craft the architecture for the family and design the initial components. Other groups within the divisions created components consistent with this architecture or developed applications using them. A final group was established to support and maintain the components. To initiate and coordinate the efforts of these several divisions required involvement of senior management.

Senior management must make a strategic decision to establish one or more reuse-driven business units and create a context in which they will work together. These units will produce multiple, related applications optimized around the production and reuse of components, forming an explicit component-based product-line.

An organization will only change because of an appropriate level of management commitment (for example, a strategic statement from senior management to improve the speed with which new products are developed with the appropriation of an adequate long-term budget). Business trade-offs, such as expense, time-to–market, and profit must be managed using well-defined economic, product, and process measures.

9.4.1 Model-Driven Development Using a Standard Modeling Language

Figure 9-1 summarizes the key elements of the RSEB using the UML (Booch, Rumbaugh, and Jacobson, 1999), an established OMG standard modeling language. The ellipses are business use cases representing software engineering processes, while the tabbed rectangles are systems, representing sets of UML model elements. The stick figures are actors, representing people or organizations with which the RSEB interacts.

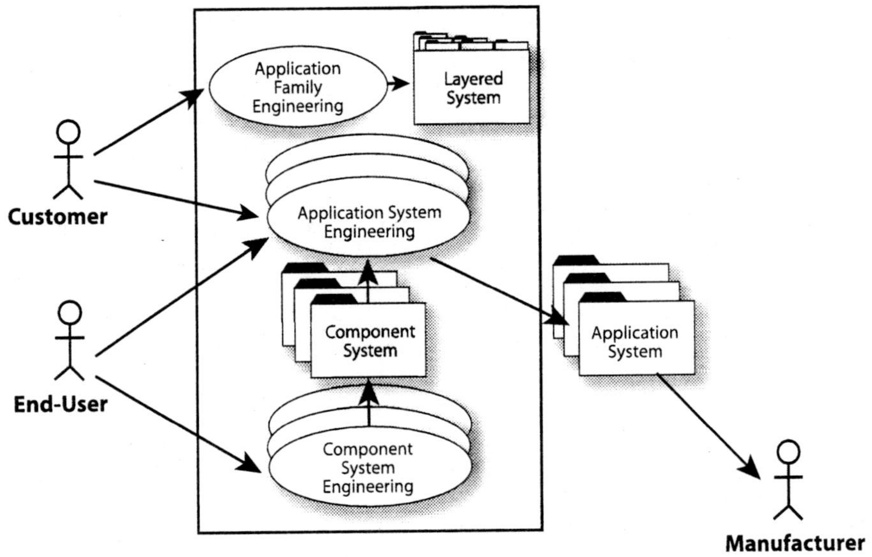

Figure 9-1: *The elements of the reuse-driven software engineering business.*

Each system in Figure 9-1 is expressed as a set of UML models. The UML provides software designers an unprecedented opportunity to develop and reuse precise and widely understood blueprints for software designs and reusable infrastructures. As described below, we use the same notation to model the RSEB processes.

9.4.1.1 Architecture

While I have tried to adjust my terminology to that of Chapter 1, there remain some inevitable inconsistencies because the field of CBSE is still immature. There is a awareness in the software engineering community of the importance of software architecture ([Jacobson et al., 1997] [Garlan and Shaw, 1996] [Kruchten, 1995] [Buschmann et al., 1996] [Mowbray and Malveau, 1997]). Architecture "describes the static organization of software into subsystems interconnected through interfaces and defines at a significant level how these software subsystems interact with each other" (Garlan and Shaw, 1996). Others include some of the essential behavior and key mechanisms in the definition of architecture as well, using use cases and interaction diagrams to capture these.

Similar to how a building architect works with customers and suppliers to analyze requirements and technology trends to design a building, a *software architect* "defines and maintains the architecture of a system, that is, the essential part of the use case, design, implementation and test models; the architect decides on which architectural styles and patterns to use in the system" (Jacobson, Ericsson, and Jacobson, 1995). I believe this distinct role of architect and architecture is especially important for families of large-scale systems and product-lines.

9.4.1.2 Components and Component Systems

In my book I use the term *component* for any reusable element of a development model that is loosely coupled to other elements and is designed and packaged for reuse. Since this expands on the definition in Chapter 1 and might be confusing with other chapters in this book, I will use a slightly modified terminology that distinguishes reusable components from other reusable elements. Reusable elements are part of the full specification and elaboration of components. Any model element or software engineering work product can be designed for reuse and reused when a new work product is developed. Work products intended for systematic reuse must be designed, packaged, and documented for reuse. Candidates include

- Use cases
- Classes
- Interfaces
- Patterns
- Tests
- Source code (such as Java Beans, Ada packages, C++ code, and VB script)

A component system is a group of reusable components and component elements connected by relationships and interfaces that interact with each other within a layered component infrastructure. A component system exposes to potential reusers though a façade, the minimal information and model elements needed to effectively reuse the component system. A façade is a stereotyped package containing only references to model elements owned by another package. It is used to provide a "public view" of some of the contents of a package (see UML 1.3, *www.rational.com/uml*).

The commonality and variability in a product-line is made explicit through variation points and variants in the components and other reusable component elements. Some reusable work products can be used "as is"; others must be specialized before use. A variety of mechanisms can be used to implement variability (such as parameters, inheritance, extensions, templates, or generators), as described below.

9.4.1.3 Layered Component Infrastructure

It is difficult to create a coherent set of compatible, reusable, maintainable parts through ad hoc reuse of existing software, or even by the use of common platforms and libraries. You can create reusable parts only by developing and maintaining a reuse infrastructure (architecture, frameworks, and components) as an organizational asset.

We construct applications as layered systems with a modular, layered architecture as shown in Figure 9-2. Each application is represented as a separate application system (a consistent set of models and other work products) built using lower-level components and component elements drawn from lower-level component systems. Layers below the application layer contain components targeted for specific business or application domain areas (such as banking systems or microwave instruments), common middleware cross-business components (including object request brokers [ORBs], databases, and graphical user interfaces [GUIs]), and platform-specific (hardware and software) software components and interfaces (such as operating system, networking, and specialized devices).

This layered architecture and component infrastructure provides components and a roadmap to help each person in the organization understand and apply the desired engineering practice. The component infrastructure supports platform-independent *interfaces* providing openness and flexibility. Different implementations of the same interfaces can be plug-compatible. Provided and needed interfaces will typically be packaged with other, related reusable model elements

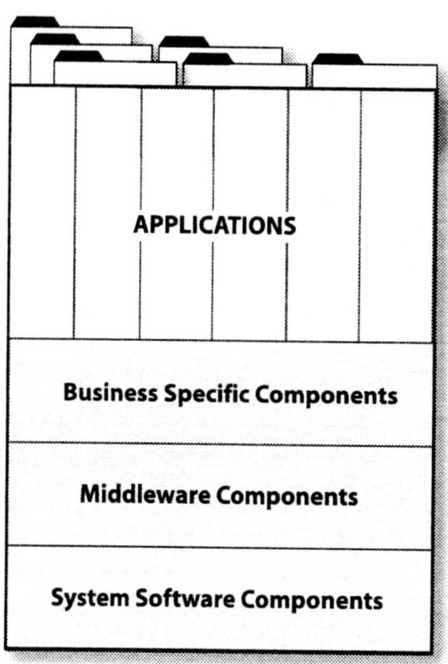

Figure 9-2: *The RSEB component infrastructure contains three layers of component types.*

in one or more facades. Finally, the infrastructure allows component systems to evolve independently as new technologies and opportunities arise.

9.4.1.4 Applications and Application Systems

Applications are defined by a set of connected UML models and other work products called an application system. Application engineers (architects, designers, and implementers) and other "reusers" (such as component engineers) construct software applications by selecting components and integrating them to form a complete system. At an early stage of software development the reuse team will work with reusable use cases. At later stages they work with reusable design components or code classes. It is important for developers to try to integrate the use cases from multiple components, because in doing so they will uncover problems that would have occurred when the respective components were integrated.

9.5 Product-Line CBSE Process and Organization

A product-line CBSE creates component systems by one or more teams for reuse by other teams. Instead of building each related application independently, the organization purposefully and proactively creates reusable assets that are then used to build applications more rapidly and cost effectively. The RSEB links previously independent projects, introduces new component infrastructures, changes development processes, introduces reusable component management and funding activities, and changes the roles of designers, process engineers, development engineers, and managers. Significant organizational change is involved.

RSEB applies business engineering to the software engineering organization itself. Business use cases model the core software development processes such as those followed by component engineers and application engineers. These models are further refined to define the roles and responsibilities of the workers, the workflows they enact, and the information systems and tools they use. Different structures of the business models allow us to model various organizations.

Shown as a business use case in Figure 9-1, the three main categories of software engineering processes within an RSEB are

- Application Family Engineering
- Application System Engineering
- Component System Engineering

9.5.1.5 Application Family Engineering

The application family engineering process creates the layered system architecture and component infrastructures for the product-line and determines how to decompose the overall set of applications into application systems and supporting component systems. This architectural process is a design endeavor that creates the layers, façades, and interfaces of the subsystems and component systems that support the complete product-line. The application family engineer (an architect or senior designer) must:

- Understand the requirements that current users of similar systems know they need now, and determine what potential users think they might want to have in future applications

- Develop a layered infrastructure robust enough to survive the inevitable changes that will occur
- Identify component systems as well as individual applications
- And wrap, reengineer, or interface with existing software, such as legacy systems and/or component producer systems

9.5.1.6 Application System Engineering

The application system engineering process selects, specializes, and assembles components and component elements from one or more component systems (made visible through an appropriate façade) into complete application systems. Application system engineering uses appropriate tools, methods, processes, and instructions provided explicitly with the component system.

The process begins when a customer requests a new version of an application. Developers (sometimes including architects) first elicit the requirements from a few sources, primarily customers and end-users. Then the developers express the requirements in terms of available component infrastructures. Certain requirements are met by directly reusing some components or specializing others. If the overall infrastructure is well-designed, and if a comprehensive set of components is available, developers (aided by librarians) can find an appropriate component or existing component elements to reuse. When no appropriate reusable components or other work products are available, the developers may have to design new components and software to meet the requirements.

A reuser may exploit variability mechanisms to adapt components to the particular application. During the modeling and implementation of an application or component system, the reuser can insert presupplied or custom-built variants (which could be a complete subsidiary component, a reusable component element, or some other software element) at designated variation points to produce a specialized element. For example, if the variability mechanism has explicit parameters for a black-box component, then setting the parameters to specific values, including binding references to other components, is the "attaching." Instead, if the component defines explicitly required interfaces, smaller components or other computational elements that match these interfaces must be "plugged in."

Finally, if the component is a framework that defines abstract or concrete classes, then concrete subclasses must be supplied that inherit from these base classes to complete the application. Thus, an application system is both customizable and configurable.

9.5.1.7 Component System Engineering

During the component system engineering process, designers will design, construct, and package components into component systems. The process uses appropriate code, templates, models, dictionaries, documents, and perhaps custom tools. The process begins when a reuse business identifies a new component system to design. The architects and designers must elicit and analyze requirements about current needs and future trends from multiple sources, including

- Business models
- Architects
- Domain experts
- Application users

The goal is to create a set of reusable components that expresses commonality and variability appropriate to the family of applications. Architects and developers (depending on the scope of the decision) should calculate costs and benefits for the amount of functionality and variability to incorporate in the components. Many components will be designed with variation points and prebuilt variants to increase the components' intended uses. In addition to using inheritance as a well known (and unfortunately, sometimes overused) specialization mechanism, you can also use problem-oriented languages, aspects, parameterized templates, and generators ([Bassett, 1996] [Griss, 2000]).

The process concludes with the certification (including internal testing, final inspection, and acceptance testing) and packaging (including documentation, classification, examples, and comparisons with other components) of the component system for retrieval by potential reusers (see Chapter 2).

9.6 Incremental Transition To an RSEB

The RSEB uses a business reengineering approach developed to systematically transition an existing software organization into an RSEB (Jacobson, Ericsson, and Jacobson, 1995). Each step in the process includes specific organizational change management guidelines, such as the use of champions, and some reuse pragmatics, such as the use of incremental, pilot-driven reuse adoption, and distinct reuse-maturity stages. To develop the appropriate transition schedule an organization must assess important business and domain drivers as well as its organization and process maturity.

9.6.1 Reuse and Process Maturity

A key question that arises when considering the transition to systematic CBSE is that of organizational process maturity, specifically the implications of software engineering process maturity as expressed by the SEI CMM ([Humphrey, 1996] [Paulk et al., 1993]). Indeed, reuse and the CMM are strongly related because introducing systematic software reuse is a significant process improvement driven by critical business need. The CMM is a process improvement framework that summarizes key guidelines about mature software process that can be directly applied to improved reuse practices.

The change to a set of concurrent, managed, and supported multi-project processes demands significant organization changes and standardized processes throughout the organization. In general, it makes good business sense for an effective plan to address the incremental reuse adoption program together with the SEI process improvement program (Griss, 1998a and 1998b). Many software engineers and managers who know the CMM believe that they should delay reuse until CMM Level 3 (Defined Process) is achieved, that is, when the entire organization is able to follow an explicitly defined process. Although cost-effective, organization-wide reuse requires the discipline and formal processes characteristic of CMM Level 3 or higher. However, significant progress to increased reuse can be made with lower CMM levels. Even a lesser amount of reuse can be of significant value in reaching critical business goals such as reduced time to market. For more details, see Griss (1998a and 1998b).

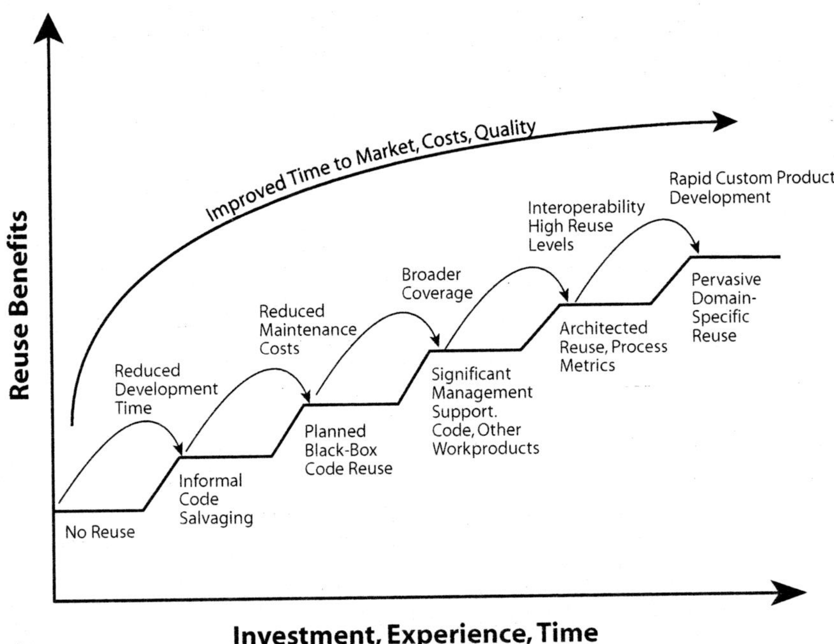

Figure 9-3: *Incremental adoption of reuse is driven by compelling business need.*

9.6.2 Incremental Adoption of CBSE

I have found it is best to introduce CBSE incrementally, making organization and process changes in a series of steps. For most organizations it is best to focus staged improvement steps on a set of pilot projects. The stages are summarized by a simplified Reuse Maturity Model (RMM), shown in Figure 9-3, based in part on experience gained from work at HP and the use of the CMM. An organization becomes ready for a transition from one stage to another when its business needs are compelling enough to motivate change.

These stages are

RMM 1: No reuse—Some code sharing may occur, but people work independently on unrelated projects. They do not communicate about their code and often take pride in "doing it all" themselves. Management may even mistakenly provide incentives for programmers to develop code independently; their pay may be associated to productivity measured by lines of code per day or week.

RMM 2: Informal code salvaging—When developers trust each other and their code, they begin to copy and adapt chunks of code from one system into new systems. Although they might prefer to rewrite the software, they copy the code to reduce time spent on a project.

RMM 3: Planned black-box code reuse—While informal code salvaging reduces development time and testing, maintenance problems soon increase. Multiple copies of components, each slightly different, have to be managed. Defects found in one copy have to be found and fixed multiple times. The next stage is a planned "black-box" code reuse strategy in which carefully chosen instances of code are reengineered into components, tested and documented for reuse, and reused without change.

RMM 4: Managed work product reuse—To increase organization-wide reuse, you need a process that supports an increasing number of reusers. Should everyone be "forced" to use only the standard version? Should multiple versions be maintained? Should adaptation be allowed? Who decides? What else should be reused? This stage leads to a defined component management process with distinct creator and reuse projects and a support organization. Employees need education and help in using these components. Strong configuration management processes and tools are needed.

RMM 5: Architected reuse—To achieve higher levels of reuse and gain increased coverage from design to implementation, it is important to design the components and the infrastructure that will use them. Developing and adhering to common architectures and component infrastructures involves even more organizational commitment and structure than ad hoc reuse of unrelated components. Groups of developers have to work together to agree on, and then enforce, interfaces and feature sets. Modeling notations become critical.

RMM 6: Pervasive domain-specific product-line CBSE—Product-lines are planned and component infrastructures and components are defined to ensure maximum reuse. Component development is carefully scheduled and resourced to ensure the quickest return on the reuse investment. People specialize in different roles, such as design for reuse, domain engineering, component engineering, and reuse library management. Separate teams operate in a concurrent, coordinated way.

Benefits, such as improved time-to-market, higher-quality systems, or lower overall development costs increase as the levels of reuse and the sophistication of the reuse program increase. Organizations cannot easily jump steps needed to achieve mastery at a particular level, although they can begin to master and institutionalize skills on one level while exploring the higher levels.

9.7 Conclusion

Effective systematic reuse is directly related to increased organizational process maturity. An organization can evolve a product-line CBSE reuse business by becoming more skilled and disciplined in following standard processes, as well as using and creating standard templates, documents, and software work products. Effective product-line CBSE requires a coherent approach that designs a product-line component infrastructure and components, organizes the workforce, and enables the transition of the development and business processes. I recommend the following key steps to ensure your own "CBSE success story."

1. Clarify the business goals that motivate product-line CBSE. Customize the CBSE program to meet these goals. Assure that senior management supports CBSE and reuse throughout the organization.
2. Address a significant segment of the product-line or key domain with enough projected reuse of the components to justify the extra technical and management effort. Ensure that senior management and the engineering staff understand that the payoff will occur only if there is repeated use.
3. Assess process maturity, experience, and readiness of the organization, and plan an incremental adoption roadmap to move the organization to mature CBSE. Use fast-paced pilot projects and reengineer existing software into initial components as appropriate. This will test and demonstrate the CBSE program for an important subset of the desired architecture, components, and product-line.
4. Design and incrementally implement a layered architecture and infrastructure for the product family. Develop components and component systems, exploiting variability mechanisms appropri-

ate to the domain or product-line variability and to the developer process and tool maturity.

5. Match the organization to the product-line structure. Assign key component and application systems to distinct parts of the organization.

Part II

Summary

Part II is a thoroughly enjoyable collection of related chapters. The chapters are educational, experiential, witty, and most of all, state-of-the-art. John Williams sets the tone by clearly establishing the various business cases for selecting CBD and CBSE. Will Tracz, in a cleverly presented chapter, exposes the myths of COTS components and provides a pithy statement on reality. Yet the dose of reality is just enough to question false impressions that might lead to the inappropriate adoption of COTS components. Paul Allen and Stuart Frost describe the team roles, and thus the personnel needs, for CBD projects.

Wojtek Kozaczynski provides a real-life story of the pitfalls of CBD and CBSE. The chapter should be read and reread because the same mistakes Wojtek describes can happen on any project, despite managers' distant memory of similar problems. Wojtek should be commended for his courage and conviction to publish a negative story of software development. Few ever print their mistakes, thus we are denied the opportunity to learn from others' mistakes and just retread them.

Martin Griss describes in detail all that is required to establish product-line component reuse. Martin describes the process, organization, and requirements for maturity necessary for successful component reuse.

Problems and Solutions

John Williams establishes a number of problems and solutions for the implementation of component technology for businesses. The first is total cost of ownership (TCO). Simply, businesses should not adopt component technology because it is the newest fad. The business must determine its commitment to CBD and CBSE and ascertain its TCO to demonstrate the savings in costs of development and maintenance.

John states that quality based on reuse is another reason to adopt component technology. He then divides components into three levels of sophistication based on four characteristics: quality, infrastructure, organization readiness, and cost. He emphasizes that it is difficult to create a single business case for the three levels of components.

- GUI components
- Service components
- Domain components

After describing the needs for organizational readiness and reuse, John identifies three key problem areas, which you will read about in detail throughout the book.

- Wrong culture
- Wrong goals
- Wrong purpose

The wrong culture is not prepared to make use of components. As you have likely learned in Martin Griss' chapter, the organization does not have sufficient repeatable processes, at a minimum, to develop components or establish a reuse program. The business may desire to implement component technology, but financial and personnel resources are diverted to other high-priority projects. In addition, businesses often reward developers according to the amount of source code they write. This form of reward will inhibit reuse.

John declares that because businesses change, especially in today's economy, domain components have a short life. Even domain components that are designed with an anticipation of the business' future are likely to require redesign. He states that, "In dynamic markets infrastructure services may remain more stable than the domains they serve."

Will Tracz initiates his list of myths with one that most information technology managers have to consider when purchasing any technology, but none so much as COTS components.

> **Myth #1:** *It's important to know what COTS components can do* for *you.*
>
> **Reality:** *It's important to know what COTS components can do* to *you.*

Will then explains that the dependencies and interactions among COTS components can lead to intractable problems when trying to resolve difficulties among various component producers. He then describes that nonfunctional requirements such as security, fault tolerance, and error handling may not be uniformly supported by all COTS components (if at all) and may affect optimal system performance. Another of his exceptionally important myths and realities is

> **Myth #5:** *COTS product selections are based on extensive evaluation and analysis.*
>
> **Reality:** *COTS product selections are often based on slick demos, Web searches, or reading trade journals.*

In Chapter 28 you will read about the importance of testing COTS components and in Chapter 38, the necessity of, and the methodology for, third-party certification of COTS components. Yet Will has determined that system integrators, component consumers, and purchasing end-users have difficulty staying current with component technology and the software component literature. There are two appropriate strategies for selecting components. Either you evaluate the total cost of ownership (TCO) as suggested by John Williams in Chapter 5 or you rely on the advice of a trusted third party. Will finds, instead, that components are often selected and purchased on impulse. Most engineering disciplines will experience the same phenomena until standards or laws are established that preempt *caveat emptor* (let the buyer beware).

Paul Allen and Stuart Frost's chapter is one of only a few reprinted chapters in this book. The chapter partially derives from their studies of the needs for new roles and positions for CBD and CBSE. They studied and consulted with numerous organizations about establishing team roles for CBD and CBSE. The chapter is a revelation concerning the roles and personnel required to function effectively once CBSE is adopted. Martin Griss' chapter certainly supports Paul and Stuart's contention that CBD and product-line development require significantly more positions than object-oriented or other forms of software development.

As with other forms of engineering or manufacturing, CBD and CBSE indeed are labor intensive. For too long project managers have had to slight one or more of the following controls on software projects' primary resources.

- Quality
- Schedule
- Budget

With an insufficient budget the project manager cannot hire an experienced staff in the right numbers. The schedule, therefore, cannot be met. Quality becomes something the manager hopes the test team can find and developers can fix in time to meet the schedule. Yet, to roll out a functioning system on schedule, the application is likely to have defects and may fail to satisfy some requirements that did not make it into the system, which will likely will prevent a fully functioning application for quite some time.

When engineers and building contractors construct a building, it is not satisfactory, nor will the building inspectors accept, that in retrospect the initial budget was insufficient. Therefore, the occupants of the high-rise building will have to learn to live without access to the building, that is, until the defects in the iron support structure are rewelded to within standard allowances for a building of that height and supporting weight per floor. In similar fashion, software managers should not initiate component-based software projects without sufficient funds and commitment from upper management.

Paul and Stuart argue that there must be an executive sponsor who convinces senior management to adopt component technology. Such a visionary would construct a cost model, following the approach of John Williams, to justify the start-up costs for both a pilot project and a full scale product-line reuse program.

Too often software development has been drastically undersold. At the time that CBD and CBSE is to be sold based on initial cost figures and TCO, those financial numbers will probably be suspect. In Chapter 24 Reifer presents methods to effectively counter those who oppose CBSE and reuse. Yet be prepared in advance for senior management's reluctance to change the status quo.

The chapter written by Wojtek will help you avoid the most common mistakes in applying CBSE. Wojtek offers solutions from often-painful experience. After many managers complete a project that did not succeed as planned, the tendency is to forget their errors. Those with courage to confront the memories, who desire to learn from them, profit beyond any educational experience. Wojtek not only shares the pitfalls with us, but the solutions he would introduce today. We thank him for an excellent learning experience that we, as coeditors, do not wish to embellish.

Finally, Martin offers a success story based on his experiences at Hewlett-Packard during many years in its laboratories. He starts by examining the obstacles to component reuse. We have discussed many of those already; Martin assembles those obstacles into a convenient list. Once you read it, the list overwhelms you with any deficiencies in your program that you might not have wanted to consider.

A product-line CBSE creates component systems by one or more teams for reuse by other teams. Instead of building each related application independently, the organization purposefully and proactively creates reusable assets that are then used to build applications more rapidly and cost effectively. The RSEB links previously independent projects, introduces new component infrastructures, changes development processes, introduces reusable component management and funding activities, and changes the roles of designers, process engineers, development engineers, and managers. Significant organizational change is involved.

Though other authors in this book may use somewhat different terminology, this concept runs through this Part like a thread. CBD and CBSE are not methodologies for the development of components for one-time use. Components are designed for reuse and not just for reuse in very similar products, but in a product-line where there are similarities at some layers and few or no similarities at other layers. Infrastructures can be reused. Documentation most certainly will be reused.

The emphasis of Martin's statement is that significant organizational change is involved. Senior business management has to believe that competitive pressures such as expenses, time-to-market, and enhanced profitability will result from such drastic measures. As we declared previously, a strong, well-trained manager must be able to support senior management's expectations over the long-term, especially when new fads that promise increased profitability and productivity receive considerable, expensive television air time as well as effective magazine placements. Alternatively, hiring the best and brightest for the newly created positions takes longer than anticipated.

Conclusion

This Part's chapters are placed early in this book for one reason. They provide the best reasons to adopt CBD and CBSE and offer reality about the state-of-the-art of the discipline. There are many good reasons to transition to CBSE; the question is whether the time is now. The time will come, we believe, when the technology will improve substantially, as you will read later, and CBSE will mature immeasurably in a few years. The public demands improvements in software and CBSE is the only way to meet the demands of a public continually dissatisfied with the quality and reliability of software.

You are among that public. You have read how software reuse improves the reliability and quality of software. Like the editors, you probably tire of rebooting your operating system at least once or more per day. Your tolerance for restarting applications because of application errors is diminishing. CBSE and software reuse, you read, can improve the quality of your software as standards and certification have improved safety-critical appliances, such as wall sockets, outside Christmas lights, and medical devices. This Part shows how some experts have achieved success and how they avoid failure. Subsequent chapters will elaborate on these perspectives.

Part II

References

P. Allen and S. Frost, *Component-Based Development for Enterprise Systems: Applying The SELECT Perspective*, Cambridge University Press—SIGS Publications, Cambridge, UK, 1998.

J. August, *Joint Application Design: The Group Session Approach to System Design*, Prentice-Hall, Upper Saddle River, NJ, 1991.

L. Bass, P. Clements, and R. Kazman, *Software Architecture in Practice*, Addison-Wesley, Reading, MA, 1998.

P. Bassett, *Framing Reuse: Lessons from the Real World*, Prentice-Hall, Upper Saddle River, NJ, 1996.

G. Booch, J. Rumbaugh, and I. Jacobson, *The Unified Modeling Language: User Guide*, Addison-Wesley, Reading, MA, 1999.

J. Bosch, "Product-Line Architectures and Industry: A Case Study," Proceedings, 21st International Conference on Software Engineering (ICSE), ACM Press, Los Angeles, CA, 1999, pp. 544-554.

F. Brooks, *The Mythical Man-Month: Essays on Software Engineering*, Addison-Wesley, Reading, MA, 1995.

F. Buschmann, R. Meunier, H. Rohnert, P. Sommerlad, and M. Stal, *Pattern-Oriented Software Architecture, Volume I: A System of Patterns*, John Wiley & Sons, Chichester, England, 1996.

IPESO/DISA, DII COE Defense Information Infrastructure Common Operating Environment, *diicoe.disa.mil/coe/*, 2001.

DSDM Consortium, *DSDM Version 3*, Tesseract Publishing, 1997.

J. Favaro, K. Favaro, and P. Favaro, "Value Based Software Reuse Investment," *Annals of Software Engineering*, Vol. 5, 1998, pp. 5-52.

W. Frakes and S. Isoda, "Success Factors of Systematic Reuse," *IEEE Software*, Vol. 11, No. 5, Sept., 1994, pp. 15-19.

D. Garlan and M. Shaw, *Software Architecture: Perspectives on an Emerging Discipline*, Prentice-Hall, Upper Saddle River, NJ, 1996.

M. Griss, "Software Reuse: A Process of Getting Organized," *Object Magazine*, Vol. 5, No. 2, May, 1995, pp. 76-78.

M. Griss, "Improved Cycle Time in the Reuse-driven Software Engineering Business," *Object Magazine*, Vol. 7, No. 6, Aug., 1997, pp. 23-30.

M. Griss, "Reuse Strategies—Models and Patterns of Success," *Component Strategies*, SIGS, Oct., 1998.

M. Griss, "CMM as a Framework for Systematic Reuse: Part 1," *Object Magazine*, Vol. 8, No. 1, Mar., 1998a, pp. 60-69.

M. Griss, "CMM, PSP and TSP as a Framework for Adopting Systematic Reuse: Part 2," *Object Magazine*, June 1998b.

M. Griss, "Implementing Product-Line Features with Component Reuse," Proceedings, 6th International Conference on Software Reuse, Lecture Notes in Computer Science (LNCS), No. 1844, Springer-Verlag, Heidelberg, Germany, June 2000, pp. 137-152.

P. Herzum and O. Sims, *Business Component Factory: A Comprehensive Overview of Component-Based Development for the Enterprise*, John Wiley & Sons, New York, NY, 2000.

W. Humphrey, *Introduction to the Personal Software Process*, Addison-Wesley, Reading, MA, 1996.

M. Jackson, "Some Complexities in Computer-based Systems and Their Implications for System Development," Proceedings, International Conference on Computer Systems and Software Engineering (CompEuro), IEEE Computer Society Press, Tel-Aviv, Israel, 1990, pp. 344-351.

I. Jacobson, M. Ericsson, and A. Jacobson, *The Object Advantage: Business Process Reengineering with Object Technology*, Addison-Wesley, Reading, MA, 1995.

I. Jacobson, *Object-Oriented Software Engineering: A Use Case Driven Approach*, Addison-Wesley, Reading, MA, 1994.

I. Jacobson, M. Griss, and P. Jonsson, *Software Reuse: Architecture, Process and Organization for Business Success*, Addison-Wesley, Reading, MA, 1997.

P. Kruchten, "The 4+1 View Model of Architecture," *IEEE Software*, Vol. 12, No. 6, Nov., 1995, pp. 42-50.

P. Kruchten, *The Rational Unified Process: An Introduction*, 2nd ed. Addison-Wesley, Reading, MA, 1998.

T. Mowbray and R. Malveau, *CORBA Design Patterns*, John Wiley & Sons, New York, NY, 1997.

M. Paulk, B. Curtis, M. Chrissis, and C. Weber, "Capability Maturity Model, Version 1.1," *IEEE Software*, Vol. 10, No. 4, July 1993, pp. 18-27.

G. Pour, "Component-Based Software Development: New Opportunities and Challenges," Proceedings, 26th International Conference on Technology of Object-Oriented Systems and Languages (TOOLS USA'98), IEEE Computer Society, Santa Barbara, CA, Aug., 1998, pp. 375-383.

E. Rechtin, *System Architecting: Creating and Building Complex Systems*, Prentice-Hall, Upper Saddle River, NJ, 1991.

SEI, COTS-Based Systems (CBS) Initiative, *www.sei.cmu.edu/cbs*, 2001.

J. Wood and D. Silver, *Joint Application Development*, John Wiley & Sons, New York, NY, 1995.

Part III

Software Engineering Practices

As we have described briefly before and will advocate later, software engineering is not an engineering discipline. The practice of each discipline of engineering is defined by a body of knowledge that is supported by the practice in the "one best way," Frederick Taylor's method for breaking large problems into smaller problems and implementing solutions as discrete components to resolve efficiency issues (Kanigel, 1997).

This book is the first to develop a useful body of knowledge for a subset of software engineering, a desired goal (see *www.acm.org/serving/se_policy/papers.html*, for example). It is a state-of-the-art text on CBSE, produced to serve as the first in a series of editions that will eventually become sufficiently empirical to serve the CBSE community as a handbook.

Part III establishes the state-of-the-art of CBSE, ranging from histories of software engineering and software components in the United

States to the present, then to recent and current practices of CBSE in the European Union and Japan. Each chapter is like a small, gift-wrapped package; once opened, you find a big surprise, a surprise that makes the package very special.

George Heineman is a coeditor of this book. He is also an author and coauthor. In his chapter on the practice of software engineering, Heineman describes the first published use of the term *software engineering* at a 1968 NASA conference. Even at that time, many software practitioners were already trying to move the manufacture of software to become based on sound engineering foundations.

George concludes that eventually the government will determine the quality of software products if software engineering does not establish and conform to standards. He cites the Uniform Computer Information Transactions Act, commonly referred to as UCITA, stating that, as theoretical and practical work on testing and quality assurance improve software development, standards will emerge to reflect software quality evaluations. As industry standards evolve, what the law deems commercially acceptable will be measured by those standards. Although the software engineering community has not widely embraced empiricism, it must preempt government intervention by establishing programs for the statistical measurement of software quality improvements. Measurement and metrics is especially necessary in the commerce of trusted software components.

Chapter 11, by Paul C. Clements, is a classic of the CBSE literature. This chapter has been published previously, once in a journal and again in a book. The work deserves to be published again. He describes the history of software components from a technological perspective and presents the assets and liabilities of CBD. Paul takes us back to 1968 when Edsger Dijkstra published his work on the separation of concerns, that is, pieces of programs that could be developed independently. Four years later David Parnas introduced the concept of information-hiding, a design principle for decomposing a system into parts that hide design decisions. The whole system could be changed by replacing a module with a different one satisfying the same interface. Object-oriented design and development and component-based design evolved from Parnas' methodology.

In Chapter 12 Barry McGibbon presents the state-of-the-art of CBD and CBSE from a European perspective. Barry explores the successes and failures of CBSE in the European Union from his experience. The most interesting of his observations is his assessment of the current skill set of European developers. The risk-averse inclination of the majority of European organizations has prevented developers from learning and implementing object-oriented methods, a prerequisite for learning CBD. The learning curve to CBD will be steep in the European Union.

Mikio Aoyama describes the recent restructuring of computing in Japan. He explains that software reuse and product-lines have been the standard for over a decade in Japanese software factories. He presents a variety of government and joint industrial and academic research projects, the first initiated in 1995. Mikio further describes advanced CBSE technologies developed by three of the large Japanese computer companies. Finally, he provides information about CBSE initiatives in the Asia-Pacific region.

All of these chapters build on one another. George Heineman traces software engineering from its first presented use at a 1968 NASA conference to CBSE. Paul C. Clements presents the technological history of the precursors of components to component reuse in product-lines. Barry McGibbon and Mikio Aoyama describe the status of CBSE in two diverse parts of the world. They too provide a brief history, and then present two very different approaches and levels of support for CBSE. Based on history and current development, how long will it take for the mainstream software engineering community to adopt CBSE ? What obstructions or new fads will intervene as CBD and CBSE mature? Is it possible that IT organizations, component producers, and component consumers will find the procurement of financial and personnel resources prohibitive? Currently we can only answer these questions with slightly optimistic anecdotal evidence. As more empirical studies become available, we believe software development organizations will rapidly embrace CBSE.

Chapter 10

Practices of Software Engineering

George T. Heineman

10.1 Introduction

This quote from the Uniform Computer Information Transactions Act (UCITA) is a shot across the bow to the software engineering community:

> "It is often literally impossible or commercially unreasonable to guarantee that software of any complexity contains no errors that might cause unexpected behavior or intermittent malfunctions, so-called "bugs." The presence of such minor errors is fully within common expectation." (UCITA, 2000)[1]

This surprising statement reveals the mediocre state in which software engineering finds itself at the turn of the millennium. In no other profession do we find such an endemic acceptance of low quality; we should wonder about the reasons that motivate such legal statements.

1. For more information on UCITA, read Chapter 40 and the overview provided in *www.nccusl.org/uniformact_overview/uniformacts-ov-ucita.htm.*

The core of the problem can best be summed up as the "software gap," the gap between ambitions and achievements in software engineering. David and Fraser first observed this phenomena in the original 1968 NATO conference:

> "This gap appears in several dimensions: between promises to users and performance achieved by software, between what seems to be ultimately possible and what is achievable now and between estimates of software costs and expenditures. The gap is arising at a time when the consequences of software failure in all its aspects are becoming increasingly serious." (Naur and Randell, 1968).

This thirty-year-old observation still holds true today.

In this chapter I make the case that component-based software engineering represents the best practices of the past thirty years of software engineering research and development. As Bill Councill and I edited this book we resolved not to fall into the traps of promoting a specific programming language, recommending a particular tool to solve your problems, or arguing that a specific process will cure your ills. However, there is a growing understanding that the software engineering community will only achieve the professionalism to which its name aspires by increasing the use of component-based software engineering.

It is imperative that the software engineering community find ways to improve both the overall quality of software assets and the productivity of organizations developing software. The following statistics highlight the scale of the problem. In 1985, the world software market was estimated to be US$40 billion; the world software industry has grown annually by 8% since 1990. By 2001, the industry is expected to grow to approximately $513.8 billion (*www.american.edu/carmel/SL3913A/sm.HTML*) and some project a $2 trillion dollar industry by 2008 (*www.nic.in/rrtd/ITcover.htm*). With such investments and opportunities at stake, we must find solutions to increase the quality of software and productivity of our industry and continually validate our results with empirical studies.

10.2 Brief History

The participants at the 1968 NATO Conference on Software Engineering coined the term *software engineering* (Naur and Randell, 1968). They included an impressive collection of academic scholars and industrial practitioners who met to address the issues faced in developing large, complex software systems. In the report resulting from the conference, the participants disagreed as to whether there was a "software crisis" or simply a widening gap between expectations and actual accomplishments. In addition, software engineering was considered a goal to achieve.

> "The phrase 'software engineering' was deliberately chosen as being provocative, in implying the need for software manufacture to be based on the types of theoretical foundations and practical disciplines, that are traditional in the established branches of engineering." (Naur and Randell, 1968)

In the intervening years, however, software engineering has come to mean the body of knowledge that has developed through computer science research and industrial practice and experience. There is not enough space in this short chapter to list the many research and practical software engineering results. Instead, I divide the past thirty years into software engineering in-the-small and in-the-large, as first identified by DeRemer and Kron (1976).

10.2.1 Software Engineering In-The-Small

A recent special issue of *IEEE Software* is focused on "Software Engineering in-the-Small." (Laitinen, Fayad, and Ward, 2000). Its attention, however, is devoted to the growing number of companies with fewer than 50 employees developing software. The original definition of software *engineering in-the-small*, by DeRemer and Kron (1976), is detailed programming such as data structures and algorithms. These topics are firmly within the sphere of computer science, and decades of research have produced numerous efficient algorithms with proven execution times and memory requirements.

I consider in-the-small engineering to include two parts: (1) the specification and design of the interface(s) for a component based upon existing requirements; and (2) the implementation, testing, and maintenance of that component. Such a description is consistent with the way in which software engineering is taught in most American colleges and universities. It is only by combining both of these parts that software is engineered, as we have described in Chapter 1.

The term "in-the-small" is often used negatively. For the most part, however, the software engineering community often uses immature specification techniques, and design—even on a small scale—is a demanding intellectual exercise. The challenge facing the lead engineer on a software engineering project is to design the software component infrastructure so that each individual component has clearly defined performance requirements. Another challenge is to incorporate existing software components into the design of a software component infrastructure.

10.2.2 Software Engineering In-The-Large

As software systems grew in size and complexity, it became essential to assure desired system properties of the resultant system. Naturally, this is the domain of software engineering *in-the-large.* There have been many proposed solutions for developing large, complex software systems that are reliable, easy to maintain, and efficient. Today, however, we need proven solutions. For example, nearly one-third of software projects exceed their cost or schedule (Putnam and Meyers, 1997). In this section, I outline the major solutions proposed over the past thirty years.

10.2.2.1 Language-Oriented Solutions

One strategy for developing larger software systems is to increase the power of each line of code written. Many software engineering texts show the increased productivity of modern programming languages, such as C and Fortran, over assembler languages. Computer scientists have endeavored to develop the next generation of programming languages to achieve better performance than previous languages by an order of magnitude. The goal of these so-called Fourth Generation Languages (4GLs) languages was to: 1) build applications more rapidly; 2) make the programs written in these languages easier to change; 3) generate robust code from "higher-level" statements; and 4) make it easier for users to write programs to solve their own problems (Martin, 1986). The most common examples of 4GLs are database languages, such as the Standard Query Language (SQL). Some even consider the use of visual programming as a fifth-generation language. Those who design new programming languages often believe that more descriptive languages will solve the problems facing software engineering. However, any solution solely based on a language will not be able to scale to address large-scale software endeavors.

Object-oriented programming languages (OOPLs) have become widely accepted because they allow developers to develop units of software, called classes, that map directly to the real-word entities in a particular domain. Object-oriented frameworks (Gamma et al., 1995) have been the greatest achievement of OOPLs because they provide well-designed partial solutions that can be completed to build applications. However, a class hierarchy developed using OOPLs can often be complicated and over time, developers become increasingly resistant to change the hierarchy. To use the terminology from Chapter 16, OOPLs are exceptionally well suited to developing fine-grained business components, but great care must be taken when attempting large-scale OOPL systems (Lakos, 1996).

Many claimed that object-oriented programming languages would address large-scale programming issues. As Kevin Sullivan shows in Chapter 19, however, C++ failed to realize this promise. More advanced research in object-oriented solutions, such as subject-oriented programming (*www.research.ibm.com/sop*), aspect-oriented programming (*www.parc.xerox.com/csl/projects/aop*), and agent-oriented software engineering (Jennings, 2000) are still years away from practical applications. The reason that large-scale OOPL systems exist today is because the designers and developers naturally decomposed their solution into components, that is, the language itself was not the reason for success.

Another approach is to develop specialized interconnection languages, often called Module Interconnection Languages (MILs) after DeRemer and Kron (1976). Using an MIL, a programmer captures the intent regarding the overall program structure. The concepts in Architectural Description Languages (ADLs) can be traced back to this work (Medvidovic, 1997). A similar concept, called *Megaprogramming*, was developed by Gio Widerhold and his colleagues to increase modeling power and software productivity by conceptualizing very large software systems in terms of interactions among very large components (Wiederhold, Wegner, and Ceri, 1992).

The primary weakness of language-oriented solutions for programming in-the-large is that they do not include a component model. Without a standard to which individual units conform, it is incredibly difficult to ensure desired system properties and the integration of the constituent parts (again, see Chapter 19). In addition, the reuse community has shown that you cannot guarantee reusability of a software unit simply by ensuring that all units are developed using the same language. To move towards a component marketplace, we clearly need solutions that address these problems.

10.2.2.2 CASE Tools

John Manley reportedly coined the term Computer Assisted Software Engineering (CASE) in 1981 while he was the head of the Software Engineering Institute. The premise of CASE is that software systems could be used to assist in the development of software systems of ever-increasing complexity. The early contributions of CASE were in supporting: 1) Analysis and Design; 2) Coding; and 3) Project Control (Russell, 1989). Organizations that adopted CASE often had to change their processes to be more focused around the CASE tools. In Europe the CASE experience evolved to be less tied to a specific language and more focused on Integrated Project Support Environments (IPSEs). These provided a means for a specific methodology and process to be imposed across entire projects, which, on average, did not occur in the way CASE was applied within United States' organizations.

After the widespread adoption of CASE, vendors sought ways to integrate and share data among different software products. In Europe, this trend led to the development and adoption of the Portable Common Tool Environment (PCTE), an offspring of the ESPRIT funding. The ECMA/NIST Reference Model (more commonly referred to as the "Toaster Model") was adopted by CASE vendors.

I believe that CASE tools can only support creative endeavors, not serve as a replacement. Their main contributions were: 1) The widespread acceptance of configuration management tools, such as Revision Control Systems (RCS) and Source Code Control System (SCCS); and 2) An increased use of analysis tools, such as StateMate or Petri network tools for analysis. A fortunate side effect of CASE was an increasing awareness that tools should use only agreed-upon standards for representing and storing data.

10.2.2.3 Process-Oriented Solutions

Many software developers realized that no single technical solution would solve the problems of software engineering (Brooks, 1995), so researchers turned to focus on *process*. This is a natural direction to investigate because of the close relationship between three factors: process, people, and technology. A process, loosely speaking, is a sequence of steps for achieving a goal. Any organization that seeks to repeat past successes should seek to document processes that have worked in the past and institute a climate of continual process improvement. Some of the initial efforts at applying process to software were decidedly CASE-oriented; tools were developed to enforce processes. For example, if a process requested managerial approval for modifying code after a code freeze, the automated configuration management tool would prevent modified code from being submitted to the code repository without some form of authorization. Some of these tools were overly criticized for being too proscriptive (Heimbigner, 1990).

Another approach focuses more on the organizational aspects of process. The two most influential models for evaluating the maturity of a process (and, one would hope, its quality) were the International Standards Organization (ISO) 9001 (ISO, 1991) and the Capability Maturity Model (CMM) developed by the Software Engineering Institute (Paulk, Weber, and Curtis, 1995). The CMM can be used to evaluate current process maturity for an organization (on a five-point scale with five being the best) and for process improvement. For the most recent statistics on the CMM, read *www.sei.cmu.edu/sema/profile.html*. From 1987-1991, the initial years of reporting (130 organizations) showed that 80% of organizations were CMM-1 while only 0.8% (apparently just one organization) were CMM-5, the highest rating. The latest study in August 2000 (with 1269 organizations) indicated that 45.9% were CMM-1 while 2.2% (about 28 organizations) were CMM-5. The trouble with blindly applying CMM to all organizations is the variability of software engineering organizations. As pointed out by Councill (1999), 99% of all IT companies in the US are officially small business with less than 500 employees. CMM is arguably best applied to large organizations and the full benefit may not be realized on small organizations (Laitinen, Fayad, and Ward, 2000).

In recent years there has been a backlash against strict, process-oriented software engineering. This is certainly a cause for concern. Software engineers should feel free to disagree with the extent to which the software process affects the quality of software. However, to discard process entirely is a mistake. The increasing acceptance of the "Free Software" movement, communities of programmers contributing to software projects, indicates the decreasing emphasis on processes.

The most visible text for the "Free Software" movement is Eric Raymond's (1999) extended essay on the Cathedral and the Bazaar. The growth of the "Free Software" movement has certainly increased the number of quality software packages available, but this is mostly because of the increased volunteerism of highly skilled computer programmers. Still, an important weakness inherent in Free Software is the lack of attention to design. For a more in-depth analysis of the weaknesses of Free Software, read Bezroukov (1999).

Another trend is to construct a lightweight "extreme" process. Here at least there is truth in advertising; following an extreme process can be as exhilarating as snowboarding down a glacier, and just as hazardous. The proponents of Extreme Programming (XP) describe it as "a lightweight discipline of software development based on principles of simplicity, communication, feedback, and courage" (*xprogramming.com*). Emphasis is on courage, apparently. The most commonly cited XP success story is the C3 payroll project for DaimlerChrysler (Waters, 2000). The success of the first XP project can be based on several aspects, such as user-centered design and better communication. However, there is a danger that the term XP will become synonymous with seat-of-your-pants, rushed implementation. This is no cause for optimism.

It is certainly true that the software development community has had mixed feelings about the merits of the disciplines software development and maintenance processes. However, for software engineering to achieve the engineering designation to which it aspires, there must be rigorous, tested, and quantifiable processes in place.

10.2.3 Government and Military-Sponsored Research

Numerous software engineering research is supported by research grants from governmental organizations, such as the National Science Foundation (NSF), and military agencies, such as the Defense Advanced Research Projects Agency (DARPA). Over the past few decades some of this work has successfully been transitioned into industrial practice. In this short space I would like to mention a few of the major initiatives. The Software Engineering Institute (SEI) is a federally funded research and development center sponsored by the U.S. Department of Defense. The SEI contract was competitively awarded to Carnegie Mellon University in December 1984. The mission of the SEI is to change the development of software from an ad hoc, labor-intensive activity to a managed discipline supported by technology, industry, and academia (*www.sei.cmu.edu*). Clearly, the SEI has had a great impact on the way software is developed and maintained within the United States military. Surprisingly, through the CMM the SEI has been able to affect the development of software in the industrial sector. Admittedly, such impact is typically limited to software organizations contracting or subcontracting for military contracts (Fayad, Laitinen, and Ward, 2000).

Two major initiatives in Europe are the ESPRIT (*www.cordis.lu/esprit*) and EUREKA (*www3.eureka.be/Home*) research and development efforts to foster collaboration between organizations from two or more European countries (McGettrick, 1993). The scale of this effort is vast. As reported by Tully (1993), during the period 1984-1989 these two funding initiatives represent roughly 50,000 person years of effort.

Japan has a long history of initiatives jointly sponsored by government funding and industrial partnerships, especially the Ministry of Posts & Telecommunications (MPT) and the Ministry of International Trade and Industry (MITI). As you will read in Mikio Aoyama's chapter, component-based software engineering is thriving in Japan (see Chapter 13). Basili argues that the average Japanese software company is actually more productive than its American counterpart (Basili, 1990).

10.3 Education

There is one basic question that has no satisfactory answer to date: is software engineering a separate discipline in its own right (Engle, 1989)? The *Guide to the Software Engineering Body of Knowledge* project (*www.swebok.org*) seeks to define the relationship between software engineering and disciplines such as computer science, project management, mathematics, and computer engineering. This question is certainly important to colleges and universities with computer science departments seeking to train their undergraduates in the latest, most relevant skills. The question is also important to engineering bodies. In 1997 The Canadian Council of Professional Engineers (CCPE) initiated a law suit to prevent Memorial University of Newfoundland from using the term "software engineering" to describe a program taught outside the school of engineering (*www.ccpe.ca/ccpe.cfm?page=softwareEngineering*).

The training of software engineers must not be confined solely to academia, simply because the need in industry is too great. In 1995, only 26% of U.S. high school graduates received a bachelor's degree (Freeman, 1995). While this is a larger percentage than in other industrialized countries, there are continual proclamations of a shortage of skilled workers (*Computer Weekly News*, 1998 and Handel, 1999). Because software systems are becoming increasingly essential in all industrial sectors, I believe that governments and industry together have a vested interest in ensuring that employees have sufficient skills to succeed in their careers. In some cases the worker only needs to become familiar with computer programming, but there are an increasing number of proponents of licensing software engineers. The following discussion is similarly divided into education in-the-small and in-the-large.

10.3.1 Academia (Education In-The-Small)

Many observers point out the shift in the relationship between academia and industry. There was initially a perception that academics were focused on principled education, and the use of structured programming was commonly seen as better practice than an industry dominated by large programming systems in COBOL or other proprietary languages. In short, the belief was that computer scientists graduating from colleges and universities had better skills than the average employee in industry. In 1984, Zelkowitz and his colleagues assessed the state of software engineering practice in industry to be about ten years behind academic research (Zelkowitz et al., 1984). I doubt anyone in academia would draw similar conclusions today.

First, industry demands increasing skills from its new employees, but, more importantly, the skills of new graduates are sometimes considered by industry as insufficient. Second, the rate of technological advancement has outpaced the resources of all but the most well funded colleges and universities. Third, true software engineering, I believe, must include practical experience. As an analogy, consider the medical profession. Prospective American doctors pursue years of education in the human body and known surgical methods and drugs, culminating in a residency program where they are evaluated, in part, on their ability to carry out the duties for which they have been trained. I suspect that such an approach would develop the most capable software engineers. I hope empirical research will validate this hunch.

10.3.1.1 Professional Degrees in Software Engineering

Some academic institutions have taken the lead in software engineering education, without waiting for consensus. In the December 1999 issue of the Forum for Advancing Software Engineering Education newsletter, the editors highlighted the accomplishments of the first U.S. Master's Programs in Software Engineering at the Wang Institute, Seattle University and Texas Christian University in 1978-79 (FASE, 1999). According to Tomayko (1998), these three programs normalized a curriculum that has been used as the basis for many other software engineering programs. Tomayko argues further that software will not achieve its professional status solely through efforts within the academic community. This is an important point to realize. The very structure of academic institutions that encourages advanced scholarship also makes it difficult to update the curriculum until an agreed-upon body of knowledge is clearly identified. There will be disagreement on the way software engineering professional degrees should be structured; Parnas (1999) has already proposed such a curriculum. I expect that the Accreditation Board for Engineering and Technology (*www.abet.org*) will soon turn its attention towards resolving this issue.

Some of the major computing associations are as yet undecided on the issue of licensing software engineers; the Institute of Electrical and Electronics Engineers (IEEE) declared in November 2000 that it was officially neutral on licensing software engineers. The IEEE and the Association for Computing Machinery (ACM) have a joint steering committee on the issue of the professionalization of software engineering (*www.computer.org/tab/seprof*).

10.3.2 Corporate Training (Education In-The-Large)

Most software engineering education in industry is actually Information Technology (IT) training, for example Microsoft Technical Certifications (*www.microsoft.com/trainingandservices*) or Novell Certification (*www.novell.com/education/certinfo*). Such certification, however, only ensures that professionals have working knowledge of specific products and does not necessarily provide the engineering foundation necessary for these employees to succeed as software engineers. There are, of course, more general certification bodies in existence. Most notably, the Institute for Certification of Computing Professionals (ICCP) has been licensing computing professionals since 1973 (*www.iccp.org*).

The most well-known corporate initiatives to teaching software engineering have typically occurred at large companies. For example, the Motorola University, initiated in 1991, teaches courses to increase the level of maturity of software development at Motorola (Coker et al, 1992). IBM also has a Software Engineering Education program. The need for skilled software engineers, however, cannot be met by the educational efforts of individual companies. There is a pressing need for industry and government to collectively fund efforts. In this respect, much can be learned by the experience of the Japanese industry (Basili, 1990).

I believe that the major reason for the continuing "software gap" in industry is that we have not solved the problem of education in-the-large. The problem will not resolve itself; the software engineering community must take immediate action to avoid an imposed regulatory oversight. By analogy, consider the profession of accounting. In the Securities Exchange Act of 1934, Congress vested the SEC with the authority to establish financial accounting and reporting standards for publicly-held companies. This body was created in response to the widespread belief that fraudulent and unfair practices in the sale of stocks and bonds greatly increased the impact of the decline in securities after October 1929 (which led to the Great Depression of the 1930s). The SEC mandates full disclosure to investors of facts about securities offered and sold (with stiff penalties as deterrents). Not surprisingly, the financial community vehemently opposed these regulations, believing that they would impede the ability for the financial industry to raise capital. In hindsight we can see that these regulations led to transparency of markets and engendered trust, thus increasing the ability to raise capital.

In 1973, the SEC officially designated the Financial Accounting Standards Board (FASB) to be the private sector organization that establishes financial accounting standards. The FASB establishes and improves standards of financial accounting and reporting, called Generally Accepted Accounting Principles (GAAP). The SEC has relied on the FASB in the belief that accounting standards developed by the private sector would become accepted more easily than government-regulated standards. Indeed, the Institute of Certified Public Accountants (CPAs) recognizes the authority of the FASB to establish such accounting standards.

The FASB and the SEC are examples of successful regulatory oversight of private sectors. If the software engineering community fails to solve its problems on its own, then a regulatory infrastructure may be imposed on it.

10.4 Conclusion

No single chapter can summarize the practice of software engineering. What I have tried to show is the limitation of individual point solutions proposed by computer scientists and software engineers. First, the programming languages used today are certainly more expressive and powerful than those used twenty years ago, but the use of a specific language will not solve the problems faced by the software engineering community. Second, sophisticated CASE tool support will certainly make it easier for programmers to develop software, but by themselves, tools will not solve our problems either. Third, an organization cannot expect to produce quality software simply because it follows a process. The software engineering community must identify and apply the best of these individual solutions if we are to see demonstrated improvement in software quality.

I believe that CBSE truly has the opportunity to codify the best practices of software engineering and thereby provide a solid foundation for the community to move forward to address the "software gap." I close this chapter with a forward-looking quote from UCITA that should help motivate the software engineering community:

> A great deal of theoretical and practical work is currently focused on techniques to reduce the time and cost needed to determine program "correctness." Professional standards also exist for software quality evaluation. Reasonable use of existing testing techniques that are commercially available can be one benchmark of whether a computer program is merchantable in law. As industry standards evolve, what constitutes a merchantable program will evolve along with those standards. (UCITA, 2000)

Chapter 11

From Subroutines to Subsystems: Component-Based Software Development

Paul C. Clements[1]

Editor's Introduction—*Paul Clements' article is the second of only two invited chapters in this book. While conducting research for the book, this article captured our attention in a variety of ways. The article is well written. It presents the history of components in interesting, brief, yet sufficient detail. Paul presents the reason for*

1. Reprinted from *The American Programmer*, vol. 8, no. 11, November 1995. This work is sponsored by the U.S. Department of Defense.

software components, that is, reuse. Paul describes how product-lines are dependent on both third-party and in-house generic components in a layered structure (see Chapter 15). Further, based on experience, he describes the successes and pitfalls of CBSE. Reading this chapter will help you get a "feel" for the history and present of CBSE. The chapter will give you a perspective of CBSE that you will not have without taking the time to read it.

11.1 Subroutines and Software Engineering

In the early days of programming, when machines were hard-wired and every byte of storage was precious, subroutines were invented to conserve memory. Their function was to allow programmers to execute code segments more than once and under different (parameterized) circumstances without having to duplicate that code in each physical location where it was needed. Thus, software reuse was born. However, this was a different breed of reuse than what we know today: This was reuse to serve the machine, to conserve mechanical resources. Reuse to save human resources was yet to come.

Programmers soon observed that they could insert subroutines extracted from their previous programs, or even written by other programmers, and take advantage of the functionality without having to concern themselves with the details of coding. Generally useful subroutines were collected into libraries, and soon very few people had to worry about how to implement, for example, a numerically-well-behaved double-precision cosine routine.

This phenomenon represented a powerful and fundamental paradigm shift in how we regarded software. Invoking a subroutine from a library became indistinguishable from writing any other statement that was built into the programming language being used. Conceptually, this was a great unburdening. We viewed the subroutine as an atomic statement—a *component*—and could be blissfully unconcerned with its implementation, its development history, its storage management, and so forth.

Over the last few decades most of what we now think of as software engineering blossomed into existence as a direct result of this phenomenon. In 1968, Edsger Dijkstra pointed out that how a program was structured was as important as making it produce the correct answer (Dijkstra, 1968). Teaching the principle of separation of concerns, Dijkstra showed that pieces of programs could be developed independently. Soon after, David Parnas introduced the concept of information-hiding (Parnas, 1972) for decomposing a system into parts that hide implementation details behind interfaces. In such a system, any module can be replaced by a different one satisfying the same interface. Design methodologists taught us how to craft our components so that they could live up to their promise. Prohibiting side effects, carefully specifying interfaces that guard implementation details, providing predictable behavior in the face of incorrect usage, and other design rules all contributed to components that could be plugged into existing systems. Object-oriented development was a direct, rather recent result of this trend.

11.1.1 Software Engineering for Components

Today much of software engineering is still devoted to exploring, growing, and applying this paradigm. *Software reuse* is about methods and techniques that enhance the reusability of software, including the management of component repositories. *Domain engineering* is about finding commonalties among systems in order to identify components that can be applied to many systems and to identify program families that are positioned to take fullest advantage of those components. *Software architecture* studies ways to structure systems so that they can be built from reusable components, evolved quickly, and analyzed reliably. Software architecture also concerns itself with the ways in which components are interconnected so that we can move beyond the humble subroutine call as the primary mechanism for sending data to and initiating the execution of a component. Mechanisms from the process world such as event signaling or time-based invocation are examples. Some approaches can "wrap" stand-alone systems in software to make them behave as components, or wrap components to make them behave as stand-alone systems. The *open systems* community is working to produce and adopt standards so that components of a particular type (for example, operating systems developed by different vendors) can be seamlessly interchanged. That community is also working on how to structure systems so they are positioned to take advantage of open standards (for example, eschewing nonstandard operating system features that would make the system dependent on a single vendor's product). The emerging *design patterns* community is trying to codify solutions to recurring application problems, a precursor for producing general components that implement those solutions.

11.1.2 CBD: Buy, Don't Build

This paradigm has now been anointed with the name *Component-based software development* (CBD). CBD is changing the way large software systems are developed. CBD embodies the "buy, don't build" philosophy espoused by Fred Brooks (1987) and others. In the same way that early subroutines liberated the programmer from thinking about details, CBD shifts the emphasis from *programming software* to *composing software systems.* Implementation has given way to integration as the focus. At its foundation is the assumption that there is sufficient commonality in many large software systems to justify developing reusable components to exploit and satisfy that commonality.

11.2 What's New?

In some ways, there is little new about CBD; it is just a reiteration of decades-old ideas coming to fruition. There are, however, some exciting new aspects.

11.2.1 Increasing Component Size and Complexity

Today available off-the-shelf components occupy a wide range of functionality. They include operating systems, compilers, network managers, database systems, CASE tools, and domain-specific varieties such as aircraft navigation algorithms and banking system transaction handlers. As they grow in functionality, so does the challenge to make them generally useful across a broad variety of systems. Math subroutines are conceptually simple; they produce a result that is an easily-specified function of their inputs. Even databases, which can have breathtakingly complex implementations, have a conceptually simple functionality: data goes in and data comes out via any of several well-understood search or composition strategies. This conceptual simplicity leads to interface simplicity, making such components easy to integrate with existing software. But what if the component has many interfaces, with information flowing across each one that cannot be described simply? What if, for example, the component is an avionics system for a warplane that takes input from a myriad of sensors and manages the aircraft's flight controls, weapons systems, and navigation displays? From one point of view, this software is a stand-alone system. However, from the point of view of, say, an air battle simulator, the avionics software for each of the participating aircraft is just a component. The simulator must stimulate the avionics with simulated sensor readings and absorb its flight control and weapons commands in order to represent the behavior of the aircraft in the overall simulation. Is it possible to make a plug-in component from such a complex entity? The Department of Defense is working on standards for just such a purpose, to make sure that simulators developed completely independently can interoperate with each other in massive new distributed simulation programs in which the individual vehicle simulators are simply plug-in components.

11.2.2 Coordination Among Components

Traditionally, components are plugged into a skeletal software infrastructure that invokes each component and handles communication and coordination among components. Recently, however, the coordination infrastructure itself is being acknowledged as a component that is potentially available in prepackaged form. David Garlan and Mary Shaw (1993) have laid the groundwork for studying these infrastructures in their work that catalogues *architectural styles*. An architectural style is determined by a set of component types (such as a data repository or a component that computes a mathematical function), a topological layout of these components indicating their interrelationships, and a set of interaction mechanisms (for example, a subroutine call or an event-subscriber blackboard) that determine how they coordinate. The Common Object Request Broker Architecture (CORBA) is an embodiment of one such style, complete with software that implements the coordination infrastructure and standards that define what components can be plugged into it.

11.2.3 Nontechnical Issues

Organizations are discovering that more than technical issues must be solved in order to make a CBD approach work. While the right *architecture* (roughly speaking, a system structure and allocation of functionality to components) is critical, there are also organizational, process, and economic and marketing issues that must be addressed before CBD is a viable approach. Personnel issues include deciding on the best training and shifting the expertise in the work force from implementation to integration and domain knowledge. For organizations building reusable components for sale, customer interaction is very different than when building one-at-a-time customized systems. It is to the organization's advantage if the component that the customer needs is most like the component the organization has on the shelf. This suggests a different style of negotiation. Also, customers can form user groups to collectively drive the organization to evolve their components in a particular direction, and the organization must be able to deal effectively with and be responsive to such groups. The organization must structure itself to efficiently produce the reusable components, while still being able to offer variations to important customers. And the organization must stay productive while it is first developing the reusable components. Finally, there are a host of legal issues that are beyond the scope of this paper and beyond the imagination (let alone the expertise) of the author.

11.3 Buying or Selling?

Different organizations may view CBD from different viewpoints. A single organization might be a component supplier, a component consumer, or both. The combination case arises when an organization consumes components in order to produce a product that is but a component in some larger system.

Suppose an organization is producing a *product-line,* which is a family of related systems positioned to take advantage of a market niche via reusable production assets. In this case, one part of the organization might be producing components that are generic (generally useful) across all members of the product-line. The organization may be buying some of the components from outside vendors. Other parts of the organization integrate the components into different products, adapting them if necessary to meet the needs of specific customers. From a component vendor's point of view, product-line development is often a viable approach to CBD because it amortizes the cost of the components (whether purchased or developed internally) across more than one system.

11.4 Structuring a System to Accept Components

From a consumer's perspective CBD requires a planned and disciplined approach to the architecture of the system being built. Purchasing components at random will result in a collection of mismatched parts that will have no hope of working in unison. Even a carefully-considered set of components may be unlikely to successfully operate with each other, as David Garlan and his colleagues (1995) have pointed out in their paper on architectural mismatch. Often, a component designer may make subtle (and undocumented) assumptions about the way in which a component is to be used. When component producers attempt to integrate that component into a software component infrastructure with different assumptions, unexpected errors may occur. These assumptions are embodied in the designs. Specific and precise interface specifications can attack this problem but are hard to produce for complicated components. Still harder is achieving consensus on an interface that applies across an entire set of components built by different suppliers.

An architectural approach to building systems that are positioned to take advantage of the CBD approach is the *layered system*. Software components are divided into groups (layers) based on the separation of concerns principle. Some components that are conceptually "close" to the underlying computing platform (that is, would have to be replaced if the computer were switched) form the lowest layer. However, these components are required to be independent of the particular application. Conversely, components that are application-sensitive (that is, would have to be switched if the details of the application requirements changed) constitute another layer. These components are not allowed to be sensitive to the underlying computing or communications platform. Other components occupy different layers depending on whether they are more closely tied to the computing infrastructure or the details of the application. The unifying principle of the layered approach is that a component at a particular layer is allowed to make use only of components at the same or next lower layer. Thus, components at each layer are insulated from change when components at distant layers are replaced or modified.

Figure 11-1 is an example of a layered scheme proposed by Patricia Oberndorf, an open systems expert at the Software Engineering Institute. In this scheme computer-specific software components compose the lowest layer and are independent of the application domain. Above that lie components that would be generally useful across most application domains. Above that are components belonging to domains related to the application being built. Above that are components specific to the domain at hand, and finally, special-purpose components for the system being built.

For example, suppose the system being built is the avionics software for the F-22 fighter aircraft. The domain is avionics software. Related domains are real-time systems, embedded systems, and human-in-the-loop systems. Figure 11-1 shows components that might reside at each layer in the diagram.

The triangle reflects the relative abundance or scarcity of components at each level. A system developer should not expect to find many components that appear to have been developed exactly for the system under construction. It will be easier to find and choose from components that are less domain-specific. For mid-level components, adopting data format and data interchange standards may aid in the search for components that can interoperate with each other.

Domain analysis techniques such as Feature-Oriented Domain Analysis (FODA) (Kang et al., 1990) can be of assistance in identifying the domain of the system, identifying related domains, and understanding the commonality and variation among programs in the domain of interest.

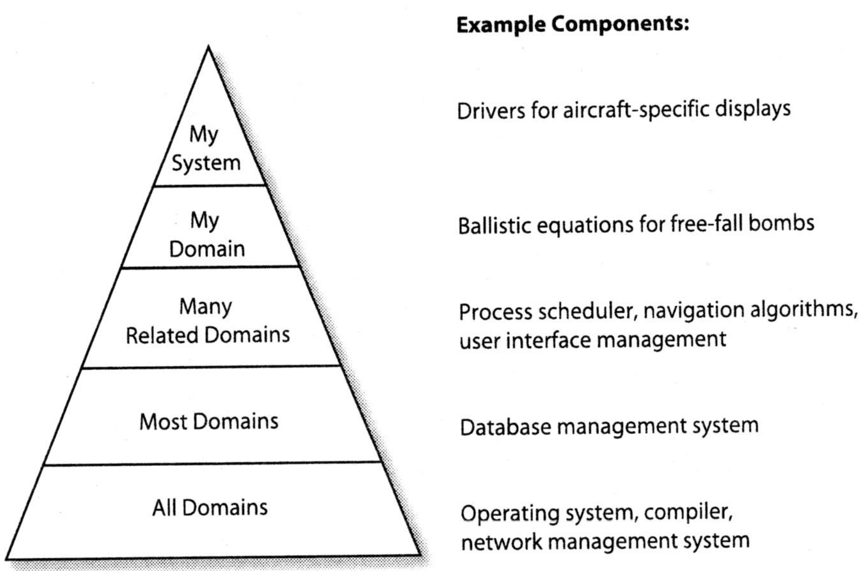

Figure 11-1: *A domain-sensitive layered software architecture.*

11.5 The Payoff and the Pitfalls

The potential advantages to successful CBD are compelling. They include

- *Reduced development time*—It takes much less time to buy a component than it does to design it, code it, test it, debug it, and document it—assuming that the search for a suitable component does not consume inordinate time.
- *Increased reliability of systems*—An off-the-shelf component will have been used in many other systems and should therefore have had more bugs shaken out of it—unless you happen to be an early customer or the supplier of the component has low quality standards.
- *Increased flexibility*—Positioning a system to accommodate off-the-shelf components means that the system is built to be immune from the details of the implementation of those components. This

in turn means that any component satisfying the requirements will do the job, so there are more components from which to choose, which means that competitive market forces should drive the price down--unless your system occupies a market too small to attract the attention of competing suppliers or there has been no consensus reached on a common interface for those components.

Obviously, the road to CBD success features a few deep potholes. Consider the questions that a consumer must face when building a system from off-the-shelf components.

- If the primary supplier goes out of business or stops making the component, will others step in to fill the gap?
- What happens if the vendor stops supporting the current version of the component and the new versions are incompatible with the old?
- If the system demands high reliability or high availability, how can the consumer be sure that the component will allow the satisfaction of those requirements?

These and other concerns make CBD a trap for the naive developer. It requires careful preparation and planning to achieve success. Interface standards, open architectures, market analysis, personnel issues, and organizational concerns all must be addressed. However, the benefits of CBD are real and are being demonstrated on real projects of significant size. CBD may be the most important paradigm shift in software development in decades—or at least since the invention of the subroutine.

Chapter 12

Status of CBSE in Europe

Barry McGibbon, MBCS

12.1 Introduction

Despite what you may read about the unity of the European Union, Europe is still a collection of nation states with significantly different languages, cultures, and technology skills. These differences act as barriers to the widespread adoption of any new technology or software development approach. Different languages impede the flow of new ideas through mainstream software development organizations. While computer languages and the Unified Modeling Language (UML) provide a lingua franca for the technologist, the majority of technological advances are published in English, often excluding the majority of European developers. Each region has a strong culture that is reflected in its approach to software development. For example, Germany, the United Kingdom, Scandinavia, and other 'northern' regions have a strong engineering bias, so CBSE has enjoyed an earlier and wider adoption there. Finally, technology skills vary greatly depending on the technology base—usually hardware-related—which precludes many developers from using modern technology; most computer systems in European countries are based on a mainframe-dominated development environment (Ovum, 2000) which may limit the adoption of CBSE.

12.2 CBSE Initiatives

However, components and CBSE are not ignored. There are many CBSE initiatives throughout Europe ranging from 'toe in the water' projects to mature decentralized CBSE. The majority of organizations are in the very early stages of adopting components (Sprott, 2000). In marketing terms, they are known as early adopters (Moore, 1991). Because of the excitement shown during this early stage there has been an explosion of information about components and CBSE. Major developer conferences in England and Germany have tracks devoted to CBSE with sessions such as "Choosing Between COM+, EJB, and CCM", "Interface-Based Development," "CBD as a Vehicle for Distributed Software Engineering," and "Loosely-Coupled Lightweight Distributed Component Frameworks" (*www.101com.com/conferences/sigs*).

A key focus for the European debate on components is the Component-Based Development and Integration (CBD*i*) Forum (*www.cbdiforum.com*) Recent topics include: "Open Market Components," "Scaling NT Up and Out," and "Building a DNS Application Based on BizTalk." Another key European resource is the Cetus Web site that devotes a complete section of its 18,500+ links to distributed objects and components (*www.cetus-links.org*).

12.3 McKinsey Indicators

I have organized this status report on CBSE in Europe using the powerful set of indicators known as the McKinsey Seven Ss: *strategy, structure, systems, staff, style, skills,* and *shared values*. (Pascale and Athos, 1981). Each of the following sections explores an indicator and details my observations, based on my experience as a consultant to large and small organizations throughout Europe. Working on the "front line" of software development—that is, helping project teams adopt CBSE—means that I have explored the successes and failures of software component-based development on a regular basis across a wide variety of businesses and technologies in Europe.

12.3.1 Strategy

> You must plan a course of action to reach identified goals that will allocate a business's scarce resources over time.

Organizations perceive risks differently, and that determines their response towards CBSE. Part of this response is a lack of trust in third-party components that is now being challenged by the explosion of demand for Internet-ready applications. Can organizations plot a strategy in such a changing world?

I find that many chief technology officers and software development managers do declare their commitment to CBSE. Unfortunately, that's often as far as it goes. Strategy documents are produced, presentations are made, marketing releases are announced, and then it's back to business as usual: update the legacy application and roll out a new service pack.

12.3.1.1 Manage Risk

Perceived risk—both in technology and in business culture—remains a major barrier to CBSE for many European organizations. Risk-averse organizations will ensure that their transition to CBSE is as controlled and managed as practical. This means that the focus is on adoption at the project level rather than the enterprise level. I observed large organizations with a centralized culture that initially attempted enterprise-scale adoption of components. After months of research, consultancy support, confusion, and deliberation, these organizations eventually found that they needed to focus at the project level to explore and understand the issues involved with CBSE.

Those risk-averse organizations that have successfully adopted CBSE recognized that whatever their different starting points—whether structured or object-oriented development—they find a common path through project-based CBD (with legacy wrapping) to their own particular goal, whether that was a distributed or enterprise scale development. Attempts to use CBSE to leap from their current environment to a more mature development environment without project-based experience resulted in higher risks and eventual failure. Figure 12-1 shows the various low-risk transitions through project-based CBD.

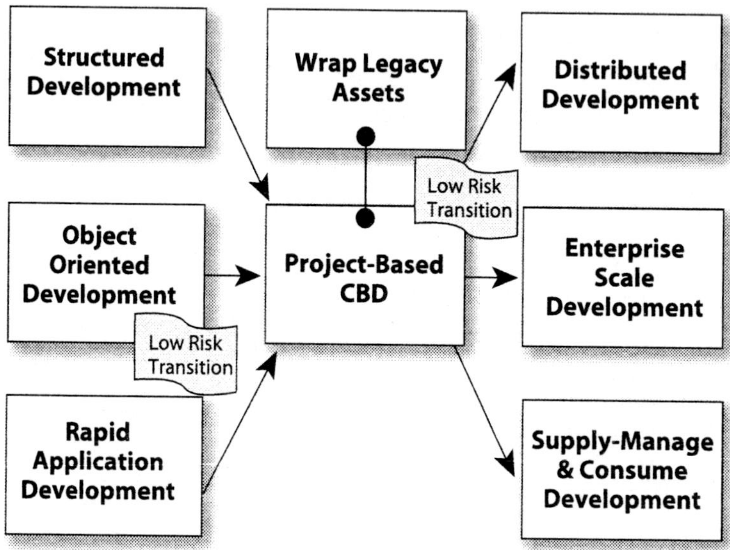

Figure 12-1: *Low risk transitions of project-based CBD.*

Of course, there are organizations that accept risk as part of their business culture. For example, in financial services organizations such as banking, rapid product development and responsiveness to customer demands are crucial to success. In these organizations—many of which have a global presence—the search for increased productivity, rapid evolution, flexibility, and quality parts provide a fertile ground for the transition to component-based development. However, in many cases the production of components is at the technology level rather than the business level. Visual Basic screen widgets, data access wrappers, and message handlers have been the preferred form of components, with few, if any, customer, market order, trader, or investment portfolio components. This technology-based adoption is usually the result of vendor-led initiatives that exploit a desire for novelty in technology and systems by visionaries and early adopters. Because many of these organizations have a "just do it" development approach, encouraging coding rather than design, technology components become more important than the discipline of software engineering.

12.3.1.2 Produce Quality Parts

CBSE emphasizes the production of quality parts. In Europe many customers state that they will have confidence only in components that have been produced under a recognized quality control standard such as ISO 9001 (*www.iso.ch*), BS 5750 (a collection of UK standards for all aspects of quality-driven manufacturing, testing, and installation), and AQAP (a fading standard used by NATO countries on defense contracts). Many software development organizations claim to follow quality standards but fail to deliver quality parts. Although many companies claim an increased use in purchased components, I find that few companies trust components from other component producers. In general, in today's European Union organizations rely only on their own components.

12.3.1.3 Reuse

Another common strategy goal is reuse. Reusability is more than the ability of software elements to serve the construction of different applications; software reuse also includes extensibility, the ease of adapting software to changes in specification. It is currently far more common for business components to evolve through refactoring and extension than it is for them to be reused as a "black box." Refactoring is the process of changing a software system in such a way that it does not alter the external behavior of the software, yet the refactoring improves its internal structure (Fowler, 1999). This approach reflects the controlled adoption of CBSE within large organizations that do not want to wait for the perfect all-encompassing component from a component producer, especially when they need it immediately. It also reflects a value-based approach to component development that is gaining supporters among European project stakeholders: If the cost of building a feature for a component involves uncertainty regarding its technical risk or the return on the investment, then it may be better to defer the cost until the uncertainty is eliminated.

In both risk-averse and risk-embracing organizations, e-commerce and e-business initiatives have forced a profound and significant change that encourages businesses to adopt components. The desire to provide new business channels through the Internet has reached fever pitch. Most businesses in Europe have lagged behind the USA in establishing a Web presence (Kee et al., 2000). This delay, however, is actually an opportunity because they have avoided many of the costly pitfalls of the new business paradigm and many are well positioned to move rapidly into cyberspace. In order to achieve this move, software components are seen as the way to combine new applications with legacy systems. It is understood that software components and software component infrastructures are the best mechanisms for constructing and deploying complex systems that integrate front office and back office services.

12.3.2 Structure

The character of the organization chart (for example, functional or decentralized) reflects the culture of the organization.

Boundaries between business units within an organization can change when decentralized service groups are created to provide service-oriented components. Mature European component-based organizations recognized that the different skills shown by component developers have changed the structure of the development teams. Instead of the ultimate delivery of an application by a single large project team supported by domain experts, CBSE encourages a loose affiliation of service producers: software component producers, software component infrastructure producers, solution producers, and component brokers (a term that should not be confused with object request brokers).

- Software component producers use a specification of component services to design and implement components. The focus of component producers is on quality parts based on an agreed specification.
- Software component infrastructure producers provide a robust technical design solution for a multi-tier environment. The focus for software component infrastructure producers is a robust and generic solution—generally based on design patterns (Princeton Softech, 2000)—that can be adapted and modified without significant cost.

- Solution producers, otherwise known as software component consumers, define the business requirements and identify the components with their services. Solution producers combine software components, software component infrastructure support, and additional components to deliver the specific application. The focus of solution producers is meeting the customers' business needs in a timely and acceptable fashion.
- Component brokers act as agents that publish the products from component and software component infrastructure producers to solution producers. The broker may be a third-party organization, for example, Component Source (*www.componentsource.com*), but in the majority of cases, the broker is an internal resource—people, tools, shared libraries—treated as a corporate asset.

I perceive that there is a reluctance to use external component brokers at the present time. Many organizations forbid the use of outside software without stringent procurement and quality checks. This reluctance also occurs, I believe, because the U.S. is the primary source of components. Many technical components are used, but for business components—the ones that add real value to the application—the U.S. dominates. European businesses are willing to use American businesses for technical reasons, but it is their unsuitability to the European market that limits software component adoption. For example, setting up a payment by direct debit mandate, validating bank codes, and calculating sales tax is common to all organizations but specific to each country. Such payment components from the United States offered as black box products by a broker are unlikely to be useful in Europe.

One of the major benefits of separating responsibilities among component producers is the possibility of decentralizing development. With component specifications for both business and component infrastructure development, organizations are no longer restricted to project teams that work in a single location. For example, SCALA International AB, a provider of Web-enabled ERP products, has decentralized on a global scale: product and component specification are performed in Sweden, component design and construction are conducted in Russia and India, and solution assembly is performed in America. Software component development decentralization offers the benefits of lower development costs and an integration staff close to the customer base.

12.3.3 Systems

> The routine processes, such as development methods, and procedural reports indicate the maturity of the organization.

Because software engineering is not widespread among developers of business systems, this community has only partially adopted the more rigorous approach required by CBD. Success depends on applying proven techniques and conforming to recognized practice standards.

One reason for this attitude is that the majority of software development processes for object-oriented and component-based systems are considered too complicated. I find that many European project managers believe there is too much risk in following a complex process that may slow development.

Component consumers, that is, organizations that want to purchase packaged software products or search for components, usually commit to the initial scoping stage—business process models, use cases, and perhaps candidate component models—to provide an invitation to tender (ITT) or identify the gaps in a possible solution. This approach has been successful in achieving the right solution for a number of large European organizations.

Quality, however, improves with each reuse of the component. A given component may not exactly fit the requirements of a new project, but any adaptation and alteration within the component or extension to its services will be tested within the new and the older production systems; errors are evident immediately. This approach to demonstrating quality through repeated delivery of production components (within and across projects) is more readily accepted by European component developers than relying on rigorous quality processes.

The planning of component-based projects is still an art rather than a science. Europeans generally do not have the "blue book" used by building construction workers, as described by Tom DeMarco (Love, 1993), nor are we likely to have one. Successful planning and delivery of component systems relies on the *time box* approach. In this approach three key attributes are fixed—quality, cost, and schedule—and the only factor that can be altered is scope (identified in use case scenarios). Project managers, representing the business' needs, and developers agree on the priorities, and if the time box is likely to be exceeded then the lower priority items are deferred.

12.3.4 Staff

> You must be aware of the demographic description of important personnel categories within the development group (for example, designers, coders, analysts).

Few European organizations have identified unique roles and responsibilities for their development staff undertaking CBSE. One practical reason is the difficulty in changing the existing titles and job descriptions, and perhaps the remuneration package, within large organizations. The traditional roles of business analyst, technical analyst, analyst/designer, designer/programmer, and database administrator still remain. Strong resistance can be met when encouraging business analysts to define components and services, as they do not identify component analysis as part of their jobs. I have spent many hours encouraging trained and knowledgeable analysts to produce interaction diagrams to show the threads of control among components for a particular use case.

Though forward engineering—building from scratch—is widespread, specific roles for reverse-engineering, that is, reuse or shared use, are not well-established. Projects cannot afford the time to develop generic software components to meet the possible needs of other projects, so delivered components usually have a specific solution model. To make components suitable for other projects, further effort and resources need to be provided; there is little evidence of this extra spending in European organizations.

Coaching and mentoring are necessary for software organizations implementing CBD and CBSE. Generally, businesses lack experienced help for new teams embarking on CBSE. For pilot projects, outside help in the form of consultants is needed and recommended. At present there are few European companies that can provide experienced CBD consultants to meet the demand for coaches and mentors.

12.3.5 Style

> The cultural style of an organization reflects how key managers behave in achieving business goals.

Many European developers are frustrated engineers at heart. Engineers are highly regarded in some European countries and disregarded in others. Frustration occurs when a developer wishes to engineer software within a culture or organization that will not afford the time for "engineered" solutions to business problems. Innovation is another dominant theme in many countries, but innovation tends to drive out the engineer, at least until the concepts are more concrete. With software—the most malleable of engineering material—the concrete never appears to set!

As we work to better understand CBSE, I believe it is inappropriate to use physical engineering as the model for software development. The term "soft" means it can be changed, sometimes easily and quickly. The paradigm for software is that it is adaptable to the changing needs of the business. Parts can be engineered to a high quality if, and only if, the application requires such expensive software components. As a result, CBD represents more of the "industrialization" of software development than the engineering of software.

Adopting the component-based development model has turned some software development shops in large European organizations into internal software houses, that is, supplier and customer roles have become well-established. The customers are the business units, the suppliers are the various Information Technology (IT) groups that deliver solutions to the business units. Although part of the same organization, IT development is viewed as an external resource and treated accordingly. Work is estimated against specifications, developers bid for the work (sometimes with outside suppliers) quality criteria becomes more important, and enhancements and alterations are agreed.

While this new style of software development raises the energy of the development group and encourages them to adopt CBD to better respond to the demands of the business, it has introduced new roles that must be fulfilled: a technical help desk, customer support engineers, instructors for training courses, "sales" staff to bid for work, and project trackers to monitor progress. These extra needs increase the budget for the development group but are necessary to ensure success of the software house style of CBD and solution building in large European organizations.

12.3.6 Skills

You must acknowledge that key personnel will need distinctive skills.

Before the new skills for components can be acquired, two prerequisites must be achieved: an understanding of the evolution of software components and a refocusing on design rather than coding.

12.3.6.1 CBD Skills Naturally Evolve from Object-Oriented Skills

CBD is an evolution of technology and engineering skills and one of the major barriers to the widespread adoption of CBD is that the developer community lacks the necessary skills. Many find that understanding object-oriented technology is necessary for developers to comfortably adopt a CBD approach. While components do not have to be constructed using an object-oriented model, the object paradigm is crucial to the understanding of component interfaces, services, delegation, encapsulation, and message passing.

Europe has been slow in the adoption of objects (Masters, 1998). This is not because of apathy in the developer community, but is a symptom of the risk-averse nature of the majority of organizations. An increasing number of new systems are now developed as client-server applications using graphical user interfaces (GUIs). This means that objects and components are becoming more common, but it does not mean that the developer skill base has improved to the level of CBSE.

12.3.6.2 Focus On Design Rather Than Coding

Coding predominates for software developers in Europe. Programming is mainly performed using Visual Basic or C++ in a Microsoft-dominated environment. The use of Java is increasing for Internet solutions, but its utilization is nowhere near U.S. levels. Smalltalk is popular with a few organizations—generally subsidiaries of a U.S. parent—but is not considered to be mainstream. Because coding dominates, the preferred skill set centers around the language, knowledge of the object and component libraries, understanding the chosen integrated development environment (IDE), and the ability to refactor code (Fowler, 1999) in the light of changing requirements.

CBSE demands a formalized approach to design and construction. This is generally a model-driven approach based around a common set of deliverables, for example, use cases, component models, class models, and interaction models. In Europe the Unified Modeling Language (UML) has become the standard notation for all models, although given the complexity of the standard, few CASE tools support the full set of diagrams, decorations, and elaborations.

Knowledge of an iterative and incremental development lifecycle is also a critical requirement for software developers. Most European developers follow an ad-hoc approach, applying techniques as appropriate, while organizations alter and adapt published methods to meet their own conditions.

12.3.7 Shared Values

> The goals, significant meaning or guiding concepts must be clearly understood by all members of an organization.

Software components redraw the lines of responsibility between business and development, which include ownership of components and the need to accept change.

Europe is in the early adopter stage of CBD and CBSE. Therefore, little movement towards the assembly-style of development has occurred. Many organizations have not even initiated large-scale object-development projects; therefore, the priority is to establish and agree about the values of component-based development and issues such as component ownership.

There are two distinct views on component ownership: 1) components are allocated to individuals for design and delivery; and 2) components are allocated to teams for design and delivery. The most common approach is for developers in their individual capacities to have sole responsibility for one or more components. This encourages a unified design and coding model, focuses expertise, builds local knowledge, and identifies the long-term maintainer of that component. However, the developer-centric approach also restricts knowledge of the system as a whole, inhibits learning, and constrains personal growth. More European organizations are adopting the common ownership model where the expertise and learning are shared among all team members. Components are held as a group and individuals—analysts, designers, programmers, and testers—are expected to contribute, enhance, and correct any component as necessary.

12.4 Conclusion

CBSE is currently restricted to systems integrators, middleware, and tools development in Europe. These development groups usually comprise the early adopter market, as they seek any approach that improves the economics of software development. Moving to components is inevitable for such software development organizations, and others are starting to realize the benefits.

There is an increasing use of blueprints, engineering handbooks, templates, and design patterns amongst the CBD community. Standards have also become more important. These standards include the different types of interface technology such as Microsoft's Component Object Model (COM) and the Object Management Group's (OMG) Common Object Request Broker Architecture (CORBA). There is also an increasing use of Enterprise Java Beans (EJB), as Java becomes more popular in Europe. The eXtensible Markup Language (XML) is gaining notice as the medium for inter-component communication.

Those organizations with poorly-defined software component infrastructures are experiencing uncontrolled growth in *technical software components*. Technical software components are those that provide application control, such as data access, user interface interaction, and are readily available with language IDEs. If there is no guiding software component infrastructure group, each developer and team will assemble their own personal toolkit, thus making the long-term maintainability of such systems difficult. No benefit is achieved for using components.

Business pressures ensure that only tactical solutions are provided for software components, often making it difficult to engineer components for quality. Initial designs are often abandoned when increased pressure force producers to deliver a component within a shortened time frame. Legacy engineering processes are well understood and declared as the main method for developing software, yet these have not been updated to cope with components. Development teams are often distributed to employ underutilized skilled resources. The distributed resource model makes the need for components more urgent. With this distribution, the need for a common tool set that allows easy communication of designs, specifications, and code between interested parties becomes apparent.

Like any early adopter market, Europe is experiencing significant changes in the search for solutions that deliver lower product costs, faster time to market, and more complete customer service. Those European organizations that are embracing this change expect a discontinuity between the old ways (structured methods or data-centric development) and the new approaches of CBSE. Organizations that have adopted CBSE are prepared to champion the cause of components against entrenched resistance. This means that these organizations are eager to accept new products and services based on a component view of development. After these early adopters become successful, the next wave, known as the early majority (Moore, 1991), will seek further products and services that provide an evolutionary path from their present position. I foresee many great opportunities for CBSE in Europe in the next few years.

Chapter 13

CBSE in Japan and Asia

Mikio Aoyama

13.1 Introduction

The Japanese software and information service market has been growing rapidly since 1995. According to the Japan Information Service industry Association (JISA), in 1999 the market exceeded ten trillion yen (US$100 billion) as illustrated in Figure 13-1 (JISA, 2000). During the same period the Internet changed the computing paradigm and almost all Japanese industries underwent restructuring, both organizationally and among their computing systems. For example, nine large banks merged into four in 1999 and planned to invest some $6 billion in fiscal year 2000 alone for reengineering their computing systems. Japanese businesses now demand agility and dynamic evolution of software systems.

Unlike most other countries, the Japanese software market has been dominated by custom software. Customers in almost all business domains develop their own software systems to comply with their specific requirements. However, the size of the software need is continually increasing. Custom software is costly and lacks the flexibility to meet rapid changes in the business infrastructures of customers. Because of the need for businesses and consortia to develop custom software applications, CBSE is gaining important adherents among industry.

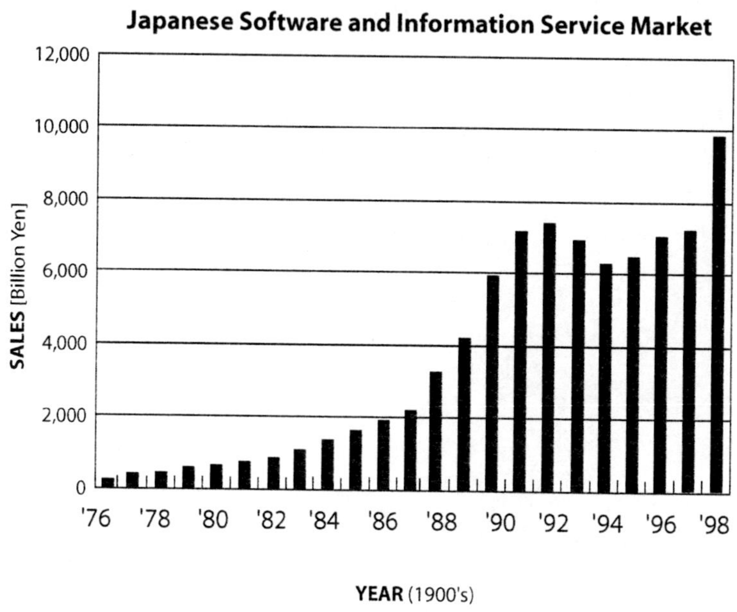

Figure 13-1: *Japanese software and information service market.*

13.2 The Changing Japanese Software Market and Industry

Since the late 1990s the Japanese software market and industry have dramatically changed, as follows.

- *Software market structure*—From custom software to shrink-wrapped package software and component-based software
- *Software industry structure*—From a hierarchical structure to an open, competitive structure

13.2.1 Software Market Structure

Corporate customers and their demands for custom software have dominated the Japanese software industry. Corporate customers tend to differentiate their requirements from other companies'. Since major software vendors in Japan are also computer vendors, software for corporate use is generally delivered with the vendor's hardware. Based on this vertically-integrated business model, hardware vendors tend to use software as a bargaining tool to meet customers' specific needs. However, while hardware has become more cost-effective, custom software is becoming less cost-effective and more difficult to evolve as fast as demands change. Customers prefer a rapid and more cost-effective evolution of software and services. Thus, application packages and component-based software are finally gaining ground. Application packages such as ERP (Enterprise Resource Planning) and SCM (Supply Chain Management) are increasingly deployed in corporate environments. Sales of custom software, which accounted for 80% of software development in the 1980s, dropped to 52.5% in 1998. For personal and office use, PC sales reached 10 million units a year in 1999. Package software such as Microsoft Office and others are commonly used.

Two unique and ever-increasing software markets are embedded software and computer game applications. In the so-called post-PC era, the pervasive use of embedded software is an emerging market in Japan. Major computer companies in Japan produce a wide variety of micro-controllers for embedded computing. Automobiles, electronic appliances, PDAs, and mobile phones are just a few examples of where programmable software components are used in embedded software. Introduced in mid-1999, Internet access from mobile phones has quickly spread across Japan. Software inside mobile phones well exceeds one million lines of code and new software versions are released every three months. NTT DoCoMo, the largest mobile phone operator, introduced a Java-enabled mobile phone in December 2000. Game software is another big market in Japan including the games played on the SONY Play Station, NINTENDO, and the SEGA Saturn.

13.2.2 Software Industry Structure

Besides foreign-based companies such as IBM Japan, there are three major native computer vendors (Fujitsu, Hitachi, and NEC) with full product-lines extending from super-computers and mainframes to mid-range servers and PCs. Other Japanese computer vendors, including Toshiba and Mitsubishi, are also selling mid-range servers and PCs. These computer companies are also major software vendors that operate subsidiary software companies. For example, Fujitsu has some 100 software development subsidiaries. This hierarchical structure is unique to the Japanese software industry. There are a large number of software houses; some work with large computer companies while others independently develop custom-applications and packages.

Since the rapid deployment of the Internet and the shift from hardware to software and services, computer and software companies as well as software houses are focusing on Internet-based software and services. They provide software for electronic commerce as well as system integration (SI) and application service provider (ASP) services.

13.3 The Evolution of Software Reuse and CBSE Technologies in Japan

13.3.1 Japanese Software Factory and Software Reuse

Software reuse is a norm in so-called Japanese software factories (Cusumano, 1991). Japanese software factories generally offer integrated processes, programming environments, and organization (Aoyama, 1996). For reuse the factories focus on domain-specific and fostered reuse of products along with a product-line. Thus, reuse across product-lines is rare. On the other hand, a number of research and development projects utilizing software reuse have been initiated in Japan, but with little success. While there are some successes, most of the projects are either specific to narrow application domains or fail after heroic efforts.

While reuse is important, companies achieve a competitive edge in software development by improving time-to-market of its software. Many in Japan advocate an agile software development process (Aoyama, 1998a). In the 1990s software development organizations gradually adopted object-orientation and recognized the importance of software infrastructures, patterns, and components. One major driving force is high-demand Windows-based software, where COM (Component Object Model)-based GUI components are popular. To meet the demand, a number of new component vendors emerged. The component producers are mostly startup software houses specializing in component development. Component-based development is gaining ground in relatively small-scale applications. On the other hand, large corporations such as banks and telecommunications are implementing distributed object environments (for example, CORBA) to mission-critical applications.

Businesses now require many corporate applications to adapt to the Internet in a short period. For example, large banks started Internet banking services by integrating mainframe-based legacy applications with Web-based application servers. Component-based development is penetrating into the large-scale corporate applications.

13.3.2 CBSE Research and Development Programs

Around 1995, the following list of research and development programs on CBSE were initiated.

1. *Software CALS (Continuous Acquisition and Lifecycle Support) Program*—A variety of CBSE research and development programs began from 1996 to 1998 as a part of the Software CALS program sponsored by the government's Information Technology Promotion Agency (IPA) with 21 major computer and software companies. Named a next-generation software engineering program, parts of this research were published by Aoyama (1997), Aoyama and Yamashita (1998), and Sato et al. (1998).
2. *Information Technology Consortium Program*—From 1998 to 1999 the ITC, another industry consortium of 12 major software houses (*www.itc.co.jp/index.html*), conducted a series of pilot developments of applications, infrastructures, and components.
3. *Japan Information Service Industry Association (JISA) Working Group*—From 1996 to 2000, JISA (*www.jisa.or.jp/index-e.html*), the largest industry association of software development organizations (also referred to as software houses) in Japan, formed a working group to transfer CBSE technology to its 600-odd member-companies.

4. *Strategic Software Research (SSR) Working Group*—SSR is a research consortium involving both academia and industry and is focused on information technology (*www.iisf.or.jp/index-en.html*). From 1998 to 2000 a working group conducted an intensive study of CBSE and software architecture design.
5. *Others*—There are a few additional collaborative research projects bridging academia and industry. One of them surveyed major CBSE technologies and case studies of CBSE in Japan, resulting in the book *Componentware* by Aoyama et al. (1998). Another industry consortium named the Consortium for Business Object Promotion (CBOP) has operated since 1997.

13.4 CBSE Technologies in Japan

13.4.1 Major CBSE Technologies in Japan

Major Japanese computer companies are delivering a variety of technologies for component-based development as summarized in Table 13-1.

13.4.1.1 Fujitsu

Fujitsu is developing a wide spectrum of CBSE technologies under the name Component-based Application Architecture (ComponentAA) ranging from

- An analysis and design methodology
- Tools for analysis and design as well as component assembly
- Consulting and education services

The company provides some 140 components, including domain-independent and domain-specific ones, for both (Enterprise) JavaBeans and ActiveX. Figure 13-2 illustrates the infrastructure of Fujitsu's CBSE technologies (*www.fujitsu.com*). Fujitsu is also providing an OMG CORBA-compliant object request broker named INTERSTAGE. The company plans to provide various services and tools for enterprise application integration (EAI) and component certification.

Table 13.1: *Major CBSE Technologies in Japan*

Vendor	Tools	Client Components	Server Components
Fujitsu	• CAA/BR MODELER • CAA/EJBean Development Kit • APWORKS • SIMPLIA NeOtune • PowerGEM plus	• CAA/Client X (ActiveX) • CAA/Client J (Java) • CAA/Gkit Web Development (ActiveX)	• CAA/Server Key Components • CAA/Business EJBean
Hitachi	• APPGALLERY • APPGALLERY Enterprise • APPGALLERY for Lotus Notes	• APPGALLERY Object • Standard Data Object • Multimedia Object • EUR (End-User Reporting)	• Business Components • Technical Components
NEC	• HolonEnterprise • ABL (Application Builder Language)	• GUI Components	• HOLON-DB

13.4.1.2 Hitachi

Hitachi initiated CBSE with APPGALLERY, a visual CBD environment running on Windows (*www.hitachi.co.jp/Prod/comp/soft1/open-e/appgal/appgal.htm*). An example of a screen display is shown in Figure 13-3. A labeled icon represents a component. Two components are linked together by a connector with a rounded box indicating the function of the connector. By drawing a connector, a module of script programs gluing components is generated automatically. A glue script may include method invocations, event handling and database accesses. APPGALLERY comes with a set of components, a set of tools for developing and customizing components, and a visual debugger on which the application designer can run component-based applications. Hitachi also provides various technical support and training services. APPGALLERY was successfully applied in a number of component-based development projects in Japan. Hitachi also provides a wide range of technologies for building application servers on distributed object environments.

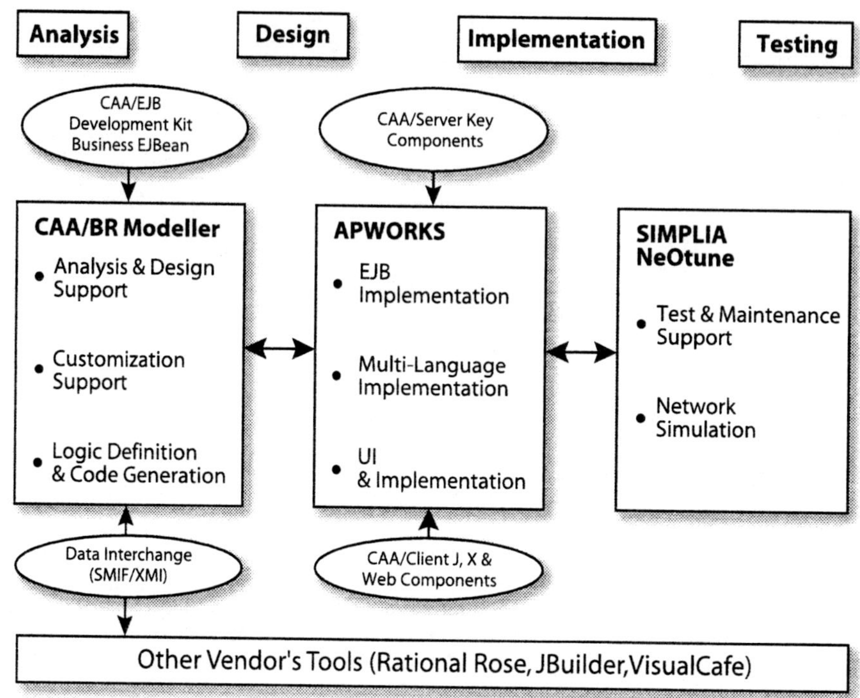

Figure 13-2: *Architecture of CBD technologies from Fujitsu.*

13.4.1.3 NEC

NEC developed a set of CBD technologies consisting of infrastructures, components and visual CBD tools. Among them, the visual CBD tool named HolonEnterprise was used on a number of component-based applications. HolonEnterprise was used on a store management and point-of-sales (POS) system for 7-Eleven Japan, the largest chain of convenience stores across Japan. The system, deployed in 1998, used infrastructures and components assembled by HolonEnterprise. The infrastructure consists of a number of design patterns intensively. A mediator pattern is used to plug components into the infrastructure as illustrated in Figure 13-4 (Ishii et al., 1999). Design patterns are usually used to design local object-oriented structures, but in specific cases they can also be applied to components.

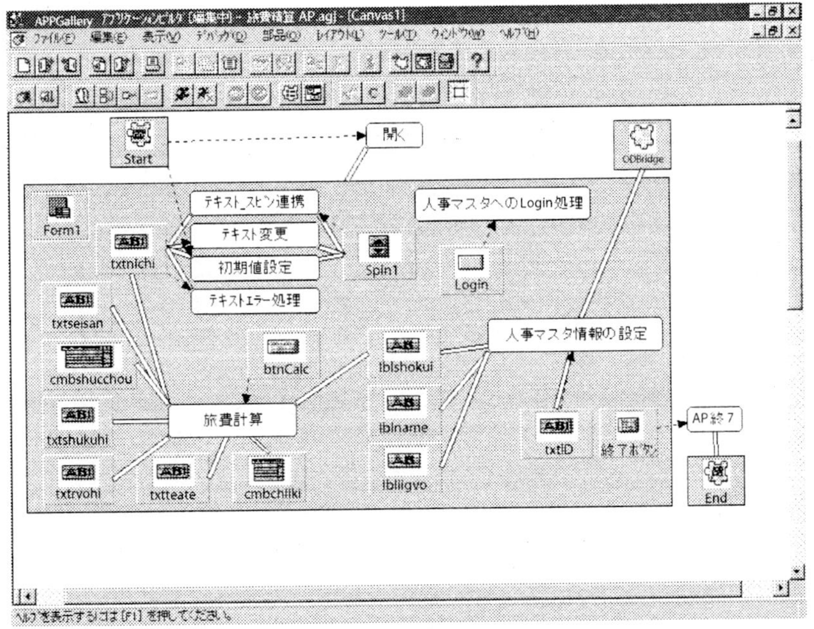

Figure 13-3: *Sample screen of APPGALLERY*

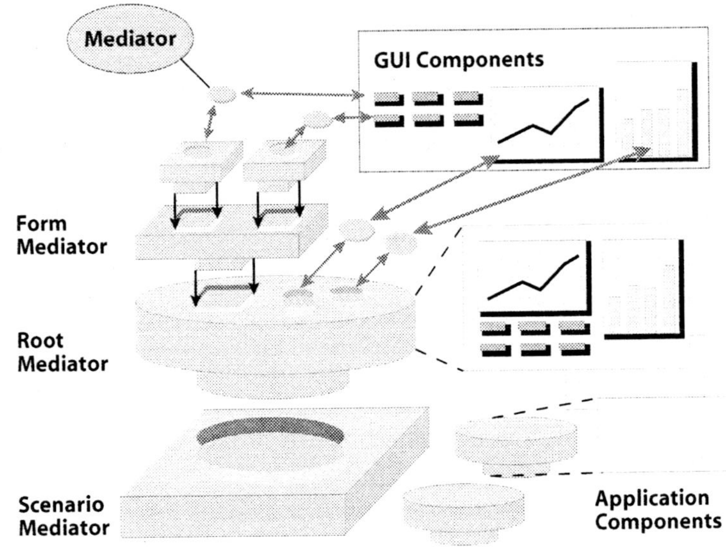

Figure 13-4: *Mediator-based software architecture of POS framework.*

13.4.2 Component Vendors

Most independent software component vendors in Japan are either relatively small companies or start-up companies. Additionally, several large computer and software companies that develop software components exist. Since escrow services are not widely established in Japan, there is a perceived risk in purchasing components from small or start-up companies because many doubt the ability of those companies to provide long-term component support. Until such confidence is achieved, this perception is a major obstacle to the growth of the software component marketplace in Japan. To facilitate the software component marketplace, 30 Japanese COM component vendors formed the ActiveX Vendors Association (AVA) in 1997. AVA invites component-user companies to be members and provides them with technical support and maintenance information through the Web. AVA has attempted to increase the confidence in long-term support of vendor components.

13.4.3 Component Distribution

Some Japanese component vendors distribute their components on their Web sites. However, independent component distribution is still in an early stage, except for shareware and open-source software distribution. For shareware, one of the on-line distributors, Vector Inc. (*www.vector.co.jp*), lists more than 50,000 individual shareware and open-source items for download on their Web site. Further, Vector reports that it has distributed more than 160 million copies of shareware and open-source software.

13.5 Research Projects

13.5.1 Software CALS Next Generation Software Engineering Program

The Next Generation Software Engineering (NGSE) project of the Software CALS program explored a wide range of CBD technologies by conducting research and pilot projects ([Aoyama, 1997] [Sato et al., 1998]). Major topics include:

- Component specification and distribution over the Internet
- Composition of COM and CORBA components with visual CBD tools
- Interoperability across multiple distributed object environments from multiple vendors
- Web-enabled interoperation between client components and server components
- Security of application integration over a VPN (Virtual Private Network)

A result of the component specification and distribution research project, a component specification language named the Software specification and Commerce Language (SCL) was developed based on HTML. SCL was extended to eXtensible SCL (XSCL) based on XML. The Software Commerce Broker (SCB) was developed with SCL/XSCL, a prototype for trading components over the Internet. Figure 13.5 illustrates the infrastructure of SCB and an example of an SCL description of component specification. Since the interface specification of SCL is upward compatible to CORBA IDL, the IDL description can be automatically generated from SCL/XSCL. The Component Player for JavaBeans was implemented so that an application designer can invoke the component through the SCL/XSCL description over the Internet (Aoyama and Yamashita, 1998).

13.5.2 ITC Next Generation Componentware Program

ITC conducted a series of research and development projects on CBSE from 1998 to 2000, partly sponsored by the IPA (ITC, 2000). The program includes the following research topics.

- *Component Development*—Development of infrastructures and components
- *Component-Based Applications Development*—Use Case-driven component identification, composing infrastructures, patterns, and components

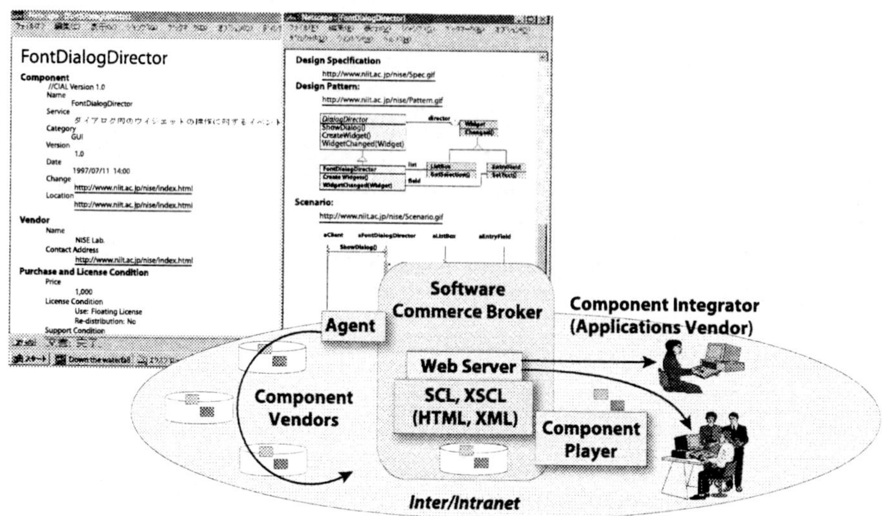

Figure 13-5: *Architecture of Software Commerce Broker.*

- *Business Collaboration with Workflow and Components*—One of the interesting results is a composition of a number of patterns into a POS infrastructure (Aoyama, 1999)

13.6 CBSE in the Asia-Pacific Region

Besides Japan, many Asian countries are actively working on CBSE. For example, the Korean government initiated a three-year research and development program on CBSE in 1999 with a total budget of $34 million. They intend to develop CBSE technology and its supporting infrastructure.

The Institute for Information Industry (III) in Taiwan commenced a research and development program on CBSE in 1996. The institute is scheduled to complete the program in 2001. The III aims at developing a reusable infrastructure using component technologies.

These research results were presented at the Asia-Pacific Software Engineering Conference (APSEC), an annual representative conference on software engineering in the Asia-Pacific region. APSEC began in 1994 and is hosted by countries in the Asia-Pacific region. The workshop on Software Architecture and Components (WSAC) was held in conjunction with APSEC '99 (*apsec99-www.cs.titech.ac.jp/apsec99/index.html*). Papers were published on the workshop proceedings (Han, Kim, and Kishi, 1999). During the previous year, the first International Workshop on Component-Based Software Engineering was held in Kyoto in conjunction with the International Conference on Software Engineering (ICSE) (Brown and Wallnau, 1998a and 1998b).

13.7 Conclusion

A big wave from the Internet and e-commerce is washing down upon the coast of Japan and the other Asia-Pacific countries. To keep up with the increased pace of business on the Internet, many application developers and customers consider CBSE to be a promising technology (Aoyama, 1998b). Thus, CBSE is a strategic research and development issue in these countries. However, the maturity of software technology is at different levels in the various countries. Even in Japan, the adoption of object-oriented technology varies from company to company. I believe CBSE will provide the competitive edge that will enable software development organizations to more rapidly produce quality software.

Part III

Summary

Introduction

CBSE is a microcosm for software engineering issues. Currently, software engineering is too broad to attempt a state-of-the-art text. CBSE is sufficiently limited in scope—although 42 chapters are required to describe the contents within the boundaries of our discipline—so that a state-of-the-art book can capture the current knowledge of the field. Although not what an engineer would call a body of knowledge, continued editions of this text published every two to three years will result in enhanced empiricism and eventually—who knows when?—a handbook describing CBSE's body of knowledge.

Much of this book's content is the result of experience, generally many years of experience, and anecdotes. This cannot be viewed as negative. Simply, the current state-of-the-art is experiential and anecdotal. In numerous medical journals today editors still permit space for anecdotal reports because those anecdotal reports stimulate the next round of funding for medical research and treatment trials. In this part, we gather anecdotal experience from around the world that indicates the ascendance of CBSE within the software engineering community and the larger industrial context.

Problems and Solutions

Paul C. Clements describes David Garlan's (1995) concept of architectural mismatch. Because of subtle, undocumented interactions among carefully selected components, or expectations about the services or behaviors about those or other components, the components may be unable to operate with each other. He then described the layered system of CBD, later presented in detail in Chapter 15. Based on Edsger Dijkstra's separation of concerns principle, software components are divided into groups or layers with other components for which they have an affinity. Components at the lowest level (closest to the operating system) are required to be independent of the application. Application-based components, such as business components, would have to be replaced if the requirements for the application change. These components constitute another layer. Business components would not have access to the underlying computing layer or communications layers.

Components at any layer can only interact with components at the same layer or the next lower level. Components at each level are insulated from change when components at distant layers are replaced or modified. Although architectural mismatch can occur within two levels, mismatch cannot become pervasive within an application. Thus, a partial solution to architectural mismatch has offered greater reliability to component-based design and development.

To resolve problems involving interfaces among variously purchased or replaced components, international standards must be established. Barry McGibbon describes how the European market is willing to use technical components developed in the United States, but finds business components developed in the U.S. unsuitable. Assurance of high reliability and mission-critical component-based applications requires standards. Other industries have developed standards for new and replacement products and prospered because of the standards. Standards, additionally, assist component producers and component consumers through the third-party certification process.

For example, various commercial building and construction industry parts are offered as choices for new buildings and as replacement parts for existing buildings. Since 1925, the Builders Hardware Manufacturers Association (BHMA) has served as the sole United States organization accredited to develop performance standards for architectural hardware and is the only group sponsoring independent certification of builders' hardware products (*www.buildershardware.com*). BHMA is the only U.S. organization accredited by the American National Standards Institute (ANSI) to develop and maintain performance standards for builders' hardware.

Barry does not create a false image for software engineering in the European Union. He clearly states engineering of software has been a constant theme for the last thirty years and yet few systems, particularly those in the business world, can claim to be engineered. This is not to imply that they are poorly designed nor contain quality code, but that most systems, based on his experience, have not been subject to rigor and discipline at every stage. The evidence is that developers and managers often revert to their previous practices when confronted by the challenges of CBD and CBSE in particular. Barry's revealing remarks must be considered beyond the European Union. While he describes other problems, such as developers' general lack of object-oriented programming experience, a requirement for the transition to CBD, for the purposes of this summary we believe it necessary to focus on the reversion to previous practices when challenged.

Later, in Chapter 24 Don Reifer describes the need for a change agent and a champion from senior management to sell an organization on CBD and CBSE. Even a pilot CBD and reuse project will require an increased budget and more staff than an object-oriented project. Once a CBD program is in place, reusable components are stored in the component library and an organization can design a product-line. Over time, the organization must manage the extra investment and staffing costs because there is always a tendency to revert to previous practices when CBSE projects encounter difficulties. The change agent and champion may be at a loss when a budget for the product-line is presented to senior management, especially once they have heard that the purchase of components is down and the construction of new components by the team has slowed significantly. In addition, developers may have difficulty maintaining the first component-based system that, at first, looked to be such a success.

An exceptionally well-trained manager is required to prevent this group behavior from occurring. Only an engineering-trained software engineer or a component-based software project manager (Chapters 27 and 37) can prevent the group from reverting to previous practices.

The engineer or manager is able to guide the group because of past experience gained from organizing subprojects.

A more unsettling problem occurs when the manager recognizes that the CBD and CBSE staff is overwhelmed. The manager assesses the staff's needs for additional training and mentoring. When presented to the project team, the staff will feel motivated to become proficient in the required tasks. However, the requested funding is denied. The manager is told to buy some training tapes and set aside a room on a full-time basis so that the CBD and CBSE staff can get just-in-time training at a fraction of the price of a consulting organization. But whenever training and mentoring on subjects as complex as CBD and CBSE is considered necessary by a manager or a consultant, such as Barry McGibbon, it is our experience that the costs of withholding training are greater than the costs of the training.

Mikio Aoyama describes a number of government and industry-funded research and development projects in Japan. Two of the programs involve academia and industry. He describes three CBD and CBSE analysis, design, and assembly products. At least two of the technologies appear exceptional and could be beneficial to design and development staffs in the U.S.. Our views of the Japanese research efforts, especially of the academia-industry research and development efforts, and the sophisticated design and assembly tools is that the world has something to learn from Japanese technological cooperation.

Mikio presents a universal topic worthy of consideration and resolution. Many software houses in Japan are small component producers. Because they are small or start-up companies, the component producers are perceived as risks in their ability to provide long-term support of their components. Since escrow services are limited in Japan, as they are in the United States, conducting commerce in components with small or start-up software houses is considered precarious. Many companies in Japan are forming consortia to directly address this weakness.

Certification

In Japan, Fujitsu plans to offer component certification services. For many years Underwriters Laboratories has offered third-party certification services for safety-critical software for programmable components (embedded software). Whereas standards currently address only software for non-networked embedded programmable components and medical devices, the same or similar standards can be used to validate operating systems and applications (see Chapter 38). The certification process would have access to all analysis, design, and testing documentation. The third-party certification organization would likely not have access to the source code.

Source code placed in escrow is of little value if the component producer were underfunded and designers and developers were laid off, or the component producer declares bankruptcy. Large companies negotiating with smaller companies or start-ups should negotiate on a quarterly basis for both the source code and any changes made to the code.

In consideration, the larger company should agree to provide all changes made to the source code to the component producer on a quarterly basis. The transfer of source code every three months permits both organizations to evaluate the status of the code as well as review the financial health of the other party. It may be in the larger company's best interest to invest in the component producer so that the organization can remain stable.

Another strategy that small companies might consider, based on the open software and free software movements, is to offer the source code for free, as well as all documentation. Initial purchasers of the components would purchase the third-party certification, which would be returned in the form of a loan plus interest once the component producer starts to sell its services. This strategy would be especially valuable for small component producers that have developed sophisticated middleware or business components. In addition, offering the source code for the component and its interfaces would resolve some of the problems associated with architectural mismatch.

Otherwise, negotiating an agreement with component producers for a notice of financial instability as specified by your company's attorney could establish a series of events that would protect your organization. For a component producer that is unwilling to provide source code under any circumstances, the triggering event could cause the producer to place all documentation and source code pertinent to the component in escrow. Once in escrow, the materials can be thoroughly inspected by your designers, developers, and testers most knowledgeable with the component.

Conclusion

For every problem in this part, there is at least a partial solution. Nevertheless, the state-of-the-art of CBSE is largely experiential. Japan holds out hope for all the forms of research and development in which government, academia, and industry participate. Still, the field has years to go before experience will yield scientific results. In Chapter 10, George Heineman describes several approaches developed over the past thirty years for solving the problems facing software engineering. The software engineering community must draw from its successes to identify the best practices of the field. Future best practices, however, will only be discovered by sustained research funded jointly by government and industry. Accepting the state-of-the-art, research should be funded in the following areas:

- Developing of standards that enable ease of interaction among components and provides effective means for separating concerns
- Establishing industrial consortia for the transfer of knowledge and research in CBD and CBSE
- Conducting research to determine the most cost-effective training and mentoring methods for CBD and CBSE
- Determining if state and federal governments should fund universities to offer training to qualified small business component producers and component consumers
- Conducting research to ascertain the cost-effectiveness and long-term success of producers and consumers offered training by government funded universities
- Finding means to protect component producers and purchasing end-users from the financial failure of start-up producers and small companies

Research in these areas requires commitment that we hope and believe will stimulate academic and industrial researchers to advance the discipline.

Part III

References

M. Aoyama and T. Yamashita, "A Commerce Broker of Software Components and Its Experience," Proceedings, 2nd IEEE International Enterprise Distributed Object Computing Workshop (EDOC), IEEE Communications Society Press, Los Alamitos, CA, 1998, pp. 155-161.

M. Aoyama et al., eds., *Componentware*, Kyoritsu Pub (in Japanese), 1998.

M. Aoyama, "Beyond Software Factories: Concurrent-Development and An Evolution of Software Process Technology In Japan," *Journal of Information and Software Technology*, Vol. 38, No. 3, Mar., 1996, pp. 133-143.

M. Aoyama, "Process and Economic Model of Component-Based Software Development," Proceedings, 5th IEEE International Symposium on Assessment of Software Tools (SAST), IEEE Computer Society Press, Los Alamitos, CA, 1997, pp. 100-103.

M. Aoyama, "Agile Software Process and Its Experience," Proceedings, 20th International Conference on Software Engineering (ICSE), IEEE Computer Society Press, Los Alamitos, CA, 1998a, pp. 3-12.

M. Aoyama, "Component-Based Software Engineering: Can it Change the Way of Software Development?" Proceedings, 20th International Conference on Software Engineering (ICSE), IEEE Computer Society Press, Los Alamitos, CA, 1998b, pp. 24-27.

M. Aoyama, "Evolutionary Patterns of Design Patterns," Proceedings, International Workshop on Software Architecture and Components (WSAC), IEEE Computer Society Press, Los Alamitos, CA, Dec., 1999, pp. 37-40.

V. Basili, "The Software Factory (The Experience Factory: Packaging Software Experience)," Video Notes, IEEE Computer Society Press, Los Alamitos, CA, 1990.

N. Bezroukov, "A Second Look at the Cathedral and the Bazaar," *First Monday: Peer-reviewed Journal of the Internet*, Vol. 4, No. 12, *www.firstmonday.dk/issues/issue4_12/bezroukov*, Dec., 1999.

F. Brooks, "No Silver Bullet: Essence and Accidents of Software Engineering," *IEEE Computer*, Vol. 20, No. 4, Apr., 1987, pp. 10-19.

F. Brooks, *The Mythical Man-Month: Essays on Software Engineering*, Addison-Wesley, Reading, MA, 1995.

A. Brown and K. Wallnau, "The Current State of CBSE," *IEEE Software*, Vol. 15, No. 5, Sept., 1998a, pp. 37-46.

A. Brown and K. Wallnau, eds., Proceedings, 2nd International Workshop on Component-Based Software Engineering (CBSE), IEEE Computer Society Press, Los Alamitos, CA, 1998b.

S. Coker, B. Glick, L. Green, and A. von Mayrhauser, "Corporate Software Engineering Education for Six Sigma: Course Development and Assessment of Success," SEI Software Engineering Conference, C. Sledge, ed., Lecture Notes in Computer Science (LNCS) No. 640, Springer-Verlag, San Diego, CA, 1992, pp. 360-379.

B. Councill, "Third-Party Testing and the Quality of Software Components," *IEEE Software*, Vol. 16, No. 4, July/Aug., 1999, pp. 55-57.

M. Cusumano, *Japan's Software Factories*, Oxford University Press, Oxford, UK, 1991.

F. DeRemer and H. Kron, "Programming-in-the-large Versus Programming-in-the-small," *IEEE Transactions on Software Engineering*, Vol. 2, No. 2, June 1976, pp. 80-87.

E. Dijkstra, "The Structure of the 'T.H.E.' Multiprogramming System," *Communications of the Association of Computing Machinery*, Vol. 11, No. 5, May, 1968, pp. 453-457.

C. Engle, Jr., "Software Engineering is Not Computer Science," Software Engineering Education, SEI Conference, N. Gibbs, ed., Lecture Notes in Computer Science, No. 376, Springer-Verlag, Pittsburgh, PA, 1989, pp. 257-262.

M. Fayad, M. Laitinen, and R. Ward, "Software Engineering in the Small," *Communications of the ACM*, Vol. 43, No. 3, Sept./Oct., 2000, pp. 115-118.

Forum For Advancing Software Engineering Education (FASE), Vol. 9 No. 12, *www.cs.ttu.edu/fase/v9n12.html* Dec. 15, 1999.

M. Fowler, *Refactoring: Improving the Design of Existing Code*, Addison-Wesley, Reading, MA, 1999.

E. Gamma, R. Helm, R. Johnson, and J. Vlissides, *Design Patterns: Elements of Reusable Object-Oriented Software*, Addison-Wesley, Reading, MA, 1995.

J. Freeman, "What's Right with Schools," *ERIC Digest*, Number 93, *www.ed.gov/databases/ERIC_Digests/ed378665.html*, Feb., 1995.

D. Garlan and M. Shaw, "An Introduction to Software Architecture," in *Advances in Software Engineering and Knowledge Engineering*, Vol. I, World Scientific Publishing Company, 1993.

D. Garlan, R. Allen, and J. Ockerbloom, "Architectural Mismatch or Why It's Hard to Build Systems Out of Existing Parts," *IEEE Software*, Vol. 12, No. 6, Nov., 1995, pp. 17-26.

J. Han, S. Kim, and T. Kishi, eds., Proceedings, Workshop on Software Architecture and Components (WSAC), IEEE Computer Society Press, Los Alamitos, CA, Dec., 1999.

M. Handel, "Is There a Skills Crisis? Trends in Job Skill Requirements, Technology, and Wage Inequality in the United States," Jerome Levy Economics Institute of Bard College, Working Paper 295, *www.levy.org/docs/wrkpap/papers/295.html*, Oct., 1999.

D. Heimbigner, "Proscription versus prescription in process-centered environments," Proceedings, 6th International Software Process Workshop, Hokkaido, Japan, IEEE Computer Society Press, Los Alamitos, CA, 1990, pp. 99-102.

S. Ishii, A. Tsubotani, A. Sano, A. Kobor, A. Koyamada, and A. Uchida, "Applying Object Technology for the Development of Convenience Store System: Development and Deployment of Application Framework and Middleware for Convenience Store System," *IPSJ (Information Processing Society of Japan) Magazine* (in Japanese), Vol. 40, No. 1, Jan., 1999.

International Standards Organization, *ISO 9000-3, Guidelines for the Application of ISO9001 to the Development, Supply, and Maintenance of Software, www.iso.ch*, 1991.

Japan Information Service industry Association, Information Service Industry in Japan 1999, *www.jisa.or.jp/index-e.html*, 2000.

N. Jennings, "On Agent-Based Software Engineering," *Artificial Intelligence*, Vol. 117, No. 2, Apr., 2000, pp. 277-296.

K. Kang, S. Cohen, J. Hess, R. Novak, and S. Peterson, "Feature-Oriented Domain Analysis Feasibility Study: Interim Report", Technical Report, CMU/SEI-90-TR-21, *www.sei.cmu.edu/publications/documents/90.reports/90.tr.021.html*, Aug., 1990.

R. Kanigel, *The One Best Way: Frederick Taylor and the Enigma of Efficiency*, Viking Penguin, New York, NY, 1997.

R. Kee, H. Dransfield, R. Walton, and N. Harman, "An Ovum Report: Ovum Forecasts the Internet and E-commerce", *www.ovum.co.uk*, July 2000.

M. Laitinen, M. Fayad, and R. Ward, eds., "Software Engineering in the small," *IEEE Software*, Vol. 17, No. 5, Sept./Oct., 2000.

J. Lakos, *Large-Scale C++ Software Design*, Addison-Wesley, Reading, MA, 1996.

T. Love, *Object Lessons: Lessons Learned in Object-Oriented Development Projects*, SIGS Books, Inc., 1993.

J. Martin, *4GL: Fourth-Generation Languages*, Vol. I-III, Prentice-Hall Press, Upper Saddle River, NJ, 1986.

S. Masters, "Perspective: Sticky tape holding back the revolution," *www.vnunet.com/News/66554*, Oct. 21, 1998.

A. McGettrick, "Software Technology within ESPRIT," in *Software Engineering: A European Perspective*, R. Thayer and A. McGettrick, eds., IEEE Computer Society Press, 1993, pp. 14-16.

N. Medvidovic, "A Framework for Classifying and Comparing Architecture Description Languages," Proceedings, 6th European Software Engineering Conference, Number 1301 in LNCS, Springer-Verlag, Zurich, Switzerland, 1997, pp. 60-76.

G. Moore, *Crossing the Chasm*, Harper Business Books, 1991.

P. Naur and B. Randell, eds., "Software Engineering: Concepts," Report on a conference sponsored by the NATO Science Committee, NATO Science Division, Brussels, Belgium, Oct., 1968.

Ovum, "Ovum Evaluates: Enterprise Business Applications," *www.ovum.co.uk*, Sept. 2000.

D. Parnas, "On the criteria for decomposing systems into modules," *Communications of the Association of Computing Machinery*, Vol. 15, No. 12, Dec., 1972, pp. 1053-1058.

D. Parnas, "Software Engineering Programs Are Not Computer Science Programs," *IEEE Software*, Vol. 16, No. 6, Nov./Dec., 1999, pp. 19-30.

R. Pascale and A. Athos, *The Art of Japanese Management: Applications For American Executives*, Simon & Schuster, New York, NY, 1981.

M. Paulk, C. Weber, and B. Curtis, *The Capability Maturity Model for Software: Guidelines for Improving the Software Process*, Addison-Wesley, Reading, MA, 1995.

Princeton Softech, "Perspective Patterns," A White Paper from Princeton Softech, *www.princetonsoftech.com/news/press/ebusinessdev.htm*, Mar., 2000.

L. Putnam and W. Myers, *Industrial Strength Software—Effective Management Using Measurement*, IEEE Computer Society Press, 1997.

E. Raymond, *The Cathedral and the Bazaar: Musings on Linux and Open Source by an Accidental Revolutionary*, O'Reilly & Associates, Oct., 1999.

F. Russell, "The Case for CASE," *ICL Technical Journal*, Vol. 6, No. 3, May, 1989, pp. 479-495.

Y. Sato, T. Yamashita, K. Murayama, K. Takahara, Y. Yasutake, and M. Aoyama, "Experiment of Component-Based Software Development on Multiple Distributed Object Environments," Proceedings, 5th APSEC (Asia-Pacific Software Engineering Conference), IEEE Computer Society Press, Taipei, Taiwan, 1998, pp. 12-19.

D. Sprott, "Buying and Selling Components," *Interact—The Journal of Component-based Development and Integration*, *www.cbdiforum.com/inter1999.php3*, Sept., 2000.

J. Tomayko, "Forging a Discipline: An Outline History of Software Engineering Education," *Annals of Software Engineering*, Vol. 6, 1998, pp. 3-18.

C. Tully, "European Collaborative Research and Development Projects in Sofware Engineering, 1984-1989: A Brief Guide," in *Software Engineering: A European Perspective*, R. Thayer and A. McGettrick, eds., IEEE Computer Society Press, Los Alamitos, CA, 1993, pp. 17-41.

Uniform Computer Information Transactions Act (UCITA), Article 2b, *www.law.upenn.edu/bll/ulc/ucita/ucita600c.htm*, 2000.

J. Waters, "'Extreme' Method Simplifies Development Puzzle," Application Development Trends, *www.adtmag.com/Pub/article.asp?ArticleID=879*, Vol. 7, No. 7, July 2000.

G. Wiederhold, P. Wegner, and S. Ceri, "Towards Megaprogramming," *Communications of the ACM*, Vol. 35, No. 11, June 1992, pp. 89-99.

M. Zelkowitz, R. Yeh, R. Hamlet, J. Gannon, and V. Basili, "Software Engineering Practices in the US and Japan," *IEEE Computer*, Vol. 17, No. 6, June 1984, pp. 57-66.

Part IV

The Design of Software Component Infrastructures

The development of a successful component-based software system is a complicated activity. You can increase your chance of success by designing the *software component infrastructure* of your system with the same care in which you design each individual component. In Chapter 1 we defined a software component infrastructure as:

> A *software component infrastructure* is a set of interacting software components designed to ensure that a software system or subsystem constructed using those components and interfaces will satisfy clearly defined performance specifications.

The design of a component-based system starts with stated performance objectives and results in the design of a set of software components that will form the infrastructure for the final software system. As with any engineering endeavor, the design of the infrastructure must meet or exceed its performance objectives. Through increasingly refined design, the software component infrastructure is decomposed into its individual components. We have identified the software component infrastructure as a distinct product because it is common for component-based software systems to include software assets, such as existing code libraries or wrapped legacy systems that are non-components.

Chapter 14, "Software Components and the UML," written by Kelli Houston and Davyd Norris, describes in detail and with numerous diagrams how the Unified Modeling Language (UML) can be used to model software components and component infrastructures. UML has become the *de jure* standard for object-oriented modeling, and the authors propose that UML become the standard method for modeling components. Kelli and Davyd present the strengths and weaknesses of using the UML for modeling component infrastructures and documenting components for reuse.

Next, Steve Latchem, in Chapter 15, "Component Infrastructures: Placing Software Components in Context," describes that a component infrastructure can be designed in layers, with each layer having different responsibilities. The stereotypes for a layer determine the set of components that can exist in that layer of the infrastructure. Steve further explains the four common layers used when designing component infrastructures. An important contribution of his chapter is a series of tables that present a large variety of component stereotypes and their logical position layering.

In Chapter 16 James Carey and Brent Carlson describe two types of business components based on their many years with the SanFrancisco project. The authors differentiate between business fine-grained components from business course-grained components. Although the book's editors and authors demonstrate an obvious preference for the black box reuse of components, James and Brent make a persuasive case for the use of white box (fine-grained) components. They argue that such components are required for business domains where well-defined dependencies can be carefully managed. They then describe how the fine-grained components are deployed in accordance with a component model and present their method for deployment. You will find that components come in all shapes and sizes, and this chapter explains why.

In Chapter 17, "Components and Connectors: Catalysis Techniques for Designing Component Infrastructures," Alan Cameron Wills provides a practical, demonstrative chapter on the design of interfaces and connectors among components operating within a software component infrastructure. The author starts the chapter with an interesting analogy, comparing an electronics starter kit to software component infrastructures and their "carefully designed" interactions. Alan stresses that, in CBD, connectors generally must be designed before components and explains why with a rationale and examples.

Brian Henderson-Sellers, in Chapter 18, "An OPEN Process for Component-Based Development," describes a metamodel for creating the rules for building a component-based software life cycle process, as well as industry-specific and domain-specific process instances. Brian then presents how the current OPEN tasks support CBD and proposes numerous detailed activities, tasks, and subtasks that, if added to OPEN, would provide significantly more support for CBD and CBSE in the OPEN metamodel. A standardized metamodel for CBD and CBSE similar to the Reference Model for Open Distributed Processing (RM-ODP) would go far to advance CBSE. The author presents one such metamodel for consideration and debate.

In Chapter 19, "The Design of Component Models for Integration," Kevin Sullivan writes on a topic rarely presented at conferences or published in the CBSE literature. He makes the case for standardized design rules that are usually complex, logical software-like structures. The chapter continues on to answer two dimensions of how to develop successful design rules for CBD: (1) What are known or likely success conditions for such design rules; and (2) In what sense do traditional software design concepts, tools, and methods apply in particular to the creation of design rules for component software?

You will only achieve the full benefits of CBSE by assembling software components to form component infrastructures. By itself, a component is nothing more than a software asset that, presumably, can be reused more easily because it has well-defined interfaces. As an analogy, consider fax machines. Fax machines were not useful until a critical mass of people and businesses had fax machines; their utility increased with each use and each purchase.

The challenge for the lead engineer of a project is to design a component infrastructure that can be used to solve the project at hand, but is also powerful and flexible enough to be used for any number of foreseeable projects. Part of the challenge for the lead engineer is to clearly specify, and distribute among all stakeholders, the services that each component in the component infrastructure must provide.

Put together, these chapters form the basis for an engineering approach towards careful specification and design. Many practitioners have found that CBSE addresses the important need for developing reusable software assets in specific business domains. The key to successfully developing business components is using business requirements to drive the creation of the business components, as described in Chapter 16. Finally, Chapter 19 describes the importance of understanding exactly how components can be integrated and what services and responsibilities will be provided by the component model implementation.

Chapter 14

Software Components and the UML

Kelli Houston
Davyd Norris

14.1 Introduction

In this chapter we describe an approach for modeling software components using the Unified Modeling Language (UML). To date, there is no standard for modeling components. This directly affects the ability to document software components completely and consistently, thereby hindering their effective reuse. Now that the UML has emerged as the industry standard for software-modeling notation, we show how to use it as a standard way to model components. We present two separate aspects of modeling components: using the UML to model the design and implementation representations of a component, and using the UML to document components for reuse. We conclude by evaluating the strengths and weaknesses of the UML in support of component-based software engineering (CBSE), and examine how some of the intended revisions to the UML will increase support for CBSE.

14.2 The Problem: Effective Modeling of Components

CBSE has largely delivered on its promise of better management of complexity, encapsulation, and separation of concerns, but it has failed spectacularly (with only a few exceptions) to deliver on its promise of better reuse (Meyer, 1997). Based on our experience, we believe there are several reasons why the large-scale reuse of software components has not occurred.

- Developers focus their reuse efforts at the implementation level, where technology changes rapidly and standards are only just emerging, rather than at the design level
- Appropriate components are too hard to find and evaluate for goodness-of-fit
- Once found, documentation is often inadequate to enable developers to integrate components into the rest of the system
- Component implementations often differ in their execution of the interface's key responsibilities. This leads to insidious, hard-to-detect errors when the components are reused in a similar but different context; for example, the Ariane 5 rocket malfunction (see **Ariane Rocket Malfunction** sidebar)

We need a way to express the design of software components in an implementation-neutral fashion, a level above the latest language fads and programmer prejudices. Whether the system is implemented in C++ or Java does not change a component's fundamental internal design, nor does it change the contracts stated in its interfaces. Our goal should be to specify the entire realization of a component in such a way that the generation of a particular implementation style can be automated. We draw a distinction between realizing a component's interfaces as a detailed design and its implementation in a chosen language.

Ariane Rocket Malfunction

The Ariane 5 rocket guidance system reused software components from the Ariane 4 program, but their internal mechanisms were not documented completely. As a result, a single uncaught exception shut down the entire control system in mid-air.

This same neutral design could then be used as the basis for a component's formal documentation in catalogues and libraries. Extracts from the internal design specification would clarify the execution semantics of the interface by showing how key responsibilities have been realized. Extracts from the external design specification would provide a developers' user guide and rationale for component selection by demonstrating the use of the component's interfaces in context. Effective modeling of components using the UML brings us closer to this ideal.

14.3 The Solution: Use the UML to Model Components

CBSE promises several advantages to the software development community—complexity management, encapsulation, separation of concerns, and reuse. None of these promises will truly be realized until a standard component representation is adopted, and the UML can satisfy this need. Moreover, the UML can model a component's design and implementation, and can be used as the basis for its reuse documentation.

14.3.1 Designing Components

A component has a logical and a physical (implementation) aspect. Each must be considered and represented to completely define the component. In this section we show how to use the UML to model the logical and implementation aspects of a component.

14.3.1.1 Modeling the Logical Representation of a Component

The logical representation of a component is concerned with its logical abstraction, its relationship with other logical elements, and its assigned responsibilities. The logical representation of a component is modeled using a *UML subsystem*, which can be thought of as the design view of a component.

In the UML metamodel a subsystem is shown as a subtype of a UML classifier. Therefore, it can realize interfaces as well as have its own operations; these together define the subsystem's specification. By realizing an interface the subsystem agrees to carry out the contract defined by the interface in addition to its own responsibilities. A subsystem is also shown as a subtype of UML package, so it can contain other design elements. These elements realize the operations in the subsystem's specification and are encapsulated within it, thus isolating clients from the subsystem implementation details. This separation of specification and implementation exemplifies the object-oriented concepts of modularity and encapsulation.

An interface may be realized by multiple subsystems and a subsystem may realize multiple interfaces; therefore, interfaces are distinct entities and are not "owned" by the subsystems that realize them. Subsystems (and their interfaces) define the potential flexibility of the system, that is, what can be exchanged and replaced. Any two subsystems that realize the same interfaces can be substituted for one another; this is the basis for "plug-and-play" software systems, one of the major benefits of component-based development.

When drawing subsystems and their interfaces on UML class diagrams:

- A subsystem is modeled as a package annotated with the special keyword `«subsystem»`
- An interface is modeled as a circle, as a full rectangle with a small circle in the top-right corner, or as a full rectangle with the special keyword `«interface»`. A circle is the elided, or abbreviated, form for an interface, so you must use one of the rectangle forms if you wish to display the interface's operations.
- A subsystem is related to the interfaces it realizes via the realization relationship. The realization relationship may be modeled as a dashed line with a hollow arrowhead pointing at the rectangle form of the contract interface (canonical form), or when combined with the circular form of an interface, as a "lollipop" (elided form). Refer to Figures 14-1 and 14-2.

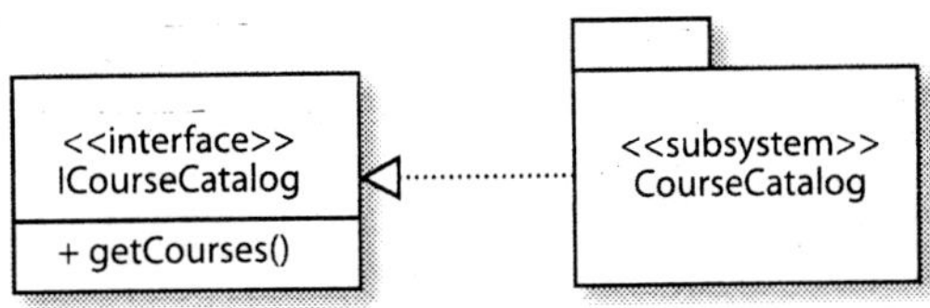

Figure 14-1: *Canonical form.*

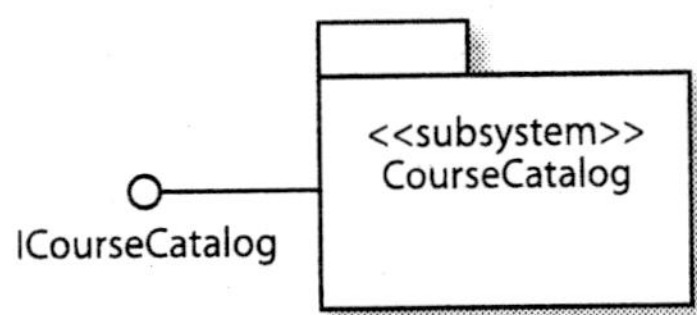

Figure 14-2: *Elided form.*

The UML can also be used to model the internal subsystem design. For each realized interface, UML `«realization»` collaborations are created within the subsystem to demonstrate how the subsystem elements interact to satisfy the interface contract (see The UML Collaboration sidebar on page 250). Inside the collaboration UML diagrams are used to document both the structural and behavioral aspects of the solution.

- Class diagrams show major relationships between internal subsystem elements as well as between other subsystems or packages
- Statechart or activity diagrams show important behavioral aspects of the subsystem as a whole
- Interaction (that is, Sequence or Collaboration) diagrams show how the subsystem elements implement the major interface operations

The following figures are taken from an interface `«realization»` inside the `CourseCatalog` design subsystem, showing how it realizes the `ICourseCatalog` interface. Figure 14-3 shows an internal structural view of the `CourseCatalog` subsystem, as well as external dependencies (dependencies on `IDatabase`, `ITransaction` and `IPersistent`). We will revisit these "outgoing interfaces" (that is, dependencies) when we discuss documenting components for reuse. Figure 14-4 is a sequence diagram showing how the subsystem implements the `ICourseCatalog::getCourses()` operation.

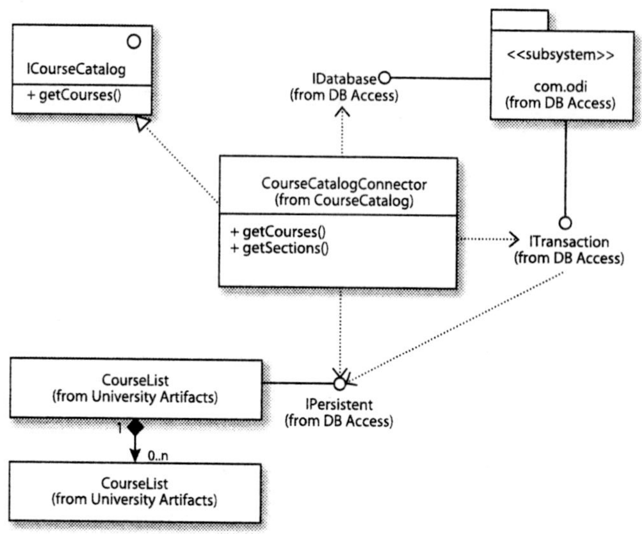

Figure 14-3: *Internal structural view of the CourseCatalog subsystem, showing external dependencies.*

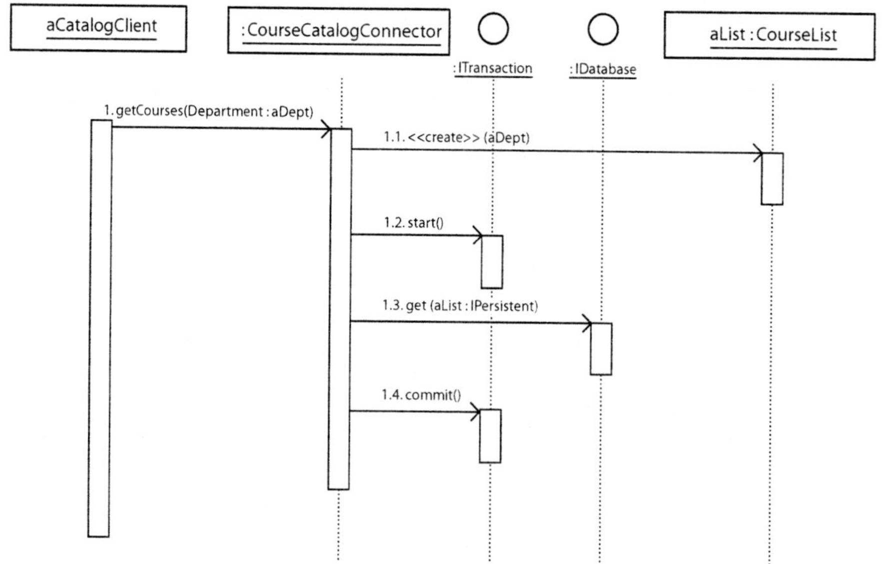

Figure 14-4: *The CourseCatalog subsystem's implementation of ICourseCatalog::getCourses().*

14.3.1.2 Modeling the Implementation Representation of a Component

The implementation representation of a component defines how its logical representation is implemented in the chosen environment. As discussed earlier, a component's logical representation is modeled using a UML subsystem. The implementation representation of a component is modeled using a UML *component*. Different UML component stereotypes can be used to distinguish different types of implementation elements, such as «.CPP», «.H», «.EXE», «.DLL», «.DOC», «table», or «file».

The implementation representation defines the mapping between subsystems and components in the chosen environment, that is, a UML *component* is the physical realization of one or more UML subsystems. The implementation representation of a component is optional if there is an obvious, documented mapping between the logical representation and the implementation representation.

The transformation from design subsystem to component is affected by:

- The chosen implementation language and development environment
- The chosen component model, if any
- How the component is to be deployed
- And the source of the component (bought, developed, or open source)

The component implementation representation also documents any implementation dependencies between components. For example, a component designed for a particular component model may have dependencies on infrastructure components.

When modeling the implementation representation of a component, two aspects must be considered: the development aspect and the deployment aspect (Booch, Rumbaugh, and Jacobson, 1998) for the three categories of UML components.

- Work Product
- Deployment
- Execution Component

The development aspect is how the component is to be developed, as opposed to being bought or reused "as is." The deployment aspect

The UML Collaboration

The UML collaboration is used to document a "solution to a problem" and is one of the most useful elements in the UML, but in practice is also one of the least used or understood. Similar to a package, collaborations allow component designers to group together a set of UML diagrams in order to document how their design satisfies key requirements. Also similar to a package, collaborations may import and use elements from other namespaces in a model. However, unlike a package, a collaboration may not own any elements except for a set of placeholders that define its specific participants, along with the required subset of their structure and behavior. These placeholders are known as *roles* and can be bound permanently to existing design elements outside the collaboration or can be left free, in which case the collaboration is shown as parameterized and the unbound roles are shown as arguments that must be supplied at a later stage. Roles and imported elements can be used together on any of the contained diagrams, resulting in a tremendously powerful way to express generic behavior.

Various stereotypes of the collaboration have been identified as:

1. The `«realization»`, in which all the participants are either imported elements or permanently bound roles. A use-case `«realization»` is used to show how a design model meets the system functional requirements, while an interface `«realization»` is used to show how a subsystem implements the requirements of an interface contract.
2. The `«mechanism»`, in which some of the participants are unbound roles. An architectural `«mechanism»` is used to express a specific partial solution to a design problem, such as the way an architect wishes the team to implement persistence, security, or distribution. A `«mechanism»` may also be used to show how to use a component's interfaces in the correct context.
3. And the `«pattern»`, in which all participants are unbound roles. This is the most generic form of collaboration, expressing an abstract solution to a generic set of problems.

A good discussion and examples of how to use the various types of collaborations can be found in The *Unified Modeling Language User Guide* (Booch, Rumbaugh, and Jacobson, 1998).

describes the final form in which the component will be deployed. If the component is not being developed then there is no need to model the component development aspect.

The *component development aspect* is modeled using *work product* components. Work products depict the "residue" of the development process—for example, the source code files, data files, build files, and all the other intermediate artifacts that are compiled to create the final deployed component (see later discussion on deployment components). Modeling the work products enables you to visually represent the compilation dependencies among the source code elements, which is important for their configuration management and version control. Each element contained within a UML subsystem is mapped to some work product by using a «trace» dependency relationship from the UML component representing the work product to the subsystem element, as shown in Figure 14-5.

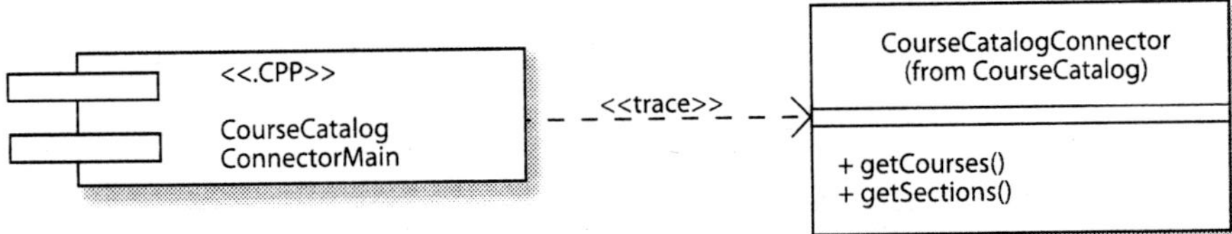

Figure 14-5: *Mapping from a work product to a subsystem element.*

The *component deployment aspect* is modeled using *deployment* components, which depict the elements that need to be delivered as part of a particular release of the software—those parts needed to deploy and configure a running system. Deployment components are the software assets that end up on the nodes (run-time computational resources) of the physical system. These include executables and shared libraries as well as nonexecutable resources that are critical to the deployment of the system. Deployment components define the physical flexibility of the system—that is, what parts can be updated/upgraded independently—and are the primary physical reusable elements of CBSE. Examples include: executable files, shared libraries, COM components, Java JAR files, database tables, data files, scripts, initialization files, applets (.class files), and Web pages (.html files). Modeling the deployment representation of a component allows you to visually understand and control the physical configuration of the system.

Because both work product components and deployment components are modeled using the same UML element, they will typically reside in separate package hierarchies within the model, and will often be stereotyped to differentiate their use. They are typically viewed along with their dependencies as a directed graph on UML component diagrams. Since deployment representations are also a type of UML Classifier, they may additionally be shown on UML class diagrams when you need to demonstrate the dependencies between design level and implementation level elements, as in Figure 14-5.

UML subsystems and their interfaces are mapped to deployment components; multiple subsystems may be mapped to the same deployment component to satisfy the needs of the overall system. For example, suppose that two pieces of the solution are in logically different subsystems (for example, Data Formatting and Data Recording), but the interface between these two subsystems carries a high volume of data. Rather than implementing these as two separate executable components, forcing all communication via Inter-Process Communication (IPC), both subsystems could be implemented in the same executable component to enhance performance.

The mapping from a subsystem to its associated deployment component is shown using a «trace» dependency relationship from the UML component to the subsystem, as shown in Figure 14-6.

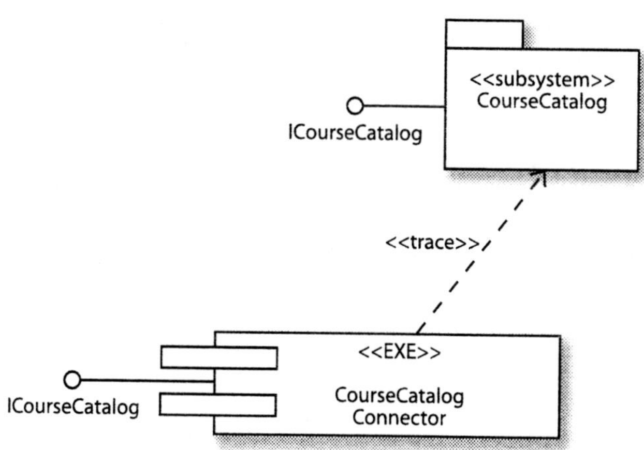

Figure 14-6: *Deployment component to subsystem mapping.*

UML interfaces span both logical and implementation representations, so subsystems and their deployment components both realize the same interface(s). Therefore, no mapping is necessary. Once the development aspect of a component has been modeled, the relationship between the deployment component and the work products used to create it are modeled as UML dependency relationships. The relationship initiates from the deployment component to the work products, as shown in Figure 14-7.

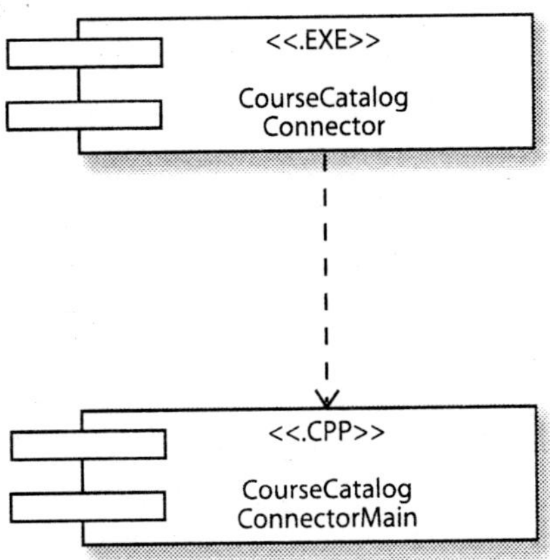

Figure 14-7: *Deployment component to work products mapping.*

14.3.2 Documenting Components for Reuse

It is difficult to find and reuse appropriate software components. To make the reuse task easier you need documentation that describes how a component actually implements its interfaces (what assumptions, preconditions, postconditions, or requirements were considered important during design), as well as documentation that describes how and where the component should be used. The latter information provides the correct reuse context for the component. Supplying implementation documentation may seem to violate the principle of encapsulation, but we are really only interested in the *contractual semantics* of the component, not its actual implementation.

The method described in this section is part of a more generic approach to extracting and documenting any reusable asset set from within a software system description, the Reusable Assets Framework (RAF) Draft 0.3 (Rational Software, 2000a), and provides a standard for UML component documentation. We use the Rational Architecture Description Standard (ADS) Draft 0.5 (Rational Software, 2000b), which is an evolution of the well known "4+1 Views" architecture description (Kruchten, 1995). The same approach can be used with other formats such as the Reference Model of Open Distributed Processing ([RM-ODP][Kerry, 1995]), or indeed any other description based on the *IEEE P1471 – Recommended Practice for Architecture Description* (IEEE, 1999).

The following sections describe the primary steps in a process for documenting a component for reuse. Guidelines for interface and component documentation can be found in the "Interface Documentation Guidelines" and "Component Documentation Guidelines" sidebars.

14.3.2.1 Identify and Extract the Primary Artifacts

In this case, the primary reuse artifact is the deployment component extracted from the implementation representation, along with the definition of any realized interfaces (incoming interfaces), required interfaces (outgoing interfaces) and the component's key properties. Unfortunately, documenting the deployment component is typically where most component reuse efforts stop, thereby providing only the barest glimpse of the reason or purpose for the component.

14.3.2.2 Identify and Extract All Related/Secondary Artifacts

Secondary artifacts are those supplementary assets that help describe the context in which a component was designed, and are important if we want to reuse the component properly. Secondary artifacts include elements from other parts of the system model, as well as the component's key requirements (related use case realizations), preconditions and postconditions, quality factors, and contextual information, all of which serve as the component's reuse context. Additional secondary artifacts include the component's logical representation (UML subsystems, their associated interface realizations, any major structural elements), and, if the component was developed, the set of all related work products (from the component's implementation representation).

14.3.2.3 Document the Internal Component Functionality

The internal subsystem or component design is documented using UML collaborations (one UML `«realization»` collaboration for each interface realized by the subsystem or component). Thus, the production of the reuse documentation for the internal component functionality will consist mostly of refining existing interface `«realization»` diagrams to capture the essence of the component (the entire realiza-

Component Documentation Guidelines

Because a component is a reusable element, its documentation is very important. *Specifying just the component interfaces does not adequately express the behavioral interactions with a component* (an interface is a one-way protocol). The following are metadata that should be included in the component documentation.

- What the component is and does, that is, the realized interface(s) and the provided functionality. The component description should allow easy matching of a problem to a solution; the problem, context, and solution (functionality) should be clearly stated. This is the component's *provided* interface(s), as described in Chapter 1 and in the **Interface Documentation Guidelines** sidebar on page 256.
- Run-time characteristics—The performance, error handling, propagation, concurrency (thread safety) and other characteristics should be clearly stated.
- Constraints or limitations—Although the functionality may match what is needed, there may be some limitations that invalidate its potential use. For example, the component may not be binary interoperable or may require too much adaptation.
- Any requirements on what the component needs from the environment to operate, such as dependencies on external components. A heavyweight component is self-contained while a lightweight component might depend on functionality provided by the environment. The component may have resource needs that must be met by the environment for it to operate properly. In total, these requirements form the component's *required* interface(s), as described in Chapter 1.
- Instructions for use, such as descriptive text, sample interaction diagrams, statechart diagrams, or class diagrams. This information is necessary so that users of the component can integrate it properly with other components. It provides a measure of the complexity of the component and how well it is documented.
- How the component fulfils its responsibilities (that is, the interface realizations). This is necessary to understand if the component will work within the current design and implementation context.

tion is not included in the reuse documentation). Too much information will violate encapsulation, while too little may leave essential assertions and preconditions unstated; both will result in potential component misuse. For more information on UML collaborations, see **The UML Collaboration** sidebar on page 250.

Rigorous encapsulation enforcement is critical at the source code/binary level and is fundamental to CBSE. However, the higher up the abstraction level you go, the more internal detail you are able to publish without giving away too much information. For example, you can

Interface Documentation Guidelines

The interface defines a contract for a subsystem and component. Therefore, interface documentation is very important. The following are metadata that should be documented for the interface.

Interface name—The interface name should concisely reflect the role the interface plays in the system.

Interface description—The interface description should describe the responsibilities of the interface. It should be several sentences long, up to a short paragraph. It should not simply restate the name of the interface, but should illuminate the role the interface plays in the system.

Operation definition—The operation definition should include a unique and well-defined set of operations. The operation name should reflect the operation result. The operation definition should describe what the operation does, including key algorithms and return values, as well as the meaning or semantics of those values. The operation parameter names should indicate what information is passed to the operation and the type of the parameter should also be identified.

Interface documentation—The behavior defined by the interface is specified as a set of operations. Additional information may need to be conveyed. Some examples include:

- How the operations are used, and the order in which they are performed (illustrated by example statechart and/or interaction diagrams)
- Possible externally observable states in which a model element realizing the interface may exist (illustrated by example statechart diagrams)

Test documentation—The test documentation should include test cases and scripts which test the behavior of any model element realizing the interface.

To group and manage this information, a package should be created that contains the interface as well as one or more `«mechanism»` collaborations that define the additional Interface and Test Documentation above.

publish a great deal of information about the detailed architecture of J2EE without losing the competitive advantage that a good EJB server implementation would provide. With reuse there is a tradeoff, and the loss of encapsulation at the design abstraction level gives the designer greater confidence at the implementation level.

14.3.2.4 Document and Categorize the External Component Functionality

Many component producers supply a user's manual with their software components; component designers can do the same using UML collaborations. The difference between this approach and a simple user's manual is that designers have detailed information about the original design context, that is, the way the component was originally designed to be used, and the architectural considerations that were taken into account during its design. When you design components for reuse, you should record such detailed design information using `«mechanism»` to provide a "How To" guide for the subsequent reuse of the component. For more information on `«mechanism»` collaborations, see **The UML Collaboration** sidebar on page 250.

When documenting the outside of the component, a less formal approach is typically taken by creating class diagrams that show the interfaces in their accompanying context and interaction diagrams that are descriptive rather than rigorous. These diagrams should strictly observe encapsulation and only show the externally visible parts of the component, such as clients interacting with sets of interfaces and dependencies emanating from the component or subsystem itself to other system packages. They should also demonstrate the key responsibilities assigned to each interface in such a way that the original design context is preserved and exposed.

14.3.2.5 Parameterize Any Dependencies If Necessary

Sometimes developers need to indicate where variation points exist in a component's design in order to document exactly how it may be extended. At other times they may not wish to release, or may be prohibited from distributing, certain parts of a component (for example, designers may have to leave out proprietary algorithms or encryption routines). Before the component can be catalogued, it is important to identify which elements are not included in the component's distribution unit or may require extending before the component can be effectively reused. This is where collaboration roles are useful—if there are any parts of the design that will not be in the final distribution unit, they should be replaced in the collaborations with unbound roles. All unbound roles appear as parameters on the collaboration and must be bound to concrete elements before the component can be considered fully realized. Using unbound collaboration roles allows you to fully document your component and still explicitly indicate any points of variability. It also allows for the possibility of automating the subsequent reintroduction of the component into new systems.

UML diagrams may still be insufficient to explain the context and rules for what may bind to the collaboration roles when you attempt to reuse the component, in which case supplemental information may need to be provided. These may take the form of simple text notes or Object Constraint Language (OCL) declarations if more formality and rigor is required (Warmer and Kleppe, 1999). Figure 14-8 shows the `CourseCatalog «mechanism»` with its extracted key requirements. The mechanism has been parameterized, showing that the developer must supply some sort of `CatalogClient` as well as some database routines.

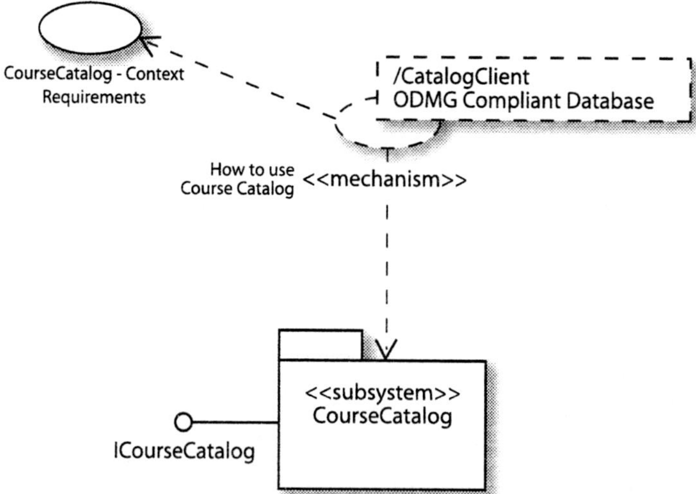

Figure 14-8: *CourseCatalog «mechanism» showing associated requirements.*

Figure 14-9 shows the external structural view of the `CourseCatalog «mechanism»`. The slash '/' in the names of some of the elements indicates that these elements are roles. Note the correspondence between the mechanism parameters in Figure 14-8 and the roles in Figure 14-9.

14.3.2.6 Catalogue the Component

All this information may now be used to create a searchable catalogue entry for the component. This catalogue may be a proprietary repository-based product, or it can even be as simple as publishing your model on the Web and adding its pages to a search engine.

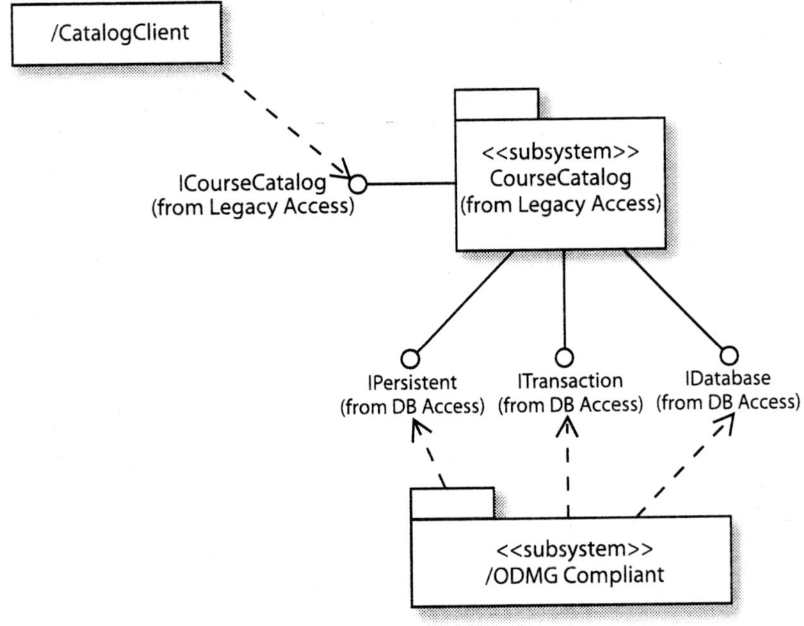

Figure 14-9: *CourseCatalog «mechanism» – an external structural view showing specific outgoing interface requirements for the parameterized subsystem. Any reuse effort will require a compatible ODMG subsystem to supply these interfaces.*

14.4 UML - Strengths and Weaknesses in Support of CBSE

The UML offers a rich set of semantics to support the design of component-based software systems. In particular:

- UML subsystems allow you to model the logical representation of a component
- UML components permit modeling the implementation representation of a component

- And UML collaborations give you the ability to document the context in which component interfaces are used, as well as how those interfaces are realized internally

Such modeling will make a dramatic difference to the level of component reuse we are presently able to achieve.

However, the exact semantics of UML collaborations need further clarification. Subsystems as they currently stand in the UML are not required to completely encapsulate their contents, which is one of the tenets of CBSE. Also, the UML does not provide any formal enforcement of "outgoing" interfaces. In practice, it is recommended that a subsystem's outgoing dependencies be *only* on other interfaces (if the subsystem's dependencies are on packages, the outgoing interfaces are not explicit and additional information is needed). More rigor in this area is required and the proposed real-time profile for the UML attempts to address this with the introduction of the *capsule*, a modeling element analogous to the *actor* of the Real-Time Object-Oriented Modeling (ROOM) method (Selic et al., 1994).

Another major weakness, as far as our goal for CBSE is concerned, is that there is no UML "pseudo-code" element. This means that there is currently no way to completely describe executable component systems solely in UML, or at the very least, to create a mechanism that will take a UML model and generate complete implementations in various languages.

Finally, there is no standard for large-scale commercial documentation and categorization of reusable assets. These standards are necessary for effective component reuse programs, but the UML does not provide guidelines for what is a necessary and sufficient set of diagrams and properties for documenting a component in order to reuse it effectively. This is not the UML's fault—by its very nature it is descriptive, not prescriptive, but additional standards that use the UML need to be put in place to support such categorization. Thankfully, the authors of the UML had the foresight to include several standard extension mechanisms such as stereotypes, tagged values, and properties that can be used to this end.

14.5 UML - Intended Revisions to Support CBSE

The UML has undergone several revisions and will continue to be revised as its use increases. To date, most of the changes have been minor clarifications or defect fixes with only a few externally visible modifications.

Planning for the next major release of the UML (version 2.0) is also underway. Comments on the Request for Information indicate that several existing areas related to component description may undergo some change. Most notable is the possible strengthening of the semantics of various high-level grouping constructs such as subsystems, packages, and components. Collaboration semantics may also be refined to provide a clearer understanding of how to express interactions more succinctly, resulting in better documentation of component mechanisms for reuse.

For the area of CBSE the most exciting initiative is the proposed introduction of action semantics. The objective of this proposal is to provide a mechanism to express the executable semantics of UML model elements in an implementation-independent fashion. The proposal is currently concerned with semantics for actions on UML states (of which an activity is one kind) and UML operations. Acceptance of this proposal will allow the UML to be more precise in both the external definition of an interface's responsibilities and the internal definition of its realization within a subsystem. The action semantics will also bring us closer to the goal of producing executable UML components.

Numerous UML profiles are also being submitted that provide a set of standard extension elements for describing Enterprise Java Beans, data modeling entities, real-time components, Web components, and XML components. Not all of these profiles are directly related to component-based development, but all will impact the ability to document the elements necessary to provide the correct context for component integration into existing models—for example, documenting components that implement business objects and including the definitions of the database tables required to persist them.

14.6 Conclusion

A standard representation for modeling a component must be defined to exploit the benefits and reusable aspects of software components. Our solution is to use the UML to model a component's design, implementation, and use. In this approach, UML subsystems and their associated interfaces are used to model the logical representation of a component, UML components are used to model the physical/implementation representation, and UML collaborations are used to model a component's internal realization, as well as its usage in context. In all cases UML interfaces serve as a contract for incoming and outgoing behavior, isolating the component from the rest of the system and making it easier to create "plug-and-play" component systems, one of the major benefits of CBSE.

Just defining an interface does not make a component a reusable asset; therefore, we also presented an approach for documenting components for reuse. Different types of UML collaboration are used for documenting the internals of a component's design and the context in which the component can be used—both of which are necessary for effective reuse documentation. Parameterized collaborations also permit designers to concisely specify variation points or even exclude parts of a component's implementation without compromising either the documentation or the subsequent reuse effort.

As with any approach, the use of the UML for modeling components is not without its limitations and we examined the current strengths and weaknesses of the UML in support of CBSE, as well as intended revisions to the UML that will enhance our ability to model components.

Chapter 15

Component Infrastructures: Placing Software Components in Context

Steve Latchem

15.1 Introduction

This chapter describes component infrastructures for CBD development. As with all software, the component infrastructure must be carefully designed to separate responsibilities and ensure that the logical connections between the components do not result in unnecessary coupling.

The most effective method to ensure needless coupling is to establish a series of layers into which various types of components with preset responsibilities will exist. I will specify the component stereotypes for each layer and describe their behavior.

Deployed component-based development (CBD) applications contain many components, each fulfilling a designed responsibility in the component infrastructure. I use the term *component stereotype* to reflect an intended behavioral responsibility for a component in a component infrastructure. In the context of the Unified Modeling Language (UML), a stereotype extends the semantic information known about a software artifact. At its simplest a component infrastructure can be designed in layers with each layer having different responsibilities (Figure 15-1). In this case, the stereotypes for a layer determine the set of components that can exist in that layer of the infrastructure. More frequently, however, you will need to define substereotypes to specify additional responsibilities and domain-specific constraints upon the component itself. You may also design your component infrastructure to use components that are composites of several distinct components (Figure 15-2).

The four common layers I use when designing component infrastructures are :

- User
- Workflow and Process Control
- Business Services and Legacy Wrapping
- Data and Operating System Services

After describing these layers in more detail I present a short compilation of component stereotypes that I have found useful in practice. I close this chapter by describing the changes you will need to make in your system development if you follow my approach.

15.2 Component Design Layers

Figure 15-1 presents the design layers for component infrastructures. These layers are ubiquitous in software systems and it is important to

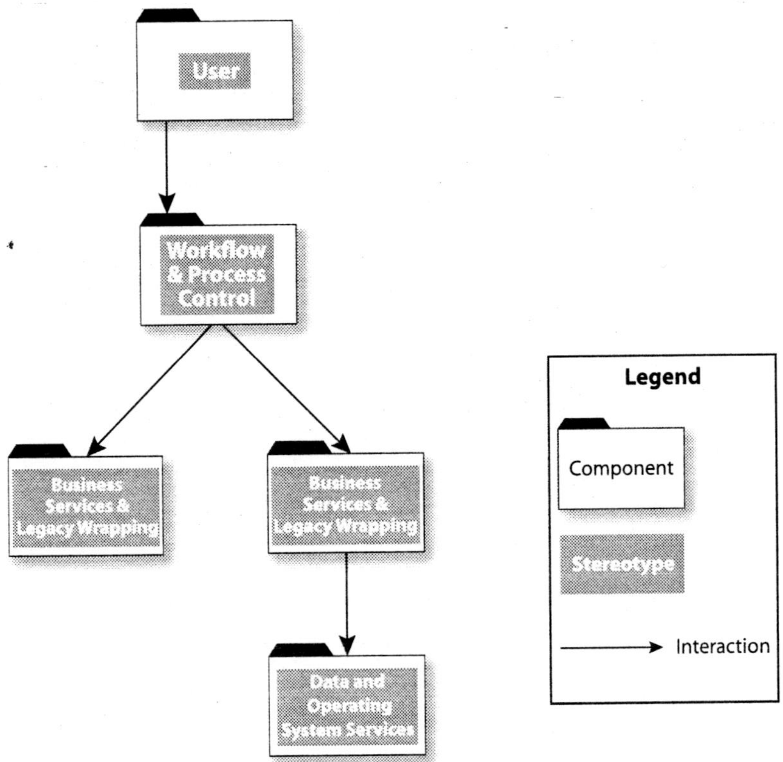

Figure 15-1: *Common component infrastructure layers.*

design component infrastructures following the principle of separating concerns.

15.2.1 User Layer

User components provide the external interface (graphical user interface (GUI), Web-based, or batch commands) and the knowledge of the user interactions (the sequence of user activities within a use case). User components request services from other components in response to commands issued by the user.

Component stereotypes included in this layer are typically: visual control, interface controller, session manager, and publish/subscribe between visual controls.

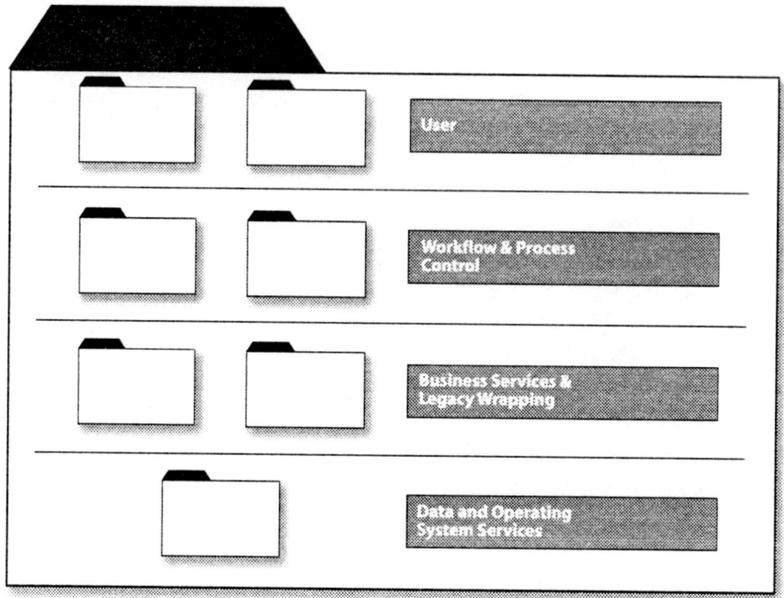

Figure 15-2: *Internal component layered design.*

15.2.2 Workflow and Process Control Layer

Workflow and process control components manage complex, automated business processes that interact with (potentially) many business services. Component stereotypes included in this layer are typically: process/workflow controller, publish/subscribe process state, process data cache, and service brokering.

15.2.3 Business Services and Legacy Wrapping Layer

Business service and legacy wrapping components provide the implementation of the business rules and the operational activity. This is accomplished by using internal business object implementations or by wrapping legacy systems behind the component interface.

Component stereotypes included in this layer are typically:

- Business object
- Collection object
- Service object (façade)

15.2.4 Data and Operating Systems Services Layer

These components provide the functionality that interacts with the persistent storage environment, including database management systems and file systems. These components are often heavily dependent on application programming interfaces (APIs) provided by the operating system on which they execute. To provide platform independence the interface for these components is generic and only the implementation is tied to a particular operating system, thus shielding other components from platform dependencies. Examples of their functionality would be the implementation of a data mapping and transaction implementation.

Component stereotypes included in this layer are typically: service object, transaction object, data object, and database connection object.

15.2.5 Middleware

I define *middleware* as an enabling technology that facilitates seamless integration of components across platforms and multiple deployments, allowing an enterprise to construct solutions by composition of existing software assets irrespective of their implementation technology. I consider middleware as "glue," rather than design; it supports the marshalling of input/output data and manages the interaction between components across process boundaries. By itself a specific middleware doesn't drive the design of components and their services; it only constrains the compiled data type libraries and interface definition language syntax for their inputs and outputs.

When conducting designs, I often compose several distinct components into a larger component by combining user interface, business logic, and persistence components together. Such a composite component is bundled together for deployment, typically through a dynamically linked library (DLL) or some other packaging mechanism. A black-box component of this type can expose a standard interface that can be implemented to multiple middleware standards (and I have done this in the past). For example, a COM+ and CORBA interface can be implemented by the same component and deployed as appropriate into the target delivery environment.

I recommend that you design component infrastructures to be independent of what I call "delivery vehicles" including middleware, any particular intergrated development environment (IDE), and specific data layer technology choices. As you can see in Table 15-1, you can design the "middle" layers of a component infrastructure (workflow and process control, business services, and legacy wrapping) to be independent from the user layer (that encapsulates the specific interactions with end-users) and the data and operating systems services layer (that encapsulates the specific interactions with hardware and other machine dependencies). In this way the component infrastructures are designed to be easily deployed to increase black-box reuse and integrated deployment. For these goals to succeed it is essential to separate components into their respective design layers. Separation allows you to rapidly change a collection of user layer components and reuse the business/data layer as is.

15.3 Component Stereotypes and Their Design Layers

Table 15-1 describes a variety of component stereotypes and positions them into their logical component layering. This effectively places the software components into their infrastructure context.

Table 15-1: *User Layer Component Stereotypes*

Stereotype Name	Design Layer	Comments
Visual Control	User	Visual control is a general name for a client-deployed form, grid, button, or menu, among others.
Server Page (ActiveX or Java)	User	While resident in the user layer, a server page manages the visual presentation of information before conversion to HTML. These pages are always server-deployed.
Interface Controller	User	Managing the navigation and sequence of visual controls, or server pages, the Interface Controller allows the decoupling of individual user display elements.

Table 15-1: *User Layer Component Stereotypes (Continued)*

Session Component	User	Holds the required user's session information, for example, process state, shopping cart contents, "skin" and format preferences. While deployed on the server, this is firmly part of the user layer's user interaction responsibilities. The Session Component may communicate with the Data/Operating System Layer to persist session information to a separate data server. When in a Web farm (a collection of web servers) that requires cross-Web server session management (as the session may traverse different web servers), the Session Component likely will communicate with the Data/Operating System Layer.
Publish/ Subscribe Component	User + Business	This component stereotype is dependent upon changes of state or data. The publish/ subscribe component might reside in the user layer in order to notify many visual controls of changes in application state or their presented data. Alternatively, the business components may behave differently or inhibit/allow their services based upon the published change events.
Error Presenter	User	Manages the presentation of errors to the user and the identification of valid resolutions to be implemented by the calling components once the user has decided which resolution is acceptable.
Applet	User (+Business?)	A client-deployed piece of Java code that is responsible for the management of certain user interactions. This component could potentially contain user and business components to provide local business logic and validation, hence the optional inclusion in the business layer.

15.4 Workflow Stereotypes and Their Design Layer

Table 15-2 shows that workflow control generally functions through an agent. Workflow is often considered an aggregate of business processes or use cases. Workflow agents control the user-side interface, as well as the process controllers and business processes.

Table 15-2: *Workflow and Process Control Component Stereotypes*

Stereotype Name	Design Layer	Comments
Process Controller	Workflow & Process Control	Manages the interaction with a number of services on one or more business components to complete a coarse-grained business process, for example, a use case, in an automated fashion.
Queue Manager	User + Workflow & Process Control	Manages the queues of requests for component services to provide an asynchronous environment. The layer that requires the asynchronous behavior defines the layer within which the components reside.
Workflow Agent	User + Workflow & Process Control	This component has two elements, the user-side control (via an Interface Controller) of the navigation of screens for a particular workflow, and the workflow/process control-side that manages the use of Process Controllers and Business Components to execute, interrupt, and manage the workflow itself. A workflow is typically considered an aggregate of a number of business processes or use cases.

15.5 Business Stereotypes and Their Design Layer

Table 15-3 demonstrates the business components required in the business layer. Notice that business code from previous applications may be inserted in this layer once wrapped; if primarily data, the information will be placed in the data/operating system layer.

Table 15-3: *Business Layer Component Stereotypes*

Stereotype Name	Design Layer	Comments
Session Bean	Business Layer	Java component or object stereotype that is the "working" business object inside a business component.
Business Component	Business Layer	Provides business logic, validation, and update services to the user layer components.
Business Component	Business Layer	Archetypal business logic and validation providing component in its own layer.
Legacy Wrapping Component	Business OR Data/ Operating System Layer	Dependent upon the kind of services the legacy-wrapping component offers. If functional, then business layer; if data only, then data/operating system layer.

15.6 Data/Operating System Layer Stereotypes

Table 15-4, fourth of the four design layers, provides the ability to transform native data types from the storage media to data types used by the business layer. In addition, this layer offers the ability to persistently store data required by the application

15.7 Other Stereotypes and Their Design Attributes

Table 15-5 provides a variety of stereotypes that support the layered component stereotypes above. The stereotypes may be found in any of the four layers supplying services to other stereotypes in the design phase and later during implementation.

Table 15-4: *Data/Operating System Component Stereotypes*

Stereotype Name	Design Layer	Comments
Data Component /Object	Data/ Operating System Layer	Provides data access and mutation services, including integration with any transactional control component(s). This component typically does some form of data transformation from the native data types returned from the storage media to the data types required by the business layer coding environment.
Entity Bean	Data/ Operating System Layer	The persistent object within the Java Environment often compared to an "active" row of the database. Provides access and mutate behavior for Session Beans and business components.
Infoware Component	Data/ Operating System Layer	These provide the ability to work with persistent data/information required by the application. Any persistent object, for example, database records, files, documents, or graphics would be available via the services of these components.
Transaction Manager	Data/ Operating System Layer	Provides the management of database/business transactions for the data components.

15.8 A Component Enterprise

As a systems engineer will happily tell a software developer, a true system consists of far more than just software. A software-intensive system consists of several different kinds of collaborating components, all of which are needed to implement the system's requirements.

- Software components
- Hardware components
- System components
- Peopleware components (personnel)
- Infoware components (data)

Table 15-5: *All Layers Component Stereotypes*

Stereotype Name	Design Layer	Comments
COTS Component	All	Dependent upon what the COTS software provides, it could reside in any of the layers, for example, if the component is a GUI widget, it would reside in the user layer. If the component is a currency calculator, it would reside in the business layer.
Hardware Component	All	Broadly there are two kinds of hardware components within the component layers: Hardware that the user interacts with, for example, scanners, that require user layer components to present and validate their input and output; and hardware components on which the component infrastructure executes; they are low-level service providers to the software components themselves, for example, Windows NT Security Component.
System Component	All	System components can provide configuration or meta data services for components in any of the design layers. As the configuration typically involves storage of metadata for retrieval, any system component will use data components to execute this retrieval and metadata maintenance.
Peopleware Component	All	Peopleware components provide user preferences or customizations for components in any of the design layers. As the configuration/customization typically involves storage of profile data for retrieval, any peopleware component will use data components to execute this retrieval and metadata maintenance.
Software Component	All	These are resident in all layers, being the generic term for a component of any design layer responsibility.

Table 15-5: *All Layers Component Stereotypes (Continued)*

Error Handler	All	Provides services to log as well as to collect errors and convert errors to meaningful explanations for later presentation to the user. This component is typically deployed in all layers as a service provider to components in these layers upon failure.
XML Parser	All	This might be an implementation of W3C's Document Object Model (DOM) or Simple API for XML (SAX). As all layers of the design potentially need to read, manipulate, or write XML documents, this component can be deployed/used in all layers.

A hardware component is a discrete unit of hardware that is reusable (its instances are intended to be used in numerous systems), independently deployed without modification, and can be treated as an encapsulated black box through its well-defined public software interfaces. There are many different kinds of hardware components and they vary depending on whether you are talking about embedded or distributed applications. These "resource-constrained" components may collaborate with other components using protocols such as the Wireless Application Protocol (WAP) and broker data contained in a version of the XML for WAP, the Wireless Markup Language (WML).

A software component can be defined as a discrete unit of system functionality that is reusable and provides black-box business functionality through an agreed, published interface. When developing the system context of the component-based system it is essential that you identify the necessary hardware components on which the software will execute.

In today's software-intensive systems, hardware is still just as critical as software—after all, without hardware the software cannot execute. In addition, there exists hardware that does not directly execute the software components but is still a critical part of the system (that is, Ethernet networks, routers). Your system model must contain hardware components and their software interface definitions.

A *system component* is a software component that configures or controls the behavior of a set of applications. It is administrative rather than operational. Administrative components support meta or configuration functions and maintain global or user-specific initiation files such as access and security profiles, XML document grammar definitions, or other metadata that configures the application. Some concrete examples of system components are

- *Access and Security Components* that maintain the security profiles for individual users of the system. They provide a service to business components that determines those users eligible to request the execution of a particular service
- *Static Data Management Components* that maintain the static data used by other business components, for example, the product and supplier codes used by an organization

A *peopleware component* is a software component that allows applications to exhibit "personalization" characteristics to its users, such as configurable user interfaces or preferred processes or workflow. These components can monitor the use and context of users' interactions with the application and configure the application characteristics to provide pertinent guidance. These are perhaps the most complicated components to design and develop; they are contextually dynamic and have some of the characteristics of artificial intelligence engines. These components are most likely to reside in the user layer. However, user-configurable business components are becoming more common within applications.

Lastly, there are *infoware components* that provide persistence services to other components, that is, the ability to access and update information in permanent storage. Infoware components are the most common generic components in today's development environment, from Microsoft's ActiveX Data Objects to Enterprise Java Beans' entity beans; the interface to a persistent component is well known and generic to all queries and updates. With the prevalence of "smart" data definitions that can define the data, its semantic and storage requirements, the most prevalent of the "smart" data technologies is W3C's XML. The World Wide Web Consortium (*www.w3.org*) is the international standards forum for developing Web technology, including XML.

15.9 Component Designers and the Design Layers

The separation of component design into the design layers has an obvious impact on the component designers and their role in the analysis, design, and implementation of components into the layers. Figure 15-3 shows the roles of component designers in the design layers.

Solution Component designers are responsible for designing the solution that is operated by the users and delivering the use cases that the application users consume. Therefore, they implement the User Design Layer using user stereotype components, for example, Visual Control, Interface Controller, and Process and Workflow Controllers that consume the component services from the Business Design Layer.

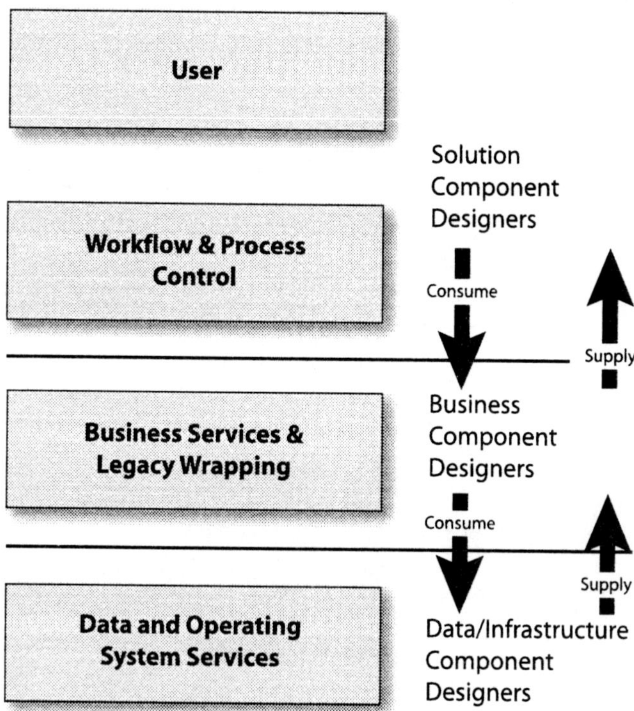

Figure 15-3: *Component designer roles.*

Business Component designers are responsible for the business design layer, implementing the business components. They expose their external component interface and design as well as build the component internals. In addition, the business component designers collaborate on other business components to supply the required functionality to the solution component designers.

Data/Operating System Component designers are responsible for the data/operating system design layer, implementing data and infrastructure components, and exposing their external interfaces for consumption by the business component designers, as well as building the component internals.

15.9.1 Additional Staff Skill Sets

As well as the component designer roles that I have discussed, the following roles, described in Table 15-6, are required on CBD projects to support the use and implementation of component business and technical design.

15.10 Impact on System Development Process

Designing layered component infrastructures will impact your software development process and will change the way you model software and how you evaluate your staff skills.

15.10.1 Software Modeling

The modeling of components within software projects is typically accomplished using UML standard notation. The modeling impact is defined here in terms of UML models.

Requirements elicitation within UML are realized using use cases. On my numerous client engagements on CBD projects, I encourage software teams to develop three types of use cases.

- Business
- Systems
- Technical

Table 15-6: *Roles and Their Required Skills*

Role	Skills
Business Architect	Quality assurance of the business infrastructure use cases and models. Owner of any business or requirements issues. Liaison with business stakeholders. Mentor/evangelist/trainer to business analysts and designer/developers.
Technical Architect (User Layer)	Definition of the object stereotypes utilized in the GUI technical infrastructure layer, for example, GUI/Window and Interface Control. Maintain documentation on GUI standards and styles, including use and purpose of visual controls and technologies, for example, form style and form types (Internet, MDI, Wizard). Investigation and prototyping of new GUI technologies. Mentor/evangelist/trainer to GUI developers across the organization. Development of base classes and templates for use by development teams. Perform and monitor quality assurance of GUI development for all software developments.
Technical Architect (Process/ Workflow and Business)	Definition of the object stereotypes utilized in the business application design layer, for example, business object, collection object, process object. Maintain documentation on business layer code standards and styles, including use and purpose of stereotypes, for example, process and business objects. Investigation and prototyping of new business layer technologies. Mentor/evangelist/trainer to user layer developers across the organization. Development of base classes and reusable assets (for example, Java Templates) for use by development teams. Perform and monitor quality assurance of business layer development for all software developments.

Table 15-6: *Roles and Their Required Skills (Continued)*

Technical Architect (Middleware)	Definition of the object stereotypes utilized in the middleware services, for example, component broker, publisher, and subscriber. Maintain documentation on middleware code standards, including use and purpose of stereotypes, for example, component broker. Investigation and prototyping of new middleware technologies. Mentor/evangelist/trainer to component/middleware developers across the organization. Development of base classes and reusable assets (for example, middleware protocol and data marshalling facilities) and templates for use by development teams. Perform and monitor quality assurance of middleware development for all software developments.
Technical Architect (Data/ Operating System)	Definition of the object stereotypes utilized in the data services application design layer, for example, data object, transaction object, or database connection object. Maintain documentation on data layer code standards, including use and purpose of stereotypes, for example, data and transaction objects. Investigation and prototyping of new data services technologies. Mentor/evangelist/trainer to data services developers across the organization. Development of base classes and reusable assets (for example, Java templates) for use by development teams. Perform and monitor quality assurance of data services development for all software developments.

Business use cases – These are the most commonly understood use cases because they capture the dialogue among actors (human user roles, other systems, and time) and the system. Business use cases are typically "operational," that is, they describe requirements for users, systems, and time using the system to deliver automation of the target business processes.

System use cases – These define the requirements for administrative support of the use of a computer system. They have the same actor types but define administrative functions. Examples of administrative requirements are static data maintenance, access, security profile maintenance, batch-scheduling maintenance, and logon/logoff. You'll notice the repetition of the word "maintenance." Maintenance is quite common to system use cases as they are derived from requirements *because* end-users will continue to use the computer system long after system deployment.

Technical use cases – These are used to define technical capabilities required for one or more applications; their actors are typically software elements of the application. These use cases, more than the prior two types, are useful for determining the components that will be used to design the component infrastructure. From these use cases designers will likely define technical components that provide services to a number of applications. Examples include error handling or access and security components. The interaction modeling within a technical use case leads to a set of classes that will be used to implement components. For successful designs, these classes should be developed using appropriate design patterns ([Gamma et al., 1995] [Mowbray and Malveau, 1997]). Also, the designer can identify base classes that contain reusable attributes and functionality.

Table 15-7 shows the relationship between the use case types and the business component stereotypes that are modeled against them.

15.10.2 Additional Phases and Activities

From the use cases described previously, we can divide the modeling of the components into *business infrastructure* and *technical infrastructure*. Business infrastructure modeling develops class and interaction diagrams from the business and system use cases to define the components and their services. Technical infrastructure modeling develops class and interaction diagrams from the technical use cases to define the patterns, base classes, and technical components that will be integrated into the business infrastructure.

During these parallel activities—requirements definition and software modeling—you will define all necessary component stereotypes and show how they work together to provide a complete component-based design for the application.

The business infrastructure process is well-documented within most software life cycles; it is concerned with the elicitation and vali-

Table 15-7: *Use Case Types and Their Component Stereotypes*

Use Case Type	Component Stereotypes
Business	Visual Control, Server Page, Applet, Session Bean, Business Component, Legacy Wrapping Component (services required from user's perspective), Data Component/Object, Entity Bean, Infoware Component, Software Component, Business Component
System	COTS Component (using the existing, available services), System Component
Technical	Interface Controller, Process Controller, Workflow Agent, Session Component, COTS Component (where a new API/Interface is required to integrate this into the component infrastructure), Hardware Component, Peopleware Component, Transaction Manager, Queue Manager, Publish/Subscribe Component, Error Handler, Error Presenter, XML Parser

dation of business requirements, identification of business components, then modeling their delivery of services via standard interfaces. The technical infrastructure may be less familiar. You can use UML modeling of the technical infrastructure to define the integration of the "technical" component stereotypes listed against technical use cases. The process for this modeling is very like the business infrastructure but can be summarized as

Planning and scoping—Where the technical high-level requirements and team activities are identified for the project or the enterprise. This includes identifying the constraints, target environments, and nonfunctional requirements for the target system.

Technical infrastructure analysis–Where the modeling starts. Beginning with technical use cases, the component infrastructure is modeled using UML notation, discovering, and identifying the patterns, as well as base or facility classes. Technical component services that the technical infrastructure will provide will be identified.

Increment planning—The technical infrastructure need not be delivered all at once, as this would significantly delay the incremental delivery of business functionality by developers who are customers! Therefore, the technical infrastructure is designed, built, and tested incrementally on a "just in time" basis when compared to the flow and sequence of the business increments. During this stage, the engineer or project manager plans the increments and the deliverables that will be achieved.

Technical infrastructure design—The physical design of the technical infrastructure. Patterns, base or facility classes, technical component services are refined using prior phases' analysis models. The analysis models are verified before the design phase; likewise, at the completion of the design phase, the design of the infrastructure is verified.

Technical infrastructure build and test—The build and test phases are vitally important. Patterns, base or facility classes, and technical component services are first built, then unit and integration tested against their designs. Once the project team considers determines the infrastructure is "fit for purpose," that is, validated to work as agreed, the project team will want to demonstrate that customers can use the infrastructure in its current form.

15.11 Conclusion

Today's component infrastructure is complex and multi-faceted. While earlier client/server implementations were developed for individual applications, the modern component landscape requires the integration and consolidation of many designed component infrastructures and the wrapped reuse of many applications.

We need to develop our world to consider our entire infrastructure as component services and their design layers that provide generic behavior that can be reused in multiple component-based applications.

The first part of the solution to this complexity is the separation of the component infrastructure into design layers, namely user, process/workflow, business, and data infrastructure. Secondly, components are stereotyped for their residence in a design layer and their functional/facility responsibilities. Finally, the process surrounding the requirements definition, analysis, and design of the software solution has two parallel streams (and UML Models): business infrastructure and technical infrastructure. These streams use component stereotyping and use cases to differentiate the requirements and the software deliverables. Then component designers work within the design layers to analyze, design, and implement components that provide the required application behavior, supply services to and consume services from other design layers.

A concrete example of the power of component design layering occurred on a recent client component-based development. The software component team started with a VB Windows/GUI user layer of controls and interface controllers that requested process controllers via COM to execute business component services, which then requested data services via CORBA requests to ICL mainframes. When the late decision was taken to go to a Web client, building the Server Pages and hooking up to the existing Process Controllers took five days. With design layer separation comes changeability!

The separation of component-based developments into collections of black-box, stereotyped components that participate and reside within design layers is critical to a successful implementation of CBD.

Chapter 16

Business Components

James Carey
Brent Carlson

16.1 Introduction

The term *business component* means many things to many people. In this chapter we define what a business component is and then, using the lessons we've learned from developing business components, we provide guidelines for developing them more effectively. We developed this chapter after many years' experience with the SanFrancisco project, a project designed to provide application families of third-party components to customers. The varieties of component-based systems were designed to closely or precisely meet customers' business rules and requirements, rather than retrofit a system to approximate the needs of the customer.

16.2 Defining Business Components

A business component is a software component that provides functions in a business domain. A business domain is the usual target for a business application; for example, an order management application is part of the Enterprise Resource Planning (ERP) business domain. In general, there are two types of business components and they provide services at different levels. A *fine-grained* component represents a business entity (a "noun" within the business domain composed of business information and related behavior). A *coarse-grained* business component provides a business process, a functional decomposition of related behaviors within a particular business domain. Typically, fine-grained components are used in a white-box manner while coarse-grained components are best used in a black-box manner (see Szyperski, 1998 for a discussion of white-box versus black-box reuse).

16.2.1 Fine-Grained Business Components

Fine-grained components are business entities that are recognizable as the "nouns" (and their related behavior) in a particular business domain. Within the ERP domain shown in Figure 16-1, for example, there is a fine-grained component that represents a product within the system. The Product component will contain information about the specific product it represents (for example, product description and SKU number). This component also provides the behavior associated with a product in the ERP domain such as lot management.

Fine-grained business components establish dependencies on other fine-grained components within their business domain. Sometimes this coupling occurs directly between business entities; at other times, an intermediary class (sometimes referred to as a "link" class) represents the coupling between two business entities. Link classes are useful when a *many-to-many* relationship exists between business entities.

In Figure 16-1 the fine-grained Product component is tightly coupled (either directly or indirectly) to a fine-grained Warehouse component. Changing this Warehouse component may have an impact on the product component (and vice-versa). Using fine-grained components may create many well-defined dependencies that we must carefully manage. Component models typically establish a strong

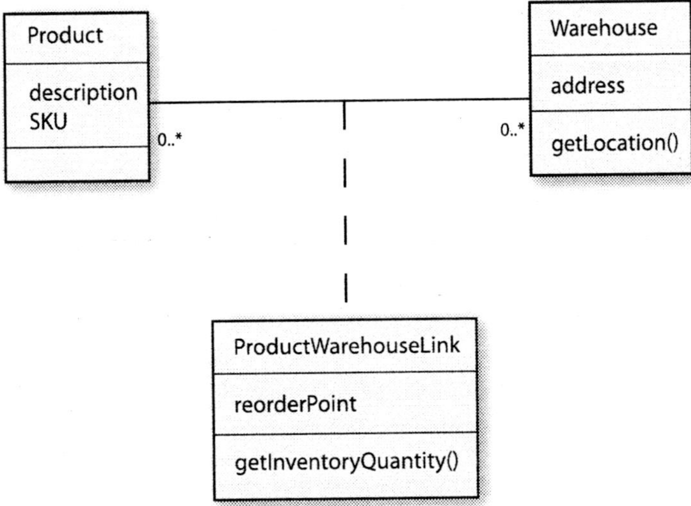

Figure 16-1: *Fine-grained components.*

distinction between type/interface and class/implementation ([D'Souza and Wills, 1999] [Monday, Carey, and Dangler, 1999]). The dependencies established between fine-grained components are at the type level, elevating this model above simple object-oriented relationships between classes.

The figures in this chapter do not explicitly make a distinction between type and class. In other words, the boxes in the figures represent logical components rather than physical instantiations within a particular component model.

16.2.1.1 Fine-Grained Business Components Are Not Data Models

Data modelers may consider fine-grained business components to be glorified data models and may view these components as simply a wrapper of a physical or logical row in a database table. However, defining fine-grained business components is a top-down activity, starting with domain requirements and driving them into the business entities. Although the data represented by a particular component may ultimately reside in one or more relational database tables, fine-grained components ensure that the appropriate behavior is associated with the data. For example, consumers should have knowledge of whether associated products are available. This functional association is not at all obvious when looking at the ERP domain from a data modeling perspective.

16.2.1.2 Fine-Grained Business Components Are Not Object Models

Fine-grained business components clearly result from an object-oriented analysis of a business domain. The key difference between a set of fine-grained business components and an object model is that designers of fine-grained business components follow two key rules to enable independent deployment and composition (see Chapter 1). First, there must be a strict separation between interface and implementation. Second, any dependencies between components are clearly identified and managed. These rules are introduced by the underlying component model used to implement the fine-grained business components ([Szyperski, 1998] [see also Chapter 3]).

16.2.2 Coarse-Grained Business Components

Coarse-grained business components provide a purely functional view of some part of a business domain, such as a subsystem or a business process within the domain. For example, Figure 16-2 shows a Dry Goods Management component that represents services such as product and warehouse definition, stock updates (increases and decreases), unit conversions to inventory in stock, and product availability calculations. Coarse-grained components establish loose relationships with other coarse-grained components and typically create only a few visible dependencies on other components. Unlike fine-grained components, coarse-grained components can effectively hide many of their dependencies as internal implementation details, that is, fine-grained components are often the implementation details hidden by a coarse-grained component. Information hiding allows coarse-grained components to incorporate existing assets such as procedural programs.

16.2.3 Fine-Grained vs. Coarse-Grained Business Components

Both types of components are needed, and the key difference between these two is the target audience and intended use. Fine-grained components, because of their dependencies, usually present a steeper

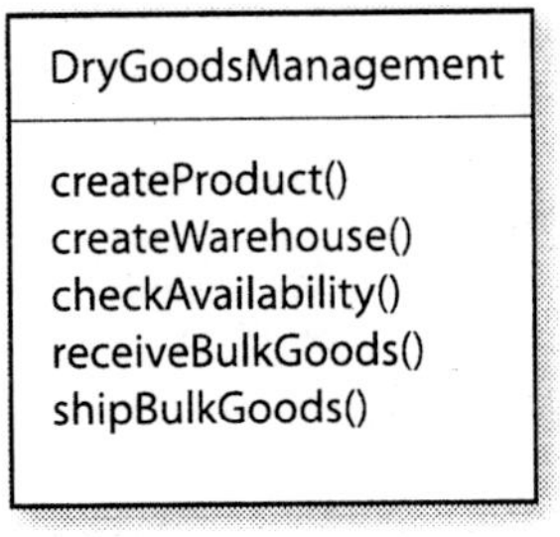

DryGoodsManagement

createProduct()
createWarehouse()
checkAvailability()
receiveBulkGoods()
shipBulkGoods()

Figure 16-2: *Coarse-grained component.*

learning curve for designers, but solve many different problems within a domain. By contrast, coarse-grained components present a shorter learning curve, but apply only to a subset of the problems in the domain. In fact, fine-grained components provide a powerful set of parts that can be used to build coarse-grained components; in Figure 16-3, the coarse-grained Dry Goods Management component is built from two fine-grained components—Product and Warehouse—and a Product Warehouse link class.

16.2.4 Applying These Definitions

Our definitions of fine-grained and coarse-grained components are independent of any specific development process or component model. However, process and infrastructure choices clearly impact how these definitions are realized. A development process establishes a discipline of component reuse and the concept of fine-grained and coarse-grained components affects the way we design and implement components.

16.2.5 Development Process

Taking into account the CBSE development process, there are two processes that need to be considered. One is the process used by component producers. This process must focus on the reusability of a particular component and enable designers to design, and developers to implement, the component in the chosen component model.

The other process is used by component consumers. This process must enable consumers to effectively locate and assemble the business components. Although the process used by component consumers is

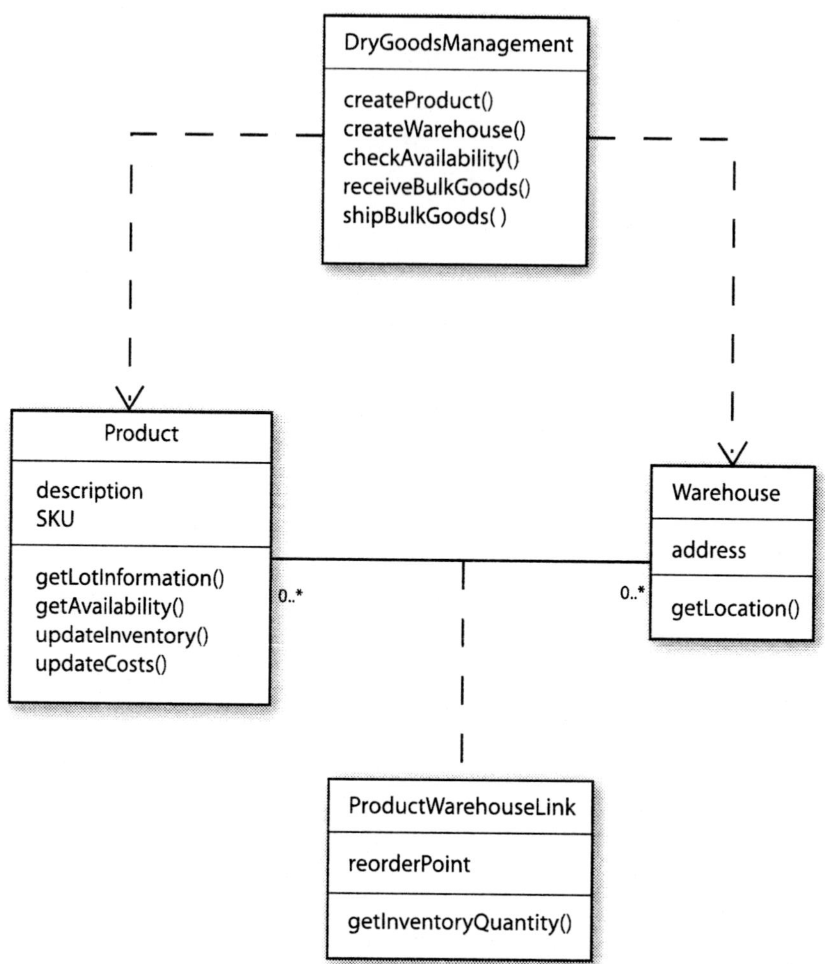

Figure 16-3: *Relationship between fine and coarse-grained component.*

important, in this chapter we focus on the development of business components. Processes for locating, deploying, and assembling components are discussed by Hedley Apperly in Chapter 29.

We must define a development process for business components that encourages and enforces a disciplined approach to reuse. In Chapter 22 Martin Griss shows how to define a development process focused on identifying the target products for the components and making the components useful for the range of products. As target products are identified, a product-line encourages designers to view the commonality and variability across those products.

During the requirements and analysis stages we identify the coarse-grained components needed to assemble the product set. We then refine these coarse-grained components to identify the fine-grained components (and, potentially, the fine-grained component infrastructure) needed to assemble them. In this way, the resulting coarse-grained and fine-grained components can be compared with existing components to determine if existing components can be reused or new components need to be developed. We may also modify software components as part of the natural iteration required to make them reusable.

As the result of experience and the continuing development of software components, the developers of coarse-grained components will leverage the growing set of powerful fine-grained components to produce coarse-grained components, and application builders (coarse-grained component assemblers) will leverage the growing set of coarse-grained components to build applications.

16.2.6 Component Model

While the requirements and analysis stages can and should be executed independently of any specific component model, the choice of a model clearly impacts the design and implementation phases of component-based development. For fine-grained and coarse-grained business components to be useful, they must be deployed within the scope of a particular component model implementation, such as EJB ([Flanagan et al, 1999] [*www.javasoft.com/ejb*]), CORBA (*www.omg.org*), or COM ([Box, 1998] [*www.microsoft.com/com*]).

We have found that EJB provides a good foundation for implementing fine-grained components because individual business components can be defined as entity beans (see Chapter 33) and can be deployed and managed independently. The coupling among fine-grained components is established by defining and persisting remote references to deployed entity beans. Because all such references are declaratively described in the deployment descriptor of the entity bean, the deployer can discover and manage inter-component dependencies (EJB 2.0 JavaBeans Specification Version 2.0, Section 19.3.1.2; see also Chapter 33 in this book). In addition, coarse-grained components can be implemented as session beans, together with the Java Messaging Service ([JMS] [*www.javasoft.com/products/jms*]) for asynchronous messaging support. Dependency relationships between coarse-grained components are declaratively described in the deployment descriptor of the session bean. Throughout this chapter, where appropriate, we map EJB and other Java-based technologies within the J2EE infrastructure (*www.javasoft.com/j2ee*) to our development principles.

16.3 Developing Business Components

We have developed a set of guidelines to construct effective business components based on our experience developing fine-grained business components as part of IBM's SanFrancisco product (Monday, Carey, and Dangler, 1999) and coarse-grained business components as part of IBM's WebSphere Business Components product (*www.ibm.com/software/components*). A disciplined development cycle is a crucial aspect of successful component-based development. This development cycle starts from the top with business rules and requirements, creating both the fine-grained business components and the coarse-grained components that compose the fine-grained components into functional business processes.

The development cycle for business components is no different than any other successful software engineering process and includes iterative cycles of business rules elicitation, requirements capture, domain analysis, design, implementation, and testing. Creating coarse-gained and fine-grained components are actually two interleaved and interdependent development cycles. Fine-grained components used to implement the coarse-gained components will be identified as part of the design of the coarse-grained component. Fine-grained components will need to be at least partially developed before the coarse-grained components are implemented. This is a trade-off between directly implementing coarse-grained components and building or reusing new fine-grained components.

To use a manufacturing analogy, when building a bicycle you could build the frame directly from raw tubing (or even form the tubing out of sheet metal), or you could use partially or fully assembled frames that come from another internal or external supplier. This is no different than a coarse-grained component developer choosing to develop a new collection class for internal use from scratch or to select a collection class from a preexisting class library. Because the component's interface and implementation are independent, we can make this type of trade-off. In addition, a developer of a coarse-grained component could first provide a prototypical, custom-built implementation and then replace that implementation with one that uses (or reuses) fine-grained components as they become available as long as the interface remains the same.

In the software component design process we have developed guidelines implemented in the following four steps of the development cycle.

1. Define the business process view, that is, developing business rules, requirements, and use case scenarios
2. Model fine-grained business components
3. Design fine-grained business components
4. Build coarse-grained business components

16.3.1 Defining the Business Process View

The key to successfully developing business components is using business rules and requirements to drive the creation of the business components. In our development model, where coarse-grained components are comprised of fine-grained components, we initially use business rules and requirements to define coarse-grained components within the business domain. The key guidelines in this step are to focus on the requirements, ensure that we have the right expertise, and apply the right amount of that expertise to the problem.

16.3.1.1 Requirements, not Implementations

Requirements should be in the form of requirements and not in the form of implementations. While this sounds painfully obvious, achieving this in practice is a difficult task. For example, while developing IBM SanFrancisco we encountered a case where the systems our financial domain experts had recently worked on maintained a base set of account balances used to quickly calculate account balances. This prior experience led them to initially define a requirement that the account components keep a base set of account balances. As we investigated this stated requirement we found that the true business requirement was that the system must make it possible to rapidly determine certain summarized account balances. Forcing the system to keep a base set would have removed the possibility of allowing users to specify which balances they wanted to maintain. Providing this level of flexibility made it possible to retrieve some balances very rapidly while reducing the system overhead by not storing unneeded balances in all cases.

16.3.1.2 Domain Expertise is Crucial

As we developed business components we found it critical to separate technical proficiency (for example, using an object-oriented language) from the domain expertise needed for the component (for example, basic accounting principles and standards). The domain expert ensures that the correct rules and requirements are identified. The technical expert ensures that the correct technical solution is achieved. Together these experts identify and resolve the trade-offs (inherent in any development project) between the two points of view. For example, during the development of IBM SanFrancisco (Monday, Carey, and Dangler, 1999) technical experts often became excited when they realized they could easily modify their design to support another use case scenario, only to discover that the domain experts had excluded that scenario on purpose because it didn't make sense from a domain perspective. Just because something is technically possible doesn't mean that it is the right thing to do—a hard lesson for most developers to learn.

We recommend establishing domain expert teams of two to three people. Having more than three domain experts is too many, as we've found that they lose focus and discussions rapidly become unproductive arguments. It is better to have a small team develop a set of requirements to be reviewed by a broader group.

16.3.1.3 More Reusable Means More Expertise

To define reusable components (especially crosscutting components as described in Chapter 22) applicable in multiple domains, we need a greater variety of domain expertise. This is a risky trade-off that has to be made depending on factors such as whether a similar reusable asset has been defined and built in the past (prior to components) and what expertise is currently available. A General Ledger product covering all five of the major Generally Accepted Accounting Principles (GAAP) needs experts in, and rules and requirements from, all five domains. If we concentrate only on the main market for our product, the components may not be able to support the other products without major modification. The need for domain expertise is especially important when developing fine-grained business components because they are intended to be applicable in more situations, allowing them to be reused in many different (and more narrowly targeted) coarse-grained components. For example, IBM SanFrancisco (Monday, Carey, and Dangler, 1999) provides fine-grained business components supporting the assembly of a General Ledger. These components were developed in Germany so that we had access to the international accounting expertise we needed. As part of this expertise we teamed up with business partners who had previously developed General Ledger applications. Two of these partners provided domain experts who worked directly with us while the others had their domain experts participate in a review board that periodically validated that they could use IBM SanFrancisco to build their applications.

16.3.2 Modeling Fine-Grained Business Components

After decomposing business rules and requirements into coarse-grained business components, we must further decompose coarse-grained business components into their underlying fine-grained business components. Again, this decomposition should be driven by the requirements as documented by use case scenarios ([Jacobson, 1994] [Jacobson et al., 1992]). As we model fine-grained business components, the scenarios we develop become part of an analysis model. The challenge is to distribute business behavior associated with the coarse-grained components across the various fine-grained business entities defined during analysis.

All guidelines in the previous section are applicable here, and, in fact, may be more crucial for two reasons. First, at this lower level it is easier to mix implementation and requirements. Second, because we are trying to produce highly reusable fine-grained components (addressing many products), we will need more diverse domain expertise. Our additional guidelines are related to reuse.

16.3.2.1 Don't Forget to Map

At this stage it is crucial to review existing fine-grained business components for reuse. This involves adding an explicit mapping stage to analysis where we look for, and map to, analysis models of existing fine-grained business components. This process can be expensive the first time through because it involves learning about your potential reusable assets. However, as we become more familiar with what is available, the mapping process becomes easier. The sooner reuse can be identified, the greater the savings in time and effort. If we delay or skip this step we may perform additional development work that will just be thrown away once the mapping is realized. An outstanding example of effective mapping to existing fine-grained components is a personnel scheduling application in development using IBM SanFrancisco's warehouse management fine-grained components (Jaufmann and Logan, 2000).

16.3.2.2 Be Reuse Aware

The flip side to reusing existing business components is defining new business components to increase their likelihood of reuse. Decisions made at this stage can dramatically impact how much reuse can occur in the future. A good way to hone this awareness of reuse potential is to investigate how others have analyzed the business domain ([Fowler, 1997] [Monday, Carey, and Dangler, 1999]). At some point we must decide how reusable a component should be (that is, what products it will support) and make the tradeoff between reusability, generality, time, and available domain expertise.

16.3.3 Designing Fine-Grained Business Components

This stage in the development cycle involves incorporating the characteristics of the selected component model with the analysis model to create the design. This is the point in the development cycle where design patterns have a key purpose. A component model such as EJB embodies a set of technical design patterns (Gamma et al., 1995) against which all components deployed into that model must conform. For example, EJB's entity bean programming model enforces a clear separation of interface and implementation by requiring the entity bean Remote interface to be specified in a separate hierarchy from the implementation class supporting that interface. On top of these technical design patterns we defined a set of functional design patterns that support both broadly-based business requirements—such as managing business information across an organizational hierarchy—as well as more narrowly-defined requirements, such as selectively overriding business algorithms based on the business information being processed. For more details of these examples refer to chapters 5 and 7 (Carey, Carlson, and Graser, 2000) concerning the controller and chain of responsibility-driven policy, respectively. We recommend using well-tested patterns during design to keep component responsibilities properly focused.

16.3.3.1 Be Pattern Aware

We became aware of available design patterns ([Gamma et al., 1995] [Carey, Carlson, and Graser, 2000]) and then applied them consistently throughout our design. Patterns represent reusable design structures, which in some cases lead to reusing specific fine-grained utility components (components that provide generic partial implementations of specific design patterns) and in others identify the fine-grained business components that need to be created.

16.3.3.2 Tor's Second Cousin

Tor was a domain expert on the SanFrancisco project who had a knack for identifying "edge cases," activities very few users of an application would want to do. We often "blamed" his fictitious (and crazy) second cousin for imagining these wild and unlikely cases. It is important to consider these potential secondary use case scenarios and test cases, both to ensure that the component meets business needs, but also to balance completeness and reusability of a particular fine-grained business component.

16.3.4 Building Coarse-Grained Business Components

Coarse-grained business components can be built in a number of ways. Because the interface is independent of the implementation, the component consumer does not have to change its usage when the implementation changes. This means that we can implement the coarse-grained component using other coarse-grained components, fine-grained components, or by wrapping other systems. Just as we have already noted for fine-grained components, a component model such as EJB defines how coarse-grained components are deployed. The EJB session bean model ensures that we maintain separation between our coarse-grained component's interface and implementation. The session bean interface can easily represent the functional behaviors specified for a coarse-grained component as well as provide the necessary transactional, security-based, and other technical characteristics required by a business application. Its associated implementation class can then delegate responsibility for business behaviors to whatever implementation approach we choose. For some components we might delegate directly to a set of fine-grained business components. Other component implementations may take advantage of Java facilities such as JMS or Java's JDBC Data Access API ([JDBC] [*www.javasoft.com/products/jdbc*]) to delegate responsibility to another (non-EJB-based) implementation.

Choosing one implementation approach over another may not be clear when the first coarse-grained components are implemented. The true power of well-designed fine-grained and coarse-grained components is evident when considering the next application (or product) in a particular business domain. With a well-composed set of reusable fine-grained and coarse-grained components in hand, the analysis mapping process (as described above) can identify many reusable business components which can then be tuned to specific needs when implementing the coarse-grained component.

16.3.4.1 Mapping Is Crucial

Once we design and implement a set of fine-grained business components, we evaluate the inventory of fine-grained and coarse-grained components to see if they can be reused. This reuse is important because we save time in developing a solution, but it also has another, less obvious benefit. Since the business components were developed with domain experts, the domain experts can recognize the reused components and are able to participate in the reuse mapping process. The domain expert can identify any misuse of the components.

16.3.5 Mapping to Fine-Grained Components

If we design fine-grained components with reuse in mind, we should be able to construct a coarse-grained component by assembling fine-grained components to meet the "narrow" needs of a specific business process as defined by the use case scenarios. Let's return to our ERP example of cooperating fine-grained Product and Warehouse components used to build a coarse-grained component that supports dry goods warehouse management. The use case scenarios place specific constraints on our fine-grained components (such as establishing valid stock types, lots, units, and conversion factors for product inventory managed by our dry goods warehouse). These specific constraints either limit what is exposed by the coarse-grained component or fix the configuration (or initial) information for the fine-grained components. We can then implement specific use case scenarios assigned to our coarse-grained component by assembling the components to support the functional interfaces exposed by that component. For example, we might implement the use case scenario "update inventory" (specified as receive Bulk Goods on the Dry Goods Management coarse-grained component in Figure 16-4) by first invoking the updateInventory and updateCosts business methods on the Product component. We might then create a separate record of the inventory transaction (perhaps defining a new fine-grained component to support this transaction record) to meet legal or business requirements for inventory tracking.

16.3.6 Mapping to Coarse-Grained Components

If we design coarse-grained components with reuse in mind, we can construct a new coarse-grained component by encapsulating and tailoring existing coarse-grained components for this particular use. Continuing with our dry goods management example, an alternative to using fine-grained components to build our Dry Goods Management coarse-grained component would be to use a prebuilt Product Management coarse-grained component as an implementation detail. We can take this approach only if the Product Management component supports enough customization to accommodate this level of reuse. If we take this approach the Dry Goods Management component must then define the configuration of this contained component as part of its

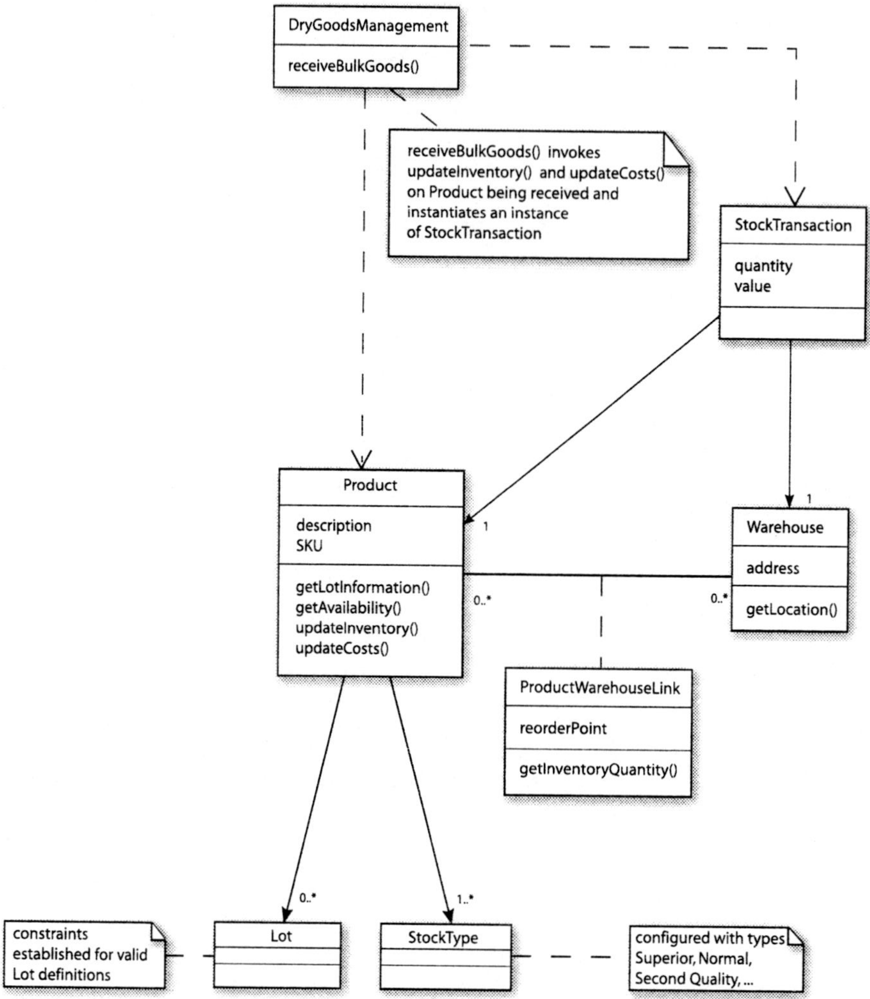

Figure 16-4: *Mapping to fine-grained components.*

implementation. Each interface of the Dry Goods Management component would then be implemented by using the functions on the contained component. For example, Dry Goods Management might support a receiveBulkGoods function that is implemented using Product Management's updateStock function, as shown in Figure 16-5.

The trade-off between mapping to coarse-grained and fine-grained components involves choosing between more rapid reuse versus flexi-

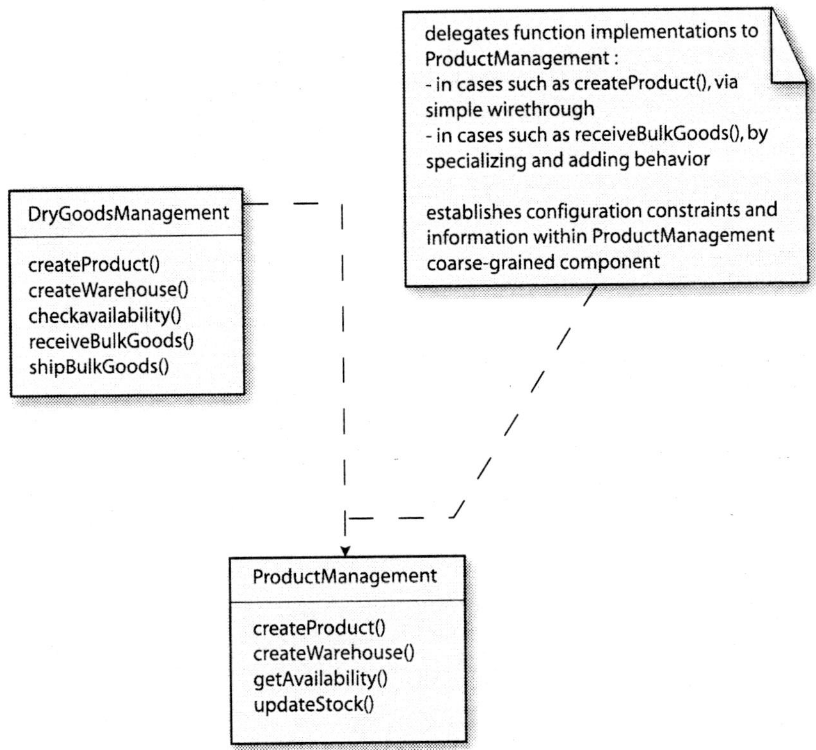

Figure 16-5: *Mapping to coarse-grained components.*

bility and also involves decisions related to the number of explicit dependencies that exist between components.

16.3.6.1 Encapsulated vs. Shared Usage

We recommend sharing the use of a business component with other components. Using our dry goods management example again, the "update inventory" use case scenario may also have specified that the necessary accounting journal entries should be created. If this were the case, our coarse-grained Dry Goods Management component would establish a dependency on a General Ledger coarse-grained component, as shown in Figure 16-6. Depending upon how our use case scenarios are written, we might have chosen an alternative approach to meet this requirement, for example, returning the accounting information to the user of the Dry Goods Management component. Unfortunately, this approach forces the users of our component to separately invoke the necessary functions on the General Ledger component to update its account information. Allowing the General Ledger component to be used in a shared manner enables the more natural model of having the Dry Goods Management component do the update. (This brief example shows how an implementation can often masquerade as a requirement. A domain expert familiar with an existing application that does not provide for integrated accounting may quite naturally describe the use case scenario in this form without realizing that a better implementation is possible.)

Although this example is one where all components should share the same General Ledger component, there are many cases where groups of components share unique instances of the shared component. For example, a component that manages information about people could be used to manage and share information about customers in a call center component and ordering component; a different instance would be used to manage the employees in a payroll component. As shown in Figure 16-7, an instance of the Person Management component, called Customer Information, can be shared by the Primary Call Center and a Consolidated Order Entry component instances. However, a different instance of the Person Management component, Employee Information, is used by the United States Payroll. Thus, when requesting the name for a particular person, such as person1, the Primary Call Center and Consolidated Order Entry components will get back the same result, George Smith. However, the United States Payroll system (assuming it used the same identifier) will get back a different result, Anne Jones, since it uses a different instance of the Person Management component.

There are cases where the use of a component must be encapsulated. In these situations the use of the other coarse-grained component is simply an implementation detail and cannot be shared with other components. Although this is similar to cases where a component has its own unshared instance of a shared component, it differs in that the encapsulated component can never be shared. Figure 16-5 in our example above shows the Dry Goods Management component built using the Product Management component. In this case, the Product Management component is encapsulated by the Dry Goods Management component, thus preventing situations such as adding a

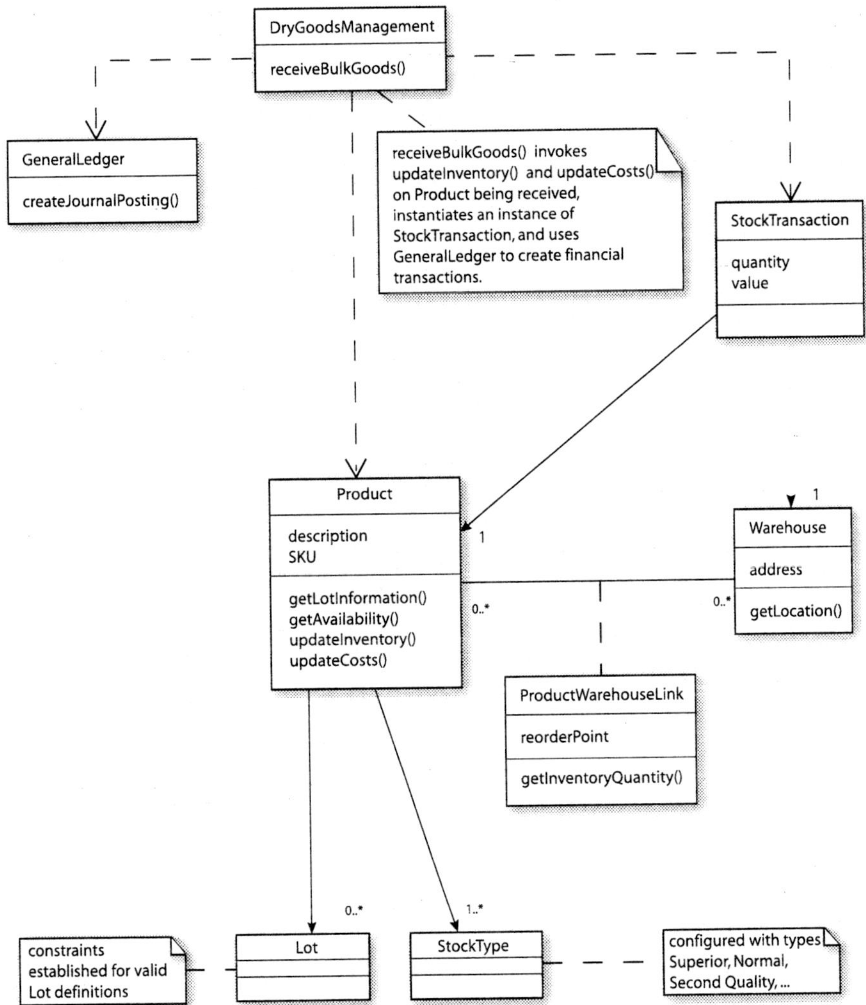

Figure 16-6: *Shared usage of coarse-grained components.*

new Dry Goods Management product and seeing that product appear in a Frozen Goods Management component (because of shared component use) from occurring.

Determining how another component needs to be used (encapsulated versus shared) is related to the time during the development cycle when the dependency was created. From our perspective, if the component is identified as part of domain analysis it is probably a

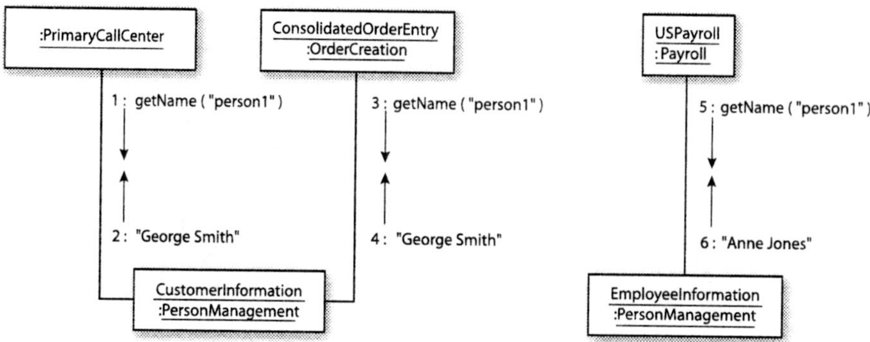

Figure 16-7: *Shared usage of coarse-grained components.*

shared usage. If it is identified as part of implementation it is probably encapsulated. In other words, if a domain expert identifies explicit dependencies between two components within the product-line, it is likely that both components should be visible in the final solution. On the other hand, if the coarse-grained component designer identifies another coarse-gained component that can provide part of the implementation for that new component, then encapsulation is probably a better choice.

16.4 Applying These Guidelines

The best way to apply these guidelines is to adopt a systematic development process. This can be a process built on the Rational Unified Process (Jacobson, Booch, and Rumbaugh, 1999), the Product-Line Architecture (see Chapter 22), Catalysis (D'Souza and Wills, 1999), or one of the new lightweight processes (Fowler, 2000). The specific process you choose is not important; its purpose is to ensure that these guidelines are applied at the correct points in the process. A well-defined process also provides a place for you to attach other guidelines as you discover them. We have focused on only the most important of the generally applicable guidelines we discovered. These guidelines are often ones we learned the hard way. We expect that as you gain experience in business component development, you will establish additional guidelines to add to those we've described in this chapter.

Using these guidelines as our starting point, we were able to more rapidly produce focused, highly reusable components that are well-partitioned. By involving domain experts we could discern the true rules and requirements and focus on the core problem to be solved. We experienced the weakness in using an implementation as the basis for designing components. Lastly, we made a concerted effort to reuse our own components. In this way we discovered (and appreciated) our customer's problems before they became problems in keeping that customer. We also validated our core (crosscutting) components because we improved our own productivity by using these components.

16.5 Conclusion

Regardless of the granularity of your business components, ensuring you get them "right" does not require a magical process. The development cycle for business components is no different than for any other successful software engineering process, and includes iterative cycles of rules and requirements capture, domain analysis, design, implementation, and testing. Within that process you should keep in mind the key guidelines we presented. Build a core team of experts with enough experience to explore the full breadth of component requirements and don't be afraid to ask these experts as many questions as necessary. Develop a culture of reuse that applies design patterns where appropriate in order to capitalize on tested approaches to solving problems and supports spending time investigating mapping; some existing components can only be reused by applying a suitable mapping. Don't over-design to create complex components that meet outlying cases. Lastly, design coarse-grained components as compositions of fine-grained components. Following the strategies in this chapter should help you create successful business components that meet the needs of your immediate business requirements and establishes a rich catalog of components for future reuse.

Chapter 17

Components and Connectors: Catalysis Techniques for Designing Component Infrastructures

Alan Cameron Wills

17.1 Introduction

The assembly of component infrastructures is enabled by the careful design of connectors that enable components to be integrated with each other. By focusing on the way components are connected, you can precisely specify a component's interface using a logical formalism, such as the Object Constraint Language (OCL).

17.2 Connector Design

A principal objective of component-based development is to rapidly develop a variety of software products from a kit of components. It should be possible to change the functionality of an assembled product just by reconfiguring its components, rather like an electronics starter kit. To illustrate the point (which I argue would apply on a large scale as well as this small scale), consider the simple electrical kit configuration in Figure 17-1 modeled using components. We've pulled a few parts out of a box and assembled them using simple connectors to produce something useful.

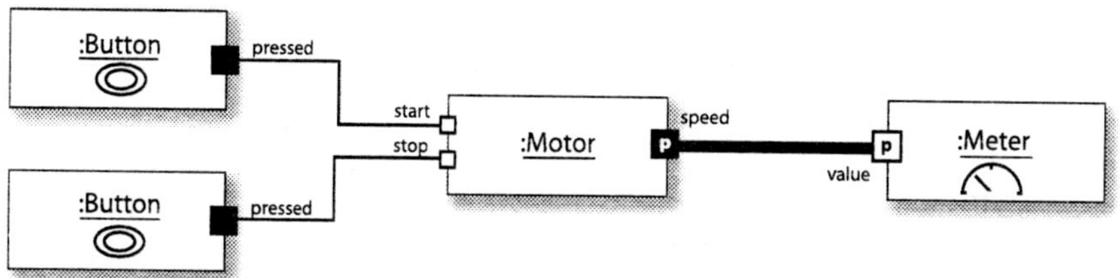

Figure 17-1: *An electrical system displayed as a set of connected components.*

The boxes represent components and a line between two components is a *connector,* an abstract representation of the interaction between those two components (Medvidovic, 1997). The specification of an interface defines a list of operations that can be performed on a component. Too often, however, there is not enough attention paid to the interaction that must exist over time between two interacting components. Using connectors to model the interactions is a powerful technique for designing component infrastructures with replaceable parts. In fact, let's combine a few more components to make something slightly more complex, as shown in Figure 17-2. Can you figure out what it does?

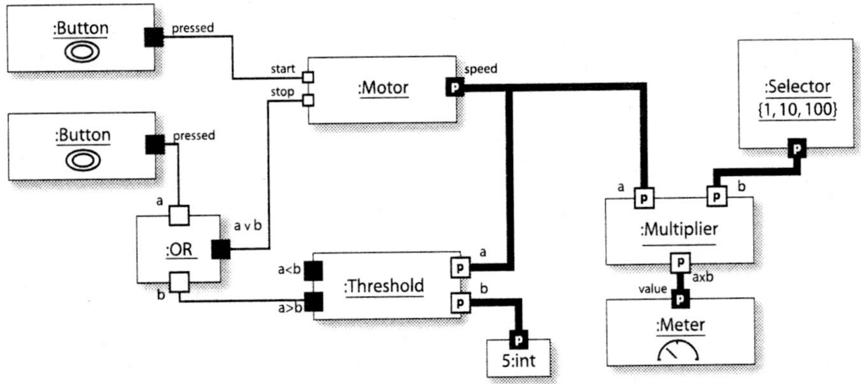

Figure 17-2: *A new electrical configuration.*

You can assemble these components into many configurations because the component interfaces conform to just a few basic types, and they can be assembled together using two basic connectors. The thin lines represent the delivery of an event from one component to another and the thick lines represent continuously-updated properties.

The interface for the Button component is a conduit that will allow voltage to flow through it when the button is closed but not when the Button is open. The Motor component will engage if sufficient voltage is applied to a metal contact. In this case the connector between these components is simply a wire that will transfer current via the Button to the Motor. If the voltage flowing through the Button is 5 V, but the motor is only capable of receiving 2 V, the connector would include a resistor to reduce the voltage. The connector introduced in Figure 17-2 is just a simple example of an interaction that must be carefully designed. We will discuss more complicated connectors in this chapter.

There are several lessons to be drawn from these simple examples of assembling configurations of components and connectors.

Families of products from kits of components—Component-based development is about producing components that can be assembled together in many different configurations. This principle works as well for software as it does in hardware, and it works as well for large components as it does for small ones. A software development organization might produce many basic components that can be assembled in different ways. Any assemblage of components can be considered to be a software component infrastructure if it is intentionally designed to enable software systems to meet specific performance requirements. But components are only half the picture; I argue that the interactions between components must be as carefully designed as the components themselves.

Minimize connector types—What makes the reconfiguration possible is the small number of connector types in relation to the number of components. The Button component can be connected to the Motor component or the OR Gate component through the same connector. In a larger-scale example the information transmitted over a connector will include rich data types or domain-specific objects, and the connectors will become more complicated.

Design of a component infrastructure—You must define the connectors separately from, and often before, individual components. Part of this definition is basic technology, such as whether the interaction between the components is through procedure calls or remote method invocations. Well-designed connectors also are domain-specific and are based on models of the business within which the components work. This is an important point, and I'll return to it shortly. In component-based development, there is a separation of roles into the following areas:

- Product building—the assembly of components into useful end-products. This can be done rapidly, once a well-designed component infrastructure has been built
- Component infrastructure design—the definition of the way in which components interact
- Component design—making components that conform to a component infrastructure

No adaptation—The component consumer should use the components "as is." When product designers use a component they are saving the cost of defining, testing, maintaining, and updating the component. If the component is modified by the product designer, much of the potential savings are lost. As a corollary, a good component design is one that is general enough to be used in several contexts. To enforce this policy of "no adaptation," component producers often sell their components in binary packaged form.

Pluggable connector definitions—The designer of a component cannot know the other components to which that component will be connected—there are countless possibilities that will be determined when the component is assembled with others to make an end-product. Therefore, the connectors must be precisely defined and the component designer must conform to them. The definition of a connector includes functional interfaces as well as the behavior to which the component must conform.

In traditional modular design, the module designers can usually discuss their interfaces and resolve any ambiguities or misunderstandings. In component-based development the designers of the component infrastructure must define the connectors precisely, and the component designers must conform to the definitions, otherwise the parts won't fit together properly.

17.3 Designing Interaction Standards

As described in Chapter 1, an interface is an abstraction of the behavior of a component that consists of a subset of the interactions of that component together with a set of constraints describing when they may occur. Each component model defines an interaction standard that describes the elements that may belong to an interface. In the example I used at the beginning of this chapter, the only interactions that could exist with a hardware component were through metal contacts; the connectors were therefore simple and the concept of "wiring together" components was reasonable.

A software component is more powerful than its hardware counterpart, and thus a component model can provide more complex interaction standards. Each software component must follow the interaction standard of the component model to which they conform. Therefore, the interaction standard must be clearly defined. The definition for an interface can include

- Resource use (in terms of allocated memory or disk usage)
- Processor use (such as CPU time and number of operating system processes or threads)
- Database use (such as database tables or specific embedded queries)

- Global variables (defined by the component or just used by the component)
- Methods (including parameters, return types, and exceptions that may occur)
- Input and Output specifications (from terminal, disk, network, or any device controlled by the operating system)
- Data types or classes that must be provided for the component to execute

The component designer must produce an accurate specification of a component's interface to allow the component to be assembled together with other components when a component infrastructure is designed. Most component models have interaction standards that are most concerned with the operations (methods) supported by an interface. Component models for real-time or resource-constrained systems (such as embedded software or hand-held devices) require component designers to explicitly declare more information about a component's interface.

17.3.1 Reconfigurable Component Infrastructures

If you wish to develop a component infrastructure that can be reconfigured without alterations, you must carefully design the interactions between the components. You must also enable an application assembler to deploy the components and specify how they will be interconnected. At a syntactic level, the component model to which these components conform defines the interaction standard that will enable the components to communicate with each other. For example, distributed components can be interconnected using remote procedure calls as support by CORBA, RMI, or DCOM. The connector encapsulates any interaction and is thus general enough to address the following interactions between component C_1 and C_2:

- C_1 updates a row in a common database and C_2 issues an SQL query to retrieve the information
- C_1 initiates a File Transfer Protocol (FTP) session to transfer information between two machines, and C_2 directly opens the file containing that information
- C_1 issues a remote method invocation of C_2

The connector models the flow of information between components as well as control flow. The important concept is that the components are designed to match the connector definitions. Not everyone has the goal of developing reconfigurable component interfaces, so I now describe the essential aspects for designing interfaces for your components.

17.4 Designing Component Interfaces

An interface will be the contract agreed to by a component. In this section I describe various aspects that you must design.

17.4.1 Business Concept Modeling

The designer of the component infrastructure has to specify to all component designers the types of objects within the business domain that may be part of the messages among the components. The Unified Modeling Language (UML) is often used to document the business domain because it has become the standard notation for documenting types and their relationships. The UML class diagram in Figure 17-3 demonstrates the relationship between a customer and purchases from the business.

Each Customer in this business has a name, address, exactly one Account, and any number of Orders (from 0 to "*"—any number). Each Account has a list of Items (payments or charges), some of which may be associated with Orders; each Item is associated with only one Account. Each Account has a balance, is billed to one Customer, and each Order is delivered to only one Customer. The Money class has an attribute, smallestUnit, that describes the smallest unit of accuracy (for example, 1/100 of a U.S. dollar) for converting currencies.

This model of business concepts is completely independent of the implementations of the components in the business and of their internal database schemas. Each component is free to use its own implementations of these common business concepts. To avoid direct coupling, the connectors may translate between the business concepts and internal implementations of those concepts. Each component is an encapsulated unit, which has certain implications as I now describe.

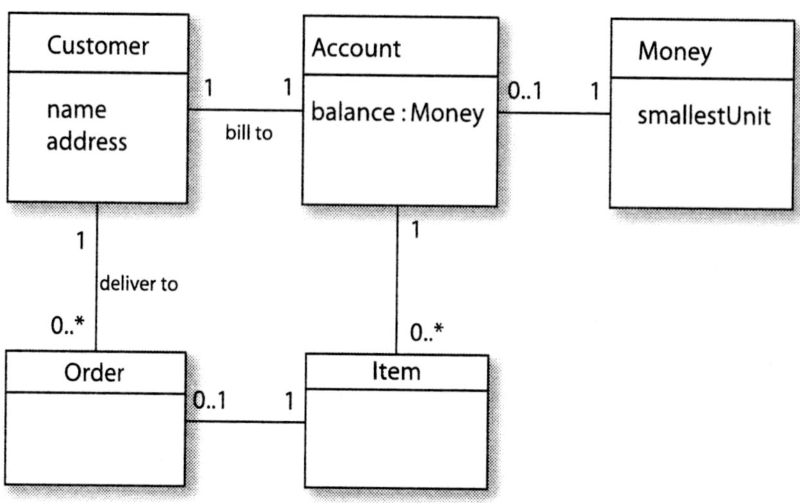

Figure 17-3: *UML diagram of customer purchases.*

17.4.1.1 Encapsulation

There should be no direct access to the data of any component from outside that component. All communication should be a request defined in an interface. This ensures that the implementation of each component is free to represent its data internally as determined by the component designer.

I once encountered a global corporation that thought that their many systems were difficult to interconnect because there was no uniform data format. They therefore mandated that all local designers would migrate the format of their customer records towards a common format; by doing so, they expected that customer records could be exchanged among any of the corporate systems. Unfortunately, it didn't work too well. For one thing, most of the existing systems couldn't be adapted. Even where they could, the local usage of customer records did not fit the corporate model in many cases. For example, where the corporate model only allowed for one address, what should a local designer do for applications that required two addresses? Different patches were applied in different localities with the result that the customer records weren't interchangeable at all.

The appropriate solution is encapsulation. The connectors define the external view of data and leave the internal implementation within each component to its designer. Each component is wrapped in an adaptor that translates from its internal representation to the common external format. The functional interface of a component defines the services it supports. In most cases these services are defined as parameterized requests. For example, a component could support the behaviors "Charge $10 for Order 534 to Customer Joe" and "Process a Customer payment" using the interface in Figure 17-4.

```
interface Billing {
     placeOrder (Order ord, Customer cust, Money mon);
     payment (Customer cust, Money mon);
}
```

Figure 17-4: *First version of an interface for a component to manage billing.*

The methods of this interface are based on domain-specific objects—what is an Order, and what is a Customer, and what can you do to them? Also, there are business rules governing these objects—can an Order refer to two Customers? What happens to an Order when a Customer makes a payment?

I have frequently seen insufficient attention given to the classes of objects referred to in interface methods; business rules in particular are forgotten. Much confusion will ensue if one component assumes that Order can have two Customers and it sends messages about them to another component that assumes there must be only one. You must find a way to describe such business constraints with the interfaces themselves, as I now show.

17.4.2 Business Constraints

The UML diagram describes constraints on the relationships between business concepts that all components must observe. For example, an Order is always associated with exactly one Item on an Account. Not all the components may understand every part of the business model. For example, components with Accounts may not know about the delivery address of an Order, while components dealing with dispatching orders may not know about Account Items. But no component can invalidate a constraint. For example, no component should send messages associating an Order with more than one Customer.

Some constraints are not so easily represented directly in UML diagrams. For example, some businesses insist that the billing address is the same as the delivery address; other businesses have no such rule. These business rules must be defined, documented, and associated with the component infrastructure. Business rules should always be written in natural language (that is, British English) so that business representatives throughout the organization can understand them easily. But convoluted rules are easily misunderstood, and each rule should be defined precisely as well.

The most direct way to verify that constraints are not broken is to develop test suites for any component that claims to conform to your component infrastructure. This must be done at some stage as part of quality assurance, but test cases are not the best form of documentation. Many designers prefer to use OCL, the Object Constraint Language, which is part of the UML. It provides a formal approach to defining constraints precisely. For example, the OCL statement

```
Order :: item.account.bill-to == deliver-to
```

is a precise way of saying:

```
For every instance of an Order, the associated item's
account's billing address should be the same as the
Order's delivery address.
```

These precise definitions are associated with the model of business concepts, the connector definitions, and component interfaces. Your testing team can use OCL constraints to develop test suites to ensure component compliance with the component infrastructure.

17.4.3 Dynamic Constraints

There are also business rules about how business concepts and their relationships are affected by the operations of components. Within a particular domain you may have a set of components that perform different tasks, yet there are some constraints to which they all adhere. I recommend that you use OCL to specify these constraints with the interface. In the next few subsections I assume there is a software element (called the client code) that invokes a method from the interface of a target component.

17.4.3.1 Invariants

An invariant is a logical statement associated with an interface that a component assumes is always true. The component ensures that its implementation will not invalidate any invariants defined by its interfaces. An invariant must be true before a method is invoked, and it will be true once the method is completed. In OCL, an invariant is specified as "**inv** logical statement".

17.4.3.2 Preconditions

A precondition is a logical statement associated with a method in an interface that must be true before that method is invoked. The responsibility of the client code requesting the method is to ensure that the precondition is true before it invokes the method. A component is only responsible for executing the methods in its interfaces whose preconditions are true. However, the implementation of a component should be robust enough that it will gracefully exit if a method is invoked improperly.

Most component models (and an increasing number of programming languages) use the concept of an *exception* to exit a method in such a way that the client code clearly understands that an error of some type occurred. The exception will be clearly documented with the interface. In general, you should develop two types of exceptions: 1) a *precondition failure* exception can be signaled by a component when the client code fails to verify the precondition before invoking a method; and 2) a *postcondition failure* exception can be signaled by a component when it is unable to process the method because of an unusual (or undocumented) circumstance.

In OCL a precondition is specified as "**pre** logical statement." The logical statement can refer to the component state or any of the parameters of the method. An interface declares that a method can signal an exception by specifying "**exception** (type) logical statement" with the method declaration.

17.4.3.3 Postconditions

A postcondition is a logical statement associated with a method in an interface that must be true after that method is invoked. The component is responsible for ensuring the postconditions of its interface methods.

In OCL a postcondition can refer to the component state or any of the parameters of the method. It can also conveniently refer to the previous value (that is, before the method was invoked) of such a component state or method parameters by using the "@pre" modifier. We shall see examples of "@pre" shortly. In OCL a postcondition is specified as "**post** logical statement."

17.4.3.4 Effects

Finally, an effect is a logical statement associated with an interface that must be true after any method in that interface is invoked. An effect is often called a "freestanding" postcondition that must be agreed to by every method of that interface. Effects are useful because they apply to all methods in an interface—even those not yet invented.

In OCL an effect is specified as "effect logical statement ➜ logical statement". That is, if the first logical statement is true, then the second one must also be true.

```
interface Billing {
effect (Customer.balance@pre > 0) and (Customer.balance <= 0) ➜
     (Customer.paidOff = true)

placeOrder (Order ord, Customer cust, Money mon)
   pre (cust.balance == 0) or (cust.balance > mon)
   post (cust.balance@pre - cust.balance - mon) <
      Money.smallestUnit)
   exception (FailCredit) cust.balance < mon
   exception (IllegalOrder) ord.deliverTo <> cust

payment (Customer cust, Money mon)
   pre mon > 0
   post (cust.balance - cust.balance@pre - mon) <
      Money.smallestUnit)
}
```

Figure 17-5: *Final billing interface.*

17.4.3.5 Some Examples

Consider the initial version of the Billing interface, as shown in Figure 17-4, and the business concepts from Figure 17-3. For example, the main effect of a customer making a payment should be to reduce the account balance. Although it may be impossible to describe the exact amount of the reduction, because there may be currency conversions involved, some facts are clear. The logical precondition for `payment` in Figure 17-5 requires a positive payment amount and the postcondition asserts that the resulting customer balance is accurate to within the smallest unit of currency available. When a customer places an order there is a business rule that requires the prior balance of the customer to be zero or that the new cost of the order is no greater than the outstanding balance. This is captured in the precondition on the method `placeOrder`. The postcondition on this method shows that the balance is accurately updated. Finally, there are two exceptions to note: the first is an exception that tells the client code that one of its preconditions failed; the second shows that the client would have invalidated the business concepts with this method request. An accurate interface specification is invaluable when determining whether components can be connected together.

17.5 Conclusion

Component-based design builds families of software products from kits of components. The assembly process is made possible by the relatively small number of connectors that are designed to enable components to be integrated with each other. For effective CBD the lead engineer must carefully design the connectors for a component infrastructure. Connector definitions include protocols of transactions between the components and a model of the business domain within which the components work. UML and OCL can be used to define the business domain concepts and the static and dynamic rules by which they behave. These rules can be used to guide the construction of test software for components that are candidate members of the kit.

Chapter 18

An OPEN Process for Component-Based Development

Brian Henderson-Sellers[1]

Editor's Introduction—*The UML and ISO 9001 series have gained momentum among large companies and defense contractors as the most effective methods to assure increasingly improved software. For many companies, these organizational processes do not stimulate the culture for quality. In many companies around the world, over 90 percent of the software businesses and independent software vendors are small businesses with less than 500 employees. Small companies just do not have the time, effort, or resources to devote to a relatively rigid, organizational software maturity plan, especially one that measures the organization's capacity to produce effective software a few days a year, rather than by product.*

1. Excerpts of this chapter appeared in "Adding CBD to OPEN", *Journal of Object-Oriented Programming*, Apr., 2001, 101communications LLC.

What makes sense for many of these software organizations, like their colleagues in safety-critical software, elevator construction, and joists for bridges is a standard against which they are measured and a series of conformance assessments to ensure the success of the status of their endeavor.

OPEN is a flexible process that is derived from a metamodel (a model of a model) that is tailored to the organization and its culture. OPEN is a series of best practices that may be implemented as needed to improve the component-based software process and its quality. As you will see, OPEN is a people-oriented approach, one that can be applied to a complex endeavor in a team context. This chapter focuses on the evaluation, acquisition, and reuse of appropriate components. Remember that Will Tracz in Chapter 6 said, "COTS product selections are often based on slick demos, Web searches, or reading trade journals." Brian's approach relies on research and comparison, and metrics.

18.1 Introduction

Creating a software-intensive system requires much more than just a notation—it requires a process. A process assists both the development and management teams in creating a software-intensive system in an orderly manner to maximize the chances for an on-time delivery and a quality product. Indeed, the most important driver for successful software development, after "having good people," is process. By imposing order and rigor, a disciplined process enables you to repeat successful outcomes and to achieve continuous improvement.

A *process* is defined as "a set of interrelated activities, which transform inputs into outputs" (ISO, 1995). It discusses what must be done, by whom, when, and how. A process should also give advice and guidelines on quality issues, overall project management, and people issues. As an example of the use of an object-oriented (OO) approach to building software, a process like OPEN (Graham, Henderson-Sellers, and Younessi, 1997) or Catalysis (D'Souza and Wills, 1999) offers broad support for all the issues mentioned above and, to document the deliverables, uses a notation like the Unified Modeling Language ([UML] [Henderson-Sellers and Unhelkar, 2000]).

Many CBD processes have a root in object-oriented processes. Creating applications from preexisting components is a necessary part of any CBD process. The emphasis shifts from synthesis with OO to integration with CBD (Seacord and Nwosu, 1999) to a prominence on creating these components as reusable assets. For component-based application development, the acquisition and integration of components becomes an activity that occurs in parallel with the design activity, resulting in the creation of new components. Thus, a CBD process has a context in which a component is developed and used and must, like its OO counterpart, be designed for a wide variety of uses, including

- Project management
- Organizational culture
- Employee skills
- Tool availability
- Reuse strategies
- Quality criteria imposed by the end-user of the software

CBD typically focuses on the use of encapsulated and pluggable components as units of deployable code (Szyperski, 1998); some approaches, such as Catalysis (D'Souza and Wills, 1999) allow components to be designs, specifications, text documents or anything that can be described by a UML package. In comparison to an object-oriented approach, a component package includes definitions of the interfaces it requires as well as what it provides. Because components are known almost exclusively by their interfaces ([Szyperski, 1998] [Digre, 1998]); these interfaces must be clearly specified, trusted, and useful. In addition, components tend to have more complex actions at their interfaces, not just individual messages, and are coarser-grained (D'Souza and Wills, 1999); indeed, a component may contain several objects inside it. Components are also more static than objects, although both work through interfaces with possibly multiple alternative implementations.

Components need to be "composable," that is, there must be easy ways of assembling them, leading to the need for minor enhancements or variations in use with current OO modeling languages. In all fairness we should note that currently there are difficulties in using or adopting UML's notions of aggregation and composition to components (Henderson-Sellers and Barbier, 1999). Fixing UML's composition support is therefore more crucial for CBD than in OO software development. A request for proposals is already scheduled for UML Version 2.0 (refer to Chapter 14 by Houston and Norris on their view of the need for enhancements to the UML's composition support).

You can therefore use existing development processes, such as those for OO, with modifications suitable for CBD. In this chapter I show how the OPEN Process has been extended to add a new focus on components. I describe only one part of an OPEN CBD process: the evaluation and selection of components from a repository, so-called "with reuse." I do not attempt to describe the important aspects of component creation, which I refer to as "for reuse." Good advice on component creation as well as component utilization can be found in D'Souza and Wills (1999), which provides a good basis for a later incorporation into OPEN of any necessary additional support "for reuse."

18.2 OPEN

OPEN (Object-oriented Process, Environment, and Notation) is a third-generation, full life cycle, process-focused, object-oriented development approach designed to support the construction of software and software-intensive applications, particularly object-oriented ones and now component-based development. OPEN was developed and is maintained by the not-for-profit OPEN Consortium, an international group of over 35 methodologists, academicians, CASE tool vendors, and developers (*www.open.org.au*).

OPEN addresses business nonsoftware-related quality, modeling, and reuse issues within its end-to-end life cycle support for software development. It also covers such management activities as project management (planning, staffing, and scheduling), metrics, team building, and training. Few other contemporary development methods emphasize these business-focused and people-related issues. For object and component technologies to be relevant to commercial component implementations, an OOD/CBD method should seriously consider these early life cycle issues. You cannot assume that the life cycle begins with a clearly defined requirements definition.

OPEN is defined by a generic *metamodel* that is flexible enough to create new industry-specific or domain-specific process instances. Thus, OPEN is *not* the process itself, but its metamodel provides the rules for building that process. The figure demonstrates that from the OPEN metamodel we can create a "family" of OPEN instances, each geared towards one specific domain, organization, or project. Although there is effort in instantiating a process from the OPEN process framework, the resulting process is carefully configured to the specific organization, problem, or domain. For example, Figure 18-1 could be instantiated to produce effective requirements. In this chapter the "specific domain" that we address is that of component-based development.

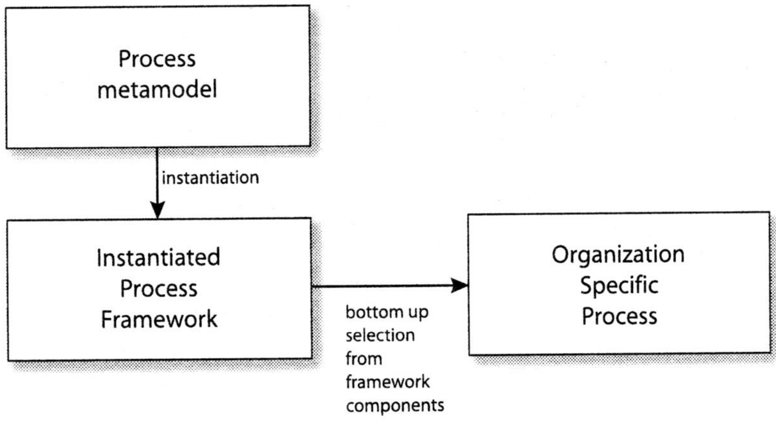

Figure 18-1: *Constructing a process from a process metamodel involves first instantiating the framework and then selecting instances of those chosen meta-elements in a bottom-up fashion (after Firesmith and Henderson-Sellers (2001) © Addison-Wesley, 2001).*

In this comprehensive approach to solution provision rather than software development, the overall OPEN Process Framework (OPF) is described in terms of a set of interrelated meta-components, each of which encapsulates some concept in the process model. In Figure 18-2, the essential elements of the OPF are Producers, Work Units, and Work Products.

Also needed, but not discussed here, are the various necessary languages (including the Unified Modeling Language [UML] or the OPEN Modeling Language [OML]) as well as the structure of the life

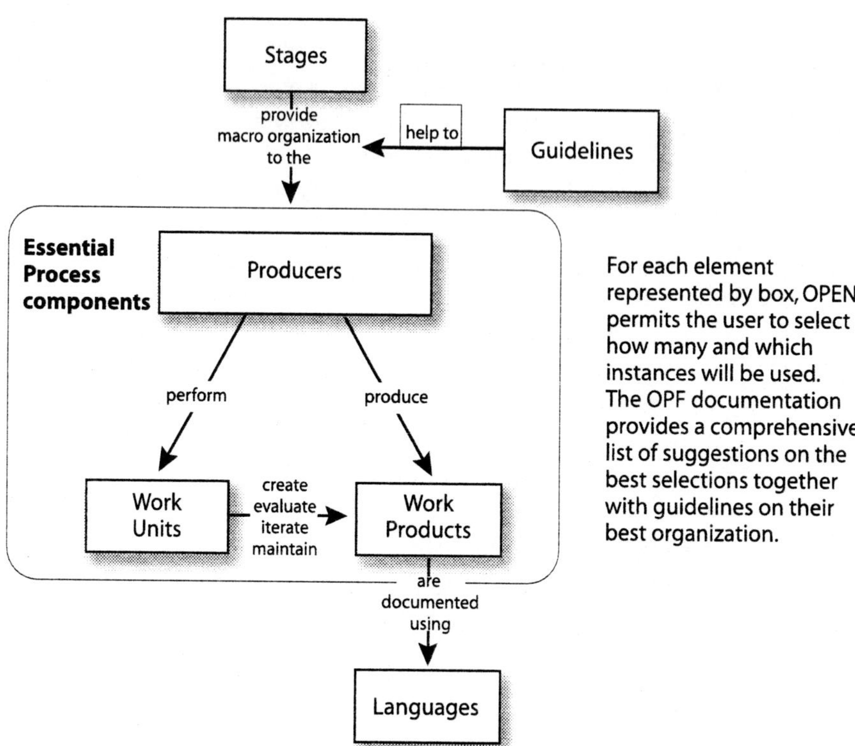

Figure 18-2: *The main three meta-types in OPEN are Producers, Work Products, and Work Units with supporting meta-types of Stages and Languages (after Firesmith and Henderson-Sellers © Addison-Wesley, 2001).*

cycle itself, described in terms of stages, milestones, phases, builds, releases, and workflows (Firesmith and Henderson-Sellers, 2001). Figure 18-3 illustrates instances of each of these elements that create a library of process components upon which the bottom-up selection of Figure 18-1 can operate.

All the elements from which to create and configure your own OPEN-compliant methodology are described in the texts on OPEN. In the next subsections I briefly outline the three key meta-components (Producers, Work Units, and Work Products) and then give a brief example of the construction of one specific OPEN instance.

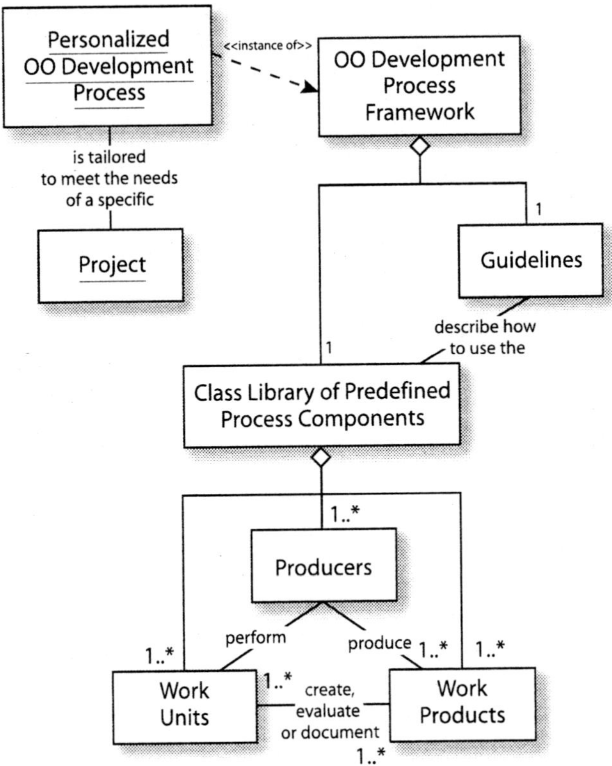

Figure 18-3: *Using the process component library to build a project-specific process (after Henderson-Sellers, © IEEE Computer Society Press 2000).*

18.2.1 Producers

A *Producer* is anything that creates Work Products. A *Direct Producer* represents a person (or more strictly a role) directly responsible for creating a Work Product. Alternatively, there may be *Indirect Producers*—teams of people (the membership of teams strictly being roles), organizations (the membership of which are teams) and *endeavors*. An endeavor is staffed by one or more organizations. Endeavors, in turn, may be classified as projects, programs, or enterprises.

18.2.2 Work Units

A *Work Unit* is defined as a functionally cohesive operation performed by a Producer during an Endeavor. Predefined Work Units in OPEN are Activities, Tasks, and Techniques. *Activities* are typically high-level descriptions of goals to be achieved, such as the need to undertake requirements engineering, architecture, design, implementation, integration, testing, and delivery. Project management at this scale is complicated because the notion of "completion" is difficult to define. Instead, project management occurs at the Task level. These smaller scale *Tasks* are elements you might find in a "to do" list. Each task represents an achievable goal and is homogeneous—in contrast to the heterogeneous nature of an activity. Together, Figure 18-4 demonstrates activities and tasks at two different granularities, the goals of the process. Both activities and tasks focus on the "what" to be done, not the "how." The "how" is described in OPEN by a collection of techniques that can be regarded as the "tools of the trade," akin to the toolkit of a plumber or electrician.

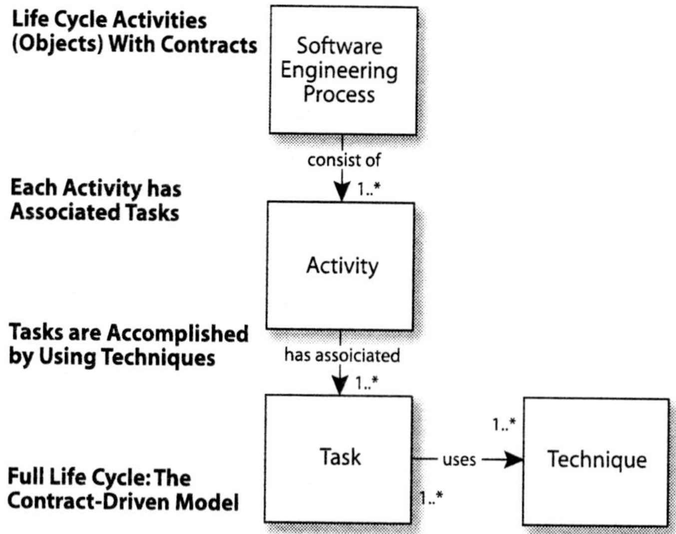

Figure 18-4: *The Software Engineering Process element of OPEN is made up of activities that are in turn decomposed into tasks. Tasks are affected by techniques.*

Figure 18-5 depicts the selection of appropriate activities and tasks together with suitable techniques that are part of the process of creating an instance of OPEN (an actual process) from OPEN's metamodel to fit an organization's specific requirements exactly (see "Example Process Instance" in section 18.2.4). This selection process is therefore largely a matter of experience, real or surrogate—although we anticipate software tool support in the near future. Finally, for any given producer a Workflow may be created as a sequence of tasks to be performed.

Task

Techniques	A	B	C	D	E	.
1	M	D	F	F	F	.
2	D	D	F	F	D	.
3	D	D	O	O	D	.
4	F	O	O	O	F	.
5	F	M	O	D	F	.
6	R	R	M	R	O	.
7	D	R	F	M	O	.
8	D	F	M	D	D	.
9	R	R	D	R	R	.
10	O	D	O	O	R	.
11	F	M	O	F	D	.
.	.	.	.	.	.	.
.						

5 Levels of Possibility

M = Mandatory
R = Recommended
O = Optional
D = Discouraged
F = Forbidden

Figure 18-5: *A core element of OPEN is a two-dimensional relationship between tasks and techniques (and a similar matrix linking tasks and activities). For each combination of Task and Technique, an assessment can be made of the likelihood of the occurrence of that combination. Some combinations can be identified as mandatory (M), others as recommended (R), some as being optional (O), some are discouraged (D) but may be used with care, and other combinations are strictly forbidden (F). Filling in the matrix values is an important part of the life cycle tailoring Task in OPEN (© Henderson-Sellers and Unhelkar, 2000).*

18.2.3 Work Products

The final key element in Figure 18-2 is the *Work Product,* any asset of significant value developed during a project, such as a document, diagram, model, class, component, or application. One or more *Producers* develop a *Work Product* while performing one or more *Work Units.* Table 18-1 shows that work products can be organized into nine sets, based on the activities that produce them.

Table 18-1: *The Nine Sets of Work Products Within OPEN*

Management Set	
Engineering Set	Process set
	Requirements set
	Architecture set
	Design set
	Implementation set
	Integration set
	Test set
	Transition set

18.2.4 Example Process Instance

OPEN's metamodel defines how work units, such as activities, tasks, and techniques, relate to each other and to other process elements, such as producers (individuals and teams), and to work products, such as design diagrams and requirements specifications. Figure 18-1 illustrates the creation of an actual process from the OPEN framework; each element in the metamodel must be instantiated one or more times, thus creating *specific* activities, tasks, techniques, and work products.

As a small, indicative example of only a portion of the full process lifecycle, we consider the case of an OO development where the requirements have already been finalized—perhaps appropriate to an outsourcing organization. Figure 18-6 demonstrates the main activities that are selected, which are Project Planning, Build (Modeling, User Review, and Consolidation), and Evaluation.

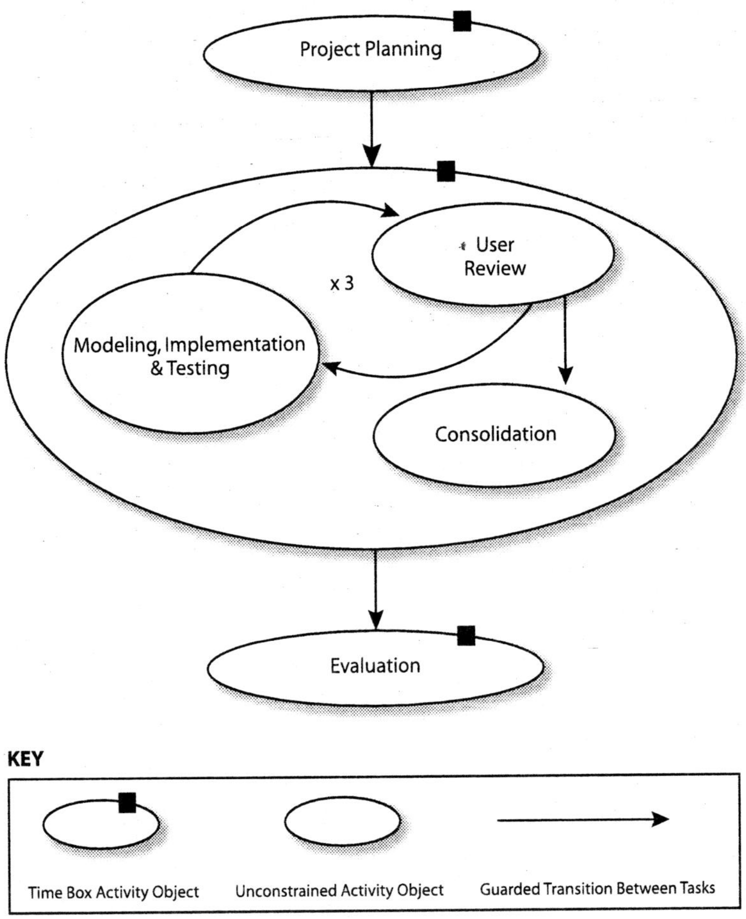

Figure 18-6: *Instance of OPEN appropriate for a small project where requirements are already "frozen." (© Henderson-Sellers and Unhelkar, 2000).*

For these activities Figure 18-7 shows that seven major tasks, together with 25 suitable techniques, have been identified during a comparative case study of the application to a small library information system. By using the two tailoring matrices, a process is *specifically created* for each individual organization or each application development project.

Technique	1	2	3	4	5	6	7
Abstract class identification		X					
Abstraction utilization		X			X		
Class internal design	X	X					
Class naming		X		X			
Collaborations analysis		X					
Complexity measurement				X			
Contract specification	X	X			X		
Coupling measurement				X			
CRC card modeling		X			X		
General &inheritance ident.		X					X
Implementation of services	X						
Implementation of structure	X					X	
Inspections				X			X
Interaction modeling		X					
Package and subsystem testing							X
Prototyping	X	X					
Relationship modeling	X	X					
Responsibility identification	X			X	X		X
Role modeling		X				X	
Service identification		X					
State modeling		X					
Textural analysis					X		
Timeboxing			X				
Unit testing							X
Walkthroughs				X			X

Key:
1. Code
2. Construct the object model
3. Develop and implement resource allocations plan
4. Evaluate quality
5. Identify CIRTs
6. Map roles on to classes
7. Test

Figure 18-7: *The linking of OPEN tasks to appropriate techniques is supported by an organization-specific version of the OPEN tailoring matrix shown in Figure 18-5 (© Henderson-Sellers and Unhelkar, 2000).*

18.3 Existing OPEN Support for CBD

OPEN will only support CBD if its activities, tasks, and techniques do. We first need to identify what support for CBD already exists in OPEN and what conditions are missing. This section identifies and introduces those previously missing elements.

There are already three OPEN tasks focusing on reuse that are immediately applicable (when enhanced with more component-focused discussion).

- Create and/or identify reusable components ("for reuse")
- Optimize reuse ("with reuse")
- Manage library of reusable components

These three elements cover the ideas of:

- Creation of reusable assets
- Management throughout the duration of their existence
- And subsequent (re)use in other applications

"For reuse" focuses on how we might successfully create components either for an organizational purpose or as a spin-off from the development of some other software application. Domain analysis is required; extra effort is necessary to ensure the reliability of the components, often leading to the creation of a software component infrastructure from the components. "With reuse" takes those existing, well-crafted components and advises how they can be used in the present project. This is partly sociological in encouraging developers to even consider using someone else's code and it is partly realizing that reuse occurs not just from the use of inheritance, as is typically the myth in object-oriented circles, but from means much more appropriate to components, notably types of composition or "aggregation."

The third task concerns management rather than technical or development issues. Managing a library of reusable components requires skills in cataloguing and classification as well as retrieval algorithms, and, ideally, a software intelligent browsing tool (Freeman and Henderson-Sellers, 1991). For more on this topic refer to Chapter 29 for a concise yet current description of component management applications and librarians.

There is also a fourth task "Develop software development context plans and strategies," which has existing subtasks to establish plans and strategies. None of these currently addresses the organization's policy on components—clearly, an extension will be needed here.

As well as the three OPEN tasks discussed above, there are also a significant number of techniques in OPEN relevant to component usage. The most relevant are those focusing on reuse, including library management, library class incorporation, and reuse measurement, together with a number of more technical techniques not focused solely on components or reuse. These include:

- Application scavenging
- CIRT (class, instance, role or type)
- Indexing
- Completion of abstractions
- Domain analysis
- Software infrastructure creation
- Genericity specification
- Idioms
- Mechanisms
- Pattern recognition
- Revision of inheritance hierarchies (generalization for reuse)

All are all described in *The OPEN Toolbox of Techniques* (Henderson-Sellers, Simons, and Younessi, 1998).

18.4 Extending the Support

In this section we identify the extent of preexisting support in OPEN for CBD. It is clear from that discussion that OPEN needs to augment several existing tasks as well as include new tasks and subtasks that are specifically focused on component selection and use.

Creating applications from preexisting components is a prime example of "with reuse." Currently in OPEN, "with reuse" is described by a task that relates to activities such as domain analysis and application building. For OO *application* development, this has been adequate. However, for CBD the whole focus of acquisition and integration of components is really a parallel for (at least part of) the Build Activity of software application development. While some components *may* be built in-house, it is my contention that the majority will likely be acquired elsewhere. It thus seems more appropriate to "elevate" OPEN's support for "with reuse" to the level of an activity rather than (merely) a task. In so doing, the activity is renamed in OPEN as "Component Selection." This new OPEN Activity has three associated tasks, based on the work of Kuruganti (1999).

- Screen the candidate list of components
- Evaluate the potential components
- Choose appropriate components

It then remains for appropriate techniques to be identified to fulfill these tasks, if necessary identifying and adding any such missing Techniques to *OPEN's Toolbox.* Secondly, we note the need for a new task: "Integrate Components" that describes how the selected components are synthesized into the application. This may be a substitute for, or a complement to, the existing OPEN task: "Code."

18.4.1 Activity: Component Selection

In transforming OPEN's existing task "Optimize reuse" to this new OPEN activity "Component Selection," we expand on the existing description (Graham, Henderson-Sellers, and Younessi, 1997) with its focus on software development, by including concerns identified by Kuruganti (1999). Component selection is described as finding pieces to fit into an underlying jigsaw puzzle, yet it remains unclear how the underlying architecture should be elucidated. Components ("jigsaw pieces") also exist at different granularities, which can have an impact on how the component-based development proceeds (Unhelkar, 1997).

Kuruganti's (1999) methodology for selecting components stresses the need to evaluate various vendors' offerings of components to identify the best-fit solution for your organization's particular problem. She notes that this may be difficult because of a lack of understanding of components, framework, and architecture issues; incomplete understanding of functional requirements and deployment constraints that must be met; and inconsistently packaged offerings from different vendors.

The three tasks identified as relevant to this new component selection activity each deal with a different aspect of component selection. Each also has prespecified inputs and outputs (Kuruganti, 1999) as well as roles.

18.4.2 Tasks to Support Component Selection Activity

Tasks to support the activity of component selection operate across three dimensions. These are functional specifications, operational and performance attributes, and deployment factors.

In addition, each task has preconditions and postconditions that are affected by individuals playing roles. Each task is comprised of a number of steps, expressed here as subtasks.

18.4.2.1 Task: "Screen the candidate list of components"

The goal of this task is to identify vendors and available components. These are then screened against a list of requirements that might themselves be simultaneously evolving. The preconditions thus relate to the draft specification for required features (services) of the components, performance constraints, target platforms, and expectations from vendors regarding business alignment.

Appropriate subtasks are identified as:

- Gather information on candidate components (which selects OPEN techniques from those already found useful in requirements engineering)
- Select candidate components
- Gather preliminary cost information on selected candidates
- Produce first (rough) assessment (which uses the new OPEN Technique "Checklist" – see section 18.4.3.2)

The postconditions of this task are a ranked list of screened components, possible revisions to requirements, and refined component specifications.

18.4.2.2 Task: "Evaluate the potential components"

The goal of this Task is to undertake a full evaluation of the candidates identified in the previous task. The preconditions are equivalent to the postconditions of that task. The producers involved are software developers, designers, and component engineers.

Appropriate subtasks are

- Generate a compliance matrix (using the new OPEN technique: "Compliance Matrix Template"—see section 18.4.3.3)

- Execute component producer-supplied examples in test mode
- (Optional) obtain independent benchmark data, that is, third-party certification (refer to Chapter 38 concerning third-party certification)
- Develop and test context-specific examples
- Document results of component evaluation
- Document interactions with component producer
- Rank the candidate components (which uses OPEN techniques "Checklist" and "QESTA"—see sections 18.4.3.2 and 18.4.3.1)

The postcondition of the task "Evaluate the Potential Components" includes evaluation results from each candidate component, revisions to software architecture and component specifications, and, finally, a ranked list of component producers and their components.

Kuruganti (1999) notes that this task is crucial and should be conducted with extreme care. Indeed, if one component (and component producer) clearly stands out from the rest and satisfies the required levels of testing or certification, then the decision-making process (task "Choose appropriate components") becomes unnecessary.

18.4.2.3 Task: "Choose appropriate components"

For this decision-making task, we need to choose the most appropriate component(s). This task is only activated if there is no clear winner already. The precondition is equivalent to the postcondition of the previous task. Producers involved are technical and product managers as well as system architects.

Appropriate subtasks are

- Compile a list of critical components
- Discuss trade-off factors and risks
- Compile a list of Producers' assessments of candidate components
- Arrive at overall score and ranked list using a normalization and weighted aggregate approach

The postconditions include a decision on the "make or buy" question and, in the latter case, the recommended component producer. Additionally, risk assessments should be attached to any decision. A mitigation plan is optional, but any evaluation plan should account for risks.

18.4.2.4 Subtask: "Establish policy on component acquisition"

One of the major project management (PM) tasks in OPEN is "Develop software development context plans and strategies." Subtasks focus on various plans, such as, contingency, security, and strategies (for example, component management). I propose the addition of one further subtask focused on CBSE, the subtask "Establish policy on component acquisition."

The use of software elements from elsewhere is often influenced by both individual and corporate mindsets. There is too often wariness about using other component producers' work, although this is beginning to change. As a supply of high quality components continues to become available in the marketplace, the trend will likely increase. At the same time an increasing number of organizations are now outsourcing their IT. This means that by downsizing the in-house IT skill set, more emphasis must be placed on developing skills related to testing and evaluation of third-party software. Policies need to be developed regarding evaluating the quality levels of component producers. The evaluation of producers has been one of the elements in a Total Quality Management (TQM) approach in manufacturing for many years, but often requires a time interval in which to build mutual trust. In other words, "buy or build" decisions need to be made, either on a high level (as a departmental policy) or on a per project basis.

18.4.3 Supporting Techniques for Component Selection Tasks

Because of these new OPEN tasks and subtasks, three new techniques need to be added to the OPEN "Toolbox." These are QESTA, checklists, and compliance matrix templates.

18.4.3.1 New OPEN Technique: QESTA

QESTA (Hansen, 1999) is described as a process and can therefore be thought of as a "way of doing things" (in OPEN terminology, a Technique). QESTA thus is an excellent candidate for an OPEN Technique that is useful not only for evaluating COTS (as originally proposed by Hansen (1999), but also for evaluating components. QESTA is an acronym that represents

- Quantification—Define the metric for each characteristic to be evaluated

- Examination—Values for each metric are found for each product under examination
- Specification—Values are interpreted as "good" or "bad"
- Transformation—Values are normalized
- Aggregation—An algorithm is used to create a single number from the set of values from the Transformation step

Results are tabulated at each step and the values may be closely linked to checklist.

18.4.3.2 New OPEN Technique: Checklist

The technique of using a checklist of criteria is straightforward. A list is compiled, probably sectional under different subheadings, of a set of criteria for assessing the attributes of components and their interfaces. Importance can be assigned, for example: critical (must have), preferable (nice to have) and optional. The actual criteria used depends on the task to which this technique is applied. For example, Kuruganti (1999) provides checklist criteria useful for the three Component Selection Tasks. A single example is provided in Table 18-2 for the task "Screen the candidate list of components."

18.4.3.3 New OPEN Technique: Compliance Matrix Template

In a compliance matrix the features of interest are listed in a column on the left side and the performance criteria are listed along the top. The performance criteria are evaluated for each feature as met or not met. Ticks or crosses are put in the matrix elements and the overall picture can be built up of whether or not (or to what extent) the proposed component complies with the requirements.

18.4.3.4 New OPEN Task: "Integrate Components"

When components already exist they do not need to be coded; the OPEN task "Code" is no longer needed. Instead, components need to be integrated together or "composed." This, in essence, is, coding at a coarser granularity. The interfaces of the components would ideally be immediately pluggable but, in many cases, an assembly strategy will need to be written, perhaps using a scripting language or creating some other form of inter-component "adapter" (D'Souza and Wills, 1999).

Table 18-2: *Example Criteria For Checklist**

Functional Specifications
Includes all "must have" features? Satisfies relevant technical standards? Does vendor documentation on interfaces match requirements?
Operational/Performance Attributes
Does component meet known minimal performance requirements? Are there any violations of required operational constraints in vendor documentation?
Deployment Factors
Availability of implementation on target platforms Support of multiple platforms and operating systems Platform and OS independent
Vendor Selection Criteria
Alignment of vendor organization with component user's business goals Market share (as indicator of market acceptance of product)? Existing customer base Experiences with vendor interactions Vendor commitment to component (product) with respect to projected R&D investment and level of marketing support

*Appropriate for component screening.
(from Kuruganti, 1999) (© IEEE Computer Society Press)

18.5 Conclusion

Although OPEN was originally developed to support object-oriented development, it has been shown to be readily adaptable and extensible to support component-based development (CBD). These extensions are introduced here for acquisition and integration of components. The ease of extending OPEN to CBD results from the metamodel that underpins the process definition. We have identified the areas in which extension will be most valuable and have contributed, largely from the existing literature, appropriate tasks and techniques for component selection that match the OPEN framework and its philosophy.

Chapter 19

Designing Models of Modularity and Integration

Kevin J. Sullivan[1]

19.1 Introduction

To *integrate* means to put parts together into a functioning whole. The parts that software designers put together are called *modules*. Integrating a collection of modules produces a *software system*. Such a system is a description of a computation to be performed by a computer. By *modularity* I mean the *structure* of this description as an integrated set of modules. Modularity and integration are two sides of one coin. In this chapter I discuss the design of *models of modularity and integration* (modularity models, for short), especially for component software.

1. This work was supported in part by the National Science Foundation under grants numbered ITR-0086003 and CCR-9804078.

A modularity model comprises a set of *design rules* that constrain how modules are formed and integrated. The purpose of such a model is to ensure that systems built from modules have certain properties. One such property is that modules can be integrated in certain ways with known cost and performance properties.

More generally, modular systems can be viewed in terms of design rules with hierarchically arranged scopes of influence (Baldwin and Clark, 2000). System-wide rules include modularity models, standard data types and representations, and programming languages. Additional design rules constrain modules. Conformance of an implementation to such rules is meant to ensure that the system goals are realized in general, and that the modules function and can be integrated successfully.

In traditional software development a single design authority is responsible for defining all design rules of a system. The distinguishing feature of component-based design is that there is no single design authority. Rather, components are obtained in a market and are specialized and integrated to meet the system goals. Without a single authority, who or what guarantees that the modules integrate successfully? Components still have to follow certain design rules in order to be integrated. Rather than flowing from within an enterprise, however, they are promoted and accepted as standards within the relevant industry sectors. Such standardized design rules—in particular the ones defining modularity models—are the subject of this chapter.

Models of modularity and integration are themselves complex software, but they generally do not appear to be designed using the best software engineering methods. Perhaps as a result, important models contain design flaws—they are hard to understand and to use aggressively without error—and concepts in component-based software design remain obscured by the details of prevailing models. Most seriously, we have yet to succeed in fostering component software methods and industry structures.

I argue that we should treat modularity models for component software as first-class software systems, and that sophisticated software design and engineering concepts, tools, and methods can help us to design and understand them. Design should be based on business models, requirements, specifications, modularity and abstraction, verification, and documentation. The evolution of such models also has to be anticipated and managed.

I use Microsoft's Component Object Model, COM—whose latest version, COM+, Tim Ewald discusses in Chapter 32—as a case study to make my ideas concrete. However, this chapter is not about COM, but about the design of such models.

The first section of this chapter provides background on models of modularity. The second section discusses important economic and technical issues that need to be considered in designing such models. The fourth section addresses some key software engineering concepts, tools and methods that have the potential to help, focusing on requirements and specification.

19.2 Background

Modularity models have always been important in software design. The developers of such models were traditionally programming language designers. In the past a programming language defined and imposed a model on developers who used it. Today such models can be decoupled from languages. Standards for component software are largely based on certain models of modularity, for example, Microsoft's COM and DCOM, CORBA, Enterprise JavaBeans, and others.

There are many questions to ask of a modularity model:

- What are its design goals?
- What technical, cost, and performance properties does it promise to systems that use it?
- Does conformance to the model deliver the promised properties?
- Are those properties adequate to achieve the intended purpose?
- What properties, important to a given developer, do not follow from the model?
- Can the model be extended to provide them?
- Does the model have undesirable consequences?
- Are the design rules adequately documented?
- Can the model designers and users understand and reason about it fully and clearly?

To make these ideas concrete and to show their relevance to model design, I now discuss some programming language models. Afterwards I turn to models for component software.

19.2.1 Programming Language Models of Modularity and Integration

Algol and Pascal were early proponents of modularity models. Their models are based on *procedural abstraction*. A module describes certain operations of an abstract, application-specific computer. Modules are integrated to create descriptions of ever more specialized operations using procedural programming abstractions. Procedural abstraction ensures two properties: first, the programmer retains intellectual control by defining new procedures that become part of the language; and second, top-down refinement leads to efficient code. These programming models largely delivered on their promises, but not in areas such as reusability and ease of evolution.

By contrast, ease of evolution and the need for reusable parts were requirements for the models of modularity in object-oriented languages such as C++ and Smalltalk. The models in these languages are based on data abstraction. These models have substantially delivered on their promise of ease of evolution relative to procedure-oriented models. However, they have generally not delivered on the promise to foster reuse markets.

Why did C++ not succeed as hoped for reuse? One reason is that it is unreasonable to demand that every development enterprise in a large market commit to one language. A more interesting reason is that the C++ modularity model is not logically strong enough to ensure that an essential property, namely the interoperability of modules developed by independent enterprises, is obtained. The C++ designers did not specify how procedure calls should be implemented. The resulting freedom provided to compiler writers led to a powerful *mismatch problem*: object codes created by different compilers can conflict on procedure call mechanisms (Box, 1998). The important procedure call interoperability property of independently developed components does not follow from conformance to the C++ model. There are three ways to interpret the failure of C++ to increase reuse markets:

1. Supporting such markets was not a design objective, and the model naturally did not achieve it. In this case, people who promoted the view that C++ could create such markets were being naïve or mischievous.
2. Creating such markets was a goal, but it was not recognized that procedure call interoperability was critical. The required properties were inadequate to meet the goals — a validation problem.
3. Interoperability was recognized as required, but the design rules of the model were too weak to ensure that it followed — a verification problem.

19.2.2 From Programming Languages to Component Object Models

Problems with language-based models led to a new focus on language-independent models and ultimately to component models. Such component models are prominent in broad-spectrum standards such as COM, CORBA, and Enterprise JavaBeans. Specialized component models also exist, for example, the U.S. Department of Defense High Level Architecture for simulation.

These component models reflect requirements critical to component marketplaces. Language independence is generally required. Support for distribution is another. Procedure call interoperability is a third. A fourth requirement, influential in the design of COM, is to ease software evolution as component instances shared among applications are changed. Performance is another important concern (for example, to minimize the cost of procedure calls).

We can analyze modularity models for component software in terms of the questions asked earlier. In work with colleagues I found analyzing COM in these terms was interesting, and that in some cases the answers were surprisingly unsatisfactory. The design objectives were not documented clearly. The documentation of the design rules was casual, erroneous in places, incomplete, ambiguous, and open to interpretation on substantive matters. We found that when we created a precise specification of the rules they had significantly undesirable, though not fatal, consequences (Sullivan, Marchukov, and Socha, 1999).

The lack of clearly defined objectives, properties and rules — which define what a model does and does not promise — allows some people to expect more from a model than it can deliver. Unrealistic expectations are ultimately dashed. COM, for instance, promises language-independent dynamic polymorphism, type casting, and procedure call interoperability, but not integration at higher levels, that is, involving user interface issues.

As discussed in Chapter 1, the lead and subproject engineers have to select suitable component models for the design of a given system. They can only make these choices with justifiable confidence if component models clearly declare their goals and the means by which they achieve them, and if these models have been validated and verified against their high-level objectives and requirements.

Despite the successes of models such as COM, CORBA, and others, the state-of-the-art in designing models of modularity is inadequate. Such models often specify complex types and protocols, and this logic is as subject to design error as any complex software. Moreover, the consequences of design flaws can be significant because such models are foundations for whole industry sectors. Better design is necessary if we are to realize our aspirations for component software.

19.3 Considerations in Designing Models of Modularity

In this section I briefly discuss some properties that we should require of almost any modularity model. Then I turn to particular properties that I believe are essential to modularity models for components if they are to foster markets in reusable components.

19.3.1 Modularity and Abstraction

First, a modularity model is based on abstraction. The model permits the module specification—module-level rules—to be separated from the implementation. The implementer need only follow, and the user need only know, the rules. Second, a model embodies mechanisms for decomposing systems into parts. These two aspects are the essential enablers of intellectual control over otherwise unmanageable complexity.

We have already discussed procedural and abstract data type (such as state machines or object-oriented classes) models for decomposition and abstraction. Recent work suggests that even the state machine model might have serious shortcomings. Structuring a system as a collection of state machines cannot adequately abstract important, conceptually coherent concerns, such as synchronization and security, because they inherently pertain to multiple state machines.

Newer models are emerging to address this problem. One example is *aspect-oriented programming* (Kiczales et al., 1997). The idea is that aspects have modular representations in *source code,* just as the individual state machines do. The effects of aspect models are integrated with those of the state machines to which they pertain when the source code is interpreted. The design objectives include further easing of software design and evolution.

19.3.2 Substitutability as a Key to Competitive Marketplaces

Also essential is the idea of *substitutability,* that all implementations that satisfy a given specification are interchangeable where their specification governs. Substitutability is critical for a modularity model to support a market in components. It is substitutability that enables competition among enterprises to provide key parts of a system, and it is competition that will tend to provide the best results over time. Among other things, it accelerates design evolution by encouraging module level experimentation in the market. Important recent work provides significant insight into the role of product modularity in the structure of the computer industry (Baldwin and Clark, 2000). The same basic dynamics appear to be applicable to software ([Sullivan et al., 1999] [Boehm and Sullivan, 2000]).

19.3.3 Support for Economical Structuring of Work Assignments

A second key link between industry structure and modularity models arises in connection to the notion of modules as work assignments. Ever since Parnas (1972) we have known that the modular structure of a system can be the basis for work assignments. The assignments are typically parceled out within one enterprise. The new emphasis on creating component software industries puts this issue in a new light. We need models that distribute work assignments economically over multiple enterprises.

19.3.4 Support for Reusable Module Implementations

We seek marketplaces to support software developed based on commercial parts because, when feasible, it is far more economical to buy software assets produced by specialized enterprises whose engineering costs have been amortized over multiple buyers than to build it "from scratch." This idea is not new. More than thirty years ago McIlroy (1968) envisioned markets for prefabricated software parts. Unfortunately, progress in reuse has not kept up with needs and is viewed as not having delivered.

I believe one of the most important reasons for reuse is that we still lack adequate modularity models for modern systems. First, we have only recently understood that reusability alone is not enough. Work on architectural mismatch (Garlan, Allen, and Orkerbloom, 1995) showed that without a shared modularity models, one cannot expect to integrate components—even reusable ones—with desired cost and performance. Second, the original Unix pipe-and-filter model still remains the standard for successful models. To this day we do not have equally good models for modern—for example, distributed, highly interactive—systems.

19.4 Designing Modularity Models for Component Software

Models of modularity for component software such as COM, CORBA, and Enterprise JavaBeans have raised hopes and provided important insights into key issues. They have advanced software development practice significantly, but they have not truly transformed routine software development or the basic structure of the software industry.

Designing modularity models that can actually succeed in fostering major component marketplaces and development practices remains a significant open problem. We need models that provide not only the traditional benefits—good mechanisms for abstraction, decomposition, and so forth—but models that successfully address very hard problems.

These problems are both technical and economic. Technical problems include the possible need for aspect abstraction and the need for models that support systematic reuse. A third problem is that, unlike computer hardware, for which component markets thrive, software systems are more diverse and they change faster; thus, these are unfavorable conditions. How should we proceed? I suggest that we first identify modularity models that have succeeded in order to understand what factors account for their success, and second, that we begin to employ the best software engineering concepts, tools, and methods available to design these models.

19.4.1 Learning from Past Successes and Failures

Any serious study of modularity models for software components should first identify and characterize successful and unsuccessful models and attempt to account for the outcomes on the basis of conditions and properties pertaining to these models. I have not undertaken a comprehensive analysis of this sort, but my work with colleagues has provided some insights. In this part I discuss three key issues: favorable economics, averting mismatch, and assuring that models provide the properties actually required.

19.4.1.1 Favorable Economics

Perhaps more than in any other area of software engineering, modularity models for software components involve complex economic issues. The design problem is not just to create a profitable software product or product-line—itself difficult—but to transform the very structure of the software industry and the design methods it uses. The economics involved are truly strategic in scope. To attract component producers and consumers in sufficient number and variety, a new model has to create compelling economic forces.

Do we have modularity models that have succeeded in this dimension? According to Lampson (1999), yes. Operating systems, database management systems, and Web browsers are successful components. They are bought for tiny fractions of their engineering costs, which are amortized over large, successful markets. In most cases, building them from scratch would be unthinkably costly. They provide enormous value to their users. They are routinely specialized and integrated to produce a dazzling variety of valuable systems. Wide acceptance of an operating system or database management systems actually creates entire industries. The design rules in modularity models for operating systems, for example, have explicit specifications, such as POSIX, to which applications must conform. Adopting such a model imposes a layer of design rules that application-specific systems include, leverage, and extend.

What lessons can we draw? One inference is that compelling economics are associated with models based on huge, mass-market components (Sullivan and Knight, 1996). Such components provide leverage to designers by reducing the number of components that have to be integrated, and to end-users by providing rich functions. In addition, mass markets support volume pricing.

Can this lesson inform the design of future modularity models? Yes. A guardedly optimistic analysis of the viability of a modularity model based on certain shrink-wrapped application packages ([Coppit and Sullivan, 2000] [Sullivan and Knight, 1996]) is based in part on the observation that it has similar economics. Certain large, mass-market application packages conform to shared modularity models, such as ActiveX and the Active Document architecture (*www.microsoft.com*); the Active Document architecture strengthens the rules of COM. These modularity models provide great leverage to designers and end-users because their functions are prohibitively expensive to reproduce.

The success of a component model creates a positive feedback loop by making it valuable for component providers to adopt the model. Thus we see products such as Mathcad (*www.mathcad.com*) following the Active Document architecture design rules. An increasing supply of software components in turn increases the incentives for potential users of the modularity model in the form of an increasingly rich supply of available components for integration.

There are other issues that could undermine this particular model, including inadequate specification of component functions and faults in implementations. Experiments with the Microsoft model (Coppit and Sullivan, 2000) show that there are many such problems, but that the basic model and even this particular instance have the potential to support component-based construction of some important classes of systems. More generally, the lesson is to look to models based on fewer large mass-market components.

19.4.1.2 Avert Component Mismatches

Conformance to given design rules must prevent critical mismatch phenomena. There are two related axioms for component-based software in this dimension. First, in general, components can only be integrated with given cost and performance properties if the components conform to a shared modularity model. Second, such a modularity model can only ensure that certain integration and performance properties follow from conformance. A designer can only expect the promised properties and no more. Thus, models are needed that are sufficiently powerful to address the specific needs of targeted system integrators.

Conformance to the rules of the COM component model, for example, ensures that components can call each other, but it does not guarantee that they handle graphical menus consistently enough to integrate peacefully. If such assurance is required, then the component producer must develop a component that conforms to the Active Document architecture. To avoid mismatch surprises it is critical for system integrators to understand just what a model provides. Thus, model designers must clearly document the assured properties.

19.4.1.3 Address Actual Requirements of System Integrators

In a related vein, the properties that follow from a given modularity model have to be strong enough to satisfy the needs of system integrators. For an integrator who must integrate windows and menus of component applications, it would be a serious mistake to merely adopt COM or CORBA. More generally, we cannot look to any single model as a silver bullet. Any one will be too weak for some, too strong for others.

One idea that can help is that modularity models can be structured. The Active Document architecture, for example, is layered on COM. Broad-spectrum models that provide modest assurances, such as COM, can provide foundations for stronger models.

19.4.2 The Software Design and Engineering of Models of Modularity

In this chapter I have established two facts. First, modularity models are software. They are not applications but complex, structured sets of design rules that constrain system designers in an attempt to ensure that integration-related and other properties are obtained. Second, designing successful modularity models for components will be hard.

My third and final contention is that we can improve our chances of success in designing such modularity models by using our best engineering concepts, tools, and methods. In particular, clearly defining design objectives and developing mathematically rigorous specifications are important. Tools can aid in such analysis and in managing the inevitable evolution of such models. I will make these ideas concrete in a brief analysis and critique of COM based on work that I have done with several colleagues over the last several years.

19.4.2.1 Documented Design Objectives

COM seeks to meet several design goals including: easing the evolution of systems of applications that share components; efficient procedure call interoperability among independently developed components; protection of intellectual property by the hiding of source code; programming language independence; and to provide a basis for stronger models such as the OLE model for integrating Microsoft Office-style applications.

These objectives, however, were not as clearly documented as desirable. Developers were forced to determine the design rationale of COM on their own, for example, from books and white papers. Future modularity models and their users can benefit from clear, comprehensive documentation of design objectives.

19.4.2.2 Clearly Specified Design Rules

To meet its goals COM defines a set of design rules that application developers who adopt COM are bound to follow. One of the innovative rules of COM is that components describe computations in binary—not source—code form. This rule helps to satisfy the COM requirements for language independence and the protection of intellectual property.

Second, COM imposes a rule stating that components support one or more interfaces. Each one provides access to a service that the component implements. Among other things, this rule anticipates that richer models will be based on COM, namely ones with design rules requiring support for particular interface types intended to support richer forms of modularity and integration, such as OLE, Active X, and Active Documents.

Third, COM requires components to negotiate for interfaces. This aspect addresses the design goal of easing evolution as shared components change. One component can never make incorrect assumptions about the interfaces of components. One must always query a component for desired interfaces. Thus if a new version of a component lacks an expected interface, requesting components discover this and can respond gracefully.

Fourth, the ability to negotiate for interfaces has to rest on minimal assumptions. Thus COM requires each interface to implement an operation, *QueryInterface*, for negotiation. A lower-level design goal was to ensure that each supported interface of a component may be obtained with a single *QueryInterface* of the object. This goal led to defining design rules for *QueryInterface* implementations. These rules require that these implementations be transitive, reflexive, and symmetric, as defined by COM. The details are not critical here. What I want to communicate is that COM consists of a set of design rules from which certain properties and assurances are expected to flow.

These rules are complex—enough so that it is not only hard to understand them but it is difficult even to get them right without the benefit of mathematical formalization. Two colleagues and I tried to use COM in an innovative way to develop an efficient, COM-based multimedia authoring system. We had a hard time deciding whether the rules of COM pertaining to interface negotiation and what is called COM aggregation even allowed the architecture that we envisioned. We were driven to develop a formal definition of the rules, not as an academic exercise, but as a practical necessity (Sullivan, Marchukov, and Socha, 1999).

What we discovered is interesting. First, the informal statements of the rules of COM published in Microsoft's COM specification were ambiguous and hard to understand. For example, critical terms such as *interface* were used with a variety of meanings. Second, some of the rules were incorrect: the desired properties of COM did not follow.

For example, the rule that *QueryInterface* must be transitive declares that if you query an interface a of type A for an interface of type B and get result b, and then query b for type C and get result c, then querying c for type A must succeed. This rule is not consistent with the usual meaning of transitivity, which would require the ability to query *a* for type *C* successfully. More importantly, it is inadequate to ensure a required property: that you can always get a supported type with just one query.

We also found that the rules of COM have some strange and unexpected consequences that arise from interactions between the rules for *QueryInterface* and those for another aspect of COM, *aggregation*. In a nutshell, interface negotiation malfunctions within aggregates. We came to this conclusion after trying to specify COM using formal methods. I believe formal methods can contribute significantly to designing modularity models.

As a final exercise, another colleague and I used a tool to check properties of formal specifications to help us to simplify my specification (Jackson and Sullivan, 2000). Our goal was to express only those rules involved in causing the problems I had discovered earlier. The result was that we found it astonishingly hard to change the form of the design rules without unintentionally changing their consequences. The support of such tools can provide invaluable help in designing and evolving modularity models.

19.5 Conclusion

This chapter contributes not a solution, but a challenge and an approach. The state-of-the-art in component software remains inadequate despite decades of effort. There are some reasons for serious concern, including the need to solve long-standing problems and the relative lack of architectural uniformity or stability for software. Nevertheless, I believe we can make progress.

I have found modularity models to be incredibly important, but the ones that we have are inadequate. Developing the ones we need requires that we view them as complex software. Designing modularity models is even more demanding than the already hard problem of designing complex applications, because they must reflect the technical and economic requirements of whole industry sectors. Developing such models emerges as a major problem in *strategic software design* (Boehm and Sullivan, 2000). In a nutshell, we can hope to make progress by studying successes and failures and using engineering concepts, tools, and methods to design new modularity models for software components.

Part IV

Summary

Introduction

The first responsibility of the lead and subproject software engineers, component-based software project managers, and component-based designers is to design a software component infrastructure whose implementation will ensure that software systems using that infrastructure meet a specific set of performance objectives. We must admit, however, that software engineers do not have the empirical tools to make such an assessment. To reach this objective, we need advances in at least three directions. First, the software engineering community will need to improve the way individual software components are specified and modeled (Chapters 14 and 17). Second, we need to develop formal approaches to analyze a topology of interacting software components to determine in advance whether certain properties are guaranteed (Chapters 15, 16, and 19). Third, we need to promote those processes that are successful in creating component-based software systems (Chapter 18). The chapters in this section describe a roadmap for achieving these goals.

Specifying and Modeling Software Components

For many years the object-oriented community was fragmented based on specific, often incompatible, object-oriented design methodologies. One of the major benefits of object-orientation is the design and implementation of object-oriented frameworks, a set of cooperating classes that make up a reusable design for a specific class of software (Gamma et al., 1995). Frameworks also revealed a weakness in object-orientation because it is nearly impossible to deploy and reuse just a single class within a framework without incorporating the entire framework. Clearly, a marketplace of objects never occurred, although there were many instances of successful object-oriented frameworks.

For component-based software engineering to truly develop a component marketplace, software engineers must develop strategies for ensuring that individual software components can be designed, implemented, marketed, and purchased as individual units. A necessary first step in this direction is for the software engineering community to reach consensus on a standard representation for modeling software components. It should be possible to achieve this goal; after all, there is already a global acceptance of the use of interface definition languages (IDLs) in describing the functional interfaces for software components.

In Chapter 14 Kelli Houston and Davyd Norris state that UML should be used to model the logical representation of a component. Most engineers would readily accept this position, but they go one step further by arguing that UML should be used to model the implementation representation of a component. They make the case that a component designer should also represent how the component is to be deployed, the component model selected, and the implementation language and development environment chosen. Some argue that revealing implementation details violates the principle of keeping the implementation hidden, but they believe it is necessary to enable prospective buyers to evaluate the feasibility of purchasing a component. Software engineers should take note that all other engineering disciplines have successfully incorporated mathematical equations and rigorous diagrams as a universal language for specifying physical components and devices.

In Chapter 17 Alan Cameron Wills argues that the interactions between software components must be carefully modeled and designed. Like Alan, many researchers and practitioners have identified the importance of *connectors*, an abstract representation of the interaction between two software components. By explicitly modeling and designing connectors Alan demonstrates that it is possible to design software component infrastructures with replaceable parts. He also describes how to model the interfaces to include logical preconditions, invariants, and postconditions. It is crucially important to attach such semantic information to functional interfaces because it enables system assemblers to evaluate the suitability of a particular component. In the future we expect there will be greater demand for annotating interfaces with logical conditions and other meta data.

Software Component Infrastructures Guarantee Properties

Because software components are diverse and are available in so many different domains, granularities, and capabilities, it is especially important that the lead engineer design the software component infrastructure in accordance with tested design principles. For example, a layered system is an approach to decomposing a complex software system into discrete layers with clearly defined communications between each layer. Further constraints are possible; for example, a layer could be restricted to only communicate with the layer directly below it. The software component infrastructure is designed to be composed of specific software components, each providing its own services to solving the overall task. In Chapter 15 Steve Latchem clearly identifies how to apply layering when designing a software component infrastructure. Such an approach assures substitutability of individual software components and increases the maintainability of the software component infrastructure; these system properties are directly supported by the design. When a lead engineer designs a software component infrastructure, the primary challenge is to decompose the problem into a set of suitable software components. We recommend that you follow the layered approaches described by Steve in Chapter 15 and Martin Griss in Chapter 9.

In Chapter 16 James Carey and Brent Carlson approach software component infrastructures by focusing broadly on two component types that they call fine-grained and coarse-grained business components. Fine-grained business components are business entities within a particular business domain while coarse-grained business components provide a purely functional view of some part of a business domain. From their business-oriented perspective, a software component infrastructure is decomposed into coarse-grained components, each of which is itself designed and implemented using fine-grained business components. Put together, Chapters 15 and 16 offer practical strategies for the critical task of designing the initial set of software components for a software component infrastructure.

Underlying the software component infrastructure is the component model to which the components in the component infrastructure conform; it is possible for multiple component models to be used, but in practice it is common for all software components to belong to the same model. As Kevin Sullivan observes in Chapter 19, there has been little attention devoted to the role of the component model in ensuring system properties when software components are integrated to form a software component infrastructure. The fundamental observation to be made is that components can only be integrated in defined ways with given cost and performance properties if the components conform to shared design rules. Another important guarantor of system properties is the component model implementation that supports the execution of components that conform to that component model. At the time of publication of this book, there was an unusual expectancy in the component technology marketplace because the major component model providers were releasing or reviewing major upgrades to their core technologies. COM+, the long-promised and only recently released update to the COM component model from Microsoft, has only just been released for use. The CORBA CCM proposal is being reviewed at the time of publication of the text. The editors do not know when the CCM proposal will reach publication; the CCM Web site provides no information for a proposal due initially on February 2000. The specification for EJB 2.0 was released in October, 2000 by the Java Community Process. The Enterprise JavaBeans Expert Group is currently discussing proposed modifictions to improve container managed persistence. In the "free software" community, GNOME's Bonobo is still undergoing development (Bonobo is currently an unstable release at version number 1.0.2). The component model implementations are critical for ensuring that software component infrastructures operate as designed.

Successful CBSE Processes

Successful CBSE processes must be described and promoted to increase the overall awareness and acceptance of CBSE. Many CBD processes are extensions of object-oriented processes. CBD processes must be able to include preexisting components when creating applications, however, for object-oriented application development there is unfortunately less emphasis on process and design than there is in CBSE. Thus, for component-based application development, the acquisition and integration of components becomes an activity that occurs in parallel with the design activity, resulting in the creation of new components. There is a shift in emphasis from synthesis (with OO) to integration (with CBD).

One of the most noticeable weaknesses of most component-based methodologies is the near absence of processes. At a time when software engineering increased the emphasis on processes, reasons for nullifying software processes enhanced. The vanishing of process—the key part of software engineering in the 1980s—can be attributable to several factors. First, over 99% of all businesses in the United States are small businesses, with fewer than 500 employees (*www.sba.gov/advo/stats/profiles*). A similar percentage of independent software vendors and software component producers, implementers, and consumers are small businesses. The Software Engineering Institute, perhaps inadvertently, has focused its Capability Maturity Model (CMM) towards large businesses and federal government contractors; however, the small business community generally has insufficient resources to implement the CMM. Second, many in the software engineering community have promoted the certification of software components as a means of assuring quality. Small businesses, as demonstrated in other industries, function effectively with a comprehensive standard and third-party certification. The standard provides much of minimal documentation for analyzing, designing, constructing, and testing a component. Certification assures that even small companies comply with the standard for each component built. Third, the increasing prominence of the "free software" movement clearly shows that many in the software engineering community are persuaded by the argument that a meritocratic, though chaotic, process results in higher quality software. Fourth, software organizations are increasingly adjusting their software development processes to time-to-market marketing pressures. In doing so there is more emphasis on finding ways to reduce the time-to-delivery; as evidence, note the increased exposure, even in respected software engineering conferences and journals, of Extreme Programming (XP).

One consistently changing process is OPEN (see Chapter 18). Originally a consortium of object-oriented methods and processes, OPEN has developed a metamodel that is flexible enough to function in most any organization, whether large or small. OPEN is a flexible process that is derived from a metamodel (a model of a model) that is tailored to an organization and its culture. OPEN is a series of best practices that may be implemented as needed to improve the component-based software process and its quality. As you will see, OPEN is a people-oriented approach, one that can be applied to a complex endeavor in a team context. Chapter 18 focuses on the evaluation, acquisition, and reuse of appropriate components.

The OPEN metamodel would advance the process of companies that have no process or require a process because of component standardization and certification. Its flexibility can allow a company to fill in the gaps between standards and everyday discipline. As OPEN becomes more recognized, especially as third-party certification becomes a reality for commerce in business to business trade in software components, OPEN will provide the processes necessary to assist component producers and consumers.

Conclusion

One of the hallmarks of an engineering discipline is the repeatability of empirically proven processes. For example, chemical engineers are responsible for designing high-yield, robust industrial processes to repeat chemical processes that occur within a research laboratory. For software engineering to achieve the same status we must share our success stories, as well as our failures, and constantly identify processes that increase the chance of successfully constructing component-based software systems. A consequence of repeatable processes is trust. For a thriving component marketplace to exist there needs to be a diverse collection of trusted software components available. The chapters in this section explain how we can achieve this goal.

Part IV

References

C. Baldwin and K. Clark, *Design Rules: The Power of Modularity*, MIT Press, Cambridge, MA, 2000.

B. Boehm and K. Sullivan, "Software Economics: A Roadmap," *The Future of Software Engineering*, A. Finkelstein, ed., ACM Press, 2000, pp. 319-344.

G. Booch, J. Rumbaugh, and I. Jacobson, *The Unified Modeling Language User Guide*, Addison-Wesley, Reading, MA, 1998.

D. Box, *Essential COM*, Addison-Wesley, Reading, MA, 1998.

J. Carey, B. Carlson, and T. Graser, *SanFrancisco Design Patterns: Blueprints for Business Software*, Addison-Wesley, Boston, MA, 2000.

D. Coppit and K. Sullivan, "Multiple Mass-Market Applications as Components,", Proceedings, 22nd International Conference on Software Engineering (ICSE), ACM Press, Limerick, Ireland, 2000, pp. 273-82.

T. Digre, "Business Object Component Architecture," *IEEE Software*, Vol. 15, No. 5, Sept., 1998, pp. 60-69.

D. D'Souza and A. Wills, *Objects, Components, and Frameworks with UML, The Catalysis[SM] Approach*, Addison-Wesley, Reading, MA, 1999.

D. Firesmith and B. Henderson-Sellers, *The OPEN Process Framework: An Introduction* (in preparation), Addison-Wesley, Reading, MA, 2001.

D. Flanagan, J. Farley, W. Crawford, and K. Magnusson, *Java Enterprise in a Nutshell: A Desktop Quick Reference*, O'Reilly and Associates, 1999.

M. Fowler, *Analysis Patterns: Reusable Object Models*, Addison-Wesley, Reading, MA, 1997.

M. Fowler, The New Methodology, *www.martinfowler.com/articles/newMethodology.html*, Nov., 2000.

C. Freeman and B. Henderson-Sellers, "OLMS: the Object Library Management System," Proceedings, Technology of Object-Oriented Languages and Systems (TOOLS), J. Potter, M. Tokoro, and B. Meyer, eds. Sydney, Australia, 1991, pp. 175-180.

E. Gamma, R. Helm, R. Johnson, and J. Vlissides, *Design Patterns: Elements of Reusable Object-Oriented Software*, Addison-Wesley, Reading, MA, 1995.

D. Garlan, R. Allen, and J. Ockerbloom, "Architectural Mismatch: Why Reuse Is So Hard," *IEEE Software*, Vol. 12, No. 6, Nov., 1995, pp. 17-26.

I. Graham, B. Henderson-Sellers, and H. Younessi, *The OPEN Process Specification*, Addison-Wesley, 1997.

W. Hansen, "A Generic Process and Terminology for Evaluating COTS Software," Proceedings, 30th Technology of Object-Oriented Languages and Systems (TOOLS), D. Firesmith, R. Riehle, G. Pour, and B. Meyer, Eds., IEEE Computer Society Press, Los Alamitos, CA, 1999, pp. 547-551.

B. Henderson-Sellers and F. Barbier, "Black and White Diamonds," Proceedings, <<UML>>'99—The Unified Modeling Language (Beyond the Standard), R. France and B. Rumpe, eds., Lecture Notes in Computer Science (LNCS), No. 1723, Springer-Verlag, Berlin, Germany, 1999, pp. 550-565.

B. Henderson-Sellers and B. Unhelkar, *OPEN Modeling with UML*, Addison-Wesley, Reading, MA, 2000.

B. Henderson-Sellers, "OPEN-ing up the UML," Proceedings, Software, Methods, and Tools (SMT), IEEE Computer Society Press, Los Alamitos, CA, 2000.

B. Henderson-Sellers, A. Simons, and H. Younessi, *The OPEN Toolbox of Techniques*, Addison-Wesley, Reading, MA, 1998.

IEEE, IEEE Recommended Practice for Architecture Description, Version 4.0 of IEEE P1471, Oct., 1999.

ISO/IEC, "Information Technology," *Software Life Cycle Processes, International Standard 12207*, Apr. 7, 1995.

D. Jackson and K. Sullivan, "COM Revisited: Tool Assisted Modeling and Analysis of Software Structures," Proceedings, ACM SIGSOFT Conference on the Foundations of Software Engineering (FSE), ACM Press, Nov., 2000.

I. Jacobson, M. Christerson, P. Jonsson, and G. Overgaaard, *Object-Oriented Software Engineering*, Addison-Wesley, Reading, MA, 1992.

I. Jacobson, *Object-Oriented Software Engineering: A Use Case Driven Approach*, Addison-Wesley, Reading, MA, 1994.

I. Jacobson, G. Booch, and J. Rumbaugh, *The Unified Software Development Process*, Addison-Wesley, Reading, MA, 1999.

E. Jaufmann Jr. and D. Logan, "The Use of IBM SanFrancisco Core Business Processes in Human Resources Scheduling," *IBM System Journal*, Vol. 39, No. 2, 2000, pp. 285-292.

R. Kerry, "Reference Model of Open Distributed Processing (RM-OOP): Introduction, CRC for Distributed Systems Technology," Centre for Information Technology Research, University of Queensland, Brisbane, Australia, *archive.dstc.edu.au/AU/research_news/odp/ref_model*, 1995.

G. Kiczales, J. Lamping, A. Mendhekar, C. Maeda, C. Lopes, J. Loingtier, and J. Irwin, "Aspect Oriented Programming," Proceedings, European Conference on Object-Oriented Programming (ECOOP), Lecture Notes in Computer Science (LNCS), No. 1241, Springer-Verlag, Heidelberg, Germany, 1997, pp. 220-242.

P. Kruchten, "The 4+1 View Model of Architecture," *IEEE Software*, Vol. 12, No. 6, Nov., 1995, pp. 42-50.

I. Kuruganti, "A Component Selection Methodology with Application to the Internet Telephony Domain," Proceedings, 30th Technology of Object-Oriented Languages and Systems (TOOLS), D. Firesmith, R. Riehle, G. Pour, and B. Meyer, eds., IEEE Computer Society Press, Los Alamitos, CA, 1999, pp. 552-556.

B. Lampson, "How Software Components Grew Up and Conquered the World," Keynote Speech, Proceedings, 21st International Conference on Software Engineering (ICSE), *research.microsoft.com/lampson/Slides/ReusableComponentsAbstract.htm*, 1999, p. 585.

M. McIlroy, "Mass-Produced Software Components," Report on a conference sponsored by the NATO Software Engineering Conference, Garmisch, Germany, Scientific Affairs Division, NATO, Brussels, Belgium, 1968, pp. 138-155.

N. Medvidovic, "A Framework for Classifying and Comparing Architecture Description Languages," Proceedings, 6th European Software Engineering Conference, Lecture Notes in Computer Science (LNCS), No. 1301, Springer-Verlag, Heidelberg, Germany, 1997, pp. 60-76.

B. Meyer, *Object-Oriented Software Construction*, 2nd ed., Prentice-Hall, Upper Saddle River, NJ, 1997.

P. Monday, J. Carey, and M. Dangler, *SanFrancisco Component Frameworks: An Introduction*, Addison-Wesley, Reading, MA, 1999.

T. Mowbray and R. Malveau, *CORBA Design Patterns*, John Wiley & Sons, New York, NY, 1997.

D. Parnas, "On the Criteria to be Used in Decomposing Systems into Modules," *Communications of the ACM*, Vol. 15, No. 12, Dec., 1972, pp. 1053-1058.

Rational Software, *Reusable Asset Framework*, Draft 0.3, *www.rational.com*, 2000a.

Rational Software, *Architecture Description Standard*, Draft 0.5, *www.rational.com*, 2000b.

R. Seacord and K. Nwosu, "Life Cycle Activity Areas for Component-Based Software Engineering Processes," Proceedings, 30th Technology of Object-Oriented Languages and Systems (TOOLS), D. Firesmith, R. Riehle, G. Pour, and B. Meyer, eds., IEEE Computer Society Press, 1999, pp. 537-541.

B. Selic, G. Gullekson, P. Ward, B. Selic, and J. McGee, *Real-Time Object-Oriented Modeling*, John Wiley & Sons, 1994.

K. Sullivan and J. Knight, "Experience Assessing an Architectural Approach to Large-Scale Systematic Reuse," Proceedings, 18th International Conference on Software Engineering (ICSE), ACM Press, Berlin, Germany, 1996, pp. 220-229.

K. Sullivan, P. Chalasani, S. Jha, and V. Sazawal, "Software Design as an Investment Activity: A Real Options Perspective," in *Real Options and Business Strategy: Applications to Decision Making*, L. Trigeorgis, consulting editor, Risk Books, Dec., 1999.

K. Sullivan, M. Marchukov, and J. Socha, "Analysis of Conflict Between Aggregation and Interface Negotiation in Microsoft's Component Object Model," *IEEE Transactions on Software Engineering*, Vol. 25, No. 4, July/Aug., 1999, pp. 584-599.

C. Szyperski, *Component Software: Beyond Object-Oriented Programming*, Addison-Wesley, Reading, MA, 1998.

B. Unhelkar, "Effect of Granularity of Object-Oriented Design on Modeling An Enterprise, and Its Application to Financial Risk Management, Ph.d. thesis, University of Technology, Sydney, Australia, 1997.

J. Warmer and A. Kleppe, *The Object Constraint Language: Precise Modeling With UML*, Addison-Wesley, Reading, MA, 1999.

Part V

From Software Component Infrastructures to Software Systems

In component-based development you will develop the final software system by building upon a well-designed component infrastructure. This component infrastructure will make it possible to build an entire family of possible software systems, often called a "product-line." Because software must continually evolve to meet changing requirements and demands for new features, it is important to design a solid foundation on which to build. However, designing the component infrastructure only makes it possible that software systems constructed using the infrastructure will meet specific performance objectives. The chapters in this section describe how you incorporate the component infrastructure into the final design for your software system.

The concept increasingly used in software engineering is considered a *software architecture*. One of the most commonly cited definitions is that software architecture is a level of design that specifies the overall system structure of a software application (Shaw and Garlan, 1996). The design of the component infrastructure addresses many of the structural concerns of how a system is composed from components. We can describe an approach to software architecture by analogy with domestic architecture. Building architects are trained to design safe, functional, and affordable houses by applying their general knowledge of materials, building codes, and aesthetic principles to a set of specific customer needs and budget constraints. A building architect may design a residential dwelling based on a standard model of the "colonial style," but is free to add an extra family room, an attached garage, or even an extra bedroom above the garage. The building architect may also design the shape and placement of the driveway, walkways, and other landscape features. Moreover, building architects must clearly communicate their designs to a wide audience that includes customers, builders, inspectors, and other architects. To reduce the risk and cost involved in design they are trained to assemble designs from familiar, well-understood components. The guiding principle the building architect follows is that no aspect of the final designed dwelling invalidates the original design of the house.

Returning to component-based software engineering, the lead engineer or project manager must ensure that the design of the final software system conforms to the original intent and that the performance objectives are met. We thus consider software architecture to describe the final structure of a software system, showing the original component infrastructure upon which it is built as well as the software entities integrated by the designer to form a complete system. In short, the software architecture may contain noncomponent-based software assets while the component infrastructure is comprised solely of designed software components.

We recommend an engineering-based approach to designing software systems. As we described in Chapter 1, the lead engineer develops a master software development plan that divides a project into discrete and manageable subprojects. The use of the term software architecture thus directly corresponds to the initial logical software component infrastructure. Through increasingly detailed design, the lead and subproject engineers refine this design, ultimately selecting the appropriate component model in which to realize the design of the software component infrastructure. The component infrastructure is the foundation for constructing a software system that will satisfy the performance requirements of the software system.

The chapters in this section provide principles for how to design component infrastructures, formally capture their structure using an architectural description language, and analyze them from different perspectives. The component infrastructure is also an important business asset because, as Martin Griss explains in Chapter 25, it forms the basis for profitably producing an entire product-line of applications.

Chapter 20

Software Architecture

Judith A. Stafford
Alexander L. Wolf

20.1 Introduction

A software system's architecture is the arrangement of its components into one or more structures defined by the functional role played by each component and the interaction relationships exhibited by the components. The lead engineer is responsible for designing, documenting, and evaluating the software component infrastructure for a software system. The lead engineer must also maintain the integrity of the original design while modifying and evolving the software system.

To manage the complexity inherent in large software systems, skilled software architects arrange components and their interactions into familiar and reliable structures. There are many common software architectures in practice, ranging from general-purpose architectures such as pipe & filter and client/server, to domain-specific architectures, such as telephone call processing and flight dynamics. As an example, a common architecture for programming language compilers is the *multi-phase translator* ([Perry and Wolf, 1992] [Shaw and Garlan, 1996]). In this architecture the compilation task is structured into three phases of lexical, syntactic, and semantic analyses, followed by optimization and target-code generation. Each phase is embodied in a functional component of the system. A formal theory and tools support this architecture for each individual phase. In fact, the adoption of this common architecture for compilation has allowed advances in individual phases, such as the creation of component generator tools such as *lex*, a lexical analyzer, and *yacc*, a tool for constructing compilers.

Building architects use various means to capture and communicate the results of their design activities, such as blueprints and scaled models. Similarly, software architects create specifications of software architectures for a variety of purposes, leading to different forms of description. For example, pictures are a convenient way of expressing the essence of the component and interconnection structure of a system, but are poor at expressing intended dynamic behavior. Textual descriptions are easy to write, but their ambiguity makes them useless for performing any kind of serious analysis.

The emerging field of software architecture seeks to make the process of architecting software systems more rigorous and the result of architecting more reliable and reusable by applying powerful specification and analysis techniques. This chapter provides an overview of the major issues and trends in architecture-based software engineering. We begin by discussing the importance to the development process of an architectural perspective, and then we discuss the formalization of linguistic and analytical aspects of software architectures. We conclude by briefly discussing several other emerging concepts in software architecture that are having an influence on the general utility of the area.

20.2 Importance of Architecture to the Development Process

When developing a software system your primary goal is to produce the "best" system that provides the required functionality. There are many ways to define "best" depending on the system being built. For a missile guidance system a higher value will likely be placed on reliability than on time-to-market. In contrast, shrink-wrapped software vendors typically value time-to-market and feature differentiation over quality, until such time that the product has captured sufficient market share. During requirements analysis the system developers will determine the appropriate evaluation criteria for the system design. Decisions at this level are critical to the success of the development process because these decisions directly affect all other aspects of the development process.

If you are able to analyze early on the correctness and completeness of a design's satisfaction of system requirements, you will reduce the number and costs of problems encountered in later stages of development and reduce the time spent revisiting prior stages to correct those problems. Such analysis demands an explicitly and formally captured software architecture. The system view provided by an architectural description is useful throughout the life of a system as a high-level reference point for evaluation and change. There are two primary benefits to be gained from including an explicit architecting stage in the development process: the system can be viewed at a higher level of abstraction, which supports increased understanding of large, complex systems, and system analysis can be performed very early in the development process.

20.2.1 Abstraction

Abstraction is a modeling activity that allows you to selectively highlight (or hide) particular characteristics of a system. An architectural specification is an abstract model of a system that highlights the *components*, the *connections* among the components, and the *behaviors* that regulate the interaction of components through connections. The benefits of viewing a system from an architectural perspective are improved communication among the stakeholders of the system and improved software understanding by the developers and maintainers of the system.

20.2.1.1 Improved Communication Among Stakeholders

The development of a software system succeeds only when the participating stakeholders communicate effectively. Stakeholders such as financiers, inspectors, system commissions, and system developers must be able to communicate about their needs and their ability to meet the needs of others. The difference in views and backgrounds is greatest among the stakeholders involved in the high-level design of a system (Gonzales and Wolf, 1996). For example, the system commissioners (those who requested that a software system be built) should know the desired functionality but they typically have no knowledge of how systems are developed. During high-level design, these commissioners must be able to communicate with the system developers who know how to build systems but may know little about the particular system domain.

Architectural specification provides a vehicle for such communication. At the simplest level a picture of the system comprised of boxes and arrows representing the components of the system and how they would interact can be drawn. This level of architectural description allows the commissioners of the system to see that their needs have been recorded and it allows the developers to consider different alternatives. At a more detailed level a formal description of components, connections, and behaviors can be formally analyzed and perhaps even simulated.

20.2.1.2 Software Understanding

To maintain or evolve a software system you have to understand it. Trying to understand a software system based solely on its implementation is difficult in moderately-sized systems and impossible in large systems. However, the ability to reason about the system based on the architectural description can greatly improve system understanding by reducing the system to its essence: the major functional components and their interactions.

To use the architecture for these purposes you must be able to map between levels of abstraction of the system. But because of the phenomenon of *architectural drift* (Perry and Wolf, 1992), it is critical that the mapping be explicit and accurate. As an analogy, consider the following scenario: a worker needs to expand the networking cables in a building and finds in the building's blueprint a shaft running between floors. If the architecture (as represented by the blueprint) did not clearly show that the shaft was designed to be a chimney, then an unintended violation of the architecture (in this case, the interconnection structure between floors) could have disastrous results. It is not hard to think of analogous situations in software architectures where communication channels are similarly abused.

Three proposed solutions that avoid architectural drift are *architecture recovery* ([Gall et al., 1996] [Murphy, Notkin, and Sullivan, 1995]), *forced consistency* ([Schwanke, Strack, and Werthmann-Auzinger, 1996] [van der Hoek, Heimbigner, and Wolf, 1998] [Oreizy, Medvidovic, and Taylor, 1998]), and *system generation* (Batory et al., 1994). Forced consistency and system generation are useful when building new systems. Architecture recovery is a reasonable alternative for systems with no architectural description or for systems whose architectures have drifted over time.

20.2.2 Architecture-Level Analysis

The goal of software architectural-level analysis is to determine the degree to which a system satisfies its requirements. This form of analysis should not be confused with "requirements analysis," the effort to elicit requirements from a problem domain. The choice of an architecture depends on many factors, both functional and extra-functional. The functional criteria are almost obvious: the architecture must satisfy the functional requirements for the system. The extra-functional criteria are less obvious, but are in some sense more critical to the choice. These include the likely reliability, performance, and security of an implementation, the extensibility of the architecture, the availability of ready-made components, and the collective experience with the architecture.

Researchers have studied how to apply analysis techniques to architectural specifications to detect the presence of errors early in development and at a high-level of abstraction ([Allen and Garlan, 1997] [Bass, Clements, and Kazman, 1998] [Compare, Inverardi, and Wolf, 1999] [Inverardi, Wolf, and Yankelevich, 2000] [Magee, Kramer, and Giannakopoulou, 1997] [Naumovich et al., 1997] [Richardson and Wolf, 1996]). Analysis techniques are also used to locate the cause of errors in the system (Stafford, Richardson, and Wolf, 1998). The techniques attempt to balance the accuracy of the method against the effort required to perform the analysis (Young and Taylor, 1991) because, in general, proving the absolute correctness of systems is intractable.

Many system properties can be analyzed for faults during the early stages in development, such as component incompatibility (Inverardi, Wolf, and Yankelevich, 2000), the possibility of deadlock (Magee,

Kramer, and Giannakopoulou, 1997), and race conditions (Naumovich et al., 1997). Stafford, Richardson, and Wolf (1998) apply a dependence analysis technique to discover failures and locate the faults causing the failures.

In general, detecting faults during the early stages, including during architectural design, results in fewer errors being propagated forward, which in turn results in increased reliability and reduced maintenance costs. It is not unusual for testing and maintenance to account for nearly 40% of a system's development costs (Pressman, 1997). In a case study involving the prediction of software quality based on the development of the JStar ground surveillance system (Khoshgoftaar et al., 1998), the number of faults created during design was 32%, yet the number of faults discovered before or during design was a mere one percent. A solid architectural design will enable stakeholders to detect errors early in the development of a system. Among the properties that can benefit from early analysis are the following.

- *Completeness*—The entire range of functionality specified in requirement documents are met
- *Liveness*—Intended system behavior (for example, computational progress) eventually occurs
- *Safety*—No unintended behavior (for example, deadlock) ever occurs
- *Component interaction*—Connected component interfaces and functionalities are compatible
- *Performance*—System performance requirements are met

A course-grained view of a system provides important benefits even after system design because it allows you to reason about the entire system. Many issues, when addressed at the code level, are intractable even with only a few thousand lines of code. Having an architectural specification can help perform such tasks as.

- *Localizing faults*—After an error has been identified in a system, the cause of the error must be investigated. This is normally done by systematically reducing the code to be inspected until the fault is eventually isolated to a specific set of statements. In a large system the first approximation to this reduction is provided by the component structure of the system's architecture.

- *Regression testing*—When a modification is made to a piece of software it is necessary to rerun tests to assure that no faults were introduced. Minimizing the tests to just those affected by the change helps reduce the cost of regression testing. Again, in a large system the first approximation to this minimal set is provided by associating test cases with the component structure inherent in the architecture.
- *Detecting drift*—Over time the structure of a system tends to drift because of undocumented enhancements and repairs. A well-maintained representation of the architecture provides a basis for detecting drift.
- *Reuse*—When a system component is recognized as being usable in other applications that component, as well as any other components it requires, can be extracted and used in other settings. This requires an understanding of the architectural context and assumptions within which the component operates.
- *Reverse engineering*—When a system has been in service for many years it often becomes difficult to make modifications because of lost engineering information describing the system. A typical and tractable starting point for recovering this information is to recapture the architecture.

Each of these tasks currently involves detailed sifting (whether manual or computer-assisted) through source code to achieve the particular goal. The architecture can be used to segregate large chunks of code (that is, components) to be either included or ignored during this examination, thus making such processes more practical.

20.3 Formalizing the Software Architecture

Software architectures have traditionally been informally described as natural-language documents. Box and arrow diagrams are often used to describe software architectures more precisely; by doing so developers are able to detect ambiguous or missing requirements. However, these diagrams are not capable of modeling all the information provided in the natural-language specification, such as system behavior. To formalize a software architecture specification you must apply model-based languages to capture structural and behavioral properties of systems. These languages provide support for a rigorous analysis of a system early in the life cycle and at a high level of abstraction. But there are also other benefits.

- You can improve communication among stakeholders by providing precise and unambiguous architectural descriptions
- You can identify commonalities among architectures with well-understood and well-documented components and connections
- You can better choose among design alternatives if the features and properties of architectures are explicit
- You can increase your ability to modify a system if it has well-documented component interfaces and if there are reliable techniques that analyze possible effects of a modification to a system
- You can use formal descriptions to capture domain-specific properties and requirements to support domain-specific architectural generalizations
- You can specify larger granularity design elements, thus improving scalability and providing better support for developing large-scale systems

One of the goals of the ISO 9000-3 guideline for applying the ISO 9001 standard to software development is to formalize at all stages of the software life cycle. However, there are two common objections to using formal methods to build quality software (Oskarsson and Glass, 1996). The first objection is that the ISO emphasis on "complete and unambiguous" specifications through formal languages is incompatible with the evolutionary nature of software development. "Complete and unambiguous," however, does not imply that a system is fixed in time. Rather, it requires that *all* system artifacts be kept synchronized with each other throughout the life of the system. More sophisticated analysis techniques should help enhance system evolution by isolating the effects of changes and by raising the developer's confidence in those changes.

The second objection is that customers and users, as well as many developers, are unable to understand formal methods. This is patently not true, considering that other engineering disciplines regularly use more sophisticated techniques than those found in software engineering. Indeed, the essence of most formal methods is a normal part of postsecondary education: set theory, graph theory, and logic. The current limitation of formal methods is that the software engineering community has not agreed on the specific techniques that should be taught, thus most software engineers currently leave their studies ill prepared to learn advanced formal methods.

20.3.1 Architecture Description Languages

Languages for describing high-level designs have been in development and use for over two decades. The recent interest in software architectures has spawned the development of a new generation of such languages, which are now referred to as Architecture Description Languages (ADLs). Most are intended to support some sort of formal analysis, but these are still rather immature and few descriptions of actual system architectures have been written using them. However, this is an active area of research focused on providing languages and tools that are practical and useful. Table 20.1 provides a list of several representative ADLs. These ADLs vary widely in their level of expressiveness. They also vary widely in maturity, as well as in the degree to which the structure and behavior of the system can be modeled.

Table 20-1: *Several Representative Architecture Description Languages*

ADL	Organization	Reference	Design Goals
Acme	Carnegie Mellon University	Garlan, Monroe, and Wile, 1997	Provide an interchange language to facilitate sharing of architectural components and analysis tools
CHAM	Universitá dell' Aquila University of Colorado	Inverardi and Wolf, 1995	Investigate a formalism for the description of architectural components and the interaction among them for the purpose of system analysis
Gestalt	Siemens Corporate Research	Schwanke, Strack, and Werthmann-Auzinger, 1996	Provide support for describing system structure, abstractions needed by developers, and communication mechanisms used in industrial software, as well as automatically checking consistency with source code

Table 20-1: *Several Representative Architecture Description Languages (Continued)*

MetaH	Honeywell Technology Center	Vestal, 1998	Specify real-time and concurrent aspects of the software and hardware of a system, and provide support for the analysis of functional and extra-functional system properties
Rapide	Stanford University	Luckham et al., 1995	Provide an executable ADL based on a rule-event execution model for prototyping, simulating, and analyzing software systems
SADL	SRI	Moriconi, Qian, and Riemenschneider, 1995	Provide support for specifying the structure and the semantics of an architecture through explicit mappings among architectures, architectural styles, and architecture refinement patterns
UniCon	Carnegie Mellon University	Shaw and Garlan, 1996	Support style-based architectural construction by interconnecting predefined or user-defined architectural components
Wright	Carnegie Mellon University	Allen and Garlan, 1997	Provide a formalism that focuses on explicit connector types and analyses associated with architectural connection

No single ADL is the best choice for all systems. One primary difference between ADLs is the model they support in a representation. Shaw and Garlan (1995) reviewed a set of model types that appear regularly in software: *structural*, *framework*, *dynamic*, *process*, and *functional*. They described how each model is more or less well supported by various ADLs. The most complete attempt to classify ADLs to date is presented by Medvidovic (1997). He classifies ADLs according to the support provided for various aspects of components, connections, and configurations as well as the types of tool support provided with the language.

20.3.2 Analysis Techniques

Formal ADLs make it possible to reason about functional and extra-functional properties of software systems early in the software life cycle and at high levels of abstraction. The premise is that the confidence gained through analysis at an architectural level will translate into confidence in other levels of the system.

Many techniques for analyzing software systems have been developed over the past decades. Most, however, are ineffective for analyzing large systems. This is particularly true for techniques aimed at analyzing concurrent systems, where state explosion problems are especially acute. Software architecture is another approach to attacking the problem by providing a particular method for abstraction and modularization.

Automated analysis techniques can differ in the levels of assurance they provide. In general, the techniques balance efficiency and tractability against precision and completeness. For example, it may be possible to guarantee some properties only under certain assumptions or conditions. Carefully chosen, those assumptions and conditions can match well with the context in which the system is expected to operate, and thus the analysis can provide useful information.

It is critical that an imprecise or incomplete analysis technique used to examine a property gives no false positive results; it should never indicate the absence of a problem when there is one. In contrast, it is permissible for a technique to indicate the possible presence of a problem, even if none truly exists, and defer further analysis to some other automated analysis technique or to a person. This characteristic is commonly referred to as *conservatism*. One goal of analysis research is to increase the precision of conservative techniques so they can be both efficient and useful.

Techniques for describing extra-functional properties are significantly less advanced than techniques for describing functionality. Therefore, the analysis techniques that are available to formally analyze the extra-functional properties of software architectures are not as well-developed as those for functional properties. Assuming it is possible to describe the extra-functional properties of individual components, the key issue in performing an extra-functional analysis is to understand how to compose the properties based on the interactions evident in the architecture. MetaH is an ADL that is well-suited to analysis of extra-functional properties (Vestal, 1998). It captures information about both software and hardware components using attributes such as safety, security, schedulability, and reliability. Analysis tools can determine which components can affect or be affected by other components in the system depending on the values of the attributes.

There are three general categories of analysis techniques intended to reveal behavioral properties of software architectures: *proofs*, *sampling*, and *reduction*.

Proof techniques can examine properties such as system safety and liveness. Safety properties say "nothing bad will ever happen," whereas liveness properties say "something good will eventually happen." Safety properties in this context should not be confused with properties associated with so-called "safety-critical systems." Although safety-critical systems and their properties are important, little work in software architecture has been targeted toward addressing their specific needs. The standard safety property of interest in concurrent systems is freedom from deadlock. Given a compositional approach to system construction, deadlock freedom becomes a serious challenge at the architectural level. The standard liveness property is continued computational progress of all, not just some, processing components.

Sampling techniques provide an attractive alternative to proof techniques when a full proof is too costly, yet you still would like to be confident that a system is correct. Sampling is most useful to understand how a system will react under specific conditions. The two main sampling techniques are *simulation* and *testing*. Simulation enables you to directly observe the abstract behavior of a system without requiring you to complete a full implementation. Of course, the simulation is made possible by making certain assumptions, and thus the quality of the results of a simulation analysis are heavily dependent on the quality of those assumptions. An architectural description is a suitable target for testing if it contains enough behavioral information to permit simulated executions. The primary difference between simulation and testing is that simulation analysis focuses on broadly illustrating system behavior, whereas testing analysis is aimed at carefully exercising the system behavior under specific conditions. Testing techniques are typically applied at a variety of levels, but it is *integration* testing, which checks for errors in the interoperability of components, that appears to be most appropriate for use with architectural descriptions (Richardson and Wolf, 1996).

One way to reduce the cost of analyzing a large system is simply to reduce the amount of the system that needs to be analyzed. The reduction process is itself a form of analysis, but one that is more appropriately characterized as a "meta-analysis," because its result is intended to be input to another analysis technique rather than a result in its own right. Dependence analysis is a reduction technique that identifies interdependent subsets of components within a system.

20.4 Other Architectural Concepts

So far we have concentrated on the role of software architecture in the design process and the characteristics of various languages and analysis techniques that support the software architect. We now present brief reviews of four other topics important to software architecture: architectural styles, domain-specific software architectures, system generation and refinement, and architectural views.

20.4.1 Architectural Styles

Architectural styles provide a standardized vocabulary to help stakeholders communicate about the high-level structure of a software system. In the domain of building architecture, style names are evocative of the building being discussed. Analogously, software architectural styles provide a succinct description of the kinds of components in a system and the constraints on the ways that the components can interact ([Garlan, Allen, and Ockerbloom, 1994] [Le Métayer, 1998] [Perry and Wolf, 1992] [Shaw and Clements, 1997]).

An architectural style defines a family of systems that shares certain properties. Among these properties are its allowed components, constraints on the interactions among those components, invariants, underlying computational model, and shared experience with systems built in the style. Styles can arbitrarily be specialized by further restricting properties such as acceptable topologies and allowable methods of communication. Choosing a particular style directly impacts both the engineering techniques used and the resources needed to build the system. In general, different application domains such as telecommunications, transaction processing, or avionics, have developed their own architectural styles appropriate to that domain. Figure 20-1 depicts several common styles found in the domain of computer systems software (for example, compilers, operating systems, database management systems, and the like).

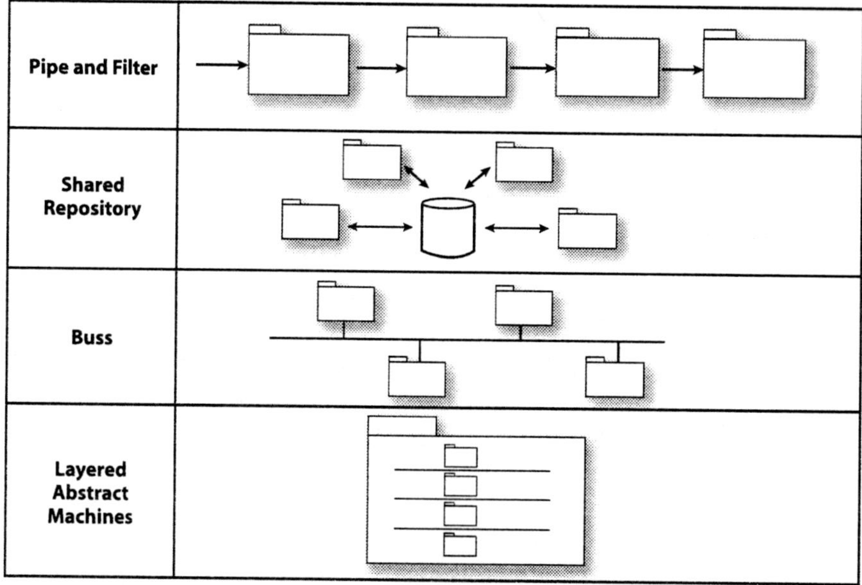

Figure 20-1: *Common architectural styles used in computer systems software.*

Their basic structures can be described quite succinctly.

- *Pipe and Filter*—Input to one component is processed and the resulting output is passed to another component for processing
- *Shared Repository*—A repository serves as a data store that may be accessed by variable numbers of other components
- *Layered Abstract Machine*—Components are stratified into layers, where data produced at one layer is available only to layers above
- *Buss*—Data is broadcast over a shared communication medium from which components can choose to withdraw or ignore the data

One effort that simplifies the choice of architectural style is the classification proposed by Shaw and Clements (1997) in which component types, connector types, data communication, control and data interactions, and compatible reasoning types are used as the basis for discrimination among styles. With such a classification it is possible to construct analysis tools to augment a style-based design environment.

An architectural style also helps simplify the architecting process by making automation possible. For example, Aesop is a system that generates design environments for families of software systems (Garlan, Allen, and Ockerbloom, 1994) from the specification of an architectural style. The generated environment is specialized to support the design of architectures using the given style. In addition, Nitpick (Jackson and Damon, 1996) is an automated analysis technique that attempts to prove the absence of a specific property for an architectural style by producing an instance of a software architecture that contains the violation.

20.4.2 Domain-Specific Software Architectures

Application domains tend to exhibit software-related, domain-specific characteristics. Although the existence of domain characteristics is easy to explain and well accepted, the means for capturing a precise understanding of the specific characteristics for a given domain is new. Domain-Specific Software Architectures (DSSAs) are intended, at least in part, to support this process. They provide a forum for the modeling and definition of domain-specific characteristics that are used to provide a reference architecture from which specific applications within that domain can be created.

20.4.3 System Generation and Architecture Refinement

System generation has been suggested for raising the level of abstraction in the development of software. Perhaps the most fully developed example is the system generation tools that develop compilers from high-level specifications of language syntax, language semantics, and hardware architecture. Recently, system generation has been applied to software architecture descriptions as a means to create rapid prototypes and implementations of system families whose architectures are well understood. System generation improves productivity when building systems and better distributes engineering effort to higher-payoff tasks such as component design and inter-component communication mechanisms.

The success of domain-specific system generators inspired the creation of GenVoca (Batory et al., 1994), a domain-independent generator for the creation of domain-specific system generators. GenVoca allows automatic customization of components to improve productivity in system building and often produces systems that perform at least as well as hand-built and optimized versions.

Architecture refinement, as described by Moriconi, Qian, and Riemenschneider (1995), is similar to system generation but does not depend on preimplemented components. It is based on the "faithful interpretation" of components as the architecture is gradually refined into an implementation. Each refinement of the system is guaranteed to be correct by only allowing provably correct refinement patterns. Thus, the highest-level system abstraction can be used during system analysis at all other levels.

20.4.4 Architectural Views

No matter what form of description is used to describe a software system's architecture, no one description can, or should, contain all the information that is important to all stakeholders in the development process. Stakeholders should have access to a description that contains only the information necessary for understanding aspects of the system relevant to their work. Perry and Wolf (1992) introduced the notion of architectural views for this purpose. The use of architectural views is similar to how views are used in building architecture, where a building is described in several ways: scale-model view, floor-plan view, and builder's detailed view. As discussed in Chapter 21, there can be many views created for different stakeholders, as well as the varied types of analyses one might want to perform. Soni, Nord, and Hofmeister (1995) discuss categories of architecture: conceptual, module, execution, and code. These categories were defined after studying the structure of a variety of industrial software systems. They feel that viewing the structure of software from different perspectives is crucial, as it will provide a basis for formal reasoning about software development. Kruchten (1995) developed the 4+1 View Model to provide guidance in capturing the architecture of a system in ways that target the needs of various stakeholders.

20.5 Conclusion

Software architecting is now recognized as a critical activity in successful software development processes. Equally important are the associated activities of architectural description and analysis. The architectural description serves a variety of purposes over the life of the product and provides an unambiguous basis for communication among the stakeholders in the project. The architectural description is available very early in the development process and can be used to reason about the fitness of the structure to fulfill its purpose before effort is expended on creating the final product. As the product ages the architecture can be used as a reference to detect undocumented changes or as an aid to maintenance activities. The formalization of architectural description and analysis techniques enables reasoning about the construction and maintenance of large and complex software systems. The challenge for the future is threefold: (1) to make sure that the techniques are practical for large-scale systems; (2) to find ways to integrate the techniques into the emerging software processes that depend upon shorter and shorter cycle times; and (3) to extend the techniques to better support the description and analysis of critical extra-functional system properties.

Chapter 21

Software Architecture Design Principles

Len Bass

21.1 Introduction

This chapter shows how to design *software component infrastructures* to achieve particular goals, both in terms of function and quality attributes for the systems built from these infrastructures. A software component infrastructure is a designed set of shared components that supports a set of applications in a particular domain or set of domains, and these applications must function within the constraints imposed by that infrastructure. When designing the software component infrastructure, you must have a *base set* of applications in mind; the design of the software component infrastructure and the base set may, up to a point, proceed in parallel. Figure 21-1 shows that the final application is constructed around the software component infrastructure.

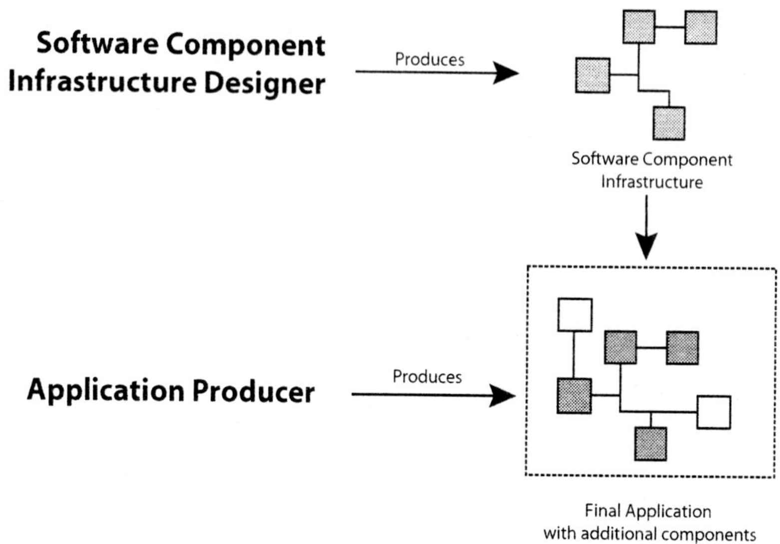

Figure 21-1: *Relationship between software component infrastructure designer and application producer.*

In the same way that the structure of a building is designed by an architect, the software component infrastructure must be designed. The title *software architect* has commonly been used in industry to describe the person who leads the design of the software component infrastructure; this is synonymous with the lead engineer introduced in Chapter 1. I use the term *software architecture* to refer to a specific software component infrastructure with an associated set of design rules. There are an increasing number of texts that provide a comprehensive introduction to software architecture ([Bass, Clements, and Kazman, 1998] [Shaw and Garlan, 1996] [Soni, Nord, and Hofmeister, 2000] [Bosch, 2000]). The Software Engineering Institute maintains a Web site (*www.sei.cmu.edu/architecture/bibliography.html*) that is also a useful source of information. In this chapter I will discuss the drivers that lead to an architecture, the concept of architectural styles, abstract and concrete functionality and qualities, and the relationship between architectural styles and functionality. Furthermore, I introduce the concept of *software templates* to capture commonalities across multiple components. I conclude by presenting eight principles to guide the design of a software component infrastructure and associated components.

21.2 Software Architecture

"The software architecture of a program or computing system is the structure or structures of the system, which comprise software components, the externally visible properties of these components, and the relationship among them" (Bass, Clements, and Kazman, 1998). Several aspects of this definition are important.

- When used by the software architecture community, the term *component* is a primitive that describes any collection of coherent computation. As such, I use the term component in a more general way than presented in Chapter 1.
- There are multiple perspectives that must be considered when designing a software component infrastructure. Some views reflect an organization of the software, such as into modules or classes, and other views represent an organization of the run-time entities of the computing system into processes. Viewing the design of a software component infrastructure from a specific perspective makes it possible to answer questions asked about systems developed using that software component infrastructure, such as whether deadlock can exist, whether performance goals can be met, or whether desired modifications will be easy to achieve (see Chapter 20). The notion of design rules is sufficiently broad to support the practical idea that there may be multiple views of the component infrastructure; I will give some example design rules shortly.
- Only the externally visible functions and behavior of the components become part of the design of the software component infrastructure. Thus, the design of a software component infrastructure is distinct from high-level design since data structures and algorithms in a component are usually not externally visible.

The software architecture for a system under development is useful in many ways. It can be used to explain proposed systems to various stakeholders and new members of the development project and it acts as a blueprint for development. This chapter is motivated by the use of the software architecture as an explanation for analysis (as further developed in Chapter 20). As described in Chapter 1, the design of the software component infrastructure is a step in an iterative design process that results in an increasingly detailed design of each component in the software component infrastructure. The principles I present in this chapter describe the information necessary to analyze the design rules of the software architecture. This ensures, as much as possible, that the designed system meets its quality and functional requirements.

In this short chapter I cannot present evidence that the use of software architecture determines whether quality attribute and functional goals can be met, but it is intuitively plausible ([Bass, Clements, and Kazman, 1998] [Bosch, 2000]). The software component infrastructure embodies the fundamental tradeoffs and decisions made during design, which are recorded as design rules. These decisions determine whether you will be able to satisfy many quality attributes, . For example, modifiability can be achieved by an appropriate division of functionality, reliability can be achieved by redundancy, and performance by how functions are allocated to processes and how processes are allocated to processors. See Table 21-1 for some examples of this relationship. The design of software component infrastructures is emerging not only in the free software market, but also in organizations that develop software product-lines (see Chapter 22). To see the practical application of the ideas from this chapter, you should investigate the Architecture Trade Off Analysis Method (Kazman, Klein, and Clements, 2000). This method was developed based on the dependence that quality attributes have on software architecture.

Table 21-1: *Some Architectural Mechanisms to Achieve Particular Qualities*

Quality Attribute	Architectural Mechanism
Modifiability	Separation, indirection
Reliability	Redundancy
Security	Firewall
Performance	Scheduler

21.3 Architectural Drivers

As every designer knows, requirements do not all have an equal impact on a design. It is important to identify those requirements that have a profound influence on the design of the software component infrastructure. *Architectural drivers* are the combination of influential functional, quality, and business requirements that "shape" the software component infrastructure for the base set of applications. The drivers are determined by examining the requirements for the purpose of the system and the critical business needs. If the important requirements can be met then the system can be satisfactorily designed. Two drivers based on the purpose of the system are

- The purpose of a flight simulator is to train aircrews
- Training aircrews dictates both high fidelity of the simulation and real-time performance

Another source of drivers might be the business goals and background of the organization constructing the systems.

- The organization shall develop a product-line and this dictates a concern for generality that might not occur in a single product-line
- The organization has an investment in prior systems in the domain and this dictates reusing components from prior systems. The organization shall either reuse software component infrastructure from prior systems or develop a new software component infrastructure that accomodates the legacy components.
- The organization shall develop a particular competence in Web-based database access. Consequently, the component infrastructure for the next system will be strongly influenced by Web-based database access.

The drivers do not depend on the details of the functional requirements, but on an abstraction of the functional requirements. In the flight simulator case, whether the simulated aircraft has two engines or four is not an architectural driver; achieving real-time performance in the face of large amounts of data transfer is driver. When designing a component-based system, the software component infrastructure must be carefully designed to satisfy all drivers.

21.4 Decomposing Software Component Infrastructures

The designer of a software component infrastructure must effectively map some subset of functionality onto a set of interacting components. The software architecture community has identified a variety of *architectural styles* to help designers in this effort. An architectural style consists of a set of architectural component types together with a description of the pattern of interaction among them ([Shaw and Garlan, 1996] [Bass, Kazman, and Clements, 1998]). Example architectural component types are *client, server,* and *process*. These architectural component types are used to model the interactions that occur in a software component infrastructure. In the same way that object-oriented design patterns (Gamma et al., 1995) help developers design classes, architectural styles provide the "rough shape" for software component infrastructures. Design patterns and architectural styles only describe functionality to the extent necessary to implement a specific pattern of interaction, but they have no application functionality associated with them. This allows design patterns and architectural styles to be applied in countless situations. Architectural drivers lead to a choice of a particular architectural style.

In the flight simulator system, for example, one architectural driver is the requirement to process large amounts of data with hard real-time performance constraints. The functional facet of the driver is the transfer of large amounts of data and the quality facet of this driver is hard real-time performance. One architectural style that results from this driver is a real-time scheduling strategy. This strategy depends on the interaction between the functional and the quality facets of the driver. For example, real-time performance could be achieved under other scheduling disciplines if the volume of data were smaller. Alternatively, if real-time performance were not an issue, the large amount of data transfer could be achieved under other scheduling disciplines. It is the combination of the two that drives the choice of style.

Once you have selected a particular style for your software component infrastructure you can begin to design the components to map the desired application functionality onto real components. For example, knowing that a real-time schedule strategy is used (for which you have selected an architectural style well-suited for real-time scheduling) does not provide any information about the schedule that will be created. Thus, in the flight simulator example specific computations must be scheduled and the number and function of these computations must be determined. The criteria for determining the number and function of these depend on consideration of the quality goals. In the flight simulator example there may be computations for each engine and these computations must exist in components defined by the real-time scheduling style. By separating the computations of each engine into different components, the overall design meets the requirements for modifiability.

21.5 Functional and Quality Requirements

It is difficult to reason about an abstract description of a system's required functionality because of special cases. Consequently, use cases have gained wide popularity as a concrete representation of requirements (Jacobson, 1994). When designing a software component infrastructure, however, use cases are not adequate without some representation of the required functionality. The base set of applications for the software component infrastructure provides the basis for developing a representation of the requirements at a more abstract level than that provided by use cases. The various functions involved in this base set should be categorized and organized into a collection of abstract requirements. Use cases can then be developed to make these categories concrete and verify that the categories cover all of the important usages of the base set.

Just as functional requirements exist in both abstract and concrete form, so should quality attribute requirements. Functional requirements often emphasize concrete needs, but quality attribute requirements, tend to be more abstract, sometimes to an unwarranted extent. Requirements of the form "the system shall be modifiable" are essentially so abstract as to be meaningless. What is needed is both abstract quality attribute requirements such as "Users shall have limited access to modify personal information" and concrete scenario versions of the quality attribute requirements, such as "Jane Fawn gets married and changes her name to Jane Doe." Both abstract and concrete representations are possible and necessary for all of the quality attribute requirements. "The system shall be secure" is too abstract. "The system shall be secure against eavesdroppers" is a good abstract requirement and "Intruders should be unable to compromise the system by listening to a particular communication channel" is a concrete representation of that requirement.

If your functional requirements are too concrete and specific you risk having increased maintenance costs by building a specific system that must be generalized in the future. If your quality requirements are too abstract you risk having a system whose quality cannot be measured objectively.

21.6 Software Quality Attributes

Quality attributes are primarily determined by decomposing an architecture into its style and its division of functionality. For example, the modifiability of a system is determined by how localized a particular set of modifications is within the divisions of functionality. The performance of a system is determined by the resource requirements of the functional divisions, the type of scheduling strategy used to allocate resources, and the number and type of data paths between the functional divisions. Vulnerability to eavesdropping is determined by the number of data communication paths and access to those paths.

This relationship between software quality and software architecture can be exploited during the design process. The division of functionality determines some aspects of the quality attribute requirements and the architectural style determines others. Figure 21-2 summarizes the process I suggest. Some abstract functional and quality requirements act as architectural drivers. This leads to a choice of style that is tailored to ensure that all quality attribute requirements are achieved. Abstract functional requirements are divided into functional blocks that are then mapped onto component types of the style.

21.7 Styles and Software Component Infrastructures

So far I have discussed the choice of architectural style and the division of functionality allocated to the style. The final goal is the design

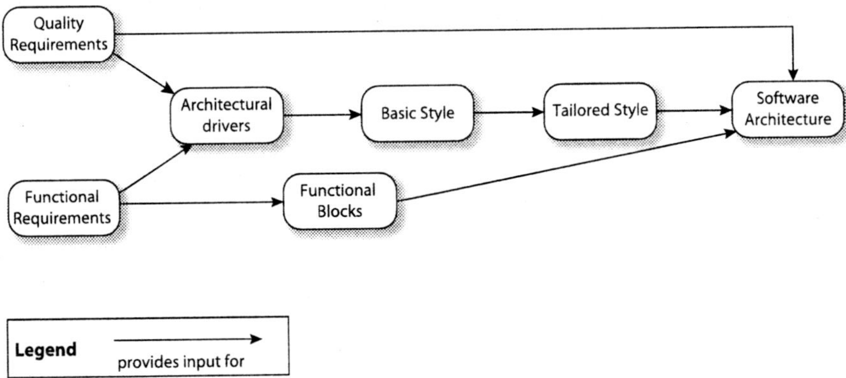

Figure 21-2: *Process for developing basic architecture from quality and functional requirements.*

of a component infrastructure and associated components. Component infrastructures represent a specific instance of an architectural style. They also implement functionality in addition to that necessary to support the pattern of interaction among the component types.

The design process shown in Figure 21-3 modifies Figure 21-2 to show that the software component infrastructure and the components are defined together instead of defining the architecture for the system directly. When you choose an architectural style with the functionality needed to support the patterns of interaction for a software component infrastructure, you decide on the shared services that will be implemented within the component infrastructure and refine them. For the functionality necessary for the base applications that is not provided by the infrastructure, you must define and refine the components.

To determine the shared services to be implemented within the software component infrastructure the base set of applications must be at least partially designed; the software component infrastructure cannot be designed in isolation. You must design how deployed components will interact with the shared services. I advocate an iterative design process that makes a first cut at defining the shared services of the software component infrastructure and then iterates through the divisions of functionality, repeating the process and refining the software component infrastructure and the deployed components.

It is worth mentioning how the construction of the final system is influenced by the software component infrastructure. If the compo-

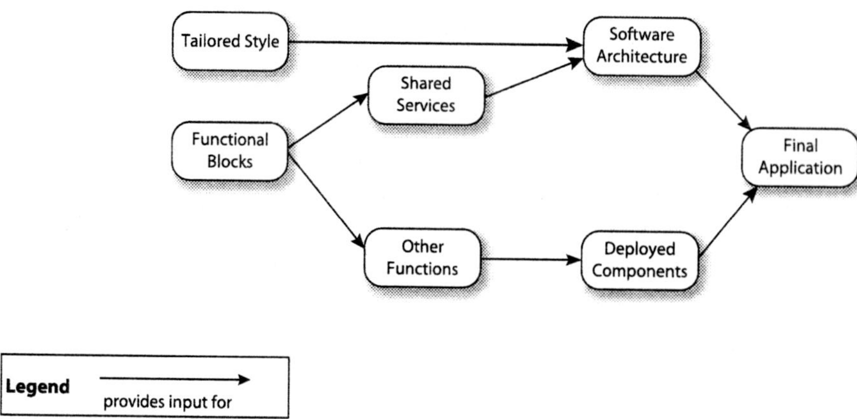

Figure 21-3: *Modification to design process to identify component infrastructure and components.*

nents are small-grained (usually as envisioned by the designers of the software component infrastructure) then the final application is dominated by the software component infrastructure. If, on the other hand, the software component infrastructure is only a small portion of the overall system (if the software component infrastructure is used as just an element of a larger system) then the structure of the final application may vary greatly beyond the structure envisioned by the software computer infrastructure designers.

This discussion of styles and software component infrastructures has focused on structural concerns independent of the domain for which the software is constructed. When designing a software component infrastructure you will often need to decide upon a set of common assumptions (most likely domain-related) understood by the component producers as they develop software components for that infrastructure. For this purpose I recommend the software template approach, which I now describe.

21.8 Software Template

I use the term *design element* to refer to a software element generated as a work product by the design process. It may be an element of the software component infrastructure or of one of the deployed components in the final application. It may also exist at different levels of granularity. That is, it may be one of the initial divisions of functionality or it may be a refinement of one of these initial divisions. I also use the concept of a *software template* (Bachmann et al., 2000) to capture the interaction that exists between the deployed components and the component infrastructure. During the design process you must identify those services that are shared among deployed components and those that should be implemented in the software component infrastructure rather than within one or more components. It is important to identify responsibilities that are assigned to each deployed component rather than the software component infrastructure. For example, components could be responsible for handling errors of a particular type or each component could report events of a particular type.

A software template is a powerful tool for assigning responsibilities to design elements. Similar to an interface, a template is typed and can be refined through inheritance rather than through decomposition.

The design process at each stage of refinement should examine all design elements within the application portion for that stage and determine services that should be included in the software component infrastructure and responsibilities associated with every deployed component. When designing the software component infrastructure you must identify all components and their responsibilities. Since the full set of responsibilities may not be known during the analysis phase, you will likely follow an iterative and incremental process life cycle during the design phase. The responsibilities are added to the software template pertaining to the affected design elements. You should analyze the quality attribute requirements for the entire system to determine additional responsibilities that should be added to a software template. At the end of the design process the software templates will determine the interface that governs interactions between the deployed components and the software component infrastructure.

21.9 Multiple Views

When reasoning about a software architecture you must examine the architecture from a variety of different perspectives. The different perspectives allow the lead engineer to reason about different properties of the architecture. For example, a static perspective that displays the organization of the functionality enables some types of reasoning about development qualities (such as maintainability or extensibility) whereas a dynamic perspective that displays activities that may take place concurrently enables some types of reasoning about performance.

The particular perspectives or views that I advocate are similar to those proposed by Kruchten (1995):

1. Logical
2. Concurrency
3. Implementation
4. Deployment

Instead of viewing these perspectives as static representations of the architecture, I believe you should dynamically evolve them during the design process. As you make decisions you should record information in these particular views. During the logical view the designer should record the responsibilities and interfaces for the design elements as they are defined during the design process. The responsibilities of the design element define its role within the system. They include functional and quality-oriented items such as "the proper implementation of this design element must execute within 50 milliseconds."

The concurrency view describes the system in terms of multiple users, resource contention, start-up, and other parallel activities. The term *concurrency* emphasizes that no commitment has been made to processes or operating system threads; this view will evolve into Kruchten's Process view once these commitments are made. The deployment view represents the physical structure of the system as deployed and the networks used to communicate among processors; this view is only used for systems that execute on multiple processors. Other views of an architecture may better enable particular analyses.

21.10 Principles of Architectural Design

To summarize the contributions outlined in this paper, I now present my eight principles for architectural design (as listed in Figure 21-4).

Table 21-2: *Eight Principles of Architectural Design*

Explicitly identify both high level and concrete functional and quality requirements
Explicitly identify architectural drivers
Choose an architectural style that best satisfies architectural drivers
Divide functionality in a manner that supports quality requirements
Use concurrency and deployment views to identify functionality not previously considered
Verify using concrete quality and functional requirements
Identify the appropriate component model
Iterate to refine the design elements

21.10.1 Identify High-Level and Concrete Functional and Quality Requirements

There are both functional and quality requirements for a system are. Each type of requirement should be expressed in abstract and concrete forms. The abstract form of the requirements is used to determine the architectural drivers and divide functionality. The concrete form of the requirements is used to verify that design decisions do not make it impossible to satisfy the requirements during more detailed design.

21.10.2 Identify Architectural Drivers

Architectural drivers are based on requirements. By explicitly identifying these drivers you can prioritize requirements. Identifying a requirement (or an abstraction of one or more requirements) as an architectural driver both assists the lead engineer in selecting the correct architectural style and informs an organization's management of those requirements that will be very difficult to either meet or change.

Thus, it provides an opportunity for negotiation between the system designers and management over the requirements.

21.10.3 Select Style and Architectural Drivers

The architectural drivers will determine the architectural style of the system. Usually it is not possible to choose a single style that will satisfy all of the architectural drivers. Typically a style is chosen that provides the best solution for the architectural drivers and then is tailored in some fashion to satisfy the other drivers. Total satisfaction of all of the architectural drivers often is not possible and tradeoffs must be made that are reflected in the overall style chosen.

21.10.4 Divide Functionality

The division of functionality will determine how well the non run-time quality attribute requirements, such as modifiability, can be satisfied. The functionality must be allocated to component types of the chosen style. Typically there are multiple iterations between the division of functionality, the choice of style, and the allocation to component types before the designers are satisfied with their design.

21.10.5 Consider Different Views

Examine your design from multiple views to identify functionality that needs to be present to handle multiple simultaneous users, resource contention, and necessary synchronization points. The new functionality that is identified through multiple views must be allocated to a design element, and this may affect the overall design.

21.10.6 Verify Requirements

The concrete quality requirements (the quality scenarios) can be used to verify a design. The design should be walked through based on each scenario to determine the extent to which the current design satisfies the requirement embodied in the scenario.

21.10.7 Identify Software Component Infrastructure Services

Services that cross multiple design elements should be considered for incorporation into the software component infrastructure and recorded in the software template. Services assumed to be provided by the component model should be recorded; these services will help designers select the appropriate component model to implement the final system. These items will often be identified while exercising the quality scenarios.

21.10.8 Refine

At each step the design elements designed thus far have a particular level of detail and contain certain information. The enumerated principles apply to designs at any level of granularity. However, higher levels are not directly suited to implementation or analysis. Thus, design elements must be refined using these principles to create a final design.

21.11 Conclusion

This chapter discusses the principles for designing software component infrastructures. A base set of applications must be considered and the systems involving those applications must be designed to some level of detail. The different applications will presumably all have the same architectural drivers and overall design. As part of the design process you should divide system functionality between the software component infrastructure and deployed components. Quality scenarios can be used as a verification mechanism to ensure that a design fulfills its quality goals. During the design process you should consider multiple views of an architecture. The principles I have identified are not magic. They depend on the realization that the design of a software component infrastructure reflects quality requirements and functional requirements.

Chapter 22

Product-Line Architectures

Martin L. Griss, Ph.D.

22.1 Introduction

A *product-line* is a set of products that share a common set of requirements but also exhibit significant variability in requirements. There are an increasing number of organizations that understand the business importance of managing related products as members of a product-line, and several of these organizations also understand how component reuse can help.

You can manage a set of products as a group, planning the whole set consistently, allocating funding and developers to several of the products at the same time and advertising the products as a set, and highlighting their common and varying features. This commonality and variability can be also exploited during development by treating the set of products as a family and decomposing the software into shared, reusable components that separate concerns (Parnas, 1976 and 1979). For example, at Hewlett-Packard several families of LaserJet printers are developed, managed, and sold as product-lines. Different models (color or black and white, personal or business, large or small) provide different capabilities, and product numbers, features, and product Web pages (*www.hp.com*) are arranged to make comparisons of commonalties and differences easy. In many cases several members of each product-line share common hardware and software components but differ in other components. For example, larger color LaserJet printers have complex paper handling systems while smaller printers do not.

Success with product-line development based on reusable components requires orchestrated attention to a variety of both technical and nontechnical issues, including

- How to design the components and the products to maximize product-line reuse
- What component technology to use
- How to define a component-based product-line development process
- And a host of issues related to organization structure, roles and culture, adoption strategies, and business strategy

Component reuse can play a significant role in reducing costs, decreasing schedule time, and ensuring commonality of features across the product-line. Business managers can make strategic investments in creating and evolving components that benefit a whole product-line, not just a single product. Common components are reused multiple times and defect repairs and enhancements to one product can rapidly be propagated to other members of the product-line.

In this chapter I will describe an approach to systematic, architected product-line development: the analysis, design, implementation, and customization of reusable components that is the essence of product-line CBSE. As in Chapter 9 I find it useful to highlight the architectural phase of product and component design—architecture is about the overall structure, subsystems, key interfaces, and key mechanisms. In particular, when considering product-line development I find it helpful to think first about the architecture of the individual products and the common architecture that underlies or shapes the entire product-line. Then I consider the component infrastructure that implements this common core to be essentially a skeletal product or so-called "framework." You must carefully design and structure the component infrastructure to express, leverage and manage the customizable properties of components.

Recent work in the mostly separate reuse, object-oriented, and software architecture communities has reached the point where I see that the integration of the activities promises to yield a new coherent approach to product-line development. This approach starts from a systematic analysis of the set of common and variable features supporting a product-line and then defines a set of reusable elements that can be customized and combined into components and component infrastructures to implement the products. More details on how this integration might proceed can be found in a series of papers by the author and colleagues ([Griss et al., 1998] [Griss, 2000a and 2000b]).

22.1.1 Product-Lines Can Exploit Reuse

Product-line CBSE delivers the promise of large-scale software reuse by promoting the use of software components built by commercial vendors or in-house developers. One of the key success factors for CBSE is that the systems produced by the organization form an obvious product-line or application family, and that the organization recognizes a compelling business imperative that can exploit product-line CBSE (see Chapter 21 for more key factors). There is a compelling business need to invest in building and managing a set of products as a family, sharing engineering effort and reusable assets. The driving business reason is the critical need to decrease time-to-market to meet competitive market forces, reduce overall costs, or improve product compatibility. Product-line CBSE then becomes strategically important, and management will pay attention. Product-line CBSE has the potential to

- Significantly reduce the cost and time-to-market of enterprise software systems by building the systems by assembling reusable components rather than from scratch
- Enhance the reliability of enterprise software systems because each reusable component has undergone several review and inspection stages in the course of its original development and previous use, and because CBSE relies on explicitly designed component infrastructures and interfaces.

- Improve the maintainability of enterprise software systems by allowing new (higher) quality components to replace old ones.
- Enhance the quality of enterprise software systems by allowing application-domain experts to develop components and allowing software engineers specializing in component-based software development to assemble the components and build enterprise software systems.
- And enhance the agility of organizations in meeting changing market demands by allowing new products to be built quickly by developing only a few new components and reusing the rest.

22.1.2 Terminology

In my work on the Reuse-driven Software Engineering Business (RSEB) and the extension to FeatuRSEB ([Jacobson et al., 1997] [Griss et al., 1998]), applications are defined by a set of connected Unified Modeling Language (UML) models and software, called an *Application System,* and constructed by an *Application System Engineering* process. Applications are engineered from customizable components imported from component groups called *component systems* that interact with each other in a layered, modular architecture. A component system refers to a set of related components that collaborate to accomplish a function too large to isolate within a single component. Component systems are engineered by a *Component System Engineering* process, described in detail in the RSEB book (Jacobson, Griss, and Jonsson, 1997).

22.2 Explicit Representation of Features for Product-Line CBSE

When we examine different applications in the same product-line or problem domain, we often compare these applications based on their features. A *feature* is a product characteristic that users and customers view as important in describing and distinguishing members of the product-line. A feature can be

- A specific requirement

- A selection among optional or alternative requirements
- Related to certain product characteristics such as functionality, usability, and performance
- Related to implementation characteristics such as size, operating system or computer, or compatibility with certain standards such as CORBA, HL7, or TCP/IP

Some features are directly related to application functionality and offered services, perhaps best expressed in use cases. Other distinguishing features might relate to the application implementation, style of graphical user interface, or operating system. When developing a product-line architecture and components for reuse it is important to understand those features that must be provided by the set of reusable assets (components, component infrastructures, models, and special tools), and how those features relate to each other.

Members of a product-line might all exist at one time or evolve with the product-line. For example, each individual member of a word processing product-line might optionally provide an outline mode, spell checking, grammar correction, or diagrams. It may run in Microsoft Windows or UNIX, be large or small, and support a small or large number of files. A product-line can be built around the set of reusable components by analyzing the products to determine the common and variable features using a technique called domain analysis. Then you develop a product structure and implementation strategy around a set of reusable components that can be composed to create a component infrastructure that can be used to implement several different products.

Some components do not need to be specialized and are reused as "black-boxes" because they match a desired problem. As described in Chapter 1, there are many ways of using components in "white-box" fashion, based on a number of ways of customizing a component. This customizability greatly expands the number of applications to which the components can be applied. For example, a component could simply be customized using parameters to account for differences in the products that are not expressible by just selecting alternative components. In other cases the components could be substantially modified to create a unique component for a specific product. More abstract components can be specialized to express key variability at well defined "variation points." Abstract components that have been implemented using an object-oriented language often can be extended through inheritance to create a concrete component that meets a particular need. A reuser exploits these mechanisms to customize the component to the particular application. If we made no provision for variability we would have to maintain a very large number of "concrete" component systems.

Each component captures some subset of features or allows features to be built up by composing components. For example, each word processor in the product-line might share a common editing component and one or more optional components for spell checking, outlining, or other features. These components may be combined to produce a variety of similar word processors, only some of which would be viable products.

22.2.1 Domain Analysis to Construct a Product-Line Feature Model

Domain analysis ([Arango, 1994] [Griss, 1996] [Griss et al., 1998]) is a technique to systematically extract features from existing or planned members of a product-line. The domain analyst uses example systems, user needs, domain expertise, and technology trends to identify and characterize elements that are common to all product-line members and to characterize and express elements that vary among product-line members.

Domain analysis is used to cluster sets of features to shape the design of a set of components that cover the product-line. The analysis will also affect the design and implementation of the product-line architecture and reusable components, infrastructure, and tools that will be used to construct the product-line. Once the variability structure has been modeled, developers can choose the overall decomposition into a component infrastructure and select an appropriate variability mechanism to produce generic components. For example, you can use a combination of inheritance and templates or a preprocessor or generator. Finally, the components are designed in detail and implemented.

In many domains quite a few of the features are already known by domain experts, which they can use to explain how different kinds of systems differ. In this case an initial feature model can be constructed without having to go through a formal domain analysis. It will often start off looking like the typical class and interface hierarchy that an experienced developer might sketch. But as the domain gets more complex, dependencies and variants will need to be carefully modeled using a well-specified and tested method. More details on how UML and FODA are used within FeatuRSEB can be found in (Griss, Favaro, and d'Allesandro, 1998).

The feature model produced by domain analysis can be represented diagrammatically in several ways. Figure 22-1 is an example of a tree-diagram of a feature model for a simple online banking domain. Distilled from many sources, it is an organized, selective, and normalized dictionary that becomes the reference for terminology used by component and product developers. The various nodes in this feature diagram show how some features are composed of lower-level features (that must always be present) while others are optional (annotated by a small circle). The model also contains alternatives (annotated by small clear and solid diamonds at variation points called *vp-features*) that can be selected at construction time or dynamically loaded at run-time.

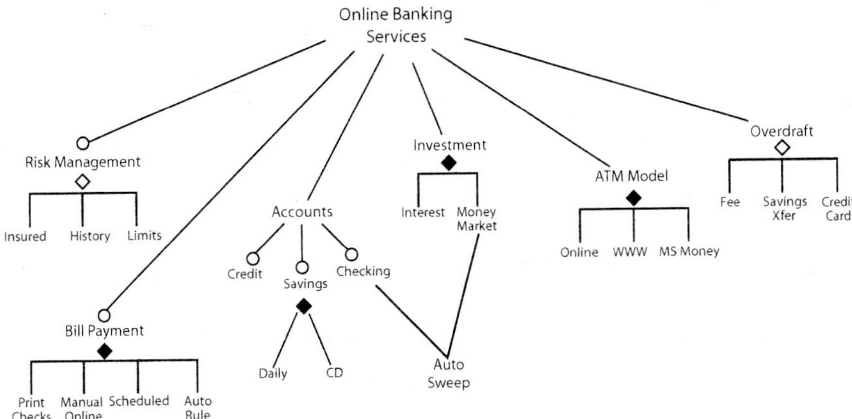

Figure 22-1: *Feature model for a simple online banking domain.*

Domain analysis is used to cluster sets of features to shape the design of a set of components that cover the product-line. The analysis will also affect the design and implementation of the product-line architecture and reusable components, infrastructure, and tools that will be used to construct the product-line. Once the variability structure has been modeled, developers can choose the overall decomposition into a component infrastructure and select an appropriate variability mechanism to produce generic components. For example, you can use a combination of inheritance and templates or a preprocessor or generator. Finally, the components are designed in detail and implemented.

In many domains quite a few of the features are already known by domain experts, which they can use to explain how different kinds of systems differ. In this case an initial feature model can be constructed without having to go through a formal domain analysis. It will often start off looking like the typical class and interface hierarchy that an experienced developer might sketch. But as the domain gets more complex, dependencies and variants will need to be carefully modeled using a well-specified and tested method. More details on how UML and FODA are used within FeatuRSEB can be found in Griss, Favaro, and d'Allesandro (1998).

Product developers rely on the feature model to understand which components to select or customize to provide the desired features. When a product developer wants to build a new system in the domain he consults the feature model to understand what can be combined, selected, and customized in the new or existing system. The feature model also expresses semantic constraints that can't be found in any of the other models—for example, "this operating system can't be selected together with that hardware," and other characteristics that are hard to express directly, such as performance constraints and other dependencies.

Component developers and product-line architects will use the feature model to determine the components to develop and how they should be customized or relate to each other. There are many different ways to cluster and decompose features into a set of components. For example, in the online banking example we could imagine the Overdraft feature being implemented in a single component, in which the choices of how to implement the overdraft (loan extra money and charge fees from account, transfer from savings, or withdraw from credit card) could be selected by a parameter. Alternatively, it may make sense to implement Risk Management and Overdraft together as a related set of components in which, for example, different limits or history would determine the fee to charge or which strategy to plug in to a Risk/Overdraft decision.

There are several different domain analysis methods that vary in how they identify the domain and represent the features and their relationships. In my work on extending RSEB into FeatuRSEB (Griss, Favaro, and d'Allesandro, 1998) I have built on FODA (Kang et al., 1990 and 1999). Kang has also extended FODA to a product-line method, FORM (Kang et al., 1998).

22.2.2 Implementing Components Corresponding to Sets of Features

The feature model serves as an index to the other models (such as UML use cases, subsystems, or classes) used during development. A major issue to be addressed is that while some features can be traced directly to specific components, other features trace to component code that is distributed across ("cuts across") multiple components. This relates to the important principle of separation of concerns and reduced component coupling.

Isolating related functionality into one or a small cluster of related components ensures that components can be changed independently of each other, usually without changing their provided or required interfaces. Just as the careful design of component interfaces and the decomposition of a system into relatively independent components is an important part of designing a robust system, so too must we carefully structure the feature model and decide how to implement the features to corresponding components.

Some features can be implemented as code that is localized to one or a small group of components. For example, features related to a language or dictionary choice for "spelling" can easily be expressed by code in the "spelling component." A change in one of these features (through product evolution or selection of a variable feature) can be localized to a small number of components.

However, in many other cases features cut across multiple components, resulting in related code that is distributed across these components. Such "crosscutting" features make it difficult to decompose separate concerns into separate components that hide details of how these features are implemented; for example, security, choice of target operating system or computer, or choice of underlying component model (such as COM or CORBA). Modifying these "crosscutting" features will have a profound impact on the system. A change in these features requires identifying the corresponding fragments of code within multiple methods in multiple components and making consistent changes. Sometimes a different decomposition into components using a different architecture, design pattern, or underlying infrastructure can reduce the crosscutting effect of some features. But it does not appear possible to do this for all features in all systems.

Managing feature and component evolution becomes extremely complicated when the code that implements a particular feature or set of closely related features needs to be spread across multiple components, particularly if this code is intertwined with the code corresponding to other features. In some cases the intertwining can be reduced by an appropriate decomposition into smaller components and well-designed interfaces, but in many cases code contributed by one feature needs to interact fairly closely with that produced by other features. For example, consider the code needed to sort a list or rows of a table. Code to access and compare the elements and code to traverse and swap list or table elements will be intermixed with code corresponding to the inner loops of the algorithm, especially for efficiency reasons. Sometimes the use of macros, inline declarations, templates and abstract data types can be used to allow these different features (choice of element, container, and algorithm) to be manipulated separately and later combined, as we will describe further below. For example, the C++ Standard Template Library (STL) goes to great lengths to factor these into separate elements that are then combined into a complete class by the C++ template preprocessor. More powerful techniques will be needed if the features interact across components, especially if these components will need to be in different applications on different computers, such as compatible choices of network protocols at both ends of client/server systems.

In general, this problem is mostly related to choosing a particular dominant decomposition into components that does not completely match the dependency and variability patterns of features. In some cases choosing a different decomposition can improve the robustness for a particular set of features. "Robust" means that for certain kinds of change in requirements and features, the consequence of the change is localized to only a few components or locations within a component.

Unfortunately, different sets of features "prefer" different decompositions, and it does not seem possible to choose a single decomposition that is robust enough for all changes and evolutions (Tarr et al.,

1999). The problem is that individual features typically do not trace directly to an individual component or cluster of components—although a product may defined as a set of features, a carefully coordinated mixture of parts of different components is involved. This "crosscutting" interaction is also referred to as the requirements traceability or feature-interaction problem. In the case of significant crosscutting variability, maintenance and evolution becomes very complicated, because the change in a particular feature may require changes all over the resulting software design and implementation.

I recommend that during use-case design you should select use cases separately and choose among variant use case features. Each use case typically translates to a collaboration of multiple components, automatically resulting in crosscutting impact. Thus, variability in a single use case typically translates into crosscutting variability in a related set of design and implementation components.

22.2.2.1 Managing Crosscutting Features

The conventional approach to managing crosscutting features and feature traceability is to build complex maps from features to components and products and manage the evolution of the features by jointly managing the evolution of the individual components. In the past this has been done manually, but more recently powerful requirements tracing and management tools have helped, such as DOORS (*www.telelogic.com/doors*) or Caliber RM (*www.tbi.com/caliberrm*) have made this somewhat easier. Even with such traceability tools, when one feature changes code in many components will have to change. To find and decide how to change this code requires developers to disentangle the code corresponding to this feature from the code for other features.

One observation is that a change to a feature (or small sets of related features) is relatively independent from other features, and thus a group of component or product code changes can be isolated to a few related features. This is similar to the near independence of well-designed use cases described above. Thus, separation of concerns is most effective at the higher level, before "tangling" and "crosscutting" into design or implementation.

In addition to the use of hyper-Web-like traceability tools to help manage or find connected pieces of code corresponding to one feature, there are two major approaches to address this problem. Typically, a combination of these is used in practice.

1. *Architecture* and *Component Design* techniques—Use tools and techniques such as patterns ([Gamma et al., 1995] [Buschmann et al., 1996]), interfaces, and styles (Shaw and Garlan, 1996), to provide a good decomposition into separate pieces that are relatively independent, localizing changes. This often leads to a better structure and a more flexible, maintainable system. However, discovering and maintaining a good design, requires skill (and some luck) in choosing a decomposition that anticipates changes. Different decompositions are more or less robust against different classes of change.
2. *Composition or "weaving" of program fragments*—The feature decomposition is used directly to produce separate code fragments (called "aspects") that are composed or woven together using a language, preprocess, or generator to produce complete components or products.

Over the last several years a number of techniques ("aspect-oriented development") have been developed to make the "composition and weaving" approach to feature-driven design and development of software practical. An *aspect* is a fragment of code (typically a statement, method, or parameterized template) that can be composed with base code and other aspects. The result of this composition is a complete component or product. The key idea is to identify a useful class of program fragments that can be mechanically combined using some formal tool and to associate these fragments with features of the software. One does not directly manage the resulting components, only the features and their aspects. One simply dynamically generates a fresh version of the component as needed.

Highly customized, fine-grained, aspect-oriented development is complementary to the more standard large-grain component-based development, in which customizable components communicating through COM/CORBA/RMI interfaces are integrated together. But well integrated systems cannot always be built from arbitrary COTS components. Many of their components must be built or tailored using fine-grained approaches, as described above. For further discussion on the relationship between customizable components and product-lines, see Bosch (1999).

22.3 A Systematic Approach to Feature-Driven Product-Line Development

The systematic approach to feature-driven, component-based product-line development becomes quite simple in concept.

1. Use a feature-driven analysis and design method to develop a feature model and high-level design with explicit variability and traceability. The feature model is developed in parallel with other models. It can be used to structure the product-line family use cases and class models. Features are traced to variability in the design and implementation models (Griss, Favaro, and d'Alessandro, 1998). The design and implementation models will show these explicit patterns of variability.
2. Select one or more aspect-oriented implementation techniques depending on the granularity of the variable design and implementation features, and the patterns of the combination they need.
3. Express the needed aspects as appropriate code fragments that will be combined into complete components using the chosen mechanism (for example, as C++ templates, parameters, or frames).
4. Design complete applications by selecting and composing features and then select and compose the corresponding aspects, composing the resulting components and complete application out of code fragments corresponding to these aspects.

22.3.1 Examples

At Hewlett-Packard Laboratories these product-line techniques are being explored in the context of several application prototypes. As described in more detail by Griss (2000b), several large-scale, domain-specific component infrastructures for families of medical and banking applications were prototyped using CORBA (and COM) as the distribution substrate and a mixture of Java and C++ for components. The same experimental component infrastructure was used for two different domains: a distributed medical system supporting doctors in interaction with patient appointments and records, and an online commercial banking system for foreign exchange trades.

The applications in each domain are comprised of several large distributed components running in a heterogeneous UNIX and WindowsNT environment. Different components handle such activities as doctor or trader authentication, interruptible session management, task lists and workflow management, and data object wrappers. The overall structure of all the components is similar across the domains and across roles within the domains. For example, all of the data object wrapper components are similar, differing only in the Standard Query Language (SQL) commands they issue to access the desired data from multiple databases and in the class-specific constructors they use to consolidate information into a single object. Each component has multiple interfaces. Some interfaces support a basic component life cycle while others support the specific function of the component (such as session keys). Several of the interfaces work together across components to support crosscutting aspects such as transactions, session key management, and data consistency.

Each component is built from one of several skeletal components to provide a shell with standard interfaces and supporting classes. Additional interfaces and classes are added for some of the domain and role- specific behavior and then the component is finished by hand. The customization of the components corresponding to the crosscutting aspects is carried out compatibly across the separate components. Component skeletons are generated by customizing and assembling different parts from a shared parts library. A simplified feature-oriented domain analysis was used to identify the requisite parts and their relationships. This used to structure a Bassett-style frame-based component generator (Bassett, 1996) that customizes and assembles the parts and components from C++ fragments. Each frame is a template that represents the code corresponding to different aspects, such as security, workflow/business process interfaces, transactions, sessions, and component life cycle. Each component interface is represented as a set of C++ classes and interfaces. Component interactions are represented as frames that are then used to generate and compose the corresponding code fragments.

The other major class of prototype applications is agent-based systems for e-commerce and applications management, described in Chapter 36 and by Griss (2000a). We have recognized the need to develop a large variety of different yet compatible agents. Changing the details of one feature (such as agent communication language, mobility, or conversation management strategy) would require compatible changes across many agents.

22.4 Conclusion

In this chapter I provided an overview of a systematic approach to component-based product-line development. Starting from the set of common and variable features needed to support a product-line, we can systematically develop and assemble the reusable elements needed to produce the customized components and component infrastructures needed to implement the members of the product-line.

Obviously, the simple prescription presented for product-line CBSE is not a complete method, but does suggest that product-line architects, domain engineers, and component and infrastructure designers should now become aware of how to use these ideas to structure their models and designs. This new approach will help designers structure their component implementations in a disciplined way to explicitly manage and compose aspects based on a product-line feature model.

Part V

Summary

This Part introduced several important concepts to help you construct software systems based on a software component infrastructure. The emerging discipline of software architecture is an important addition to software engineering. To date, however, we feel that this research area has not fully developed a coherent solution for designing, evaluating, and implementing component-based systems. The primary weaknesses are as follows. First, the software architecture community does not appear to embrace the notion of a component model. For example, the community commonly refers to a component as a primitive that describes any collection of coherent computation. Unfortunately, such a vague description makes it difficult to translate research results into practice. Also, the research examples often appear to be small, toy systems. It is not necessary to agree upon a specific component model, but we feel the community must accept that software components must conform to a component model.

Second, because the software architecture community focused much of their early research on the abstract concept of architectural styles, they missed an opportunity to focus on the problems of real component-based systems. An architectural style is defined as consisting of a set of architectural component *types* together with a description of the pattern of interaction among them. The commonly cited styles, such as Pipe/Filter or Client/Server, are too simplistic to help analyze complex systems. In addition, complex systems often have topological structures that cannot easily be mapped to a specific architectural style. Third, many different architectural definition languages (ADLs) were developed to syntactically describe topologies of components, but they were never empirically evaluated on complex, component-based software systems. Unfortunately, many ADLs have only been described and used on paper.

Even with these limitations there are indeed many research contributions by the software architecture community, and in the future we expect that there will be a transition of ideas from theory to practice. In Chapter 20, Judith Stafford and Alexander Wolf explained how the emerging field of software architecture seeks to make the process of architecting software systems more rigorous and the result of architecting more reliable and reusable by applying powerful specification and analysis techniques. They correctly observed that we need mechanisms for formalizing models of software components and software component infrastructures. The current limitation of formal methods is that the software engineering community has not agreed on the specific techniques that should be taught, thus most software engineers currently leave their studies ill prepared to learn advanced formal methods. Formalizing the architectural description and analysis techniques enables reasoning about the construction and maintenance of large and complex software systems. They identify three challenges.

- To make sure that the techniques are practical for large-scale systems
- To find ways to integrate the techniques into the emerging software processes that depend upon shorter and shorter cycle times
- To extend the techniques to better support the description and analysis of critical extra-functional system properties

In Chapter 21, Len Bass discussed the principles for designing software component infrastructures. We believe you will find it very practical to combine the concepts from Part IV with Len's principles. When designing the software component infrastructure you must consider a base set of applications that could be developed and the systems involving those applications must be designed to some level of detail. Converting the software component infrastructure into the final system will only succeed if the designer has paid attention to the architectural drivers that affect the design in the first place. Len described in detail how to design the software component infrastructure to ensure basic functional and quality requirements.

Presumably, the different applications that could be developed from the software component infrastructure will all have the same architectural drivers and the overall design for each will be the same. The principles presented in Chapter 21 describe the information necessary to analyze the design rules of the software architecture. This ensures, as much as possible, that the designed system meets its quality and functional requirements.

In Chapter 22 Martin Griss provided an overview of a systematic approach to component-based product-line development. A *product-line* is a set of products that share a common set of requirements but also exhibit significant variability in requirements. There are an increasing number of organizations that understand the business importance of managing related products as members of a product-line, and several of these organizations also understand how component reuse can help. Starting from the set of common and variable features needed to support a product-line, we can systematically develop and assemble the reusable elements needed to produce the customized software components and software component infrastructures needed to implement the members of the product-line. By emphasizing the variability inherent in a product-line, Martin makes the case for "abstract" components that can be customized, creating specialized components that can be assembled into a software component infrastructure. With no provision for variability you must maintain a very large number of "concrete" components. Follow Martin's advice to create components that can be reused in more situations because they are highly customizable.

Clearly there needs to be more empirical research in the software architecture community. One way to achieve this goal is to increase the collaboration between academic researchers and industrial practitioners. Widespread use of ADLs, for example, will only occur through studies that show repeatable benefits of using such languages to describe software systems. Another research direction is to pursue an approach similar to the one we have used in this book project. The software architecture community should seek to reach consensus on a rigorous definition and then use that definition to incorporate the concept of components. We recommend further studies showing the relationship between software architecture and UML design methods—are they compatible? In some respects UML has become widely accepted by industry because of available tools, such as Rational Rose. Can the software architecture community design and implement similar tools to promote the sorts of analyses they wish to perform?

At the original NATO Software Engineering conference there were a few comments on the perceived similarity between design and architecture. As pointed out by Naur and Randell:

> Software designers are in a similar position to architects and civil engineers.... It therefore seems natural that we should turn to these subjects for ideas about how to attack the design problem. As one single example of such a source of ideas I would like to mention: Christopher Alexander: Notes on the Synthesis of Form." (Naur and Randell, 1968).

It is illuminating to see, even at this early time, a direct reference to the architect Christopher Alexander, whom the design patterns literature commonly cites. In the follow-up Rome Conference, Sharp clarified the distinction: "Architecture is different from engineering" (Buxton and Randell, 1970). In analyzing the weakness of the OS/360 project, Sharp said, "The reason that OS is an amorphous lump of program is that it had no architect. Its design was delegated to a series of groups of engineers, each of who had to invent their own architecture. And when these lumps were nailed together they did not produce a smooth and beautiful piece of software." (Buxton and Randell, 1970). The challenge for the software architecture community is to conduct a history of the term *architecture* and demonstrate how it applies more effectively than software engineering and design to their activities.

Part V

References

R. Allen and D. Garlan, "A Formal Basis for Architectural Connection," *ACM Transactions on Software Engineering and Methodology*, Vol. 6, No. 3, July 1997, pp. 213-249.

G. Arango, "Domain Analysis Methods," in *Software Reusability*, W. Schäfer et al., eds., Ellis Horwood, 1994, pp. 17-49.

F. Bachmann, L. Bass, G. Chastek, P. Donohoe, and F. Peruzzi, "The Architecture Based Design Method," CMU/SEI-00-TR-001, Software Engineering Institute, Carnegie Mellon University, Pittsburgh, PA, Jan., 2000.

L. Bass, P. Clements, and R. Kazman, *Software Architecture in Practice*, Addison-Wesley, Reading, MA, 1998.

P. Bassett, *Framing Reuse: Lessons from the Real World*, Prentice-Hall, Upper Saddle River, NJ, 1996.

D. Batory, S. Dasari, B. Geraci, V. Singhal, M. Sirkin, and J. Thomas, "The GenVoca Model of Software System Generation," *IEEE Software*, Vol. 11, No. 5, Sept., 1994, pp. 89-94.

J. Bosch, "Product-Line Architectures and Industry: A Case Study," Proceedings, 21st International Conference on Software Engineering (ICSE), ACM Press, Los Angeles, CA, 1999, pp. 544-554.

J. Bosch, *Design and Use of Industrial Software Architectures*, Addison-Wesley, Boston, MA, 2000.

D. Compare, P. Inverardi, and A. Wolf, "Uncovering Architectural Mismatch in Dynamic Behavior," *Science of Computer Programming*, Vol. 33, No. 2, Feb., 1999, pp. 101-131.

F. Buschmann, R. Meunier, H. Rohnert, P. Sommerlad, and M. Stal, *Pattern-Oriented Software Architecture,* Vol. I: *A System of Patterns,* John Wiley & Sons, New York, NY, 1996.

H. Gall, M. Jazayeri, R. Klösch, W. Lugmayr, and G. Trausmuth, "Architecture Recovery in ARES," Proceedings, 2nd International Software Architecture Workshop, ACM Press, San Francisco, CA, 1996, pp. 111-115.

E. Gamma, R. Helm, R. Johnson, and J. Vlissides, *Design Patterns: Elements of Reusable Object-Oriented Software,* Addison-Wesley, Reading, MA, 1995.

D. Garlan, R. Allen, and J. Ockerbloom, "Exploiting Style in Architectural Design Environments," Proceedings, 2nd ACM SIGSOFT Symposium on the Foundations of Software Engineering (FSE), ACM Press, 1994, pp. 175-188.

D. Garlan, R. Monroe, and D. Wile, "ACME: An Architecture Description Interchange Language," Proceedings, IBM Center for Advanced Studies Conference (CASCON), IBM Canada, Ltd., Toronto, ON, 1997, pp. 169-183.

R. Gonzales and A. Wolf, "A Facilitator Method for Upstream Design Activities with Diverse Stakeholders," Proceedings, 2nd International Conference on Requirements Engineering (ICRE), IEEE Computer Society Press, 1996, pp. 190-197.

M. Griss, "Domain Engineering And Variability In The Reuse-Driven Software Engineering Business," *Object Magazine*, Vol. 6, No. 10, Dec., 1996, pp. 67-70.

M. Griss, "Implementing Product-Line Features with Component Reuse," Proceedings, 6th International Conference on Software Reuse (ICSR), Lecture Notes in Computer Science (LNCS), No. 1844, Springer-Verlag, Heidelerg, Germany, 2000a, pp. 137-152.

M. Griss, "How to Implement Product-Line Features By Composing Component Aspects," Proceedings, 1st Software Product-line Conference (SPLC), Kluwer Academic Publishers, 2000b, pp. 271-288.

M. Griss, J. Favaro, and M. d'Alessandro, "Integrating Feature Modeling with the RSEB," Proceedings, 5th International Conference on Software Reuse (ICSR), IEEE Computer Society Press, Los Alamitos, CA, 1998, pp. 76-85.

W. Harrison and H. Ossher, "Subject-Oriented Programming (A Critique of Pure Objects)," Proceedings, 8th Object-Oriented Programming, Languages, Systems, and Applications conference (OOPSLA), ACM Press, 1993, pp. 411-428.

C. Hofmeister, R. Nord, and P. Soni, *Applied Software Architecture*, Addison-Wesley, Boston, MA, 2000.

P. Inverardi and A. Wolf, "Formal Specification and Analysis of Software Architectures Using the Chemical Abstract Machine Model," *IEEE Transactions on Software Engineering*, Vol. 21, No. 4, Apr., 1995, pp. 373-386.

P. Inverardi, A. Wolf, and D. Yankelevich, "Static Checking of System Behaviors Using Derived Component Assumptions," *ACM Transaction on Software Engineering and Methodology*, Vol. 9, No. 3, July 2000, pp. 239-272.

D. Jackson and C. Damon, "Elements of Style: Analyzing a Software Design Feature with a Counterexample Detector," *IEEE Transactions on Software Engineering*, Vol. 22, No. 7, July 1996, pp. 484-495.

I. Jacobson, *Object-Oriented Software Engineering: A Use Case Driven Approach*, Addison-Wesley, Reading, MA, 1994.

I. Jacobson, M. Griss, and P. Jonsson, *Software Reuse: Architecture, Process and Organization for Business Success*, Addison-Wesley, Reading, MA, 1997.

K. Kang, S. Cohen, J. Hess, W. Novak, and A. Peterson, "Feature-Oriented Domain Analysis (FODA) Feasibility Study," SEI Technical Report CMU/SEI-90-TR-21, Software Engineering Institute, Pittsburgh, PA, Nov., 1990.

K. Kang, S. Kim, J. Lee, K. Kim, E. Shin, and M. Huh, "FORM: A Feature-Oriented Reuse Method with Domain-Specific Architectures," *Annals of Software Engineering*, Vol. 5, Balzer Science Publishers, *www.baltzer.nl/ansoft/contents/5.html*, 1998, pp. 143-168.

K. Kang, S. Kim, J. Lee, and K. Lee, "Feature-oriented Engineering of PBX Software for Adaptability and Reuseability," *Software—Practice and Experience*, Vol. 29, No. 10, Aug., 1999, pp. 875-896.

R. Kazman, M. Klein, and P. Clements, "ATAM—An Architecture Evaluation Method," SEI/CMU TR - 006/2000, Software Engineering Institute, Pittsburgh, PA, 2000.

T. Khoshgoftaar, E. Allen, R. Halstead, G. Trio, and R. Flass, "Using Process History to Predict Software Quality," *IEEE Computer*, Vol. 31, No. 4, Apr., 1998, pp. 66-72.

G. Kiczales, J. Lamping, A. Mendhekar, C. Maeda, L. Loitinger, and J. Irwin, "Aspect Oriented Programming," Proceedings, 11th European Conference on Object-Oriented Programming (ECOOP), Lecture Notes in Computer Science (LNCS), No. 1241, Springer-Verlag, Heidelberg, Germany, 1997, pp. 220-242.

P. Kruchten, "The 4+1 View Model of Architecture," *IEEE Software*, Vol. 12, No. 6, Nov., 1995, pp. 42-50.

D. Le Métayer, "Describing Software Architecture Styles Using Graph Grammars," *IEEE Transactions on Software Engineering*, Vol. 24, No. 7, July 1998, pp. 521-533.

D. Luckham, J. Kenney, L. Augin, J. Vera, D. Bryan, and W. Mann, "Specification and Analysis of System Architecture Using Rapide," *IEEE Transactions on Software Engineering*, Vol. 21, No. 4, Apr., 1995, pp. 336-355.

J. Magee, J. Kramer, and D. Giannakopoulou, "Analysing the Behaviour of Distributed Software Architectures: A Case Study," Proceedings, 5th IEEE Workshop on Future Trends of Distributed Computing Systems, IEEE Computer Society Press, 1997, pp. 240-247.

N. Medvidovic, "A Framework for Classifying and Comparing Architecture Description Languages," Proceedings, 6th European Software Engineering Conference (ESEC) held jointly with the 5th ACM SIGSOFT Symposium on Foundations of Software Engineering (FSE), Lecture Notes in Computer Science (LNCS), No. 1301, Springer-Verlag, Heidelberg, Germany, 1997, pp. 60-76.

M. Moriconi, X. Qian, and R. Riemenschneider, "Correct Architecture Refinement," *IEEE Transactions on Software Engineering*, Vol. 21, No. 4, Apr., 1995, pp. 356-372.

G. Murphy, D. Notkin, and K. Sullivan, "Software Reflexion Models: Bridging the Gap Between Source and High-Level Models," Proceedings, 3rd ACM SIGSOFT Symposium on the Foundations of Software Engineering (FSE), ACM Press, Washington, DC, 1995, pp. 18-28.

G. Naumovich, G. Avrunin, L. Clarke, and L. Osterweil, "Applying Static Analysis to Software Architectures," Proceedings, 6th European Software Engineering Conference (ESEC) held Jointly with the 5th ACM SIGSOFT Symposium on Foundations of Software Engineering (FSE), Lecture Notes in Computer Science (LNC), No. 1301, Springer-Verlag, 1997, pp. 77-93.

P. Naur and B. Randell, eds., "Software Engineering: Concepts," Report on a conference sponsored by the NATO Science Committee, NATO Science Division, Brussels, Belgium, Oct., 1968.

J. Buxton and B. Randell, eds., "Software Engineering Techniques," Report on a conference sponsored by the NATO Science Committee, NATO Science Division, Brussels, Belgium, Apr., 1970.

P. Oreizy, N. Medvidovic, and R. Taylor, "Architecture-Based Runtime Software Evolution," Proceedings, 20th International Conference on Software Engineering (ICSE), ACM Press, 1998, pp. 177-186.

O. Oskarsson and R. Glass, *An ISO 9000 Approach to Building Quality Software*, Prentice-Hall, Upper Saddle River, NJ, 1996.

D. Parnas, "On the Design and Development Of Program Families," *IEEE Transactions on Software Engineering*, Vol. 2, No. 16, Mar., 1976, pp. 1-9.

D. Parnas, "Designing Software for Ease of Extension and Contraction," *IEEE Transactions on Software Engineering*, Vol. 5, No. 6, Mar., 1979, pp. 310-320.

D. Perry and A. Wolf, "Foundations for the Study of Software Architecture," *SIGSOFT Software Engineering Notes*, Vol. 17, No. 4, Oct., 1992, pp. 40-52.

R. Pressman, *Software Engineering: A Practitioner's Approach*, 4th ed., McGraw-Hill, 1997.

D. Richardson and A. Wolf, "Software Testing at the Architectural Level," Proceedings, 2nd International Software Architecture Workshop (ISAW), ACM Press, 1996, pp. 68-71.

R. Schwanke, V. Strack, and T. Werthmann-Auzinger, "Industrial Software Architecture with Gestalt," Proceedings, 8th International Workshop on Software Specification and Design (IWSSD), IEEE Computer Society Press, 1996, pp. 176-180.

M. Shaw and P. Clements, "A Field Guide to Boxology: Preliminary Classification of Architectural Styles for Software Systems," Proceedings, 21st International Computer Software and Applications Conference (COMPSAC), IEEE Computer Society Press, 1997, pp. 6-13.

M. Shaw and D. Garlan, *Software Architecture: Perspectives on an Emerging Discipline*, Prentice Hall, 1996.

M. Shaw and D. Garlan, "Formulations and Formalisms in Software Architecture," *Computer Science Today: Recent Trends and Developments*, Lecture Notes in Computer Science (LNCS), No. 1000, Springer-Verlag, Heidelberg, Germany, 1995, pp. 307-323.

D. Soni, R. Nord, and C. Hofmeister, "Software Architecture In Industrial Applications," Proceedings, 17th International Conference on Software Engineering (ICSE), Seattle, WA, ACM Press, 1995, pp. 196-207.

J. Stafford, D. Richardson, and A. Wolf, "Aladdin: A Tool for Architecture-Level Dependence Analysis of Software," Technical Report CU-CS-858-98, Department of Computer Science, University of Colorado, Boulder, CO, Apr., 1998.

P. Tarr, H. Ossher, W. Harrison, and S. Sutton, Jr., "N Degrees of Separation: Multi-Dimensional Separation of Concerns," Proceedings, 21st International Conference on Software Engineering (ICSE), ACM Press, Los Angeles, CA, 1999, pp. 107-119.

A. van der Hoek, D. Heimbigner, and A. Wolf, "Versioned Software Architecture," Proceedings, 3rd International Software Architecture Workshop (ISAW), ACM Press, 1998, pp. 73-76.

M. Van Hilst and D. Notkin, "Using C++ Templates to Implement Role-Based Designs," Japan Society for Software Science and Technology (JSSST) Symposium on Object Technologies for Advanced Software, Lecture Notes in Computer Science (LNCS), No. 742, Springer-Verlag, Heidelberg, Germany, 1996, pp. 22-37.

M. Van Hilst and D. Notkin, "Decoupling Change From Design," Proceedings, 4th ACM SIGSOFT Symposium on Foundations of Software Engineering (FSE), ACM Press, 1996, pp. 58-69.

S. Vestal, *MetaH Programmer's Manual Version 1.27*, Honeywell, Inc., 1998.

M. Young and R. Taylor, "Rethinking the Taxonomy of Fault Detection Techniques," SERC TR-62-P, Department of Computer Science, Purdue University, West Lafayette, IN, Sept., 1991.

Part VI

The Management of Component-Based Software Systems

Software engineers and experienced managers must plan for and control issues—such as measurement, reuse, and configuration management—from the inception of the pilot project. Otherwise, if left unmanaged or undermanaged, the new technology could result in an organization's refusal to continue budgeting and implementing CBD and CBSE. To help with this issue we present eight chapters that comprise this "management" section.

Jeffrey Poulin makes a persuasive argument for "Measurement and Metrics for Software Components" in Chapter 23. His approach to software component measurement, especially for reuse, is reasonable and easy to implement. His measurement philosophy can be implemented immediately since it only requires what most organizations are already producing.

Don Reifer, in Chapter 24, "The Practical Reuse of Software Components," provides a guide for software component reuse advocates to prepare for successful adoption of CBSE. He describes the forms of resistance change agents are likely to experience. Don hopes to help change agents diminish resistance, or preferably, turn resistance into a successful pilot project.

Chapters 25 and 26, by Cornelius Ncube and Neil Maiden, and George Heineman, respectively, address the issues surrounding the decision of whether to buy a component or build it yourself. The chapter by Cornelius and Neil describes a requirements-based process for selecting the most appropriate component or components for a component consumer's infrastructure. In his chapter George identifies the consensus in the software engineering literature that buying components is preferable to building components. George also presents an argument that information technology organizations can benefit from developing software components. His goals are to identify weaknesses in CBSE and to determine the feasibility of the software component marketplace.

Chapter 27 "Software Component Project Management Processes," by Bill Councill is one of several chapters in the book likely to prove controversial. He argues that CBSE management should be engineering-based. With a dearth of engineers in software engineering, especially in project and product management roles, he proposes strict criteria for the selection of managers of component-based projects, especially since software project failures have been largely attributed to project management failures. In addition, Bill proposes a CBSE educational program conducted in conjunction with engineering departments as well as organizationally sanctioned certification of CBSE project and product managers.

In the highly descriptive Chapter 28 about why software component-based applications often fail, Elaine Weyuker presents the perspective of software testers and their experiences with software components. The author states her experience with reliable, reusable software components as follows:

> [I]t is doubtful that the reliability requirements mandated by many businesses will be met using CBD, and it is not clear that the cost of producing the software will be significantly cheaper than custom-designed software systems.

Because her experiences result from a different perspective from the other authors, Elaine's chapter is a "must read."

Hedley Apperly writes a chapter that describes the engineering properties of component management. In Chapter 29, "Configuration Management and Component Libraries," Hedley explains that a component management application that meets detailed criteria, as well as personnel who manage the tool according to well-defined processes, are needed. The basis of his process is the publish, manage, and consume paradigm. This chapter is required reading for those who believe they have a component management process based on an internally developed database. This chapter will certainly challenge any mistaken beliefs concerning nonengineering component management processes.

Software component maintenance is a topic that receives little attention in the CBSE literature. Mark Vigder wrote Chapter 30, "The Evolution, Maintenance, and Management of Component-Based Systems," at the editors' request. Mark argues that you must consider the costs of maintaining black-box components when you evaluate and select software components and again during the design of the component infrastructure. Describing maintenance as the longest and most expensive phase of the software development life cycle, Mark presents numerous methods to assure the appropriate selection of components for tailorability and evolution.

The chapters in this part will educate, reeducate, and continually remind us—we all need help to avoid management minefields—that CBSE management requires considerable and evolving knowledge. In addition, CBSE demands an open, questioning attitude to the nascent field, the will to challenge anecdotal "knowledge" and demand empirical studies, and the requirement to think and act like engineers, continuously searching for the one best way.

Chapter 23

Measurement and Metrics for Software Components

Jeffrey S. Poulin

23.1 Introduction

Creating quality products requires insight, control, and management throughout the component-based software engineering (CBSE) life cycle. You cannot manage a project without objective, quantitative information. Metrics provides that data and, when properly used, greatly enhance your control over the component development process and the quality of your product.

We all have some familiarity with metrics that can help determine if a reuse or CBSE project remains on time and on budget. Metrics can help estimate, plan, and identify areas to improve quality, reduce costs, enhance project management, and facilitate risk management. Ultimately, *you* must ensure the success of your CBSE project. In my experience a simple and useful set of metrics can help guide you to that success.

In this chapter I will outline some of the basic metrics you might consider for CBSE projects. I group them into areas to address issues in project management, quality, reuse, and technology—all important as part of a CBSE program. I'll also present some useful ranges for these metrics to help you assess how your project performs relative to previous, specific projects across a range of other industries.

23.2 Starting a CBSE Metrics Program

I usually work in large software development organizations with very qualified and talented supporting staffs. The staffs generally include experts in areas such as configuration management, schedule planning, development processes, and metrics. If you work in environments such as these you will find getting started with a metrics program for CBSE relatively easy. The metrics experts know what data the different tools can collect and will recommend 1) what to collect, and 2) how often to collect it. They know the key performance indicators (KPIs) that they need to report to higher management and, therefore, can immediately tell senior management what IT needs to provide to them. The experts can also provide an extensive amount of historical data that you can use to plan your project and, later, to demonstrate the benefits of CBSE as compared to non-CBSE development.

Even if you enjoy such a supporting infrastructure, you probably need some help. Surprisingly, even with metrics experts, project leaders and project managers (I use the roles interchangeably) have a huge amount of flexibility as to metrics that they use to manage their projects and can measure almost anything they want. It therefore pays to plan. I suggest considering the following when you tailor your metrics program.

1. *What do you hope to accomplish?* You want to use metrics to manage your project and provide feedback to everyone involved so they know exactly how they've done. Only you can decide what metrics you want to focus on. Whether or not we want to admit it, collecting measurement data affects how people behave. Although met-

rics should play a *descriptive* role rather than a prescriptive one, I have found that the metrics you select play an important part in reinforcing the processes you consider important.

2. *What data do you have readily available?* You want metrics to have a minimal impact on business. If used properly they can save huge amounts of money by helping you steer your team. However, metrics also represent a guaranteed resource drain because of the additional time that it takes to collect, collate, analyze, and present them. Take the time to find what data your team routinely collects and try to live within those bounds. In addition, many software-development tools automatically collect data and can generate reports for you. For example, if a test tool generates counts of problem reports by component and graphs the results for easy reference, will that meet your need without having to expend further effort?
3. *Keep it simple, stupid!* A metrics program will fall apart if people do not find the metrics simple, easy-to-understand, and meaningful. I use the "grandparent" test: a chart containing the metric should stand by itself so that an average grandparent with minimal training in mathematics should have little trouble understanding it. If you require five minutes of explanation and a degree in higher mathematics to get the point across, the metric probably won't mean much to your team. Likewise, you can only "focus" on perhaps 7±2 items at a time (Miller, 1956). Avoid trying to track too much; establish a minimal set of project KPIs and only request more data if you need to dig deeper into a specific area.
4. *Do a sanity check!* Metrics should yield consistent and repeatable values no matter who calculates them. Experts in metric theory have done a lot of analytical work on what makes a good metric and in the process have identified weaknesses ranging from how we collect raw data to how we combine that data in meaningless ways. In the end, you need to have metrics that you have faith in and can trust. You cannot trust data that comes from unrealistic assumptions or comes from sources that people can easily manipulate. Take a step back and ask yourself: "Do I feel comfortable betting my project on this information?"

Initiating a new CBSE program involves changes in organization, processes, and technology. It involves instituting a new way of doing business and requires some innovative thinking to get that business started and keep it on track. I recommend beginning with a few simple metrics or even a pilot project to help transition the organization in a nonthreatening and low-risk way. The pilot leads with new CBSE processes and then provides measures and metrics to demonstrate the benefits of CBSE. An excellent discussion on how to make this transition to a reuse-based component architecture and maintain it in a real-world development organization appears in the book by Jacobson, Griss, and Jonsson (1997).

23.2.1 Measurement for CBSE

Many descriptions of metrics programs differentiate between *measures* and *metrics*. Measures typically come from directly observable data, such as something you can count (for example, number of defects in Component A). A metric typically results from combining several measures (for example, average cost to develop a reusable component relative to normal development costs). In this chapter I will try to remain faithful to these definitions although I tend to use the terms interchangeably in everyday conversation.

23.2.2 How Should I Size My Components?

You can determine the size of your software many ways. Most people using noncommented source lines of code (SLOC). Other methods include using function points (FPs), total number of classes, total number of methods, or total number of components. Despite their shortcomings I highly favor the use of SLOC for the same reasons why almost everyone uses them. These reasons include the universality of their use, the ease of automatically counting them, and the fact that numerous studies have found that SLOC provide the most reliable indicator of overall effort on a software project ([Albrecht and Gaffney, 1983] [Boehm, 1987] [Tausworthe, 1992]).

For this chapter I will use SLOC in all text and examples. I will not define SLOC here but I roughly consider them as a count of noncommented "semicolons" in most popular programming languages. However, the points in this chapter do not depend in any way upon using SLOC as a unit. If you prefer, substitute FPs or any other unit that you choose because the principles remain the same.

23.2.3 How Detailed Should I Get?

The granularity of the data you collect will ultimately determine the accuracy of your metrics. If you collect effort in labor-months rather than labor hours you lose a huge amount of detail if you want to examine activities that take less than a month to do (and most CBSE activities do!). Likewise, if you size your effort by component rather than SLOC, you cannot differentiate between the effort and cost to build a small component versus a large, complex one.

The tools you use will help make your decision as to the level of detail that you collect. For example, if you don't have a time card system then you must decide how often you want your valuable developers sitting around counting up how many hours they spent on a particular component. I recommend collecting most data on a weekly basis. For effort, collect labor in hours. Attribute each hour to a component or equivalent activity so you can track where you spend your money. Track the size of components in SLOC, FPs, or other equivalent measures.

With this information tallied in a time card system or simple database, you have the ability to rearrange the information and generate reports in many ways. For example, you can calculate the labor expended by department or by phase of the software lifecycle. Since components form the core of component-based development (CBD), most CBSE projects will find collecting weekly data on each component sufficient.

23.2.4 How Often Should I Measure?

Frequency of measurement depends on several factors such as the size and overall duration of the project. For software development efforts involving less than 50 developers and development cycles of less than a year, I recommend tracking project KPIs on a weekly basis. I would generate monthly summaries of the weekly reports for presentation to higher-level management. The review of the measurement data with analysis should take about an hour, so it is best to plan it as a recurring meeting to ensure that the appropriate people attend. Meetings that occur more often than every week are unnecessary.

For larger projects you can review the project metrics less frequently, but I would not recommend doing so less than every two weeks. You will want to present most of your metrics as graphs so that you can easily see where you stand relative to the plan. Collecting metrics at regular intervals gives you a snapshot of the current state of your project with estimates of work remaining and potential areas of concern. Furthermore, data trends over time often give you a better indication of potential problems than snapshot values because a trend will show if a deviation appears to get worse, better, or remain constant relative to your baseline. A lot can happen in two weeks of software development, and if it takes three data points to recognize a trend towards trouble, then you have already dug a hole six weeks deep.

23.2.5 What Should I Measure?

Having discussed how detailed and how often to collect data, I will now introduce basic data elements to measure. As a starting point, I recommend the following.

1. *Schedule (planned vs. actual)*—Almost every project tracks schedule progress using a commercial scheduling tool. Each week you should update your estimated progress as milestones achieved or the ratio of work done compared to the work planned. You might also create a status of your schedule using standard earned-value reporting, such as the value of work completed compared to the budgeted cost of work scheduled. Space limitations here prevent a detailed discussion of schedule and earned-value reporting, but they make good topics of study for future project managers (Smith and Steadman, 1999).
2. *Source instructions per component*—Use your code counting tool to list the total SLOC per component.
3. *Labor hours*—I use this measure rather than staff assigned to the project because we really want to know about the work done, not the number of people working. Specifically, we need to know the effort expended per component. Note that collecting this data requires some kind of time reporting system. Lacking that, you will need a reasonable way to track what people work on, such as a spreadsheet template that you can easily distribute and collect.
4. *Classification of the component*—Classify each component in the product as
   - New code

- Changed code
- Built for reuse
- Reused code

You may want to add other categories. You will use this data to calculate the amount of reuse in a component as well as the relative costs to write reusable components, write new components, and to reuse components.

5. *Cost*—Yes, the bottom line. This information needs to link to the information in the time recording system so you can correlate time devoted to cost. You will want to generate data, such as the cost per component and the cost to develop a line of code. As a point of comparison, average software development costs fall in the range of $70-100/SLOC and about $1000/FP.
6. *Change Requests (CRs)*—Keep a count of CRs by component. This indicates the volatility of your component designs as well as the level of work you have in the pipeline.
7. *Defects*—Maintain a count of defects discovered throughout the life cycle. You will want a count of each type of defect by component (see the "Severity of Defects" sidebar for a description of how to classify defects by severity). You will use this information to indicate the quality levels of components and determine if you can safely ship a quality, trustworthy product. You can also use this data in many ways, for example, to analyze where in the life cycle you find the most defects and how much it costs to fix them.

There are several technical measurements as well.

1. *Code and design*—Many options and theories exist for measuring the quality of code and designs. We will discuss many of these potential measures below.
2. *Response time and/or Throughput*—Most metrics programs advocate tracking computer resource utilization such as CPU use, main memory use, and disk use. I prefer to track something of prime importance to customers: how fast does the system run? Whether you build embedded systems or graphical user interfaces, you must meet your performance constraints. If you cannot then you will need to investigate items such as CPU and memory utilization to identify your problem.

Severity of Defects

Assigning a severity type to defects helps prioritize the work of the development and software support teams. Table 23-1 demonstrates each type of defect associated with it, as well as a Service Level Agreement (SLA) that describes the time within which you promise to fix the problem. Obviously, the more critical errors get rapid attention. Typical customer acceptance standards for commercial software development will state that a release may have no known severity 1 or severity 2 defects in a product prior to General Availability. Consequently, you likely want your team to generate a graph each week that shows the status of severity 1 and 2 defects.

Table 23-1: *Defect Types and Associated Service Level Agreements*

Type	Description	SLA
1	Business-critical features absent or do not function; program may crash.	Fix within 4-24 hours
2	Business-critical features function most of the time. No work-around exists.	Fix within 1 week
3	Noncritical features absent or do not function. Work-arounds exist.	Fix within 2 weeks
4	Inconsequential function may not work as expected, typos in the documentation, etc.	Fix for next software release

These data should provide a good performance basis for any CBSE program. However, in past projects I have established a rule that if we did not find a piece of information useful to managing or improving our process, then we probably should not spend the time and money to track the metric. I think this guideline would serve any project well when reviewing its particular data requirements.

23.3 Metrics for CBSE

Now that we have some data to work with we will look at metrics in various areas that may form candidate KPIs for your projects.

23.3.1 Productivity

Productivity simply represents the amount of product delivered per unit time. Industry standards for productivity range from 200-500 SLOC per labor month, with a huge variation in these values. More importantly, the high levels of reuse in CBSE and product-line development can lead to 40-400% higher levels of productivity. Calculate your productivity metric by the *total development hours for the project/ total lines of code (SLOC) contained in the components that make up the product.* You can compare your CBSE data to baseline productivity numbers for your organization to show how many more lines of code your product contains compared to the amount of effort required to deliver them. By reusing large numbers of prebuilt components, this metric should indicate a very favorable argument for CBSE.

23.3.2 Quality

Quality improvement provides one of the strongest arguments for CBSE and high levels of reuse: numerous projects claim 10x higher quality (as measured by defect density) in reused components. This order of magnitude difference results from more thorough initial testing of components built for reuse as well as the enormous amount of field-testing that the components receive by virtue of appearing in many different contexts.

Calculate quality data from the types of defects found in each component. Typically you will only care about the most severe Type 1 and 2 defects. Figure 23-1 depicts the total defects for a project or component over time; this would make a good summary to present to upper level management. The lines will diverge rapidly when you begin testing and your team discovers errors faster than they can fix them. Ideally, the lines will converge by the delivery date for your product. You may want to track several variations of this chart, especially breaking down the defects by component to show where your development problems lie. You may also want to calculate density (defects per SLOC) as a normalized way of showing relative quality across components (and thereby not penalize large components for having more defects than small components).

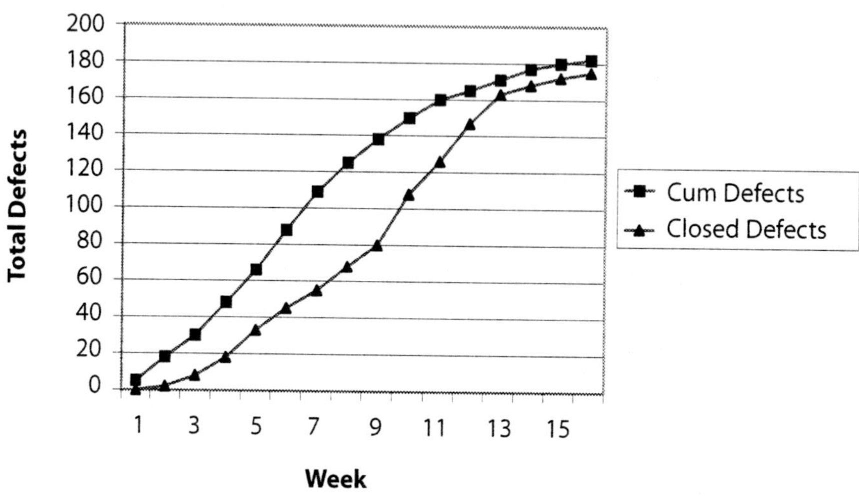

Figure 23-1: *Tracking total defects for a project or component.*

23.3.3 Product Stability

In traditional software development the customer and developers write down and agree to a set of functional requirements prior to any work beginning on the actual product implementation. Once the two parties agree to the requirements the component or reuse project team can estimate the costs of development and obtain permission from the customer to proceed to implement the product for the agreed-upon price. If the customer desires any changes to the requirements the customer will have to submit a formal Change Request (CR), for which the development team would provide a cost and schedule estimate to implement. If the customer agreed to the increased fee and schedule change the development team would make the requested change.

In this traditional environment the total number of product and component requirements gives a good indication of the overall complexity of the project. During implementation I recommend that you track the total number of open CRs and the total number of requirements (which typically grows as the customer and development team accept and agree to implement CRs). Warning signs of product instability occur when the total number of requirements plus CRs exceeds 5-10% of the baseline number of requirements. This works well when working from a firm requirements baseline.

However, the speed of modern software development and especially that of typical CBSE projects makes this approach to requirements management increasingly ridiculous. Both parties spend an inordinate amount of time up front trying to agree upon a requirements baseline, and then they spend an inordinate amount of time throughout the project estimating and arguing over the cost and timing of CRs. For this reason many current software development projects have adopted some version of iterative development. In iterative development the development team works to develop an initial version of the software from a vague functional description or minimal set of high-level requirements. The team then works closely with the customer to understand, price, implement CRs, and rapidly produce new releases of the initial product. In this environment I use *Open CRs* as the metric of choice for tracking product volatility, as demonstrated in Figure 23-2.

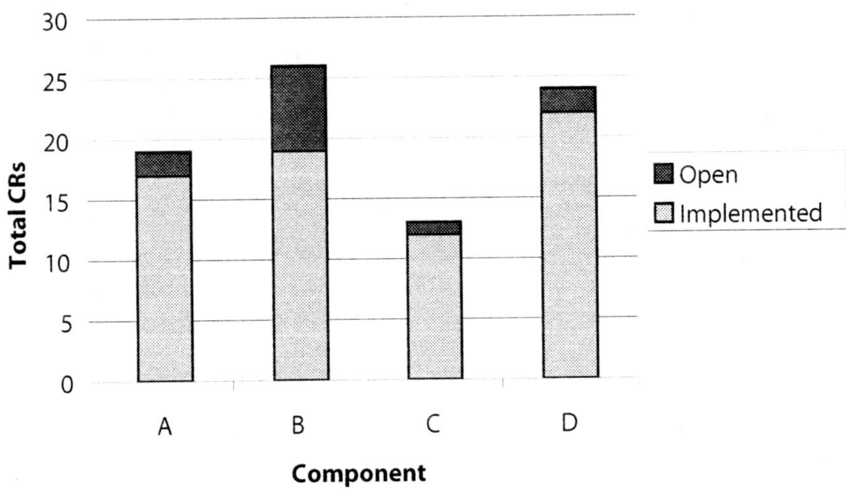

Figure 23-2: *Tracking product volatility by component.*

The chart illustrates a snapshot of how four components compare relative to the amount of function that they have implemented and the amount of function that they still need to implement. Component C is the most cohesive component due to its small number of functions and lack of changes pending. However, Component B could become a problem due to the large number of functions assigned to it and the large number of unimplemented changes pending. Incidentally, Open CRs also gives you a good indication of work that you have in the pipeline and will prove handy when laying out your future staffing requirements and schedule.

23.3.4 Reuse

On a CBSE project you look to reuse metrics to really tell you two things: first, how much reuse has your team done, and second, how much has the team saved by reuse? I call the first type of metric *measures of reuse level*, and I claim that *percent reuse* reigns as the *de facto* industry standard. It simply states what percentage of your product came from unmodified use of components created and maintained by someone else. While that appears to be exceptionally easy to visualize, in practice nothing could be more difficult to measure. If the project addresses the numerous pitfalls involved in measuring reuse described in Poulin (1997), I call this important reuse level metric *Reuse%*. Calculate Reuse% simply as *Reused Lines of Code/Total Lines of Code.* Figure 23-3 shows an example reuse level chart for a series of products in a product-line.

Notice that sometimes the reuse level declines slightly as developers add new code to a product but do not incorporate more reusable components—a common occurrence. Indications of successful CBSE design and product-line planning (refer to Chapter 22 on Product-Line Architectures) occur when the reuse levels in subsequent products and releases of products increase as those products make use of reusable components developed early in the CBSE life cycle.

The second type of reuse metric describes the costs and cost benefits of reuse. Experienced metrics analysts tend to ask these questions from the viewpoint of both the *consumer* of reusable components (the project doing the reusing) and the *producer* of the components (the project building the reusable components). Therefore, the metrics you will want to track involve the relative cost of reusing (RCR) and the

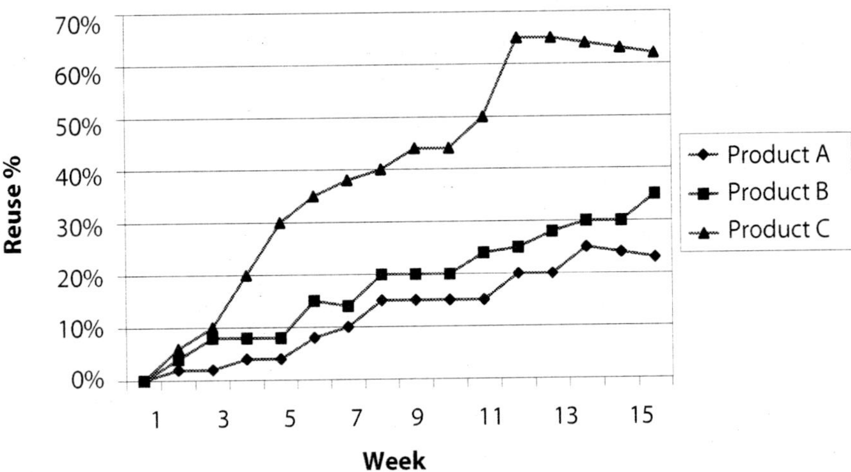

Figure 23-3: *Tracking the levels of reuse in your products.*

relative cost of writing for reuse (RCWR). These two numbers lie at the heart of any business case that you develop to show the benefits of CBSE, reuse, and product-line development. RCR represents the fraction of the effort it takes to reuse a component (without modification) as compared to what it would have cost to write a new component. For example, an RCR of 0.2 means that reusing a component costs only 20% of writing an equivalent component. RCWR represents the additional work needed to write a reusable component. For example, an RCWR of 1.5 means that it takes 50% more effort to design, code, test, and document a reusable component. Although RCR and RCWR depend on many factors, they typically lie close to 0.2 and 1.5, respectively. Fortunately, you can calculate both from the cost data that you already have and then you can use these metrics to build a CBSE business case as described in Chapter 5 of this book and sources such as Lim (1998).

23.3.5 Design and Coding

Design and coding metrics examine low-level features of component design and indicate how components might perform. These technical metrics allow you to identify high-risk components early in the life cycle and therefore significantly reduce the cost of producing a high-quality product. They require a bit more training to understand and use effectively but serve an important role in your metrics program.

To collect and analyze design and code metrics it really helps to purchase a commercial tool specialized for this area. These tools generally require little effort to use and will quickly tell you all the commonly used metrics such as size (in SLOC), depth of inheritance tree, complexity, coupling, and cohesion, among other nontrivial metrics. Of course, each tool implements slightly different metrics; for example, applications that specialize in object-oriented (OO) analysis might implement the popular design metrics introduced by Chidamber and Kemerer (1991): weighted methods per class, depth of inheritance tree, number of children, and coupling among objects, among other metrics.

I personally prefer to select just a few of the more traditional indicators. Traditional measures of good design include keeping the size of individual functions and procedures at less than 100 SLOC. Any larger SLOC leads to complex, hard-to-maintain components. Likewise, components with McCabe (Cyclomatic) Complexity metrics (McCabe, 1976) greater than 10 or Halstead Volume metrics (Halstead, 1977) greater than 30 may exhibit potential problems with errors and maintainability. The "Design Metrics Rules of Thumb" sidebar contains some excellent guidelines adapted from the experiences of Mark Lorenz and described in his book on OO software development (Lorenz, 1993).

I recommend talking with the developers on a regular basis about which components need attention. Not surprisingly, I have found that despite the huge amount of study that goes into finding statistically significant ways to identify risky components, I have scored nearly 100% by going with what developers tell me. Of course, good developers will already have initiated actions to address the areas they identify. You should verify this and stand prepared to extend additional resources in schedule, labor, and testing if necessary to help the developers eliminate this risk. You might also employ other techniques described elsewhere in this book, such as design reviews and inspections, to improve the overall quality of your product and to share experience and knowledge across your component teams.

Design Metrics Rules of Thumb

1. CBSE projects developing with OO languages could benefit from the following guidelines on how to measure the quality of their designs. This advice extends to other languages as well, and most commercial code analysis tools can easily generate these values for your project.
2. *Average Method Size*—should be less than eight SLOC for Smalltalk and 24 SLOC for C++ and Java. Bigger indicates design problems.
3. *Average Number of Methods per Class*—should be less than 20. More indicates too much responsibility in the class.
4. *Average Number of Instance Variables*—should be less than 6. More indicates too many attributes assigned to the class.
5. *Depth of Class Hierarchy*—should be less than six. Deeper leads to testing and maintenance difficulties.
6. *Number of Subsystem-to-Subsystem Relationships*—should be less than the number of class-to-class relationships (low coupling).
7. *Number of Class-to-Class Relationships Within a Subsystem*—should be high (high cohesion).
8. *Number of Comment Lines*—all code should have in-line documentation that describes the function of the component, who wrote it, change history, etc., according to your projects development standards.

23.3.6 Performance

Your customer always has performance at the top of the list of critical success factors, and will immediately notice when the system runs slower than anticipated! For all systems that have a direct human machine interface (for example, a screen with buttons on it) or an indirect interface (something that provides a service, such as database lookup), you must track *response time*. Allocate acceptable response times (latencies) to subsystems early in the project and use this metric to track against goals. I recommend having the integration and test teams collect this data.

You may also need to track another performance metric that relates to response time: *throughput*. Throughput usually gives the true picture of performance for transaction-bound systems. In these systems, we may have latency concerns over how long it takes to process an individual transaction, but your customer and you only care if the pipeline of all transactions continues to flow. This holds especially true for client/server systems and in systems that use parallel processing to speed throughput. Such systems might process two transactions at the same time, thereby having the same response time as a uni-processor system but twice the throughput.

In serial processing environments (dictated by hardware or software), latency equals one over throughput. Unfortunately, without production systems or simulators to provide adequate load, it may prove very difficult to truly test throughput. In these cases I have always successfully used latency as a surrogate metric for throughput. For non-I/O bound systems it follows that if you can meet a serial response time then you should have no trouble obtaining the necessary throughput given multiprocessing.

23.4 How to Use the Metrics

Metrics should help you achieve your primary goals of delivering your component-based project on time, on budget, and so that it performs the intended function in a quality way. During the project your metrics should not only realistically reflect the status of your project, but also help you plan for unforeseen and upcoming activities. In addition, by choosing what to measure you have the ability to influence what your team considers important and hence influence what the team does. I have found, for example, that measuring reuse levels on a project encourages developers to reuse components. Reviewing the metrics on a weekly basis also gives your team important feedback on their progress (or lack of progress) because it gives them a sense of accomplishment and mission.

As part of that feedback you will want to compare your progress against industry standards and your plan. For comparison against industry standards you will need *benchmarks* that may have appeared in professional journals, books, and in most metrics tools. Benchmarks provide a useful way of seeing how your methods and processes stack up in the industry. In short, if you can't deliver your product within the schedule, quality, and cost standards claimed by your competitors, then how can you expect to beat them in the market? Of course, you have to consider the sources of your benchmark data, and may have to take some of your competitors' claims with a bit of salt. Don Reifer does a great job of describing the uses of benchmarks in his book (Reifer, 1997a).

While comparing to industry benchmarks provides a useful comparison, you really need to know if your project performs according to your plan, or the *baseline* that you established. The baseline plan includes the schedule, resource estimates, and technical measures that tell you if you will finish on time, within budget, and whether the product will function as expected. The larger the project the more you need metrics because of the visibility they give your project, control over what you develop, and warning signs about potential problems so you can fix them before they become critical.

I traditionally use metrics to help build a business case to show the worth of an initiative such as CBSE. The data you collect can demonstrate that the investments in product-line architectures and component-based development pay off quickly and handsomely. Only metrics can give you the quantitative and objective data that you need to assess where you stand and to show the value CBSE has to your organization.

23.5 Conclusion

Implementing a metrics program for CBD requires a combination of applying what resources already exist and common sense. First, use existing data and tool support as much as possible. Provide spreadsheet templates if necessary to make data collection easier and make the metrics as unobtrusive as possible. Second, if you don't find a metric useful for managing your project or improving your process, don't use it. Collecting data for the sake of tradition does not make business sense. Choose the metrics that will help you lead your software component-based project to a successful conclusion.

Most metrics programs start with a few simple metrics or a pilot project to test the selected procedures and tools and to show success on a limited basis. Once complete the metrics program can spread into general use. However, it will continue to require support from dedicated resources to educate, train, and help collect and analyze the data. Choosing a simple set of easily understood metrics will aid in their acceptance.

In this chapter I have outlined some steps to take when developing a component-based metrics program. I have also described different areas in which to collect measurement data to give insight into the project schedule, cost, and technical progress. By comparing your data against industry benchmarks or against historical baselines from your organization, you can see how your project compares both in the large and in the small. You can then take that objective information and develop a winning business case that demonstrates the overwhelming benefits available in a component-based metrics program.

Chapter 24

Implementing a Practical Reuse Program for Software Components

Donald J. Reifer

24.1 Introduction

The current transition to the use of software components is a technologically evolutionary phenomenon. This movement follows the push made for software reuse in the early part of this decade (Reifer, 1997a). In my opinion systems will no longer be built as custom, one-of-a-kind solutions. Instead, some producers are building applications and open distributed processing systems from existing parts using product-line architectures, reusable or off-the-shelf software components, and standards-based component models. This move builds upon the experiences of early adopters in the software reuse field to cut costs and speed products to market (Poulin, 1997).

However, those making the transition to the use of software components have found that implementing change is not an easy task. In addition to dealing with several tricky technical issues, *change agents*—those committed to establishing new technologies within their organizations—must cope with the psychological aspects of change and several severe managerial obstacles that often get in the way of progress. The purpose of this chapter is to identify these obstacles and discuss what those in charge of the change can do to avoid the barriers. The proposed techniques build on those proven successful for reuse. In order to develop success-oriented, component-based reuse plans, alternatives are considered along with their potential organizational, political, and process consequences.

24.2 Barriers to Change

The top nine obstacles that I have observed when implementing software reuse adoption are summarized in Table 24-1. Each of these factors is briefly explained in the following subparagraphs under the technical, managerial, and cultural/psychological headings.

Table 24-1: *Barriers to Change*

Technical	Managerial	Cultural/ Psychological
• Structure Mismatch • Steep Learning Curves	• Infrastructure Clash • Turf Battles • Never Enough Time and Money (to do things right)	• Apathy • Not Invented Here (NIH) Syndrome • Fear of the Unknown • Ivory Towerism

24.2.1 Technical

Structure Mismatch—Most software development organizations (SDOs) have embraced paradigms, methods, and tools that do not promote the use of software components. Instead of attempting to build systems using collections of reusable components, many SDOs assume everything must be designed and developed anew. They argue that their user requirements drive them towards such unique solutions. Incorporating component concepts into such methods is difficult because the SDOs do not provide support for the types of trade-offs needed to assess the performance impacts of components. In addition, component-based development (CBD) is further complicated by the lack of tools needed to build systems using templates, software component models, software component infrastructures, and building block libraries. To address the mismatches between routine software development and CBD, guidelines need to be developed and CBD tools acquired. In addition, examples need to be developed to serve as prototypes of what is expected when the modified paradigms, methods, and tools are used to generate products.

Steep Learning Curves—Because of the conceptual mismatches severe learning curves are involved. Those trying to exploit the use of components in software systems often have to open their minds to embrace new ways of doing business. This requires organizations to provide considerable training and mentoring. Experience in the software reuse field (Lim, 1998) suggests that it can take 12-18 months to become proficient with the new development technology and software engineering process. To shorten timeframes and make schedules compatible with their product timelines, many organizations use just-in-time (JIT) training concepts and external experts to speed the transition. Change agents should inform senior managers that new component-based methods and their associated tools represent a large risk to those projects with schedules on critical paths. I recommend that projects on critical paths should not be considered candidates for technology insertion; implementation of new technologies such as software components and strategic reuse could jeopardize the ability to deliver. The integration of training and mentoring on smaller, less mission-critical CBD and reuse projects is considerably less risky.

24.2.2 Managerial

Infrastructure Clash—Most large and defense-related software organizations have also established a software management infrastructure consisting of Capability Maturity Model (CMM)-compatible processes, gating criteria, and decision rules (Paulk et al., 1995). The organizational structures, operational concepts, and reward systems in place typically were designed using this foundation. This infrastructure often has to be changed to facilitate introduction of technology such as software components. *New technology introductions tend to be major distractions because they impact the manner in which decisions are made and work is accomplished.* In addition, turmoil increases while organizational or reward system changes are implemented. Careful transition is needed in order to succeed in such a cultural change. Most small SDOs, which comprise 99% of the market, have not used, and many do not intend to use, the CMM. Yet despite the implementation of a full-scale software process, anecdotal reports indicate that changes in the organization, work distractions, and organizational turmoil are just as likely to occur.

Turf Battles—Turf battles often occur when responsibilities (and budgets) for components are assigned. As organizations compete for tasking, budget, and power, animosities may be created. Acrimony can linger after the battle appears settled. Many project managers have experienced retribution by those who harbor bad feelings because of past turf battle losses. Consequently, care must be taken to ensure that there is consensus over who wins the task of inserting components into the organization. Getting everyone to buy into the decision is essential or else lingering hostilities will impede the establishment of a CBD program.

Never Enough Time and Money (to do things right)—Most importantly, adequate resources (time, talent, people, dollars) need to be made available. Otherwise, a strong possibility exists that whomever senior management offers the authority and responsibility for implementing CBD will fail to deploy the technology throughout the organization. Schedule expectations need to be set and the proper mix of resources need to be made available for the realization of component technology to succeed. Senior management must be informed that immediate results are exceptionally unlikely. Investments need to be made and budgets appropriated based upon small, prototypical projects, that should be budgeted and launched before any large-scale project.

24.2.3 Cultural/Psychological

Apathy—"Why change when nothing is broken?" is a question change agents are bound to hear. As a proponent of CBD and software reuse you can counter this response by building both a technical and business case for components and handling the psychological issues associated with change. A well-planned, published business plan can help you convince critics that it makes sense to change and that CBSE and strategic reuse is in everyone's best interests. Otherwise, critics—generally those most comfortable with the status quo—will fight everything you do.

Not Invented Here (NIH) Syndrome—"Just because it works elsewhere does not mean it will work here," is the next comment software component advocates are likely to hear. I have heard it frequently myself. You can use success stories somewhat to counter this criticism. A recommendation for managers to visit the site of a successful software component project is in order. What works even more effectively are positive results on a pilot project. The theme, "See, components work here too" can be used to convince skeptics that the technology works in practice, especially when the pilot project is similar to projects with which critics are familiar.

Fear of the Unknown—"Why should we institute change now?" is the next question component and reuse advocates must address. You must convince senior and middle management, as well as key designers and developers that the organization is ready for technological transformation and that the most effective change is to implement CBD and reuse. You must persuade those in charge that the technical and business cases are sound, your plans are solid, upper management support is unwavering, and the effort has a high probability of success. Otherwise, those who tend to fear the unknown—and don't underestimate their numbers—might wonder why they should even consider the "new" technology.

Ivory Towerism—Because you are dealing with emerging technologies, many practitioners will argue that it might be premature to try to use something like components now. What researchers discuss does not always work in practice they will argue. Minimal tools, training, and support will be identified as pressing issues. Many academically-inclined critics will argue that immature technology drains resources from other projects. You can counter these arguments by providing proof that the technology has been successfully implemented at a variety of large and small development organizations. It would be wise to initiate phone calls to the project managers or software component advocates at some of the companies that have implemented CBD and CBSE and ask if you may use them as references within your own organization. Generally, as a change agent you will find that successful new technology programs are willing to help other companies implement the technology.

24.3 Addressing the Challenge

Although there are known techniques that address these barriers (Moore, 1991), dealing with the issues that surround change is extremely difficult. Because most organizations demand a compelling reason for change, I will offer equally convincing reasons to recommend the transition to CBD and CBSE, that is, if your organization is prepared to implement component-based technology. The opportunity for change agents is to stimulate project managers to make the decision to adopt the technology. However, this is not an easy feat. Project managers are by their very nature conservative. My experience is that they view technology change as a risk they would rather avoid than embrace. Under such circumstances, reason and sound business cases do not always overcome management's reluctance to alter how they conduct their business.

To succeed, component-based software engineers or other change agents need to create a groundswell for technological revolution. Even then, getting project managers to do things differently is not easy. Having support at both the top and bottom of the organization is a prerequisite for making a change. Having a sound set of technical and business reasons for making the change is also essential. Finally, to improve your chances of success you will need to cultivate champions at the top and get buy-in from the opinion leaders at the project team level of SDO.

Based upon experience in the reuse field, the five most promising strategies that you can use to stimulate middle management to embrace CBD are discussed in the following subparagraphs.

Pull-Push—A champion agitates for change and gets upper management to commit to an agreed-upon plan of action. The champion provides resources, understanding, and support to entice those in the middle to embrace something new. It is my experience that middle managers actively resist change. They try to resist the pressures and enlist those at the project team level to champion their cause. When project team members support the champion, they can put pressure on those in the middle to make the desired transition. This tactic is sometime called a visionary strategy because the champion, not the middle manager, acts as the force for the change.

Push-Pull—Support for change comes from the top and bottom at the same time. Those in the middle must battle both extremes as they try to resist change at all costs primarily because they view such change as a threat to their ability to deliver. Senior management and the project team wear the middle managers down in their quest for improvement. This tactic is sometimes called the "crunch" strategy because those in the middle feel the pressure as they are pushed and pulled at the same time. It is the most difficult tactic to pull off because the middle is where the operational decisions are made in most organizations. Nobody at any level in the organization wants the blame for putting a project at risk.

Rolling Wave—This approach feeds experience gained with the technology during one spiral into the next. It spawns skills that are then used during the next spiral to reduce learning curves and implement a "do a little, learn a lot" philosophy. The staff from one spiral often disseminates the knowledge and excitement to other areas. The rolling wave is an evolutionary approach that relies on timing to overcome the barriers that often challenge more revolutionary approaches. Revolutionary approaches generally rely on change agents to break down the resistance in the middle and develop champions. The rolling wave is an incremental strategy in which results are staged to make progress visible. The approach relies on success to foster further success. However, the tactic often takes years to unfold. As a result, those wanting immediate results may grow impatient and rely on other means to achieve their goals.

Win Small, Win Big—This tactic revolves around the belief that a large number of small successes can be considered a large success. To gain momentum and support a large number of highly visible, practical, low-risk activities are accomplished as quickly as possible. The perception of success is synonymous with real success in most people's minds. High visibility and the perception of winning break down barriers and overcome resistance. While this strategy buys time, the change has to be finely planned and tightly managed to ensure that you deliver what you promised and maintain the perception that you are a winner.

Big Bang—This is a more revolutionary tactic that tries to introduce change quickly before resistance can be mounted. The organization commits to making the shift and absorbing the budget and schedule as it implements the changes it deems necessary to either catch up or gain the upper hand on the competition. Those who resist change are removed from any access or position relevant to the CBD project. Action dominates, especially when the consequences involved are severe.

An outsider is typically brought in to act as the ax man. Radical changes are possible because past friendships, relationships, and loyalties do not enter into decisions. Decisions are made based upon merit alone, especially when change is the modus operandi. However, to achieve success the ax man must be empowered by those in senior management to make radical changes even when this makes the newly constituted CBD and CBSE project teams, as well as employees outside the teams, angry. In addition, the ax man has to gain the confidence of key individuals and the support of the project teams.

24.3.1 Developing a CBD Project Plan

After selecting a strategy you need to develop a CBD project plan. This plan will outline your tactics, identify pilot projects, define the tasks to be performed and their related products and schedules, identify the players and their roles, discuss communication mechanisms, summarize how progress will be assessed and reported, define measures of success and identify how you will manage risk. Implementation of this plan is influenced by many factors. Chief among these are

- The perceived need for change and the related technical and business cases
- The speed in which the change must be accomplished
- The readiness of the organization to make the change
- The degree of management commitment to the change and their involvement
- The availability of necessary talent and key personnel
- The cost of change in terms of dollars and impact on current projects
- The degree of acceptance and support for change by those impacted by it

Several pragmatic efforts were undertaken by change agents and their organizations to develop models for software reuse to help determine the readiness of organizations to attempt this transition. For example, the Software Productivity Consortium devised a reuse adoption model and related assessment scheme (SPC, 1992). The assessment scheme revolved around a set of critical success factors that were organized into the following four groupings.

- Application development factors
- Asset development factors
- Management factors
- Process and technology factors

The consortium also published a series of more technical guidebooks aimed at helping member firms insert a reuse-based synthesis method into their operations (SPC, 1993). The CARDS (Comprehensive Approach to Reusable Defense Software) took this concept one step further when they developed their reuse readiness and technology transfer framework and the related reuse success stories (DSD Labs, 1996) under DoD Software Reuse Initiative sponsorship.

This modeling work appears to be directly applicable to components. The five principal factors that were used to determine readiness in both of these models included the following.

- Whether or not there was a recognized need for the technology
- The degree of risk associated with implementing the strategies
- The organization's level of process maturity (Paulk, et al., 1995)
- Whether or not the technology was fit for use without major modifications
- The return on investment, both short and long-term, associated with the technology change

Independent of the strategy chosen, a detailed plan of action and milestones are needed to initiate the transition. Such a plan can be organized using a Work Breakdown Structure (WBS). Tasks in the WBS are defined in an associated WBS Dictionary. The recommended WBS is based upon the following underlying premises.

- The adoption life cycle is comprised of two distinct phases: startup and technology dissemination
- Establishing the management infrastructure associated with both phases is accomplished in parallel with technology adoption
- A pilot project is used to drive the adoption of the technology and demonstrate the viability of the technical and business case used for justification

Because these three assumptions are important, they deserve a brief explanation. Dividing the life cycle into two phases allows you to staff your startup activities differently. Potential team members need to be trained and mentored as skills in the new technology are developed. Teams need to be developed as the product-line infrastructure is solidified and components are acquired and programmed to populate the infrastructure and the component repository. This set of activities is aimed at developing the infrastructure that will be available through the component repository operationally after the team determines what works and what doesn't for the organization.

Treating the development of infrastructure as a separate set of tasks is also significant. The reason for this is simple. Most organizations treat the costs associated with infrastructure development as a capital or research and development expense. They do this because they do not want to penalize pilot projects with software development's return on investments. For example, a single project should not be expected to pay for the time and effort needed to insert component-based processes and develop associated best practices. However, project budgets should be expected to pay for tailoring these processes and developing the systematic procedures needed to put the best practices into action within the context of the project's charter.

Finally, using a pilot project to demonstrate the value added from a well-designed and deployed infrastructure is highly encouraged. Pilot projects force senior managers, middle-level managers, and technologists to determine how to take the technology and use it in concert with the organization's processes under real budget, schedule, and technical constraints.

24.4 Start-up Case Study

The following case study was created to communicate the lessons the reuse community has learned to help you speed the insertion of component technology into your organization. This case combines a series of my experiences. The actual name of the organization is not used to protect the innocent. This case reinforces many of the points made and startup guidelines provided in previous sections.

A large SDO recently embarked on developing a new product-line at the insistence of their investors. They were trying to penetrate the network security marketplace with a full line of products ranging from simple scanners to complicated intrusion detection and recovery packages. This market was selected because it built on their core competency in distributed operating systems and databases. The company has about 750 professional employees, of which 250 are in software engineering. The software engineering workforce was young, dedicated, and very competent. Everyone was excited about the decision to pursue a new product-line.

There was a lot of pressure on management to get the products to market quickly. Luckily, the new vice president of software engineering anticipated the go-ahead for the project and had a dedicated team develop a reference component model for the product-line during the prior six months. The component model made heavy use of infrastructures and reusable components. The team not only recommended the component model and infrastructures, it identified the specific object-oriented methods and tools that should be used to create the initial products that would form the basis of the product-line.

The recently appointed product-line manager formed an integrated product team (IPT) to develop a plan of action and milestones for product development. Members of the IPT included the product-line manager and project managers for the first three products to be built. They brainstormed a plan of attack using the recommendations of the design team as the basis.

Unfortunately, the product-line manager did not presell upper management on the plan. When the executive staff called a product-line meeting and heard the cost and schedule requirements for the project, the president told the product-line manager, "There is no way that we can put that many people to work for three years without getting some return by entering the market." The product-line manager argued that the selected team needed the time and staff to do things right. The resulting uproar was settled when the vice president of marketing stepped in and offered the following three suggestions.

1. Why don't you consider developing the scanner as the first project? Use this product to develop the processes and skills prior to starting the other two projects. Also, this would enable us to focus our resources on an initial product that we could bring to market to derive income as we developed the other two more complicated products later.
2. Why don't you enlist the support of the software process group to work the process issues? Couldn't they augment the process in parallel with the product development activities? Wouldn't this cut down the cost and months off the schedule?
3. Why not consider partnering with the component producers you have identified and ask them to make the modifications we need? This could reduce cost and time to market.

The product-line manager took these suggestions gladly. She understood that the marketing vice president was trying to help counter criticism. She quickly realized that she had come to the meeting unprepared to discuss the management and marketing issues. She asked if upper management would continue to provide advice and direction as members of a steering group. The product-line manager asked to brief the executives with a more detailed plan in a week.

The next week was hectic. Many meetings were held to pull plans together and generate cost and schedule estimates. The IPT used their internal processes and guidelines to prepare their plan of actions and milestones. The product-line manager investigated potential risks, prioritized them based upon their potential impact, and devised a risk-mitigation plan. She looked for opportunities to share and off-load costs and discussed joint investments with potential partners. In addition, the product-line manager met with key account representatives to make sure that their schedules did not impact on-going operations and were compatible with marketplace needs. She also held private meetings with each of the key executives to solicit their advice and gain their support. Because of his interest, the meeting with the marketing vice president lasted over three hours.

Most importantly, she generated a roadmap that showed how each of three planned products would be developed using the component model, infrastructure, methods, and tools that were scheduled for implementation during the first project. She met with the marketing department and reviewed their sales forecasts. In the new project plan she justified the investments to be made in terms of different levels of sales using the present worth of projected return on investment figures. In other words, she correlated the project plan to the sales plan that marketing was using to drive the effort.

The second meeting went more smoothly. The product-line manager was well-prepared for intense questioning of the new project plan. What's more important, she had presold the plans well in advance of the meeting. She had developed a champion, the vice president of marketing, and had presold senior managers on her plans. Of course, there were some battles. That was to be expected when executives meet (for example, existing empires are threatened by new products that don't fit into the existing organizational structure). However, the project won approval from senior management because the new project plan was sound and the product-line manager had developed a compelling business and technical case to continue the CBD and CBSE projects.

24.5 Conclusion

The life of a change agent advocating CBD is difficult. The organization has to have sufficient software engineering processes already established and in use by project teams in order to consider implementing a CBD pilot program. Otherwise, the change agent is required to construct a business case for a pilot project that will include the imposition of CBSE prior to, or in parallel with, the design the pilot project. As described in Chapter 23, the pilot project would start with a measurement and metrics program of existing software development projects and continue through the completion of the CBD pilot project. The metrics can be used to persuade senior management of the efficacy of CBD and CBSE.

Numerous forms of resistance will challenge the CBD change agent throughout the promotion period. Nevertheless, I believe that you can successfully make the transition to the use of components and component-based software engineering technology if you are patient, persistent, and pay attention to the details. In addition to paving the path for you, the reuse community has left rich legacy that you can build upon to make following the roadmap you've devised easier. I suggest that you review the experience base that the reuse community has left behind before embarking on your journey ([Jacobson, Griss, and Jonsson, 1997] [Karlsson, 1995] [McClure, 1997] [Tracz, 1995]). This legacy can shorten the component-based development life cycle and make it more pleasant because you will know where the roadblocks are and how to avoid them.

Chapter 25

Selecting the Right COTS Software: Why Requirements Are Important

Cornelius Ncube
Neil Maiden

25.1 Introduction

Selecting the right commercial off-the-shelf (COTS) software component is critical to the success of many CBSE processes. However, most CBSE methods support systems design and integration rather than requirements engineering and COTS component selection. You would like to select the COTS component that best satisfies your requirements, but these requirements are often difficult to acquire and model.

The lack of methods for COTS component selection is also surprising given the opportunities that CBSE offers requirements engineering.

In this chapter we describe the COTS component selection problem and present the procurement-oriented requirements engineering (PORE) method for CBSE requirements engineering. PORE integrates requirements engineering, COTS component selection, and multi-criteria decision-making techniques. We also describe recent studies of the method's use. The chapter ends with brief conclusions for requirements engineering for CBSE.

25.2 The Problem

Choosing the right COTS component is difficult because it involves two complex processes: multi-criteria decision-making (Konito, 1996) and requirements engineering (Robertson and Robertson, 2000). Requirements engineering processes are often needed to determine the selection criteria, which can be incomplete and interdependent. However, it is difficult to acquire, complete, and correct requirements (Maiden and Rugg, 1996) to model inter-dependencies and to validate criteria needed to enable effective acceptance testing (Robertson and Robertson, 2000). In addition we find that, in practice, there will be many COTS components that satisfy most of your required criteria, but there may be no single one that satisfies all criteria.

Failing to integrate multi-criteria decision-making and requirements engineering processes can lead to poor COTS component selection. On one hand, if you acquire your requirements before you select the COTS components you might not elicit sufficient requirements to discriminate between candidates (Maiden and Ncube, 1998). On the other hand, if you select the COTS component too quickly you may purchase a component that does not satisfy all requirements. Surprisingly, in spite of the need for an integrated process, there are few methods available, and organizations are often unable to conduct a complex COTS component selection process.

25.2.1 The Difference Between COTS-Based and Component-Based Development

Most of the success in COTS-based software has been in developing and reusing large-scale COTS software packages such as math libraries and domain-specific software libraries. These software assets are often not described with the degree of rigor required to define software components.

Although CBSE is usually associated with specific technologies such as CORBA, COM, or JavaBeans (Kruchten, 1998), it is primarily concerned with creating and deploying software-intensive systems assembled from components. CBSE largely involves crafting the right set of primitive components from which to build families of systems rather than the customization of larger-scale COTS software packages. An important difference is that stakeholders are more likely to select COTS software that deliver simple, even atomic software functions while nonfunctional selection criteria such as interoperability and configurability will be more difficult to evaluate.

25.3 The PORE Method

The PORE method guides a software development team during the acquisition of requirements and selection of COTS software systems that satisfy these requirements (Ncube, 2000). PORE supports an iterative process of requirements acquisition and COTS software selection as shown in Figure 25-1. During each iteration the software development team:

- *Acquires* requirements that discriminate between the COTS software candidates
- *Identifies* candidates that are not compliant with these requirements using multi-criteria decision-making
- *Rejects* COTS software candidates that are not compliant with the requirements
- *Explores* the remaining COTS software candidates to discover possible new requirements to use to discriminate further between these candidates

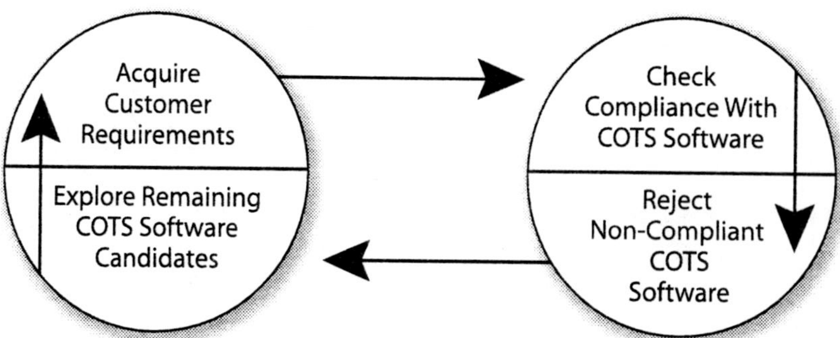

Figure 25-1: *PORE's iterative process of requirements acquisition and COTS software.*

We have successfully applied PORE to help companies select large-scale COTS software packages, but PORE is also designed to help you select smaller, fine-grained COTS components. These steps are universal in any process for selecting COTS components and your organization should find methods/tools that support these steps. PORE is one such example; in this short chapter we can only highlight the essential elements of PORE that support this COTS selection process.

25.3.1 PORE Iterations

Each iteration is divided into the four processes shown in Figure 25-2. First, the team acquires requirements and COTS software information needed to make the next selection or rejection decisions. Second, the team analyzes the requirements and other information to decide whether they are ready to make any rejection decisions. Then the team uses this information to make decisions about requirement-software compliance. Finally it rejects candidates on the basis of these decisions.

These processes are described using templates that guide the team through each process in each iteration. In template-1, for example, PORE recommends browsing the Internet, sending an invitation-to-tender to supplier Special Interest Group (SIG) mailing lists, visiting trade shows and exhibitions, and reading relevant computing journals as possible techniques to elicit information about COTS software (Maiden and Ncube, 1998). Likewise for template-2, PORE recommends that team members follow the same procedure used for tem-

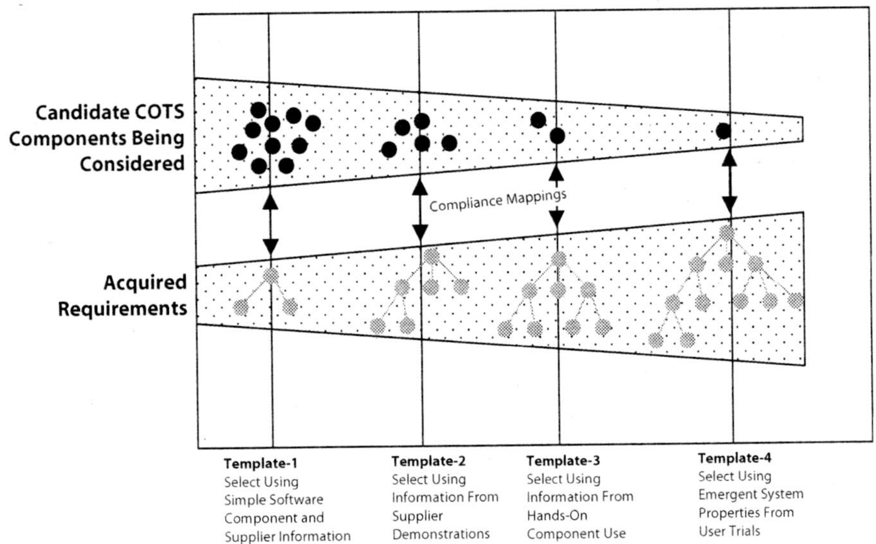

Figure 25-2: *Critical decision-making strategies to accept or reject software components in PORE.*

plate-1. Stakeholder representatives should be present to provide additional knowledge and clarification of the requirements (Maiden and Ncube, 1998).

Each iteration of PORE may acquire different requirements to better support the changing decisions that the team has to make. Ideally, the team continues these iterations until one or more candidate COTS components remain that complies with all essential requirements.

If you are familiar with the COTS components, we recommend you use the *card sorts* technique (Maiden and Rugg, 1996) as another iteration for the essential requirements. During card sorts the team writes the names of candidate COTS components on 3" x 5" cards and asks customers to sort the COTS component candidates into categories. Criteria for these sorts (for example, "Compatible with documents produced using Microsoft Word") indicate requirements that discriminate between COTS components. Categories such as "compatible" and "not compatible" indicate compliance to these requirements. A useful variation, *card sort triage*, has customers describe the similarities between two COTS component candidates and their common differences to a third candidate. Card sort techniques also fit well with *laddering* (Maiden and

Rugg, 1996), in which stakeholders discover important but nondiscriminating requirements by describing common categories of COTS components and their features. Laddering avoids wasting time acquiring less important requirements that will not affect your decision.

PORE also offers a technique based on scenarios to discover, acquire, and structure requirements to formulate test cases that can validate COTS component compliance with the requirements. As more COTS components are made available for trial use, constructing test cases is an increasingly viable way to select a COTS component. Other PORE techniques enable the team to discover and select essential COTS components before peripheral components that integrate with it. If a software demonstration of the COTS component is available, PORE recommends that stakeholder representatives are present to ask important, but unforeseen, questions and to discover missing requirements.

Each iteration of the PORE process guides the team to reject COTS software that are not compliant with these requirements. The sequence of the decisions that PORE guides the team to make is shown in Figure 25-3. More simple decisions (for example, to reject COTS component candidates for not complying with simple requirements such as cost) are made earlier in the process when there are more candidates. More complex decisions (for example, to reject candidates for noncompliance with complex requirements such as system performance) are made later in the process when the COTS component is available to explore complex emergent system properties.

25.3.1.1 How We Extended PORE to CBSE

PORE is a process for selecting any COTS software, but we have also tailored it to work with COTS components. When selecting a COTS component to be integrated into a component-based system instead of a primarily functional COTS software package, you must consider the following:

1. Does the COTS component conform to the same component model you will use for the target system? If not, is there technology available to bridge the two component models?
2. Does the COTS component need burdensome external dependencies just to function? How well will it integrate with your component infrastructure?

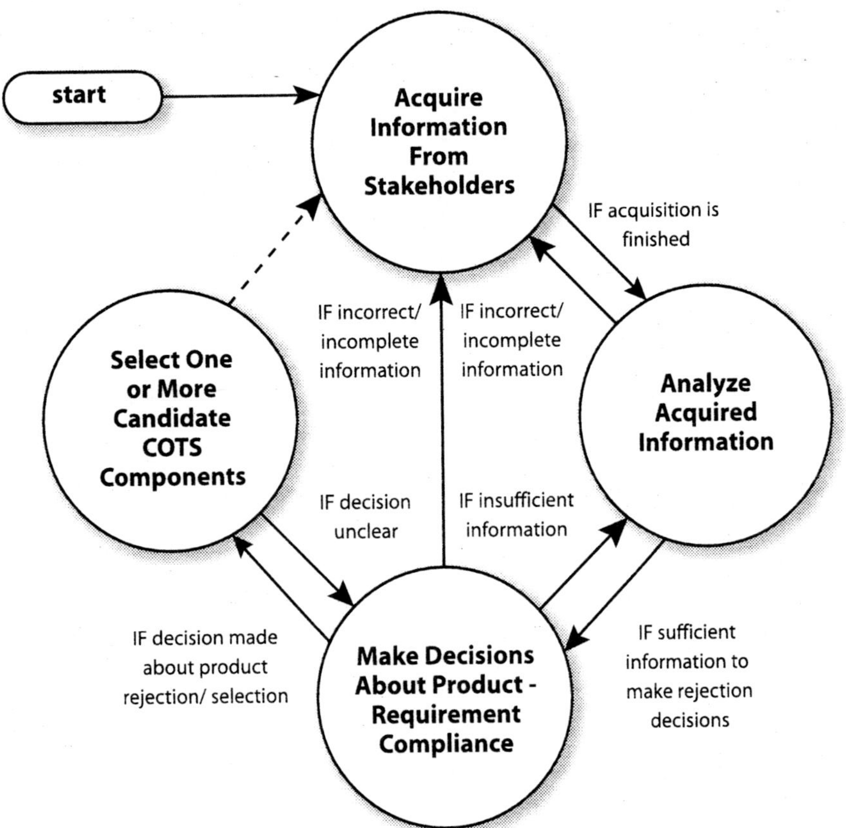

Figure 25-3: *Graphical depiction of PORE processes during decision-making.*

3. Is the COTS component compatible with the nonfunctional requirements of your target system, such as resource usage, threading policies, and security?

When using PORE for COTS components you will be inspecting the COTS component more closely than if it were simply a COTS software package. To accommodate this, two essential changes to PORE are the ordering of the process goals to be achieved by the component selection team and the emerging importance of considering software component infrastructures to enable fit with nonfunctional requirements.

25.4 PORE Method Evaluation

The design of the original PORE method was based on case studies where we observed common problems that occurred during COTS software selection ([Maiden and Ncube, 1998] [Ncube and Maiden, 1997]). PORE is a comprehensive set of templates that are continuously being enhanced to improve the method's usefulness and usability. We report two evaluations of PORE. In the ensuing discussions we make direct reference to guidelines available in the PORE templates. For example, reference T1.5 refers to guideline 5 in Template 1. Table 25-1 lists only the PORE guidelines relevant for reference purposes when reading this section.

Table 25-1: *A Partial List of Guideline Names Available in PORE Templates*

T1.1	Gather component information using recommended changes.
T1.2	Acquire first pass essential requirements using techniques such as brainstorming and interviewing.
T1.3	Develop a questionnaire to ask each supplier how much its component is compliant with each essential requirement.
T1.5	Evaluate questionnaire responses to reject COTS components that are noncompliant with essential requirements.
T2.1	Before demonstrations develop simple working prototype of the required system to discover and acquire further requirements.
T2.2	Have stakeholder representative present during product demonstration to suggest previously unforeseen requirements.
T2.3	Work with stakeholders to weight requirements.
T2.6	During the demonstrations, ask questions about the component product to discover cornerstone components first.
T2.7	During demonstrations, only allocate compliance scores if the component's properties are demonstrated.
T2.8	If it is difficult to score for compliance, use reference models.

25.4.1 Selecting COTS Dealerboard Software Systems for an International Bank

An international bank was purchasing a new dealerboard system to give traders a more efficient telecommunications system with voice-recording capabilities to trade with brokers and banks. A selection team was established to select a suitable COTS software system. The team used PORE's T1 and T2 templates to guide their COTS selection process, which included supplier-led demonstrations.

Template T1 guided the team to reject COTS software as noncompliant with requirements that were tested with supplier-provided information included in our questionnaires. The team used Internet and trade journals to identify candidate COTS software (T1.1). The project team visited other banks with similar systems (T1.1) to gather information and problems relevant to the current selection process and to observe how dealers worked with these systems. Information from these sources was integrated with initial system requirements to form a questionnaire that was sent to suppliers to request information about their COTS software systems (T1.3).

Eleven suppliers responded to the questionnaire, and based on this feedback the team rejected eight candidates for noncompliance with requirements (T1.5). Then the risk management and IT departments weighted and ranked each requirement (T2.3). The remaining three suppliers were invited to demonstrate their COTS software at the bank. One refused, narrowing the list to two. The two suppliers took eight weeks to install and configure their COTS software prior to the supplier-led demonstration phase. Finally, each supplier installed a working system that connected to the bank's switching system in order to demonstrate compliance with the compatibility requirements (T2.1).

During each demonstration numerous stakeholders were present, but only the evaluation team leader, the IT support manager, and the heads of the risk management groups were allowed to rate the COTS software for its compliance with requirements (T2.7). However, other stakeholders did contribute important questions (T2.2) that identified additional requirements (T2.6). After each demonstration the team calculated a single final compliance score for the COTS dealerboard software systems. There was only a small difference in the final compliance scores for both COTS software candidates, so the team analyzed nonfunctional requirements further, such as how well they would be able to maintain their own software if they integrated with these COTS software systems. This process ultimately resulted in the selection of a single COTS system.

The guidance provided by PORE's T1 and T2 templates was critical to the success of the COTS selection process. PORE's authors also learned some key lessons about COTS selection.

> *Lesson #1*—It is important to gather information about COTS software from many different sources early in the selection process; this will make subsequent analysis, decision-making, and COTS software rejection easier.
>
> *Lesson #2*—COTS software selection is a team effort. Having stakeholder representatives present during COTS software demonstrations identified important new requirements. Stakeholders must be involved.

PORE's templates helped guide teams through the complex processes of requirements acquisition and COTS software selection. The templates were perceived to have greatly aided the selection process.

25.4.2 Selecting COTS Document Management Software for an Insurance Syndicate

A Lloyds of London managing agent syndicate was purchasing a COTS document management software system. High-level requirements included a document scanning system and a document management system to handle hand-written claim forms. The syndicate was required to replace its paper-based, in-house software system with one that would link directly to the Lloyds' document management systems; thus interoperability and integration requirements were important. A selection team had already produced a short list of three COTS software candidates using each candidate's cost, technical specifications, supplier profiles, and recommendations from other insurance syndicates. The team applied PORE's template T2 to guide the supplier-led software demonstrations.

Before the demonstration sessions the team acquired more requirements using a paper-based prototype (T2.1) and scenarios that depicted the current sequence of stakeholder tasks affected by the new system (T2.1). The team developed graphical storyboards to depict how the stakeholders might use the future system. It also conducted interviews to acquire more detailed requirements identified with the scenarios. The team worked with stakeholders to group and rank the requirements. Another session elicited measurable fit criteria to enable system acceptance testing (Robertson and Robertson, 2000). The original scenarios were then extended with the measurable requirements to generate test cases to use during the supplier-led demonstration sessions (T2.1).

All three suppliers demonstrated their COTS software to the syndicate and stakeholder representatives from multiple business sections (underwriting, claims, and reinsurance) attended each session. Other stakeholders were also encouraged to attend to help overcome resistance to the new system. During each session team members rated the compliance of each COTS software with requirements as specified in the test cases. Other stakeholder representatives were also consulted to provide additional knowledge and clarification of requirements. After each session the evaluation team calculated overall compliance scores for each COTS documentation management software system. On the basis of these results the team recommended that the syndicate install two of the three COTS software systems for a trial period of six weeks. The purpose of the evaluation was to judge the compliance of each system with complex nonfunctional requirements such as usability and training, and to acquire further requirements from all stakeholders. The team also advised the syndicate to seek legal advice on the negotiation of a contract based on the identified requirements.

All stakeholders who completed a post-task questionnaire indicated that they would use PORE again for COTS software selection. This study showed the following lessons.

Lesson #3—Scenario walkthroughs are effective for discovering requirements, for decomposing these requirements by task, and enabling stakeholders to reach a common understanding of these requirements.

Lesson #4—Keep demonstration sessions and the overall time within which all sessions are held short; this will enable a fair comparison of all systems. One stakeholder expressed a desire to complete all demonstration sessions in the same week.

Lesson #5—The team must establish a nonaggressive attitude when questioning the COTS supplier.

Lesson #6—Design effective evaluative test cases. Compliance with one requirement was often tested several times, and this put excessive pressure on the software demonstrator. For example, demonstrators were asked to scan a document several times, index it using a reference number, and then retrieve it again. Stakeholders believed that this slowed evaluation and felt that they could have been tested at a later stage using evaluation copies of the software and the focus during the evaluation sessions should have been on core functional requirements.

25.4.3 Final Assessment

There is one final general lesson learned from PORE.

Lesson #7—You may end up selecting a COTS component from a given set of candidates that only satisfies most of your requirements. The risk of this decision is trying to use a component that was the least objectionable to the selection team. The only way you will successfully integrate and use a COTS component selected in this way is to have all stakeholders voice their position on the amount of work required to bridge the gap between what the COTS component provides and what is needed.

25.5 Conclusion

This chapter reports the key features of a method for COTS software selection and lessons learned from evaluations of that method. One lesson is clear: requirements are important for selecting the right COTS software. A remaining question is how best to integrate requirements engineering and multi-criteria decision-making techniques to support this selection. The lessons learned from our evaluations indicate incremental method improvements, which we will evaluate in future studies.

However, PORE is only a first a step to supporting buy versus build decisions. We are continually evaluating PORE's modeling and decision-making capabilities to handle the cost and risk of selection and configuration.

Chapter 26

Building Instead of Buying: A Rebuttal

George T. Heineman

26.1 Introduction

The consensus within the software engineering community is that buying a component is better than building it. The determination of "better" is based on the assumption that the costs for development, testing, and maintenance will easily exceed the cost of purchasing a component. In Chapter 6 Will Tracz exposes many myths that support this assumption. So what should you do? Before you decide to buy a component (remember that you may have to explain your reasons to upper management), you must answer the questions in this short chapter. Facing these difficult questions in advance will help you understand the risks, and may convince you to build the software component in-house.

26.2 Questions for the Consumer

First, let's assume you are interested in purchasing a software component to use in a software development effort.

Question #1: What will you do if the component's vendor goes bankrupt or ceases to support the component product?

Discussion: If you do not treat the purchase of a component as supply chain management, you are exposing your organization to inadvisable risk. When you initially selected a component, you should analyze several components from competing vendors (if there is no other vendor you may be in trouble). During the evaluation phase you should analyze the costs involved in substituting a different component if needed.

Question #2: What is your recourse if the component's producer or vendor releases a new version?

Discussion: Have you estimated the costs of a component upgrade in terms of testing, system integration, and redeployment? Are the total costs of ownership budgeted? If you decide not to upgrade if the vendor releases a new component, are you aware that this could limit your access to technical support?

Question #3: Have you determined your exact rights under the licensing agreement offered by the component producer?

Discussion: Is the license for the component for a fixed or indefinite term? Under UCITA (see Chapter 40), it is possible for a software product to be licensed for a fixed term, and then automatically deactivate or remove itself from the computer on which it is installed. Will you be granted source code access to help you detect defects during system integration? Will you be charged a royalty fee for every component instance that you redistribute with your software?

Question #4: Are you expecting to conform your application to fit the assumptions of the component or have you verified that it will work for your specific needs?

Discussion: You may have to change your existing software to enable a purchased component to be integrated. Are you budgeting for this? There have been many documented cases of "mismatch," where the component appears to be perfect, but successful integration is a time-consuming, manual process. Have you asked the component producer for information about whether other companies were able to integrate the component? Have you visited the purchasers' Web sites and asked consumers' about their experiences with the component?

Question #5: Do you have comprehensive plans to develop a small pilot project in order to validate the component with your software component infrastructure?

Discussion: In the same way that rapid prototyping helps clarify initial user requirements for software systems, you *must* carry out a pilot project. By doing so you will be able to estimate the final integration costs and determine whether the component is a good fit. If you "go live" with the component in a project essential to your company, you may create a backlash against CBD if a problem develops unexpectedly.

26.3 Questions for the Producer

Now let's assume you are interested in building a software component and selling it on the open market.

Question #1: What is the business case for developing a component in-house and selling it?

Discussion: It is commonly accepted that it is more costly to develop reusable software than to develop single-use software. Have you budgeted for the difference in costs? If you are expecting to generate revenue from selling the component, have you allocated resources for support, testing, third-party certification, and maintenance? Will the money generated from the component's revenue be used to develop future versions of the component, leading to a self-sustaining effort, or will it be diverted to other uses within the organization? Do you have a structure in place to handle licensing agreements and other legal issues that will arise?

Question #2: Is the component you wish to sell domain-specific or generic?

Discussion: If the component is generic, how do you expect to compete on the open market when you bring nothing special to the programming effort? If the component is specific, you must explain why you are offering for sale (to your competition, presumably) a component that you use in your products to maintain your competitive advantage.

Question #3: Will you use a tailored version of your for-sale component in-house?

Discussion: If you attempt to sell a "plain vanilla" version of the component but use a more sophisticated, tailored one for your competitive use, are you prepared for the increased maintenance and testing costs?

Question #4: Are you increasing the component-specific training of your developers?

Discussion: Packaging and selling a component is very different from making code libraries available. If you wish to succeed in your endeavor you must provide targeted, CBSE-specific training to make it possible to sell your component.

26.4 Questions for the Component Model Implementation Vendor

Lastly, we consider a different question. What if you are responsible for deciding whether to use an existing component model implementation or build your own?

Question #1: What is the business case for developing and maintaining a component model implementation?

Discussion: The costs of developing your own implementation for a component model are extremely high and you must have very specific reasons for choosing this option. For example, you may be unsatisfied with the real-time performance of CORBA CCM implementations from the available vendors. Without the right combination of skills—in both real-time computing as well as component model implementations—such an approach is doomed from the start. If you are intent on developing the component model implementation for your own proprietary use, do you intend to offer the resulting product for sale? Do you have sufficient marketing and support staff to allocate to make this effort succeed? In most every imaginable case, it would be better to leave the development of component model implementations to the experts.

26.5 Conclusion

In this book we consistently promote the view that you must support technological decisions with sound financial reasoning. You should neither blindly purchase components for use nor insist on developing all software in-house. CBSE offers opportunities for application assemblers to "outsource" subprojects by purchasing components, and enables component producers to profit from developing usable components. A thriving component marketplace will only exist with enough satisfied consumers and producers, and we expect such a marketplace to diversify and grow in the near-term.

Chapter 27

Software Component Project Management

Bill Councill

27.1 Introduction

If you haven't deduced it yet, software development project management and component-based software engineering management are different. The two forms of management are as different as formal organizational processes, such as the SEI CMM to assure that all projects developed by any one organization meet quality standards, and automotive engineering, where there is no room for engineering management to permit a single gear to fall outside minimally allowable tolerances.

Ideally, within CBSE project management all project managers would be first, expert in the practice of an engineering discipline, and second, in intricacies of project management as exemplified in the *Project Management Book of Knowledge* [(PMBOK) (*www.pmi.org/publictn/pmboktoc.htm*)]. Additionally, project managers should have experience in various roles during two complete component-based development life cycle projects before they are considered ready for the role of lead engineer on a CBSE project.

The field has a dearth of licensed engineers prepared to operate in the role of lead and subproject engineers. Until software engineers are trained to manage the complex designs and assemblies of software components, the CBSE discipline and software development organizations (SDOs) should ensure that project managers who will manage CBD projects have hands-on experience in almost every technical phase of the component life cycle. This form of project management is analogous to a lead automotive engineer working with subproject managers and their teams to design and manage the prototype assemblies of complex four-wheel-drive components.

27.2 Existing Software Project Management

Current software failures have been attributed to software project management failures. James H. Johnson, chairman of The Standish Group International, Inc. and publisher of the *Chaos Report,* states that information technology (IT) projects fail because, "Complexity causes confusion and costs." In the most recent Chaos Report, the Standish Group presented the following annual statistics (*standishgroup.com/visitor/chaos.htm*)

- 31.1% of application development projects are canceled before completion
- 52.7% will cost 189% of their original cost
- $81 billion in failed, and $59 billion for challenged, projects cost U.S. companies and government agencies an estimated $140 billion per year

In the same report, Tom Field (1997) reports that, "[P]roject management experts say, 'IT projects often die simply because Information Systems (IS) departments fail to follow the basic project management principles that help ensure project success in the *engineering and construction industries* (emphasis mine)'."

Don Reifer (1997b) defines the terms *project management* and *project manager* as follows:

Project management—The system of management established to focus resources on achieving project goals. [Project management] has been defined as the art of creating the illusion that any outcome is the result of a series of predetermined, deliberate acts, when, in fact, it isn't.

Project manager—The person held responsible for planning, controlling, and directing the project activities. Many times, these responsibilities involve coordinating and integrating activities and products across functional units or organizations.

Another responsibility for many project managers is to "never admit a project is a failure" (Pinto and Kharbanda, 1996). Therefore, failing projects continue while management believes the project can be completed, albeit late and, perhaps, over budget.

My experience is that too many software development project managers (SDPMs) are not trained in project management, much less the many software development life cycle (SDLC) activities required of knowledgeable project managers. Managing people, budgets, scope, risks, quality, and schedules are insufficient to ensure project managers effectively administer appropriate processes, procedures, methodologies, and policies implemented.

SDPMs must understand and have sufficient experience to conduct SDLC activities such as:

- Eliciting and modeling business rules
- Eliciting and writing requirements and use case scenarios, as well as developing use case diagrams
- Developing initial, then iterative and incremental design documentation and diagrams
- Programming code according to the criteria cited above
- Participating in test case development, starting with unit test cases and continuing through user test validation
- Participating in configuration management activities at all levels throughout the component development life cycle and continuing the maintenance phase

Additionally, Table 27-1 demonstrates that traditional SDPMs, according to Field (1997), tend to make many of the same ten signs of project failure repeatedly.

Table 27-1: *Ten Signs of IS Failure*

Project managers do not understand users' needs
Scope is not well-defined
Project changes are handled poorly
Previously selected technology changes
Business needs change
Deadlines are unrealistic
Users are resistant
Sponsorship is lost
Project lacks people with appropriate skills
Best practices and lessons are unknown to the project team or are ignored

My recommendations for SDPMs applied to CBSE exceed what most articles and books about software project management expect. Since most SDPMs do not have engineering training in project management and many, to my experience, do not have sufficient experience to manage large, complex, open distributed processing (ODP) projects, there is a shortage of experienced SDPMs. Yet where there are problems, opportunities abound.

27.2.1 Lead and Subproject Engineers

CBSE project management is considerably more precise and predictable than software development project management. The terms *component-based software project manager* (CBSPM) and *subproject CBSPMs* will be used throughout the rest of this chapter rather than the more common term *software development project manager*. These concepts of engineering management are not new; the practice of engineering has been using the hierarchy of lead and subproject engineers for decades. Frederick Taylor's search for finding the one best solution has influenced engineering, thus optimizing efficiency, minimizing costs, maintaining minimum functional requirements, and other fundamental beliefs (Kanigel, 1997).

In the practice of engineering a lead engineer is assigned a problem, otherwise perceived by many engineers and project managers as an opportunity. The problem, often referred to as a request for proposal (RFP), is to construct a new product or to revise an existing product. The lead engineer generally has the discretion to assemble a team of subproject engineers. The engineers may be trained in the same discipline, have undergone an internship, and taken the requisite licensing or certification (licensing in the U.S.; certification in many other countries) tests to ensure a minimal level of expertise in their chosen profession. Otherwise, one group of professional engineers may receive the acceptance of their RFPs and subcontract with engineers of other disciplines to complete the assignment successfully. Therefore, all or most licensed professional engineers share similar education, experiences, many of the same professional values, and management training necessary to organize and direct increasing levels of engineering management and decision-making.

As an example of engineering management performed by an automotive engineer with 10 years' experience, the lead engineer will determine the scope of the problem, that is, to design and build a prototype of a rollover-proof sport utility vehicle (SUV). The lead engineer will then apportion the apparent parts of the problem to subproject engineers (four-wheel-drive train to Al, engine to George, and steering assembly to Rustom among others), and determine the elements (subproblems) that the subproject engineers will manage. Subsequently, the lead engineer will determine what components in the vast repository of automotive parts can be reused to create and assemble management's directive for a new SUV.

It may be hard to believe, but the lead engineer does not like to assign an RFP for a new part to a subproject engineer. The RFP requires that the contracting organization develop a product (performance) specification that describes in exacting detail how the engine will interface with a newly developed chassis and reused transmission and how it will perform at a level of 20% greater horsepower and 25% greater torque than existing or competitively developing engines. The design constraints will state that when the brakes are applied at 115 mph to stop the vehicle within a specified distance, the vehicle shall not swerve greater than a fixed degree in either the left or right direction on a straight road surface and shall not rollover.

The subproject engineer must begin to design the engine with a team of veteran designers, but first the engineer will attempt to determine what components are available for reuse that fall within the range of the performance requirements for the engine. After consulting with the reuse librarian, the librarian will review the parts inventory—that is, the component repository in CBSE—for an engine that conforms as closely as possible to the performance specification. Finding a currently produced engine in inventory that produces 30% more horsepower and 25% more torque, the reuse librarian decomposes the engine into its constituent parts and searches for all meta data on the engine's components.

The subproject engineer orders a series of dynamometer tests on the engine to determine its stability and reliability under maximum stress on the engine. The engine block and crankshaft can conceivably withstand the stress declared in the performance requirements, but the camshaft cannot manage the load. The engine's cylinders will have to be bored and will require newly designed, high performance pistons, piston rings, and cylinder sleeves. A new fuel injector system also is required. The subproject engineer calls a meeting of his design team.

A new product specification must now be developed for each of the components required to satisfy the customer. The reuse librarian will be directed by the subproject manager to search the component repository for RFP documentation that closely conforms to the basic designs the design team has developed. Then the various designers can reuse RFPs to develop requests for automotive parts producers to bid on the opportunity to fulfill the exacting specifications, constraints, minimally acceptable tolerances, and cost criteria of each RFP.

27.2.2 Inter-Organizational Engineering Specialization

Unlike in most current software development projects, other engineering disciplines often cooperate on projects. The RFP for cylinder sleeves and piston rings is contracted to a manufacturer that routinely produces cylinder sleeves, pistons, and piston rings for the automobile industry. This manufacturing firm contracts with an engineering consultancy, which commences the design of the cylinder sleeves and piston rings. The lead engineer of the engineering group determines that to assist the contractor to meet its performance specifications for increased horsepower and torque, a metal unused by them but familiar to the group through the journals should be considered. The lead engineer further subcontracts with a metallurgical engineer who specializes in the use of the metal to assist them in the design and deployment of the "new" metal in the cylinder sleeves and piston rings. When the automotive lead engineer who approved the firms that were awarded contracts for feasibility studies concerning the pistons, piston rings, and cylinder sleeves is informed by the subproject engineer's weekly report of the perceived need for the new metal, he immediately arranges a conference call with the lead engineers conducting the feasibility studies and the contractor's subproject engineer. A relatively high level of risk is involved and all parties are informed that the effects of the risk must be immediately discussed. The risk, the subproject engineer warns the lead automotive engineer, could be mitigated, and at that time it is an issue of the worst circumstances. No reported cases of chafing composite metal parts, for example, the piston rings, have ever been reported. Yet no uses of the composite metal has been used continuously for long periods.

The call is made and the contractor approves the use of the new material in the prototype engine, thereby taking responsibility for the risk. The new material is the best solution to the problem of increasing horsepower and torque. Meeting with the automotive lead engineer, the subproject engineer explains the circumstances for using the "new" metal in the cylinder sleeves and piston rings. The lead engineer approves of the subproject engineer's initiative and reporting style and gives approval for contracts to the two firms conducting the feasibility studies, contingent on written reports.

27.3 CBSE Project Management

The automotive example above is similar to the best of CBSE project management today. In the next few years, when software engineers recognize the emphasis of engineering in their professional designation, component-based projects will be managed in the same manner as automotive engineers supervise their projects.

Before I describe the characteristics of an effective CBSPM, perhaps I should state and reiterate the traits of SDPMs who cannot manage CBSE projects. They:

- Have insufficient training in project management; a five day course is unacceptable
- Do not have experience in advocating for, and supporting, a measurement and metrics program
- Are not trained in the implementation of pilot programs to demonstrate the value of new technology
- Have not had experience in at least two CBD projects, preferably in all life cycle phases
- Cannot participate knowledgeably in verification meetings at each phase of the life cycle and understand the concepts and context of the presentation (for example, statechart diagrams in a design verification meeting)
- Cannot effectively manage disagreements because of the different levels of team members' knowledge, usually resulting from just-in-time (JIT) training and mentoring (see Chapter 24)
- Will not establish a engineering-style hierarchy of subproject managers
- Will not develop RFPs for a specialized component or component model because, then, it is not invented here (NIH) (see Chapter 24)
- And are subject to repetitious signs of failure with each project undertaken (refer to Table 27-1)

In my opinion, good CBSPMs are licensed as professional engineers who dedicate their work lives to the development of quality software. Since so few project managers are engineers, CBSPMs should have the following qualities.

1. Ideally, an engineering degree and license, as well a degree in software engineering; but because this quality is exceptionally rare, the following may suffice.
2. A graduate degree in an as yet established master's degree program in CBSPM. This degree program will be accredited by the Computing Accreditation Commission (CAC) of the Accreditation Board for Engineering and Technology (ABET). The CAC will be formed when the Computer Science Accreditation Board (CSAB) merges with ABET (*www.csab.org*). See Chapter 37 for more details.
3. Until the establishment of a CBSPM educational and certification program, the following skills are absolutely required.

- Study of engineering management in an accredited program offering continuing education courses. Evaluations are necessary for management
- For most project and program managers that specialize in traditional project management activities, the following academic courses should be demanded by management.
    - Measurement and metrics to demonstrate the efficiencies between pre-component development and component development, including component reuse
    - Component-based software analysis, including business rules and requirements elicitation, business process modeling, use case scenario development, and use case modeling
    - Component-based software design
    - Component construction in at least one complete object-oriented language
    - Software testing with test harnesses, including verification activities at the end of each increment for each phase of the iterative, incremental life cycle
    - Validation activities at the putative end of the project, including user acceptance testing, third-party testing, and retesting of all defects reported during system testing and user acceptance testing
    - Maintenance of black-box components, both third-party and those developed within the organization, where limited visibility is available and documentation is often unavailable

The purpose of this educational experience for current project and program managers is to ensure that CBSPMs are sufficiently knowledgeable of all phases of the CBD life cycle. If CBSPMs are lacking in knowledge of any phase or department of the incremental life cycle they cannot assist their subproject managers or project teams with the one best solution to any problem. Similarly, to return to our analogy, a lead engineer with limited or no knowledge of metallurgy would find it easy to dissuade his subproject engineer about using a new metal for automotive engine purposes because of the obvious risks. It is easier to mitigate risks early out of ignorance by denying a request than taking a chance and risking a major success because of less than optimal knowledge of the domain.

Fred Taylor in his early years experienced something similar:

> He would have liked to be able to say, "You say you can't do this job any faster? Nonsense. You're funning it way too slow. With this kind of steel, and that depth of cut and that feed, you should be able to go at twenty feet per minute, easy. Go ahead and do it at twenty. Use these pulleys here. It'll be fine." But he couldn't say that, because he didn't know for sure, anyway. Grizzled old machinists were saying, "Hell, no, that's too fast. It'll burn up the tool. It'll wreck the machine."...For all his confidence, he must have sometimes thought, who am I to say they're wrong? They knew, and he didn't (Kanigel, 1997).

27.4 Where is the Training?

In Chapter 37 John Speed, George Heineman, and I describe the immediate needs for a CBSPM educational program. While a licensure program for component-based software engineers would likely require decades to implement, a CBSPM program offered by a few core universities could be funded, accredited, and commenced within a few years.

The CBSPM educational program would require funding from governmental and business sources. Funding in the amount of $6 million each year for eight years is necessary to demonstrate the feasibility of the program. $3 million from government and $3 million dollars from the business community is required for the first year's planning phase. This phase involves the CSAB, ABET, and a core of at least five universities that pledge to offer the services of their computer science, software engineering, and engineering programs for the pilot program. Once students matriculate into the CBSPM program, seven years' funding is required for the educational course work and practica that comprise six years of the graduate degree program and a one-year internship in an accredited internship program that will complete the seventh year.

Once the accreditation organizations and core universities meet during the first year, CSAB or ABET must establish a basic body of knowledge to test the first students whose intent is advanced placement because of prior educational knowledge, work experience, or both. The accrediting organization may use this state-of-the-art text or more recent articles and books, which may include a second edition of this book that aims for more empiricism. Nevertheless, a coalescing body of knowledge must be used, no matter how unempirical, that can guide the first test for advanced placement students.

These universities will refine their curricula to construct a body of knowledge (BOK). The universities do not have the responsibility for producing this BOK; however, their curricula should reflect it. Furthermore, the accreditation organization will want to ensure that the curricula is influenced by a relatively stable BOK that is not subject to the churning fads and pseudo-knowledge prevalent in computer science and software engineering.

At the end of the internship interns who desire to work as consultants in the private sector may take an examination developed by the CSAB or ABET based on required courses of study and generally expected experiences of internship.

Until then, however, training would occur through university continuing education programs, university undergraduate and graduate courses, and apprenticeships. A senior software engineer would be charged by senior management with overseeing the progress of the CBSPM.

In addition, most CBSPMs will have to develop excellent negotiating skills and the ability to manage various forms of resistance to the ever-changing CBSE body of knowledge (Chapter 24). Even members of the organizations who supported CBD and CBSE early in the feasibility phase will resist new procedures once they have absorbed all that they consider to be CBD. Software engineers and computer scientists are used to taking directions and implementing the instructions as they prefer. Many, if not most, project team members will resist the concept of the one best way.

Engineers, following Taylor's one best way, are trained to solve each problem through discrete or simple steps until only one resolution for the problem emerges as the best method under all circumstances. For example, each of many design problems is resolved in this manner. Large problems are solved in the project team; smaller problems are resolved in the subproject groups.

CBSPMs train all subordinates in the one best way, reinforce it with training offered by their subproject managers, and ensure that the subproject managers mentor their subordinates continuously. Further, CBSPMs are required to demonstrate increasing knowledge of CBD and

CBSE. Otherwise CBSPMs unknowingly revert to their previous positions as software development project managers, with diminishing control of their projects or programs and with the frustrations of Fred Taylor and many software development project and program managers.

27.5 No CBSPM Is An Island

If you consider CBSPMs as product managers it is easy to conceive of subproject CBSPMs in a hierarchy. Lead software engineers trained in engineering or as CBSPMs can additionally manage hierarchical product-lines. Multiple products necessarily will require a hierarchy of roles and positions (see Chapters 7, 8, and 22). You may have more difficulty envisioning component-based software project management as a hierarchy of roles and positions.

Subproject engineers or sub-CBSPMs will manage each of the groups or departments traditionally associated with CBSE.

- Analysis
- Design
- Construction
- Testing
- Maintenance
- Reuse
- Component Management

The project team is comprised of the senior managers from each of these departments. Subproject teams are comprised of members of each group assigned by the department manager. The purpose of each of the project teams is to provide the lead licensed engineering software engineer or lead CBSPM with the status of each department for a period, but more importantly, to assist members in solving problems using Taylor's one best way. Just as important, managers must learn how to precisely delegate the problem to the subordinate responsible for the solution. The project team, additionally, must receive reports that the problem solution was implemented as agreed, or a deviation report is presented with remediation procedures implemented or to be exacted.

The lead software engineer or CBSPM sets the tone of the project or the program. The lead software engineer or CBSPM is responsible for selecting the software component implementation, component model, and in designing the infrastructure. An awesome responsibility, the lead engineering-trained manager will present each issue or problem to the project team for feedback as to the most effective component implementation, component model, and component infrastructure. The lead manager will work with the analysis and design teams to develop a layered design infrastructure and to identify the required components and interfaces (see Chapter 15). The results of this activity are presented to the IPT so that all department managers can consider the effects of the directed activity. Just as a gear in an automobile transmission cannot fail to comport with the performance specification's minimum allowable tolerances, no design nor construction activity can fail to correspond to analysis, design, and construction as verified at each phase of the component-based software development life cycle or the system testing and user acceptance testing activities. Component-based software project management must assure that precision by teaching the one best way in all staff members in the CBD, CBSE, and reuse teams.

27.6 Conclusion

CBSE is a state-of-the-art activity. If CBD and CBSE are to succeed, Taylorism and adoption of the one best way must become second nature to the component-based and reuse organizations. Managers must think and act like engineers. Staff members must take directions and perform their directed tasks precisely, rather than do what they consider best for the job.

Ideally, licensed engineers working as software engineers will manage CBSE projects. The numbers of licensed engineers in software engineering positions is too small. Therefore, project managers must be trained in pilot project university programs to think and work as engineers, as well as component-based software engineers. Alternatively, universities should offer engineering courses for software project managers and software engineering programs should offer CBSE programs that target education in all phases of analysis, design, programming, and testing as applied to CBSE. Project managers deserve the opportunity to earn the respect of exceptionally technically proficient staff by managing every phase of the CBSE life cycle through the project team.

Funding is required by state and federal governments and businesses to reengineer government computing processes and businesses' needs to remain competitive. Only through exceptional project management can component technology succeed. Otherwise, funds devoted to CBD and CBSE will be diverted to other projects of immediate importance, slowly and surely destroying the one technological paradigm as important to computing as Henry Ford's principle of mass production of affordable cars.

Chapter 28

The Trouble with Testing Components

Elaine J. Weyuker

28.1 Introduction

Component-based software development has been hailed as the next software revolution (Udell, 1994) and many IT organizations are changing their roles from "development shops" to "integration shops" because of the enormous cost of developing large, custom-designed, industrial-quality software systems. It is hoped that this transition will significantly decrease development costs and time to production and increase software quality.

This shift in development style implies that organizations will increasingly depend on components they did not develop themselves. The type of components used may include

- Commercial off-the-shelf software (COTS) components
- Software components specifically designed for reuse and residing in in-house software repositories

- Custom-designed components originally written explicitly for one system with no intent of being reused

In the first two cases, components are designed for no particular component consumer or end-user, and therefore no particular intended component infrastructure. In the third case there is an intended component infrastructure for which the component is presumably thoroughly tested. However, it is likely that the new component infrastructure into which the component will be integrated will have characteristics different from the original infrastructure, including different usage patterns and different components with which it must interact.

In this chapter I will investigate the implications of component-based development from a software tester's perspective. In particular I will examine issues related to validating software components that will be deployed in diverse component infrastructures. I will also consider whether anticipated savings are likely and whether or not the resulting systems built from these components are likely to meet reliability and availability standards that are routinely required in industrial settings.

I am pessimistic about the likelihood of being able to meet these requirements. For component-based software development (CBD) to revolutionize software development, developers must be able to produce software significantly cheaper and faster. At the same time, the resulting software must meet high reliability standards while being easy to maintain. Currently there is little evidence that that is the case, and plenty of reason to believe that will not be the case. From a tester's viewpoint, we mostly see the problems that CBD engenders, and see a further marginalization of test teams at the same time that testers should become even more essential to the development team. My personal experience is that, instead of increasing the test organization to compensate for decreased control over component development, management sees the movement to CBD and the associated decrease in the number of developers needed as an argument in favor of decreasing the number of testers as well. I see this as a path to disaster.

28.2 Testing Fundamentals

Using the traditional software development paradigm in which all components are custom-designed for one particular system, at least three levels of correctness testing are normally performed: unit testing, integration testing, and system testing.

Unit testing is usually performed by the person who wrote the code or others on that project's development team, and involves the testing of individual units such as functions or subroutines. The source code is almost always available during unit testing, and because developers are familiar with code details they can usually make constructive use of this information. For those reasons, and because individual units typically are small, unit testing often relies on details of the code for test case selection. For example, a tester might devise test cases that cause every statement of the code to be executed at least once or cause certain code interactions to be executed.

Members of the development team most commonly perform integration testing, although it may sometimes be performed by an independent testing organization. Integration testing involves the testing, as an entity, of the subsystems formed by integrating the units that have already been unit tested. Because these constituents have already been comprehensively unit tested, integration testing generally focuses on the interface code used to "glue" the units together. During this type of testing the component infrastructure of the final system can be tested.

An independent team of professional testers or quality assurance personnel generally performs system testing. It involves testing the entire software system formed from the tested subsystems. Perhaps for the first time, all deployed components in the software system can be tested together with the component infrastructure, in a situation identical to, or one that closely approximates, the way in which the final system will be used. Because system testers typically do not have the type of detailed understanding of the code that a programmer involved with its development would have, it is common practice for system testers to have access only to the object code rather than the source code. Also, the magnitude of the typical system' source code makes any sort of examination of the code itself impossible once the system has been fully integrated.

28.3 The Problem

Much has been written about the supposed benefits of component-based software development. The underlying assumptions of many of these articles and books is that CBD will involve substantial code-reuse and that it is possible to easily and seamlessly integrate components into new component infrastructures. Most of these arguments have relied on the following intuition:

- Costs will be decreased because components will be reused many times, allowing development costs to be amortized over many uses
- Development time will be decreased because most of the development required will now involve writing only software interfaces
- And software quality will be improved because many different projects will be using the components, and therefore defects will be caught more quickly, yielding more trustworthy software

Although these arguments have substantial intuitive appeal, there is little empirical research to validate them. There are also counter-balancing arguments that imply that the reuse of components will lead to significantly less dependable software than when systems are custom-designed. I will examine these arguments below as I explore the extent to which traditional software testing approaches can be used in component-based testing. Another goal is to determine the differences between software produced using CBD and traditional custom-designed software development. Clearly, one fundamental difference is that unit testing, as it is traditionally performed is infeasible for CBD. In the next section I will consider the implications of this fact and investigate any differences there are between the three types of components mentioned in the introduction to this chapter.

It is common for a project team to assume that components that were not developed in-house are reliable and can operate properly in many different component infrastructures; this assumption persists even though the team does not unit test these components. Integrating in-house components, especially those that have not been thoroughly tested with other components that the organization is buying or building, will likely result in escalating quality problems in a system that functioned previously. When any modifications have to be made to the components or their interfaces, significant difficulties may arise because the team does not have access to the source code and does not really understand the likely consequences of proposed modifications. The development team does not have the component producer's intimate knowledge of the code. Hopefully the project team has comprehensive specifications with which to assemble the component. Consumers must also be aware that the producers' components were not designed explicitly for their system, and therefore may include functionality that is not needed or used by the project. This may mean that the resulting system is significantly larger than it needs to be, which can lead to profound performance problems.

A recent major catastrophe resulted from a software failure caused by software reuse without adequate levels of testing. During the initial launch of the European Ariane 5 launch vehicle in June 1996, it veered off course almost immediately after takeoff and exploded. A careful investigation determined that the cause of the explosion was software that had been reused from the Ariane 4 project without sufficient testing. It had been assumed that the Ariane 4 and Ariane 5 software were sufficiently similar that they did not require substantial retesting of the components reused from the Ariane 4 software. The failure was in a 10-year-old module and was caused by a failed conversion from a 64-bit floating point value to a 16-bit signed integer; the conversion was applied to a number larger than could be represented in the 16 bit format. The failure was documented in the final report issued by Professor J.L. Lions, who chaired the Inquiry Board convened to study the accident (*www.esrin.esa.it/htdocs/tidc/Press/Press96/ariane5rep.html*).

The lesson to be drawn is that if component-based software construction becomes standard, with the associated routine reuse of components, new ways to test the resulting software must be developed so that the risk of similar disasters will be significantly reduced. If we naïvely assume that the proper behavior of a component in one component infrastructure implies its proper behavior in another, we are likely to see other tragedies occur. Furthermore, these newly developed testing techniques will need to be widely applicable even if the source code is unavailable. Finally, if we ultimately determine that there is no way to cost-effectively assure that the systems resulting from the use of these types of components meet organizations' reliability requirements, the future of CBSE is in doubt.

28.4 Testing Software When Built From Components

There are two distinct types of component reuse. In the first case the software component was custom-designed, but not for the current project. In the second case the component was not designed for any particular consumer.

28.4.1 Testing Components Developed for Another Project

If a component was developed for a particular project and then subsequently integrated with one or more different component infrastructures, I presume that the component was thoroughly tested for the original project in its intended component infrastructure.

One way to select test cases for custom-designed software components is to rely on historical usage data describing how the component was used in the past. This data may be estimated or may have been collected from an earlier version of the component, from a similar system, or from a system whose outputs serve as inputs to this system.

When selecting test cases in this way the idea is to select the most commonly occurring inputs to test. Because the number of possible inputs to a system is typically astronomically large and only a very small percentage of these possible test cases can be selected for testing, the intuitive response is to test the most commonly occurring inputs; a failure in one of these common cases will significantly impact users. Avritzer and Weyuker used this test selection approach (1995).

In 1996 I modified this approach to incorporate the consequence of failure when selecting test cases so that, in addition, the ones with the highest consequence of failure are also selected (Weyuker, 1996).

If a component were tested based on a usage profile for one component infrastructure and then reused in a significantly different one, the validity of the testing might be substantially reduced. For example, the most thoroughly tested portion of the component may not be executed in a new component infrastructure while the least tested portion may be critical. Similarly, it is possible that the most important parts of the component from the consumer's perspective correspond to extremely unlikely scenarios in the original system's behavior, and thus those parts of the component may not have been tested at all. For these reasons it is very risky to reuse software components tested for a specific project without additional testing for another project. Such behavior could lead to the types of catastrophic failures discussed earlier.

For example, consider two projects that both use a particular software component in significantly different ways. Assume both are telephone call processing systems that can handle three types of calls: c_1, c_2, and c_3. Assume for simplicity that, on average, all calls in both systems last for one minute, regardless of the call type. Table 28-1 shows that, for Project 1, three new calls of type c_1 arrive, on average, every minute. The table also shows that, on average, one new call of type c_2 arrives each minute, while type c_3 calls arrive far less frequently (1 every 3 1/3 minutes). Assume both projects can handle 1000 calls simultaneously.

Table 28-1: *Call Volume for Different Projects*

	Project 1	**Project 2**
Call Type	**Calls per minute**	**Calls per minute**
C_1	3.0	0.3
C_2	1.0	1.0
C_3	0.3	3.0

One of the central problems with testing even moderate-sized software is that the size of the input space is almost always enormous. Even for this simple example, handling only three types of calls and only 1000 simultaneous calls, I can show that there are a total of 167,668,501 distinct possible test cases, which translates to a vast amount of testing if the test group is to perform anything near exhaustive testing.

For that reason Avritzer and Weyuker (1995) developed an algorithm and tool to automatically generate test suites based on usage data of the type appearing in Table 28-1. The inputs generated correspond to the most commonly occurring scenarios that the system is expected to encounter. For Project 1 we would expect to see cases in which there are many calls of type c_1 and many fewer calls of type c_3. For Project 2 the situation is reversed.

For Project 1 the test suite generated contained a total of 88 test cases, a minute fraction of the possible inputs–roughly one test case for every 2,000,000 possible inputs. However, because the test cases were selected based on the probability of occurrence, they nevertheless covered more than 98% of the probability associated with the states. Project 2, however, had a substantially different usage pattern and the same 88-element test suite is insufficient because it covered only 24% of the probable states. From the perspective of Project 2, very few of the states that occur frequently had been tested at all by this test suite. Therefore little evidence was presented that the software component would behave properly in the new project.

For these reasons, only a significant amount of additional testing could possibly restore Project 2's confidence in the component. However, Project 2 would generally not have at its disposal all of the resources available to Project 1. For example, testers for Project 2 might not have access to the component's source code because it was written for a different project. Both detailed requirements and design specification documents might no longer be available or up-to-date, nor is there likely to be the type of detailed understanding of the system design that would be available from the component's development team. The test team might find it difficult, if not impossible, to actually perform the necessary testing for the component when it is to be integrated into Project 2, even if there were time allocated, personnel available, and the will to perform the testing. As a result, there will always be a risk (possibly leading to disastrous consequences) if this component were to be reused in Project 2.

Note that this is a fundamentally different situation than what happens during system testing of a project using a traditional development paradigm. As mentioned above, it is a common practice during system testing that the source code not be available to the testers. At that stage the development organization would normally have the source code. The reason that system testers are usually denied access to the source code is because it is not needed or useful, not because it is not available. In the case I discuss in this section, however, it would be surprising to find these artifacts available to the component consumer or the end-user.

Ideally the complete specification is available along with the source code and there is a test repository containing both test suites and test plans. In that case system testing can be performed for the new project using the component, as it would be done for any project. However, even if all of these work products are available, testing may be difficult because the original developers may no longer have the familiarity with the code that they once had or the team may have been disbanded. Additionally, the development team may feel that debugging and modification of the component is no longer their responsibility.

The customary case occurs when the component's source code is unavailable. This raises a significant testing problem: if only the object code is available, and testers do expose failures, how will the development team isolate the faults and how will they correct the faulty code? In contrast, if the traditional custom-designed software development paradigm is used, when a failure occurs during a system test the information is relayed to the development team who corrects the faults. This is possible because the development team has the source code and the detailed knowledge of the code necessary to make the changes.

28.4.2 Using Software Components Developed for No Particular Consumer

I now consider the case in which a software component is developed with the explicit intent of integration into many different component infrastructures, each having a distinct usage pattern and a unique set of other components with which it must interoperate. Note that this is similar to the product-line architectures discussed in Chapter 22. This scenario includes two different subcases.

- The software was developed with the intent that it will reside in an in-house component repository
- Commercial off-the-shelf (COTS) components

In the first case it may be possible to access the source code when needed, and it may even be possible to have access to the personnel and expertise used in the creation of the component.

This situation is fundamentally different from the one outlined in the previous section. In that case the component was developed for a particular project and it was later decided to reuse the code. In this section the component producer is developing the component to be used in many different component infrastructures. For that reason, initial testing of the component cannot depend on the expected usage patterns for the component because there are no specific, intended usage patterns.

In general, because there are likely to be many different usage patterns, the software will have to undergo comprehensive testing with software testers trying to envision many different ways that the software will be deployed. Of course, no one can foresee every possible scenario, and so prudent consumers will definitely want to spend a significant amount of resources testing the component, both in isolation and once it is integrated into their systems. Thus, even though the code itself was written only once (assuming that no modifications were made to customize it for different users) significantly more testing needs to be done. This might well offset most or all of the savings made from reusing the component, because testing and debugging without the source code or a detailed design specification might be necessary, thereby making testing significantly more expensive than if a traditional custom-designed development paradigm was used. If code modifications were implemented for the deployment of software components for the new component infrastructure, possible savings would be further reduced. Although in some cases it may be feasible to extend the functionality of a component without the source code by using a wrapper, in other cases it may be essentially impossible to modify the component or require reverse-engineering, which is typically extremely expensive.

Because the original developers of the component may be unknown or unavailable when the software is used, certain information essential for proper testing may not be available. This might prohibit certain types of testing altogether, thereby impacting the ultimate system reliability.

The second case that I discuss in this section is the use of COTS components. Recently, many sub-organizations within AT&T have begun investigating the use of COTS components as a way to deal with the enormous cost of building large software systems and the difficulty of finding sufficient numbers of developers with appropriate experience and expertise. The hope is that the use of COTS components will significantly decrease development time and thereby lead to early product deployment, which should yield a competitive advantage by being first or early to market. But each of the quality and reliability problems discussed above is even more pronounced when COTS components are integrated into a system.

Source code is usually unavailable for COTS components, making modifications difficult and expensive. There is the almost certain absence of detailed design knowledge that further compounds this problem. In addition, there is likely to be a complete lack of control over when and how COTS components are maintained and supported. Developers at AT&T report that they have found it difficult to exercise control over the frequency with which components are updated, even in cases when AT&T is a major customer (Avritzer, 2000).

Another issue with COTS components is that there may be a significant amount of functionality in off-the-shelf components that will never be used in your project. However, because the excess functionality is part of the component, it could lead to interoperability and performance problems.

Perhaps of greatest importance from the viewpoint of quality is the producer's potential to terminate support for the component. If a component producer goes out of business the situation is even worse. If your project is dependent on the component, what are your alternatives? There have been proposals to use escrow agreements to protect the component consumer or end-user in such situations, but this requires a willing producer. If you do obtain the source code as the result of such an agreement, and the vendor is no longer available to maintain it, all of the above-cited potential problems will likely make the code essentially unmaintainable from the point of view of cost and reliability. If your customers are relying on your product to provide very high levels of reliability and to meet very high availability requirements, and the software is unable to meet these requirements, it is your reputation at stake. Blaming the problems on the component producer is unacceptable; it is your responsibility to purchase components wisely and therefore your liability when the purchased component cannot be maintained. See Chapter 6 for a good summary of the risks of using COTS components.

28.5 Facilitating the Testing of Reusable Components

One of the primary reasons for moving to a component-based development paradigm is reuse. Significant preparation is required to design component repositories to enable many different projects to retrieve and use these components. In Chapter 29 Hedley Apperly describes issues related to the use of component libraries. In this section we discuss such libraries from the point of view of testing.

To improve the quality of the resulting software, software specifications and test suites should be stored with each software component and care should be taken to update them appropriately whenever modifications are made to the component. In addition, three sets of links between specific entries in the documents and code should be maintained.

1. Between each individual specified requirement and its implementation in both directions. Whenever a modification is made to the specification it is easy to keep track of the appropriate places in the code that need associated modifications. Similarly, if a change is made to the code this pointer will facilitate the update of the specification, thereby helping to assure that the specification is kept up-to-date.
2. Between each individual test case and the portion or portions of the code that the test cases were intended to validate. When the code is modified it is not difficult to identify which of the test cases are needed for regression testing. Furthermore, whenever new functionality is added it is essential to include additional test cases in the test suite. These pointers between elements of the test suite and associated parts of the code should help identify any functionality that must still be tested.
3. From the specification to individual test cases that were included to validate the functionality described in that portion of the specification, as well as pointers from the test cases into the specification. In that way it becomes evident which portions of the specification still require testing or have only been lightly or inadequately tested. In addition, when changes are made to the specification these pointers will facilitate the identification of which test cases need to be rerun or augmented.

28.6 Conclusions

I have outlined some of the potential problems to be expected when a project team decides to use a software component originally written for a different component infrastructure with different usage patterns. I have also considered the related case in which software is developed with the explicit intent that it will be used in many different component infrastructures, all or many of which may not have been known at the time of development.

Based on my personal experience, I conclude that developers and potential users should be aware that components likely will not have been adequately tested for their infrastructure. It may also be difficult to anticipate what is known about the expected behavior and performance of a component once it is installed in a project's infrastructure. This implies that the component might have to be tested as if it has not yet undergone any testing at all. In some cases, such as when the source code is unavailable to the potential new users and there is no low-level understanding of the implementation, there may be no way to adequately test and debug the software. In those cases it would be extremely unwise to use such components in a production system.

The goal for most industrial organizations is to be able to produce highly reliable software inexpensively. Many have seized upon CBD as the best route to achieve this goal. I have argued in this chapter that at this time it is doubtful that the reliability requirements mandated by many businesses will be met using CBD, and it is not clear that the cost of producing the software will be significantly cheaper than custom-designed software systems. Without significant research on testing component-based software in each of the forms outlined above, I believe it is unlikely that this status will change. We must also learn to demand adequate documentation for procured components, including evidence of the types of testing performed and the test suites, which could be used for regression testing if the software is changed.

Finally, software test managers must be included in software component project management teams. Software test managers have the experience to help make difficult build versus buy decisions. They are the most likely to argue for comprehensive documentation and source code, even if in escrow. Software test managers tend to fervently support the proper utilization of component repositories and librarians because they rely on up-to-date specifications and test cases. Effective software test managers will often tell the project team anticipated results the team does not want to hear. Nevertheless, these are predictions that are in the organization's best interests.

Without these things, I believe we are tilting at windmills.

Chapter 29

Configuration Management and Component Libraries

Hedley Apperly

29.1 Introduction

In this chapter I focus on mechanisms that enable configuration management and component libraries for component-based software engineering (CBSE). The ideas in this chapter flow naturally from the software component production, management, and consumption processes required to develop and maintain software components in both information technology organizations and commercial component producers.

29.2 Component Management

29.2.1 Why Do We Need a Component Manager?

One of the primary ways to enable a successful component development life cycle is to implement a process that includes an integrated configuration management and component library environment. As we saw from the construction analogy in Chapter 2, the warehouse or builders' yard plays a pivotal engineering role as building parts (components) are traded between producers and consumers. In many ways the quality control, storage, advertising, and shipping tasks carried out by the builder's merchant make the whole concept of component-based construction possible.

Component management is a useful engineering concept whatever the scale or complexity of the software project. You may be involved in a small team using technical components and need a process and tool to simplify communication. Alternatively, you may be involved in a large, multi-site, component-based environment with hundreds of developers and require powerful processes and supporting tools.

The key to a scalable solution is a scalable process and a scalable set of tools. The produce-manage-consume process is obviously scalable, especially since it has been proven in various industries over many years (Allen and Frost, 1998). Tools that support a CBD process are significantly more difficult to find, although examples include the Aonix Select Component Manager (*www.aonix.com*), Microsoft's Visual Component Manager (*www.microsoft.com*) and Computer Associates Component Manager (*www.ca.com*). This chapter describes the necessary features that configuration management and component library applications need to support scalable CBSE.

29.2.2 What is the Component Management Process?

The basics of the produce-manage-consume process are, not surprisingly, the production, management, and consumption of components. Component production can take the form of purchased/acquired components, producing components demanded by a solution, or the wrapping of legacy assets. Production also implies a suitable level of documentation or description. The Component Specification, defined in Chapter 1, identifies the minimum documentation necessary. Management focuses on quality control, organization, and availability. Finally, consumption includes finding and using components or their specifications.

29.2.3 What Do We Need From a Component Manager?

We need a component manager not only to manage the storage of components in a static sense, but also to enable publication (production) and consumption. The same is true for database client/server systems. In most cases, databases are useful only through the applications that are designed to connect to them. The necessary component manager services from are defined in Table 29-1.

Table 29-1: *Services for a Component Manager*

PRODUCE
• Publish undocumented or informally designed components • Use component specifications as starting point for design • Publish components with specifications • Re-publish components and specifications • Notify consumers of new components or problems
MANAGE
• Manage library repositories • Manage library users • Manage catalogues • Assure quality components • Manage components • Make components available • Manage the versioning of components
CONSUME
• Search for necessary components • Fulfill identified gaps • Specify component specifications for tender • Use or reuse component specifications • Use or reuse components • Deploy components • Register interest in components • Receive new component notification • Review new components • Refresh component specifications and components

29.2.3.1 Produce

1. Publish undocumented or informally designed components

This task refers to the components coming into the CBSE system from external sources, including components from component producers, components from other teams (who perhaps have less rigor), and from legacy renewal. Legacy renewal can include mining for components in existing solutions. Noncomponent-based solutions (or subsolutions) can be "wrapped" to provide a component-like interface. This shows that components can become available without being specifically "produced" as components.

Many components acquired by an enterprise are undocumented and have no supporting design models. To make these components available for reuse, the undocumented components need to provide enough information for potential users to determine the trustworthiness of the components in the same manner as they would evaluate homegrown components. For COM+, CORBA, and EJB components the interface definitions can be decoded fairly easily, but this is merely the beginning of the component specification. Users need information about the infrastructure and master design plan defined earlier in Chapter 1, as well as the functionality of the component and its internal algorithms. If the component producer supplies this information then it is a straightforward case of transferring the component specification into the component library while assuring all the necessary quality checks are made. If sufficient documentation is not available to satisfy your quality assurance audit, then you should question the suitability of the component for use within your organization. If your quality assurance procedures indicate that insufficient documentation is available to trust the component, then it is risky to acquire it.

2. Use component specification as starting point for design

This "design start point" process occurs when a component producer acts as a subcontractor to a solution builder or consumer. The consumer's component librarian needs to transfer the component specification to the producer, generally via a request for proposal (RFP), so that one or more producers will have a starting point (or contract) for design and development. This specification may be textual, but ideally a number of UML diagrams will be provided. A first cut class diagram with interfaces, services, and operations (with parameters) is a useful starting point for the component producer, who should develop components to the criteria detailed in a specification.

Alternatively, the component producer may define a specification in the hope that there will be a demand for a generic component. In this case it may also be useful to publish the specification for the component into the component management repository ahead of the development to allow solution designers to work in parallel.

3. Publish components with specifications

Once the component producer has completed the software component, the producer will need to make it available. If the producer has not already published a component specification, then it will need to publish the specification, implementation (optional), and executable at the same time. This form of publication allows consumers to locate components in the repository and then retrieve the physical component (executable, dynamic linked library (DLL), or other format). However, the component producer may still choose to publish only the specification; for example, if the producer plans to charge for use of the component. In this case the consumer would then use the component specification, which should provide a pointer to the producer company so that the consumer may purchase the component.

If the specification for the new component already exists in the library and represents the finished component, the two should be synchronized to form a usable component. This can be achieved by tracking the version number of component specifications. This may not be the case if the component producer has taken steps to make the component more generic or powerful. Where the specification no longer matches the finished component, the specification will need to be updated to reflect the changes. This may be achieved automatically or manually depending upon the specific component management repository. This discussion highlights the need to separate the four levels of component abstraction within the component library, as shown in Table 29-2, while maintaining links among them.

To manage all the levels of component dependency you need to define the following links.

Table 29-2: *Component Abstraction Levels*

1	**Component Specification**
2	**Component Implementation**
3	**Component Executable**
4	**Component Deployment**

- A component specification may have more than one implementation (language)
- A component implementation may have more than one executable or DLL (build)
- A component executable may have more than one deployment (be deployed on more than one *node,* to use the UML term)

This linking is particularly important for checking the impact of changes before they are made and determining in what programs software components have been used. Most source code configuration systems are not capable of managing these interdependent links.

4. Re-publish components and specifications

The component producer may need to modify software components that have already been published. To make these changes public the component producer will need to publish a new version of an existing component into the component library. This new version must also be linked to the previous versions so consumers can track the components they use. This form of tracking is also important when components are split or merged because a component used in the past may now be provided as two interdependent components. Over time components may change shape and complex components are typically split to ease understanding and facilitate use. When a component producer updates a component to provide new features for a popular commercial application, the producer must communicate the changes to all consumers. If it is hard to take advantage of updates to components, consumers may choose to stay with their current version, resulting in missed profit opportunities for the component producer.

5. Notify consumers of new components or problems

Publication and re-publication of components requires that the producer notify consumers of the availability of software components. This task may be automated with technologies such as e-mail, but there are choices to be made. New components will usually be advertised and e-mails could contain a copy of (or pointer to) the new component. If problems with components are identified or consumer feedback is required, the process can be more like a "car recall" notice. Advertising and warning are two sides of the same coin.

In summary, the component producer only needs mechanisms for putting versions of components and their specifications into a sharable component library, getting specifications for new components from the library, and notifying consumers when components change or new ones appear. The key is that the component library (or repository) is a neutral holding area between component producers and consumers. It acts as a conduit and enables the produce-manage-consume process.

29.2.3.2 Manage

The sequence of features discussed is based upon the general setup and management tasks for a component librarian.

1. Manage library repositories

As described earlier, components will need to reside in different locations for different producers and consumers. Project teams building and using components will need their own local repositories. Enterprises and even individual departments may store components. Outside the enterprise producers will advertise, sell, and distribute components worldwide. The task of managing these repositories includes setting them up and maintaining their availability.

2. Manage library users

Once you have library repositories, you will need to control who has access to them. Certain users should not be restricted from access to certain areas: others may be able to browse but not consume. At the upper end of the scale users may be able to consume from, publish into, or manage component libraries.

3. *Manage catalogues*

Within a library the contents need to be organized in such a way that housekeeping and searching are optimized. Component librarians will create hierarchies of catalogues for locating components to maintain order.

4. *Assure quality components*

Part of the role of a component librarian should be to ensure that only quality components are readily available for consumption. The component librarian or quality assurance analyst should control which components are published into a library, perhaps by implementing a holding area for quality assurance, before components are moved into an area that can be accessed by consumers.

5. *Manage components (specification, interfaces, implementation, executable, and deployment)*

Management of software components is not simply a task; component management is a component library feature required to support the four levels of component abstraction. Therefore this applies purely to the organization and protection of the published assets, which may be logical (specifications) or physical (built or compiled) components. The component library repository must be capable of holding distinct information about each of the four levels. It is also important that the links between each of the levels can be visualized and defined. This visualization should be provided graphically with a Windows-like explorer tree and ideally a dependency tree, as seen in Figure 29-1.

6. *Make components available*

Components should not only be available to users of the specific component library application or repository. I have found it useful to publish component information using alternative technologies such as documents, HTML, and the Web. Even more useful is the ability to use

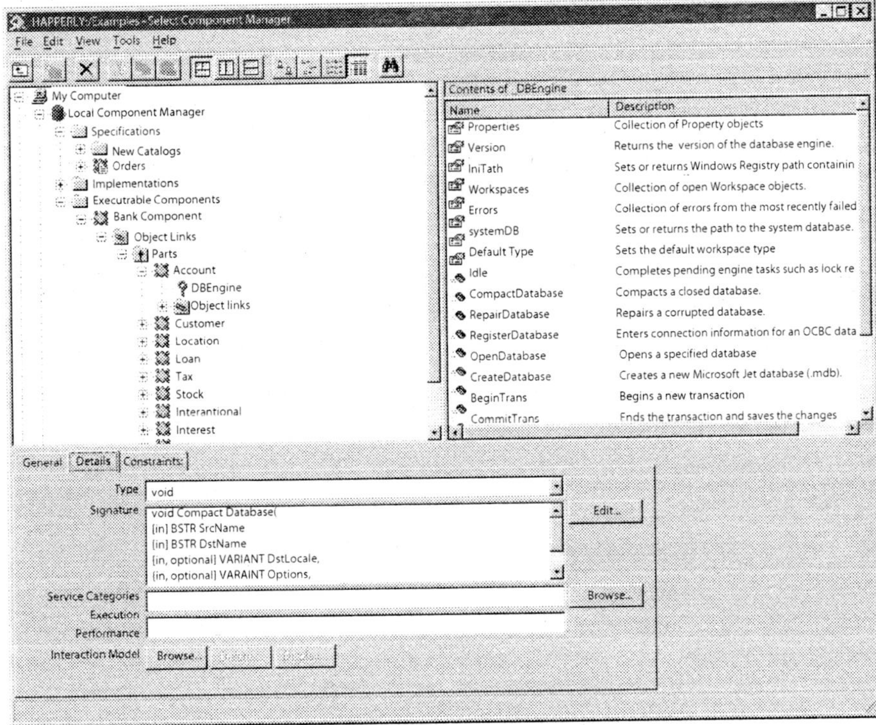

Figure 29-1: *The Aonix Select Component Manager, an example of component management.*

these forms of published libraries in searches for gap fulfillment using the same engine as the component repository at the same time.

7. Manage the versioning of components

The final level of complexity for component libraries is that each of the four levels of component abstraction will need version identification. New versions of components can be created and linked to older versions. It will also be necessary to archive and remove and old unused versions of components. This concept is similar to that of source code configuration management but refers to component specifications and completed components. The component specification exists well before any code is created and this is one of the reasons why mainstream configuration management systems are currently not suited to Component Management.

While I am on the topic of versions it is worth exploring key differences between component management tools and version control systems. From my experience there are three key differences. First, version control and configuration management systems focus on discrete artifacts, and we have clearly seen that the component concept necessitates four levels of hierarchy. This is more than purely grouping or relating items—it is an intrinsic hierarchic structure. Second, version control systems often focus on teams of developers. CBSE includes architects, designers, and reuse librarians across whole organizations, countries, and even continents. This usually implies a network of repositories with interconnected search facilities. Third, CBSE will only be possible if the availability of components is published proactively. It will be even more challenging to support CBSE if the users are always required to search through a static library of artifacts, no matter how well organized.

29.2.3.3 Consume

1. Search for necessary components

A comprehensive search utility is necessary to enable a solution builder to reuse before they buy or build. Typically, the last thing you will know about a component you are looking for is its name. You are much more likely to know in what infrastructure you will be implementing, what business function you want to perform, what programming language you use, and perhaps what services and parameters you need. These are the criteria that must be definable for searches. See Figure 29-2 for a screenshot show an example search utility in action.

2. Fulfill identified gaps

Gap fulfillment should permit you to find components that are not quite the same as your specified search. Thus, you have the option to modify your overall solution design to accommodate a component that fulfills enough of your component specifications. To enable this process step the component management system should provide a

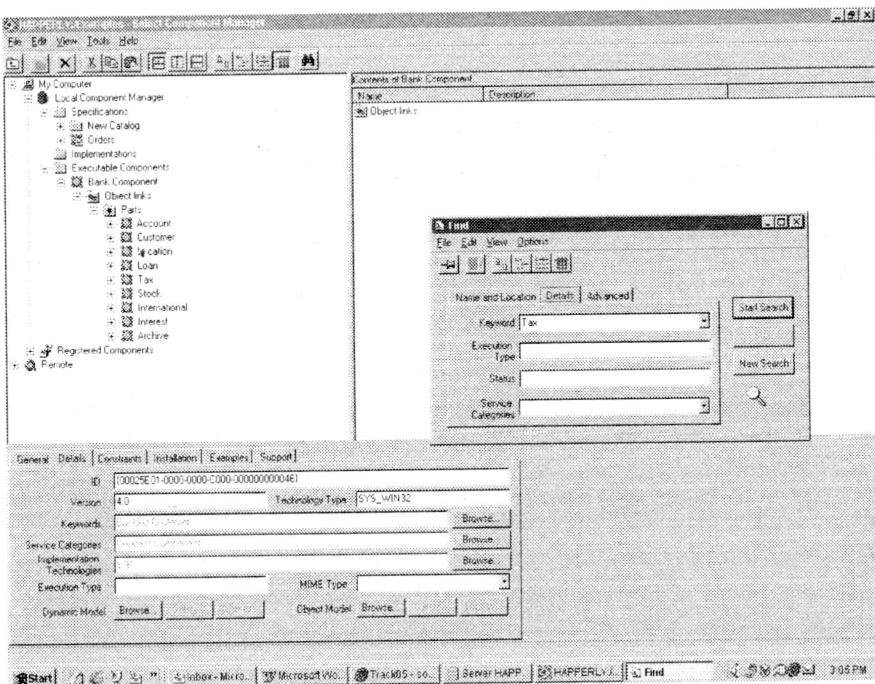

Figure 29-2: *Princeton Softech's Select Component Manager find function, an example of a search utility.*

fuzzy searching capability. Once a component that meets your needs most closely is identified, you then have the option to enhance it (if it is open source) or wrap it in your own component to add the extra functionality you need.

3. *Specify component specifications for tender*

If a component generally meets the consumer's or end-user's needs, the solution builder may choose to publish a component specification for tender. The form of the specification should be equal to the search criteria specified above. The published component specification will give a component producer information about what to build and why it should be constructed. The specified information alone may be insufficient, requiring the producer and consumer or end-user to enter into a dialogue.

4. Use or reuse component specifications

During the design stage, once you have found a suitable component you may choose to use the specification in your design. This is true even if the component has not been completed yet. However, the component executable should be stockpiled for future solution assembly if it is available when the specification is used.

5. Use or reuse components

If you are less structured in your design process or perhaps purely focused on your application build phase, you will likely need to use component implementations or component executables. This reflects the majority of current, widget-level component reuse. This in no way demeans the suitability of component management for this type of reuse. The problems encountered here are typically large numbers of small components that can be used only if found. At this level component management eases the process of communication between component vendors and direct users and reusers.

6. Deploy components

When the executable components are actually deployed onto the runtime computer, deployment details should be recorded automatically based on the machines where the components are installed. This allows you to track the complex deployment of interdependent component versions, which is necessary when auditing or upgrading deployed software components.

7. Register interest in components

Whenever components are purchased, used, or libraries searched, the consumer should be able to register an interest in the library or the component. This information should be used to inform the consumer when new components or important information become available.

8. Receive new component notification

Developers frequently register an interest in receiving notifications about new information for a component. As identified earlier, a good way to receive notification is via e-mail, possibly with the new component attached. At a minimum, a hot-link to the component in its repository should be provided so that the component can be reviewed for suitability and use or reuse.

9. Review new components

The new or modified component specification can now be reviewed to evaluate its worth. If no new benefits are obtainable the specification can be ignored. Otherwise, you may decide to take advantage of this component after conducting a quality audit and functional review.

10. Refresh component specifications and components

As you have already used this component's specification, executable, or both, you need to integrate the new version with a minimum of disruption.

29.3 Conclusion

This completes the discussion of the basic features necessary for a component manager or component repository to enable a production, management, and consumption process for CBD. As you can see, the majority of the features focus on the process of publishing, finding, and using components, not just the static management of artifacts. It is also sensible to relate the facilities needed back to the analogy provided in Chapter 2. The component management repository acts as the builders' yard and catalogue; it is the database of specifications, search facility, tracker for component use, and notifier of component updates. These are challenging responsibilities that are becoming increasingly necessary to succeed in today's CBSE-oriented world.

I have described the major steps that relate to the way in which producers and consumers want to use component management systems and component libraries. Therefore, standard features required from component management and component repository applications were described and a set of evaluation criteria was identified. These criteria are useful in the selection of component management and component library tools that enable CBSE rather than hinder it. A fair number of component management tools exist in the market today and the main differences are the level of component technology independence and their integration with design tools and IDEs. Examples include: The Aonix Select Component Manager (*www.aonix.com*) as the first independent and most mature tool of this type in the market; COOL:Jex from Computer Associates (*www.ca.com*) which now focuses on EJBs, with its links to COOL:Joe (Hunt, 2000); and Visual Component Manager from Microsoft (*www.microsoft.com*), which forms part of the COM-based Visual Developers Studio.

These processes described in this chapter apply equally to one or two-person projects and large inter-enterprise CBSE endeavors. Thus, an important fact concerning CBD is that the tools and processes you use for CBSE must be scalable in terms of application and resource complexity if you intend to achieve success through CBSE.

Chapter 30

The Evolution, Maintenance, and Management of Component-Based Systems

Mark Vigder[1]

30.1 Introduction

After deployment, software systems enter a phase of maintenance, management, and evolution that can last many years until final decommissioning. This post-deployment period is the longest and hence the most expensive phase of a system's life cycle. The ability of organizations to repair, enhance, and update systems, as well as to provide management and user support, often determines the level of success that a product achieves both functionally and financially.

Building a software system from commercial components changes neither the importance of, nor the expense associated with, maintenance, evolution, and management. Component-based systems must continue to satisfy evolving user requirements, failures of the system must be managed quickly, the system must adapt to an ever-changing environment, and managers must be able to monitor and control the deployed system.

However, the nature of the post-deployment activities changes with component-based systems. For component-based systems to be successful over many years of expected service, organizations involved in building or acquiring them must understand and accommodate these differences ([Gentleman, 1999] [Hybertson, Ta, and Thomas, 1997] [Voas, 1998 and 1999]).

30.2 Challenges in Maintaining Component-Based Systems

There are a number of reasons why component-based systems present unique maintenance challenges.

Maintenance occurs at the level of components rather than at the level of source code. Traditional maintenance involves observing and modifying lines of source code. However, in component-based systems the primary unit of construction is generally a black-box component; the custom-developed source code is typically used to tailor the components and integrate them. Although the tailoring and integration code is maintained at the source code level, maintainers must deal with most of the system at the component level. Maintenance personnel cannot "drill down" to view or change the source code of the components, but are restricted to reconfiguring and reintegrating components.

Successful components have a wide user base. One of the advantages of using components is that their cost is amortized over many users. Although amortization provides many advantages, it also means that the system builder is just one of many voices requesting changes or modification to the underlying components.

There is limited visibility into components and limited knowledge about their internal behavior. Effective maintenance involves detailed observations of the behavior of a system in order to perform functions such as troubleshooting, testing, and performance enhancements. Because system integrators have limited visibility into the component behavior, maintenance personnel must be able to monitor system behavior without observing the internal behavior of individual components.

Maintenance and evolution of the various components is under the control of diverse organizations that are outside the control of the system maintainers. When using components, particularly those provided by component producers and component consumers, system evolution may be affected by these third parties. Maintenance of the components generally remains under the control of the component developers or their agents. When a system is composed of multiple components from a variety of component producers the responsibility for maintenance is distributed across many different organizations.

30.2.1 Maintaining a Component-Based System

I have identified several key activities that will allow you to effectively maintain and manage component-based software systems. Although a number of these activities are similar to what you normally perform in noncomponent-based systems, using components means that the nature of these maintenance activities changes. You should develop strategies to support the following activities (Vigder and Dean, 1998).

Component reconfiguration—Reconfiguring is the act of replacing, adding, or deleting components within a software system. Reconfiguration is most commonly required because of the frequency with which commercial component producers release updated versions of their components, which can be as often as two or three times per year. Other reasons for reconfiguring the components include replacing components with better products from competing producers or adding and deleting components as the functional requirements of the system evolve. Unfortunately, modifying the component configuration is not as simple as installing new software. It is an expensive activity requiring integrators to complete an entire release cycle, including component evaluation, testing, design, integration, and system regression testing (Rombach, 1990).

When faced with the decision of whether to upgrade the component configuration, maintainers must weigh many trade-offs (Erdogmus and Vandergraaf, 1999).

- The financial cost of upgrading a component
- The risk of greater cost if the integrators wait through too many component releases before upgrading
- The criticality of the defect-fixes being provided in the newer releases
- The usefulness of the new functionality being offered
- The risk of new defects being introduced with the upgrade
- The risk that the vendor will stop supporting the older product

Configuration management—For component-based systems configuration management occurs at the level of components rather than at the level of source code. Maintainers must:

- Track the change history for each individual component
- Determine the availability and support level provided by the various component vendors and maintain the license and support agreements
- And manage the component configurations that are installed at each deployed site, including tracking the history of component deployments, determining the compatibility of different component sets and versions within particular environments, and managing problem reports associated with specific component sets and deployments

System tailoring—Components provide a generic functionality that can be used by many applications and organizations. System integrators must customize and tailor this functionality to satisfy any local operational requirements that are unique to the end-user organization. Successful systems are those that can be quickly modified and tailored to meet evolving user requirements.

For component-based systems tailoring involves an ongoing process of customizing and configuring components, adding new components to the system, and combining services of multiple components in novel ways. Because integrators do not have access to component internals, this must be done by integrating components to provide enhanced functionality and using vendor-supported tailoring techniques to customize the components ([Heineman, 1998] [Vigder, Gentleman, and Dean, 1996]).

Troubleshooting and repair—When a component-based system fails it is often difficult to isolate the cause of failure because maintenance personnel have little knowledge of component internals. In this case you need to experiment "at the edges" of components, watching their behavior and resource usage, to determine which component(s) is causing the problem ([Sun Microsystems, 1999] [Hissam, 1998] [Voas, 1997]).

To identify and fix a fault system builders must work closely with the support staff of the third-party component suppliers as well as the general component user community. Where faults include complex interactions involving sets of components from different component producers, many different organizations may be involved in the troubleshooting and repair of the system.

System monitoring—System managers and maintainers must continuously monitor a system during its ongoing operation. This is done to measure performance and resource usage, watch for failures, determine security violations, and monitor user behavior. Monitoring black-box components is difficult because the internal behavior is hidden. Rather than intra-component capabilities, maintainers must use inter-component and system monitoring capabilities to observe system behavior (Hissam, 1998).

30.3 Planning for Post-Deployment

A software system must be carefully designed to be maintainable and evolvable throughout its lifetime. Maintainability cannot be built in "after the fact" but must be considered during the early stages of analysis and design (Rombach, 1990).

When building a component-based system, system builders must consider maintainability and evolvability during two important phases of construction. The first is during component evaluation and selection because the components used to build the system directly impact the maintainability of the system. The second phase is the design of the component infrastructure. The approach used to integrate components determines the flexibility of the system, which directly impacts its evolvability.

30.3.1 Component Selection

There are many different criteria used to select a component, but system evolution should be one of the primary factors considered. The following factors affect the long-term evolution and maintenance of a component-based system.

Openness of components—Various characteristics determine whether a component is *open*. In my opinion component-based systems must be designed to be extensible and easily integrated into a wide array of systems. In general, the more open a component, the easier it will be for maintainers to monitor, manage, replace, test, and integrate. Many factors combine to make a component open, including adherence to standards; availability of source code, perhaps through open source licensing; and ability to interoperate with components from many different vendors.

Another desirable property of an open component is run-time support for managers. This includes a fully reflective interface to query the component at run-time to determine information such as its version, resources required, and usage history. This information is critical for configuring systems and isolating faults.

I recognize that other software component practitioners and theoreticians believe that components should be designed for the system. Only time will tell what the most effective means for the optimal design of software components is.

Tailorability of components—Much of the maintenance effort for component-based systems involves tailoring the functionality to meet evolving user requirements. A component should be selected because of the ease with which it can be tailored to satisfy local requirements. There are many techniques for component designers to create tailorable components, including scripting interfaces, data configuration files, object-oriented class hierarchies that can be extended through inheritance, and plug-ins ([Heineman, 1998] [Vigder, Gentleman, and Dean, 1996]).

Component model—As discussed in Chapter 1, a component model is needed to support component integration, with the major commercial offerings being Microsoft's Component Object Model (COM), the Object Management Group's Common Object Request Broker Architecture (CORBA), and Enterprise JavaBeans (EJB). Although there is some level of interoperability among these competing component models—for example, with CORBA components interfacing to COM+ components—designers should avoid mixing components from different component models; you will encounter difficulties when upgrading individual components or the component model implementation. The primary effect that the selection of a particular component model has on long-term maintenance is that the component model restricts the potential components that can be integrated into the system, because component producers often support only a single component model.

Another factor to consider when selecting a component model is how well it supports maintenance activities.

- How well is component reconfiguration supported? Because reconfiguration is such an expensive maintenance activity, support should be provided by the component model. One example of how this support can be provided is through CORBA's dynamic invocation (similar mechanisms exist within other component models). Using dynamic invocation, linking among components is a run-time activity, generally allowing for a much more flexible and easier reconfiguration process. Another example of supporting reconfiguration is event-driven component communication. Event-driven systems are often easier to reconfigure than synchronous-based communication mechanisms. CORBA, for example, does not provide event-based communication as part of its basic model, but as a higher-level service. Before committing to a particular CORBA implementation you must evaluate whether the producer supports the event-driven communication service efficiently and robustly.
- Does the component model implementation help you monitor the operation of the system? Monitoring system behavior is not

necessarily part of a component model, but may be provided by the component producer that developed the component model implementation. Maintainers gain insights into the system by monitoring actions such as remote method invocations, exceptions, and event broadcasts.

Available support community—System builders require extensive assistance from external organizations to support components. This support comes from the software component producer and the larger component user community. Given that successful maintenance is dependent on this support, system builders must evaluate the support available for the component. This involves evaluating both the cost and assistance provided by the producer as well as user groups, conferences, and discussion groups that may be available for the components.

The growing use of "free software" provides component users with an option that removes some of their dependence on the component supplier for support. With the source code available to all users, code modification can be performed by any user and submitted back to the controlling organization for inclusion in future releases of the software.

30.3.2 Designing for Evolution

System builders do not own third-party components, but they do own the design of the component infrastructure that integrates third-party components with components designed and developed in-house. By addressing issues of maintainability during software design, designers can build a system that facilitates the maintenance activities associated with component-based systems.

There are two major issues to face when designing component-based systems for maintainability. The first is managing component dependencies. Many uncontrolled dependencies among components make it exceedingly difficult to modify or analyze a software system. It is critical that these dependencies among components are understood and controlled by the system maintainers (see Chapter 16 for examples of dependencies between components).

The second design issue that must be addressed is the *visibility* of the system. A system is visible if maintenance personnel can instrument and monitor the system, for example, by querying the system to determine its operational characteristics, current configuration, or fault incidents. Visibility is a necessary characteristic for testing and managing systems. For component-based systems where there may be limited visibility into the individual components, software engineers and designers must design the component infrastructure to be visible.

30.3.2.1 Managing Component Dependencies

A complex software system is fragile and intricate component dependencies make it difficult to upgrade, replace, add, or remove components. Because interfaces define the only available access to the internal behavior of the component, they are the major sources of inter-component dependencies. Unfortunately, many component software engineers and designers create interfaces that do not completely satisfy component integrators' needs. The interfaces may be overly complex, they may expose too much or too little functionality, or they may not conform to appropriate standards. If a component is upgraded, all components that access that component through its interfaces will be affected. Interfaces are among the most important elements of component integration and software engineers and designers should not give up control of the interfaces to component developers.

30.3.2.2 Use Wrappers to Enable Integrators to Control Interfaces

One strategy that software integrators can use to retain control of the interface is to separate the component implementation from the interface exposed to the rest of the system. The component producer supplies the component while the integrator retains control of the interface.

One way to achieve this is to use the Adapter design pattern (Gamma et al., 1995) illustrated in Figure 30-1. In Figure 30-1a, two clients depend on the interface of a component (third-party components are represented as gray boxes in the diagrams). If the component is replaced and the interface changes, both clients will be affected. Using the Adapter design pattern designers can wrap a new interface around the component, as shown in Figure 30-1b, forcing all access to the component to occur through the wrapper. An adapter, or wrapper, separates the interface from the implementation of components and treats them as separate objects. The component dependencies are now in a wrapper that remains under the control of the integrator. As the underlying component changes, perhaps with new versions or with similar components from different producers, the maintainer can safely update the wrapper implementation with minimal impact on other components of the system. Although this may increase overhead and integration effort, the system integrator rather than the component supplier maintains control of the interface.

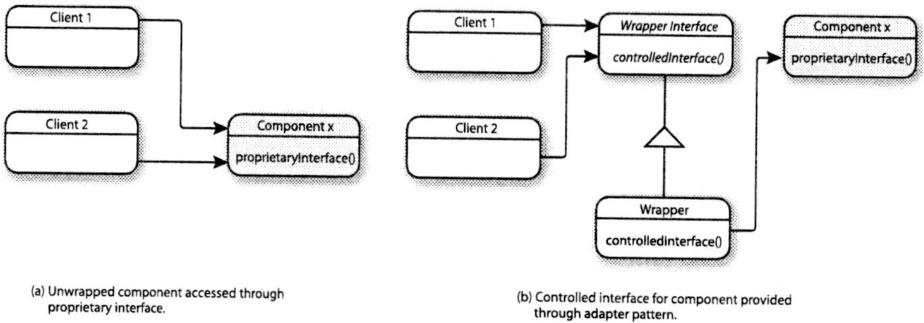

Figure 30-1: *Managing the component interface through an adapter.*

Many component dependencies are contained within the component *interconnection topology*. Two components are interconnected if there is a direct exchange of information between them. The interconnection topology is the set of all the interconnections in a system. Since an interconnection is an explicit dependency between components, simplifying the interconnection topology will make component reconfiguration easier.

The topology can be simplified in many ways, for example, minimizing the number of interconnections; minimizing the complexity of the interconnections; and hiding interconnections at different layers of abstraction. An example of hiding interconnections is the use of the Façade design pattern (Figure 30-2). In Figure 30-2a, a set of clients accesses a set of components. Because of the ad hoc nature of the interconnections it will become difficult for maintainers to understand the nature of the interconnections and to maintain them correctly over time.

In Figure 30-2b, the components are hidden behind a façade. At this level of abstraction the only visible interconnections are between the clients and the façade. The interconnections between the components are visible only at a lower level of detail by looking behind the

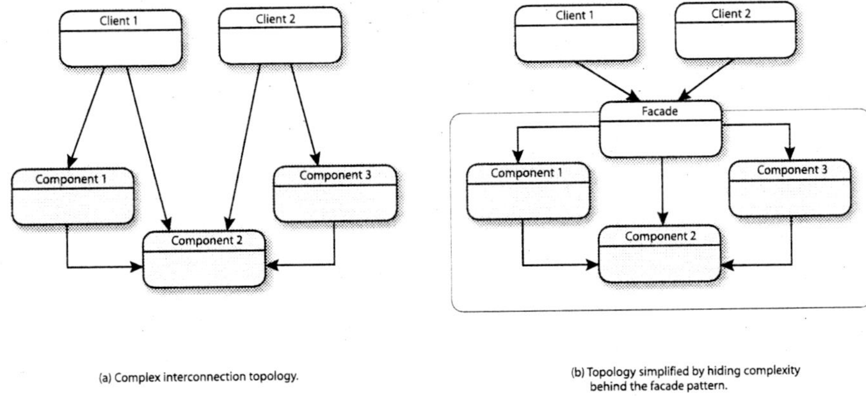

(a) Complex interconnection topology.

(b) Topology simplified by hiding complexity behind the facade pattern.

Figure 30-2: *Simplifying interconnection topology with a façade pattern.*

façade. From a maintenance perspective, this allows maintainers to modify and change components behind the façade with minimal impact on the rest of the system.

In addition to structural dependencies components also have behavioral dependencies. Complex behavior requires components to collaborate in ongoing patterns of behavior. Collaborations create strong dependencies between the components; often these dependencies are distributed and implicit within the collaboration, making component reconfiguration a difficult task. To overcome this difficulty designers should encapsulate all component collaborations within a single object, for example by using the Mediator design pattern ([Gamma et al., 1995] [Sullivan and Knight, 1996]).

As with the Adapter pattern, the Mediator pattern prevents components from interacting directly with each other and encapsulates the dependencies within an integrator-controlled object. A simple example is shown in Figure 30-3 where a service requires the combined functionality provided by three different components. One design option is shown in Figure 30-3a where Component 1 executes its part of the collaboration and passes control to Component 2, which then passes control to Component 3. The problem with this approach is that any change to the service, such as replacing one of the components, has an unpredictable impact on other components of the collaboration and on the service itself. With no centralized control and many direct component interactions it is difficult to manage the service through its evolution.

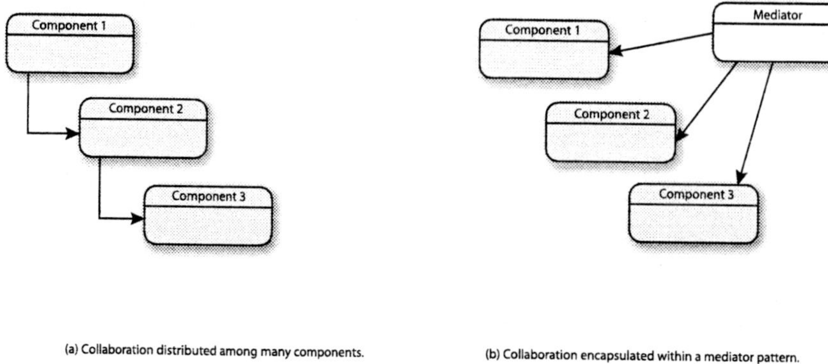

Figure 30-3: *Encapsulating collaborations within a mediator.*

Figure 30-3b illustrates an alternative design for providing the same service, where control is centralized within a mediator object. The mediator invokes the components as required and the components do not interact directly with each other. The advantage of such an approach is that when changing the service provided by the collaboration, that is, by adding new functionality or replacing a component, the inter-component dependencies are minimized and much of the impact can be restricted to the mediator.

30.3.2.3 Designing for Visibility

In addition to the visibility provided by individual components, software engineers and designers can take advantage of the custom-built integration and tailoring code to include management functionality and improve the overall system visibility. An example of how this can be done is shown in Figure 30-4. By using a mediator to control a collaboration involving three components and then implementing a management interface as part of the mediator, maintainers gain visibility into the three components and the collaboration. The management interface can gather information about the collaboration among the components such as the events generated and received by the components, the current state of the collaboration, or activations of the components.

A number of standard management interfaces and designs have been proposed; some of these are appropriate for use with component-based systems (Sun Microsystems, 1999). The solutions provided by

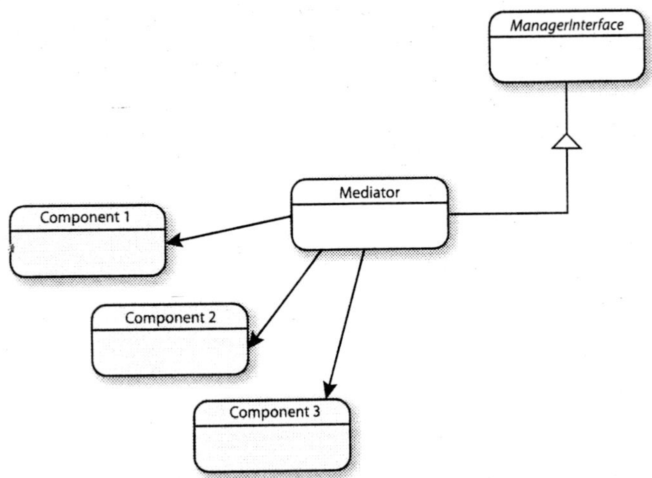

Figure 30-4: *Adding an interface to glue for visibility.*

the standards have the advantage of support from commercial developers and software. However, these solutions are often expensive and heavyweight; for many situations a small, custom-designed interface that provides visibility will be more practical.

30.4 Conclusions

Although component-based software systems provide many advantages, designers and maintainers must still expect that the majority of the life cycle cost will be incurred after the initial deployment of the system. That you are using a system built from components rather from source code does not change the need for maintenance, but it does change the nature of the maintenance activities. Reducing the maintenance and management costs and easing the effort requires software engineers and designers to consider the post-deployment activities during the earliest stages of software development. You can make systems more cost-effective by identifying the activities that maintenance personnel perform to support component-based systems and using design criteria and a component selection process that support these activities.

Part VI

Summary

Project management for CBSE is unlike project management for routine software development projects. Component-based software project management (CBSPM) requires a thorough understanding of engineering management and of Frederick Taylor's principle of "the one best way." As Taylorism has guided various engineering disciplines in the past and currently, CBSE must adopt the approach so that, "Both sides (management and workers) must recognize as essential the substitution of exact scientific investigation and knowledge for the old individual judgment or opinion," in all matters bearing on work. "This applies both as to the methods to be employed in doing the work and the time in which each job should be done." An essential requirement is

> [T]he deliberate gathering in on the part of those on the management's side of all the great mass to traditional knowledge, which in the past has been in the heads of the workmen, and in the physical skill and knack of the workmen, which he has acquired through years of experience (Kanigel, 1997).

Compared with the other engineering disciplines of his day, Taylor's recommendations from 1912 are relevant to the software engineering of today. It is a prescription we have not bothered to study or heed. Therefore, we have no common form of communication for software engineering and CBSE management. Yet, as the Chaos study demonstrates, software failure is software project management failure (*standishgroup.com/visitor/chaos.htm*). Software Engineering must improve its dismal track record where 40% of projects are canceled before completion and 33% of the remaining projects are challenged by cost or time overruns or changes in scope.

Traditional forms of software development can continue to operate without engineering management; CBSE simply cannot. While developers are designers and can continually "dig down" into source code to repair defects, managing for the best solution to a problem will always be difficult. When CBD is adopted, and with it CBSE, management will require an exceptionally well-trained CBSPM and a supporting staff of subproject engineers or subproject CBSPMs. Together, these trained employees will ensure that problems are resolved with one solution and that the solution indeed is implemented.

The only way that an engineering approach will be implemented and the stated goal of the next version of this book—that of greater empiricism both in CBSE and in the edited text—will be achieved is when measurement and metrics are taken seriously. In Chapter 23 Jeffrey Poulin demonstrated in easily readable prose that starting a pilot project with metrics is not difficult. Commencement of a metrics program does not require data that most organizations are not already collecting. Because the institution of a metrics program necessarily implements a new way of conducting business and requires innovative thinking to keep the business on track, Jeffrey recommends only a few simple metrics in order to demonstrate the efficacy of CBSE and metrics. As CBD and CBSE mature within the organization and software reuse is demanded by senior management, the requirements for more discrete metrics intensifies. Within a year or two of adopting CBD metrics can be used as empirical data to form the foundation for an engineering-based CBSE.

Compare our engineering endeavor with a field known as industrial environmental performance metrics, sponsored by the National Academy of Engineering. The purpose was to identify a set of metrics that would assist in the setting of both national and industrial environmental goals. The U.S.-focused study was to be the American contribution to a larger effort by the Asia Pacific Economic Cooperation on industrial environmental indicators and clean production. (National Academy Press, 1999)

> The committee launched a study to gather evidence and explore present efforts in the development and use of industrial environmental performance metrics. The study investigated such issues as the motivation for improved environmental performance, normalization of metrics, standards for reporting, aggregation of metrics, and weighting of metrics. Looking ahead at the changing needs in this area, the committee also delved into the role of metrics as a tool to both drive and measure aspects of sustainable development. (National Academy Press, 1999)

Establishing a CBD and reuse program can, and often does, meet with considerable resistance. Senior management might not approve because they don't understand the concept or do not want the extra costs. Mid-level management will likely oppose CBD and CBSE because both require new learning and continued time pressures. Some designers, developers, and testers will support the new program and others will resist it. In Chapter 24 Don Reifer described how a change agent, that is, an advocate for CBD and CBSE as well as reuse, can manage the resistance using a variety of approaches and still establish a pilot project with sufficient funding and staff. With Don's approaches to resistance management the pilot project can come in on time, on budget, and with successfully tested, reusable software components designed as the foundation of a product-line.

Chapters 25 and 26 appear to be engineering-based at first. As organizations consider purchasing COTS components they must develop methodical plans based on carefully elicited and verified requirements. Organizations should purchase the software components that meets users' needs, as well as the design requirements of the software component infrastructure. The problem with COTS component-based requirements elicitation such as PORE is that the requirements for maintenance and evolvability are not identified as necessary requirements for purchasing COTS components. As Mark Vigder (Chapter 30) stated the maintenance, management, and evolvability phase of the life cycle is the longest and costliest phase. Requirements that do not address the maintenance phase may prevent the early design or selection of software components that support maintenance and evolvability features. Maintainability cannot be built in after analysis and design; maintenance must be purposefully designed and include the following criteria

- Openness of components
- Run-time management support
- Tailorability of components
- Stable component model (with no mixing of components among component models)
- Support for reconfiguration by component model
- Monitoring support by component model
- Community support for component model

When designing or selecting components for evolution the selection criteria must include

- Limited dependencies among components
- And visibility of the system by querying the components to determine each component's operation characteristics, current configuration, and fault incidents

For systems that were designed to provide limited visibility to the components, the design of the software component infrastructure must be visible. We describe the need for discrete maintenance, management, and evolution requirements because of the inherent and often unsuspected problems that are likely to occur during the maintenance life cycle. If problems during the maintenance phase are anticipated, solutions will not be discovered later than necessary, and the one best way for each problem will not be considered during analysis and design.

As in Elaine Weyuker's grim assessment of CBD, because of lax CBSE, especially COTS component selection and testing, CBSE requires much more maturity before it attains uniform success. Weyuker and Vigder agree that source code is beneficial—Weyuker would argue necessary—during the various testing phases of a COTS component gone awry. Using the requirements system developed by Ncube and Maiden is a start in the right direction—because, as they recognize, many COTS components are purchased without criteria. It is incumbent now that project managers consult with their test organizations to determine the requisite test criteria for purchasing a COTS component, or even designing an in-house component. For every requirement or use case step, a concomitant test case will validate or invalidate the component.

In Chapter 27 Bill Councill's project team would include, at a minimum, a lead software engineer or CBSPM, a designer, component developer, component tester, component configuration manager/librarian, maintenance developer, and maintenance tester. At the commencement of a pilot project analysts would use a method for the selection of COTS components such as PORE to develop requirements and use cases that reflect the needs of users. Designers and analysts will determine if the component complies with the documentation and run-time needs of the software component infrastructure, as well as the component model, throughout brief period (of the component-based system. The IPT can determine if the correct problems have been identified, and if they have, whether the analysts have reached the right solutions. For those problems with inappropriate solutions the IPT will assist the analysts with the one best way. With members from each of the groups that contribute to CBD in a project team, development of optimal analysis and design is enhanced so long as analysts and designers meet with the right groups of users (see Chapter 7).

Component-based software component project or program management (CBSPM) is based on decades of engineering management. The assembly of components within a software component infrastructure is similar to other engineering endeavors, each requiring the precise assembly of components (Chapters 1 and 2). Ideally, component-based software engineers would be licensed as engineers (see Chapter 37). Licensure of component-based software engineers can take decades; yet, the need for engineering trained project and program managers is immediate. University education of CBSPMs resulting in a graduate degree and certification would help to ensure software engineers and other component-based staff would learn to think and work with the structure of engineers—striving to solve problems using Frederick Taylor's one best way.

Hedley Apperly, an engineer and software engineer, wrote a truly engineering-based chapter on component management in Chapter 2. Comparing construction warehouses or builders' yards to component managers serves to make a complex subject much easier to understand. A well accepted engineering concept, component management makes it possible for teams to work in parallel by breaking large problems into smaller, more manageable chunks. That is the basis of Taylorism, which has permeated engineering and much of business theory.

Hedley then describes the produce-manage-consume process that underlies the component management process in Chapter 29. Describing each of the processes in detail, he provides examples of who and why a consumer would access the library of components. Further, he describes which consumers would have write access to access to a component, as well as who would have security access at the following abstraction levels.

- Component specification
- Component implementation
- Component executable
- Component deployment

Hedley then describes who in the organization would have security privileges to consume the component for maintenance purposes.

Elaine Weyuker states in Chapter 28 that to assume that a component designed for use in one component infrastructure, when applied to another infrastructure, likely will not be cost-effective, reliable, and predicts "the future of CBSE is in doubt." She further explains that components generally are insufficiently tested for the intended infrastructure. When the component is sold in the COTS component market the component is even less likely to receive adequate testing, despite sufficient documentation, for the new project's infrastructure. Test managers, she explained, must participate in high level project teams and have input into the purchase of COTS components.

An example of Elaine's reality is the case of the Orbix daemon. An award-winning component consumer integrated a third-party Orbix daemon into its application for client-to-database communications. In the application's first versions, the daemon worked flawlessly. The component daemon producer then recommended to its consumers an upgrade to a more efficient version. Of course, the small but successful startup could not test the intricacies of the daemon. Trust had developed between the producer and consumer; the consumer with little testing implemented the daemon into its next version. Customers were made aware of the upgrade and most anticipated increased performance. The new daemon was exceptionally defective and application's mean time between failures at some customers' sites decreased from months to hours. The problem was not resolved for months despite the consumer's best efforts. No patch was forthcoming. All consumers and customers had to wait for the next upgrade (Councill, 1999). It is important that you read and understand Elaine's chapter. Without expert management, excellent and verified comprehensive analysis and design, and access to source code, one bad version of a software component, can prevent or diminish access to a mission-critical application.

The problem is that the component-based software life cycle has not adopted Taylor's one best way approach. In our experience many analysis, design, and construction meetings have been conducted as groups or as a multi-group project teams (see Chapter 27) where members left with no direct understanding of what solution to implement for a particular problem. This is an untenable and unacceptable management result. Just as the engine subproject engineer (see Chapter 27) on the SUV project contracted with another organization for cylinder sleeves and piston rings that subcontracted with an engineering firm, CBSE organizations must learn from engineering organizations to consult with other engineering firms with specialized knowledge.

First, we must know ourselves and our limitations. Measurements and metrics are a prerequisite for gaining knowledge of our strengths and weaknesses as well as improving on our CBSE and reuse processes progressively. Metrics are also a method for developing a body of empirical knowledge necessary for statistical measurement of especially subtle changes and for publication to enhance the status of engineering science. Our limitations will become evident at various stages of maturity of the CBSE process.

This Part on management is demonstrative of the deficiency of empiricism in software and CBSE project management. The discipline must capture data on all aspects of CBSE, none more so than project management. The first study to examine CBSE should compare organizations with standard project management practices with those whose project managers and staff are influenced by Taylorism and engineering management.

Part VI

References

A. Albrecht and J. Gaffney, "Software Function, Source Lines of Code, and Development Effort Prediction: A Software Science Validation," *IEEE Transactions on Software Engineering*, Vol. SE-9, No. 6, Nov., 1983, pp. 639-648.

P. Allen and S. Frost, *Component-Based Development for Enterprise Systems, Applying the Select Perspective*, Cambridge University Press, Cambridge, UK, 1998.

A. Avritzer and E. Weyuker, "The Automatic Generation of Load Test Suites and the Assessment of the Resulting Software," *IEEE Transactions on Software Engineering*, Vol. 21, No. 9, Sept., 1995, pp. 705-716.

A. Avritzer, personal communication, 2000.

B. Boehm, "Improving Software Productivity," *IEEE Computer*, Vol. 20, No. 8, Sept., 1987, pp. 43-57.

S. Chidamber, and C. Kemerer, "Towards a Metrics Suite for Object-Oriented Design," Proceedings, Object-Oriented Programming, Systems, Languages, and Applications (OOPSLA), ACM Press, 1991, pp. 197-211.

DSD Labs, Software Reuse Initiative Reuse Readiness and Technology Transfer Framework, STARS-VC-AA12/002/00, *dii-sw.ncr.disa.mil/reuseic/pol-hist/history/visstrat/2-12-96.html*, Defense Information Systems Agency, Feb., 1996.

H. Erdogmus and J. Vandergraaf, "Quantitative Approaches for Assessing the Value of COTS-centric Development," Proceedings, 6th International

Symposium on Software Metrics (METRICS), IEEE Computer Society Press, Boca Raton, FL, 1999, pp. 279-290.

T. Field, "When Bad Things Happen to Good Projects," CIO Magazine, *www.cio.com*, Oct., 1997.

E. Gamma, R. Helm, R. Johnson, and J. Vlissides, *Design Patterns: Elements of Reusable Object-Oriented Software*, Addison-Wesley, Reading, MA, 1995.

W. Gentleman, "Architecture for Software Construction by Unrelated Developers," Proceedings, Software Architecture: TC2 First Working IFIP Conference on Software Architecture (WICSA1), Kluwer Academic Publishers, 1999, pp. 423-435.

M. Halstead, *Elements of Software Science*, Elsevier, 1977.

G. Heineman, "A Model for Designing Adaptable Software Components," Proceedings, 22nd International Computer Science and Application Conference (COMPSAC), IEEE Computer Society Press, 1998, pp. 121-127.

S. Hissam, "Correcting System Failure in a COTS Information System," Proceedings, International Conference on Software Maintenance (ICSM), IEEE Computer Society Press, 1998, pp. 170-176.

J. Hunt, Product Focus, SIGS Application Development Advisor, *www.appdevadvisor.com*, May-June, 2000, pp. 31-33.

D. Hybertson, A. Ta, and W. Thomas, "Maintenance of COTS-Intensive Software Systems," *Journal of Software Maintenance*, Vol. 9, No. 4, 1997, pp. 203-216.

I. Jacobson, M. Griss, and P. Jonsson, *Software Reuse: Architecture, Process and Organization for Business Success*, Addison-Wesley, Reading, MA, 1997.

R. Kanigel, *The One Best Way: Frederick Taylor and the Enigma of Efficiency*, Viking Penguin, 1997.

E. Karlsson, *Software Reuse: A Holistic Approach*, John Wiley & Sons, 1995.

J. Konito, "A Case Study in Applying a Systematic Method for COTS Selection," Proceedings, 18th International Conference on Software Engineering (ICSE), IEEE Computer Society Press, 1996, pp. 201-209.

P. Kruchten, "Modeling Component Systems with the Unified Modeling Language," Proceedings, 2nd International Workshop on Component-Based Software Engineering (CBSE), ACM Press, Kyoto, Japan, 1998.

W. Lim, *Managing Software Reuse*, Prentice-Hall, Upper Saddle River, NJ, 1998.

J. Lions, *Ariane 5, Flight 501 Failure, Report by the Inquiry Board, www.esrin.esa.it/htdocs/tidc/Press/Press96/ariane5rep.html*, July 19, 1996.

M. Lorenz, *Object-Oriented Software Development: A Practical Guide*, Prentice-Hall, Upper Saddle River, NJ, 1993.

N. Maiden and C. Ncube, "Acquiring Requirements for Commercial Off-The-Shelf Package Selection," *IEEE Software*, Vol. 15, No. 2, Mar., 1998, pp. 46-56.

N. Maiden and G. Rugg, "ACRE: Selecting Methods For Requirements Acquisition," *IEE Software Engineering Journal*, Vol. 11, No. 3, May, 1996, pp. 183-192.

T. McCabe, "A Complexity Measure," *IEEE Transactions on Software Engineering*, Vol. SE-2, No. 4, Dec., 1976, pp. 308-320.

C. McClure, *Software Reuse Techniques*, Prentice-Hall, Upper Saddle River, NJ, 1997.

G. Miller, "The Magical Number Seven, Plus or Minus Two: Some Limits on our Capacity for Processing Information," *The Psychological Review*, Vol. 63, No. 2, Mar., 1956, pp. 81-97.

G. Moore, *Crossing the Chasm*, HarperBusiness, 1991.

National Academy Press, *Industrial Environmental Performance Metrics: Challenges and Opportunities*, Committee on Industrial Environmental Performance Metrics, National Academy of Engineering, National Research Council, Washington, D.C., 1999.

C. Ncube and N. Maiden, "Procuring Software Systems: Current Problems and Solutions," Proceedings, 3rd International Workshop on Requirements Engineering: Foundation for Software Quality (REFSQ), CAiSE Proceedings, Barcelona, Spain, 1997.

C. Ncube, A Requirements Engineering Method for COTS-Based Systems Development, Ph.D. thesis, City University,London, UK, May 2000.

M. Paulk, C. Weber, B. Curtis, and M. Chrises, *The Capability Maturity Model: Guidelines for Improving the Software Process*, Addison-Wesley, Reading, MA, 1995.

J. Pinto and O. Kharbanda, "How to Fail in Project Management (Without Really Trying)," *Business Horizons*, Vol. 39, No. 4, Indiana University Kelley School of Business, Bloomington, IN, July/Aug., 1996, pp. 45-53.

J. Poulin, *Measuring Software Reuse: Principles, Practices, and Economic Models*, Addison-Wesley, Reading, MA, 1997.

D. Reifer, *Practical Software Reuse*, John Wiley and Sons, 1997a.

D. Reifer, "The 3P's of Software Management," *Software Management, 5th ed.*, IEEE Computer Society Press, 1997b, pp. 10-16.

S. Robertson and J. Robertson, *Mastering the Requirements Engineering Process*, Addison-Wesley, Reading, MA, 2000.

H. Rombach, "Design Measurement: Some Lessons Learned," *IEEE Software*, Vol. 7, No. 2, Mar., 1990, pp. 17-25.

L. Smith and A. Steadman, "Gaining Confidence in Using Return on Investment and Earned Value," *Crosstalk, The Journal of Defense Software Engineering*, Vol. 12, No. 4, *stsc.hill.af.mil/crosstalk*, Apr., 1999, pp. 18-24.

SPC, Software Productivity Consortium, *Reuse Adoption Guidebook*, SPC-92019-CMC, *www.software.org*, Dec., 1992.

SPC, Software Productivity Consortium, *ADARTS Guidebook*, SPC-91104-MC, Version 03.00.09, *www.software.org*, Mar., 1993.

K. Sullivan and J. Knight, "Experience Assessing an Architectural Approach to Large-Scale Systematic Reuse," Proceedings, 18th International Conference on Software Engineering (ICSE), IEEE Computer Society Press, Los Alamitos, CA, 1996, pp. 220-229.

Sun Microsystems, Java Management Extension White Paper, *java.sun.com/products/JavaManagement/wp/JMXwhitepaper.pdf*, June 1999.

R. Tausworthe, "Information Models of Software Productivity: Limits on Productivity Growth," *Journal of System Software*, Vol. 19, No. 2, Oct., 1992, pp. 185-201.

W. Tracz, *Confessions of a Used Program Salesman*, Addison-Wesley, Reading, MA, 1995.

J. Udell, "ComponentWare," *Byte Magazine*, Vol. 19, No. 5, May, 1994, pp. 46-56.

M. Vigder and J. Dean, "Building Maintainable COTS-Based Systems," Proceedings, 14th International Conference on Software Maintenance (ICSM), IEEE Computer Society Press, Los Alamitos, CA, 1998, pp. 132-138.

M. Vigder, W. Gentleman, and J. Dean, "COTS Software Integration: State of the Art," National Research Council of Canada, Institute for Information Technology Technical Report 39198 VI, Ottawa, Ontario, Canada, Nov., 1998, pp. 132-138.

J. Voas, "Error Propogation Analysis For COTS Systems," *Computing and Control Engineering Journal*, Vol. 8, No. 6, Dec., 1997, pp. 69-72.

J. Voas, "Maintaining Component-Based Systems," *IEEE Software*, Vol. 15, No. 4, July 1998, pp. 22-27.

J. Voas, "Disposable Information Systems: The Future of Software Maintenance?" *Journal of Software Maintenance: Research and Practice*, Vol. 11, John Wiley & Sons, New York, NY, 1999, pp. 143-150.

E. Weyuker, "Using Failure Cost Information for Testing and Reliability Assessment," *ACM Transactions on Software Engineering and Methodology*, Vol. 5, No. 2, Apr., 1996, pp. 87-98.

Part VII

Component Technologies

One approach for solving difficult problems is to present a technology that addresses the issues inherent in the problem and seek wider support for that technology. Many books on the market today follow this strategy by describing how to use a particular technology, such as Microsoft's Component Object Model (COM). However, these books are more like tutorials in a particular technology than ways to learn the concepts, principles, and issues in component-based software engineering. If you wanted to become familiar with the most popular component technologies, you would have to read several books, totaling thousands of pages. In this section, we provide a primer on the leading component technologies at the time of publication.

The broad support CBSE has enjoyed has resulted in a wide battery of technologies, some in direct competition with each other. This section presents the main technologies to provide a concise introduction to the most popular component technologies. Readers interested in learning about any of these technologies should pursue the references at the end of this section. The authors discuss the most relevant technologies, such as Microsoft's COM+, the latest evolution of Microsoft's

Component Object Model (COM), Sun's Enterprise JavaBeans (EJB), and the Common Object Request Broker Architecture (CORBA) Component Model (CCM).

The lead chapter in this section, by the renowned CORBA expert Douglas Schmidt and coauthors Nanbor Wang and Carlos O'Ryan, introduces the most recent CORBA standard, the CORBA Component Model. The CCM is planned to be included in the CORBA 3.0 specification, which the Object Management Group (OMG) should release during 2001. CORBA made it possible for organizations to construct robust enterprise of distributed objects. CCM retains backward compatibility with existing CORBA objects, while enabling component producers to develop powerful CCM components.

In "Overview of COM+," Tim Ewald, the author of a forthcoming book on the same subject, introduces the latest evolution of Microsoft's COM. He clearly shows how Microsoft has converted COM, a technology for linking objects together, into a robust, enterprise-ready technology for developing distributed applications. Together with Microsoft's .NET Framework, Microsoft's next generation Web application development platform, COM+ will alter the way readers and authors alike develop components.

In his chapter "The Enterprise JavaBeans Component Model," David Blevins summarizes the component model that simplifies the development of middleware components that are transactional, scalable, and portable. Enterprise JavaBeans is also a key part in the Java 2 Enterprise Edition (J2EE), which specifies a larger component infrastructure that defines the interaction between EJB and other component models such as Java Servlets. Read David's chapter to learn how to apply Java to your resolve your enterprise needs.

As you are undoubtedly aware, the free software movement has changed the way we perceive software and software development. The GNOME project (www.gnome.org) was founded as an effort to create an entirely free desktop environment for free systems. In his chapter "Bonobo and Free Software GNOME Components," Michael Meeks presents the Bonobo component model, the *de facto* component model for free software. Bonobo and free software as a whole have recently received the support of Sun Microsystems' decision to make its StarOffice suite freely available and rearchitect it with Bonobo components (*www.sun.com/software/white-papers/wp-gnome-sunjoins/#benefit*). It is clear that Bonobo will be a key technology for GNOME. Less clear, however, is whether it will achieve widespread use.

We have provided an exceptionally well written chapter by Andy Longshaw to help readers understand which component technology is right for them. In "Choosing Between COM+, EJB, and CCM," Andy provides a set of criteria that compares these three technologies. This chapter may be the most important chapter in the book for many of our readers, since it is designed to assist technology-based readers in understanding the differences between these popular component models, as well as their similarities.

In his third chapter for the book, Martin Griss explains in "Software Agents as Next Generation Software Components" the relationship between software components and software agents. Martin makes the convincing argument that software agents must be as rigorously defined as software components before they will ever achieve the widespread impact that many foresee. There is a growing trend to describing and encoding semantic information, as evidenced by the increased popularity of the eXtensible Markup Language (XML). The benefit for having an XML-aware component is clearly capturing dependencies and constraints among data artifacts. The danger, however, is that it may be impossible to determine at assembly time whether a particular set of components will operate successfully. For XML to be truly integrated with components, we need tools to help analyze and detect errors during assembly of components whose interfaces are XML-aware.

These component technologies are all based on the same premise, namely, to achieve widespread component reuse, you need a well-designed component model and a robust component model implementation. The component model implementation makes it possible to deploy and execute components. A well-designed component model enables software engineers to map a logical design of a component infrastructure onto a set of software components that conform to that model.

At the time of publication, there are several changes to the component technologies landscape. The CORBA CCM specification has not yet been finalized; it will be released as part of the CORBA 3.0 specification (*www.omg.org/technology/corba/corba3releaseinfo.htm*), which is scheduled to be released later this year. On 25 October 2000, Sun Microsystems released the EJB 2.0 specification Final Proposed Draft through the Java Community Process. Several vendors have compliant implementations in beta form (*www.weblogic.com/docs51/classdocs/API_ejb20/whatsnew.html* is an example). On 21 June 2000 at Forum 2000, Microsoft unveiled its .NET strategy, (*www.zdnet.com/zdnn/stories/news/0,4586,2592779,00.html*) and COM+ will play a major role in the way in which services and components will be integrated. Clearly there is great interest in these often-competing technologies—we expect improved performance and robustness of the component model implementations to increase the use of components.

Conclusion

This section provides a starting point in your journey to understand CBD and CBSE by introducing the key component technologies that are most influential today. The chapters in this section describe their essential features and direct you to references that will help you learn all you need to successfully develop robust enterprise, component-based applications. In addition, you can always access the book's Web site (*www.cbseng.com*) for more references that will be added to the sections on a routine basis, as well as revisions to the chapters to ensure that they are always as up-to-date as possible.

Chapter 31

Overview of the CORBA Component Model

Nanbor Wang
Douglas C. Schmidt
Carlos O'Ryan

31.1 Introduction

In today's globally competitive software market it is becoming increasingly important to develop, deploy, and maintain complex, distributed software systems. Many companies have developed proprietary software to enable the distribution of applications over a network, but this solution can be prohibitively expensive and time-consuming over the life cycle of complex software systems. Since 1989, the Object Management Group (OMG) has been standardizing an open middleware specification to support distributed applications. The traditional OMG

Common Object Request Broker Architecture (CORBA) (Object Management Group, 2000a) shown in Figure 31-1 enables software applications to invoke operations on distributed objects without concern for object location, programming language, operating system, communication protocols, interconnections, or hardware platform (Henning and Vinoski, 1999).

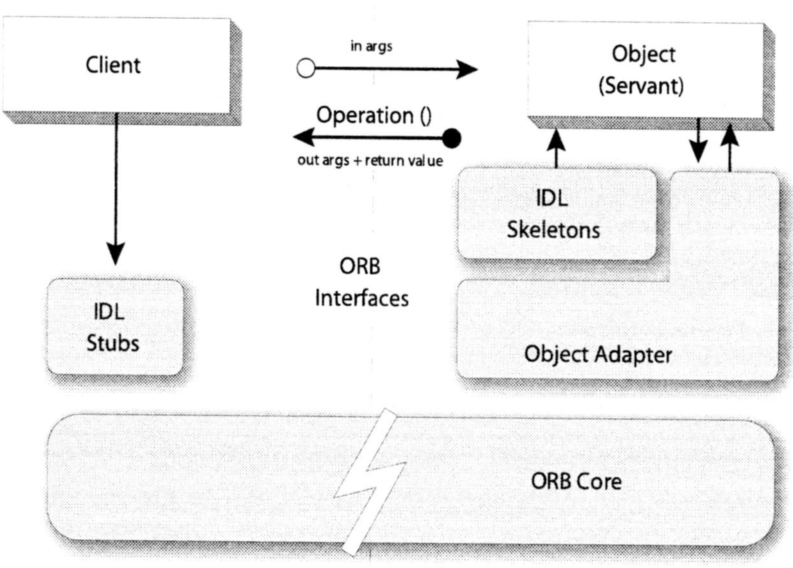

Figure 31-1: *Traditional CORBA object model.*

To provide higher-level reusable components, the OMG also specifies a set of CORBA Object Services that define standard interfaces to access common distribution services, such as naming, trading, and event notification. By using CORBA and its Object Services, system developers can integrate and assemble large, complex distributed applications and systems using features and services from different providers.

Unfortunately, the traditional CORBA object model, as defined by CORBA 2.4 (Object Management Group, 2000a), has the following limitations.

1. *No standard way to deploy object implementations.* The earlier CORBA specification did not define a standard for deployment of object implementations in server processes. Deployment involves distributing object implementations, installing those implementations in their execution contexts, and activating the implementations in an Object Request Broker (ORB). Thus, system designers developed *ad hoc* strategies to instantiate all objects in a system. Moreover, since objects may depend on one another, the deployment and instantiation of objects in a large-scale distributed system is complicated and non-portable.
2. *Limited standard support for common CORBA server programming patterns.* The CORBA family of specifications provides a rich set of features to implement servers. For example, the CORBA 2.2 specification introduced the *Portable Object Adapter* (POA), which is the ORB mechanism that forwards client requests to concrete object implementations. The POA specification provides standard application programming interfaces (APIs) to register object implementations with the ORB, to deactivate those objects, and to activate object implementations on demand. The POA is flexible and provides numerous policies to configure its behavior. In many application domains, however, only a limited subset of these features is ever used repeatedly; yet server developers face a steep learning curve to understand how to configure POA policies *selectively* to obtain their desired behavior.
3. *Limited extension of object functionality.* In the traditional CORBA object model, objects can be extended only via inheritance. To support new interfaces, therefore, application developers must: (1) use CORBA's Interface Definition Language (IDL) to define a new interface that inherits from all the required interfaces; (2) implement the new interface; and (3) deploy the new implementation across all their servers. Multiple inheritance in CORBA IDL is fragile, because overloading is not supported in CORBA; therefore, multiple inheritance has limited applicability. Moreover, applications may need to expose the same IDL interface multiple times to allow developers to either provide multiple implementations or multiple instances of the service through a single access point. Unfortunately, multiple inheritance cannot expose the same inter-

face more than once, nor can it alone determine which interface should be exported to clients (Henning and Vinoski, 1999).

4. *Availability of CORBA Object Services not defined in advance.* The CORBA specification does not mandate which Object Services are available at run-time. Thus, object developers used *ad hoc* strategies to configure and activate these services when deploying a system.
5. *No standard object life cycle management.* Although the CORBA Object Service defines a Life Cycle Service, its use is not mandated. Therefore, clients often manage the life cycle of an object explicitly in *ad hoc* ways. Moreover, the developers of CORBA objects controlled through the life cycle service must define auxiliary interfaces to control the object life cycle. Defining these interfaces is tedious and should be automated when possible, but earlier CORBA specifications lacked the capabilities required to implement such automation.

In summary, the inadequacies outlined above of the CORBA specification, prior to and including version 2.4, often yield tightly coupled, *ad hoc* implementations of objects that are hard to design, reuse, deploy, maintain, and extend.

31.1.1 Overview of the CORBA Component Model (CCM)

To address the limitations with the earlier CORBA object model, the OMG adopted the CORBA Component Model (CCM) (Object Management Group, 1999) to extend and subsume the CORBA Object Model. The CCM is planned for inclusion in the CORBA 3.0 specification, which the OMG should release during 2001. The CCM extends the CORBA object model by defining features and services that enable application developers to implement, manage, configure, and deploy components that integrate commonly used CORBA services—such as transaction, security, persistent state, and event notification services—in a standard environment. In addition, the CCM standard allows greater software reuse for servers and provides greater flexibility for dynamic configuration of CORBA applications. With the increasing acceptance of CORBA in a wide range of application domains ([O'Ryan et al., 2001] [Levine, Gill, and Schmidt, 1998] [O'Ryan and Schmidt, 1999] [Object Management Group, 2000b]), CCM is well positioned for use in scalable, mission-critical client/server applications.

31.1.2 Component Overview

CCM components are the basic building blocks in a CCM system. A major contribution of CCM derives from standardizing the component development cycle using CORBA as its middleware infrastructure. Component developers using CCM define the IDL interfaces that component implementations will support. Next, they implement components using tools that CCM providers supply. The resulting component implementations can then be packaged into an assembly file, such as a shared library, a Java Archive File (JAR) file, or a Dynamically Linked Library (DLL), and linked dynamically. Finally, a CCM provider supplies a deployment mechanism used to deploy the component in a *component server* that hosts component implementations by loading their assembly files. Thus, components execute in component servers and are available to process client requests. Figure 31-2 shows an example CCM component implementing a stock exchange and its corresponding IDL definition.

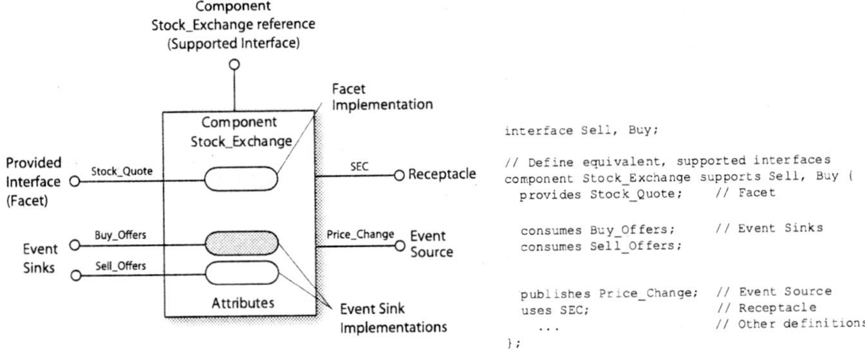

Figure 31-2: *An example CCM component with IDL specification.*

A CORBA object reference is an abstract handle referring to an instance of a CORBA object. An object reference hides the location where the actual object resides and contains protocol information defined by the CORBA specification, as well as an opaque, vendor-specific *object key* used to identify a servant that implements the object. To developer end-users, the format of a reference to a `Stock_Exchange` component is identical to the format of a reference to a `Stock_Exchange` interface. Thus, existing component-unaware software can invoke operations via an object reference to a component's *equivalent interface*, which is the interface that identifies the component instance uniquely. As with a regular CORBA object, a component's equivalent interface can inherit from other interfaces, called the component's *supported interfaces*. In our example, the supported interfaces perform transactions to buy and sell stock.

As mentioned earlier, it is inflexible to extend CORBA objects solely using inheritance. Thus, CCM components provide four types of mechanisms called *ports* to interact with other CORBA programming artifacts, such as clients or collaborating components. These port mechanisms specify different views and required interfaces that a component exposes to clients (Marvie, Merle, and Geib, 2000). Along with component attributes, these port mechanisms define the following capabilities of a component

1. *Facets*—Facets, also known as *provided interfaces*, are interfaces that a component provides, yet which are not necessarily related to its supported interfaces via inheritance. Facets allow a component to expose different views to its clients by providing different interfaces that can be invoked synchronously via CORBA's two-way operations or asynchronously via CORBA's asynchronous method invocations (AMI) that are part of the forthcoming CORBA 3 specification. For instance, the `Stock_Quote` interface in Figure 31-2 provides a stock price querying capability to the component. CCM facets apply the Extension Interface pattern (Schmidt et al., 2000) and are similar to component *interfaces* in Microsoft's Component Object Model (COM) (Box, 1998).
2. *Receptacles*—Before a component can delegate operations to other components, it must obtain object references to the instances of the other components it uses. In CCM, these references are "object connections," and the port names of these connections are called receptacles. Receptacles provide a standard way to specify interfaces required for the component to function correctly. In Figure 31-2, the `Stock_Exchange` component uses the `SEC` (Securities and Exchange Commission) interface to function correctly. Using these receptacles, components may *connect* to other objects, including those of other components, and invoke operations upon those objects synchronously or asynchronously (via AMI).

3. *Event sources/sinks*—Components can also interact by monitoring asynchronous events. These loosely coupled interactions, based on the Observer pattern (Gamma et al., 1995), are commonly used in distributed applications (Pyarali, O'Ryan, and Schmidt, 2000). A component declares its interest to publish or subscribe to events by specifying *event sources* and *event sinks* in its definition. For example, the `Stock_Exchange` component can be an event sink that processes `Buy_Offers` and `Sell_Offers` events, and it can be an event source that publishes `Price_Change` events.
4. *Attributes*—To enable component configuration, CCM extends the notion of *attributes* defined in the traditional CORBA object model. Configuration tools can use attributes to preset configuration values of a component. Unlike previous versions of CORBA, CCM allows operations that access and modify attribute values to raise exceptions. The component developer can use this feature to raise an exception if an attempt is made to change a configuration attribute after the system configuration has completed. As with previous versions of the CORBA specification, component developers must decide whether an attribute implementation is part of the transient or persistent state of the component.

These new port mechanisms significantly enhance component reusability when compared to the traditional CORBA object model. For instance, a new component that extends the original component definition by adding new interfaces without affecting existing clients of the component can replace an existing component. Moreover, new clients can check whether a component provides a certain interface by using the CCM Navigation interface, which enumerates all facets provided by a component. In addition, since CCM allows the *binding* of several unrelated interfaces with a component implementation entity, clients need not have explicit knowledge of a component's implementation details to access the alternative interfaces that it offers.

To standardize the component life cycle management interface, CCM introduces the `home` IDL keyword that specifies the life cycle management strategy of each component. Each `home` interface is specific to the component it is defined for and manages exactly one type of component. A client can access the `home` interface to control the life cycle of each component instance it uses. For example, the `home` interface can create and remove component instances.

To use a component, a client first acquires the home interface of the component. Naturally, a standard bootstrapping mechanism must locate the home interface of a specific component. To simplify this bootstrapping process, a centralized database accessed through a HomeFinder interface similar to the CORBA Interoperable Naming Service (INS) can store references to available component homes. A client first uses resolve_initial_references—the standard CORBA API—to acquire the object reference to a HomeFinder interface. HomeFinder enables clients to acquire a reference to the desired home interface of the component. After a client acquires a reference to the home interface of the desired component, the client can invoke the appropriate factory operation (Gamma et al., 1995) to create or find the target component reference.

31.1.3 Development and Run-Time Support Mechanisms for CCM

CCM addresses a significant weakness in CORBA specifications prior to version 3.0 by defining common techniques to implement CORBA servers. We now describe how CCM behaves from a *component developer's* perspective, allowing the developer to generate many types of server applications automatically.

CCM extends the CORBA IDL to support *components*. Component developers use IDL definitions to specify the operations a component supports, just as object interfaces are defined in the traditional CORBA object model. A CCM component can compose together unrelated interfaces and support interface navigation, as described in the "Component Overview" section.

Components can be deployed in component servers that have no advance knowledge of how to configure and instantiate these deployed components. Therefore, components need generic interfaces to assist component servers that install and manage them. CCM components can interact with external entities, such as services provided by an ORB, other components, or clients via *ports*, which can be enumerated using the introspection mechanism. Ports enable standard configuration mechanisms to modify component configurations. Figure 31-3 shows how the CCM port mechanism can be used to compose the components of our stock exchange example.

The CCM port mechanisms provide interfaces to configure a component, set up object connections, subscribe or publish events, and

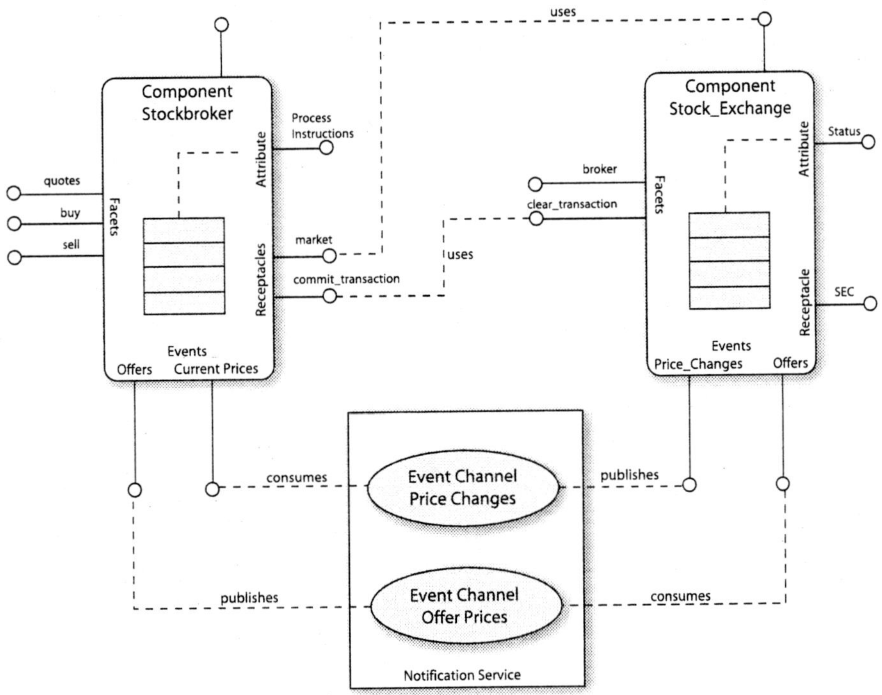

Figure 31-3: *CCM components interact with one another through port mechanisms.*

establish component attributes. For a developer to assemble components into a software component infrastructure or integrate a component into an application, however, there must be a mechanism to express a concrete configuration for a component; in particular they need to designate what component(s) must be connected and how the events published and received by a component relate to each other. Therefore, CCM defines a standard component configuration interface, called `Components::StandardConfigurator`, to help component servers configure components. Component developers can extend this configuration interface to specify how to improve the flexibility of their component implementations.

A component's `home` interface can optionally accept a component configuration object reference that performs the component configuration on a component instance. All CCM components support introspection interfaces, which these configurators use to discover the capabilities of components. The configurator then constructs the component instance by making the necessary interconnections with other components or ORB services.

CCM defines several interfaces to support the structure and functionality of components. Many of these interfaces can be generated automatically via tools supplied by CCM providers. Moreover, life cycle management and the state management implementations can be factored out and reused. The CORBA Component Implementation Framework (CIF) is designed to shield component developers from these tedious tasks by automating common component implementation activities.

Many business applications use components to model "real world" entities, such as employees, bank accounts, and stockbrokers (refer to Chapter 16). These entities may persist over time and are often represented as database entries. Components with persistent state are mapped to a persistent data store that can be used to reconstitute component state whenever the component instance is activated. For example, when a bank account component is instantiated, the CCM component model implementation is able to reconstitute the previous status of the account from a database. The CIF defines a set of APIs that manage the persistent state of components and construct the implementation of a software component.

CCM defines a declarative language, the *Component Implementation Definition Language* (CIDL), to describe implementations and persistent state of components and component homes. As shown in Figure 31-4 the CIF uses the CIDL descriptions to generate programming skeletons that automate core component behaviors, such as navigation, identity inquiries, activation, and state management.

Implementations generated by a CIDL compiler are called *executors*. Executors contain the previously mentioned auto-generated implementations and provide hook methods (Gamma et al., 1995) that allow component developers to add custom component-specific behavior. Executors can be packaged in so-called *assembly files* and installed in a *component server* that supports a particular target platform, such as Windows NT or Linux, and programming language, such as C++ or Java. The component server is part of a CCM component model implementation. In addition, the CIDL is responsible for generating *component descriptors* that define component capabilities, such as descriptions of component's interfaces, threading policy, or

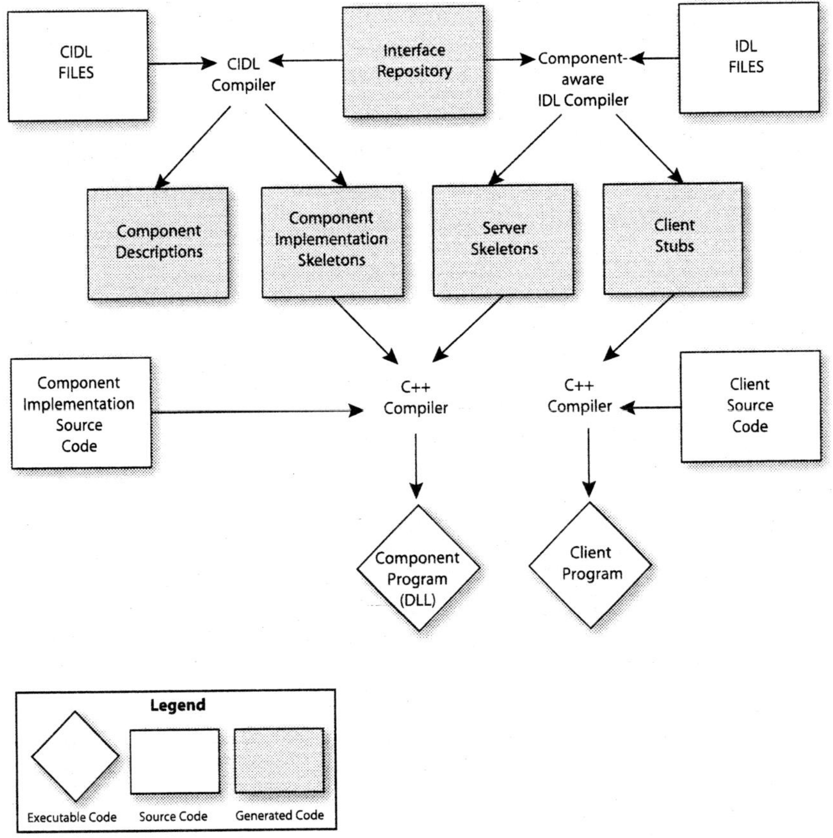

Figure 31-4: *Implementing components using the Component Implementation Definition Language (CIDL).*

transaction policy, along with the type of services required by the component being described.

Component implementations depend upon the standard CORBA Portable Object Adapter (POA) to dispatch incoming client requests to their corresponding servants. However, unlike with previous versions of CORBA, the application developer is no longer responsible for creating the POA hierarchy. The CCM component model implementation uses the component description to create and configure the POA hierarchy automatically and to locate the common services defined by CCM. Moreover, components may require notification via *callbacks* when certain events occur. To support the functionality outlined above in a reusable manner, component servers instantiate *containers,* which perform these tasks on behalf of components they manage. The CCM *container programming model* defines a set of interface APIs that simplify the task of developing and/or configuring CORBA applications. A container encapsulates a component implementation and provides a run-time environment for the component it manages that can

- Activate or deactivate component implementations to preserve limited system resources, such as main memory
- Forward client requests to the four commonly used CORBA Object Services (COS): Transaction, Security, Persistent State, and Notification services, thereby freeing clients from having to locate these services
- Provide adaptation layers (Gamma et al., 1995) for callbacks used by the container and ORB to inform the component about interesting events, such as messages from the Transaction or the Notification Service
- Manage POA policies to determine how to create component references. Figure 31-5 shows the CCM container programming model in more detail

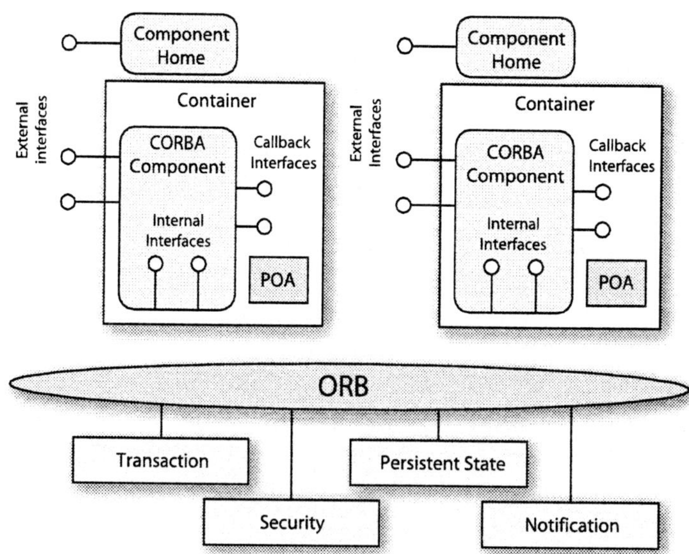

Figure 31-5: *The CCM container programming model.*

Clients directly access external component interfaces, such as the *equivalent interface*, *facets*, and the *home interface*. In contrast, components access the ORB functionality via their container APIs, which include the *internal interfaces* that the component can invoke to access the services provided by the container, as well as the *callback interfaces* that the container can invoke on the component. Each container manages one component implementation defined by the CIF. A container creates its own POA for all the interfaces it manages.

CCM containers also manage the lifetime of component servants. A CCM provider defines a `ServantLocator` that is responsible for supporting these policies. When a `ServantLocator` is installed, a POA delegates the responsibility of activating and deactivating servants to it. Four types of servant lifetime policies control the timing of activating and deactivating components: *method*, *session*, *component*, and *container*. Method and session policies cause `ServantLocators` to activate and passivate components on every method invocation or session, whereas *component* and *container* policies delegate the servant lifetime policies to components and containers, respectively.

In large-scale distributed systems, component implementations may be deployed across multiple servers, often using different implementation languages, operating systems, and programming language compilers. In addition, component implementations may depend on other software component implementations. Thus, the packaging and deploying of components can become complicated. To simplify the effort of developing components, CCM defines standard techniques that developers can apply to simplify component packaging and deployment. CCM describes components, and their dependencies using Open Software Description (OSD), which is an XML Document Type Definition (DTD) defined by the WWW Consortium. Components are packaged in assembly files and package descriptors are XML documents conforming to the Open Software Description DTD that describe the contents of an assembly file and their dependencies. A component may depend on other components and may require these components to be colocated in a common address space.

31.1.4 Related technologies

CCM is modeled closely on the Enterprise JavaBeans (EJB) specification (Matena and Hapner, 1999). Unlike EJB, however, CCM uses the

CORBA object model as its underlying object interoperability architecture and thus is not bound to a particular programming language. Since the two technologies are similar, CCM also defines the standard mappings between the two standards. Therefore, a CCM component can appear as an EJB bean to EJB clients, and an EJB bean can appear as a CCM component by using appropriate bridging techniques. EJB also support CORBA IIOP as its communication framework. We believe the CCM and EJB are mutually complementary.

CCM and CORBA are also related to the Microsoft COM family of middleware technologies. Unlike CORBA, however, Microsoft's COM was designed to support a colocated component programming model initially and later DCOM added the ability to distribute COM objects. The most recent version of Microsoft's technology, COM+, includes commonly used business services, such as the Microsoft Transaction Service (MTS). The CORBA specification defines a bridging mechanism between CORBA objects and DCOM components. However, unlike CORBA and EJB, COM+ is limited mostly to Microsoft platforms.

31.2 Conclusion

The CORBA object model is increasingly gaining acceptance as the industry standard, cross-platform, cross-language distributed object computing model. The recent addition of the CORBA Component Model (CCM) integrates a successful component programming model from EJB, while maintaining the interoperability and language-neutrality of CORBA. The CCM programming model is thus suitable for leveraging proven technologies and existing services to develop the next-generation of highly scalable distributed applications. However, the CCM specification is large and complex. Therefore, ORB providers have only started implementing the specification recently. As with first-generation CORBA implementations several years ago, it is still hard to evaluate the quality and performance of CCM implementations. Moreover, the interoperability of components and containers from different providers is not well understood yet.

By the end of next year, we expect that CCM providers will implement the complete specification, as well as support value-added enhancements to their implementations, just as operating system and

ORB providers have done historically. In particular, containers provided by the CCM component model implementation provide quality of service (QoS) capabilities for CCM components, and can be extended to provide more services to components to relieve components from implementing these functionalities in an *ad hoc* way (Wang, 2000a and 2000b). These container QoS extensions provide services that can monitor and control certain aspects of components behaviors that crosscut different programming layers or require close interaction among components, containers, and operating systems. As CORBA and the CCM evolve, we expect some of these enhancements will be incorporated into the CCM specification.

Chapter 32

Overview of COM+

Tim Ewald[1]

32.1 Introduction

COM+ is the latest incarnation of Microsoft's Component Object Model (COM). The COM+ component model implementation serves as the foundation for many higher-level technologies, including Internet Information Server (IIS), Active Server Pages (ASP), Site Server, Application Center 2000, and Biztalk Server 2000. COM+ components can be implemented in C++, Visual Basic 6, or any other COM-friendly language today and in C#, Visual Basic 7, or any other Common Language Runtime (CLR)-friendly language tomorrow. Many experts believe that COM+ makes the development of scalable Windows 2000 applications easier. In this chapter I will explain the essence of COM+ to help you better understand how you can apply this technology in your own organizations.

1. Portions of this chapter are excerpted from *Transaction COM+: Designing Scalable Applications* by Tim Ewald, Addison-Wesley, 2001.

32.2 A Quick Review of COM+

You cannot understand what COM+ is about unless you are at least familiar with COM, so here is a brief review; for more information on COM, see *Essential COM* by Box (1998) or *Inside COM* by Rogerson (1997). Microsoft introduced COM as a way to expose type-safe component code from a dynamic link library (DLL), a reusable unit executable code that multiple applications can share. COM DLLs export one or more concrete COM classes. Each concrete COM class implements one or more abstract COM interfaces. A client loads a COM component by instantiating a class of a given type. A client communicates with that instance of a COM class using the abstract COM interfaces it implements. Together, COM classes and interfaces form a type system that is both compiler- and language-independent. The types a COM component exports are documented in binary form using a type library—often called a *typelib* – that is embedded directly in the DLL. A component's typelib can be examined at development time to aid in the build process. Clients can also examine the typelib at run-time to dynamically discover types they did not know about at compile time.

COM's class loader is called the Service Control Manager (SCM). The SCM is part of the COM component model implementation. When a client calls `CoCreateInstance` to instantiate a class, the SCM locates and loads the appropriate COM component DLL. The SCM finds COM DLLs using a standard class registration database stored in the Windows Registry. COM DLLs can be declaratively mapped to server processes using entries in the Registry (it is also possible to export COM classes directly from an executable server). If a client instantiates a class in another process, the SCM returns a reference to a proxy object that communicates with the real object using the Distributed COM (DCOM) wire protocol. For more details on the SCM, see Box (1998).

32.3 COM+

COM+ is the cornerstone of a framework of technologies designed to support the development of large-scale distributed applications on the Windows platform. The current, shipping version of the framework is called Windows Distributed Internet Applications Architecture (DNA). The next version is called .NET. Both versions of the framework have similar overall architectures that are based on three assumptions about the needs of scalable systems

- Multiple users running browser-based or custom applications access distributed systems from different machines on internal corporate networks and the Internet
- Distributed systems use multiple servers to handle the volume of client requests
- Distributed systems must be reliable in the event of failure

These assumptions lead to the following design principles

- System logic should be concentrated on servers, not on clients. Servers can share resources (such as database connections), encapsulate database schemas and access mechanisms, and offer a more tightly controlled security environment
- Transactions are at the center of the programming model. They provide a standard model for protecting the integrity of distributed system state in the face of both concurrent access and system failure. The majority of system state must be kept under transactional control
- The components in a distributed system communicate use a variety of protocols. Clients typically communicate with server-side components using HyperText Transfer Protocol (HTTP) and the Simple Object Access Protocol (SOAP), but DCOM and Microsoft Message Queue (MSMQ) are also sometimes used. Server components typically communicate using DCOM, MSMQ and database-specific data access protocols (but HTTP and SOAP are also used). Figure 32-1 illustrates

COM+ is designed to make it easier to develop systems that adhere to these principles by providing run-time services such as distributed transaction management.

32.3.1 Contexts and Causalities

COM+ is based on two basic concepts, *contexts* and *causalities*. A context is an object within an operating system process that provides a

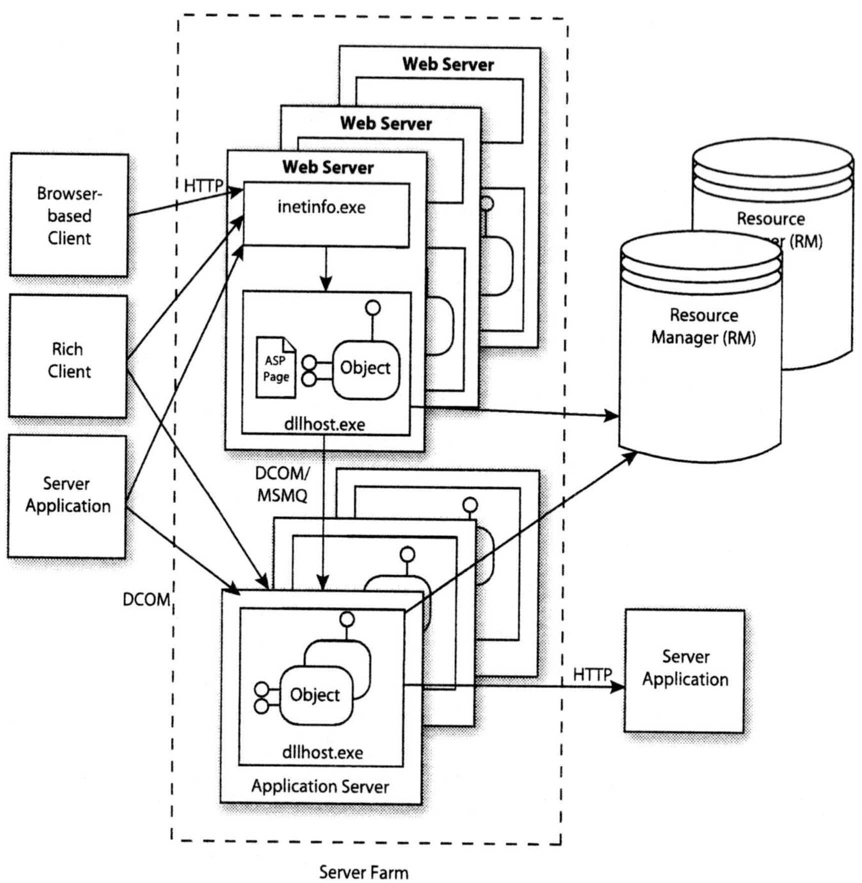

Figure 32-1: *Communication in a distributed system.*

specific set of run-time services. Every object created in a COM+ process belongs in exactly one context that is configured to meet the object's needs. A COM+ method call between objects in different contexts is intercepted by the COM+ component model implementation so that COM+ has the opportunity to invoke arbitrary service code before a method call to an object is dispatched. This generic mechanism is used throughout COM+ to provide value-added services, such as security and transactions.

For example, each operating system process in Figure 32-2 is divided into COM+ contexts. Process M contains a single context A. Process N contains two contexts, B and C. There are two objects in each context. Each pair of objects within each context uses the same set of services. In this case, each context also includes a proxy to an object in another context. Proxies are constructed automatically as object references are passed from one context to another. The three dashed ovals indicate the points where the COM+ plumbing intercepts method calls and triggers the services that the target context wants to use. It is important to note that services are mapped to contexts, not objects; this design principle makes it easier to construct COM+ components because the contexts will contain the complicated logic to access the services.

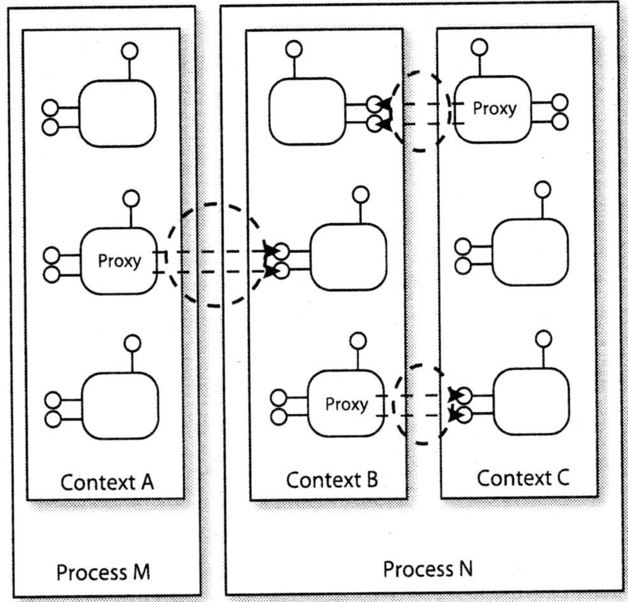

Figure 32-2: *Relationship between processes, contexts, and COM+ objects.*

Some services need to know whether multiple method calls across context boundaries are *causally* related, that is, whether one method call caused another method call. Within a single process using multiple operating system threads, the causal relationship between method calls can be determined by using the unique thread identifier. But in COM+ method calls may be dispatched on different threads, perhaps in different processes. COM+ detects the relationships between method calls by using an abstraction that is similar to a thread, but is not bound to any particular process. In COM+ this abstraction is called a *causality* (COM+ actually inherited causality from classic COM, which has had it from the beginning). A causality is a distributed chain of COM+ method calls that spans any number of contexts in any number of processes, possibly involving multiple machines. Each causality represents a single *logical* thread of action within the distributed system as COM+ method calls are invoked across contexts. Where contexts are static spatial constructs, causalities are dynamic temporal constructs. Each causality is uniquely identified by a causality id, or CID; in a way, CIDs are logical thread identifiers. Each causality can involve any number of physical threads, as shown in Figure 32-3.

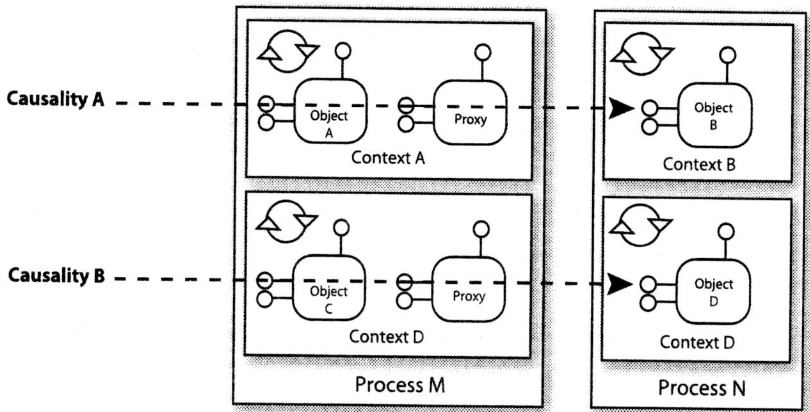

Figure 32-3: *The interaction between causalities and threads.*

Whenever a thread that *is not* currently processing a COM+ method call makes a COM+ method call, it is by definition starting a *new* call chain and therefore a new causality; the COM+ component model implementation detects new causalities and assigns CIDs. A causality's CID is automatically propagated from context to context as COM+ method calls occur. A CID will identify a causality for as long as it is running. Support for this is built into the DCOM wire protocol. (The CID is embedded in each DCOM request message as part of the implicit `ORPCTHIS` parameter. See the DCOM Wire Protocol Specification for more information.) Whenever a thread that *is* currently processing a COM+ method call makes another COM+ method call, it is by definition *continuing* an existing call chain and therefore simply participating in the ongoing causality; the CID of the ongoing causality is automatically propagated as part of the call.

32.3.2 Contexts and Causalities as Objects

COM+ implements its run-time services by pre- and post-processing cross-context method invocations. If services are implemented transparently via call interception, however, how does an object interact with these services? For instance, if a COM+ object is in a context that provides a declarative transaction (a declarative transaction is simply a distributed transaction managed by COM+), how can the object influence the outcome of the transaction? The COM+ component model implementation solves this problem by representing each context as an object called an *object context*. The COM+ component model implementation maintains a unique object context for each context in a process. Each object context implements interfaces that allow an object to interact with the runtime services its context provides. From an object's perspective, its object context represents the world the object lives in. If an object's context includes a declarative transaction, the object can use object context to detect the transaction's presence and to influence its outcome.

An object can acquire a reference to its context's object context by calling the `CoGetObjectContext` method (or the `GetObjectContext` method in Visual Basic):

```
HRESULT GoGetObjectContext([in] REFIID riid,
                           [out, iid_is(riid)] void **ppv) ;
```

`CoGetObjectContext` always returns a reference to the object context of the context the calling thread is currently in. The COM+ component model implementation tracks the context in which a thread executes. It updates this information dynamically when a thread makes a COM+ method call that crosses from one context to another through a proxy. Because the COM+ component model implementation always knows the context for a thread, `CoGetObjectContext` can accurately return a reference to the appropriate object context. In Figure 32-4 two threads, A and B, are simultaneously executing code in two different contexts, A and B respectively. Thread A has invoked a method from an interface of object A; thread B has invoked a method (in a different interface of object A) that makes a method call to another COM+ object, Object B, that resides in a different context. The threads are associated with the two *different* object contexts. If thread B finished its work in context B and returned to context A, the COM+ interception plumbing would make sure both threads were associated with the *same* object context.

Similar to contexts, causalities are represented as *call context* objects. Call contexts are just like object contexts, except that, where object contexts model the space an object lives in, call contexts model work being done in that space. An object can acquire a reference to a call context object representing the current causality by calling the `CoGetCallContext` method (or the `GetSecurityCallContext` method in Visual Basic):

```
HRESULT GoGetCallContext([in] REFIID riid,
                         [out, iid_is(riid)] void **ppv) ;
```

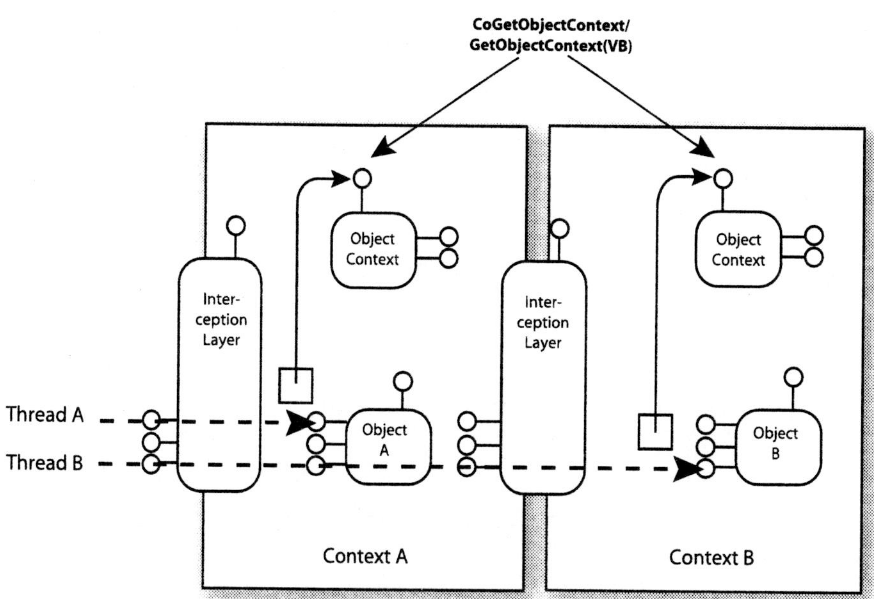

Figure 32-4: *Interaction between threads and contexts.*

`CoGetCallContext` will return a reference to a call context for the causality in which the calling thread is participating. The COM+ component model implementation tracks the causality in which a thread is executing. It updates this information dynamically as a thread is used to service different COM+ method calls. Figure 32-5 illustrates the relationship between object context and call context.

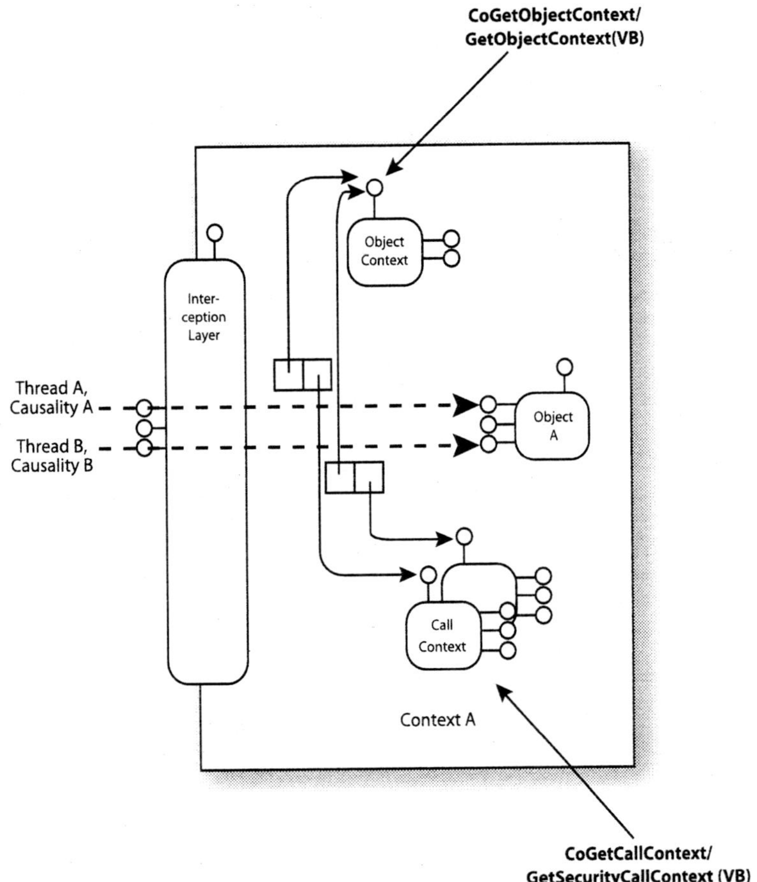

Figure 32-5: *Relationship between object context and call context.*

32.3.3 Declarative Services

Contexts often seem intangible because there is no documented mechanism for creating them. There is no COM+ `CoCreateContext` method to explicitly manufacture new contexts. Instead, the COM+ component model implementation creates new contexts implicitly, as they are needed, to house new COM+ objects whose needs cannot be met by the context in which the COM+ objects are created. In other words, context creation is tied directly to object creation.

The COM+ component model implementation offers run-time services for COM+ objects to use. To do so, a COM+ class (from which that COM+ object is instantiated) must declare its intent to use these services. If a class indicates that it requires a service, COM+ instances of that class execute within a context that makes that service an intrinsic part of the object's runtime environment. Each service's behavior—whether or not it is used, and the form that behavior will take—is controlled by one or more *declarative attributes*, as listed in Table 32-1. A COM+ class indicates its desire to use a service by declaring the appropriate attribute(s) when it is registered with the COM+ component model implementation. This information is stored in the COM+ Catalog, a registration database similar to but separate from the Registry used by classic COM. COM+ classes that declare one or more attributes—and use one or more services—are called *configured classes.* Classes that do not specify any of these attributes are called *nonconfigured classes.* All classic COM classes are by default assumed to be nonconfigured COM+ classes to ensure backward compatibility with existing COM components.

When an instance of a COM+ class is created using the SCM, the SCM checks the declarative attributes defined by that COM+ class. Then the SCM examines the context of the creator, the code that called `CoCreateInstance` (or the `CreateObject` method in Visual Basic) is executing. If the SCM decides that the current context *can* meet the needs of the new COM+ object without additional interception, the SCM assigns the new object to the current context and returns a reference to the actual object to the creator. If the SCM decides the current context *cannot* meet the environmental needs of the new object without additional interception, SCM constructs a new context, assigns the new object to the newly created context, and returns a reference to a proxy to the creator. The proxy belongs to the context of the creator and supports cross-context communication, as described in earlier. The creation of contexts occurs transparently within the scope of the object creation call.

Table 32-1: *Full Set of COM+ Declarative Services*

Declarative attribute	For a COM+ object, controls the ...
`ApplicationID`	mapping to a particular process
`ThreadingModel`	degree of thread affinity
`Synchronization`	degree of synchronization
`Transaction`	use of distributed transactions
`ObjectPoolingEnabled` `JustInTimeActivation`	life cycle relative to the lifetime of a client's reference

32.3.3.1 Applications

A COM+ class's `ApplicationID` attribute indicates which *application* it belongs to. COM+ divides configured classes into applications that define how the classes are mapped to processes. If a configured class is part of a server application, its code will be loaded into, and its instances will be created in, a dedicated process. If a configured class is part of a library application, its code will be loaded into, and its instances will be created in, the caller's process.

32.3.3.2 Thread Affinity

A COM+ class's `ThreadingModel` attribute defines the degree of *thread affinity* for its instances. COM+ has inherited the `ThreadingModel` declarative attribute from classic COM. Instances of COM+ classes with high thread affinity must always be accessed using the same thread. Instances of COM+ classes with low thread affinity can be accessed by different threads over time. The COM+ component model implementation controls the mapping of threads to contexts (and the objects in those contexts) using *apartments*. An *apartment* is a group of contexts within a process that share the same degree of thread affinity. Method calls into a context are always serviced by a thread within that context's apartment; this may force a thread switch. Every context created in a COM+ process is associated with exactly one apartment that provides the degree of thread affinity it needs.

A process can contain multiple apartments with differing degrees of thread affinity, as shown in Figure 32-6. Apartments W and X are Single-Threaded Apartments (STA), and only one thread can be processing within the apartment. Apartment Y is a multithreaded apartment (MTA), while apartment Z is a Thread Neutral Apartment (TNA) in which any thread can enter but no thread is associated with the apartment.

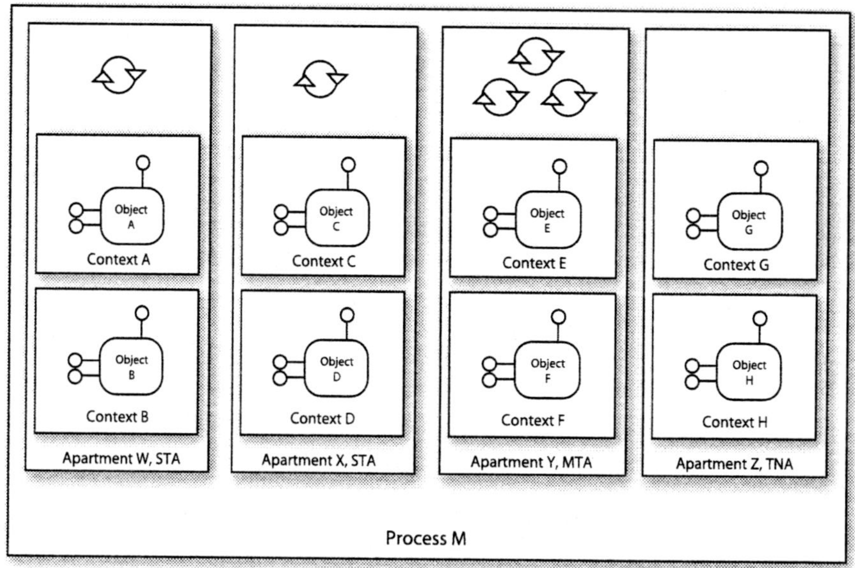

Figure 32-6: *Thread affinity in COM+.*

32.3.3.3 Synchronization

A COM+ class's `Synchronization` attribute defines the degree of *synchronization* for its instances. An instance of a COM+ class that requires synchronization can only be accessed by a single causality at a time. The COM+ component model implementation controls the mapping of causalities to contexts (and the objects in those contexts) using *activities*. An *activity* is a group of contexts within a process that can only be entered by a single causality at a time. Specifically, method calls into a context in an activity must acquire a causality-based lock before they can be processed. Every context created in a COM+ process is associated with at most one activity. A process can contain multiple activities, as shown in Figure 32-7.

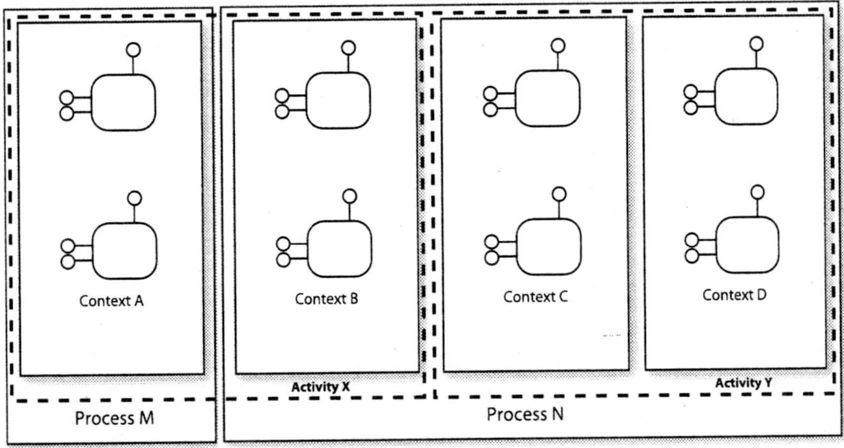

Figure 32-7: *Relationship between processes and activities.*

32.3.3.4 Transactions

A COM+ class's `Transaction` attribute determines whether or not its instances use distributed transactions. The COM+ component model implementation controls the mapping of distributed transactions to contexts (and the objects in those contexts) using *transaction streams*. A transaction stream is a group of contexts within a process that have access to a runtime-managed distributed transaction. If an object in a context in a transaction stream opens a database connection, the connection is implicitly assigned to the stream's distributed transaction. An object can also affect the outcome of its stream's distributed transaction, that is, whether the transaction commits or terminates. Every context created in a COM+ process is associated with at most one transaction stream. A process can contain multiple streams, as shown in Figure 32-8.

32.3.3.5 Object Pooling and Just-in-Time Activation

A COM+ class's `ObjectPoolingEnabled` and `JustInTimeActivation` attributes determine how an instance's life cycle relates to the life cycles of its client's proxy. In classic COM, a client controls an object's life cycle. Specifically, an object remains in existence as long as its client holds a reference to it, and when the client releases its reference, the object goes away. If a COM+ class uses object pooling, its instances can outlive their clients' references and be reused by multiple clients over time. If a COM+ class uses just-in-time activation (JITA), its instances can detach themselves from their clients before they release their references.

32.3.3.6 Additional Services

Beyond the core services that are designed as a foundation for the development of scalable systems, COM+ adds several features. Most important among them is integration with HTTP. IIS, the standard Web server on Windows 2000, is heavily integrated with COM+. Specifically, IIS processes HTTP request messages that target dynamic code – that is, either ASP pages or Internet Server API (ISAPI) DLLs, within an appropriately configured COM+ context. COM+ also provides a more flexible security model based on roles. Roles are collections of users or groups that have permission to do certain tasks. A COM+ class can declare which roles are allowed to access its methods, and the COM+ component model implementation will enforce these rules via interception. An object can also test the role memberships of the current caller programmatically.

32.4 The Common Language Runtime

COM is Microsoft's basic component technology. COM+ is a framework that provides advanced runtime services to instances of COM classes to make it easier to build large distributed systems. At the time of this writing, Microsoft is in the early stages of creating a replacement for COM. This next-generation component technology is part of the company's .NET initiative. It is based on a central component called the Common Language Runtime (CLR). The CLR is the heir-apparent to—and completely backward compatible with—COM. CLR-based components are called *assemblies*. Assemblies are reusable binary units that expose type-safe code.

The motivation for moving to the CLR is type information. Although COM is able to merge language type systems with its own component-technology type system, it doesn't go far enough, and many well-known deficiencies have hindered COM developers for years. First, not all languages can use all COM data types, so component designers have to target particular languages when they write their code. Second, the information in a COM typelib is not complete and does not accurately reflect everything that can be expressed in the interface definition language (IDL) developers use to define COM types. Third, the information in a component's typelib only reflects the types that component exposes, not the types it relies on, making it difficult to track dependencies between components. Finally, the information in a component's typelib only reflects the external details of that component's types—that is, the signatures of its interfaces' methods and the names of its concrete classes, not the internal implementation details. Many might argue that this last point is not a weakness, because exposing a component's implementation details violates the principles of encapsulation. However, the lack of binary type information about a component's classes data members makes it impossible to implement useful services, such as automatic persistence of object graphs to a database or to XML. The CLR fixes all of these problems by making type information ubiquitous. CLR components include metadata that describes everything about them. The meta data is accessible via reflection and extensible via custom attributes.

The CLR is a replacement for COM, but not for COM+. CLR components will use COM+ runtime services the same way COM components do (this works because the CLR is backward compatible with COM). The next version of Windows (Whistler, or Windows.NET) includes several new COM+ features intended to simplify configuration management for clusters of systems. In short, the only thing about COM+ that is likely to be radically different in the near future is its name. By the time the CLR ships, COM+ is likely to be called .NET Component Services.

32.5 Conclusion

COM+ provides run-time services to objects based on their classes' declared needs. COM+ implements its services by intercepting calls between contexts within a single process or across process boundaries. Objects interact with run-time services using object context and call context. COM+ works with both classic COM and the new CLR. Developers can use the COM+ runtime environment as a foundation for building scalable distributed enterprise applications.

Chapter 33

Overview of the Enterprise JavaBeans Component Model

David Blevins

33.1 Introduction

Enterprise JavaBeans (EJB) is a software component model for developing and deploying enterprise-wide business applications. The model consists of an open specification (Matena and Hapner, 1999) that software component producers, consumers, and end-users and software component model producers can use to develop their software products. Using EJB *servers, containers,* and *components,* businesses can write applications that can be deployed in any EJB-compliant system. The specification defines a simple contract among the components—enterprise beans—and the component model implementation, the container, and server. Also defined are basic component types that reflect common needs of distributed software applications such as persistent business objects, process objects, and client session state. The component model clearly defines the *life cycle* for each component type and how the container and server manage a component over its lifetime.

EJB is designed to provide application developers with a robust distributed environment that is responsible for many of the complex features of distributed computing, such as

- Transaction management
- Connection pooling
- State management
- Multi-threading

The complex features of EJB distributed computing simplify the responsibilities of the component and allow developers to focus on providing the core functionality the business application requires.

In this chapter I introduce the two most important parts in the EJB component model: enterprise beans and EJB containers. We'll talk about the two different types of enterprise beans, their abilities, and how each type is managed. I also describe the roles the EJB component model defines for bean creation, deployment, application assembly, and server platform support. These roles demonstrate how the software development team in your business would benefit from implementing EJB enterprise systems.

33.2 The Problem

As software systems expand into the enterprise and separate network systems and services become available, it becomes necessary to find a component model that allows business applications to utilize these separate systems and services in a simple, yet flexible, way. As mentioned in the CORBA chapter (see Chapter 31), there are numerous disadvantages to developing or adopting a proprietary component model. While CORBA itself is a powerful component model, it contains many language and operating system interoperability features that applications written in Java do not need. These features are a fundamental part of CORBA's design and make it more difficult to use.

The Java language is already platform-independent and contains many standard application programming interfaces (APIs) that allow common software systems to be integrated and used by applications written in Java. Businesses developing Java-based enterprise applications need a robust component model that serves their needs. I propose that EJB is best suited for their needs.

33.3 An Enterprise Bean Component

Enterprise beans are reusable, server-side components that clients can remotely access and execute. When composed and deployed in an EJB container, a bean is fully configurable and executable. Enterprise beans are modeled after the processes and entities in your business, such as an online shopping cart, payment process, or customer. Enterprise beans come in a few basic types and each component consists of a few simple parts. First I must explain the notion of an EJB container.

33.3.1 An EJB Container

The EJB container exists on the server-side of an enterprise system and is the core part of the EJB component model implementation. An enterprise bean is deployed and executed in a container. The container notifies the bean at important stages during its life cycle and provides the bean with information regarding the environment in which the bean executes. The primary responsibility of the container is to apply transactional rules and to enforce security of the bean's execution at run-time. The container initiates and terminates transactions and grants or denies access using transactional attributes and security roles defined by the bean. The container is responsible for low-level functionality and restricts the bean's access to certain aspects of the Java APIs. Resources such as the file system, Abstract Windowing Toolkit (AWT), native libraries, and thread management, as well as sockets or class loaders, are forbidden to a bean in any environment.

33.4 Component Types

There are two distinct types of enterprise beans: entity beans and session beans. Each provides its own type of functionality and provides the option of enabling the container to manage that functionality or managing it itself. Beans that manage their own functionality are more complex, but also have more options that are not otherwise available. Session beans and entity beans both come in two distinct subtypes that bring with them new responsibilities and options.

33.4.1 Session Beans

Session beans are modeled to perform the various processes of a business. They can update data in a database and participate in transactions. They can be either stateful or stateless.

33.4.1.1 Stateful Session Beans

A stateful session bean represents processes that involve many interactions with a client. A stateful session bean maintains its state between calls by the client and typically stores information for a relatively short amount of time, usually for the lifetime of the client or just long enough for the client to finish a set of related tasks. Stateful session beans are dedicated to a single client and cannot be accessed by other clients.

A good example of a stateful session bean is a Web-based shopping cart. As the user of a client application browses through a catalog of items, a stateful session bean can track the items the user would like to purchase. If the user quits the application without purchasing any of the selected items, the shopping cart session bean can roll back the transaction and discard all selected items or store the items in a database for later access.

33.4.1.2 Stateless Session Beans

A stateless session bean provides business methods that execute one logical unit of work. When a stateless session bean returns from a call made by the client, its work is done. These beans do not maintain a conversational state and are not dedicated to a single client. The bean immediately processes information it receives from the client or external resources such as a database system. A good example of a stateless session bean is a cashier for a Web-based business. The cashier can have methods such as `applyDiscount`, `totalAllItems`, `calculateTax` and `processPayment`. The shopping cart bean might invoke these methods when the user checks out.

33.4.1.3 Transaction Management

The EJB container provides powerful transaction APIs that session beans can use. Transactions may be automatically managed by the container (container-managed transaction demarcation) or explicitly managed by the bean itself (bean-managed demarcation).

Container-Managed Transaction Demarcation

A session bean can choose to have the container enforce all the transactional rules for the session bean based upon information specified when the component was deployed. Each method of a session bean can be assigned a transactional attribute. For example, if a bean's method specifies that it does not support transactions, the container will suspend the current transaction before invoking the method and then resume that transaction after the method has returned. If a bean method declares it must always be executed with a new transaction, for example, the container will suspend the current transaction and start a new transaction before invoking the bean's method. When the method completes the container will commit the transaction before returning the method's result to the client and resuming the transaction that was previously in progress. At any time during a method's execution the bean may tell the container that the current transaction must be rolled back. The container is responsible for rolling back all work performed during the transaction. The use of transactions is one of the major strengths of the EJB model and a major reason for its popularity. The transaction mechanism in EJB has many options. In all, there are six different transaction attributes that are available to select for beans with container-managed transaction demarcation (Tyagi, 2000).

Bean-Managed Transaction Demarcation

Session beans of the bean-managed transaction demarcation type receive no help from the container and must initiate and terminate transactions for themselves using the Java Transaction API. Although use of the Java Transaction API is more work for the bean, the API allows greater flexibility in the way transactions are managed. Session beans with bean-managed transaction demarcation are not confined to demarcating transactions just at the beginning and end of methods, as are beans with container-managed transaction demarcation. These session beans can begin a transaction in one method and commit it later in a different method. Similarly they can begin and commit a transaction many times in one method. The EJB specification does not allow session beans to nest transactions; the bean must commit or roll back the current transaction before a new one can be started.

33.4.2 Entity Beans

Entity beans are certainly the most complex component type in the EJB model. Entity beans operate as business objects and represent data in a database or any other persistent data source such as a legacy application. Entity beans are not bound to one client and multiple users can share them concurrently. Entity beans are persistent and represent the data even as it changes over time. Because the data the bean represents can change, the bean will need to be periodically synchronized with the data source. The container or the bean itself can take responsibility for synchronizing and persisting the entity bean with the data source. To achieve this, entity beans come in two types: bean-managed persistence and container-managed persistence.

33.4.2.1 Bean-Managed Persistence

Entity beans with bean-managed persistence are responsible for making all the necessary calls to synchronize its data to a persistent data source. The Bean Provider (see Table 33-2) must program this logic within the bean itself; the container will notify the bean when it should synchronize its state. For example, the container will call `ejbLoad` on the bean instance when a new transaction is started. This occurs before any of the bean's business methods are executed in the transaction and allows the bean instance to retrieve data that will be needed during the transaction. When the transaction completes the container will call the bean's `ejbStore` method to notify the bean that it is time to synchronize.

33.4.2.2 Container-Managed Persistence

Bean providers of entity beans can choose to have the container be responsible for synchronizing the bean's data to a persistent data source. The Bean Deployer (see Table 33-2) must map the bean's data to an available persistent data source. The container provides the sophisticated tools that will generate the necessary code, scripts, or SQL statements to synchronize the entity bean's data to a persistent data source. While the bean executes the container will automatically synchronize the entity bean's data. The tools that the container provides for deploying a bean are not defined by the EJB specification and will differ between vendors and the data sources they support.

33.4.3 Distributed Objects

Enterprise beans are distributable and accessible by clients running remotely over the network as well as by clients running on the same computer. The bean itself never leaves the container and the EJB server must provide a way for clients to access and execute the bean's methods remotely. The exact technology the server should use to achieve this is not defined by the EJB specification, but is typically a distributed object technology such as CORBA (see Chapter 31) or Java Remote Method Invocation (RMI). These technologies provide a basic stub and skeleton that, when applied with EJB, allow clients to invoke a bean's methods over the network. A stub is a network-aware object that exists at the client and accepts method calls on behalf of the component. A skeleton resides on the server and listens for requests from its stub. Figure 33-1 illustrates the basics of the technique.

When a client invokes a method on a stub, the stub sends the request across the network to the skeleton where the method is invoked on the actual component. The result of the method invocation then travels from the skeleton back to the stub.

In EJB the stub implements a Java interface that defines the methods that can be remotely executed on the bean. Client applications can only see and use the interface and are unaware of the stub behind it.

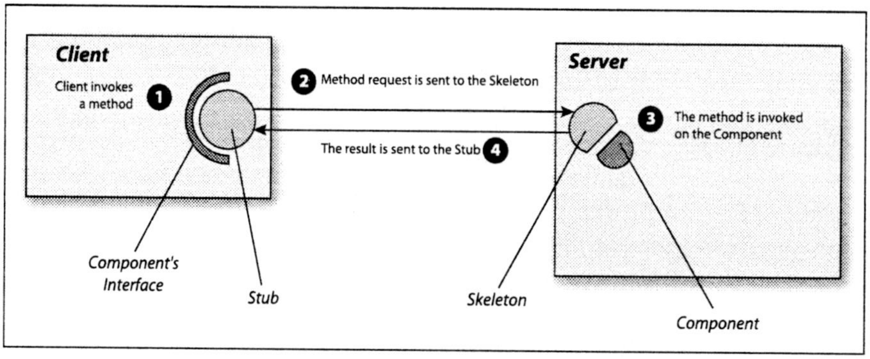

Figure 33-1: *Stub-skeleton scenario.*

This allows the client application to use the bean as if it were running locally. The distributed technology that the EJB server uses to provide the client with access to the bean is unknown to the client application. This frees up the client application from having to write distributed technology-specific code that would bind it to a specific implementation of an EJB server.

33.5 The Structure of an Enterprise Bean

Enterprise bean components are made up of a few basic parts. An enterprise bean is not executable until it has gone through the three steps of production, assembly, and deployment. A bean that is fully deployed into a container will have at least six basic parts that are created at various stages during bean composition. Fortunately, not all of these parts are the responsibility of the Bean Provider, the one who creates the bean. The EJB container and server are responsible for generating the parts they need to make the bean distributed. Table 33-1 shows the various parts of an enterprise bean and who is responsible for them.

The parts are actual `.class` and `.xml` files. To get a better understanding of how these parts are used at run-time, consider the logical view of an enterprise bean component shown in Figure 33-2.

Every enterprise bean consists of an EJBHome, EJBObject, Enterprise Bean class, and a deployment descriptor. Together these parts make a component that is accessible by the client, executable within a

Table 33-1: *Parts of an Enterprise Bean Component*

Role	Enterprise Bean Component Parts Required to Produce	Example Bean

Bean Provider	Home interface (EJBHome)
	Remote interface (EJBObject)
	Enterprise bean class
	Primary key class*
	XML Deployment Descriptor**
		`ShoppingCartHome.class`
		`ShoppingCart.class`
		`ShoppingCartBean.class`
		`ShoppingCartPK.class`
		`ShoppingCart.xml`

EJB Container or EJB Server	Home interface implementation (EJBHome)
	Remote interface implementation (EJBObject)
		`ShoppingCartHomeStub.class`
		`ShoppingCartHomeSkel.class`
		`ShoppingCartStub.class`
		`ShoppingCartSkel.class`

*Only entity beans need to supply a primary key class.
** The Assembler and Deployer will need to modify the deployment descriptor at their stages during composition.

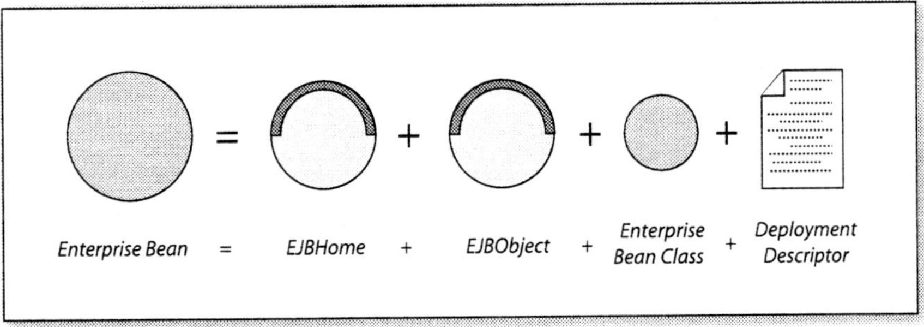

Figure 33-2: *Logical view of an enterprise bean.*

container on the server, and properly configured to meet the needs of the business and run in the business' environment.

33.5.1 The Enterprise Bean Class

The bean class is the core part of an enterprise bean that contains all the business logic and code that models the processes and entities of the business. Figure 33-3 is an example of a session bean called `Shopping-`

`CartBean`. The bean class resides in the container and is instantiated, executed, and managed by the container according to the policies the EJB specification defines. The bean class implements one of the `javax.ejb.EnterpriseBean` interfaces, either `javax.ejb.EntityBean` or `javax.ejb.SessionBean`. The methods in these interfaces are used to notify the bean when it is entering or exiting new stages of its life cycle. The container will notify the bean by actually calling the methods, at which point the bean can perform any actions it deems necessary. These methods are called *callback* methods. If you are familiar with event driven programming, it may help you to think of these methods in a similar way. Think of the container as the user triggering the event and the bean class as the object listening for the event. The `ejbLoad` and `ejbStore` methods described in the Entity Beans section are examples of callback methods. In a callback method the bean class can implement complex code and perform critical tasks or leave the methods empty.

```
public interface ShoppingCartBean extends javax.ejb.SessionBean {
   // Required create method for the EJBHome
   public void ejbCreate() {...}
   public void ejbRemove() {...}

   // Business methods available to the EJBObject
   public void addItem(int skuNumber) throws RemoteException {...}
   public void addItem(String name) throws RemoteException {...}
   public void removeItem(String name) throws RemoteException {...}
   public void checkout() throws RemoteException {...}
   ...
}
```

Figure 33-3: *Example of ShoppingCartBean session bean.*

33.5.2 EJBObject and EJBHome Objects

When deploying an enterprise bean in an EJB container, the Bean Deployer uses the container-specific deployment tools to generate producer-specific implementations of the bean's home and remote interfaces, called the *EJBHome* and *EJBObject*. Each of these objects will typically be an auto-generated stub and skeleton (as shown in Figure 33-1) that serve as adapters to integrate the bean's class with the EJB server and container. Using the *EJBHome* and *EJBObject*, the container exposes the methods of the bean class to clients and manages instances of the bean at runtime.

33.5.2.1 EJBObject

The EJBObject provides a way for the client to access and execute the business methods of a bean class. The EJBObject consists of two parts, as shown in Figure 33-4: a remote interface created by the Bean Provider and a distributable object generated by the EJB container and server that implements the remote interface.

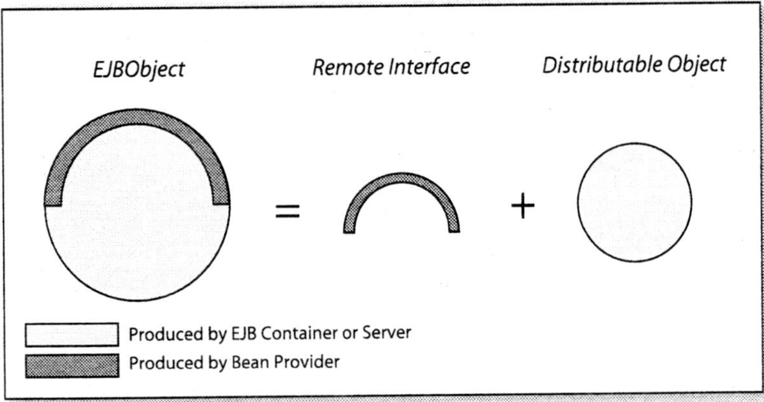

Figure 33-4: *Makeup of an EJBObject.*

The remote interface is a Java interface that extends `javax.ejb.EJBObject` and defines the business methods that are available to a client. Figure 33-5 contains a sample remote interface.

Every business method in the Bean Provider's remote interface maps directly to a method in the bean class. When the container receives a request to execute a method on a bean instance, it verifies that the client is authorized to execute the method and applies the transaction policy as defined by the bean's deployment descriptor.

33.5.2.2 EJBHome

The EJBHome acts like a factory for creating, finding, or removing EJBObjects. Clients use an EJBHome to create and remove references

```
public interface ShoppingCart extends javax.ejb.EDJBObject {
   public void addItem(int skuNumber) throws RemoteException;
   public void addItem(String name) throws RemoteException;
   public void removeItem(String name) throws RemoteException;
   public void checkout() throws RemoteException;
}
```

Figure 33-5: *Sample remote interface for EJBObject.*

to beans deployed in a particular container. An EJBHome consists of two parts, as shown in Figure 33-6: a home interface created by the Bean Provider and a distributable object generated by the EJB container and server that implements the bean's home interface.

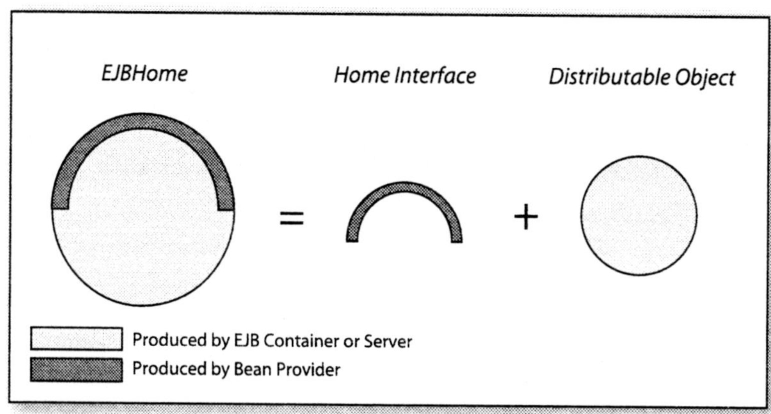

Figure 33-6: *The makeup of an EJBHome.*

In the bean's home interface the Bean Provider defines methods that create and remove beans. The home interface is a Java interface that extends `javax.ejb.EJBHome`. Figure 33-7 contains a sample home interface.

```
public interface ShoppingCartHome extends javax.ejb.EJBHome {
   public ShoppingCart create(String name);
   public ShoppingCart create(String name, int a);
   public void remove(String name);
}
```

Figure 33-7: *Sample home interface.*

All create and remove methods defined in the bean's home interface map directly to an equivalent method in the bean class. For every `create` method in the home interface there must be an `ejbCreate` method in the bean class with the same parameters. The same rule applies for `remove` methods. When a client calls `create(String name)`, for example, the container will call `ejbCreate(String name)` on an instance of the bean class. A new EJBObject is then created by the container and sent back to the client.

Figure 33-8 contains a simplified fragment of a client application that uses the EJBHome and EJBObject of the `ShoppingCartBean` to make a purchase; the EJBHome is `ShoppingCartHome` and EJBObject is `ShoppingCart`. The client uses a `ShoppingCartHome` instance to create a new `ShoppingCart` EJBObject for a customer called John Smith. The EJBObject instance is then used to order two items and check out. Once the checkout is complete the `ShoppingCartHome` instance is used again to remove John Smith's `ShoppingCart`.

```
ShoppingCartHome cartHome = ...;
ShoppingCart cart = cartHome.create("John Smith");
cart.addItem(1234);
cart.addItem("Book=CBSE: Putting the Pieces Together");
```

Figure 33-8: *Code fragment from a sample client application.*

To summarize this discussion, Figure 33-9 shows how an enterprise bean is fully deployed. Note how the client accesses the home interface and remote interface, while the bean class instance executes on the server.

33.5.3 The XML Deployment Descriptor

The last part of an enterprise bean is the deployment descriptor. A bean's deployment descriptor is an XML file (*www.w3c.org/XML*) that contains the configuration information and properties of the bean, such as

- Information about the component's classes
- Transactional attributes
- Security roles
- Settings that dictate the component's behavior

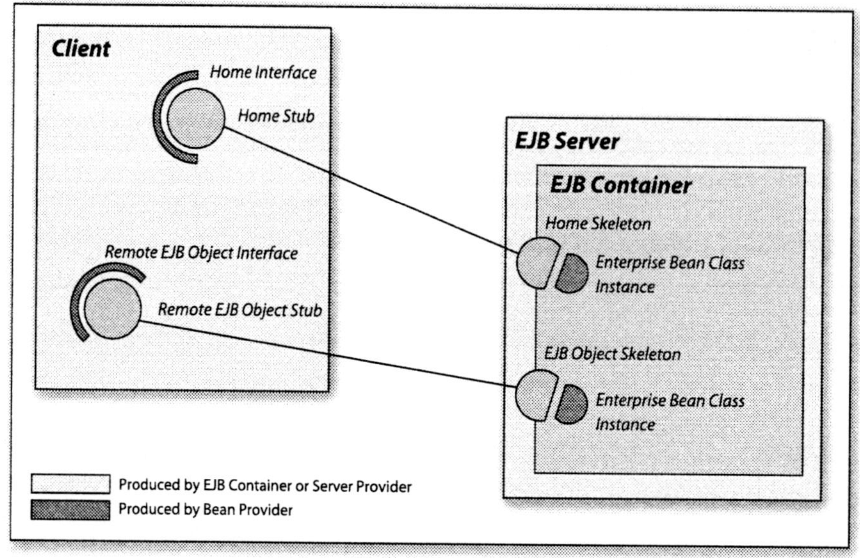

Figure 33-9: *View of a fully deployed enterprise bean.*

The deployment descriptor is part of what makes an enterprise bean a unique component. If you change the information in the deployment descriptor, you *greatly* change the bean's behavior and identity. Two beans with identical EJBHomes, EJBObjects, and bean classes but with different deployment descriptors are considered to be two different beans. A business may purchase a single bean component from a vendor and deploy it many times in a container. Each time the bean is deployed the result is a new and unique bean component that clients can create, access, and remove.

33.6 Roles in the EJB Model

The EJB specification clearly defines the responsibilities that component producers, component consumers, vendors, and end-users fulfill. As shown in Table 33-2, there are six roles defined for the EJB component model: Enterprise Bean Provider, Application Assembler, Bean Deployer, EJB Container Provider, EJB Server Provider, and System Administrator.

33.6.1 The Bean Provider

The Bean Provider produces a reusable component that adheres to the EJB component model. The Bean Provider can be a component producer that sells enterprise beans targeted for industry-specific applications or a developer creating enterprise beans for a custom application. Because enterprise beans are modeled after the processes and entities in businesses, they should be easily reusable. The Bean Provider must provide a single deployment file called an *ejb-jar* file. The ejb-jar file is a Java Archive (JAR) file that is identical to an ordinary zip file and contains the enterprise bean classes, its home interface, the remote interface, and an XML deployment descriptor.

Table 33-2: *Roles in the EJB Component Model*

Role	Description
Enterprise Bean Provider	Produces the enterprise bean component
Application Assembler	Writes an application using enterprise beans
Bean Deployer	Deploys the beans and application into an EJB container and server
EJB Container Provider	Provides an EJB container and deployment tools
EJB Server Provider	Provides a server that distributes the enterprise beans in a container to clients
System Administrator	Configures and tunes the server and container for optimum performance

33.6.2 The Application Assembler

Application Assemblers construct an application using enterprise beans. They package applications with the *ejb-jar files* of all beans used and supply specifications for assembling and deploying the application in an EJB-compliant platform. The deployment descriptors of beans used in the application are customized to link beans that reference each other and the value of parameters used by each bean are modified.

33.6.3 The Bean Deployer

The Bean Deployer installs the beans and applications in the target software component implementation using the information in the beans' deployment descriptors and assembly specifications. At this point all the bean's properties must be set and its required resources must be resolved. Everything the bean declares in its deployment descriptor such as Java Database Connectivity (JDBC) connections or security roles must map directly to actual systems and entities in the target component implementation. The Bean Deployer deploys the bean into an EJB container using the deployment tools the container provides. When a bean is deployed the container uses the deployment descriptor and information the deployer provides to generate implementations of the EJBHome and EJBObject. These implementations will be specific to the EJB container and are not a permanent part of the enterprise bean.

33.6.4 The EJB Container and EJB Server Providers

The EJB Container Provider and EJB Server Provider are typically developed by the same component model implementation vendor. At the time of this writing the EJB specification does not yet define a clear separation between the EJB container and the EJB server. Therefore, most producers have developed them as one inseparable product. Table 33-3 lists some of the major commercial EJB Server Providers on the market.

Commercial products are not the only choice when selecting an EJB server. There are a number of open source EJB servers that are available to download and use for free. The development of open source software is available to the public and anyone may observe (generally via a list server) or participate. Your company can dedicate or sponsor programmers to develop features that you may need in an EJB server. Table 33-4 lists the open source EJB server projects in development.

I am a cofounder of the OpenEJB open source project, which is currently the only EJB Container Provider on the market. Open source EJB software in general has grown in popularity and receives increasing support from developers and business alike.

Table 33-3: *EJB Server Providers—Commercial*

Vendor	Product	Additional Information
BEA Systems	BEA WebLogic Server	*www.beasys.com*
Gemstone Systems	GemStone/J	*www.gemstone.com*
IBM	WebSphere Application Server	*www.software.ibm.com*
Silverstream	SilverStream Application Server	*www.silverstream.com*
Sun Microsystems	NetDynamics Application Server	*www.netdynamics.com*
Sun-Netscape Alliance	iPlanet Application Server	*www.iplanet.com*

Table 33-4: *EJB Server Providers—Open Source*

Sponsor	Project	Additional Information
Intalio	OpenEJB (EJB Container Provider)	*www.openejb.org*
Telkel	jBoss	*www.jboss.org*
Evidian	JOnAS	*www.evidian.com/jonas*
Lutris	Enhydra (based on JOnAS)	*www.enhydra.org*

33.6.5 The System Administrator

The System Administrator installs, configures, and maintains the EJB container and EJB server. The System Administrator is also responsible for tuning the server and container for optimum performance. Most servers and containers allow the System Administrator to set pool sizes, cache sizes, connection limits, and other features that help the server and container meet the needs of the environment. A container may delegate transaction and security responsibilities to external systems. In this case the System Administer would use the tools that the component producer of the EJB container provides to connect the systems together.

33.7 Conclusion

Enterprise JavaBeans currently offers four component types: stateful session beans, stateless session beans, bean-managed persistence entity beans, and container-managed persistence entity beans. The four component types were chosen carefully and reflect the common needs of typical software applications. The Enterprise JavaBeans component model has quickly been adopted as the component model of choice for Java applications. To date a number of vendors provide EJB support in their server platforms. Enterprise JavaBeans is also a key part in the Java 2 Enterprise Edition (J2EE), which specifies a larger component infrastructure that defines interaction between EJB and other component models such as Java Servlets. With Enterprise JavaBeans you can engineer the simplest software or the largest enterprise applications.

The Enterprise JavaBeans specification continues to evolve to meet the needs of its community. With Enterprise JavaBeans' clever marketing, robust component model and infrastructure, EJB should continue to lead the pack in component-based software in Java.

Chapter 34

Bonobo and Free Software GNOME Components

Michael Meeks

34.1 Introduction

This chapter describes the impact that the growing phenomenon of free software has on component-based software engineering. For more details on the "free" philosophy see *www.gnu.org/philosophy*. Free software improved the quality of software components in the marketplace and created an open component model, called Bonobo, that I believe will become a standard for free software components.

The GNU Network Object Model Environment (GNOME) Project (*www.gnome.org*) is developing a free desktop operating environment supported by Bonobo, a CORBA-based component model. Bonobo and free software as a whole have recently received the support of Sun Microsystem's decision (refer to Part III Preface) to make its StarOffice suite freely available and rearchitect it with Bonobo components. Since StarOffice will be available under a General Public License (GPL), these feature-rich components will become available for desktop environments on many different hardware platforms, such as Windows, Linux, and UNIX. This news is exciting because it will provide an opportunity for independent software vendors (ISVs) to construct extremely powerful applications that can run anywhere without the burden of purchasing extra office components.

34.2 Free Software Model

There is a growing realization that the traditional per-box sales revenue for software is an inappropriate financial model for software. This change has happened not because of any particular marketing flaws, but from the incredible power and flexibility of the open source alternative development model.

34.2.1 Revenue

In the free software model the source code is available for every application and revenue is generated from software services. For more information on how to generate revenues from free software either individually or corporately, refer to *www.ibm.com/developerworks/library/license.html*. Because software, in general, continues to be sold shrink-wrapped as a commodity, companies will find it difficult to transition to a service-based model. Many free software companies bootstrap their service business by generating revenue from sales of CDs and manuals. Such opportunities will vanish, however, as the Internet makes increasing bandwidth available.

34.2.2 Quality From Chaos

As more companies transition to a service model, the developing situation might appear to lead to a chaotic environment of conflicting, incompatible versions of lower-quality software. What emerges instead is a marketplace of decommoditized software typified by quality and support in which brand equity is paramount. This appears to be achieved through two mechanisms.

1. Free software attracts a community of extremely competent programmers and encourages peer scrutiny of code, abstraction (instead of quick hacks), and massively parallel bug fixing. Companies can hire from this talented community when seeking to expand their service development.
2. Since there may be many competing versions of a free software project with different features, a trusted and familiar company can stabilize and support specific components, creating order for their clients from the many options. Clearly, the number of nontechnical consumers of software vastly outnumbers the highly technical developers described above.

Free software development typically follows the development axiom *release early, release often*. Consequently, there are often several parallel streams of development with different levels of stability. For example, Ximian's system manager will allow the user to select groups of packages on the basis of their stability. Much free software is assigned a version number that conforms to the numbering standard adopted by the developers of the Linux kernel (*www.linux.org/dist/kernel.html*). A *stable* release has an even second digit (that is, "4.2"), and there can be multiple minor "bug fix releases" with a third digit; for example, version "4.2.3" is the third release that fixes minor problems with stable version "4.2". Most developers will use stable versions and companies generally will only support stable releases.

Market forces and greater economies of scale solve many of the conventional problems of product quality and testing. Consumers use software they find to be stable and quickly become disillusioned with unstable software, especially when competing versions exist. This new model of development produces excellent-quality software and fosters a sense of community and mutual help surrounding the software. However, to see only this is to misunderstand the phenomenon. This misunderstanding is rooted in the term *open source*.

34.2.3 Open Source versus Free Software

Eric Raymond, co-author of *The Cathedral and the Bazaar* (Raymond and Young, 2001) coined the term *open source*. Open source software (OSS) advocates attempt to create communities of developers by providing restricted access to the source code. However, they stop short at fully freeing it (under a GPL license) because they still wish to sell the software as a commodity. The expectation is that talented programmers will be happy to develop a product and then buy it in certain situations.

Richard Stallman of The Free Software Foundation (*www.gnu.org*) has strongly criticized closed licenses. Over the years the Gnu Public License (GPL) has evolved to grant protection to patents secured by companies, yet provide the freedom that programmers have come to expect in software (*www.gnu.org/copyleft*). The GPL also wisely restricts people from denying these freedoms to others. This licensing structure provides a far more attractive license for distributing decommoditized software than OSS licenses.

Luckily, the open source software phenomenon has been short-lived for two reasons. First, the average talented programmer realizes that OSS could force him to buy back his own contributions. Second, complicating the variety of different source code licenses makes code sharing difficult, thus OSS is unable to leverage its resources. The decline of OSS is reflected in the list of companies now colicensing their code under GPL. For example, Netscape switched from the OSS Mozilla Public License (MPL) (*www.mozilla.org/MPL*), Sun will license StarOffice under the GPL, and Troll Tech switched from the Q Public License (QPL) (*www.troll.no/qpl*).

34.2.4 Open Standards

As the World Wide Web (WWW) becomes pervasive, and as the limitations of HTML (HyperText Markup Language)-based content become apparent, open standards are in danger. A company can clearly provide richer content by integrating services into the desktop environment on top of native operating systems. Microsoft's .NET strategy (*www.microsoft.com/net*) appears to follow this approach. .NET is supported by C# (Trupin, 2000), COM+, Exchange Server, and other Microsoft technologies, and will provide a powerful environment to develop distributed software applications. If Microsoft succeeds in leveraging their desktop monopoly to dominate the server market there will be two consequences. First, there would be no alternative component models to the underlying component model implementations so critical for component-based applications. Second, one company would dominate and own the protocol and component model standards for distributed computing, stifling innovation in such an important area.

Of course, another alternative is free software and the Bonobo component model environment. Free software is beginning to provide equivalent functionality to the current level of component technology. The diversity of free software and its openness allows developers to inspect the protocols and port the software to whatever operating system (OS) and hardware they choose, thus creating a marketplace in which everyone can compete.

34.3 GNOME

The GNOME project, founded by Miguel De Icaza and Federico Mena in 1997, has been working to make UNIX a more attractive graphical user interface-based OS. GNOME intends to create a component model to develop productivity applications that will help solve many usability and consistency problems.

A major motivation for the GNOME project is to bring innovation back to UNIX, a characteristic missing in recent years (de Icaza, 2000). Although there are many successful projects enjoying widespread popularity in the free software community, such as Apache, bind, sendmail, and samba, none of these projects share a single line of code. Furthermore as projects grow in size their source code becomes increasingly complex, making it nearly impossible for newer programmers to contribute effectively to the project. Bonobo aims to remove these problems by allowing free software to be componentized and providing clear interface contracts that define functionality. Bonobo is also language-independent, so developers can implement and share their code as components using widely disparate programming languages.

34.4 Bonobo[1]

Bonobo is the component model for the GNOME project. It is comprised of a set of CORBA interfaces designed to standardize component programming for UNIX, and an implementation of these interfaces based on the Gtk+ object model (*www.gtk.org*).

1. The Bonobo is an endangered species and the animal that is most genetically similar to human beings.

34.4.1 CORBA—ORBit

The foundation for Bonobo is the OMG's CORBA. CORBA was selected because it is a public standard implemented by a number of free Object Request Brokers (ORBs). It was also well specified and not tied to any particular manufacturer, and it provides location transparency for distributed components. The C language was chosen for implementation because of its superior portability and its ability to interface nicely with the multiple language bindings gained in the Gtk+ project.

When the GNOME project started using CORBA, however, we soon realized that all the free implementations were too resource-intensive and slow or did not implement the C bindings we desired. Solving this problem involved writing a new ORB called ORBit (*www.labs.redhat.com/orbit*). ORBit provides a nominally CORBA (2.2)-compatible ORB with some necessarily efficient features. First, since the GNOME vision requires adding CORBA interfaces to all system functionality, the ORB must be small. Second, the ORB must be efficient because it is a core component of the system. ORBit features a dynamic linking mode, enabling trusted components to share the same address space and greatly improving efficiency of the ORB. Software written in any of the languages supported by the CORBA bindings, including Java, Perl, Python, C, and C++, can create and invoke Bonobo components by using CORBA.

34.4.1.1 Overview

We present Bonobo by describing its essential features.

- *Interfaces*—These define Bonobo and are specified in CORBA IDL. They are language, widget set, and platform independent.
- *Wrappers*—These provide a simple abstraction that hides the CORBA layer, and they dramatically simplify the task of programming with Bonobo.
- *Implementation*—The GNOME implementation of Bonobo is available from *developer.gnome.org/arch/component*.
- *Components*—These form the basic unit of functionality and support document and view abstractions.

- *Controls*—They provide single-view "rich widgets" customizable via property interfaces similar to Java Beans.
- *Compound Document*—This code integrates supporting interfaces for structured storage, printing, monikers for linking, and more.

34.4.2 Interfaces—Handling the Unknown

The basis of the Bonobo component model is very similar to that of Microsoft COM (see Chapter 32). Every interface inherits extends from *Unknown*. The Unknown interface provides methods for interface introspection and a reflexive, transitive, and symmetric aggregation mechanism. The Unknown interface also provides reference-counting semantics. As with COM, reference counting can be used to automatically release component resources when they are no longer needed.

34.4.3 Oaf Activation

While CORBA is ideal for distributed programming, there was no convenient mechanism in CORBA 2.2 for locating a remote component by name. This problem is analogous to finding the first Domain Name Server to translate a domain name—such as changing *www.cnn.com* into a physical Internet Port Address such as `207.25.71.26`. Initially GNOME provided a desktop environment with a centralized registry that stored such information (similar to the Windows 9x registry). While this was an easy solution, it tied GNOME to a single desktop. To overcome this the Object Activation Framework (Oaf) was written to allow object activation by both unique ID and by capability. To download Oaf see *ftp://ftp.gnome.org/pub/GNOME/stable*.

Capability-based activation satisfies the needs of component programming far more closely than other approaches. Oaf allows a software system to locate a component that provides a desired service without activating the object in advance. For example, Oaf can locate a component that handles a certain Multi-Purpose Internet Mail Extensions (MIME) type, implements certain named interfaces, is editable, and renders a certain version of HTML.

34.4.4 Wrappers—Making Life Easy

There is a perception in the free software community that CORBA is hard to use and difficult to understand. The primary reason appears to be that developers do not like the granularity of exception handling, which can make simple blocks of code rather verbose and difficult to read. Furthermore, because the user is seldom interested in the explicit reason for failure, it seems reasonable to simplify many common method invocations with wrappers.

Bonobo wrappers provide a simple interface to create powerful, network-transparent objects with little knowledge of CORBA. The fine-grained exception handling is still available, but we anticipate that it will not be heavily used. The wrappers typically flag an exception with a `NULL` return value and cover much of the core Bonobo interfaces. The code fragment in Figure 34-1, for example, creates a new control containing a button and binds a persistent stream to it.

Consequently, someone invoking `query_interface` on the associated CORBA object could get either a Control or `PersistStream` interface from this aggregate.

```
BonoboObject *a = bonobo_control_new (gtk_button_new_with_label
   ("Hello World"));
BonoboObject *b = bonobo_persist_stream_new (my_load_fn,
   my_save_fn, NULL, NULL);
bonobo_object_add_interface (a, b);
```

Figure 34-1: *A simple Bonobo wrapper.*

Another important wrapper is that for controls, allowing trivial integration with the Gtk+ widget set. The code fragment in Figure 34-2 creates an animator widget, that happens to run in a separate process, and asks it to load a certain file. The widget can then be inserted into a Gtk+ container in the normal way and acts in every respect like a standard widget.

```
GtkWidget *widget = bonobo_widget_new_control ("OAFIID:animator",
   NULL);
bonobo_sidget_set_property (widget, "filename", "/demo/an.gif");
```

Figure 34-2: *Simple control wrapper.*

34.4.5 Implementation

As with all free software, a vendor could provide a high-performance commercial implementation that supports the Bonobo interfaces. The current Bonobo implementation, written in C, is small, extremely portable, and reasonably efficient. There is a tutorial to help you learn more about Bonobo's design and how to adapt your software to take advantage of its power (Ruiz, Lacage, and Binnema, 2000).

34.5 Examples

Currently three companies have started to develop free components for the Bonobo component model. These are Ximian (*www.ximian.com*), Sun Microsystems' StarOffice division, and Eazel (*www.eazel.com*). Eazel is developing a componentized file manager and generic component shell called Nautilus. Sun will port its StarOffice software to the GNOME environment, using Bonobo components in particular. Ximian has produced an ambitious set of components for groupware applications development. Ximian currently integrates e-mail, calendaring, and contact management in the evolution project. These companies are releasing their components under a GPL license and have received widespread support from the developer community in terms of technical bug reports and patches to add features and fix bugs. This process is expected to accelerate as usage increases and will also produce a set of common core business components.

The GNOME project implements a growing number of controls suitable for Rapid Application Development. In addition to the controls provided by Evolution and Nautilus such as calendar and file view controls, there are controls for tasks ranging from animation through database access. Many of the additional controls have been in development and were released in stable form with GNOME 2.

34.6 Issues and Advantages

Bonobo provides powerful support for compound document creation reminiscent of OpenDoc (Apple Computer, 2000). However, many interfaces are not yet provided. Bonobo is still under development but, in my opinion, it is clearly the component model of choice for free software. In the next few years I expect Bonobo to be a viable technology rivaling COM+ and EJB. In this section I describe the process for upgrading Bonobo and planned changes for the future.

34.6.1 Bonobo is an Open Standard

Much of the power of an interface is derived from its standardization, hence it is important to understand how an interface can become part of Bonobo. Free software is typically maintained by a group of developers in a meritocratic hierarchy. This essentially means that the more an individual or organization contributes to a project in terms of repairing defects, adding new features, or providing support, the more access they have. Development is driven purely by technical prowess, motivated by recognition of the maintainers and the hope for future opportunities. Project participants meticulously read and review the code and discuss the design (sometimes exhaustively) before some contributions are accepted. Design and development peer review conducted worldwide using `listserver` is one of the greatest strengths of free software. In practice interfaces tend to be developed in Evolution and Nautilus and when they are sufficiently mature they are moved into Bonobo to extend the standard.

The OMG has a similar process to update the CORBA standard, but the process is more complicated and considerably lengthier, taking many months. The OMG standards process is considerably more bureaucratic.

Another great advantage of free software is that of parallelizing bug fixing. The free model offers a wealth of capable early adopters who provide excellent defect reports, making early diagnosis easy. The people who detect the defects often provide the repairs.

As the product grows more stable more people feel comfortable enough to use it—still at a prerelease stage—and consequently more bugs are fixed. Also, because of the nature of concurrent development and the culture of constant upgrading, beta software rapidly evolves through many incremental fixes.

The decoupling provided by the component model provides a safe encapsulation mechanism and frees development time-scales. It is possible to have totally disparate release schedules across projects. This is important because monolithic systems are far less likely to fully stabilize.

With Bonobo less frequently used components can have their release schedules slip indefinitely with no real impact on the main product.

The contracts provided by the interfaces and the splitting of large complicated applications into comprehensible components also makes it possible to rewrite components. Many large-scale software applications become encumbered by years of software maintenance that complicates the addition of new features as well as the performance of defect repairs. It is my experience that the redesign of large applications into Bonobo components automatically increases the scriptability and applicability of the legacy code to many new situations.

34.6.2 The Future of Bonobo

There are several major changes planned for Bonobo in the future, yet the primary change is in transaction processing. The transaction processing interfaces are especially important since EJB and CORBA have transactional APIs and Microsoft's Transaction Server makes transactions available for COM+ components. Clearly, the transaction processing interfaces will have to work closely with the interfaces managing the life cycle of Bonobo components.

34.7 Engineering Free Software

The best way to add value to the free software market is to deploy your software as a component. This has the benefit of avoiding the large engineering task of creating a distribution while leveraging the specific skills that your business can bring to market. There are many ways of creating free software components. The shared library approach enables a developer to deploy a component as a code library such as a dynamically linked library. However, while it is possible to build a component model based on dynamic linking of components, this approach has stability problems since a fault in a single component will impact the whole system.

Even without the need for intellectual property protection, it is helpful to deploy software as separate components. A free component is used as a black-box that can be opened during design and development. Its interfaces provide the contracts and specifications for the component. In the free software market it is common for volunteer programmers to program actively for perhaps a year and then move into the commercial world. In this situation the learning curve for these programmers is much smaller if the software has clearly specified interfaces. Consequently, there is no need for a prolonged adaptation process to understand a massive monolithic system. In addition, a component can easily be substituted with a more efficient (or easier to maintain) equivalent component that provides the same functional interface.

34.8 Conclusion

To survive in the software industry of tomorrow it will become increasingly important to develop free software. It is not sufficient to simply release source code; there needs to be strategies for code reuse and programmer freedom. The GPL license (the yardstick of software freedom) works towards this goal. Free software flourishes in an unstructured manner, making it necessary to have trusted companies to package and distribute stable versions of software. Trusted companies will likely retain third-party certifiers (refer to Chapter 38) to assure users that the software meets process standards, and is implemented as designed. A component model will impose some degree of order while giving all the benefits of increased value through integration.

The community and companies working with the community are developing many free components, although quite how many components StarOffice will be split into is unknown and how overlapping GNOME projects will be fused is inscrutable. Table 34-1 shows the number of companies and their products that are expected to ship following the release of Bonobo 2.0. When Bonobo stabilizes these projects will release and ultimately result in a powerful and flexible suite of components available on every UNIX system.

Free component development will accelerate the development of apparently complex software and keep the implementation details of individual components simple and public. This will lead to a growing, competitive market in both free and nonfree components, middleware, and integrated Internet services. The Bonobo project is rapidly becoming an efficient, stable, distributed component platform that is an industry standard in the free software community.

Table 34-1: *Bonobo-Related Products*

Company	Products
Evolution	Composed entirely of components: Calender, Contact Manager, lightweight HTML editor, event server
Nautilus	Similarly, for file manipulation, File trees, icon views, et cetera
StarOffice	Spreadsheet, Word processor, Presentation, Database components
SodiPodi	Vector graphics
Dia	Diagramming
Gnumeric	Spreadsheet
Guppi3	Large dataset charting/analysis
Gpdf	PDF viewer
EoG	Animation and quality image view
Gnome-DB	Database abstraction
Achtung	Presentation

Chapter 35

Choosing Between COM+, EJB, and CCM

Andy Longshaw

35.1 Introduction

The users of computer systems are a demanding group to satisfy. This applies to internal enterprise systems as much as to external e-commerce systems. Customers, both internal and external to the organization, demand functionality that is increasingly sophisticated and accessible at all times. These demands place increasing requirements for flexibility, scalability, and robustness on the software systems underpinning this functionality. Although the decomposition of monolithic applications into components helps to deliver some of the required flexibility, this alone is not sufficient. Most modern systems are distributed, largely because of the distributed nature of the users and the information that they bring together. Even if this were not the case, the need for scalability and robustness would mandate a solution that was distributed across multiple machines. This has led to the adoption of a *multi-tier architecture* that all major vendors promote. The multi-tier architecture separates the management of data from the business logic, which in turn is separated from the user interface handling. These "logical" tiers are usually mapped onto separate physical tiers, or groups of machines, to assist with flexibility and robustness.

A key factor in the scalability delivered by this architecture is the use of transactional components on the business, or middle, tier. It becomes easier to develop business components if the component model supports *transactions*, a concept from the database community that has been used for years to develop robust applications. This chapter compares the three main component model contenders: Sun's Enterprise JavaBeans (EJB), Microsoft's latest Component Object Model (COM+) and the CORBA Component Model (CCM).

Note: because of the order in which the chapter is written, and the discussion of the mechanisms employed by the component model implementations, COM+ receives more space. The sole reason for this is that it appears first (hence more concepts need explaining) and does not reflect a bias either for or against it.

35.2 Why Use a Middle-Tier Component Model Implementation?

Understanding the architecture, terminology, and motivation that lies behind multi-tier systems will assist in defining the benefits and features of middle-tier component model implementations. Multi-tier systems have their origins in two-tier, client/server systems that separate out the data tier from the presentation and logic. Such systems, typical of traditional Visual Basic development, face fundamental scalability and deployment issues when used on a large scale. Adding another tier to house the business logic independently from the presentation (client) layer can bring several advantages, namely

- *Flexibility* – Relocating the business logic onto a middle-tier server means that the same business services can be accessed from many different types of clients. These clients can potentially use one of multiple, interchangeable middle-tier servers that offer the same services. These servers can be upgraded, or more servers added, as the application scales.
- *Scalability* – All applications contend for certain scarce resources, such as database connections. By concentrating these resources in the middle tier, caching and recycling strategies can ensure that many clients share these resources optimally between them.
- *Robustness* – By delivering business services from interchangeable servers as described above, a server failure is no longer catastrophic. Clients of the failed server can be redirected to another server providing the same services.

The services that ensure these qualities are part of the component model implementation and provide a uniform environment on which applications can be developed and deployed. Each component that conforms to a specific component model can be deployed into the appropriate component model implementation running on a middle tier server.

35.2.1 Middle-Tier Component Architecture

Figure 35-1 shows the standard application architecture of a multi-tier application. This architecture is vendor-neutral in that all three of the major component models are intended to operate in such an environment. The application clients are either thin (simple Web clients), rich (Web clients with some additional processing such as Java applets or ActiveX controls), or fat (distributed object clients).

The clients of the middle-tier components themselves are either executables, such as Visual Basic applications or Java applications, or Web server plug-ins, such as servlets (*java.sun.com/products/servlet*), Active Server Pages (ASP), or CGI scripts. The components implement the application's business logic and provide a layer of abstraction between the client and the data tier or Enterprise Information Services (EIS).

As with any technology, middle-tier components will only solve certain problems. They simplify the creation of secure, scalable, and transactional systems but more design decisions must be applied to

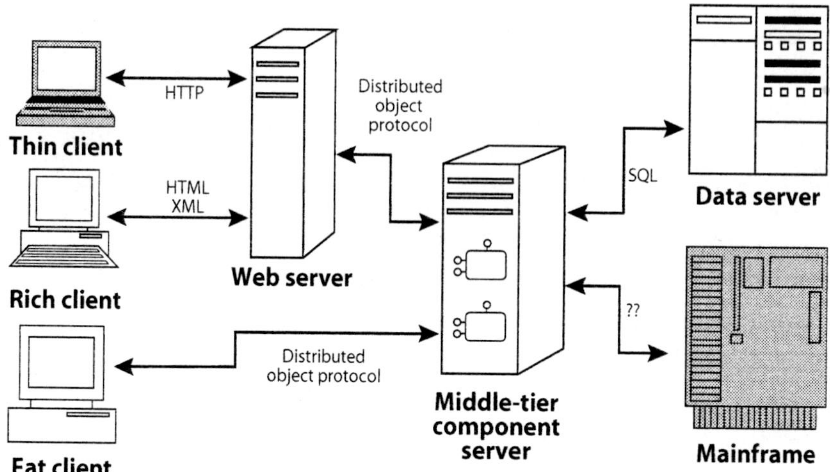

Figure 35-1: *Application architecture for middle-tier components.*

create a meaningful application. It is not only the architectures in which the components operate that are common across middle-tier component models. There is also a generic mode of operation as shown in Figure 35-2.

In Figure 35-2, a proxy (or wrapper) intercepts all method calls between the client application and component. This wrapper can then automatically apply component services, such as transactions or security. The client believes that it is talking to the component and is unaware of the interception. The component behaves as if the method calls received originate from the client. However, the component is still aware of the interception since it will use the wrapper to communicate with the underlying component model implementation, such as when querying for client security credentials. The component model implementation creates instances of the component as required, and controls the lifetime of the component and its wrapper.

35.3 A Framework for Comparison

The strengths and weaknesses of the competing component model implementations can be compared by building a set of requirements for

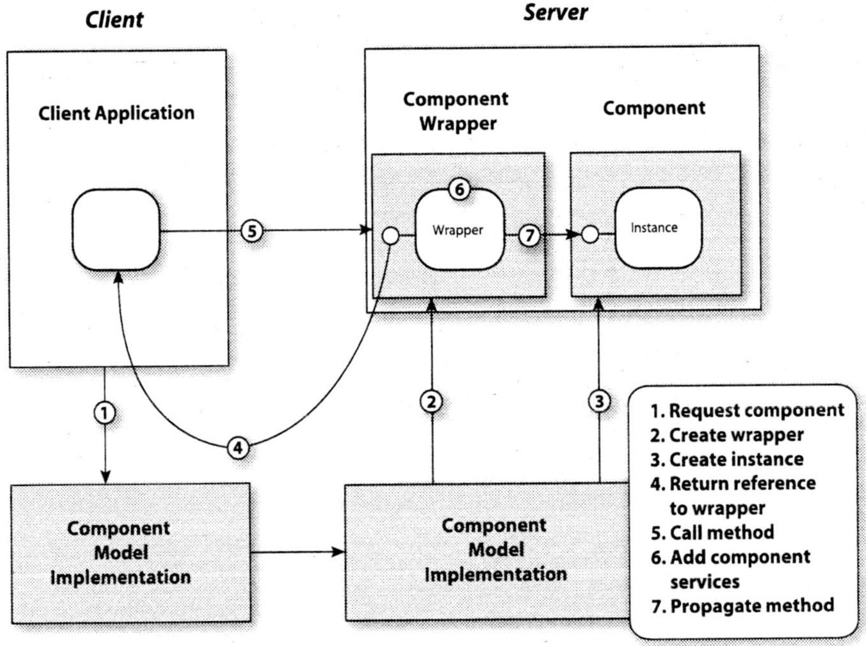

Figure 35-2: *Generic middle-tier component platform.*

such a platform as shown in Table 35-1. The rest of this chapter will evaluate these component models based on the qualities outlined earlier.

35.3.2 COM+

COM+ is built on the foundation of Microsoft's Component Object Model (COM). COM is a flexible, but non-distributed, component model under which components are described in terms of the interfaces they implement. As COM evolved, the ability to distribute functionality among machines was added based on Distributed COM ([DCOM] [*www.microsoft.com/com/tech/DCOM.asp*]), Microsoft's distributed object transport protocol based on Remote Procedure Calls (RPC).

To effectively enable development of enterprise applications, Microsoft delivered Microsoft Transaction Server ([MTS], [*www.microsoft.com/com/tech/MTS.asp*]) on top of COM. MTS provides transaction support, ORB-style instantiation, and component wrappers.

Table 35-1: *Framework for Comparison*

What do I get?	Why do I care?
Scalability	How many users will your system support? Local workgroup Intranet or enterprise Extranet or Internet Thin client means potential for unlimited users What level of service is needed?
State management	Maintain the integrity of data Guarantee updates Prevent corruption of data if update fails Simplify data persistence Provide coherent caching to operate on correct data
Simpler security	Programmatic security has flaws Environment controlled security eases management Support for audit and usage statistics
Fault tolerance	Mission critical systems must always be available Poor customer interaction can lose business
Ease of development	Distributed system development is too complex Experienced developers are rare and expensive Development is slow and unpredictable Need to even out differences between platforms This has all been done before . . . by middle-tier environment vendors
Help with deployment	Remote deployment of components Creating client support package No deployment for thin client Remote management

To simplify the development of secure, transactional applications, MTS also provides a declarative syntax for defining transaction and security requirements. The code required to implement transactions and security in a distributed environment has always been complex and error-prone. Use of declarative attributes devolves responsibility for transaction and security control to the respective services. For example, under MTS a method on a COM object may be marked as requiring a transaction. The wrapper will intercept that method call and ensure that the call is made in the context of a transaction. If not, the wrapper will initiate a transaction in whose context the method will run. All of this potentially takes place without any extra transaction code being required in the client or COM object, hence reducing the complexity of both. Declarative attributes also place more control in the hands of the application deployer or integrator since they can be altered without having to resort to recoding and recompilation.

To deliver scalability, MTS relies on Just-In-Time (JIT) instantiation and As-Soon-As-Possible (ASAP) destruction of COM object instances. However, a developer is unable to dissociate this mode of operation from the rest of the transactional support - it is very much an all-or-nothing decision. Since the MTS model does not fit all requirements, Microsoft perceived a need to deliver more fine-grained control of such features. COM+ delivers such fine-grained control in addition to new features and services. COM+ components are intended to operate under the Windows multi-tier Distributed Networking Application Architecture (DNA) that maps to the application environment shown in Figure 35-1. For more details on COM+, see Chapter 32. Given the information above, COM+ can now be evaluated against the criteria in Table 35-1.

35.3.3 Scalability

To be scalable, any system must recycle resources quickly and efficiently. Resources are held by the component model implementation in central resource pools. Rapid recycling thus ensures that the maximum number of resources is available in these pools at any one time. The JIT/ASAP life cycle ensures that all resources are recycled at the end of a transaction. Large scalability improvements can be obtained by pooling certain types of resources, such as database connections. The pooling of other resources under COM+, such as component instances, will deliver a lesser benefit unless they must load a large amount of nontransactional data on startup.

If multiple component servers are available, an even distribution of clients across those servers will also aid scalability. The COM+ Load Balancing service can direct new clients to lightly loaded servers. A configurable algorithm can determine the level of loading. One caveat on the use of COM+ Load Balancing is that once a component has been allocated to a server, it is locked into that server, so short component lifespans are of great benefit.

35.3.4 State Management

In COM+, component state and transactions are interrelated. COM+ provides data integrity by ensuring that another transaction cannot access data pertaining to one transaction until the first transaction has completed. To achieve this, database locks and other resource locks are held until the transaction ends. This ensures that any state changes within that transaction are isolated, but the holding of the locks does restrict access to the application's data. Such a restriction will limit scalability, so to overcome this problem, COM+ requires transactional components to be stateless. Transactional components must also use a JIT/ASAP lifecycle. Note, however that nontransactional COM+ components can be both long-lived and stateful.

COM+ provides no automated state management that can be used by the component provider. All access to data, including the retrieval and storing of state, must be performed explicitly by the component using a data access mechanism such as ADO or OLE DB. Any state that changes as the result of a transaction must be programmatically stored in a database before the ASAP destruction takes place at the end of the transaction.

35.3.5 Simpler Security

COM+ security is built on top of the Windows 2000 security infrastructure (Ewald, 2001) which provides a hierarchy of authentication levels. COM+ also builds on the original COM security mechanism that provides access control to a component's methods and control over the creation of component instances. COM+ refines this model so that access controls can be defined on a per-interface or per-method basis.

In addition to underlying security mechanisms, COM+ delivers role-based security that allows access rights to be assigned to named roles, such as "administrators" or "managers." Such roles are typically discovered at design time as actors interacting with the system along with their associated interfaces. At deployment time, the roles can be associated with principals (commonly users or groups) defined in the underlying operating system security infrastructure. Interface security and roles are strongly related since all methods on an interface will usually share the same access permissions for the same roles. Since the roles should be discovered in parallel with the interfaces, a requirement for per-method access control may well represent poor interface design. Declarative security cannot handle all security requirements, such as the need to restrict access to functionality to certain times of day. Security-based code in the component is still required to impose such restrictions.

In MTS (and COM itself) there were various issues relating to the identity of the caller and the propagation of client credentials to other servers that restricted access to server-side resources. With the arrival of Kerberos-based security in Windows 2000, a client's credentials can be propagated successfully. Some identity issues still remain however, such as the identity used to access pooled resources. Each pooled resource must have the same security credentials associated with it, which makes auditing resource access more difficult.

35.3.6 Fault Tolerance

COM+ has a set of features that assist in building robust applications. Traditional DCOM was rather fragile in the face of failure since many applications stored fixed server locations in the registry. If a particular server failed, the client had no alternative. This could be somewhat improved by storing server connections in Active Directory ComConnectionPoints or by mapping many servers to the same name using intelligent DNS name servers.

For a more robust solution, COM+ Component Load Balancing will compensate for a server failure by sending new clients to alternative servers. However, existing clients of the failed server must reconnect to continue working. The use of Queued Components can also help to compensate for server failures. The queued calls can be delivered when the server is back up again.

35.3.7 Ease of Development

Making a component transactional is fairly simple under COM+. The component calls the `SetComplete` and `SetAbort` methods on its wrapper to indicate the required transaction outcome. These calls are available in any COM-aware development language such as Visual Basic, Visual C++, and VBScript.

Declarative attributes allow the developer to concentrate on business logic rather than "plumbing." Such external configuration can allow existing COM components to be used as COM+ components without the need for recoding (as long as certain criteria are met). So, for example, transactions can be configured to auto-commit or auto-abort based on return values instead of the component instance explicitly informing its wrapper of the failure. This is not always ideal, since components that were not written to be transactional can perform poorly as part of a transaction. Other limits to scalability include methods that cross COM+ contexts, such as transaction or apartment boundaries since they will usually have high overheads.

35.3.8 Help With Deployment

From the client perspective, a COM+ component appears the same as an ordinary COM component. Hence, COM+ applications can be used from any COM-enabled platform, primarily Windows 98, Windows NT, and Windows 2000. However, COM+ servers can only run on Windows 2000 itself.

Once developed, a COM+ application can be exported as a Windows Installer package to be deployed on the required system(s). During installation, the component's declarative attributes can be adjusted to change the behavior of the application. The client part of a COM+ application can be deployed on Windows 2000 via the Active Directory Class Store. This includes registry settings and COM+ proxies. Clients on non-Windows 2000 platforms will require a manual installation process such as InstallShield (*www.installshield.com*).

35.4 Enterprise JavaBeans

Enterprise JavaBeans (EJB) is a Java-specific component model that operates in the context of the Java 2 Enterprise Edition ([J2EE] [*java.sun.com/j2ee*]) application architecture. Unlike COM+, EJB is based on a specification rather than being delivered as a specific implementation. The EJB specification is defined through the Java Community Process (JCP). Once approved, this specification can be implemented by a variety of server environments, including application servers (such as BEA WebLogic, IBM WebSphere, iPlanet Application Server) and databases (such as Oracle 8i, Sybase Jaguar, IBM DB2). To encourage widespread adoption of EJB, the first EJB specification (version 1.0) was rather loose. Version 1.1 endeavored to provide a more standard platform and to deliver a more consistent development and deployment environment. In October, 2000, the EJB version 2.0 specification was released in final form under the acronym JCP (*java.sun.com/products/ejb/2.0.html*). EJB 2.0 aims to make EJBs more flexible (such as providing message-driven EJBs) and to make EJBs more portable (such as introducing an EJB query syntax to replace proprietary mechanisms).

The component model implementation for EJB is split into two parts. The first part is the EJB Server, which provides the underlying support for security, transactions, and so on, and is shared between all EJBs. Each type of EJB will then have a wrapper, or container, generated for it by tools provided by the component model implementation. This container acts as an intermediary between the EJB and the EJB server - providing a consistent, server-independent API for the bean while integrating with the EJB Server to provide the required services. Each EJB has a single business interface and an associated home, or factory, interface. There are two primary types of EJBs: session beans, which are conceptually similar to transactional COM+ components, and entity beans, which are typically a mapping of underlying data and are intended to be longer-lived than session beans. The EJB lifecycle is broadly similar to that of a COM+ component. The main differences are

- Most EJB home (factory) interfaces will have EJB-specific creation methods rather than the single `CreateInstance` method provided by COM+
- EJBs are registered in a centralized naming service rather than the local registry. The client queries the naming service for the EJBs it needs
- There is no `SetComplete` equivalent in EJB to indicate transaction success. An EJB will only indicate if it requires a transaction to be rolled back. Otherwise, the container will presume that the method was successful and continue the transaction

The EJB component model is described in more depth in Chapter 33. Since the mechanisms involved in the EJB component model implementation are quite similar to those in COM+, we can proceed by highlighting the differences.

35.4.1 Scalability

The EJB specification requires that EJB servers provide pooling both for database connections and EJB instances. The database connection pooling provided by the Java Database Connectivity (JDBC) 2.0 Standard Extension is essential for scalability. The database code required to use connection pools is similar to normal JDBC code except that the EJB must look up the connection pool first.

Since entity EJBs represent underlying data and are relatively long-lived (more than one method call), they present particular challenges for scalability. If an entity is transactional, then its internal state must form part of the transaction. This means that the container must prevent other transactions from entering that EJB until the first transaction commits or aborts. Hence, a long-running transaction could potentially "lock" that entity until the original transaction commits or aborts. The container needs to employ similar mechanisms to those used by databases to avoid "locked" beans from becoming a bottleneck.

As discussed for COM+ earlier, the benefit of instance pooling depends very much on the type of component instance involved. If state cannot be usefully retained while in the pool, then many benefits are lost. However, one variation that is useful for scalability is the caching of entity EJBs so that they can be easily retrieved if they are requested again shortly after being returned to the pool.

35.4.2 State Management

As with COM+, the management of state and transactions is intertwined. Transactions are the primary mechanism for preserving the integrity of state persisted to multiple resource managers, such as databases. The EJB wrapper determines the outcome of any transaction and by default will commit the transaction unless the EJB calls `setRollbackOnly` on its context or a method raises an unchecked exception.

Different types of EJB have different state management models.

- Stateless session beans are equivalent to typical COM+ components and retain no state between method calls
- Stateful session beans retain state between method calls until the container passivates them. At that point, any necessary state must be persisted by the bean or the container. This is analogous to a Web shopping cart

- An entity bean is stateful, and that state persists over time. The container will prompt the bean to save and load its state when required

Bean producers will use the appropriate model based on their state management requirements. Note, however, that there is a certain amount of debate regarding the use of entity beans as opposed to direct database access (Larman, 2000). If designed correctly, an entity bean can be a useful data representation, but almost all business logic resides in session beans.

Using Container Managed Persistence (CMP) for entity beans can make state management easier. Under CMP, the container is responsible for the saving and loading of state between the bean and the underlying data store. Simple entity beans will map to a single row in a single database table. In this case, CMP is straightforward and serves to reduce the amount of JDBC code needed. Complex bean mappings involving multiple tables or joins have traditionally required a specially designed container or an object database. The mapping of state between database and component instance variables defined in the EJB specification has evolved over time from a simple, but container-specific, mechanism under EJB 1.0 to a sophisticated, but container-independent, mechanism in EJB 2.0 called Persistence Manager to address such issues. The Persistence Manager will facilitate complex data mapping to ensure that CMP entity beans are truly portable.

35.4.3 Simpler Security

EJB security is based on the security provided by the underlying J2EE platform, which in turn uses the security infrastructure of the underlying operating system. This serves to provide credentials for the calling security principal that can be used as a basis for access control.

As with COM+, EJB security is role-based. A given role can be granted access permission to one or more methods on an EJB interface. Underlying security principals can be assigned to the defined roles at deployment time. EJB must specify security down to the method level since each EJB has only one business interface. There is no ability to create separate, role-based interfaces with differing security requirements.

As with persistence, EJB security has evolved with subsequent specifications to the degree that certain features, such as the "run as" identity that can be specified for a component in COM+, has been dropped, and then reinstated, in subsequent specifications.

The issues relating to pooled resources and identity described earlier in COM+ also affect EJB; each resource in the pool must share the same security context. This makes it more difficult to track resource usage based on identity. The EJB specification defines per-principal pools to try to alleviate this problem, but this assumes the available resources can be split between the different principals.

35.4.4 Fault Tolerance

Although the EJB specification does not address load balancing, vendors of EJB component model implementations will frequently provide this capability. Some vendors provide very good load balancing mechanisms, typically applied by the home interface implementation when an EJB is created. However, load balancing remains an area of inconsistency. Load balancing can also be provided through the registration of factories in the Java Naming and Directory Interface (JNDI). The ability to register a new server with the naming service in place of a failed one can also be used to provide a measure of robustness.

As with load balancing, there is no explicit requirement in the EJB specification to provide any other fault tolerance and robustness features. Again, most vendors will provide this functionality as part of their product differentiation.

35.4.5 Ease of Development

One of the stated aims of EJB is to allow bean producers to concentrate on writing business logic rather than low-level "plumbing." On the one hand, declarative attributes are provided, as in COM+, to reduce the amount of security or transaction code required. On the other hand, an EJB producer must implement the life cycle methods that form the contract between the bean and its container. The number and style of life cycle methods depends on the type of bean implemented, varying from stateless session bean (simple) to entity bean (relatively complex). However, much of this code is "boilerplate" code that developer tools can generate automatically. Container Managed Persistence also serves to reduce the amount of code required.

From the client perspective, EJB-aware code is required to locate the home interface of the required EJB via the naming service. The home interface is then used to explicitly find or create the required EJB instance. Once the specific instance has been located, the client/server interaction is identical to that between a client and server using the standard Java distributed object protocol Remote Method Invocation ([RMI] [*java.sun.com/products/rmi*]).

35.4.6 Help With Deployment

The availability of multiple component model implementations for EJB is both a blessing and a curse. On the positive side, different products address different requirements (they each have strengths or "sweet spots" in their functionality). However, this is also a great disadvantage since implementation differences can cause portability problems for EJBs. This is especially true for more complex EJBs.

Until EJB 2.0, there has been no requirement for different EJB component model implementations to interoperate. The RMI/IIOP (Internet Inter-ORB Protocol) interoperability protocol for security and transaction context was introduced, but not mandated, in EJB 1.1. Prior to this, vendor-specific protocols would have effectively locked clients into specific servers.

To deploy an EJB, an EJB-JAR file (Java Archive file) is created containing the bean, helper classes, other resources, and a deployment descriptor containing deployment-related information. When this EJB-JAR is deployed into a specific EJB component model implementation, tools provided by the EJB component model implementation generate the container classes for that particular EJB server. These containers cannot be carried with the EJB since the interface between container and server is not currently specified. Once deployed, the deployer can alter the bean's declarative attributes if necessary. The client requires practically no installation since almost all of the required Java classes can be dynamically downloaded on demand.

35.5 CORBA Component Model (CCM)

The CORBA Component Model (CCM) is built on the Common Object Request Broker Architecture (CORBA) as specified by the Object Management Group (OMG). CORBA itself is a powerful and robust distributed systems platform (or middleware) that has proven itself over many years to be capable of delivering enterprise scale systems. The platform provides a variety of distributed services such as ORB functionality, naming service, security service, and transaction service. Clients and servers aimed at the CORBA platform can be written in many languages since the interfaces are defined in a language-neutral interface definition language (IDL).

The CCM forms part of the CORBA 3.0 platform. It defines a component model that includes component contracts, component life cycle definitions, state management, and multiple interface support. In many ways the specification draws together many of the features that have proven popular in EJB and COM+. The specification also notably emphasizes the need for interoperability with EJBs. For more information on the CCM, see Chapter 31.

Many of the features of the CCM are common to both of the other component models.

- The Component Implementation Framework (CIF) is a definition of a component model implementation that includes component wrappers that deliver component services based on declarative attributes
- A deployment descriptor defines component requirements and relationships
- Common CORBA services such as transaction and security are used to provide transactions and security

In addition, CCM also delivers functionality that is only available in one or the other competing component model.

- A home interface is defined that provides factory operations to create, destroy, or find the desired component
- Each component can have multiple interfaces or facets
- The CORBA persistence service is used to provide container-managed persistence
- A distributed event model is defined

Now let us consider how the CCM compares to the other component models and the comparison framework.

35.5.1 Scalability and State Management

The CCM provides more flexibility in defining component lifetimes and state management than either EJB or COM+. It provides five different types of containers that deliver different levels of statefulness, identity, and state management.

Similarly, the CCM specification defines a choice of component lifetimes so that the producer can specify when the component instance should be passivated.

- At the end of a method
- At the end of a transaction
- At the request of the instance itself
- By the container when the instance pool becomes empty

Mixing and matching (where sensible) the container type and component lifetime should allow a producer to address state management and scalability for almost any application scenario.

35.5.2 Simpler Security

CORBA's security model is well proven, and CCM can take advantage of it through declarative attributes and role-based security using a similar paradigm to EJB and COM+.

35.5.3 Fault Tolerance

The approach to robustness, fault-tolerance, and load balancing taken by CCM is the same as that of EJB. The CCM specification does not mandate specific mechanisms for such functionality but leaves it up to the individual component model implementation vendor. Since there were no shrink-wrapped commercial products available that implement CCM at the time this book was published, no judgment can be made on this. However, the CORBA vendors have a good track record in providing such enterprise-level functionality.

35.5.4 Ease of Development

To deliver a powerful distributed environment, CORBA requires a lot of "plumbing" code to be developed or generated. One of the objectives of CCM is to eliminate much of this code by providing services as part of a higher-level component model. Developing a CCM component is, again, very similar developing an EJB. The component producer

- Defines home and business interfaces
- Implements those interfaces and writes the business logic behind them
- Implements the interfaces of the component contract with the container (such as life cycle management)
- Defines the application's resource requirements and relationships in the deployment descriptor, including any declarative attributes

As with EJB and COM+, tools provided by the component model implementation will generate all the logic for the component wrapper.

A client can be written specifically to use the CCM component, using component-related methods to access a particular component's facets (interfaces), receptacles, event sources, and event sinks. If the specific component functionality is not required, or the client must be backward compatible with non-CCM CORBA objects, the client can access a CCM component as if it were a standard CORBA server using the component's default CORBA interface.

35.5.5 Help With Deployment

The deployment descriptor for a CCM component shares some of the aspects of a J2EE application assembly in that it defines more relationships between application components than an EJB deployment descriptor currently does.

35.5.6 CORBA Components Caveat

Currently, the CCM is a paper specification. Until it has been implemented and delivered as a commercial product, many questions remain unanswered. An environment containing as many options as the CCM will require powerful tool support to help developers to make the right choices. These tools will follow once the component model implementations have been accepted. However, regardless of tool support, the main question is whether the EJB Server vendors (who include all of the main CORBA vendors) will support both component models. Without a variety of implementations, the CCM will not be a realistic choice of component model.

35.6 The Final Word

Any rating of tools or platforms will always be somewhat subjective. However, based on the discussions above, Table 35-2 provides an "at a glance" comparison between the different environments (subject to the notes beneath).

Table 35-2: *Side-By-Side Assessment of COM+, EJB and CCM*

	COM+	EJB	CORBA Components
Scalability	****	****	****
Ease of Development	*****	****	***
Security	****	****	****
State Management	***	****	****
Deployment	***	**	****
Robustness	***	**	**
Platform Support	**	*****	None
Implementation	****	***	None

Each matrix entry represents the extent to which a component technology satisfies a criteria (on a scale of 1 to 5, with 5 being the best).

The main things to note are

- COM+ is marked down in state management since it has no container-managed persistence

- EJB is marked down for deployment because of the current platform inconsistencies. This mark should rise as EJB 2.0 compliant platforms appear
- EJB is marked down for robustness since it is not explicitly covered or mandated in the specification. However, some individual EJB products would rate higher than COM+ for robustness
- It is difficult to give an overall rating for consistency of implementation for EJB since it varies from vendor to vendor
- Aspects of CORBA Components such as ease of development and robustness are difficult to judge until products ship and have therefore been marked down
- No presumptions have been made about the platform support or consistency of implementation of CORBA Components

So, in summary

- COM+ has a single, consistent implementation (service packs allowing) from a single vendor. However, this implementation is limited to a single platform (Windows 2000). Also, it is too early to judge certain COM+ services, such as the Event Service and Queued Components
- EJB is available on many platforms and can exploit long-standing, proven technology to implement its features. However, issues persist regarding cross-vendor interoperability and porting between platforms
- CORBA Components are still to be proven in the market

Chapter 36

Software Agents as Next Generation Software Components

Martin L. Griss, Ph.D.[1]

36.1 Introduction

The increasing volume of Business-to-Consumer (B2C) and Business-to-Business (B2B) Internet traffic provides great opportunity to delegate information search, analysis, and negotiation to automated assistants. These new classes of applications demand flexible, intelligent solutions. Distributed software agents offer great promise, building on

1. An earlier, shorter version of this chapter appeared in the *Software Development Magazine*, Feb. 2000

increasingly pervasive message-based middleware and component technology, Java, the Extensible Markup Language (XML), and the HyperText Transfer Protocol (HTTP). Agents are specialized kinds of components, offering greater flexibility than traditional components. As will be explained, agents use dynamically adaptable rich message-based interaction, and flexible knowledge-based techniques to make it much easier to build and evolve systems as requirements and technologies change. At HP Laboratories, our e-commerce research focuses on simulation, agent communication, mobile appliances, and personal agents, as well as multi-agent systems ([Griss, 2000b] [Chen, 2000]). We are interested in how agents are defined and constructed, how they communicate, and how collaborations among groups of agents can be established and controlled. We combine agents and workflow to provide significant benefits beyond those traditionally associated with components and scripting. There are many kinds of software agents, with differing characteristics such as mobility, autonomy, collaboration, persistence, and intelligence. This chapter surveys some of these agent capabilities. More details can be found in books ([Huhns, Singh, and Gasser, 1998] [Jennings and Wooldridge, 1998] [Bradshaw, 1997]), papers ([Genesereth and Ketchpel, 1994] [Maes, Guttman, and Moukas, 1999] [Griss, 2000a]) and Web sites ([*agents.umbc.edu*] [*www.hpl.hp.com/reuse/agents*]).

36.1.1 E-Commerce Requires Flexible Implementation

To integrate B2B business processes across enterprises, the next generation of e-commerce applications will need to be larger, more complex, and flexible (Sharma, 1999). Because these applications will be assembled using components written at different times by different developers, the developers need powerful ways to quickly build flexible systems and services to provide more compelling user experiences to more users.

Agent-oriented e-commerce systems have great potential for these e-commerce applications. Agents can dynamically discover and compose e-services and mediate interactions. Agents can serve as delegates to handle routine tasks, monitor activities, establish contracts, execute business processes, and find the best services ([Maes, Guttman, and Moukas, 1999] [Chen, 1998]). Agents can use the latest Web-based technologies, such as Java, XML, and HTTP. These technologies are simple to use, ubiquitous, heterogeneous, and platform neutral. XML will probably become the standard language for agent-oriented e-commerce interaction to encode exchanged messages, documents, invoices, orders, service descriptions, and other information ([Glushko, Tenenbaum, and Meltzer, 1999] [Meltzer and Glushko, 1998] [*www.w3c.org/XML*]). HTTP, the dominant World Wide Web (WWW) protocol, provides many services, such as robust and scalable Web servers, firewall access, and levels of security.

36.1.2 Agent Types

There are many definitions of agents, but many experts agree that "an autonomous software agent is a component that interacts with its environment and with other agents on a user's behalf." Some definitions emphasize one or another characteristic, such as mobility, collaboration, intelligence, or flexible user interaction. Organizations such as the Foundation for Intelligent Physical Agents (FIPA) define reference models, mechanisms, and agent communication language standards ([O'Brien and Nicol, 1998] [*www.fipa.org*]). There are several different kinds of agents.

- *Personal agents* interact directly with a user, presenting some "personality" or "character-monitoring and adapting to the user's activities, learning the user's style and preferences, and automating or simplifying certain rote tasks. Toolkits such as Microsoft Agent (*msdn.microsoft.com/workshop/imedia/agent*), which is a set of software services that supports the presentation of software agents as interactive personalities, includes natural language and animation capabilities. Microsoft's agents "Bob" or "Paper Clip" are simple examples built using this technology. The site, *www.bottechnology.com*, provides a survey of some personal agent technologies and *www.redwhale.com* describes personalizable interfaces using aspects of agent technology. Many of the information agents explored at MIT fall into this category.
- *Mobile agents* are sent to remote sites to collect information or perform actions and then return with results. "Touring" agents visit sites to aggregate and analyze data, or perform local control. They are typically implemented in Java, Tcl (Ousterhout, 1994), VB Script, Perl, or Python (*www.python.org*). Such data-intensive analy-

sis is often better performed at the source of the data rather than shipping raw data. Examples include network management agents and Internet spiders.

- *Collaborative agents* communicate and interact in groups, representing users, organizations, and services. Multiple agents exchange messages to negotiate or share information. Examples include online auctions (for example, Michigan Auction Bot or Pricebots at *www.priceline.com*), planning, negotiation, logistics, and supply chain and telecom service provisioning. COBALT (Bénech, Desprats, and Renaud, 1998) uses the Knowledge Query and Manipulation Language (KQML), CORBA, and the XML for cooperative service and network management.

More than 100 agent system and toolkits have been developed and described in the literature or on the WWW, ranging from A to Z (for example, Agent-TCL, Aglets, Concordia, FIPA-OS, Grasshopper, Jackal, JADE, JATLite, Jumping Beans, Voyager, and Zeus), with different mixes of mobility, adaptability, intelligence, agent communication language (ACL), and multi-language support. Agents are often implemented using distributed objects, active objects, and scriptable components. Agents are usually driven by goals and plans (rather than procedural code), and have "business" or "domain" knowledge. Often, agents differ more from each other by the knowledge they have and roles they play, than from differences in their implementing classes and methods.

In the rest of the chapter, I explain how agents are really next-generation components and discuss some features and variants of typical agent systems. I then show how agents communicate using XML-encoded messages, and finally how agent conversations can be "choreographed."

36.2 Agents Are Next-Generation Components

Agent-oriented software development extends conventional component development, promising more flexible, component-based systems, less design and implementation time, and decreased coupling among agents. In the same way that models, collaborations, interaction diagrams, patterns, and aspect-oriented programming help build more robust and flexible components and component systems, the same techniques can be applied to agents and agent systems ([Kendall, 1999] [Gschwind, Feridun, and Pleisch, 1999] [Griss, 2000b]).

Agents rely on an infrastructure that provides services and mechanisms, allowing agents to have simpler interfaces and be more composable. Agent-oriented programming (AOP) (Shoham, 1993) decomposes large, complex distributed systems into relatively autonomous agents, each driven by a set of *beliefs*, *desires*, and *intentions* (BDI). An agent-oriented developer creates a set of agents (each with its own beliefs and intentions) that collaborate among themselves by exchanging carefully structured messages. Some agents may be implemented using Artificial Intelligence (AI) technology; others will use conventional component technology. As we shall see, agent technology based on autonomous, communicating, adaptable agent components promises quicker, more flexible development of complex, distributed, evolving systems.

36.3 Major Characteristics of Different Kinds of Agents

An agent system is essentially a component system exhibiting several of the characteristics pictured in Figure 36-1. The greater the area enclosed on the diagram, the more "agent-like" the component system. These six orthogonal characteristics work together to make agent-oriented systems more flexible and robust to change. These characteristics are supported by mechanisms and interfaces in the underlying infrastructure and by models and policies configured in each agent or group of agents.

- *Adaptability*—the degree to which an agent's behavior may change after it has been deployed
- *Autonomy*—the degree to which an agent is responsible for its own thread of control and can pursue its own goal largely independent of messages sent from other agents

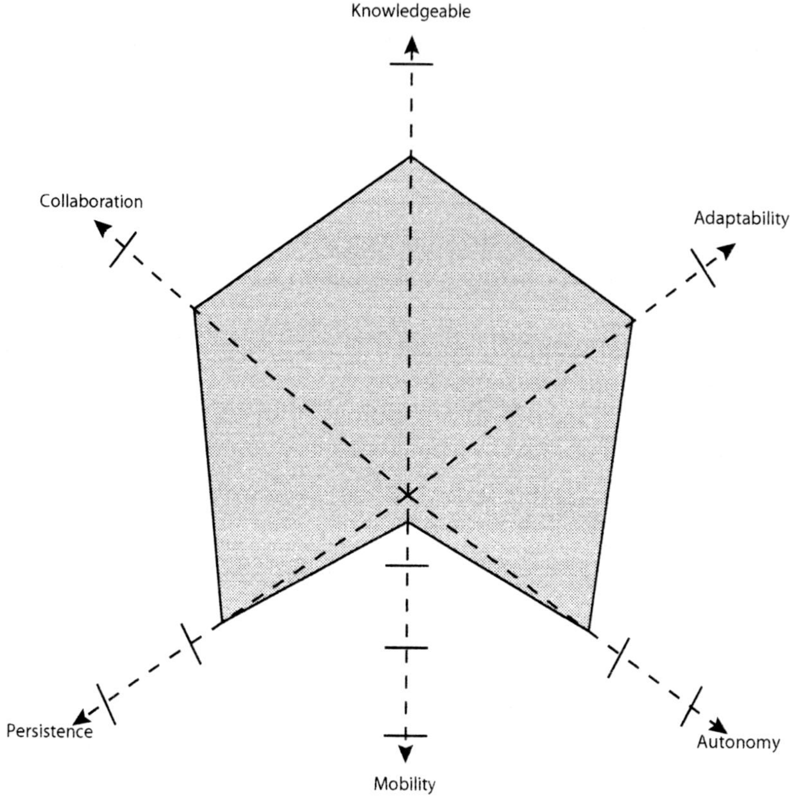

Figure 36-1: *Agent dimensions.*

- *Collaboration*—the degree to which agents communicate and work cooperatively with other agents to form multi-agent systems working together on some task
- *Knowledgeability*—the degree to which an agent is capable of reasoning about its goals and knowledge
- *Mobility*—the ability for an agent to move from one executing context to another, either by moving the agent's code and starting the agent afresh, or by serializing code and state, allowing the agent to continue execution in a new context, retaining its state to continue its work
- *Persistence*—the degree to which the infrastructure enables agents to retain knowledge and state over extended periods, including robustness in the face of possible runtime failures

36.4 The Structure of an Agent System

The term *Agency* refers to the conceptual and physical location in which agents reside and execute. Using the terms of this book, the heart of the agency is the *agent platform*, the component model implementation that provides local services for agents and includes proxies to access remote services. An agent system can provide particular services using *service agents*, such as a broker, auctioneer or community maker agents (for example, refer to Hewlett Packard (HP) E-Speak *www.hp.com/e-speak*). These service agents form the component infrastructure.

As described in Chapter 1, the interaction standard of a component model defines the nature of an interface. An agent system is composed of components with simple interfaces, but complex behavior results from the messages that the components process and communicate with each other. The agents can only communicate with each other because they all conform to some common, well-defined interaction standard.

The agency serves as a "home base" for locating and messaging mobile and detached agents, and collecting knowledge about groups of agents. Services include agent management, security, communication, persistence, naming, and agent transport in the case of mobile agents. In addition to basic agent infrastructure and agent communication, a FIPA compliant agent system, such as Zeus (Nwana, 1999), provides additional services in the form of specialized agents, residing in some (possibly remote) agency, such as Figure 36-2.

- *Agent Management System (AMS)*—controls creation, deletion, suspension, resumption, authentication, persistence, and migration of agents; provides "white pages" to name and locate agents
- *Agent Communication Channel (ACC)*—routes messages among local and remote FIPA agents, realizing messages using an agent communication language
- *Directory Facilitator (DF)*—provides "yellow pages" service for FIPA agents that register agent capabilities so an appropriate task-specific agent to handle the task can be found
- *Internal Platform Message Transport*—provides communication infrastructure

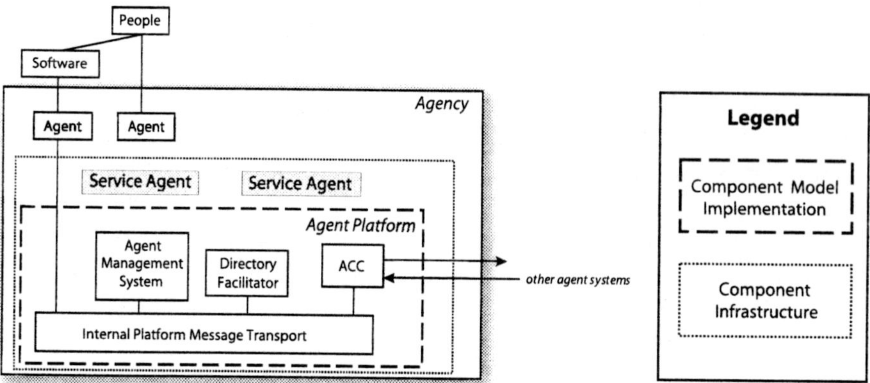

Figure 36-2: *Agency reference model.*

Many agent capabilities for naming and communication can be implemented by using HTTP and XML, such as XML-structured documents for messages, and Uniform Resource Locators (URLs) for naming and locating. Agents may have a globally unique name, or they may have one or more local names based on the agency or agent group. To provide a systematic and consistent way for agents to exchange messages with each other, most agent systems use a special Agent Communication Language (ACL). The ACL becomes associated with the component model. The agent platform and additional service agents can monitor and control these message exchanges to ensure that they conform to a desired protocol, or at least do not violate "rules of engagement."

36.5 The Language Problem

The interaction that a component supports is generally described by interfaces, defined using an IDL (refer to Chapter 1), that contains a syntactic description of each method, its parameter names and types, return values, and possible exceptions. The semantic knowledge of these interfaces, however, must be understood from documentation, though a protocol may be used to provide precise specification of the ordering and interaction of methods. As a component-based system increases in size and complexity, the designer often creates standardized interfaces in the component infrastructure, making it increasingly rigid and difficult to extend to meet needed change.

Instead of defining many interfaces and methods, the agent approach is to use a simple interface with more complex, structured messages. These messages can be extended dynamically as the system evolves, avoiding a costly re-design and re-implementation. XML provides an attractive way to encode these messages with structure defined by an XML Document Type Definition (DTD). It is easy to define an *ad hoc* XML-based language for each application or domain. However, these *ad hoc* languages have no well-understood relationship to each other, are hard to extend, and quickly lead to a large number of incompatible languages.

36.5.1 Multi-Agent Communication Languages

A standard ACL carefully defines the overall structure and standard patterns of interaction between agents in an extensible way. An ACL factors messages into several relatively independent parts.

- Message type
- Addressing
- Context
- Content of the message

Some parts of the message indicate the domain being described, and others describe the expected conversation pattern. This approach makes it easier to dynamically extend agents to new problem areas, yet still have the system check conformance to expectations, and enable the component model implementation to manage messages and agents.

Most ACLs are loosely based on Speech Act Theory (Bach, 1979), a linguistic theory concerning how people communicate and engage in stylized conversations using typed messages. The type indicates the key intent of a message (e.g., request, command, information, or error), suggesting how messages should be processed individually, and how they should be handled as part of a multi-agent conversation. There are a number of agent communication languages, with KQML (Finin, Labrou, and Mayfield, 1997) and FIPA ACL (*www.fipa.org*), the most well known. Some ACLs are intended to support the BDI model, while others make it easy to check that agents conform to organizational conventions and display acceptable behavior (Moore, 1998). Each ACL factors messages in different ways and provides different standard reusable parts. KQML has more than thirty standard types, while FIPA ACL has fewer, but they can be combined in more ways.

We use an XML encoding, combining aspects of several ACLs, which we call *KXML 1.0*. Figure 36-3 contains a sample message.

Each part of the message has a distinct role.

- *Message type*—These building blocks of conversations, such as ADVERTISE, BROKER, ASK-IF, TELL, SORRY, ERROR, REQUEST, INFORM, REFUSE, and FAILURE, are used with specified conversation protocols to allow the system to monitor and control the progress of conversations, and confirm the compatibility with conventions, with a need to examine detailed content
- *Address*—*Sender* and *receiver* identify the participants in the conversation. *Originator* is used for forwarded or brokered messages

```
<message type = "REQUEST" version="kxml 1.0">
      <address sender="//hplmlg3/martin" receiver="//hpbooks/seller">
      <context protocol="english-auction" conversation-id="c12"
                         reply-with="m123" in-reply-to="m17"
                        reply-by="10/9/99 3pm pst"/>
     <content language="Xpression" vocabulary="book-buying">
       <expression op="offer-to-buy">
            <price currency="USD">30</price>
            <item code="27345" units="3"/>
       </expression>
     </content>
</message>
```

Figure 36-3: *Sample KXML message.*

- *Context*—*Reply-with* and *in-reply-to* are used to connect a series of messages to a specific conversation and to each other. *Conversation-id* connects a set of related messages, and *reply-by* sets a deadline for a timeout and *protocol* identifies a specific conversation type, which details an expected pattern message exchange between agents
- *Content*—*Vocabulary* (also called ontology), identifies the domain of the message, for example "buying," "payment," or "banking." The vocabulary defines objects and legal data types, action words, and attributes. *Language* specifies the how the content is expressed, using an AI language (LISP, Knowledge Interchange Format (KIF),

or PROLOG), an agent language (FIPA-SL or KQML), or a scripting language (Tcl, Perl or VB Script), perhaps encoded in XML. Finally, the content is a statement or an expression in the chosen language using terms from the chosen vocabulary, or a nested message

KXML 1.0 provides the syntax of the messages and lists all the legal message types, additional constraints on the attributes, and the explicit expression and statement structure (Griss, 2000a).

36.5.1.1 Vocabulary—What the Words Mean

Agents communicate using words that are meaningful and understood in the given context. The set of words, their relationships, and their meanings is known as an *ontology* or *vocabulary*. It is not enough to know the syntax of the message, nor is it enough to know just the list of legal words. The agent sending the message and the agent receiving the message (or at least the programmers creating each of the agents) must understand what the words mean. Some words can be defined formally in terms of other words, but others must be described in a standard "dictionary," telling the agent programmer how they are to be used.

For example, the word "charge" could be used when talking about finance, battles, or electrical batteries—and would mean different things in each case. Similar words can have distinct meanings. For example, in banking, the words "charge," "fee," "levy," "settlement," "payment," and "interest" have distinct meanings and relationships.

The vocabulary specifies the concepts in a domain and defines the meaning and intent of each word. The vocabulary defines key relationships among words, such as synonyms or generalizations. A vocabulary can be created by using agreed terminology from an international standards committee (for example, UML), or created for specific markets by industry groups (for example, "banking," or "auto parts exchange"). Vocabularies from different sources will be used, and so the ACL needs to specify the selected vocabulary using the *vocabulary* attribute. Several organizations are standardizing vocabularies and related e-commerce frameworks—for example, BizTalk (*www.biztalk.org*), Ontology.org (*www.ontology.org*), CommerceNet (*www.commercenet.com*), CommerceOne's (*www.commerceone.com*), and RosettaNet (*www.rosettanet.org*).

HP E-Speak provides a basic vocabulary for describing and managing other vocabularies (*www.e-speak.hp.com*).

A useful vocabulary may be represented in several ways.

- A natural language "dictionary" listing terms, their meanings, and intended uses.
- An XML DTD defining terms, and some relationships (attribute syntax and some typing). Comments or an external dictionary explain the meaning, additional relationships, and intent. A DTD alone cannot completely define meaning or fully model all data types or multiplicity.
- An object-oriented XML Schema can more precisely define structured data types, can use element inheritance, and provide more precise control over how many of each type of element and attribute are permitted. CommerceOne has used this approach.
- A full modeling language and tool, such as UML or Ontolingua, defining vocabulary elements (classes or types), relationships (inheritance or associations), and semantics and constraints, using OCL and comments. For example, RosettaNet uses UML to precisely model elements in its technical dictionary.

36.5.2 Multi-Agent Coordination

While some agents are used individually, several agents can collaborate to perform tasks that are more complex. For example, to purchase books, a group of agents will exchange messages in a conversation to find the best deal, bid in an auction, arrange financing, select a shipper, and track the order.

Multi-agent systems (groups of agents collaborating to achieve some purpose) are critical for large-scale e-commerce, especially B2B interactions such as service provisioning, supply chain, negotiation, and fulfillment. The grouping can be static or dynamic. The conversation can include interactions between people and agents, or between agents. We need to coordinate the interactions between the agents to achieve a higher-level task, such as requesting, offering, and accepting a contract for some services. We call this "choreography" or "conversation management." An agent group will have a series of stylized message exchanges to accomplish this task, perhaps by advertising and using a brokered service (Figure 36-4), bidding during an auction, responding to a call for proposals, or negotiating a price.

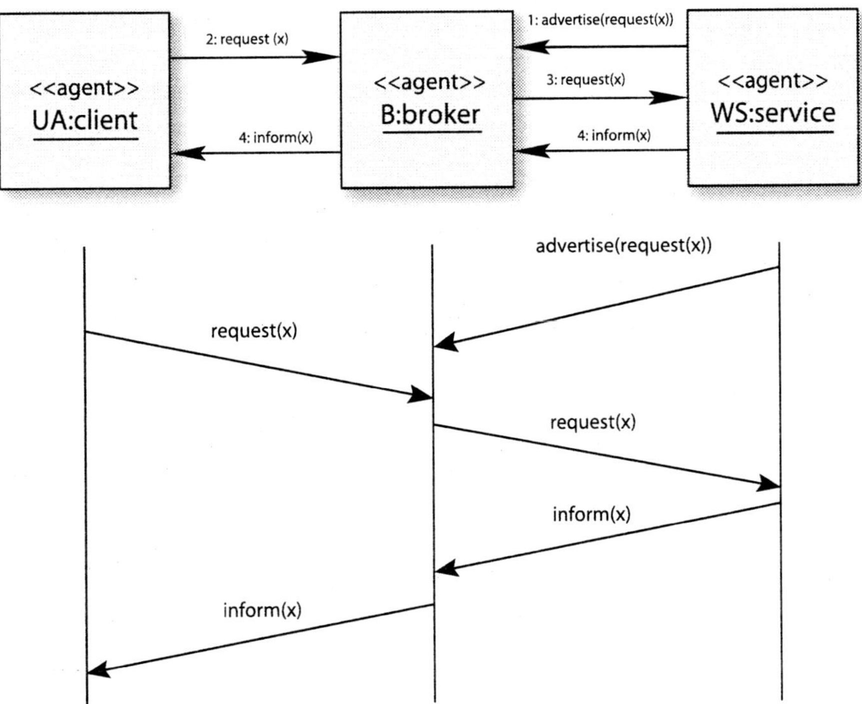

Figure 36-4: *Message sequencing.*

There are several possible levels of choreography of the expected message sequences, depending on the need for a relatively "loose" or more "tight" control of allowed interactions (Griss, 2000a). These include

1. *Built-in message type assumptions*—The message type itself directly suggests a standard expected message sequence. The agent system can monitor compliance. For example, an agent might issue a "request" to one or more agents. Other agents would respond, either to "inform" of their ability to provide this service, or to indicate that they "did not understand" the message. The system can also monitor timeouts, using the "reply-by".
2. *Rules*—A set of rules can be defined for any agent, or community of agents. For example, one could customize an agent's time to wait

for a response, the number of other agents it can talk to at one time, and what sort of responses to make to a specific message from various types of agent. Not all request/response patterns are constrained by the rules (Moore, 2000). A standard rule language can be used, such as the forward chaining rule system provided by Zeus (Nwana et al., 1999).

3. *Conversation protocols*—Often a group of agents must "lock-step" through a standard protocol of messages, for example. If A says x then B says y, bidding during an auction, or responding to a call for proposals. These protocols can be expressed as finite state machines, UML state charts or Petri Networks. Each participant can have the same or a compatible model, stepped through explicitly to determine the action and response any incoming message. Figure 36-3 shows UML diagrams of the "broker" message type, used by a weather service agent, WS. First, WS advertises to broker B that it can respond to certain requests by sending the message `advertise(request(x))` to B. User agent, UA, issues a `broker(request(x));` it will obtain the answer from WS, via a `request(x)` which then responds with `inform(answer)`. B relays this to UA with its own `inform(answer)`.
4. *Workflow*—When the conversation coordination for interactions of multiple agents and humans needs to be more complex and precise, a workflow system can be used. A workflow system allows the explicit definition (e.g. as a graphical model) and control of a group of participants that execute a process, such as a business process (Schmidt, 1999). Many e-commerce applications involve some form of inter-organizational or intra-organizational workflow. A workflow system automates part of a business process, passing documents, information, or tasks from one participant to another for action, according to a set of rules. Workflow systems such as ActionWorks Metro, Endeavors, HP ChangeEngine, IBM FlowMark, Little-JIL, or Verve Workflow describe allowed connections between participants, desired and exceptional processing conditions, the assignment of roles, and the request and allocation of resources. For example, a telecom management workflow system would alert a human operator, or assign a repair to a provisioning engineer. This use of workflow can be seen as a "next generation scripting language" (Griss, 2000a). A single coordinat-

ing agent ("workflow manager") with full workflow, could assign tasks and monitor progress for each member of the group; alternatively a piece of the workflow structure could be assigned to an agent with the role it is to play (say as "buyer" or "seller").

Workflow and agents can be combined in several ways ([Chen, 2000] [Griss, 2000a]). Agents can collaborate to perform a workflow, for example, *telecom provisioning,* or *service provisioning.* Agents can represent the participants and resources or the society of agents to collaborate, thus enacting the workflow. Agent systems have been used to implement new workflow systems (Jennings and Wooldridge, 1998) or augment existing workflow systems (Shepherdson, Thompson, and Odgers, 1999). Agents can be used to make workflow more intelligent, that is, by adding negotiation or reasoning at decision points. Other examples include the Little-JIL process programming language, which demonstrates how a workflow language can be used to coordinate agents (Sutton and Osterweil, 1997). Worklets is an agent-like lightweight process workflow system implemented in Java and the JPython. (Kaiser, Stone, and Dossick, 1999).

36.6 Related Work

At HP Labs in Palo Alto and Bristol, we have several experimental agent projects focusing on e-commerce and application management. The CWave lightweight mobile agent system and visual toolkit was developed for application management and process control using Microsoft COM, a publish-subscribe bus and VB Script ([Griss and Kessler, 1996] [Mueller-Planitz, 2000]). Agents include standard libraries of measurement objects and methods to initiate, change, and dynamically update measurement (see *beast.cs.utah.edu*). We have implemented a lightweight, dynamic agent infrastructure in Java (Chen, 1998 and 2000), used for data mining and dynamic workflow integration and provisioning. Dynamic agents support "on demand" dynamic loading of new classes to extend agents with domain-specific XML interpreters, new vocabulary parsers, or workflow. Several projects have focused on the agent-mediated e-commerce, looking at negotiation in task allocation (Preist, 1999), implementing a new facilitator architecture (Pearson et al., 1997), and playing a key role in the FIPA97 ACL specification. The team has developed and analyzed negotiation algorithms for agents participating in electronic marketplaces ([Cliff and Bruten, 1998] [Preist, 1999a]). My group is developing an experimental Web-based economic simulation environment for a shopping mall, and integrating that with personal agents and mobile appliances based on HP CoolTown ([*www.cooltown.com*] [Griss, 2000b]), using Zeus (Nwana, 1999) as base. We also plan to incorporate HP's technology for constructing e-services, E-Speak, (*www.e-speak.hp.com*).

Agents can perform a range of simple or complex tasks, such as automatic notification via e-mail of the availability of a report, sending a reminder or rescheduling a meeting (Bolcer and Taylor, 1996), or negotiating on a user's behalf (Maes, Guttman, and Moukas, 1999). The Iconic Modeling Tool (Falchuk and Karmouch, 1998) uses visual techniques and UML to assemble and control mobile agent programs and itinerary. Microsoft BizTalk is an XML-based platform neutral e-commerce set of guidelines (see *www.biztalk.org*). The BizTalk "framework" is composed of: schema, products, and services.

36.7 Conclusions

As agent technologies and multi-agent systems become more widely used for constructing e-commerce systems, carefully constructed XML-based agent communication languages, more formal vocabularies, modeling techniques to specify properties of individual agents and groups, and workflow methods and technologies to provide agent choreography will provide significant advantages.

Technologies such as HTTP, XML, agents, e-services, KQML/FIPA ACL, and workflow will combine to produce the next generation of flexible, component software technologies appropriate to rapidly construct these new applications. The rapid evolution of the XML/HTTP-based eCo, BizTalk, UUDI, .NET, and E-Speak specifications, communication, and vocabulary repositories give the flavor of how the future will unfold.

Research is needed to make it easier to define and implement different agent systems directly in terms of their capabilities. An agent, or set of compatible agents, will be constructed by combining aspects and components representing key capabilities. UML models of vocabularies, workflow, role diagrams, patterns, and feature trees will drive aspect-oriented generators to create highly customized agent systems ([Kendall, 1999] [Gschwind, Feridun, and Pleisch, 1999] [Griss, 2000b]). See Chapter 14 for discussion of some of these technologies.

Multi-agent systems can reveal interesting kinds of "emergent behavior," in which autonomous agents can work together in ways that have not been explicitly programmed, potentially producing unpredictable or unexpected results. Agents can discover other agents and form dynamic groups, new behavior modules can be downloaded to adapt the basic behavior of an agent, new vocabularies and protocols can be installed, and knowledgeable, adaptive agents can use machine learning techniques to change their responses to events and messages. Research is being directed at ways of predicting, simulating, exploiting, and controlling this emergent behavior. Techniques based on rules of engagement, monitoring agents, and simulators are being explored to understand and manage these effects. For example, see the Swarm multi-agent simulation system at *www.swarm.org*.

In summary, agent technology has the potential to be more flexible than programming with traditional, more static components. Most agent and e-service systems offer several capabilities that work together to provide this flexibility, and that promises quick development of flexible, complex systems and more effective handling of evolution, distribution, and complexity. First, all agents use the same, albeit simple interfaces, with major differences in behavior provided by richly structured messages and dynamically grown databases of knowledge within the agents. Second, message structure and interaction between agents is factored into relatively independent pieces, described and controlled by dynamically loadable protocols and vocabularies. This means that a particular agent or group of agents can be changed dynamically, adding new capabilities without changing other agents. Finally, agents register and discover each other dynamically using the white pages and yellow pages naming services, which means it is easy to add a new agent with new capabilities into a system, and to have other agents find when requesting services from directory and facilitator agents. Furthermore, some of the agents can act as mediators, or intermediaries, transforming and delegating requests to other agents, and transforming and aggregating responses. All of these capabilities make it much easier to grow and evolve a system as requirements, technology, and business change.

Part VII

Summary

In this section, we presented an overview of the main component technologies available at the time of publication. These technologies all have several things in common. First, there is a standard that describes how to implement components that conform to a specific component model. Second, the component model implementation is necessary for these components to execute. There may be multiple component model implementations for a given component model, and it is hoped that such competition will improve the robustness and quality of the component model implementations. Third, as with any proven technology, a well-defined component model, together with a robust component model implementation, is capable of creating an entire component-based industry.

There are many forecasts for the economic growth of component marketplaces. According to the Giga Information Group (*www.thestandard.com*) the market for ActiveX controls amounted to US$240 million in 1996 and is forecast to grow to US$3.3 billion by 2001, a per-annum growth of 66 percent. By contrast, PriceWaterhouseCoopers predicts that the open market for software components will be worth US$1Billion by 2002 (*www.componentsource.com/build/OpenMarket.asp*). It is not clear, however, how to calculate the market share of each component technology. COM/COM+ is one of the oldest, most stable component technologies, and it should naturally hold the largest percentage of the market because Microsoft has successfully encouraged backward compatibility through all its evolutions of COM. One limitation on EJB market penetration is that the components must be implemented in Java. Over time, as more organizations develop their code initially in Java, this limitation will no longer have a serious impact. Lastly, CORBA has clearly proven that it is capable of building large, complex systems (*www.corba.org*). In most cases, CORBA was used as a platform for developing enterprise systems using distributed objects, and developers may not have thought of developing and selling CORBA components in an open marketplace. The advent of CCM should change this attitude, but we shall have to wait until OMG formally accepts the CORBA 3.0 specification.

We are sure that many readers at this point would like to be told which is the "best" component technology to adopt for their next project. The bad news is that we cannot possibly give a blanket recommendation for any technology until we know your requirements. The good news is that the chapters in this section should help you reach an educated decision. If pressed, however, we would recommend the technologies in the following order: COM+, EJB, and then CORBA. COM+ has a single, consistent implementation (service packs allowing) from a single vendor. It also has strong tool support, and future versions of Microsoft Visual Studio will be strongly integrated with COM+. For enterprise organizations, COM+ also is Internet-ready, with transaction and security support. However, the COM+ implementation is limited to a single platform (Windows 2000) and there will likely be turmoil as the Department of Justice case against Microsoft proceeds. Also, it is too early to judge certain COM+ services, such as the Event Service and Queued Components. EJB and CORBA will easily interoperate with each other, and because CORBA CCM is still not available, we recommend that you consider EJB next. EJB is available on many platforms and can exploit longstanding, proven technology to implement its features. Numerous companies are developing EJB component model implementations, and some are available free of charge. However, issues persist regarding cross-vendor interoperability and porting between platforms.

We would certainly feel more comfortable with our recommendation if COM+ were an open standard with multiple component model implementations. The "Free Software" movement has successfully produced robust code through its meritocratic process of code review, bug fixes, and voluntarism. Bonobo is the community's best candidate for a component model to rival the dominance of COM. However, at the time of publication, there has been no stable release of Bonobo (*ftp://ftp.gnome.org/pub/GNOME/unstable/sources/bonobo*); that is, Bonobo is only truly available for developers. To date, the Gnumeric spreadsheet application (*www.gnome.org/applist/view.php3?name=Gnumeric*) is the best example application built using Bonobo. We expect that the recent partnership with Sun Microsystems and the GNOME project will hasten the day when a stable release of Bonobo is available. Without further evidence of widespread use, Bonobo's impact will continue to be small.

As Kevin Sullivan argued in Chapter 19, component models must be carefully designed. In his analysis of the COM specification, he found that there is an unexpected interaction that leads to malfunction. COM objects are integrated using both aggregation and interface negotiation (Sullivan, Marchukov, and Socha, 1999b). Fortunately, the situation is uncommon and the defect is not serious. However, there needs to be further research into the properties that each component technology will ensure, and into whether the component model definitions themselves are consistent and complete. In the same way that different drugs are evaluated using double-blind studies in pharmaceuticals, we recommend that more studies should be carried out to evaluate the use of these component technologies in specific domains, such as real-time software, or embedded or resource-constrained systems. Only by empirically carrying out such research will confidence in the technologies be assured.

One of the most visible sources for components is ComponentSource.com (*www.componentsource.com*). On 10 January 2001, a search of their Web site revealed that one could purchase and download 1,018 software components. Of these, 55 percent (566) were Microsoft COM components (and related technology, such as ActiveX) while EJB components represented slightly more than 10 percent of the total (108) were EJB/Java components. The remaining components for sale were Visual Basic, Delphi, C++, or Visual Studio components. Although this is only one data point, it highlights the apparent dominance of COM component technology. Much of this success, admittedly, occurred because of the dominance of the Microsoft Windows Operating Systems and the widespread use of Integrated Development Environments (IDEs) like Visual Studio for Windows-based personal computers. John Williams estimates there were about 4,000 components available in October 2000 (Williams, 2000). Williams cites ComponentSource's president Sam Patterson as stating that 20,000 to 40,000 components are needed for a component marketplace to reach critical mass. With current growth rates, this may be achieved by 2003.

This is certainly an exciting time to be involved in component technologies. We hope that the chapters in this section will inspire you to contribute to the growing understanding of component technologies within the software engineering community.

Part VII

References

K. Bach and R. Harnish, *Linguistic Communication and Speech Acts*, MIT Press, Camgbridge, MA, 1979.

D. Bénech, T. Desprats, and Y. Renaud, "A KQML-CORBA Based Architecture for Intelligent Agents, Communication in Cooperative Service and Network Management," R. Boutaba, A. Hafid, eds., Proceedings, 1st IFIP Conference on Management of Multimedia Networks and Services, Kluwer Academic Publishers, 1998, pp. 95-106.

G. Bolcer and R. Taylor, "Endeavors: A Process System Integration Infrastructure," Proceedings, 4th International Conference on Software Process (ICSP), ACM Press, Brighton, UK, 1996, pp. 137-147.

D. Box, *Essential COM*, Addison-Wesley, Reading, MA, 1998.

J. Bradshaw, ed., *Software Agents*, MIT Press, Cambridge, MA, 1997.

D. Chappell, *The Next Wave: Component Software Enters the Mainstream*, Chappel & Associates, *www.rational.com/products/whitepapers/354.jsp, Apr., 1997*

Q. Chen, P. Chundi, U. Dayal, and M. Hsu, "Dynamic Agents for Dynamic Service Provisioning," Proceedings, International Conference on Cooperative Information Systems, IFCIS, The International Foundation on Cooperative Information Systems, IEEE Computer Society Press, New York, NY, 1998, pp. 95–104.

Q. Chen, M. Hsu, U. Dayal, and M. Griss, "Multi-Agent Cooperation, Dynamic Workflow and XML for E-Commerce Automation," Proceedings, 4th International Conference on Autonomous Agents, Barcelona, Spain, 2000, pp. 255-256.

D. Cliff and J. Bruten, "Market Trading Interactions as Collective Adaptive Behaviour," Proceedings, 5th International Conference on Simulation of Adaptive Behavior, MIT Press, Boston, MA, 1998, pp. 417–426.

M. de Icaza, Bonobo, *www.ximian.com/tech/bonobo.php3*, 1999.

M. de Icaza, "Lets Make Unix Not Suck," Ottawa Linux Symposium, *www.ximian.com/~miguel/bongo-bong.html*, Ottawa, Canada, July 2000.

T. Ewald, "Application Servers: The Next Silver Bullet?" *Component Strategies Magazine* (SIGS), Mar., 1999.

T. Ewald, *Transactional COM+: Building Scalable Applications* (The DevelopMentor Series), Addison-Wesley, Boston, MA, 2001.

B. Falchuk and A. Karmouch, "Visual Modeling for Agent-Based Applications," *IEEE Computer*, Vol. 31, No. 12, Dec., 1998, pp. 31–37.

T. Finin, Y. Labrou, and J. Mayfield, "KQML as an Agent Communication Language," in *Software Agents*, J. M. Bradshaw, ed., MIT Press, 1997, pp. 291–316.

E. Gamma, R. Helm, R. Johnson, and J. Vlissides, *Design Patterns: Elements of Reusable Object-Oriented Software*, Addison-Wesley, Reading, MA, 1995.

M. Genesereth and S. Ketchpel, "Software Agents," *Communications of the Association for Computing Machinery*, Vol. 37, No. 7, July 1994, pp. 48–53.

R. Glushko, J. Tenenbaum, and B. Meltzer, "An XML Framework for Agent-based E-commerce," *Communications of the Association for Computing Machinery*, Vol. 42, No. 3, Mar., 1999, pp. 106-114.

M. Griss and R. Kessler, "Building Object-Oriented Instrument Kits," *Object Magazine*, Vol. 6, No. 2, Apr., 1996.

M. Griss and R. Letsinger, "Games at Work—Agent-Mediated E-Commerce Simulation," Proceedings, Agents in Industry Workshop, associated with Autonomous Agents Conference, ACM Press, Barcelona, Spain, June 2000.

M. Griss, "My Agent Will Call Your Agent," *Software Development Magazine*, *www.sdmagazine.com/articles/2000/0002/0002toc.htm*, Feb., 2000a.

M. Griss, "Implementing Product-Line Features By Composing Component Aspects," Proceedings, First International Software Product Line Conference (SPLC), *www.sei.cmu.edu/plp/conf/SPLC.html*, ACM Press, Aug., 2000b.

T. Gschwind, M. Feridun, and S. Pleisch, "ADK—Building Mobile Agents for Network and Systems Management from Reusable Components," Joint Proceedings, 1st International Symposium on Agent Systems and Applications (ASA) and 3rd International Symposium on Mobile Agents (MA), Palm Springs, CA, *www.infosys.tuwien.ac.at/ADK*, IEEE Computer Society Press, Oct., 1999, pp. 13–21.

M. Henning and S. Vinoski, *Advance CORBA Programming with C++*, Addison-Wesley, Reading, MA, 1999.

M. Huhns, M. Singh, and L. Gasser, *Readings in Agents*, Morgan-Kaufmann Publishers, 1998.

N. Jennings and M. Wooldridge, eds., *Agent Technology: Foundations, Applications, and Markets*, Springer-Verlag, 1998.

G. Kaiser, A. Stone, and S. Dossick, "A Mobile Agent Approach to Light-Weight Process Workflow," Proceedings, International Process Technology Workshop (IPTW), Electronic Proceedings: *www-adele.imag.fr/IPTW*, Villard de Lans, France, Sept., 1999.

E. Kendall, "Role Model Designs and Implementations with Aspect-oriented Programming," Proceedings, 14th Object-Oriented Programming, Systems, Languages, and Applications (OOPSLA), ACM Press, Dallas, Texas, Oct., 1999, pp. 353–369.

C. Larman, "Enterprise JavaBeans 201: The Aggregate Entity Pattern," *Software Development Online, www.sdmagazine.com/articles/2000/0004/0004c/0004c.htm*, Apr., 2000.

D. Levine, C. Gill, and D. Schmidt, "Dynamic Scheduling Strategies for Avionics Mission Computing," Proceedings, 17th IEEE/AIAA Digital Avionics Systems Conference (DASC), IEEE Computer Society Press, Seattle, WA, 1998.

P. Maes, R. Guttman, and A. Moukas, "Agents That Buy and Sell," *Communications of the Association of Computing Machinery*, Vol. 42, No. 3, Mar., 1999, pp. 81-91.

R. Marvie, P. Merle, and J. Geib, "Towards a Dynamic CORBA Component Platform," Proceedings, 2nd Symposium of Distributed Objects & Applications, IEEE Computer Society Press, Antwerp, Belgium, Sept., 2000.

V. Matena and M. Hapner, Enterprise JavaBeans Specification, v1.1, Sun Microsystems, *java.sun.com/products/ejb/docs.html*, May, 1999.

B. Meltzer and R. Glushko, "XML and Electronic Commerce: Enabling the Network Economy," *ACM Special Interest Group on Management of Data (SIGMOD) Record*, Vol. 27, No. 4, Dec., 1998, pp. 21-24.

Microsoft, COM+ Component model, *www.microsoft.com/com*, 2000.

S. Moore, "KQML and FLBC: Contrasting Agent Communication Languages," *International Journal of Electronic Commerce*, Vol. 5, No. 1, Fall, 2000, pp. 109-124.

C. Mueller-Planitz, CWave 2000—A Visual Workbench for Distributed Measurement Agents, Ph.D. thesis, Computer Science Department, University of Utah, Salt Lake City, UT, May, 2000.

H. Nwana, D. Ndumu, L. Lee, and J. Collis, "ZEUS: A Toolkit for Building Distributed Multi-Agent Systems," *Applied Artificial Intelligence Journal*, Vol. 13, No. 1, Nov., 1999, pp. 129-186.

P. O'Brien and R. Nicol, "FIPA: Towards a Standard For Intelligent Agents," *British Telecommunications (BT) Technical Journal, www.bt.com/bttj*, Vol. 16, No. 3, July 1998.

Object Management Group, *CORBA Component Model Joint Revised Submission*, 1999.

Object Management Group, *The Common Object Request Broker: Architecture and Specification*, Version 2.4, 2000a.

Object Management Group, *CORBA Success Stories, www.corba.org/success.htm*, 2000b.

Apple Computer, Inc., OpenDoc, *devworld.apple.com/techpubs/macos8/Legacy/OpenDoc/opendoc.html*, 2000.

C. O'Ryan and D. Schmidt, "Applying a Scalable CORBA Events Service to Large-scale Distributed Interactive Simulations," Proceedings, 5th International Workshop on Object-Oriented Real-Time Dependable Systems (WORDS), IEEE Computer Society Press, Monterey, CA, 1999.

C. O'Ryan, D. Schmidt, F. Kuhns, M. SPivak, J. Parsons, I. Pyarali, and D. Levine, "Evaluating Policies and Mechanisms to Support Distributed Real-Time Applications with CORBA," *Evaluating Policies and Mechanisms to Support Distributed Real-Time Applications with CORBA* (Special Issue on Distributed Objects and Applications), John Wiley & Sons, Vol. 13, No. 2, Feb., 2001.

J. Ousterhout, *Tcl and the Tk Toolkit*, Addison-Wesley, Reading, MA, 1994.

S. Pearson, C. Preist, T. Dahl, and E. de Kroon, "An Agent-Based Approach to Task Allocation in a Computer Support Team," Proceedings, 2nd International Conference on Practical Application of Intelligent Agent and Multi Agent Technology (PAAM), The Practical Application Company, Ltd., Blackpool, UK, 1997.

C. Preist and M. Tol, "Adaptive Agents in a Persistent Shout Double Auction", Proceedings, 1st International Conference on Information and Computation Economics (ICE), Elsevier Science, The Netherlands, 1999, pp. 11–18.

C. Preist, "Economic Agents for Automated Trading," in A. Hayzelden & J.Bigham, eds., *Software Agents for Future Communications Systems*, Springer-Verlag, 1999.

I. Pyarali, C. O'Ryan, and D. Schmidt, "A Pattern Language for Efficient, Predictable, Scalable, and Flexible Dispatching Mechanisms for Distributed

Object Computing Middleware," Proceedings, IEEE/IFIP International Symposium on Object-Oriented Real-time Distributed Computing, Newport Beach, CA, 2000.

E. Raymond and B. Young, *The Cathedral and the Bazaar: Musings on Linux and Open Source by an Accidental Revolutionary*, O'Reilly & Associates, 2001.

T. Rizzo, "Build a Better Web with Microsoft Exchange Server," Microsoft Internet Developer, *www.microsoft.com/Mind/0599/webExchange/webExchange.htm*, May, 1999.

D. Rogerson, *Inside COM* (Programming Series), Microsoft Press, 1997.

D. Rosenberg, "How to Make Money With Open-Source," Stromian Technologies, *www.ibm.com/software/developer/library/license.html*, Aug., 1999.

D. Ruiz, M. Lacage, and D. Binnema, GNOME & CORBA, *developer.gnome.org/doc/guides/corba*, 2000.

D. Schmidt, T. Harrison, and I. Pyarali, "Object-Oriented Framework for High-Performance Electronic Medical Imaging," Proceedings, SPIE Vol. 2663, Very High Resolution and Quality Imaging, V. Algazi, S. Ono, and A. Tescher, eds., The International Society for Optical Engineering, *www.spie.org*, 1995, p. 260-271.

D. Schmidt, M. Stal, H. Rohnert, and F. Buschmann, *Pattern-Oriented Software Architecture*, Vol. 2, *Patterns for Concurrency and Distributed Objects*, John Wiley & Sons, New York, NY, 2000.

M. Schmidt, "The Evolution of Workflow Standards," *IEEE Concurrency*, Vol. 7, No. 3, July/Sept., 1999, pp. 44-52.

T. Sharma, "E-Commerce Components", *Software Development Online*, Vol. 7, *www.sdmagazine.com/articles/1999/9908/9908a/9908a.htm*, Aug., 1999.

J. Shepherdson, S. Thompson, and B. Odgers, "Cross-Organizational Workflow Coordinated by Software Agents," BT Laboratories, Work Activity Coordination and Collaboration (WACC), *www.labs.bt.com/projects/agents.htm*, Feb., 1999.

Y. Shoham, "Agent-Oriented Programming," *Artificial Intelligence*, Vol. 60, No. 1, Nov., 1993, pp. 51-92.

S. Sutton Jr. and L. Osterweil, "The Design of a Next Generation Process Programming Language," Proceedings, Joint 6th European Software Engineering Conference (ESEC) and 5th Symposium on the Foundations of Software Engineering (FSE), Lecture Notes in Computer Science (LNCS), No. 1301, Springer-Verlag, 1997, pp. 142–158.

J. Trupin, "Sharp New Language: C# Offers the Power of C++ and Simplicity of Visual Basic," *MSDN Magazine*, *msdn.microsoft.com/msdnmag/issues/0900/csharp/csharp.asp*, Vol. 15, No. 9, Sept., 2000.

S. Tyagi, "Understanding EJB Transactions," *Java Developers Journal*, *www.javadevelopersjournal.com*, Vol. 5, No. 4, Apr., 2000, pp. 26-35.

N. Wang, D. Schmidt, K. Parameswaran, and M. Kircher, "Applying Reflective Middleware Techniques to Optimize a QoS-enabled CORBA Component Model Implementation", Proceedings, 24th Computer Software and Applications Conference (COMPSAC), IEEE Computer Society Press, 2000.

N. Wang, M. Kircher, K. Parameswaran, D. Schmidt, "Towards a Reflective Middleware Framework for QoS-enabled CORBA Component Model Applications," Proceedings, Reflective Middleware Workshop (RM), ACM Press, 2000.

J. Williams, "Consuming Components," *Application Development Trends*, Vol. 7, No. 10, Oct., 2000, pp. 95–96.

Part VIII

Legal and Regulatory Component Issues

Part VIII will be a welcome surprise for readers who take the opportunity to read even one chapter. It would be easy to dismiss a part entitled "Legal and Regulatory Component Issues" as dry and uninteresting. However, these chapters are anything but bland. Each is full of the author's enthusiasm for the subject matter. More than sharing the collective authors' excitement, the chapters contain information that most readers generally don't know, and, moreover, in the content of these chapters, what you don't know will hurt you.

John Speed was previously the executive director of the Texas Board of Professional Engineers. During his tenure at the board, he managed the state's regulation of the engineering profession, including the development of regulations concerning the licensure of professional consulting software engineers (*www.tbpe.state.tx.us/sofupdt.htm*). In his chapter entitled "CBSE As a Unique Engineering Discipline," Speed and the coeditors argue that all engineering disciplines are component-based. They then present Frederick Taylor's concept of the "one best way" for each problem that can be divided into discrete and simple steps. The authors explain how Taylor's one best way has become a central tenet of all forms of engineering, except in software engineering. While first considering the option of licensure for component-based software engineers, the authors concede that licensure will take decades to establish.

Subsequently, the authors propose an engineering-based educational program for project and product managers. The need for managers trained in engineering, mathematics, computer science, and CBSE is immediate. Current software engineering and CBSE staff could apply for advanced placement in core pilot university programs accredited by the Computer Science Accreditation Board (CSAB) and the Accreditation Board of Engineering and Technology (ABET). After graduation with a master's degree and a one-year internship, the graduate would take a certification test to practice as a component-based software project manager.

In "The Future of Software Components: Standards and Certification," Janet Flynt and Manoj Desai describe the significant role that third-party certification will play in the future of relations among component producers, component consumers, and end-users. Currently, third-party certification is used primarily for safety-critical software for programmable components (such as embedded software). Flynt and Desai, as well as the coeditors, believe that considerable third-party certification activities will involve business-to-business commerce in software components, software component infrastructures, and software component models. Without third-party certification, there can be no assurance of trusted components. After reading Elaine Weyuker's chapter (Chapter 28), the need for certification before purchasing expensive components or components that likely will require considerable evolvability (Chapter 30) will become evident.

The next two chapters are written by Stephen Chow, an internationally recognized intellectual property and computer law attorney. First, Stephen writes about historical and current laws that affect transactions among software developers and those who license software. Second, he writes about a newly proposed and recently enacted law (in some states) entitled, the Uniform Commercial Information Transactions Act (UCITA). Stephen Chow has the ability to make otherwise arcane statutory law and court decisions comprehensible for readers who have never even read an abstract of a court case. The first chapter, entitled "Commercial Law Applicable to Component-Based Software," provides an historical perspective on

- Intellectual property law
- Trade secrets
- Copyright law
- Patent law

Then, he offers advice to component producers and consumers on how to protect their property rights in software components.

In Stephen's chapter on "The Effects of UCITA on Software Component Development and Marketing," the author describes the history of software commercial transactions under the Uniform Commercial Code (UCC) and then explains the politics behind UCITA. Stephen demonstrates how UCITA emerged and then explains its benefits and liabilities for component producers, component consumers, and purchasing endusers. In both chapters where legal citations are found, the editors have attempted to provide Web citations to make it easier for you to further research the statutory and case law, should you have an interest.

We believe you will find these chapters some of the most helpful in the book. This part will not help you design better UML diagrams or write better CBD components and interfaces. The chapters, however, will help you protect your interests in the sale of your quality, certified component-based products and assist you when you have purchased a defective component. In addition, when you have knowledge concerning the trustworthiness of a component producer or a component, or discover that a producer's project management is ineffective to produce component-based products on time, on budget, and within acceptable quality tolerances, the chapters provide much needed advice.

Chapter 37

Component-Based Software Engineering As a Unique Engineering Discipline

John Speed
Bill Councill
George T. Heineman

37.1 Introduction

In this chapter, we discuss component-based software engineering in relation to more traditional engineering disciplines. We will review

CBSE among traditional disciplines and other historical engineering practices, and will present ways in which component-based software engineering may develop independently. We argue that to create CBSE as a true engineering discipline, we must develop a mechanism for educating future practitioners, and must boldly join the ranks of traditional engineering disciplines by adopting rigorous engineering practices and procedures.

For many software engineers, we are assuming an antithetical position. However, we are not recommending an engineering approach for all software engineers. Our position is that if you manage a CBSE project or subproject, you must understand and implement the practices and follow the standards for CBSE certification. CBSE is an assembly-based product delivery system. Managers of engineering projects must have knowledge of every phase of the engineering life cycle. For CBSE managers, this is especially true—once a project team decision is made, it is too easy for programmers to implement code as they would like to. The programmer's subproject engineer must perform quality assurance on that particular "one best way" to ensure that the subproject teams are participating with the project team to produce the best product possible.

37.2 Component-Based Engineering

All traditional engineering is based upon the premise that a physical or chemical problem can be resolved by assembling the right materials and machines—the right *components*—into a system that resolves the problem. Using that premise, all traditional engineering is *component-based*. Depending upon the situation, some components are more complex than others are, but the concept is still valid.

A component-based solution to an engineering problem may take a variety of forms, depending upon the discipline of engineering. For example, a civil engineering problem might require the transport of large quantities of fluid between two locations. A wide range of solutions, each using a variety of off-the-shelf components, can be arranged to resolve the problem. One solution might include components such as storage tanks, pumps, and pipelines. Another might include the storage tanks, but replace the pipeline with a dedicated rail line or trucking route. Still another might transport the fluid using open-air channels, locks, and weirs. The possible permutations of available components are, theoretically, endless.

In the same way that civil engineers investigate various components to transport fluid, well-trained, experienced software engineers will investigate the use of available software components in the creation of a robust solution to a distributed systems problem. The components may appear different, but they are employed for the same reason—to resolve the problem in the best way.

37.2.1 The One Best Way

Robert Kanigel's recent biography of Frederick Taylor, the creator of the scientific management system, was entitled, *The One Best Way* (1997). The book refers to Taylor's dogged, lifelong insistence that one method of solving an industrial engineering problem had to be the "best" method. For Taylor, the best solution for each problem was one that provided discrete and simple steps—or components—that maximized efficiency and minimized material waste. The traditional engineering community embraced the one best method concept that forms the basis for engineers' fundamental problem-solving approach. The notion has so permeated society as a whole that almost every business setting, from industrial manufacturing to fast food preparation, still searches for "one best way" of doing things. Most importantly for the purposes of component-based software engineering, Taylor's process for resolving efficiency problems involved breaking large problems into smaller ones and implementing solutions as discrete "components."

Is one solution truly better than another? If so, what makes it better? What makes the other solutions inferior? When asked these types of questions, a group of traditional mechanical, electrical, or civil engineers will provide remarkably similar answers. They will speak of optimizing efficiency, minimizing costs, maintaining minimum functional requirements, and other fundamental tenets gleaned from their traditional engineering education.

However, these same questions asked of group of software engineering practitioners will result in answers that are anything *but* consistent. This, we believe, is one of the most fundamental challenges facing the software engineering profession today—a large number of software engineering practitioners have not been educated to recognize or generate optimal solutions to problems.

Does this mean that software development must conform to Taylor's scientific management principles to be performed at the highest possible levels? Absolutely not! Just because Taylorism was one of the first tools used in traditional engineering processes does not mean that it is the only tool. Taylorism is important simply because it has been so heavily used by traditional engineers that it now serves as a common procedural tool for collaboration.

Software engineers, on the other hand, come from diverse backgrounds and work in even more diverse settings. While the diversity certainly brings new ideas to problem solving, diversity fails to convey common goals, methods, and understandings to a collaborative process. In short, many software engineering practitioners do not agree that a "best" solution exists. They do not agree about the technology that must be in place to achieve a "best" solution, and they agree even less about the processes needed to ensure that "best" solution.

Unfortunately, component-based software engineering can easily make this situation even worse because of the ready availability of software components. Practitioners are often tempted to "stack" off-the-shelf products onto an application, even if it creates inefficiencies or user complications (see Chapter 28). The use, or misuse, of software components in this manner allows less-than-optimal solutions to be implemented. As this type of scene is repeated, some practitioners come to consider the practice acceptable. The net result is that an unacceptably large percentage of software engineering practitioners settle for lower standards of professional performance than their counterparts in traditional engineering disciplines.

If software engineering—especially component-based software engineering—is to be performed at the highest possible levels, it must adopt some common tools that virtually all practitioners understand. Probably the easiest place to start searching for common ground is to look at a professional setting where common ground already exists—traditional engineering.

37.2.2 Common Traits of Traditional Engineering Practice

Traditional engineering performance has not always been well-defined. Over the past century however, traditional engineering practitioners and engineering universities have developed systematic approaches to collecting the components needed for a solution. Based on Taylor's scientific management, analysis and design processes have been created for new technologies as they appeared. As the processes developed for each technology, those processes soon became known as its own discipline. Evolving from the civil engineering discipline, specialists in machines developed processes that became known as mechanical engineering. Specialists in electricity developed processes that became electrical engineering. Each discipline came to be defined by the unique "bodies of knowledge" and processes that helped to define it. Collectively, the bodies of knowledge have become the foundation of collegiate engineering education. The systematic procedures of the bodies of knowledge are known as the "practice of engineering."

The practice of engineering is a collection of systematic approaches to engineering problems. Many of these practices can be generalized. Whether the discipline is a traditional one (such as mechanical, civil, chemical, industrial, or electrical) or a nontraditional one (such as software, safety, materials, or systems), engineering practices will usually include some combination of the following.

- *A problem description* – While this may seem obvious, it is probably the most commonly skipped step in the practice of engineering. A complete problem statement will not only establish a picture of the solution being sought, but will also establish the problem boundaries to exclude those things that are not being sought. Of critical importance, the problem description also defines the characteristics of an optimal – or "best" – solution
- *An analysis model* – Even the most complex problems can be broken into solvable subproblems. Each subproblem should be established in a manner such that, when it is resolved, it will contribute to the process of designing an overall solution to the complex problem. The engineer's challenge is to establish a procedure for solving these subproblems that is consistent with acceptable scientific and mathematical procedures. The most successful engineers are able to optimize the procedure to minimize the effort needed to complete the work. Once the technical issues have been defined during analysis, possible solutions begin to evolve
- *A series of possible solution options* – A preliminary list of components needed for implementing the solution will accompany each

possible solution, and the solution usually includes a cost component. Cost effectiveness is the single most common solution criteria in traditional engineering, and it is utilized at this stage to narrow the field of alternatives to those that minimize cost without sacrificing effectiveness. Each possible solution is compared against the others and against the standard of performance established in the problem description. Once a single solution emerges as the most promising, the process moves to the design phase. In actual practice, engineers may need to create preliminary designs of several possible solutions during this step to better define the potential or weaknesses of each.

- *An optimized design for the solution* – After a single alternative is selected, the engineer begins the process of designing a system that will minimize the cost of building and operating the system and still provide all of the features of a "best" solution defined in the problem description. A complete design will be well documented, and those documents can be used by a person who is not familiar with the project to construct/install the system
- *A plan for operating and maintaining the system* – The engineer's job is not complete until the user is able to fully implement the system in a routine manner. Depending upon the complexity of the system, the effort expended in developing an operations and maintenance plan may surpass the effort expended to design the system

One additional factor must also be included when discussing common traits in traditional engineering practice—that factor is the law. In the United States and Canada, state and provincial laws that are fairly common across jurisdictions regulate engineering practice. These laws establish a license requirement for engineers offering services to a third party or who otherwise portray themselves as engineers. The minimum requirements for a professional engineering license usually include an engineering education, a period of post-graduation internship, and (in the United States) passage of national examinations.

One of the most interesting aspects of these laws is the way in which they define the practice of engineering. The practice of engineering is considered to be the actual performance of those concepts that engineers learned in engineering school. While this definition may seem circular at first, it provides insight into the strong links between an engineering education and active practice. Practitioners must understand that this legal reality will play a role in the successful emergence of component-based software engineering as a unique engineering discipline. We must recognize that the current lack of an identifiable component-based software engineering education at an accredited university will hinder—and possibly prevent—the discipline from being recognized in its own right.

Because component-based software engineering lacks a well-defined body of knowledge, the development of an accredited education in the discipline will evolve slowly. This book is an excellent first step in defining the body of knowledge unique to component-based software engineering, but consensus must be achieved on a broader base for the profession to grow. The body of knowledge cannot be static. It must be subject to continuous scrutiny by professional organizations and the academic community. The processes associated with the body of knowledge must involve participation by the accepted leaders of the field.

The legal aspects of defining any engineering discipline lead to an even more fundamental challenge concerning the continued development of component-based software engineering as a unique discipline. Each of these challenges must be resolved collectively among practitioners if the profession is to prosper.

1. First, we must conclude that our field is really engineering
2. Second, we must develop a mechanism for educating future practitioners
3. Third, we must boldly join the ranks of traditional engineering disciplines by adopting practices and procedures that compare favorably with those disciplines

If we are successful, within the next few decades, we believe that CBSE will be viewed as another "traditional" engineering discipline alongside the "newcomers" of decades past.

37.2.3 Is Component-Based Software Engineering Really Engineering?

The best way to approach this question is to compare it to traditional engineering practices. Can the practice of component-based software engineering be defined in the same way that other traditional engineering disciplines have been defined? Without a formal component-based software engineering education, the answer would be no. However, the actual processes that make up the practice *can* be compared to the general traits of traditional engineering as a first step in evaluating the current state of the practice. While this evaluation process is quite extensive and will not be covered in this essay, we believe that any such comparison will identify significant common traits with traditional engineering disciplines.

Many have argued that component-based software engineering—indeed software engineering in general—is different from other types of engineering. To emphasize this difference, a group of software engineers chooses to call their practice of design, "architecture." Despite the terminology turf wars, we firmly believe that the practice of component-based software design must be considered an engineering practice. Our reasoning is simple. Optimal software solutions can only be consistently achieved by applying a process that is intended to provide optimal results. Traditional engineering practice has successfully employed these processes for decades, and component-based software engineering can utilize similar processes to improve the consistency of its product. All of the other terms used in the software field refer to endeavors where professional practices emphasize form (architecture) or uniqueness (design).

By its very nature, only the practice of engineering provides a set of procedures from which practitioners can derive consistent software products. Only the practice of engineering provides procedures designed to optimize results. Currently, the practices and procedures of component-based software engineering are not yet well developed. However, acceptably rigorous practices and procedures can be easily developed by emulating traditional engineering practice.

37.2.4 Developing an Education Program for Component-Based Software Engineering

The second challenge is to develop a component-based software engineering education. This effort will take cooperation from a variety of sectors. We will now briefly overview the traditional engineering education system in search of meaningful parallels with component-based software engineering.

In traditional engineering disciplines, the responsibility for developing an engineering education is held jointly by accrediting organizations, professional societies, and universities. Without question, United States engineering programs have had the most rapid development of any programs in the world. In our opinion, there are more top-tier engineering programs per citizen in the United States universities than in any other nation except Canada. Because the engineering programs at Canadian and United States universities are similar, we will arbitrarily look at United States engineering education programs as a point of reference.

In the United States, the official accrediting body for engineering education is the Accreditation Board of Engineering and Technology (ABET). It is divided into subgroups, two of which are responsible for the bulk of the accreditation process: the Engineering Accreditation Commission (EAC) and the Technology Accreditation Commission (TAC). These commissions recruit volunteer engineers to physically visit universities who wish to accredit a particular engineering or technology degree program. The visiting engineers evaluate the curriculum, the quality of the facilities and faculty, and the program's ability to produce an educated student. Many of these visiting engineers are active practitioners involved in professional societies. Most are current or former engineering faculty at other universities. The societies actively support the accreditation process by training a pool of practicing engineers and engineering faculty to participate as evaluators, and the universities support the process by encouraging faculty to participate in evaluating similar programs at other universities.

Professional societies such as the American Society of Mechanical Engineers (ASME), the Institute of Electrical and Electronics Engineers (IEEE), and the American Society of Civil Engineers (ASCE), have been supporting accreditation for decades. In addition to supplying evaluators, most societies have large internal committees dedicated to monitoring and establishing trends in engineering education. Many committee members are themselves engineering faculty members, providing direct communication links between practitioners and the universities. One of the most important roles the professional societies play is to establish and maintain the discipline's body of knowledge documents. The body of knowledge establishes the scope of the discipline, which then translates into the scope of the university education. The National Council of Examiners for Engineering and Surveying

(NCEES) also monitors and maintains discipline-specific body of knowledge documents, which are used to develop professional examinations used by state licensing boards.

The primary responsibility for maintaining a healthy system of engineering education still falls to the universities. A natural, healthy competition exists among schools for the best students, research funding, and the finest facilities. The purpose of the competition is to recruit the best faculty—the heart and soul of any program. By recruiting the best faculty, the universities can then recruit better students, research funding, and facilities. This circle of recruiting can create, under the best of circumstances, a kind of synergy that results in prestigious engineering programs.

Most universities believe that this synergistic cycle starts by establishing an accredited program. Therefore, universities actively support well-established and universally recognized accreditation programs such as ABET. Professional societies are a direct link to practitioners, and those practitioners hire graduates and provide research and facility funding. Universities often actively support society programs by supplying key logistic support such as clerical help, meeting space, and access to speakers and informative programs. Most also expect their faculty to maintain membership and actively participate in their discipline's professional society.

If we are to successfully translate the success of traditional engineering education into the component-based software engineering discipline, we must begin the process by filling in the missing elements. Those elements are

- *Common professional society* – Without a common forum for handling technical and professional concerns, our efforts at developing a meaningful educational program will be disjointed and ineffective
- *An accreditation process* – The Computer Science Accreditation Board (CSAB) has recently formed an alliance with ABET (*csab.org*). Software engineering and CBSE must seek to meet ABET's standards for a robust educational experience through representation of CSAB. In other nations, it will be equally important to establish relationships with the existing accreditation boards to achieve a higher level of educational excellence
- *A "flagship" university program in component-based software engineering* – The educational process must start somewhere. Regardless of

the number of "virtual" educational experiences available, a true engineering education must have face-to-face contact with top-tier faculty located in a real university. One of the most critical parts of any educational experience is the opportunity to share experiences with other students and faculty. Which university will take the lead by establishing the first program?

- *A body of knowledge* – The scope of the profession must be established as a cooperative effort of practitioners, a professional society, ABET, and NCEES. While much has already been written to define various aspects of component-based software engineering practice, much remains to be done to achieve the consensus necessary to create a comprehensive body of knowledge. A body of knowledge document will be a crucial first step in the development of university education programs and accreditation processes, and in the establishment of national certification/licensing programs

37.2.5 Developing Professional Practices and Procedures

The third challenge is one that must be undertaken concurrently with the second. The development of professional practices and procedures is a part of the development of the body of knowledge needed for a successful collegiate educational program. One professional society that intends to use the results as a part of an education accreditation process must sponsor the effort. This will create the highest probability that the resulting practices and procedures will reasonably conform to the practices and procedures utilized in other engineering disciplines.

Now, we must discuss professional practices. All too often, practitioners view ISO 9000 series standards and the Capability Maturity Model (CMM) as standards of professional practice. While these tools may be a useful method of quantifying results of processes, they are woefully inadequate in providing the underlying professional logic needed to optimize a solution to a problem. The ISO 9000 series and CMM processes are useful in environments where the desired results are already established. However, the real role of a professional engineer must include the assessment of a *specific* problem and the establishment of quantitative and quality standards *for a particular, previously unsolved problem*. ISO 9000 series tools may be a part of that process, but by no means should such standards be allowed to supplant the professional logic of a competent engineer.

37.2.6 The Next Steps

Thus far, we have described the requirements for establishing a licensure program for component-based software engineers. We also explained that it may take decades to institute a component-based software engineering licensing program commensurate with the other recognized engineering disciplines. However, well-trained software engineers with a basis in engineering are needed immediately. We therefore recommend that we focus on developing an IEEE-certified program for component-based software project managers (CBSPM). There are precedents for this idea. The American Counselors Association (ACA), similar to our proposal, once certified counselors through the National Board of Certified Counselors ([NBCC] [*www.nbcc.org/aboutnbcc.htm*]) and the National Association of Social Workers (NASW) certifies and provides other distinctions upon its members (*www.naswdc.org*). These two forms of certification are quite different than what we propose and the proposed software engineering certifications offered by the IEEE Computer Society ([*www.computer.org/education/cstrain.htm*] [*www.computer.org/education/sestrain.htm*]).

We have demonstrated the similarities between CBSE and the engineering disciplines. In addition, we have established the need for the precision and reliability of software components, especially since many will be used in devices that will affect the health, safety, and well being of the public. Currently, the training of managers with specialized engineering courses is crucial. Generally, the failure of software projects is the failure of software management. Therefore, training component-based software project engineers is paramount to success in CBSE as more organizations adopt CBD and CBSE. These potential program managers would receive the following training, at a minimum.

- *Education* – Students would graduate with five years' education culminating in a master's degree in software engineering from an accredited university with ABET-accredited computer science and engineering departments. Courses from computer science, software engineering, and engineering would commence early in the curriculum and continue throughout the course of study

- *Best practices* – Students would work on research projects or with industrial partners who have adopted CBSE best practices. Students should engage in a practicum with faculty members on laboratory projects or industrial software component projects for two consecutive semesters. They would take accompanying courses at night. At a minimum, students should be exposed to component analysis, design, construction, and testing
- *Internship* – Following graduation, students would participate with a certified internship organization for a period of one year. During this year, the student will work closely with the lead engineer (preferably the lead software engineer) on an engineering project. Note that this *mentor* must have an engineering degree. In the event that a lead engineer or lead software engineer is unavailable for the complete year, the student may, with the program chairman's permission, work with a senior subproject engineer. The emphasis of the internship is that the intern would learn to think and work like an engineer. Ideally, the intern would learn to think and work like a software engineer as preparation for the position of CBSPM (see Chapter 27)

CBSE is moving too fast and is too important to our economy for even a few years to pass without the establishment of a core of universities, working with the IEEE and ABET to develop a program for CBSPMs. The body of knowledge for CBSE is sufficiently circumscribed currently that this book provides coverage for most of the major subject matter. Make no mistake, however—the body of knowledge is increasing significantly.

We further recommend that the IEEE and CSAB immediately represent the needs of the CBSE community with ABET to determine the correct ratio of software engineering and computer science courses to engineering courses. ABET could propose the most effective engineering courses for a CBSE graduate degree. Subsequently, the IEEE and ABET should meet with a core group of universities interested immediately in establishing a multi-department graduate program for CBSPMs. All parties should determine a curriculum with the universities that will serve to

- Provide a minimum engineering education necessary for CBSE project managers to understand and manage each phase of the general engineering life cycle

- Determine the minimum number and type of engineering and mathematics courses (Parnas, 1999) project managers should take to function effectively in this transitional engineering discipline. For example,
  - Introductory Mechanics
  - Waves, Electricity, and Magnetic Fields
  - Engineering Mathematics (depth to be determined by committee)
  - Introduction to the Structure and Properties of Engineering Materials
  - Introduction to Dynamics and Control of Physical Systems
  - Introduction to Thermodynamics and Heat Transfer
- Determine the number and type of computer science and software engineering courses (Parnas, 1999) required for an effective software engineering education. Some of those courses follow.
  - Software Design I: Programming to Meet Precise Specifications
  - Software Design II: Structure and Documentation of Software
  - Design and Selection of Computer Algorithms and Data Structures
  - Data Management Techniques
  - Software and Social Responsibility
  - Design of Parallel and Distributed Computer Systems and Computations
- Decide on a curriculum in CBSE, in addition to Parnas' software engineering courses, from the following examples
  - Business Analysis Incorporating Business Rules, Requirements, and Use Cases
  - Infrastructure Design, using the Unified Modeling Language
  - Configuration Management and Component Libraries
  - (Software) Engineering-based Team Management
  - Unit, Integration, and System Testing COTS Components and Organizationally Developed Components
  - Maintenance of COTS and Organizationally Developed Components

Recent graduates of computer science departments and software engineering departments must submit their university transcripts to receive credits for courses similar to those offered by the CBSPM program. In addition, they will have to take a test to determine where in the program they will commence their studies. Others who have not received a degree in computer science, software engineering, or engineering, but have worked in software analysis and design, software development, or software testing for a period of five years or more, must submit their college transcripts as evidence of their grade point average (GPA). A minimum GPA must be established for consideration to take a comprehensive software engineering test to establish their matriculation status. For both groups, test scores likely will benefit those most who have solid software engineering experience.

We recommend that the IEEE and ABET, as well as members of the core universities, assign members to meet with U.S. government funding agencies to propose the need for significant funding for the component-based software project manager program. The funding for the small number of core universities must be sufficient to implement a substantive five-year program from inception of the program. Adequate funding must be available for the research and development programs at each university so that students can participate in next-generation projects from commencement through completion. Universities should receive significant funds to recruit and retain the finest researchers and practitioners in the field, many of whom have written chapters for this book. Funding also must be available for the IEEE, ABET, and the core universities to establish a body of knowledge as they anticipate students' needs for courses from the commencement of the program. Adjustments can be made throughout the first five years from matriculation to graduation, and thereafter.

37.2.7 The One Best Way and the Issue of Trust

Ask most software engineers what their primary duty is and they will respond with any number of answers. In most businesses, however, senior management will reply with only one answer: Software engineers are responsible for assuring the production of quality software on time that precisely meets users' needs. The corollary is that software engineers serve in their appropriate business-related role: fiduciaries for their company's board of directors and shareholders with the responsibility to maintain profits, and avoid financial losses because of non-implemented, delayed, over-budgeted, and terminated projects.

CBSPMs will have the same responsibility, but with certification, they are liable for managing CBSE according to the body of knowledge that is established during the period the university programs are training their first students. In addition, CBSPMs must manage the life cycle phases and new processes that present substantial problems for CBSE. Weyuker (Chapter 28) describes the difficulty in testing organizationally developed component-based applications, as well as COTS components integrated into applications. Vigder (Chapter 30) explains that maintenance of software components, if maintainability and evolvability are not realized during design, is restricted to reconfiguring and reintegrating components, because of components' limited visibility and maintainers' limited knowledge of their internal behavior. Further, Flynt and Desai (Chapter 38) detail how third-party certification can assure that component consumers and end-users will receive the products for which they contracted or that they purchased in the stream of commerce. CBSPMs must avoid the problems described so effectively by Weyuker and plan for maintenance management activities clarified by Vigder and Tracz (Chapter 6), while preparing for third-party certification that must be designed into the process (Chapter 38) and accounting for all certification activities proposed by Flynt and Desai.

In a trusted marketplace of third-party components, CBSPMs must assure their senior managers, directors, and shareholders that their components or component infrastructures comply with the requirements of contractors and with the needs of the market. Far more important than the type of software component—general ledger, inventory control, manufacturing control system—is the belief that the market views the component as trustworthy.

It would seem that third-party certification, the ISO 9000 series of standards, or the Capability Maturity Model (CMM) would provide sufficient processes to assure trustworthy software components. Third-party certification would result in sufficiently verified and validated software components and negate the need for an engineering-trained CBSPM. Third-party certification reviews the process, as well as validates the finished product against the initial, risk-addressed requirements. As we stated earlier, the ISO 9000 series of standards and CMM are effective when the desired results are already established. The problem is that few, if any of the members of the project team understand the concept of the one best way. Most are prepared to demonstrate collegial acceptance of the manager's directives and to continue conducting longstanding practices. Precisely because of these stable state behaviors, CBSPMs are required to learn every aspect of the CBD life cycle. The manager cannot rely on the existing subproject managers' practices. The CBSPM must verify CBSE processes and procedures and determine the extent to which the subproject managers are participating in the project team using the one best way for their department and life cycle phase.

Therefore, the CBSPM is the most effectively trained manager for CBSE projects, and for implementing engineering management practices to achieve practical solutions to complex, component-based problems. It is hoped that the heterogeneous education will enable the CBSPM and component-based organization to deliver trusted products on time and on or below budget.

Ensuring the design and development of trusted components requires adherence to the following properties.

- A CBSPM knowledgeable in the ever-changing requirements of trust in the intellectual property of software components and component infrastructures
- Project members who are continually trained by the CBSPM in the elements of trust in the members' specialty
- Project members who continually mentor their subordinates in the elements of trust in the subordinates' particular specialties
- Adherence to standards for software component implementations and component models, which, by default, provide the basis for standards for software infrastructures
- Documentation standards for components, interfaces, and software component infrastructures, specifying the meta data necessary to query the component library for a productive search, as well as for information developers need to reconfigure, replace, or customize the component during maintenance
- Test cases, based on
    - Business rules or standards existent at the time of the design of the component

- Business process models derived from senior management at the time of the component design from standards, laws, regulations, or business practices
- Functional and nonfunctional requirements developed by information technology managers (internal development) or marketers, business analysts, and designers for components developed by software component producers
- Incremental analysis, design, development, and testing
- Incremental verification activities
- Incremental third-party certification
- System testing and defect repair
- Internal validation
- Third-party validation, perhaps with other components
- When successful, third-party execution of documentation, and award of an appropriate seal of validation

In a subproject group, decisions must be made about the one best way to accomplish each task assigned the during the life cycle phase. Opposition to problem solving using Taylor's one best way will manifest itself in many of the same resistance patterns identified by Reifer (Chapter 24). Nevertheless, lead and subproject engineers have encountered and succeeded at implementing the one best way approach for many years.

The CBSPM must demonstrate knowledge of managing resistance. Unlike many project managers, CBSPMs should not be surprised by subordinates who expect the project manager to negotiate budgets, schedules, call meetings, report discrepancies in budgets and schedules to management, and issue directives. CBSPMs are trained in computer science, CBSE, and engineering. When designers argue for a method that is overly complex, or will present problems for component consumers during maintenance, the CBSPM has to understand the problem and assist the designers in arriving at the best solution for the problem. Engineering management prepares the CBSPM to understand, without reprimand, that technologists like to implement the newest methods, often without thinking the total life cycle problem through. Later, the same solution will be the right answer to a problem.

37.3 Conclusion

Ideally, software engineers practicing CBSE would require licensing. CBSE and the various disciplines of engineering are responsible for assembling components. CBSE is an engineering activity that has not yet developed a body of knowledge. This book serves as a compilation of the state-of-the-art of CBSE and in future editions may become CBSE's body of knowledge. Licensure of software engineers practicing CBSE is dependent on a body of knowledge.

For a complete engineering discipline, CBSE will need to establish its own professional society or its own unique identity within an existing society, and an accreditation board to evaluate emergent and established universities offering approved courses in engineering and CBSE. A flagship university must undertake responsibility for offering an excellent faculty. Internships must be established for members of the first graduating class and retained for subsequent graduating classes. Finally, a test based on the accreditation board's approved curriculum and anticipated experience gained through the internship must be prepared before completion of the first internship.

Establishing a licensure process for software engineers practicing CBSE could take decades. The need for component-based engineering trained project managers is immediate. We propose a five-year graduate program for CBSPMs that would provide education in the following disciplines

- Computer science
- CBSE
- Engineering

We urge the IEEE, CSAB, and ABET to meet on behalf of the proposal set forth in this chapter and one that we will make independently to establish a sufficiently funded core of universities to provide a master's degree graduate program in CBSPM. The program will provide certification through the CSAB until state licensure or state certification is mandated. The program is not designed to train engineers. The CBSPM graduate program is intended to provide component-based project and program managers with a sufficient background in engineering to recognize a problem and derive the one best solution considering all factors. In addition, the program is designed to ensure that component-based project and program managers have an adequate understanding of all phases of the software component life cycle, including reuse.

Chapter 38

The Future of Software Components: Standards and Certification

Janet Flynt
Manoj Desai

38.1 Introduction

Since Y2K is still relatively fresh in our memories, consider a few simple questions.

- Why was Y2K so difficult to resolve?
- Was it a system or a component (module) problem?
- Would a software standard and certification have made any difference?

Of course, answers to these and other similar questions are not that simple. One could argue that in a global, market-driven environment, where economy and efficiency determine winners and losers, a phenomenon like Y2K was bound to happen. But intuitively, having better standards and requiring compliance could have significantly reduced the frequency of Y2K problems and the efforts required to fix them.

Without engaging in philosophical debate, it would be safe to say that the Y2K experience has moved the pendulum in the direction of identifying risk earlier to understand software's limitations, constraints, and intended use. It has also convinced many about the importance of testing, documentation, and change control.

In the book *Awakening* (Laddon, Atlee, and Shook, 1998), Reverend Dacia Reid estimated that there are 25 to 50 billion embedded computer chips in existence, or about four to eight chips per person. Of course, some of us do not own any integrated circuits (ICs) at all, but many of us purchase products with the latest ICs. Because of the proliferation of computer chips, all of us will experience, at some time, some aspect of computer problems. For many years, we have been writing software upon which the world economy and society now depends. Failure of a single component or even a single misplaced line of code can cause an entire system to crash, leading to unavailable resources or even creating a safety hazard. With consumer awareness raised by the Y2K crisis and improvements in software engineering methods, it is important that we provide for the future by building high-integrity systems (that is, fault-tolerant and failsafe systems) and meeting certification standards (Underwriters Laboratories, 1999).

38.2 A Chain Is No Stronger Than Its Weakest Link

We believe that to develop systems that are market-worthy using a CBSE approach, the software component project team must design to standards and use certified components. Standards and certification are necessary preconditions for CBSE to be successfully adopted and to achieve the associated economic and social benefits that CBSE could yield. With the success of CBSE, software developers will have more time to develop, instead of spending their time addressing problems associated with understanding and fixing someone else's code. Certified components used during development will have predetermined and well-established criteria, thus reducing the risk of system failure and increasing the likelihood that the system will comply with design standards.

38.3 The Issue

Advances in computer technology have yielded computers that are smaller, cheaper, and faster. To take advantage of this tremendous power, software vendors are now developing programs that are longer (in terms of lines of code), more complex, and highly specialized. In today's marketplace, it is common to have four different vendors develop one appliance assembled from microelectronic hardware, operating systems, and networking systems, as well as applications. Consumers have every right to expect all components to function seamlessly without any malfunctions or failures. To establish that a system performs its intended function, each component and its interfaces must perform in accordance with comprehensive specifications.

With the CBSE approach, developers use components derived from component libraries to rapidly build applications (Chapter 29). If the components in the component libraries are not adequately described or do not comply with the stated functional specifications, the trustworthiness of these components diminishes and the potential for nonconformance with system standards increases. Without standards and certification, extensive reuse of components from component libraries will probably not occur. The situation would be similar to populating reuse repositories without qualifying components (Scheper et al., 1997).

One proposed alternative for component certification is to require source code to be available. However, making changes to the source without documented specifications and testing can introduce unanticipated side effects. These side effects may result in a loss of system availability and potential for injury. Additionally, the amount of time it takes to understand and integrate source code into producers' applications may eliminate any savings in development costs and life cycle time.

38.4 Standards and Certification: The Missing Pieces

38.4.1 Design to Standards

Several studies have provided data that show that a large portion of software failures are errors in specification, or more specifically, that the scope of the design did not meet the requirements. For a discussion of incidents that occurred in computer-controlled plants and equipment, see *Computer Control and Human Error* (Kletz et al., 1995). These studies, together with the growing use of software in safety-related applications, have resulted in further interpretation of regulations to require consideration of the potential failure of "logic." The result is the emergence of International Electro-Technical Commission ([IEC] [*www.iec.ch*]) and American National Standards Institution ([ANSI] [*www.ansi.org*]) standards applied to software that require demonstrated compliance with regulations. Table 38-1 identifies several existing standards that contain requirements to improve software development practices when software is used in safety-related applications.

Table 38-1: *Published Standards That Reference Software Requirements*

IEC 60601-1-4	Medical Electrical Equipment, Part I: General requirements for safety, 4. Collateral Standard: Safety requirements for programmable electronic medical systems
IEC 61508	Functional Safety of Electrical/Electronic/ Programmable Electronic Safety-Related Systems
ANSI/UL 1998	Standard for Software in Programmable Components

Table 38-1: *Published Standards That Reference Software Requirements*

ANSI/ISA-S84.01	Application of Safety Instrumented Systems for the Process Industries

Given the functional complexity inherent in software and programmable components, the requirements in the ANSI/UL 1998 Standard (*www.ul.com/pscs/ansi.html*) address issues important to system components that result in an end product. The standard addresses the entire product life cycle, from the requirements phase through the maintenance phase, specifying both process and design criteria ([Councill, 1999] [Desai, 2000]).

As such, the ANSI/UL 1998 Standard emphasizes the need for

- Risk-based analysis and design
- Consideration of provisions for hardware malfunctions
- Test planning and coverage
- Usability considerations
- Comprehensive documentation
- Processes for handling software changes
- Qualifications for off-the-shelf software
- Labeling that uniquely identifies the specifics of the product interface
- The hardware platform
- The software configuration

If the requirements in the standard are considered early in the process, then the system under development is more likely to meet marketability requirements. When the system is developed using a CBSE approach, the use of certified components could provide objective evidence that the components meet rigorous specifications including data on intended use. This approach does not permit the designer to forego inherently safe system design practices. Instead, certification reduces the risk of system failure by providing information about a software component's risk mitigation procedures, such as the anticipation of a failure state and return to the last stable state with notice to the system administrator. The objective is to build safe systems from well-documented and proven components. If these components are independently certified, then we have more confidence that the information accompanying the software component meets requirements.

38.4.2 Balancing Interests

The Underwriter's Laboratory (UL) follows the ANSI Accredited Organization Method (AOM) process as one approach for developing consensus for UL's *Standards for Safety*. This approach involves the formation of Standards Technical Panels (STPs) – knowledgeable, interested parties – who will serve as the main standards development forum. Features of the AOM process include an open process and meetings, input on standard development from a balanced range of participants, and ANSI approval of the UL Standard upon publication.

The UL 1998 Standard was first published in 1994 as the *UL 1998 Standard for Safety-Related Software.* The scope of the standard applied to software whose failure could result in a risk of injury to persons or loss of property. In May 1998, the second edition of UL 1998 was published, and ANSI recognition soon followed in February of 1999. With the publication of the second edition, the title of the standard became *UL 1998 Standard for Software in Programmable Components.*

To maintain this document, UL has formed the ANSI/UL 1998 STP. The STP membership represents a balance of interests among participants according to the ANSI categories of Producer, User, and General Interest. A Producer participant is anyone who is predominately involved with producing products, materials, or services (usually manufacturers and trade associations). A General Interest participant is usually a professional, a layperson employed by an academic or scientific institution, an expert, or an employee of a government research agency, among other offices. To achieve a balanced and functioning STP, membership is limited to not more than twenty participants, including a chair and secretary. However, the STP will establish working groups to address specific technical issues related to product sector requirements (for example, appliances, industrial control devices, electromedical devices) and technology (for example, requirements for networked systems, languages/tools, etc). Working group membership is open to anyone with credentials appropriate to the purpose of the working group.

38.4.3 Develop Certifiably Reusable Components

By definition, a component must be independently deployable, composed without modification according to a composition standard, and have clearly defined and documented interfaces in accordance with a vendor-specific interface standard. Components may be written in different programming languages. They may have low complexity. For example, a software component could implement a simple, repetitious loop that senses temperature and signals an event when a temperature exceeds boundary values. Alternatively, components may have high complexity. For example, a software component might implement repetitious and parallel sensing of the multiple temperature indicators and signaling of multiple events when differing combinations of sensors exceeds preset values.

Components may have pre-established functionality or functionality that evolves based on application or product-specific needs. For example, components are developed to provide functionality based on accepted algorithms, such as those found in mathematical and statistical libraries and I/O utilities, and for graphical data display. Components with functionality that evolves may result in producer-specific standards by default, as is the case with network protocol standards.

38.4.4 Benefits of Standards and Certification

The decision to invest in standards development and certification depends on the product and the intended market. The cost of certification varies significantly, as it is based on market requirements, product size, complexity, criticality, development process capability, and comprehensiveness of the documentation. However, by certifying software components to meet standards, the risk of the component-based software application not working in accordance with its specification can be reduced. These standards contain minimal requirements for design, testing, and documentation. Thus, the purchaser will have certified information available (including "conditions of use") to support purchasing decisions. Whereas standards and certification will not obviate the need for the Uniform Commercial Code Article 2B requirements, standards can be used as a preventative approach toward reducing the need for litigation.

38.5 Certification in the Electrical Safety Domain

For more than a century, certification of electrical components has provided objective evidence that an electrical component in a product meets standards of safety. Product acceptability is achieved through either voluntary compliance with industry consensus standards or required compliance with standards specified by regulation or statutory law.

Applying certification to electrical components has reduced the likelihood of safety-related failure in consumer products. Shielding wires and spacing them according to predetermined and well-established criteria is a proven requirement for avoiding burn injury and fire hazards. In the same way that a shorted wire may potentially result in a burn injury or a fire, a software component that continues to output an "on" signal after a temperature limit has been reached may also potentially result in a burn injury or fire. Software components, likewise, require predetermined and well-established criteria for engineering.

The *National Electrical Code* (*www.cssinfo.com/1999NEC.html*) used in the United States specifies requirements for electrical safety that have to be met for electrical components used in buildings. This code requires third-party certification, and if an electrical component with programmable software is to be used in a building, it must have associated evidence that it meets the electrical safety code. Certification means that the electrical component supplier, the software component producer, the authority having jurisdiction, and the consumer recognize that the UL mark on the product provides confidence that the code's standards have been met and the likelihood of electrical fire has been reduced.

A technical report or safety file contains the engineering evidence that these standards have been met. This report or file may be cumbersome to reproduce, especially if the intent is to demonstrate compliance with a specified set of requirements. Thus, product markings on a component quickly communicate conformance with safety-related requirements, including use limitations.

Product markings reduce the engineering data to easily recognizable and meaningful symbols. In the hardware industry, symbols are internationally specified and recognized for electrical safety. For example, the back of a power supply has a UL mark together with symbols that communicate conditions of use, as shown in Figure 38-1. The user can consult the technical file to obtain additional qualifying information.

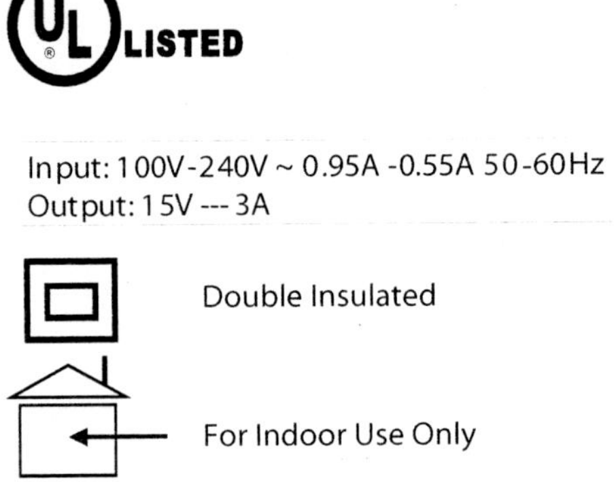

Figure 38-1: *Example markings used to convey information about a laptop power supply (IEC 60417-2).*

38.6 Certification in the Software Component Domain

The *STB610.12-1990, IEEE Standard Glossary of Software Engineering Terminology* defines certification as a written guarantee, a formal demonstration, or the process of confirming "that a system or component complies with its specified requirements and is acceptable for operational use." The expression of this confirmation could be a signature on a test summary form or report, a mark applied to the product, or a certificate that accompanies the product. If these specified requirements are explicitly defined in generally recognized standards, then the certification generally has more acceptability.

Figure 38-2 shows an example of one possible scenario of how a software component could be developed, tested, certified, and then used. Later in the chapter we will discuss some key questions that must be addressed before the successful deployment of a component. Standards play an important role in addressing how a component fits into an application environment and in how a component interacts with other local or remote components. Certification provides a mechanism for verifying compliance to the applicable standard.

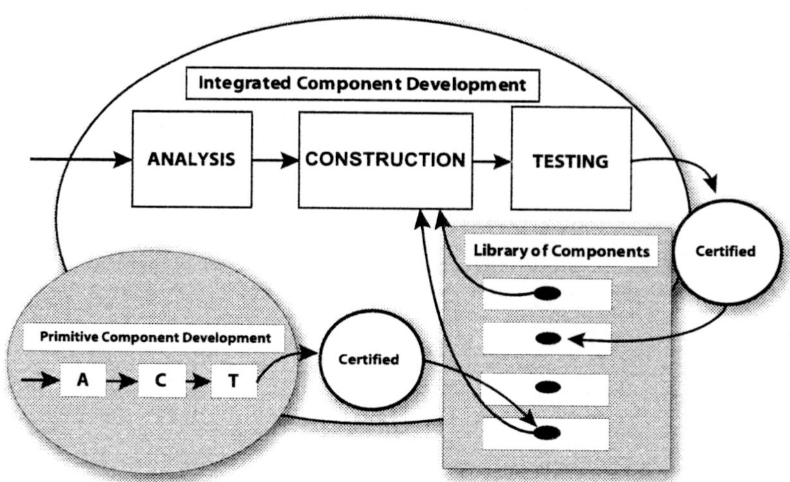

Figure 38-2: *A possible scenario of development, certification, and use of a component.*

We would like to discuss a commonly used term—*third-party* testing or certification. As the name suggests, it is testing or certification that an organization, independent of the producer, supplier, seller, buyer, government, or any other regulating body performs. Typically, a buyer or a regulator requires or requests certification to satisfy the purchaser about the product's acceptance or compliance with the contractor's precise requirements often according to standards—especially when safety and security are primary concerns. With the privatization of governmental functions, there is increasing use of third parties for testing that is independent, but recognized by the government. Third parties are also used to address business-to-business concerns, for example, to demonstrate interoperability among components.

The purpose of software component certification, then, would be to provide information about the component which 1) results in a software consumer reusing the component and 2) supports compliance with applicable standards. We believe that use of a third party to certify the relevance of the producer's answers to the questions shown in Questionnaires 38-1 and 38-2 will achieve this purpose with confidence. We also state with assurance that the answers do not come easily and require significant auditing.

For software certification, a mark, or certificate points to an online technical file that can be made accessible to users of the component, the technical file contains meta data about the component.

Specifications 38-1 provides examples of the type of information that could be included in the technical file. Additionally, standardized symbols—for example a symbol that indicates conformance with a particular interface definition language (IDL) specification—can be used to further reduce this information for rapid, meaningful conveyance. For example, markings associated with the standards shown in Specifications 38-1 could be developed if they do not already exist. Table 38-2 lists several component interface standards that could be used for marking.

Questionnaire 38-1
Questions That Are Of Interest to a Third-Party Certification Body

(Answered by the Component Producer)

- To what specification is the component designed, developed, tested?
- What kind of software life cycle was used? Did it include thorough risk analysis?
- What functionality does the software component provide and what is its intended use?
- Do the component's functions meet the design objectives without modification?
- Are there comprehensive test requirements, objectives, plans, scope, methodologies, and results? Please provide them in writing and UML diagrams, if applicable.
- Has the component been tested in established stress conditions, and, if so, how and for what intended uses?
- With what other components will the software components establish associations and dependencies?
- Demonstrate all associations and dependencies in UML diagrams.
- What is its memory space and execution time requirements, and to what workloads do they apply?
- What composition and interaction standards are adhered to? Demonstrate composition and interaction standards in UML diagrams.
- What use dependencies are not easily discernible?
- What assumptions about underlying microelectronic hardware and electrical/ mechanical hardware interfaces have been made? (For embedded systems)

The information in Specifications 38-1 in its entirety will not always be needed to successfully test a component. Nonetheless, if this information is made available, then consumers have more details for use during design, construction, and maintenance than if standardization and certification regulations were not available.

We have explained most of the key elements and critical variables associated with software components. We also described standards and their importance in determining suitability of a component in a given infrastructure. We also presented the role of third-party testing in verifying compliance to the applicable standards and the value of independent certification.

To a buyer or a user of the software component, all these are extremely important. It is also important to be aware of information needs and level of details for different group of users. For example, a component producer or a system integrator could benefit from considerable details about components, interfaces, infrastructures, component models, and component model implementation (see Chapter 1), while a user could be satisfied to know that some well respected, independent test laboratory has tested or certified the product. Figure 38-3 illustrates an example of a certificate that could be used to provide information that both could readily understand and use.

Questionnaire 38-2
Questions That Are Of Interest to A Consumer Of The Component

(Answered by the Seller of the Software Component)

- Who is the producer of the component and what is their contact information?
- Does the developer have an ISO 9000 registration, TickIt or SEI CMM assessment?
- Is the component functionality certified by a third party? By whom/when and what is the type of certification?
- What/Where/How can you find technical documentation? Provide all documentation for us.
- Is the role of component librarian established? Does someone function in that role *de facto*? Can this person find component versions for various releases of the product, along with associated interfaces, specifications, and design constraints?
- In what form are the specifications?
- What functionality does the component offer?
- What is its intended use?
- What are the limitations, restrictions, dependencies, and coexistence requirements?
- What are the environment assumptions (HW, SW, OS, CPU, User)?
- What composition and interaction standards are adhered to?

Specifications 38-1: *Examples of Meta DataThat Could Reside in a Technical File*

Description of the intended functionality and use of the component
Specification of interface, including conformance with interface definition languages (IDLs)
Data dictionary with semantic and type information
Package information
Specification of class libraries required for use
Specification of hardware dependencies and environmental assumptions
Component diagram
Specification of uses (for example, use case diagrams or usage models)
Activity diagram
Class diagram
Object diagram
Timing diagram
State transition diagram, for example, Statechart diagram
Description of producer design and verification activities
Summary and detailed results of producer verification activities

38.2 Conclusion

Some individuals will always oppose spending time, energy, and resources to do just a little more than absolutely required. It may even be very tempting to omit the extra steps, but in the end, it may not be the smartest choice. As Y2K crisis showed us all, standards can help in the long-term by making products safer and easier to maintain.

It is time that we, as software engineers, awaken and create a legacy for the future by developing standard-compliant designs and certifiably reusable components. The emergence of IEC and ANSI standards that contain requirements for application and embedded

Table 38-1: *Example Component Interface Standards That Could Be Used For Certification and Marking*

Software Component Certification Standards					
	OLE	SOM/ DSOM	OpenDoc	Corba	ALL+
Packaging					
Architectural Systems	x	x		x	
Component Access	x	x		x	
Naming Conventions	?	?		x	
Messaging/ Notification	x	x	x	x	
Object Versioning	x				
Functional Performance					
Register with Environment	x				
Performs to Specifications					x
Handles Exceptions	x				x
Communicates with Other Components	x		x	x	
Shares/Uses Data of Other Components	x		x	x	
No Functional Degradation with Other Components					x

software, in addition to the possible extension of ANSI/UL 1998 to the non-safety related CBSE approach, is certainly pushing us in this direction. Over the past 30 years, the field of computing has evolved tremendously, and the lessons learned from prior experience are not always carried forward from generation to generation. By following a defined process such as that required for a standard to achieve ANSI

Underwriters Laboratories, Inc.®

Programmable Systems Certificate

UL File EXXXXXX.EXXXX | Cert. No. 00PSCXXXX | Issued: (Project Completion Date)

ABD Corp.
1 Technology Lane
Research Triangle Park, NC 27709

is authorized to display this Certificate under the conditions stated in the Underwriters Laboratories Inc. Certification Report(s) for the product described as follows:

Product: : (Name of Programmable Industrial Control Equipment)

Product Description: : (Configuration Specification) - XXXX

Software Description: (Description of Configuration Specification)

Base Standards Profile: List of Standards Used) Example: UL 1998, First Edition, UL 508, Din V VDE 0801.01.90 and Amendment A1, 10.94

Software Standards Profile: (for use with software standards)

The above-described product meets the requirements of the standards specified above as long as the conditions stated in the Certification Report(s) are satisfied. The award of this Certificate is based upon document review and on-site assessment.

The name of Underwriters Laboratories Inc., any abbreviation thereof or any symbol, shall not be used on or in connection with the product or any marketing activities unless and until specifically authorized by the certification organization as a result of establishment of appropriate service.

Underwriters Laboratories Inc., issuing this Declaration of Programmable Systems Conformity, in recognizing the reviews, assessment and tests conducted, does not assume or undertake to discharge any responsibility of the above-named company to any other party(ies). The opinions and findings of Underwriters Laboratories Inc. represent its judgment given, with due consideration to the necessary limitations of practical operation and in accordance with its objects and purposes and Underwriters Laboratories Inc. does not warrant or guarantee the correctness of its opinions or that its finding will be recognized or accepted.

Figure 38-1: *Example of a certificate.*

status, a baseline set of practices can be codified. Through open communication with industry and technical associations, data studies, and previous experience, a practical and solid technical basis for the standard can be formed.

In the future, the marketplace may eventually not permit embedded or application software, including operating system products, that have not demonstrated compliance to software standards. The safety and quality concerns of retailers and consumers are a strong impetus driving the realization of such a drastic measure against potentially substandard products. People in some of the highest levels of government hear and share these concerns, as is evidenced by the European Union Directives and U.S. Codes. Another driving force behind the move toward standardization is business-to-business concerns associated with security and confidentiality. It is to this end that we can strive to effect meaningful software component certifications.

About Underwriter's Laboratories

Underwriters Laboratories Inc. (UL) is an independent, not-for-profit product safety testing and certification organization. We have tested products for public safety for more than a century. Each year, more than 16 billion UL marks are applied to products worldwide.

Since our founding in 1894, we have held the undisputed reputation as the leader in U.S. product safety and certification. Building on our household name in the United States, UL is becoming one of the most recognized, reputable conformity assessment providers in the world. Today, our services extend to helping companies achieve global acceptance, whether it is an electrical device, a programmable system, or a company's quality process.

- Estimated UL Marks appearing on new products in 1999: **16.1 billion**
- Product evaluations in 1999: **94,396**
- Follow-up service visits in 1999 to audit compliance with product certification requirements: **509,442**
- Consumers UL reached with safety messages in the U.S. and Canada during 1999: **110 million**
- Total number of current UL Standards: **748**
- Countries with UL customers: **89**
- Staff of the UL family of companies ready to serve customers: **5,644**
- UL Inspection Centers: **193** in 71 countries
- Laboratory testing and certification facilities in the UL family of companies: **46**
- Number of product types UL evaluates: **18,059**
- Total number of facilities registered by UL to a management system standard as of 1999: **4,089**
- Number of manufacturers producing UL-certified products: **58,684**

Chapter 39

Commercial Law Applicable to Component-Based Software

Stephen Y. Chow

39.1 Introduction

Even as CBSE is perceived as the next step in software engineering towards the "real world" of manufacturing nuts and bolts, "digital convergence" is forcing that world to change. The essentially perfect and virtually costless reproducibility and transmissibility of digital information makes it difficult to cleanly apply the existing laws for developing, transferring, and using that information. Two bodies of law, intellectual property law and commercial law, have intersected—some say collided—in application to this new world.

39.2 Intellectual Property and Commercial Law

Information products are "public goods" that once created are not inherently limited to a few consumers by relative scarcity of production or by exhaustion of the products or their raw materials, as are "ordinary" goods such as toasters. Historically, intellectual property laws such as the federal Copyright Act (*www.legal.gsa.gov/fedfra23.htm*) have been applied to limit distribution of, and by such "propertization" allow collection of "rent" for information products such as printed books. The distribution of information through the vehicle of a book is limited because of the number of copies printed and the degrading of physical material (ink, paper, and book covers) over time. There are no such limitations for digital information. Thus, intellectual property laws carry more of the burden of providing a framework in which the producers and distributors of digital information products can extract compensation for their investments and efforts.

In further contrast to information products published in print, digital information products typically include *functionality* in digital computer code as an important part of the value added, and sought to be collected, by the producer. The assessment of the value of functionality of a digital information product is made the same way as it is for traditional goods—by posing questions such as, "Does it work? How well does it work? Does it meet the expectations of the buyer or the representations of the vendor?" For some digital information products such as DVD movies or multimedia content, these questions are simply about the functionality of the vehicle, with that deterministic functionality being evaluated objectively (does the DVD work?) and the aesthetically oriented "content" being evaluated more subjectively (is the movie good?).

In other digital information products, however, the aesthetic element is subsidiary to the function of the product, such as in digital computer programs for "number-crunching." The function of accuracy is essential, although the aesthetic aspects of the user interface may be important just as the typography and quality of paper for a book is. In each of these cases, components of the digital information products—software components, the subject of this book—must function with other computer programs with less tolerance for error than most "physical" components. Because functionality is a primary issue, the commercial law applicable to the sale of goods, Uniform Commercial Code Article 2 ([UCC Article 2] [*www.law.cornell.edu/ucc/ucc.table.html*]) has been applied to computer programs. Thus, both intellectual law and commercial law have been applied to computer program transactions, depending on whether an issue arises as to the product's creation or distribution or to its performance or functionality.

There have been no "market failures" universally recognized as caused by the dual application of these two bodies of laws. Nonetheless, well before the rise of the Internet, large software and database publishers, such as Microsoft and the National Association of Securities Dealers Automated Quotation (NASDAQ) system, which receives significant revenues from licensing of trading data, promoted the revision of UCC Article 2 for their industries. In 1999, this modification became the Uniform Computer Information Transactions Act ([UCITA] [*www.law.upenn.edu/bll/ulc/ulc.htm*]). Billed as an "economic statute" to attract information industries, UCITA was enacted in 2000 in the rival states of Virginia and Maryland, and has been introduced in seven other states and the District of Columbia.

This chapter reviews the intellectual property law considerations applicable to software component developers and distributors, including the development of an intellectual property portfolio. Chapter 40 reviews the commercial law considerations, including UCITA, applicable to writing and negotiating contracts involving software components.

39.3 Applicability of Intellectual Property Law to Software

Property law is the body of law by which a property owner may prevail upon the courts or administrative agencies of a government to aid the owner in excluding others from exercising or "trespassing" upon its property rights recognized under the law. While real property law involves rights to occupation and use of land, intellectual property law involves specific rights to various activities relating to "intellectual" pursuits, such as the activities recognized under the United States Constitution that authorized Congress to enact statutes "[t]o promote the progress of science and the useful arts, by securing for limited times to authors and inventors the exclusive right to their respective writings and discoveries"

([Article 1, section 8, clause 9, U.S. Constitution] [*www.law.cornell.edu/constitution/constitution.articlei.html*]). Accordingly, the first versions of the federal Patent Act and Copyright Act were enacted in 1790. Interestingly, however, protection of the fruits of software development was not fully available under patent law until relatively recently.

39.3.1 Trade Secrets and the Origin of Licensing

Traditionally, the branch of intellectual property law most applicable to software was trade secret law, that is, the "common law" created by state courts that protected the expectations of trade secret owners against intrusions or breaches of confidence that offended local standards of business conduct. These are considered "misappropriation" of trade secrets.

The sale of software prior to the mid-1970s was usually part of hardware sales or leases. During this heavy antitrust-enforcement era, patents were disfavored as "monopolistic" by most federal courts. The Uniform Trade Secrets Act (UTSA) was written and promoted to the states by NCCUSL as the favored way to protect technological advances. To bring a lawsuit under UTSA, a software development organization (SDO) needs to show an intentional misappropriation of valuable confidential information for which reasonable steps were taken since the property owner's "promise not to sue" for use of what otherwise would have been the exclusive "right" or "property" of the owner. Nonexclusive licenses were thus "personal" to the purchaser of the software license ("the *licensee*"), so that without additional grants, the nonexclusive licensee could not transfer to another party the property owner's promise not to sue the licensee. This was different from other personal property, such as movable goods, for which Anglo-Saxon common law had established a presumption against restraints on transfer in favor of free commerce.

The state of intellectual property law concerning software underwent significant change in the late 1970s, making copyright law the most relevant body of law, and again in the late 1990s. Therefore, patent law became a major factor in developing and marketing software.

39.3.2 Copyright Law and "Licensing" as Nonsale

As the market for computer software expanded in the 1970s and "off-the-shelf" computer programs became available separately from their hardware platforms, vendors saw their roles as publishers and thus followed the model of the print publishers who relied on the Copyright Act. This coincided with the disfavoring of patents and the enactment of a major modification of the copyright law in the Copyright Revision Act of 1976 (*lcweb.loc.gov/copyright/title17*).

Under preexisting practice, codified in the 1976 Act, copyright law gives the copyright owner exclusive rights to reproduce, distribute, and make "derivative works" from the copyrighted "works." Only "expressions" of ideas rather than the ideas themselves or the functionality of the works are protected. Prior to 1978, when the 1976 act took effect, a federal copyright of twenty-eight years (renewable for another twenty-eight years) vested upon publication of a copyrightable work with a copyright notice. This scheme shared with the federal patent scheme the same constitutional basis of an "economic bargain" in which one could obtain a limited monopoly from the federal government in return for disclosure to the public. Beginning in 1978, under the new law, a copyright was automatically created upon the recording of an eligible "work" on a tangible medium. Since 1988, copyright notices have not been required at all, although it may be useful to provide actual notice of a claim to copyright.

"Computer programs" were not previously mentioned in the text of the 1976 Act, but were recognized as copyrightable in a backhanded way when, in 1980, Congress amended the 1976 Copyright Act to provide exceptions to the exclusive rights of the owner of copyrights in computer programs to allow an owner of a *copy* of a computer program to make an archival copy and to modify the copy "as an essential step in the utilization of the computer program in conjunction with a machine"(Pub. L. No. 96-517, 94 Stat 3015, 3028, Dec. 12, 1980). This and the "fair use" and "first sale" provisions of the 1976 Copyright Act (17 U.S.C. 107 and 109) have led to subsequent disputes over the extent to which "reverse engineering" of a copyright computer program is allowed.

The purchaser of a product protected by intellectual property ordinarily has an implied license to use the product for its intended purpose, and an intellectual property owner, having once received payment for use of the product, ordinarily has "exhausted its monopoly" with respect to that product upon that "first sale." The 1976 Copyright Act expressly provided for first sale rights for the owner of a copy to transfer (but not duplicate) the copy without requiring permission from the copyright owner. A secondary rental market developed for videotapes under these first sale rights, but has been avoided for computer programs through 1990 legislation specifically excluding under the first sale provision any right to rent by the owner of a copy of a computer program other than a video game for "limited purpose" computers, such as game consoles ([Computer Software Rental Amendments Act of 1990, Pub. L. 100-617, 102 Stat. 3194] [Dec. 1, 1990]).

The rise of the mass-market software publishing industry presented a number of difficulties for its lawyers, most of whom either had an intellectual property law background or a commercial law background, but not both. One issue that needed to be addressed was the relationship between the software publisher and the end-user within a mediated distribution chain. The existing intellectual property paradigm, including software licensing as licensing of "know-how," was one of licensing and sublicensing down the chain. In the retail sale of goods, the concept of a remote contract formed between the producer and the ultimate user was and remains strained, with theories of "pass-through" warranties and limitations of those warranties. In the 1980s, the industry developed the concept of a "shrinkwrap" license, where license terms could be viewed through the cellophane shrinkwrap around the package containing the software (such as a package of 5-1/4" floppy disks) along with a warning that opening would result in agreement to those terms. The marketers soon prevailed in putting the terms inside the box, out of view, to allow for more marketing material on the outside of the box.

The difficulty then arose that a purchaser on the open market would have paid for the copy along with sales tax and certainly believed he owned at least the copy. The industry at least half-believed that consumers had first sale rights, since it succeeded in having Congress limit those rights in 1990. Notices that the phrase "this software is licensed" would appear the same as a videotape notice, "licensed for home use only," thus having no more effect than prior notices in books that "this book may not be resold for less than a dollar." Any ambiguous limitation on ownership of the copy would be read against the publisher and in favor of first sale rights. A state law validating shrinkwrap contracts—enacted by the Louisiana legislature to attract software developers to their state—was found unconstitutional in 1988 by a federal appellate court as contrary to the elimination of state common law copyright by the 1976 Copyright Act (*Vault Corp. v. Quaid Software, Ltd.*, 847 F.2d 255 [5th Cir. 1988]).

Throughout the 1980s and up until 1995, software was protected by trade secrets and copyrights. Source code and algorithms were kept secret, while copyrights were asserted against those who copied user interfaces. Globally, the United States Trade Representative was able to force other countries to grant copyright protection to software even where the source code was held secret. The Free Software Foundation, with its General Public License, sometimes called a "copyleft" license (*www.gnu.org/philosophy*), notably departed from this pattern by offering a free license as long as the original source code were transmitted along the distribution chain at cost with appropriate notices.

The high-water mark for copyright protection for software was reached in two federal court decisions. First, in 1986, the Philadelphia federal court of appeals ruled that the copyright of the "structure, sequence, and organization" of a dental office program was infringed by the writing of a program with the same functionality for a different hardware platform ([*Whelan Associates, Inc. v. Jaslow Laboratory, Inc.*, 797 F.2d 1222 3rd Cir. 1986, *cert. denied*, 479 U.S. 1031 1987] [*www.columbia.edu/~law9023/whelan_v_jaslow*]). Second, in 1993, a Massachusetts federal district court decided that Borland's Quattro Pro product, compatible with Lotus's then-popular "1-2-3" spreadsheet product, violated Lotus's alleged copyright in the "look and feel" of Lotus's user interface (*Lotus Development Corp. v. Borland International, Inc.*, 831 F. Supp. 223 D. Mass. 1993, *rev'd*, 49 F.3d 807 [1st Cir. 1995], *aff'd by equally divided Court*, 516 U.S. 233 [1996]).

In 1995, however, the Boston federal court of appeals reversed the *Borland* decision. It found the user interface uncopyrightable because it was dictated too much by functionality and contained too little of what is protected by copyright, namely "original expression." (*Lotus Development Corp. v. Borland International, Inc.*, 49 F.3d 807 [1st Cir. 1995], *aff'd by equally divided Court*, 516 U.S. 233 [1996]). An equally divided Supreme Court allowed the decision to stand.

The current state of copyright law for determining whether a computer program violates a copyright in another application, where the alleged copying is not "literal," involves the "abstraction-filtration-comparison" test set down in 1991 by the New York federal court of appeals (*Computer Associates International, Inc. v. Altai, Inc.*, 982 F.2d 693 [2nd Cir. 1991]; *www.columbia.edu/~law9023/altai.wl*). In that test, alleged similarities are first sorted into "levels of abstraction" ranging from uncopyrightable "idea" to detailed, copyrightable "expression." Then, alleged similarities dictated by functional requirements of the level of abstraction are filtered out. Finally, comparisons are made. If there remain substantial similarities, infringement may be found.

39.3.3 The New Relevance of Patent Law

The United States Patent and Trademark Office (USPTO) responded in 1996 to the diminished copyright protection of software under *Borland* by relaxing the artificial barriers that had evolved to screen unpatentable "mathematical algorithms" from patentable "computer-related inventions" (software disguised as hardware [*www.uspto.gov*]). Previously, patent practitioners had to be careful that claims to software inventions somehow acted on a physical article or involved some physical structure. The Federal Circuit Court of Appeals, created in 1982 to consolidate all patent appeals cases among the regional circuit courts of appeals, generally approved the USPTO's approach, finding computer programs patentable as creating "useful, concrete, tangible result(s)."

A turning point in the use of patents to protect software was the December 1999 injunction that Amazon.com obtained against rival Barnesandnoble.com for infringing on their "one-click" patent (*amazon.com, Inc. v. Barnesandnoble.com, Inc.*, 73 F. Supp. 2d 1228). Soon after, many venture capital fund managers, particularly on the West Coast, changed their prior admonition of "don't reinvent the wheel, just copy what's working" and demanded that their portfolio companies and prospective investees establish "patent positions" by filing provisional patent applications to stake a claim to their business plans. This put in place the current conditions under which enterprises with new technologies are well advised to stake their own claims at least defensively to preempt a competitor filing or to have a "bargaining chip" for cross-licensing. (The second entrant often has a more optimal approach to a marketplace that is rapidly changing and, with a patent stake, can say, "If you don't let me practice your patent, you can't practice my patent, which covers the practical way of doing this.") One positive side benefit of the patent process is that it forces the software developer to provide some documentation of the operation of the code.

39.4 Conclusion

This review of how the "property" interest in software is protected provides an outline for how companies should develop contracts for the development and distribution of technology. A software component producer or consumer should be careful to understand and protect its property rights in a product to

- Obtain nondisclosure and technology transfer agreements from key personnel and trading partners
- Establish a culture of carefully managing valuable information
- Register copyrights in every substantive release of code
- Keep inventor notebooks witnessed periodically
- Consider filing patent applications for important advances in the product, even in the development and distribution models

A strong intellectual property portfolio provides leverage in negotiations with suppliers, customers, and investors. It provides a basis for taking advantage of the new "licensing" model of reserving rights in the use of software in the hands of customers.

Chapter 40

The Effects of UCITA on Software Component Development and Marketing

Stephen Y. Chow

40.1 Introduction

The previous chapter summarizes the principal ways available under United States law to protect the production and distribution rights of software component producers. This chapter presents how written contracts protect the rights of both component producers and component consumers. The basic dilemma in writing a contract for selling a software component is whether the courts view the component as "goods" or "services," because different legal principles protect each.

40.1.1 The Uniform Commercial Code Framework

Since the late nineteenth century, the National Conference of Commissioners on Uniform State Laws (NCCUSL) has drafted uniform laws that it promotes for uniform enactment in the states to enhance commerce (*www.nccusl.org*). The most successful of the uniform laws is the Uniform Commercial Code (UCC), which has been adopted by every state of the Union (with some differences in such places as Louisiana, which has a civil law tradition; see *www.lasc.org/history.html*), and has simplified commerce for two generations. UCC Article 2 on the sale of goods has been extended internationally in the Convention on International Sale of Goods ([CISG] [*www.cisg.law.pace.edu*]). Parties must expressly opt out of CISG, which distributors of products should do if they are unsure of their rights under the CISG.

UCC Article 2 governs various aspects of the sale of goods from formation of a contract through performance of the contract and remedies for breach. Article 2 provides default rules ("gap-fillers") where the parties have not expressly agreed on terms. Because it is a product of the late 1940s through 1960s, UCC Article 2 was informed by the rise of mass production of manufactured goods and their distribution often as "fungible" (replaceable by one equal part or quantity) goods to a developing retail market that may be viewed as a "mass-market." What was important was whether products in fact worked. Thus, provisions are included in UCC Article 2 for implied warranties of "merchantability" and "fitness (for a particular purpose)."

Moreover, Article 2 introduced the concept of "blanket assent." The concept of "a meeting of the minds" to support a "contract" was difficult to apply to a world where some deals were done on a handshake or over the counter in exchange for immediate payment, although the concept persists today in the nonretail situation. UCC Article 2 tends to "save deals" by recognizing the existence of a contract, even if terms set forth in the parties' respective writings (such as a purchase order or an invoice) differ. All terms consistent with the agreement are made part of the contract, and subsequent materially different terms are treated as counter-offers. The "battle of the forms" was resolved more than two generations ago by standard forms commercial lawyers drafted for their clients.

Other parts of the UCC that NCCUSL and its partner on UCC matters since the 1970s, the American Law Institute (ALI), intermittently review include provisions for payment systems, letters of credit, warehouse receipts, and other commercial transaction issues (see *www.nccusl.org*).

40.2 Software Components as Goods Versus Services

UCC Article 2 covers complicated nonconsumer goods, such as airplanes or electrostatic precipitators for air pollution control. Such products are "movable," that is, not a fixture attached to real property (that is considered unique), and the main object of the underlying contract is to obtain services (considered personal). Characterizing a product as a UCC Article 2 good subjected it to such default rules as the "perfect tender rule," under which a product could be rejected if it did not comport perfectly with the performance required under contract. Characterizing the product as the result of a service contract, however, subjected the performance to a test of "substantial performance" often measured by a standard of reasonable care by the service provider. The view was that the vendee specifically chose the service provider, so that the relationship was "personal" and not easily transferable.

When software was distributed on magnetic tapes, a contract for providing software was often treated as a service contract and often provided for professional attention to installation and testing. The service contract conformed to the traditional model of technology transfer through "licensing" of trade secrets, as discussed in Chapter 39. This concept of licensing was not expressly included under the federal Robinson-Patman Act ([15 U.S.C. sec. 13] [see *www.law.cornell.edu/topics/antitrust.html*]), which largely prohibited discrimination in prices charged for goods sold or leased. Thus began the tradition of software "licensing," which has come to mean something other than simply licensing under intellectual property law.

With the advent of off-the-shelf computer programs, courts began to find that computer programs were either "goods" or very much like "goods," and thus governed by UCC Article 2. Subsequently, most software vendors followed commercial practice and disclaimed implied warranties and limited modification according to the standard rules of practice under UCC Article 2. For more than a generation, this treatment of software as "goods" did not result in any recognized harm to the software industry.

In 1991, in the *Step-Saver* decision of the federal appellate court in Philadelphia that UCC Article 2 applied to the case where off-the-shelf software had been ordered under one set of terms and was delivered with a different terms inside the box, the court found the terms in the box that were materially different from those presented leading to shipment of the software unenforceable ([*Step-Saver Data Systems, Inc. v. Wyse Step-Saver Data Systems, Inc.*, 939 F.2d 91] [3rd Cir. 1991]). This decision appeared to firmly place noncustom software within the scope of UCC Article 2.

In 1996, the Chicago federal appellate court, in its *ProCD* decision, reached a different conclusion and enforced the provisions of a "click wrap" agreement restricting a CD-resident telephone directory that was alphabetically organized to nonbusiness use. That directory was "licensed" in both business and nonbusiness versions at significantly different prices (*ProCD, Inc., v. Zeidenberg*, 86 F.3d 1447 [7th Cir. 1996]). The *ProCD* court nonetheless applied UCC Article 2 principles in a "rolling contract" approach, finding that the "click wrap" terms were proposed modifications accepted by the vendee, who clearly knew of the restriction from multiple notices both in paper and electronic form and his purchase and use of multiple copies.

As of the mid-1990s (although there was some grumbling from "computer law" practitioners), it was generally assumed that UCC Article 2 would apply to computer programs that were marketed as products with minimal customization required. In more developmental projects, the service component dominated, and the common law of service contracts applied.

40.3 The Uniform Computer Information Transactions Act

Apparently in response to the 1991 *Step-Saver* decision and other cases following it, and with the rapid rise of the mass-market software industry in the same time period, the Business Software Alliance ([BSA] [*www.bsa.org*]), dominated by Microsoft Corporation, joined in the revision of UCC Article 2 by NCCUSL and ALI. In 1995, the BSA succeeded in spinning out of the revision process a proposed new UCC Article 2B addressed to "licensing" (*www.law.upenn.edu/bll/ulc/ucc2/ucc2b296.htm*).

The same questions faced the mass-market software industry as faced mass producers of "traditional goods": What is the contract? Does the product work as warranted? Proposed UCC Article 2B provided different answers to the same UCC Article 2 questions that BSA said reflected the inherent "bugginess" of software, particularly software provided at low prices that fueled the recent advances in the American economy. In their words, "the perfect tender rule [should] be abolished with respect to software contracts because of the complexity of the software product and the fact that minor flaws ("bugs") are common in virtually all software. The perfect tender rule is not well suited to this technology."

The UCC Article 2B paradigm of "license of information" rather than the "sale-of-a-copy-plus-license-of-copyright" understood by most intellectual property lawyers also would support the argument that a vendee would have no "first sale" right to resell the copy or modify it for interoperability (as discussed in Chapter 39).

Early proponents for the project included NASDAQ and the New York Stock Exchange (NYSE), who sought to buttress their contractual restrictions on retransmitting securities trading data within the first fifteen minutes of trade. The enforceability of these contractual restrictions was deemed necessary to maintain fees charged for such data in light of the Supreme Court's preclusion of copyright protection for factual information organized in obvious ways (such as an alphabetical list of phone numbers [*Feist Publications, Inc. v. Rural Telephone Service Co.*, 499 U.S. 340] [1991]) and the New York federal appellate court's limitation of protection of "hot news" to cases of actual competition (which did not exist between Motorola and the National Basketball Association (NBA) in the case of near-real-time broadcast to personal pagers of basketball scores [*National Basketball Association v. Motorola, Inc.*, 105 F.3d 841 [2nd Cir. 1997]).

Early opponents to the project included the motion picture industry, which was concerned that the extension of UCC Article 2 to "digital information" would implicate their motion pictures on warranty issues previously applicable only to "functional" products. Although these particular concerns have been neutralized by exclusions of the studios' "core" transactions and other inducements, their concerns remain for other information-oriented enterprises that do not share their lobbying prowess.

Partly because of the broad and vague scope of proposed UCC Article 2B, the ALI refused to endorse it, thereby preventing Article 2B from becoming part of the Uniform Commercial Code. NCCUSL renamed the proposed statute the Uniform Computer Information Transactions Act (UCITA) and put it out for a field test in 1999 following intense and continuing opposition. As of July 2000, Virginia and Maryland enacted UCITA with amendments, while Iowa enacted a UCITA "bomb shelter" invalidating the choice of UCITA as law. As of April 2001, seven other states are actively considering UCITA, as well as the District of Columbia.

UCITA favors software and other digital information *publishers* (at the expense of "upstream" authors and downstream users) for at least the following reasons.

1. UCITA provides a mechanism for a digital information publisher to present additional contractual terms at the "click wrap" stage, when the consumer accesses the information for the first time. These terms may be materially different from those of any earlier deal, thereby preventing the contract from being formed prior to clicking. The materially different terms need not be enforced, but should be unlikely to be part of an earlier deal, for example, an agreement not to comment on the performance of a product.
2. UCITA generally allows any term that is not substantively unconscionable (found in no more than a dozen cases in the forty years of UCC Article 2) and that does not "violate the fundamental public policies of the state" (which enacted UCITA). The common "fair use" defense to a federal copyright infringement action would be subjected to much higher hurdles in a state breach of contract case under UCITA.
3. UCITA provides for "releases" from upstream authors to publishers without compensation and limits the possibility of implied contracts in submissions of ideas. UCITA treats all digital information as manufactured products for the purposes of title and non-

infringement warranties, thereby imposing such warranties on unsuspecting upstream authors.

4. To appease the motion picture industry, UCITA now provides that contracts for submissions of ideas are not enforceable unless the ideas are "confidential, concrete, and novel to the business, trade, or industry or the party receiving the disclosure otherwise expressly agreed." Licenses of know-how that do not expressly provide for effectiveness even if the know-how is not "concrete" might be subject to challenge. On the other hand, nondisclosure agreements that expressly restrict disclosure of nonconfidential information may be unenforceable on other grounds.

5. UCITA is not necessarily good for component consumers or integrators of components, hardware, or other software at least because of the above reasons and for the following additional reasons.

   - UCITA creates "remote privity," that is, a direct contract between the "licensor" of digital information and the user "licensee," even if there are intervening sellers, to bind the licensee to license restrictions. This may allow remote downstream users to sue upstream producers directly on warranty matters. Even the users are indirect purchasers and, therefore, without traditional contractual privity.
   - UCITA authorizes "electronic self-help," that is, the remote activation of software devices to disable software products, sometimes used by smaller developers when they believe a user is in breach of a license agreement, for example, by late payment. UCITA authorizes this highly controversial procedure subject to "safeguards," including the imposition of consequential damages, not waivable by contract, for improper use of the procedure. However, smaller developers do not have the means to pay such damages, so that, faced with an environment in which electronic self-help is authorized, a prudent customer would avoid the smaller developers or require a bond to cover such damages.
   - UCITA enables stand-alone software producers to embed their contract terms as "click wrap" and keep those terms away from the eyes of "whistleblowers" (the producers could argue that it is too expensive or "impractical" to reveal these terms in

advance). Component producers, on the other hand, typically must disclose all their specifications and contractual terms for their customers to be assured that the components are appropriate for the job: trusted components are only components that have sufficient documentation of the component and its interfaces to permit the end user to maintain or modify the component for its own particular purposes.

- UCITA establishes a baseline of low quality from those with the market power to impose terms through "click wrap" agreements. Upstream developers who do not have such market power may still be held to higher standards.

In any case, it is likely that CBSE must measure up to the quality standards similar to that for hardware components. The acceptability of software components will turn on whether components meet the expectations of users, namely that the components function reliably, predictably, and deterministically. Components used in consumer products, both hardware and software, have been held to high standards, while application and system software for the mass market have not. Because UCITA has been driven by the mass-market publishers, it sets a low standard for those publishers but a higher one for upstream developers. It would be in the interest of the component producer for the software component consumer to be held to the same standards of quality, lest end-user lawsuits be funneled to the component producer.

40.4 Contract Issues in CBSE Transactions

Whether or not UCITA will be widely adopted remains an open issue. UCITA is a very complex statute with multiple redundancies. It stands in stark contrast to the Uniform Electronic Transactions Act (UETA) also promoted by the NCCUSL, which has enjoyed many more state adoptions(*www.nccusl.org/uniformact_summaries/uniformacts-s-ueta.htm*). There, the drafting approach was guided by the principle that law should not precede the development of technology and the marketplace. The recent federal Electronic Signature in Global and National

Commerce Act adopted much of UETA and arguably preempts UCITA's electronic contracting provisions.

However, UCITA has already had some effect, for example, by negating "first sale" rights where an agreement referring to "sales" of software nonetheless had enough restrictions on post-sale use to convince a court to treat the agreement as a "license." Component-based software developers may similarly "license" their components, but questions remain on whether that is an appropriate model for many licensees (the mass market) and what restrictions should be applied.

It is not likely that the use of "click wrap" contract terms would help component-based software developers gain acceptance in the marketplace, but some form of "click wrap" may be necessary in some cases to balance the new risk of liability to remote purchasers. The component consumer may address this risk through indemnification. The underlying question is whether the software component vendor wishes to

- Establish multiple remote contractual relationships to control use of the component
- Rely only on the component consumer to protect the component contractually from copying
- Protect the component through intellectual property, such as a patent. This alternative provides the most autonomy for the component vendor by limiting contractual privity and its attendant potential liability. It has the further advantage of creating asset value in the company

To the extent possible, the component producer should seek licensing-back of improvements or new uses of its components. The producer should also have the consumer disclose the intended use of the component to determine whether use restrictions have been violated or intellectual property infringed, and potential liability should be identified.

A joint development agreement with a component producer may be appropriate under certain circumstances. In such a case, a fair allocation of the fruits of development is crucial and should be reduced to writing. Often, both producer and consumer expend extensive resources beyond those originally anticipated to produce a marketable end-product, but a supply agreement may reserve all intellectual property to one or the other party, resulting in an adversarial situation that may be destructive to both parties. Such conditions should be anticipated to the extent possible.

40.5 Liability in CBSE Transactions

A computer program is generally treated as a manufactured good for the purposes of product liability. Attempts to disclaim such liability have had a mixed history of success because product liability is based on expectations rather than formal agreements. In the mass market, warranty obligations typically are passed through to the user.

UCITA exacerbates the liability issue for a component vendor. Because the component consumer will disclaim all liabilities as may be the custom in distribution to users, the component vendor becomes an important target. The component vendor should ask for allocation of various risks according to the expectations between them. Thus, the vendor should require indemnification, that is, to be "made whole," by the consumer for any liability of the vendor caused by use of the components in contexts other than the ones disclosed by the consumer, while indemnifying the consumer for errors caused by the components in normal use.

40.6 Putting It Together

A typical "long form" contract, negotiated by the parties for development/supply of software components will have the following provisions.

1. Recitals of the objects of the agreement, often referring to the intellectual property involved
2. Definitions, particularly of the product and often with specifications appended
3. Any developmental obligations such as consulting time, documentation, and confidential treatment and return of documentation

4. A grant of an intellectual property license (recall that unless otherwise stated, nonexclusive licenses are deemed nontransferable and non-sublicensable. If treated as a sale, traditionally, the property right is exhausted, but in today's world of software license, one might treat distribution to end-users with a sublicense, and obligate the consumer/licensee to provide sublicense terms to the producer/licensor's satisfaction as a condition of the license)
5. Delivery terms (who bears risk in transport), possible escrowing of source code
6. Payment terms, record keeping, audit rights, financing terms (the producer may authorize a third-party lender to take a security interest)
7. Representations and warranties. Typically for components, a warranty to meet the specification and regulations (including export) or to remedy to the specification. Because of UCITA, the consumer should require that the producer warrant that there is no electronic self-help device for disablement of the component controlled by anyone except the user
8. Disclaimers of other warranties, including implied warranties, and limitation of liability. Usually the producer warrants noninfringement, although in the software industry, often there is only a representation of "no knowledge" of infringement of patents (which may be in gestation). The obligation to remedy may be limited to negotiating a license or providing alternative technology, and liability may be limited to the contract price, typically in software transactions. Both parties disclaim liability for consequential and incidental damages
9. Confidentiality obligations (restriction to need-to-know, possibly financing professionals, continuing obligation unless information publicly available through no fault of the obliged party)
10. Term, natural termination, cancellation for breach, what survives (typically confidentiality)
11. Notices. Because of the possibility of "click wrap" modifications to the terms, these should be to specific people by specific means
12. Integration. This is the entire agreement, there are no "handshake" agreements

13. Modification only in writing notified to specific people by specific means
14. Choice of law and forum, typically the law and forum most comfortable for the party with better leverage, possibly a UCITA jurisdiction for producer and a non-UCITA jurisdiction for a consumer, disclaimer of CISG, possible submission to arbitration, with rules of the American Arbitration Association or the International Chamber of Commerce selected

"Short form" agreements may be used in "click wraps." These typically include the grant of a license, a disclaimer of warranties and limitation of liability, and the choice of law and forum. In component licensing, the consumer usually includes such agreements in distribution to the user. The producer should reserve the right to review these agreements.

40.7 Conclusion

Although UCITA is unlikely to be uniformly or even widely enacted, software component producers are well advised to select a state that has enacted UCITA as providing the applicable law for "construction" or interpretation of a contract and as the forum for resolution of disputes, as UCITA's rules tend to favor publishers of "computer information" (*www.law.upenn.edu/bll/ulc/ucita/ucita600c.htm*). For the same reason, software consumers and end-users, to the extent that they are able, should resist.

Part VIII

Summary

Introduction

We are concerned that this part of the book could be the most overlooked. However, in many ways, the chapters in this part are some of the most important. Below are some of the "what ifs" that make the chapters so vital to the book.

- What if I were to prepared to enter into a contract, but the contract required that I had to have a licensed software engineer managing the CBSE process for the component or infrastructure subject to commerce?
- What if I had to demonstrate that my company's software component infrastructure and required components were subject to prior patents or patents pending?
- What if during a patent search, a student's dissertation was discovered as patent pending, and while the dissertation is a theoretical work, my company's infrastructure and components are real and marketable? Can I sell my component products without fear of liability? Can I close the deal with my purchaser when I disclose the pending patent, or will the purchaser wait for a settlement or trial decision?

- The Uniform Commercial Information Transaction Act (UCITA) is passed in my state and I'm a component consumer. I assemble components and write interfaces and wrappers to legacy code for customers. What if the consumer sues me for defects that I know are attributable to the component producer? What are my rights?
- What if one of my customers demands third-party certification before the customer is willing to purchase an expensive software component-based system with a significant number of reusable components? What do I have to do to comply with third-party certification? Is it just testing, or does the certifier want to do more? So far, I haven't produced a lot of documentation with my components. Will I have to produce lots of documentation to satisfy the certifiers?

These chapters intend to answer each question and many more in extensive detail. The authors of the chapters respond to the needs of a technical audience by answering those technical questions with engineering, business, and legal answers in an informal language we all can understand.

One Best Way and Project Management

John Speed and the coeditors tackle the issues of professionalism of component-based software engineers and the minimum training to perform as manager of a CBSE project or product-line reuse program. Because of the uniformity of engineering training, whether chemical or mechanical engineering, one form of problem-solving binds engineers together—Frederick Taylor's "the one best way" (Kanigel, 1997). In addition, each discipline of engineering is bound to the practice of a body of knowledge.

Until CBSE adopts the one best way, which Speed, Councill, and Heineman (see Chapter 37) identify as a process for resolving problems that involves breaking large problems into smaller ones and implementing solutions as discrete "components," the emerging discipline will have difficulty developing a body of knowledge. Our experience with organizations that want to transition from object-orientation to CBD without first implementing a measurement and metrics program indicates resistance to measuring the success of breaking problems into smaller, manageable problems and then selecting a solution. The simple metrics of success or failure with the one best way provides the organization with considerable information about the project team or the subproject team, as well as the verification of managers' precise directives by subordinates concerning the selected solution.

A New Educational Curriculum Including Engineering

Engineering-trained component-based software engineers are ideal for managing component-based projects and product-lines. If they are not now in great demand, the demand soon will far exceed the supply. With a vacuum of engineering-trained component-based software engineers, Speed and the coeditors have proposed a university program of six years resulting in a master's degree in component-based software project management. Although a bachelor's degree may be accepted during the educational path towards the master's degree, the program is not designed as a two-step program. From the beginning, students take courses in engineering, mathematics, computer science, and CBSE. The program is rigorous, requiring thorough training in all aspects of the CBD life cycle, as well as engineering and engineering management. The universities must be accredited to offer the program, and the students must take a one-year internship before completing the program with a comprehensive test in all aspects of their education.

The New Education and Its New Certification Paradigm

One reason CBSPMs are required to manage component-based projects and product-line programs is that they will learn to understand the needs of commerce for the assurance of trusted components and component infrastructures. As a CBSPM, that job is your responsibility. It is also your responsibility to work cooperatively with third-party certification organizations to help your component producer business meet the requirements of a potential purchaser or governmental agency. Therefore, you must provide the verification and validation necessary to assure the putative purchaser with knowledge of your processes. Third-party verification of your processes is considerably preferable to your report about the efficacy of your CBSE processes. In addition, the certification organization will want access to documentation of functional and nonfunctional requirements, design documentation (often in the latest version of the Unified Modeling Language [UML]) software components, interfaces, software component infrastructures, test harnesses, results of testing and methods of testing, among other forms of documentation required by the certification organization.

The certification organization likely will validate the final product, whether a component, a component infrastructure, or even a component model by comparing the functionality of the product with the requirements and design. If more than one component is involved in the transaction or the potential purchaser has developed a component infrastructure and software components, the third-party certifier may determine whether the producer's component documentation is sufficient to permit the potential purchaser to assemble the component and interfaces into the software infrastructure with limited modifications to the interfaces. This scenario is more likely to occur with custom-designed components, purchased through a request for proposal (RFP). It is also likely for graphical user interface (GUI) components and middleware when designers specifically know or purchase the specifications, incorporate the specifications into the design of the component infrastructure, and purchase or develop other components to interface with the original components.

Third-party certification is similar to the building inspector going into Apperly's (Chapter 2) high-rise building at various stages of construction to ensure that it meets "the code," that is, the building code. Defectively welded interfaces between vertical and horizontal beams could cause catastrophic effects later. The building inspector, a third-party representing a governmental agency, is responsible for the public safety and welfare that might use that building. Third-party certification organizations are responsible now for more than the safety and welfare of users of safety-critical software for programmable components (such as embedded software). These organizations can serve in business-to-business certifications for potential purchases. Because of the precision required of black-box components, the needs to test the components under a variety of conditions, and the maintenance, tailorability needs, and evolution of components, certification is vitally important for nonsafety-critical applications. Managers, the ultimate purchasers of components, owe a fiduciary duty to their boards of directors, and the company's shareholders, to protect the business from failure of component-based projects and reuse-based product-lines. Engineering-trained managers and third-party certification certainly can mitigate risks, but make no mistake—both are required for success.

Component-Based Software Engineering and Project Leadership

Stephen Chow's first chapter is about the history of the law applied to commerce in software. Interestingly, most of the laws that were written by state legislatures and the federal government still govern the trade in software. Some laws have gained popularity over the years because of court decisions. The basis for intellectual property laws is the United States Constitution, which authorizes Congress to enact statutes to

> [P]romote the progress of science and the useful arts, by securing for limited times to authors and inventors the exclusive right to their respective writings and discoveries"(Article 1, section 8, clause 9, United States Constitution).

Prior to the mid-1970s, the states provided protection of technological advances, including software development, through the Uniform Trade Secrets Act (UTSA). To bring a lawsuit under the UTSA, an intentional misappropriation of valuable confidential information had to occur. It was not until the mid-1970s that patent law was applied to software. Then in 1976, the copyright law gave software owners the right to protect the "expressions" of their copyrightable works.

In 1991, a federal court of appeals in New York established an "abstraction-filtration-comparison" test for copyrightable expression. As a result, the United States Patent and Trademark Office (USPTO) responded to the diminished copyright protection of the New York federal court of appeals and relaxed barriers to patents on software. Patent law has changed to the point where investees establish patent positions by filing provision patent applications for claims in their business plans.

Stephen's next chapter describes in detail how the Uniform Commercial Code Article 2 (UCC) provided the same protection for the production and distribution of software as it did for other goods and services. In contracts made on a handshake, by phone, or over the counter in exchange for immediate payment, even when there are forms (such as a purchase order or an invoice), all terms consistent with the agreement are made part of the contract, and materially different terms are treated as counter-offers.

The UCC treated off-the-shelf software as goods, and software vendors could disclaim warranties of merchantability and fitness for a particular purpose. Vendors were permitted limited modification of their contracts according to the standard rules of practice of the UCC.

The UCC served the software vendors and purchasers well and perpetuated no harm to the software industry. In 1991, in the *Step-Saver* case, an important federal court case, off-the-shelf software was ordered with one set of terms, but delivered with materially different terms in the box. The court found the terms in the box unenforceable.

Opponents to the 1991 case, as well as subsequent cases, the Business Software Alliance (BSA), dominated by Microsoft Corporation, joined in the rewriting of UCC Article 2 to 2B focusing on the "license of information" rather than the "sale-of-a-copy-plus-license-of-copyright." When the American Law Institute (ALI) refused to endorse UCC Article 2B as a proposed statute for enactment by the states, the committee's direct parent, which reports to the ALI, renamed the proposed statute the Uniform Computer Information Transactions Act (UCITA) following intense and continuing opposition. UCITA is a complicated act that has been enacted into law in Virginia and Maryland. A component producer's concerns are different from those a component consumer would face. A purchasing end-user would have yet a different set of concerns under UCITA. For example, a component producer would be advised to select a state that has enacted UCITA for interpretation of a contract and as a forum for resolution of disputes. UCITA's rules tend to favor producers of "computer information." Software component consumers and purchasing end-users, to the extent that they are able, should resist.

Additionally, in states that have enacted UCITA, we advise that component consumers and purchasing end-users demand third-party certification during the request for proposal process. Component producers that want your business will have to abandon many of the protections of UCITA and submit to certification, which certainly is a great equalizer. You will have access to process and design information, defects, and whether self-help (the ability to turn your software off for nonpayment of renewal fees) is implemented. If the component producer desires to hide behind UCITA, you probably can accept that the producer has more to hide.

Part VIII

References

W. Councill, "Third-Party Testing and the Quality of Software Components," *IEEE Software*, Vol. 16, No. 4, July/Aug., 1999, pp. 55-57.

M. Desai, "UL 1998—Software in Programmable Components," Proceedings, Embedded Systems Conference (ESC), *www.esconline.com*, Spring, 2000.

R. Kanigel, *The One Best Way: Frederick Taylor and the Enigma of Efficiency*, Viking Penguin, New York, NY, 1997.

T. Kletz, P. Chung, E. Broomfield, and C. Shen-Orr, *Hazard and Operability (HAZOP) Studies Applied to Computer-controlled Process Plants, Computer Control and Human Error*, Chapter 2, Institution of Chemical Engineers, Gulf Publishing Company, Houston, TX, 1995, pp. 45-80.

J. Laddon, T. Atlee, and L. Shook, *Awakening, The Upside of Y2K*, The Printed Word, 1998.

D. Parnas, "Software Engineering Programs Are Not Computer Science Programs," *IEEE Software*, Vol. 16, No. 6, Nov./Dec., 1999, pp. 19-30.

C. Scheper, J. Flynt, S. Smith, C. Jones, and J. Torres, "An Independent Evaluation of the Rome Laboratory Framework for Certification of Reusable Software Components," Rome Laboratory, Air Force Material Command, Rome, New York, Oct., 1997.

Underwriters Laboratories Inc., "Clients With Non-Y2K Compliant Products Urged to Contact UL," *On The Mark*, Vol. 5, No. 2, *www.ul.com/about/otm/otmv5n2/y2k.html*, Summer, 1999.

Part IX

Conclusion

Chapter 41

Summary

Bill Councill
George T. Heineman

41.1 Introduction

We hope you will return to this book again and again as you try to harness the power of CBSE in your professional careers. Each part can be read as a standalone unit and we have provided introductions and summaries to capture our editorial vision. Yet we believe you would benefit from an impressionistic summary of the entire book from our perspective. We learned much about CBSE during the past eighteen months, more than we could possibly describe in a single short chapter. We hope that you will join us on the discussion forum hosted on this book's Web site to continue the journey begun with this work. We look forward to your impressions, which may be quite different from our own. Feel free to support or contend with our opinions and the authors' views on the discussion forum. The discipline of CBSE will grow only through such discussions and, finally, through the empiricism we seek.

One motivation for initiating this book project was our hope that the software engineering community would avoid repeating past mistakes. We believe that object-oriented (OO) analysis, design, and programming were over-hyped and over-sold. Early courses and seminars in OO described the technology as an elixir for all that was wrong with years of poor analysis, design, and programming practices. It didn't take long for information technology (IT) departments and many independent software vendors (ISVs) to realize that OO was a very expensive methodology that, ironically, had been sold to senior management as a way to save money. Training was limited, mentoring was relatively nonexistent, and most designers and developers learned on their own through books and tireless practice. If authors and advocates are not careful CBSE will also be marketed as OO was.

As you have no doubt realized, for every benefit of CBSE our authors have identified there is almost always a warning or a liability. No author has tried to convince you to drop your current design and development processes and adopt CBD and CBSE. Our uniform message is the following: if your organization has sufficient processes in place to support a radical new technology, and if your senior management is prepared to participate in the business engineering that is required of component technology and software reuse, then the time may be right to introduce a pilot CBSE program.

41.2 History

As you've learned, a long history of reuse has preceded us. In 1972 David Parnas taught us how to divide a system into parts so the whole system would not have to change when one module replaced another satisfying the same interface. We still have problems with the practice of information hiding, although the theory is widely accepted. Modules have given way to software components, and perhaps for the first time with this book, components are uniformly defined.

Preceding the development of information hiding by a few years, in 1968 a NATO conference established the term *software engineering*. However, for years the discipline displayed no real interest in investing its students with the time and effort required to learn and think like engineers. Once again Parnas was a leader in the engineering trained-software engineering field (Parnas, 1999). The design, implementation, deployment, and maintenance of CBD, using CBSE, require an engineering approach. As John Speed and the editors stated in Chapter 37, all disciplines of engineering require the assembly of components.

The assembly of software components through interfaces requires just as much precision as the assembly of an automotive engine and a transmission. Both must be designed with all problems identified and resolved. Multiple transmissions and the engines from various manufacturers are designed for assembly and disassembly with ease. As the transmission is upgraded, its new parts must integrate with the engine and either maintain or increase performance. Evolvability should not diminish the ease of reassembly. In the same way, software component assembly and the reuse of software components must expand and become equally well-designed and precise as automotive design and inventory reuse.

41.3 Learning CBSE

Many books teach us about specific technologies, practices, and processes of component technologies. Often the authors of such books promote technologies they have devoted considerable time to learning, even beyond the limitations the authors then describe. Read enough CBD and CBSE books and you will surely become confused because all the technologies have great success, greater promises, and few limitations. One of our motivations in compiling this book was to produce an unbiased view of CBD and CBSE. We brought together CBD and CBSE specialists and these authors, speaking from their own experiences, summarized and assessed (both positively and negatively) their topics with an honesty no one can contest.

There are many communities with an interest in CBSE. The software architecture community often minimizes the sophistication of software components. On the one hand, software architecture has too many perspectives to affect the business and industrial communities that are drawn to CBD and CBSE. Software reuse, on the other hand, preceded CBSE in organization and empiricism. The reuse community is well organized, the defining books for reuse have effectively designed measurement and metrics models, and empiricism is an intended outgrowth of the metrics models.

Product-lines and product-line architectures are a natural extension of software reuse and they also provide an industrial metaphor to better explain the concepts of CBSE. As stated in a 1998 Department of Defense (DoD) Product Line Practice Workshop, "refocusing the reuse target on strategic, large-grained reuse at the level of a product-line … can result in remarkable efficiency and productivity improvements and time economies." There is clearly great synergy between CBSE and product-lines, as revealed by the summary from this DoD Workshop: "… construct and articulate a solid business case for the product-line … Adopt a metrics collection plan before the project begins," and "Ensure an appropriate and enduring funding model." The CBSE community can build on the strengths of product-line approaches as we move towards a global, self-sustaining component marketplace.

The time has come for component-based software engineering to establish its own discipline, while allowing other related fields to retain their own identities and contribute to CBSE. Professional meetings could occur at software engineering or OO programming conferences in the near-term until a conference series is founded focused entirely on CBSE. CBSE has made great advances in the private sector despite its limited visibility in academia. This book is written largely by consultants to industry and well-established CBSE leading-edge practitioners and authors in business. We are fortunate, however, that academics are well represented in the contribution of chapters. Only through the combined effort of academia and industry will CBSE change the way software is developed.

41.4 CBSE: The Revolution

Business and industry should be encouraged to participate in the proposed discipline in large numbers. At one time academia was considered years ahead of business in knowledge and experience with new technologies including application tools. In our opinion, and those of many of our authors, business is now ahead in practical knowledge of, and experience with, new technologies. This divergence in new technology transfer creates problems for business. In past years industry required students graduating from computer science programs to bring their knowledge of new technologies to the IT organization.

Today the business IT organization discovers that it must train students in components, and often in object-oriented analysis and design, before they can be productive.

In an interesting article, "Components: What if They Gave a Revolution and Nobody Came?" (Maurer, 2000), the author identifies three great revolutions in computing technology in the past fifty years: the stored-program computer, high-level languages, and component-level programming. Maurer then reports that academic researchers are doing little or nothing with CBD or CBSE. He states, "The revolution has already happened, and in the academic community, nobody came." In Japan academia embraces CBSE and industry and academia have established consortia for research and development. With the revolution of software components upon us, academia must establish CBSE programs to prepare students to meet the needs of business and industry.

Because strong, knowledgeable management is required for CBSE, current software project management is generally insufficient to manage CBSE projects, reuse projects, and product-lines. In Chapter 37 we proposed a graduate program in component-based software project management. The program requires computer science, engineering, and software engineering courses. A one-year practica is required during the five-year program that results in a master's degree. Following graduation, a one-year internship with a software engineering program, managed by an engineering-trained software engineer, or in an engineering business, is required. The purpose is for graduates to learn to think and work like engineering managers.

The software industry has embraced OO on the whole; less clear is the overall impact that OO has on all forms of industry, including engineering and manufacturing. OO is certainly successful in conducting software engineering in-the-small. OO allows developers to develop units of software (called classes) that map directly to the real-world entities in a particular domain. OO frameworks (Gamma et al., 1995) were the greatest achievement of OO because they provide well-designed partial solutions that can be completed to build applications. However, the class hierarchies developed using OO can often be complicated and developers likely will increase their resistance to change the hierarchy over time. Also, developing code libraries, the standard for reusing code in OO, is not as rigorous as designing the interfaces for, and the implementation of, a component. To use the terminology from Chapter 16, OO programming languages are exceptionally well suited to developing fine-grained business components, but great care must be taken when attempting large-scale OO systems (Lakos, 1996). There is also an undeniable problem with interoperation among independently developed classes. Lastly, the barrier of entry to nonsoftware industries for OO is high.

41.4.1 The Commitment to CBD and CBSE

Because we established that businesses must provide the training for CBD and CBSE, businesses must commit to CBSE organizationally. Businesses must be willing to reengineer their processes as the IT organization trains its staff in CBD and CBSE. Although the organization may have trained the IT staff previously in object-orientation, the transition to proficient design, implementation, deployment, and maintenance of components is difficult for many staff. Therefore many, if not all, employees require mentoring. The cost from the beginning of the pilot project is steep. The problem is that businesses under competitive pressure may find it easy to divert the funds from CBD and CBSE to other projects that may appear to offer short-term gains. Well-trained project managers must prepare senior managers for competitive risks and work to modify the organization's business plan to include a clause concerning business engineering that is central to the organization and shall not be changed except for an exceptionally unfortunate downturn in the business' financial condition. In addition, continuing education is required as CBSE continues to mature and become more empirical, and thus, trustworthy.

We learned from the Standish Group's *Chaos Report* (*standishgroup.com/visitor/chaos.htm*) that 31% of all application projects are canceled before completion; the costs are staggering. The lesson is that software project failures are project management failures. Because CBD and component-based software project management are considerably more complex than previous software development technologies, the opportunities for failure are even greater, we believe, than those reported by the Standish Group.

41.4.2 The One Best Way

We advocate an engineering approach proposed by Frederick Taylor (Kanigel, 1997) and referred to as *the one best way*. The one best way, adopted by all disciplines of engineering and by groups of businesses, is a method for decomposing large problems into smaller problems and then implementing solutions as discrete components. The traditional engineering community embraced Taylor's method as the basis for engineers' fundamental problem-solving approach.

When asked what makes one solution better or another inferior, a group of traditional mechanical, electrical, or civil engineers will provide remarkably similar answers. They will speak of optimizing efficiency, minimizing costs, maintaining minimum functional requirements, and other fundamental beliefs gained during their engineering educations. Ask the same questions of a group of software engineering practitioners and the answers are anything *but* consistent. This, we believe, is one of the most fundamental challenges facing the software engineering profession today: *a large number of software engineering practitioners have not been educated to recognize or generate optimal solutions to problems.* We believe that the inability to solve problems in a systematic, scientific manner requires an immediate solution: as described before, a new graduate program for component-based software project managers who can then teach and mentor subordinates in the one best way.

Taylorism shows how component engineers and designers can design components that bridge between design in-the-large and design in-the-small. Many claimed that OO programming languages would address large-scale programming issues. However, we believe the reason that large-scale OO systems exist today is because the designers and developers naturally decomposed their solution into components—that is, the language itself was not the reason for success. OO and CBSE make an adequate match but OO is not a precondition for CBSE. Only CBSE, with widespread support for standards and its ability to accommodate independently developed software components, will be able to assist software engineers as they design complex software systems. Such standards, at a minimum, must declare the proper way to document a component and its elements, as shown in Chapter 38.

41.4.3 The Marketplace and Trust

The current Internet component marketplace includes Web sites that permit you to try components before you purchase them. In the United States, approximately 4,000 components are currently available for sale, yet many of the types of components you may need are not available. Purchase of the components off the Web or through an advertisement in a trade journal can result in risks to the system. Sometimes these risks do not become known until maintenance or operation. Components should only be purchased after a thorough evaluation and analysis, including a total cost of ownership (see Chapter 6). Components on trial from any source should be tested thoroughly, either by your own organization, or by a third-party testing and certification organization. A good test for components is the documentation made available, such as that mentioned in Chapter 38. If the component producer cannot, or will not, provide adequate documentation, you can presume that you will have difficulty with the component at some phase of the component development life cycle.

We identify three necessary precursors to a marketplace of trusted components. First, there must be accurate documentation of components and their dependencies. Second, there must be a sufficient number of trained software engineers and component-based software project managers. Third, the CBSE community must develop and promote independent, nonbiased bodies capable of third-party certification. For many years third-party certification organizations such as Underwriters Laboratories have been certifying safety-critical software for programmable components (such as embedded software). Third-party certification organizations evaluate process, requirements, design, implementation, verification, testing, and validation of the product against the initial requirements.

Trust is established when a component producer receives a certificate from a certification organization, or better yet, when through a voluntary certification arrangement, two businesses have their components certified for interaction with the other. Let us make the concept of trust clear. Trusted components require three things.

1. Considerable comprehensive, well-structured documentation about the component or component infrastructure.
2. Component-based software management, either:

- Engineering-trained software engineers
- Component-based software project managers

3. Third-party certification, managed by a trusted organization with many years in the field.

41.4.4 Design and Assembly Analogies

An ideal design tool permits designers to thoroughly design components or component infrastructures. Application assemblers will use specialized tools to assemble their software system from internally stored components or patterns that will yield the correct components. In Japan, Hitachi developed APPGALLERY, a "visual CBD environment" that allows designers to draw a connector between two components automatically generating a module of script programs that glue the components. A glue script may include method invocations, event handling, and database access. APPGALLERY comes with a set of software components, tools for developing and customizing components, and a visual debugger that can run component applications. APPGALLERY was successfully used to construct an insurance management application of 97 KLOC, where 95% of the code came from preexisting components (Aoyama et al., 1998). A competitive set of CBD technologies is NEC's HolonEnterprise. The technologies consist of an infrastructure, software components, and a visual CBD tool. A store management and point of sale system, deployed in 1998, intensively used infrastructures and components assembled by HolonEnterprise. The infrastructure consists of a number of design patterns. A mediator pattern is used to plug components into the infrastructure. As most are aware, design patterns are used to design local object-oriented structures. However, HolonEnterprise clearly demonstrates that design patterns can be used to assemble components by replacing objects with components (see Chapter 13).

Computer Aided Design (CAD) fundamentally changed the way engineers performed design. The slide rule and the drafting board have given way to CAD systems. Thirty years ago, only crude two-dimensional CAD drawings were available. One has only to look at the diverse set of CAD programs available today to sense their impact. Engineers from all disciplines can design models, not just sketches, in two and three dimensions. These models can be analyzed for an amazing array of properties, such as thermodynamic performance, ergonomics, ease of manufacturing, or composability. Engineers can simulate the assembly process, the way in which the molds and dies are machined. There are even companies that automatically build three-dimensional models from CAD files (*www.zcorp.com*).

Even as CAD is revolutionizing manufacturing, there are still many concerns. For example, a recent National Institute of Science and Technology report states that U.S. $1 billion dollars of profit is lost in the U.S. automotive industry because of interoperability problems in CAD files, the representation of the CAD models (Fowler, 1999). As this important sector of industry struggles to solve the interoperability problem, it is rapidly converging on a standards-based approach. The CBSE community should learn from the advances and limitations achieved by the CAD industry.

41.5 Conclusion

We find it easy to make comparisons between CBSE and the automotive industry for two reasons. First, evolution within the industry occurred in three stages: 1) early craftsmanship; 2) A fledgling industry whose quality products were only available to the very rich; 3) An industry generating quality, mass-produced, and affordable automobiles. Second, the tremendous investment in infrastructure, such as roads, bridges, and tunnels enabled the automobile to have such a profound impact on all aspects of our lives, from where we live to the reduced cost of goods because of cheap transport. The automobile was a revolution indeed. We believe CBSE has the same power to transform the development of software, and in doing so, impact our lives because of the increasing dependence that modern society has on software.

After reading the book how do you rate the sophistication of CBSE in comparison with the automotive industry? In reality CBSE is somewhere between a Model T and a 1950 Ford. CBSE is the modern day equivalent of the moving assembly line revolution.

By adopting the CBSE techniques and principles from this book, you will be able to introduce CBSE into your organization. Many software engineering texts focus on the triangle of project management. The three project management elements

- Time
- Costs
- Human resources

are especially important to CBSE, as to all projects. Routinely, projects succeed only by providing "creative" or heroic solutions when one or two of the elements become unavailable. For example, the organization decides to channel one-third of the component pilot project's remaining funding to another project halfway through the project. As we've seen before, only the heroics of the project team working 12 to 16 hour days will complete the project on time. To ensure that CBSE is successfully adopted within your organization, you must push for a one-year pilot project similar to an existing project you have already completed. Building on its success, the second CBSE project should develop a software system that previously would have been developed using traditional means, but this time metrics are recorded. You will provide measurement information to management to increase their confidence in CBD and CBSE. To convince your organization to incrementally adopt CBSE enterprise-wide, you must use the skills you learned in Chapters 23, 24, and 27 to negotiate your budget up front. Only sufficiently funded CBSE initiatives, with well-trained personnel, reasonable schedules, and a supportive upper management will succeed. Once your negotiations are complete, commit your agreements to writing and encourage the most senior managers, that is, the president and CEO if possible, to execute the agreement. The agreement is not binding, but agreements confer a sense of importance and longevity that a word and a handshake don't confer.

- Teams must have sufficient training, mentoring, and experience to produce a speculative schedule (reuse and product-lines are business engineering projects too). Experienced managers will not provide senior management with a schedule until all collaborating teams have produced their schedules
- The organization must provide sufficient funding needed for completion of the project, including all identified risk factors
- All roles and positions should be recruited, trained, mentored, and deemed comfortable in the CBD and CBSE before moving the new staff members to a major project (mentoring might continue for months)

- Project and product management must have knowledge of every position and phase of the CBD life cycle and establish rapport with subordinates and senior management alike

The management triangle is being replaced by a more complicated set of relationships that must be managed hands-on, not behind a desk. If business organizations are unwilling to reengineer their businesses for product-line use that provides the companies with identified organizational competitive advantages, then CBSE will not become the revolution the authors and editors expect. As the Web becomes ubiquitous, we expect that businesses will hire only the most adept management, demand a structured engineering management process, and invest in continuous training and mentoring. Most importantly, businesses must be prepared to reengineer not just the IT department but also the whole company. The world of software engineering will change in ways that we cannot even fathom. What a time to practice CBSE!

Chapter 42

The Near-Term Future of Component-Based Software Engineering

Hedley Apperly
Grady Booch
Bill Councill
Martin Griss
George T. Heineman
Ivar Jacobson
Steve Latchem
Barry McGibbon
Davyd Norris
Jeffrey Poulin

42.1 Introduction

To paraphrase Edmund Burke (1790), software engineers will not look ahead with any sense of realism who never look backward to their ancestors. As we now turn our vision to the near-term future of CBSE, the next three years, we must admit that many in our discipline have not even recognized the struggles and accomplishments of the past. Far too many computer scientists and software engineers believe that they need to understand only the latest technology to advance in their profession. This book describes the state-of-the-practice of CBSE and contains specific knowledge needed today by developers and managers. In this forward-looking chapter we discuss our perspectives on the future direction of CBSE. We invited several authors to present their forecasts of the near-term future. We expect many of these predictions to be realized in this short time period. We also recognize our collective humiliations because of past predictions and hopes and their concomitant pitfalls and failures. To succeed, we must avoid the errors of software engineering's past, as well as the history of engineering's failures. Therefore, we focus only on the short-term future.

42.1.1 Return on Investment

By now Henry Ford's resolute search for a way to lower the price of his automobile may sound clichéd, but his example emerges as the closest match to CBSE and the software reuse revolution. Unfortunately, the revolution has not found its way into most of the world's innovative software development companies.

One reason for the slow acceptance of CBSE in the business world is the extent of spending on Year 2000 (Y2K) repairs. Y2K-related costs diverted investments that could have been used to initiate CBSE pilot studies. According to the Cutter Consortium's Survey of 150 IT Professionals in 1997, the average year 2000 IT budget was projected to be \$25 million. In the United States we now spend more than \$250 billion each year on IT application development of approximately 175,000 projects. The average cost of a development project for a large company is \$2,322,000; for a medium company, \$1,331,000; and for a small company, \$434,000 (*standishgroup.com/visitor/chaos.htm*). Y2K repairs were estimated at between \$300 and \$600 billion by the Gartner

Group. Capers Jones estimated Y2K spending of $1.6 trillion, including all hardware, software, and other related expenses and not including litigation (*www.ciras.iastate.edu/Y2K/year2kcost.html*). Because of the focus on Y2K many companies have not discovered the benefits of CBSE. Adopting CBSE during Y2K would have made the necessary repairs easier and diminished the costs of instituting a necessary step in software development. This book is largely written for those who have to manage their skyrocketing IT costs to remain competitive.

We divided this chapter into four sections. Authors Apperly, Latchem, and McGibbon recommended the following themes for this chapter: Cultural Change, Market Dynamics and Economics, Measurement and Metrics, and Standards. We agree that these four themes sum up the near-term future of CBSE. Our authors will continue to be active and will participate in future activities, consult with progressive companies, and work in research and development laboratories. Their jobs are to anticipate and shape the future we predict here.

42.2 Cultural Change

You have repeatedly read that the state of software management is inadequate. We consider software failure to be the failure of software managers to promote, embrace, and adhere to the best practices of software engineering (see Chapter 27). As competition in software markets increases companies will be driven to adopt CBSE. We expect major companies such as IBM, HP, and Motorola will report the productivity gains and cost savings realized by adopting CBSE. This will be reminiscent of the way that software companies in the 1980s and early 1990s reported the benefits of documentation and adherence to specific software engineering processes. CBSE will replace software process improvement as the best way to increase productivity.

Ironically, the future of CBSE *is not* in the hands of IT departments or independent software vendors. Despite the difficulties we experience today—most are described in the pages of this book—technology is not the problem. Proper funding will make CBSE successful. In the near-term major Fortune 500 companies that have yet to adopt CBSE will likely do so or lose ground to competitors that have initiated or actually made the transition. CBD and CBSE are smart investments in companies' futures and future profits.

42.2.1 Funding

Component technology is expensive. Initiating a pilot project with appropriate staffing is costly compared to pilot projects for new software technologies such as metrics, effective project management, or effective verification activities. A small pilot project will lead to larger pilot projects, which form the basis for an enterprise-wide reuse program. Instituting such a software reuse program, compared with today's software development programs, requires significantly greater organizational costs and other resources, only some represented below:

- Hiring
- Funding
- Training time
- Mentoring
- Quality assurance
- Metrics
- Metrics reporting
- Continued hiring
- Significant senior management oversight

You will only be able to secure funds for your CBSE transformation by considering the return on investment (ROI) that CBSE promises.

42.2.2 Training

Academic software engineering and software development project management courses train students to be computer programmers, not software engineers or software project managers. Project managers often supervise other programmers who are only a few years younger than themselves. Managers often exercise their responsibilities without any preparation and they are rewarded, usually, when projects are completed on schedule, regardless of whether the schedule was reasonable. A new development manager generally has no experience in any phase of the life cycle except coding. Analysis and design may be foreign concepts and the manager may consider testing as an impediment to meeting scheduled deadlines. In short, "management" can degrade into a situation where a project manager accedes to whatever requests come from upper management. This would not occur on an engineering project such as a suspension bridge, nor should it occur on a software project.

Project managers responsible for component-based software development projects must show competence in all phases of the component-based software life cycle (CSLC). On the whole, industry believes that a successful manager on one project could be transferred to another project and achieve similar success. The well-documented evidence of failing software projects disproves this belief in the software domain. As we have described throughout the book, CBSE is an engineering activity. CBSE managers must demonstrate that they can manage the complete CSLC process with hands-on knowledge of all phases.

Licensure and certification are two forms of professional recognition available for project managers to demonstrate their competence. Licensure is a mandatory process administered by a governmental authority. Performance as an engineering consultant without a license is illegal. Certification is generally a voluntary process administered by a profession. Nevertheless, states reserve the right to certify professions, although the same profession certifies its own members.

We do not expect licensure to be adopted to promote CBSE. We believe that it is imperative to undertake a multi-year grant to initiate a one-year study on the curriculum for a component-based software project manager (CBSPM) academic program and establish five core universities to initiate a curriculum similar to that described in Chapter 37. The program would have three tracks as shown in Table 42-1.

Hedley Apperly demonstrated in Chapter 2 that there is great similarity between constructing a high-rise building and assembling a complex, distributed component-based system. Indeed, both require the same skills. Many project managers and some businesses will object to a rigid educational curriculum. However, to assure reuse projects that complete on time, within budget, with the originally planned resources requires a manager trained in computer science, CBSE, and a sampling of engineering, especially engineering management. With multiple levels of CBSPMs we anticipate we can start training the first class within three years, especially those with technical bachelors degrees and five years' experience. Within six years, the first

Table 42-1: *CBSPM Education Tracks*

	Toe-in-the-Sand	Full Commitment-Nights	Full Commitment-Days
Target Audience	Managers and business not sure of their commitment to CBD, CBSE, and engineering management.	Full-time equivalent manager.	Young, committed student or an organizationally sponsored student.
Description	Taught only at nights. Each course is "an introduction to" class, but not an introductory course.	Combines class and distance learning with lab assignments. May opt out of classes through testing. Generally a four-year master's degree program including a one-year internship while taking classes. Computer science, CBSE, and engineering taken from first year.	Classes generally taken on campus. Students may test out of courses because of experience. Generally, a four-year master's degree program including a one-year internship while taking classes. Computer science, CBSE, and engineering taken from first year.

students will graduate, complete an internship, and earn certification as a CBSPM. The goal is achievable and, with governmental and industrial funding, we can diminish the software failures we've all grown to accept. Because our critical national infrastructure is dependent on software, we can no longer accept academic programs ill-prepared to graduate software engineers.

42.2.3 Development

The majority of software development projects develop end-user applications or large-scale systems. As more components become available, companies will want to license these components for use. Before purchasing and incorporating a component in over 10,000 applications, the component consumer organization will likely execute a contract requesting the component producer to certify the component. The component consumer may pay for the certification. If the component consumer is a small organization without funds to purchase the certification, it can negotiate with the larger organization to subsidize part or all of the costs. If the larger organization has some trust in the consumer, funding the certification of the component would be worthwhile to assure the purchase of large numbers of trusted components. Such certification will ultimately be a service provided by well known independent organizations, such as Underwriters Laboratories (UL), using known applicable standards. Until then the component consumers and producers could select a mutually trusted third party to evaluate the component.

Many software companies were involved in mergers and acquisitions during the 1990s. Such expansion is not sustainable. In many cases the mergers were attempts to improve a company's market position, allowing them to buy their share of a market. This approach is an enterprise-scale example of buy versus build, as discussed in Chapters 25-26. The purchasing company clearly has increased their productivity by acquiring the assets of the purchased company, but they have also shouldered the future burden of integration and maintenance. Many mergers and acquisitions were enabled by easy access to venture capital; in times of economic downturn such capital will be harder to secure.

Instead of acquisitions, we project software companies will only increase their productivity by reusing software components that conform to industry-accepted standards. Each component model ultimately leads to an entire industry of producers, vendors, and consumers. Fortune 500 companies will increasingly demand components that conform to specific component models, creating an opportunity for component vendors to compete in niche component-based industries.

42.3 Market Dynamics and Economics

Many in the software engineering community write about a component marketplace as if it is already here. We must first admit that one does not currently exist. We must accept the responsibility for creating such a market—it will not come about on its own. This book will be read by technical people who must realize that the nascent forces of a technological revolution have emerged. However, as pointed out by Peter Maurer (1999), leading researchers in academia have been slow to embrace the latest advances in component technology. You can participate in the growth of the software component industry by convincing your organization to purchase and sell components. As John Williams states in Chapter 5, reusing components can have a significant impact on your productivity, but you may encounter resistance as you implement CBSE processes. Developing a business case may be the only way to convince skeptics in your organization. CBSE will capture the attention of millions of programmers in the same way that the Free Software movement has done.

Industries are formed top-down from products built from specialized parts. To achieve the economy of scale to make mass production profitable, entire industries are formed around each specialized part. Once standardized, a specialized part forms an industry. For example, a group of manufacturers decides that a standard window size for high-rise windows would enhance safety during storms, increase structural support for the building, and ease design because all window interfaces would be the same size, as well as other important reasons. The group is comprised of glass companies, metal interface firms, installation businesses, business yards, and a variety of other, related organizations, including the major window manufacturing groups, which meet to determine the ideal size for most high-rise building windows.

After many meetings a decision is made and the majority of the group executes a document stating the height, breadth, and thickness of high-rise window interfaces. One of the groups agrees to take the information to an American National Standards Institute (ANSI) meeting for incorporation in an ANSI standard. Once the standard is published, conformity assessments are performed (*www.ansi.org/public/ca_act.html*) to assure compliance with the standards, and the public is safer because of ANSI's promotion of the quality of life.

There is a convergence evident in component models today. Each of the component models discussed in Part VII of this book has a devoted following and will coexist with each other. In addition, consumers of all component models benefit if component model implementations enable interoperability across component models. For example, IBM's WebSphere Application Server (*www.ibm.com/websphere*) is compatible with J2EE, Enterprise JavaBeans (EJB), and CORBA 2.0. It also enables COM and ActiveX clients to interoperate with CORBA based objects. CORBA CCM will be compatible with EJB. The converging technologies will mitigate the risk that a lead software engineer must face when selecting a specific component technology to use for development. From a market perspective, however, companies would typically wish to compete with each other by differentiating themselves from their competitors by the features they add to a commonly accepted core standard.

42.3.1 Scale of Components

Booch and Norris observe that the smaller the component, the easier it is to understand and apply, but the less likely it will be reused because the individual developer will often find that building the component from scratch is still easier. Furthermore, the larger the component, the more difficult it is to understand and apply. At the limit the largest components offer the most opportunity for reuse, but there is rarely incentive for organizations to make the investment in such components and then sell them on the open market. Instead, they will find a greater ROI by using those components as a competitive advantage for dominating one particular vertical market. As a result some of the best components are underutilized. Practically, this means that the marketplace appears to support only two types of components: components at the level of design patterns and slightly higher and larger platform-specific frameworks. .NET and J2EE represent such frameworks and can truly be considered to be assemblies of components, since they both offer parts upon which other systems may be built.

For the public market—which does have the potential for being a vibrant market place—Booch and Norris observe that one of the most interesting possibilities in this area is remote component services. Application Service Providers (ASPs) are only just beginning to investigate the possibility of client software remotely accessing component services either by download on demand or through a micro-payment system. With appropriate standardization ASPs could either define a standard distributed execution model or they could publish component interfaces in both formats using a middleware bridge like J-Integra (*www.linar.com*) to translate calls between them.

42.3.2 Legal Issues

In business the purpose of the law is to allow competing and cooperating businesses to reach agreements that are mutually beneficial and support the public good. When two companies cannot trust each other or their products, they will sign no contracts. We can envision a company choosing only to enter into a contract to purchase a software component that has received the mark of rigid certification. We foresee no radical shift in the way that the law is applied, but there is an ongoing vigorous debate in mass-market software industry. What is the contract? How can one verify or ensure that a software product works as warranted?

The National Conference of Commissioners on Uniform State Laws (NCCUSL) has drafted uniform laws that it promotes for uniform enactment in the United States to enhance commerce (*www.nccusl.org*). The most successful of the uniform laws is the Uniform Commercial Code (UCC), which has been adopted by every state of the Union. UCC Article 2 governs various aspects of the sale of goods from formation of a contract through performance of the contract and remedies for a breach. In most states UCC Article 2 applies to computer programs that were marketed as products requiring minimal customization. Recently the NCCUSL has sought to update key provisions in Article 2 with the Uniform Computer Information Transactions Act (UCITA). Essentially, UCITA would abolish the "perfect tender rule" (under which a product could be rejected if it did not comport perfectly with the performance required under a contract) for software. The rationale given by UCITA proponents is that software is complex and "minor flaws are common in virtually all software." The closing sections of Chapters 39 and 40 contain specific advice that will become increasingly relevant for component producers and consumers. We expect UCITA will become known for the way consumers and industry resist its adoption.

42.4 Measurement and Metrics

This state-of-the-art book is not a handbook. Engineering handbooks generally contain both precise textual specifications and mathematical equations. For the most part this book recounts the authors' experiences with CBD and CBSE. The state-of-the-art of software engineering and CBSE is not empirical. Science and engineering take a back seat to experiences and anecdotes. This lack of empiricism is untenable. CBSE must become an engineering discipline.

The next edition of this book will emphasize an empirical approach to the practice of CBSE. The "practice of engineering" or "practice of professional engineering," as defined by the Texas Board of Professional Engineers, is any service or creative work, either public or private, the adequate performance of which requires engineering education, training or experience in the application of special knowledge or judgment of the mathematical, physical, or engineering sciences to such services or creative work (*www.tbpe.state.tx.us*).

The foundation for the practice of engineering is a rigid, scientific methodology. Underlying civil engineering is physics; the basis of chemical engineering is chemistry. For CBSE to continue to expand and benefit society, computer science must indeed become a science whose principles are applied by software engineers. Computer science must emphasize mathematics and general science and the discipline required for laboratory rigor. CBSE can become an engineering discipline through: requirements for built-in testability and maintainability; significant, precise documentation that is updated as the components and interfaces change; and risk-acceptable procedures to address failures. Engineers and CBSPMs must adopt metrics to establish a baseline for both their precomponent projects and their first pilot and subsequent enterprise CBD projects. Component-based software engineers must supplement the above procedures by practicing the complexities of all forms of software testing.

One weakness of existing metrics is the lack of follow-up reports detailing reuse experiences as evaluated by the models. It seems that few organizations actually use the metrics to properly assess progress and accomplishments within their organizations. We can assess the progress and accomplishments in the wider CBSE profession by funding a consortium of companies that report metrics on a routine basis. As the most important (and easiest to gather) metrics are determined, the consortium can extend to a larger number of organizations. Please note that metrics should not be used to determine compensation or prestige within an organization, otherwise people will alter their behavior simply to receive these benefits.

Business leadership will likely demand return on investment (ROI), total cost of ownership (TCO), and other financial metrics to assist management to continue to support their extensive investment in CBSE or decide against the use of CBD or CBSE. For many years senior management expected managers of the various business departments to produce and present reports on the precise state-of-affairs of their departments. Other business managers are prepared to answer negative questions nondefensively because of their training and experience. Many CIOs escape accountability by claiming they have insufficient data to inform senior management of the financial status of software projects. As CBSE matures, effective metrics will enable organizations to monitor and improve their productivity.

Without developing an empirical foundation for CBSE, the chances are rare indeed that competitive organizations will share data. With an emphasis on manufacturing and scientific efficiency, especially if promoted by governmental funding agencies and industrial consortia, anonymous data can be made available within three years. The problem is that the field of CBSE and reuse metrics requires experimental data and information based on comparable experiences to assess our models and quantitatively research the factors leading to successful reuse. Analytical research could identify these factors by using population studies to determine the effects on projects that do and do not practice reuse. This approach, developed in the social sciences, measures the statistical similarity of issues and gives a probability that an outcome will occur. Allowing for the degree of similarity between projects and given enough data points, funding agencies and organizations can develop a statistical correlation between reuse and results.

42.4.1 Moore's Law—A Lesson in Metrics

In April 1965 Gordon E. Moore, the Director of Research and Development Laboratories of Fairchild Semiconductor, wrote the article "Cramming more components onto integrated circuits" for *Electronics Magazine* (Moore, 1965). He was asked to predict what changes would occur over a ten-year period in the semiconductor industry. Based on three data points he projected that the complexity of each integrated circuit would roughly double each year. In 1975, after ten years of empirical results confirming his projection, he revised his estimates slightly to the now familiar "law" that the complexity of integrated circuits (and thus their computational power) would double every 18 months. Michael Malone considers Moore's law a technical barometer, because "it tells you that if you take the information processing power you have today and multiply by two, that will be what your competition will be doing 18 months from now. And that is where you too will have to be" (Malone, 1996).

With a few data points it is likely we could develop a similar observation concerning team productivity and software components. Currently we have merely anecdotal evidence regarding organizational productivity. In Chapter 23 Jeffrey Poulin cited industry statistics that programmers develop between 200-500 industry-quality source lines of code per month, but these figures are hotly debated. If the CBSE community can agree on a baseline for programmer productivity and make multi-year projections, we can provide a standard of what is possible for those organizations that initiate CBSE metrics projects. We are in desperate need of more empirical evidence.

More importantly, organizational productivity can be measured in reused components. Poulin's measure, relative cost of reuse (RCR) is exceptionally important when assessing the productivity of reuse. RCR is the portion of the effort it takes to reuse a component without modification versus writing a new one. The organization from the top down has to take the position that reuse supersedes designing and writing new code. In most cases that requires a visit to the component repository or the librarian before even considering the design of code. Repeated use of the component repository and reuse of components by project teams is a positive sign that the organization values reuse over writing new code: the organization has successfully inculcated the advantages of reuse to its software project teams.

42.5 Standards and Product Certifications

Certified standards are an attribute of a mature commercial trade, science, or engineering practice. The IEEE has devoted considerable time and effort to developing wide-ranging software standards. However, the organization has not developed a policy to perform conformity assessments to assure adherence to these standards. Standards promote the quality of life by assuring "conformity assessment systems and promoting their integrity" (*web.ansi.org/public/about.html*). The public should not accept the level of software defects that we thrust upon them today. If we were to produce a report showing the total loss (both time and money) incurred by industry because of defective software, it is likely that the Federal or local governments would enact regulations. The applications and operating system (OS) software industries have launched an effective public relations effort saying that software will inherently contain defects. UCITA is an interesting study in the construction of a model law attesting to necessarily defective software. Clearly, software can be engineered to operate properly because safety-critical software, often exceptionally complex, is relatively defect-free.

Conformity assessments and certification are synonyms. Both are third-party review activities that include the evaluation of testing and development processes as well as assessments of the product under the relevant standards. Such certification evaluates a wide range of elements and at a minimum should include the document described in Table 42-1.

Table 42-2: *Certification Scope*

1. Analysis plan
   - Business rules
   - Functional and nonfunctional requirements
   - Use case scenarios and use case diagrams
2. Various forms of design diagrams
3. Development processes and practices, configuration management, and component library management
4. Evaluation of verification activities
5. Design plan
6. Risk analysis and risk mitigation plans
7. Evaluation of, or participation in, validation activities
   - Assurance that the product under certification actually satisfies the requirements established at the negotiation of the contract or the voluntary business-to-business certification activities for the component or components, the subject of the commerce

Chapter 38 describes the forms of documentation required for UL certification of a software component. Table 42-2 lists concrete documentation from the UL 1998 Standard, Sections 3.1-3.4.

Table 42-3: *Concrete Documentation According to UL 1998, Sections 3.1-3.4*

3.1 A risk analysis shall be conducted to determine:

a) The set of risk, and

b) That the software addresses the identified risks

3.2 The risk analysis shall be based on the safety requirement for the programmable component

3.3 An analysis shall be conducted to identify the critical, noncritical, and supervisory sections of the software

3.4 An analysis shall be conducted to identify states for transitions that are capable of resulting in a risk

Standards assure specific requirements and offer additional analytic and design elements. Standards present a roadmap describing the building blocks required to construct software components, the process required to build components correctly, and the timetable when documents of one component phase will be verified against the documents of the directly preceding phase. In addition, future component standards, it is hoped, like most standards, will specify when and how to record potential risks and their mitigation during the component-based software life cycle (CSLC), or in design (ANSI/UL 1998). These standards will establish the means for a component, including an application and OS component, to return to its previous, stable, steady state once it enters a risk-addressed state. Therefore, an unstable, safety-critical, or *revenue-critical* state will not be maintained, the component monitor will be notified, and eventually a human system administrator will be contacted. In today's business economy, the chief financial officer (CFO) of a company is not just responsible for established income and disbursements by the company; the CFO is a fiduciary for the financial health and well being of the board of directors and shareholders. The chief information officer (CIO) likewise is a fiduciary liable for the financial and the intellectual capital of the company. The CFO relies on the CIO for consistently reliable applications. Too many unstable, unreliable components and applications may have severe financial repercussions on the company. A knowledgeable component-based project team can adopt CBSE processes to verify safety-critical properties during analysis and design.

Similar to the safety critical example described in Chapter 4, the CIO must be aware of the performance of the component-based applications of the company (whether adequate or inadequate). The CIO should receive timely reports showing reported defects by customers, maintenance costs, open change requests, and similar information by which the quality of the components can be measured. We can imagine a company notifying (via alarm, page, or personal screen message box) both the CIO and CFO of potential events that have financial repercussions.

As a fiduciary of the company, the CIO should assure that applications are developed with components that can roll back to the previous "safe" state or monitor vital components' activities. The application should be as reliable and fault tolerant as a pacemaker. Domain specialists, well versed in CBSE, will assist in the analysis and design of financially critical states. Just as the CFO may have third-party international accountants on whom the CFO relies for the benefit of the company and its shareholders, the CIO will have specialists backed by third-party certification to validate the component-based software upon which the CFO's financial reports depend.

This behavior should not apply to only safety critical and financial applications, but to any feature users consider necessary for the continuous performance of work. With software components, reliability and fault tolerant behavior can be located in a cluster of components and interact with a large number of other components.

42.5.1 Documentation

Booch and Norris observed that there is still no standard approach to documenting and cataloguing design subsystems, components, and other reusable assets. Because the Unified Modeling Language (UML) is being adopted as the standard way to express software designs, we now have the "electronic symbols" to use in specifications, but there is no accepted format. To this end Rational has instigated work on a Reusable Assets Specification (RAS) to define a standard way of documenting valuable assets that may be harvested for reuse from a software project. Companies such as Microsoft, IBM, and ComponentSource have joined Rational in proposing to Object Management Group (OMG) the use of the RAS as a future standard. The specification uses both textual meta data and UML elements to specify the component interfaces and define the context for correct reuse. Members of the consortium are working to provide examples to test the specification and a draft document is published on Rational's Web site (*www.rational.com/eda/ras/preview/index.htm*). RAS builds upon the UML and helps developers express the component parts of a system. Perhaps the most interesting aspect of the RAS is that it is not limited to just code components; instead, it takes the view that there are many nonsoftware assets that can be reused.

42.5.2 Certification

One essential aspect of CBSE will be the precise specification of software components. With a standard specification format third-party certification organizations can operate and help build trust in components. Component vendors can market and sell components and component consumers can accurately specify and locate components to suit their unique purposes. Standard component models are only the first phase. Next, the software engineering community must standardize the meta data to be associated with components.

If you incorporate third-party components, you should contract with your component producer or vendor, specify all documentation you will provide and all that you expect the producer to make available in a carefully crafted request for proposal (RFP), and then execute an agreement. The agreement should clearly state your expectations and the use of a third-party certification organization. The component producer's milestones and the certifier's milestones should be synchronized, which will provide much feedback into the component's proposed progress by the producer. Since the third-party certifier is unbiased, you will learn the facts, but subjected to no speculation or rumors.

We believe the only way to protect investments in costly software components and their elements are to ensure unbiased third-party certification. Today, as Will Tracz stated (see Chapter 6), organizations purchase COTS components "because of slick demos, Web searches, and trade journals." Organizations should only contractually purchase software components using thorough and well-founded evaluations, including tests designed by test managers and their teams—that is, unless you prefer to trust your judgment to the third-party certifier. As

Janet Flynt stated in Chapter 38, the safety and quality concerns of retailers and consumers are a strong impetus driving the realization of such a drastic measure against potentially substandard products.

42.6 Tools and Technology

We're sure you have heard that the only constant in life is change. Even during the original 1968 NATO meeting on software engineering, a participant stated: "Just once, I would like to be able to build a software system incrementally" (Naur and Randell, 1968). CBSE provides some ability to mitigate the impact of rapid advances in technology, but there has been some turmoil within component technologies as they have evolved. In many ways it is not possible to stand still with a particular technology without falling behind. In this closing section we identify trends that will directly affect CBSE in the near-term.

42.6.1 Advances in Networking and Operating System Technology

We anticipate that Message Oriented Middleware and Message Queuing Middleware (MQM) will develop component models suitable for their asynchronous domains. MQM provides the powerful ability to enable applications to communicate with each other over a network with messages whose delivery is guaranteed by the MQM infrastructure (Dickman, 1998). MQM is asynchronous and uses persistent message queues to guarantee message delivery. MQM enables the loose integration of Internet-based e-commerce applications through asynchronous, secure channels. MQM departs from the point-to-point, synchronous communication between remote software components common to the component models described in Part VII. We expect a new MQM component model will appear or, at the very least, component model implementation vendors will bridge component models and MQM.

OSs are also evolving, mostly under pressure from the burgeoning Linux movement. For most of the personal computer (PC) era the connection between an OS and hardware was very strong; consider the Wintel integration of Microsoft Windows and Intel processing chips. We expect this connection to be severed and desktop PCs will run multiple OSs, and effortlessly switch among them. The Amiga computer, in an amazing display of resilience, is making a resurgence with its componentized OS that executes on both Amiga computers and other PCs (*www.amiga.com*). Amiga also provides a software development kit that uses a Virtual Processor technology to enable binary programs to run without modification on every platform supported by Amiga, including Linux, Windows, PowerPC, and Embedded Linux (*www.amiga.com/products/SDK.shtml*).

42.6.2 Advances in Computing Technology

There are an amazing array of computing devices currently on the market and planned for release in the near term. The use of Personal Digital Assistant (PDAs) and other mobile devices will continue to increase. Currently, Palm computing (*palm.com*) maintains the dominant market share in this industry with PDAs that execute a proprietary operating system, PalmOS. Most market watchers focus on the number of applications available for the Palm, but the real payoff will occur when component model implementations are available for the Palm. For example, Inmotion (*www.inmotion.se/TechnologyCenter*) has a component model designed specifically for the PalmOS. Pocket computing expands on the popularity of the PDA market with devices with extra functionality. The Itsy Project (*research.compaq.com/wrl/projects/itsy*) spearheaded by Compaq's Western Research Lab, for example, has developed a prototype with considerably more computing power and memory than other PDAs. Itsy is targeted for CPU-intensive applications such as speech recognition, multimedia e-mail, and desktop applications.

42.6.3 Evolution of Component Models

Now that component technologies have achieved widespread use vendors are adding more functionality to the component model implementations. For example, transaction support and security are the two most common "additions" to a component model. You must be prepared for component models to continually evolve and change. In addition, vendors will likely add specialized features to their component model implementations to differentiate their product from the competition. We anticipate that component models in the near term will embrace standardized approaches to distributed resource management, load-balancing, and fault tolerant redundancy. Component models will continue to evolve and layering of specialized component models will exist for niche markets. So long as there are multiple, popular component models there will be a need for interoperability. Sometimes this interoperability will occur at the component model level. For example, CORBA Internet Inter-Orb Protocol and Java Remote Method Invocation are designed to coexist. However, because standards are often slow to change, individual component model implementation vendors may support interoperability to enhance the functionality of their technology. Consider IBM's WebSphere Application Server discussed earlier. As more vendors develop component model implementations there will be standards bodies that ensure compliance-testing to the component model.

42.6.4 Advances in Tools

Jacobson and Griss emphasized the increasing need for tools that support CBSE. Without powerful tools analysts, designers, and developers will find it very hard to effectively customize and assemble applications from the large-scale components. We need tools to allow them to incorporate components described by a set of models so that they can build new applications by reusing those models. The tools will come from still another group of companies, the tool builders.

We first need tools to support component reuse, enabling application builders to import a set of components into a component infrastructure to construct an application. This approach would naturally be layered, allowing developers to build on top of several such underlying components coming from different component factories. An essential capability would be to enable reusers to specialize the reused component without modification. Rich UML models and effective descriptions will be used for this task.

The first generation of CBSE-aware tools are available today and will only improve in their functionality and capability. APPGALLERY from Hitachi is a visual CBD environment running on Windows (*www.hitachi.co.jp/Prod/comp/soft1/open-e/appgal/appgal.htm*). APPGALLERY comes with a set of components, a set of tools for developing and customizing components, and a visual debugger on which the application designer can run component-based applications. Hitachi also provides various technical support and training services. The Aonix Select Component Manager supports publishing, managing, and using software components across the enterprise. Components and specifications are kept in Select Component Manager's shared repository and repository managers can track the location and use of each component and its elements. It supports automatic notification when a component or element is updated or the catalog is changed.

We also need tools that help search a catalog of components and then instantiate a component in our development environment to test it for suitability. We find that cataloging components is often over-engineered—the lesson here is that simple catalogs seem to be sufficient, especially if meta data is kept with components as they are cataloged (namely, rationale, use cases, and test cases). As for instantiation, component models such as .NET and J2EE establish a run-time environment within which one may assemble suitable components and provide a wealth of services we would previously have created ourselves.

Traditional system testing is used to detect errors between individual software components. Such an approach is too costly because it detects most problems after significant investment in installing, deploying, and integrating the component into your software system. We need tools that can perform static analyses of a component to detect in advance the suitability of using that component. We need tools for dynamic analyses for detecting inconsistencies in behavior. Chapters 20 and 21 provided preliminary results towards solving these problems.

We need more Integrated Development Environments to support component-based concepts, including design time assembly, deployment, and evolution of components. These development tools will improve the productivity of component-based software engineers by automating mundane, often error-prone, tasks.

42.7 Conclusion

The ROI for CBSE is equivalent in scale to the return on Henry Ford's tremendous investment in building moving assembly line factories. We believe CBSE encompasses the best practices of software engineering and holds the only promise for improving the quality of software and the productivity of the software industry. CBSE follows the tried and true methods of Ford and engineering and while these processes continue to improve, we can invest in the first steps of their successes. We also have to follow their public relation successes and raise the funding necessary to implement CBSE on a large scale. With a stream of high profile software failures, the memory of Y2K, and news about UCITA, the public will demand a more successful methodology for developing software. We must establish a society to promote CBSE to businesses and the public. Ironically, the society should derive its funding from organizations where CBSE is an unqualified success.

There have been countless attempts in software engineering to identify a specific programming language, tool, computer, or process to solve the challenges of writing quality software without significant investments. We have seen that this does not succeed. If the software engineering community cannot apply the principles of CBSE, then it is our opinion that the state of software cannot be improved from its current situation. No other industry continues to develop all the specialized parts of a product in-house with existing failure rates. We can do better. We must do better. This book provides numerous ways to move forward. Let's roll up our sleeves and get to work!

Part IX

References

M. Aoyama et al., eds., *Componentware,* Kyoritsu Pub (in Japanese), 1998.

A. Brown, "The Many Flavors of Open," *Mechanical Engineering Magazine Online, www.memagazine.org/backissues/march00/features/flavors/flavors.html,* Mar., 2000.

A. Dickman, *Designing Applications with MSMQ: Message Queueing for Developers,* Addison-Wesley, Reading, MA, 1998

J. Fowler, "Systems Integration for Manufacturing Applications Program Review," *www.mel.nist.gov/div826/msid/sima/99ovwvis/tsld001.htm,* July 1999.

P. Maurer, "Components: What If They Gave a Revolution and Nobody Came?" IEEE Computer, Vol. 33, No. 6, Jun., 2000, pp. 28-34.

M. Malone, "Chips Triumphant," *Forbes ASAP, www.forbes.com/asap,* Feb. 26, 1996, pp. 53-82.

G. Moore, "Cramming More Components Onto Integrated Circuits," Electronics Magazine, Vol. 38, No. 8, Apr., 1965, pp. 114-117.

DoD Product Line Practice Workshop Report, *Software Engineering Institute Technical Report, CMU/SEI-98-TR-007, www.sei.cmu.edu/publications/documents/98.reports/98tr007/98tr007abstract.html,* May 1998.

Glossary and Acronyms

Abstract Component	The design and partial implementation of a component that must be completed to create a software component. Such a component is also a white-box component.
Abstraction	The act of identifying the essential characteristics of a thing that distinguishes it from all other kinds of things.
Architectural Description Language	A language for describing the structure of a component-based system into its relevant components and connectors.
Architectural Driver	A functional, quality, or business requirement that greatly influences the composition of the software component infrastructure for an application.
Aspect	A fragment of code, typically a statement, method, or template, perhaps parameterized, that will be composed with base code and other aspects into a complete method, class, or component to create complete components or products.
Bespoke	A term used to describe a custom-made product or process. Applies to applications as well as components.
Black-box Component	A component that can be used by understanding its interface and without knowing the details of how its internals are constructed or by modifying the details.
Black-Box Reuse	The reuse of a component with no knowledge of its internal construction, relying on the published interfaces only.
Component Assembly	The process of composing components to form larger software elements.

Component Consumer	An experienced organization capable of deploying trusted components for use within a component-based software application or system.
Component Customization	The ability for a consumer to customize a component prior to its installation and use.
Component Management	The publication and re-publication of components and specifications, management of components, users, and versioning, and use and reuse of components and specifications for internal use or for license.
Component Model	A model that defines an interaction and composition standard.
Component Model Implementation	The dedicated set of executable software elements required to support the execution of components that conform to a component model.
Component Producer	An experienced organization capable of developing trusted components for distribution.
Component-based software life cycle	The development process for a software component with an emphasis on business rules, business process modeling, design, construction, continuous testing, deployment, evolution, and subsequent reuse and maintenance.
Composition	The combination of two or more software components yielding a new component behavior, at a different level of abstraction. The characteristics of the new component behavior are determined by the components being combined and by the way they are combined
Composition Standard	Mandatory requirements employed and enforced to enable software elements to be composed to create larger software elements
Connector	An abstract representation of the interaction between two components.
Crosscutting	A term used to describe fragments of software that appear in (cuts across) many components.
Deployment	The process of preparing a component for execution, including installation and any necessary configuration.

Design Element	A software element generated as a work product during design.
Domain	A systematic reuse term that refers to a conceptual space of applications.
Domain Analysis	A systematic reuse term that describes the modeling of a domain into its commonalities and variabilities.
Exception	When an operation is invoked on a method contained in a component's interface, the component can raise an exception; this means the caller is notified that the operation has prematurely terminated.
Context Dependency	A relationship between two software elements, in which a change to one software element (the independent element) will affect the other (the dependent element).
Feature	Product characteristic that users and customers view as important in describing and distinguishing members of a product-line.
Glue	A technique for composing components by writing a small amount of special purpose code to enable the components to interact with each other
Data Interaction	An interaction that transmits data from one software element to another
Dependency Interaction	An interaction that defines a relationship between the behavior of two or more software elements.
Functional Interaction	An interaction that causes a function to execute
Information Hiding	Decomposing a design into code units whose implementations have interfaces that reveal as little as possible about their inner workings.
Interaction	An action between two or more software elements.
Interaction Standard	Mandatory requirements employed and enforced to enable software elements to directly and indirectly interact with other software elements

Interface An abstraction of the behavior of a component that consists of a subset of the interactions of that component together with a set of constraints describing when they may occur.

Interface Standard Mandatory requirements employed and enforced to enable software elements to directly interact with other software elements

Interchangeable A condition that exists when two or more elements possess such functional and physical characteristics as to be equivalent in performance and durability and are capable of being exchanged one for the other without alteration of the elements themselves or of any interacting elements.

Introspection The ability for an executing program to examine the meta data for a software element, including its interfaces and methods.

Marshalling The process of gathering information contained in one or more parameters of a remote method call, linearizing the data pieces into a message buffer, and organizing or converting the data into a wire format that is prescribed for a particular receiver or programming interface.

Master Software Development Plan The methods adopted by the lead software engineer or manager for a system's composition and interaction. It is a conceptual plan that defines the boundaries of the system, its elements, interactions, and constraints on these elements and interactions. The master software development plan consists of a global design that identifies discrete and manageable subprojects.

Meta data Minimally sufficient information about a component, its interfaces, and their relationships that distinguish the component from any previous or competitor's version of an almost identical component.

Model Mandatory requirements employed and enforced to prescribe a disciplined uniform approach for a domain or profession. A model is a standard.

Object-Oriented Framework A well-designed set of collaborating object-oriented classes that provide a partial solution for a specific domain and can be completed to construct an application.

Performance Requirement Any condition, characteristic, or capability that must be achieved and is essential to the end item's ability to perform its mission in the environment in which it must operate. Requirements must be verifiable.

Performance Specification A document that states requirements in terms of the required results and provides criteria for verifying compliance, but it does not state methods for achieving results. It defines the functional requirements for the product, the environment in which it must operate, and the interface and interchangeability requirements.

Plug-and-Play The concept that components should be designed to be easily composable through standardized interfaces.

Postcondition A logical condition that will be true after an operation has been invoked. In most cases, the code containing the operation is responsible for ensure the condition to be true.

Precondition A logical condition that must be true for an operation to succeed. In most cases, the code invoking the operation is responsible for ensuring the condition is true

Product-Line A family of applications that share a common collection of requirements but also exhibit significant variability in requirements.

Project A set of activities that organizes and employs resources to create or maintain a work product (or part of a work product).

Provided Interface An interface whose operations are implemented by a component; the component is said to support the interface.

Proxy object A software element that implements an interface corresponding to the interface provided by a component remote to the caller.

Refactoring The process of changing a software system to improve its internal structure without altering the external behavior of the software.

Relative Cost of Reuse (RCR) The portion of the effort that it takes to reuse a component without modification versus writing it.

Relative Cost of Writing for Reuse (RCWR)	The portion of the effort that it takes to write a reusable component versus writing it for one-time use only
Required Interface	An interface whose operations are requested by a component that does not contain an implementation of these operations; the component is said to need the interface and it expects some other software element to support the interface.
Reuse	The incorporation into an application of unmodified software components obtained from other programs external to the application. These external sources typically include other applications, other organizations, and reuse libraries.
Skeleton	The software element that receives a request from its partner stub to invoke a specified operation; the skeleton and stub are often generated by a compiler.
Software Architecture	The fundamental organization of a software system embodied in its components, their relationships to each other and to the environment, and the principles guiding its design and evolution
Software Component	A software element that conforms to a component model and can be independently deployed and composed without modification according to a composition standard.
Software Component Infrastructure	A set of interacting software components designed by the lead engineer, with assistance of selected subproject engineers and component designers, to ensures that a software system or subsystem constructed using those components and interfaces will satisfy clearly defined performance specifications.
Software Development Life Cycle	The period of time that begins with the decision to develop a software product and ends when the software is delivered. This cycle typically includes a requirements phase, design phase, implementation phase, test phase, and sometimes, installation and deployment phase.

Software Element	A sequence of abstract program statements that describe computations to be performed by a machine
Software Engineering	The application of a systematic, disciplined, quantifiable approach to the development, operation, and maintenance of software; that is, the application of engineering to software.
Software Template	A description of the responsibilities for a component within a software component infrastructure. A software template captures the interactions that shall exist between deployed components in a software component infrastructure.
Stakeholder	A party or individual that has a great stake in the success of a software system being developed and has some direct or indirect influence on the system requirements.
Standard	An object or quality or measure serving as a basis to which others should conform, or by which the accuracy or quality of others is judged (by present-day standards). Mandatory conventions and practices are in fact standards.
Stepwise Refinement	An incremental process of increasingly detailed design resulting in a complete implementation.
Stub	The software element that requests an operation to be invoked on a software element by communicating with its partner skeleton; the skeleton and stub are often generated by a compiler.
Subproject	A self-contained process of analysis and design that produces design elements that will be incorporated through to a final design.
Technical File	A component descriptive file describing the behavior, assumptions, and structure of the component.
Transaction	Often associated with databases, a transaction is a sequence of operations that forms an atomic unit; that is, all operations in the transaction are executed or none of them are.

Variation point	An explicitly designated location within a component at which a variability mechanism may be used to create a customized component.
White-box Reuse	The reuse of a component by inspecting and possibly modifying its source code.
White-box component	A component whose source code is fully available, and can be studied, reused, or even modified.

Acronyms

4GL	Fourth Generation Language
ADA	Active Document Architecture
ADL	Architectural Description Language
ANSI	American National Standards Institute
API	Application Programming Interface
CASE	Computer Assisted Software Engineering
CMM	SEI's Capability Maturity Model
COM	Microsoft Component Object Model
COM+	The latest incarnation of Microsoft's COM
CORBA	Common Object Request Broker Architecture
COTS	Commercial Off-The-Shelf
CRM	Customer Relationship Management
DCE	Distributed Computing Environment
DCOM	Microsoft Distributed Component Object Model
DLL	Dynamically Linked Library
DOM	Document Object Model

EAI	Enterprise Application Integration
EJB	Enterprise JavaBeans
ERP	Enterprise Resource Planning
FODA	Feature-Oriented Domain Analysis
GUI	Graphical User Interface
GUID	Global Unique Identifiers
HTML	HyperText Markup Language
HTTP	HyperText Transfer Protocol
IDE	Integrated Development Environment
IDL	Interface Definition Language
IIOP	Internet Inter-Orb Protocol. A CORBA technology
IPSE	Integrated Project Support Environment
IPC	Interprocess Communication
IPT	Integrated Project Team
ISO	International Standards Organization
IT	Information Technology
J2EE	Java 2 Enterprise Edition
JAD	Joint Application Development
JDBC	Java Database Connectivity
MIL	Module Interconnection Language
MOM	Message-oriented Middleware
OCL	Object Constraint Language
OLE	Microsoft Object Linking and Embedding
OMA	Object Management Architecture

OOPL	Object-Oriented Programming Language
OS	Operating System
OSF	Open Software Foundation
PDA	Personal Digital Assistant
PES	Programmable Electronic System
POSIX	Portable Operating System Interface
RMC	Remote Method Call
RMI	Remote Method Invocation. A Java technology
RM-ODP	Reference Model of Open Distributed Processing
RPC	Remote Procedural Call
RSEB	Reuse-Driven Software Engineering Business
SCM	Supply Chain Management
SOAP	Simple Object Access Protocol
SQL	Standard Query Language
TCL	Tool Control Language
TCO	Total Cost of Ownership
UCITA	Uniform Computer Information Transactions Act
UML	Unified Modeling Language
UUID	Universally Unique Identifiers (OSF/DCE)
W3C	World Wide Web Consortium
WAP	Wireless Application Protocol
WML	Wireless Markup Language
XML	eXtensible Markup Language

About the Editors

George T. Heineman

George T. Heineman is an Assistant Professor of Computer Science at Worcester Polytechnic Institute in Worcester, MA. He has worked as a Research Scientist at the IBM Center for Advanced Studies (Toronto, Canada), Bull Electronics (Billerica, MA), and AT&T Bell Laboratories (Murray Hill, NJ).

George received a prestigious National Science Foundation Early Faculty Career Development Award in Software Engineering in 1998. This research grant funds the ADAPT project investigating the design of adaptable software components. He also receives funding from the Defense Advanced Research Projects Agency. Besides government funding his lab has received funding and hardware donations from Natural Microsystems and Intellution, Inc.

George has authored or coauthored over 20 articles and papers on software engineering topics including component adaptation techniques, component-based software engineering, software development environments, and software engineering processes. He also has interests in advanced concurrency control techniques.

George received his Ph.D. (1996) and M.S. (1990) from the Computer Science Department of Columbia University. His advisor was Gail Kaiser, Ph.D. George earned his BA (1989) in Computer Science from Dartmouth College.

William T. Councill

Bill Councill is a partner in TQC in Dallas, Texas. Previously he was Systems and Software Process Manager for Mannatech, Inc in Coppell, Texas. His experience includes the development of systems and software processes and component-based software life cycle processes and methodologies as well as:

Business Analysis—including business rules elicitation and management

Requirements engineering using requirements management applications, use case development and liaison with the software design team

Configuration Management

Measurement and metrics using function points and well-accepted FP applications

Quality Assurance

Risk Management

Software Change Impact Analysis

Bill dedicated the last 10 years to absorbing and practicing knowledge from the emerging field of software engineering. He has an M.S. from Nova University, earned in 1975—one of the first behavioral graduate programs in the United States specializing in behavioral counseling--and devoted 18 years to counseling patients in chronic pain and those with difficult psychiatric diagnoses. Additionally, he earned a J.D. in 1990 at the Birmingham of School of Law. After earning the law degree Bill worked in health care consulting and administrative lobbying. He graduated from the University of North Carolina with majors in anthropology and Radio-TV-Films in 1972.

Bill entered the discipline of software engineering in 1992 as the founder of PenKnowledge, Inc in Birmingham, Alabama and was the creator and project manager of Doctor's Office 3.0, a computer-based patient record system. The system incorporated Microsoft Windows for Workgroups, pen computing across a radio frequency LAN, and the replication of data among client and server SQL databases. Bill participated in the development of the slowly emerging standards for computer-based patient record systems by contributing to the work on digital signatures, confidentiality and security, and the functionality of computer-based record-keeping systems.

About the Authors

Paul Allen joined Sterling Software in April 1999 from SELECT Software Tools, where he was VP of Methods and a key player in shaping and implementing their CBD vision. Over his 25 years in the IT industry, Paul has worked as project manager and consultant on a variety of large commercial systems. He coauthored the book *Component-Based Development for Enterprise Systems*, published by SIGS-Cambridge University Press.

Mikio Aoyama has been a professor at the Niigata Institute of Technology in Japan since 1995. Before that, he worked for Fujitsu Limited for 15 years. His current research interests include component-based software engineering, real-time distributed object computing, and agile software process. He is the author of more than 10 books and numerous articles. Contact him at *mikio@iee.niit.ac.jp*

Hedley Apperly has 18 years experience in design and IT, covering engineering, relational, object-orientation, and components. He was recently involved in the development of the Select Perspective for component-based development. For the last three years he has taken the lead in setting product direction for Select Component Factory, the world-leading product set for component-based design and development.

Len Bass is a Senior Member of the Technical Staff at the Software Engineering Institute (SEI) and splits his time with the School of Computer Science. He has led efforts that developed a software architecture used by the U.S. Air Force in multiple flight training simulators, created a user interface implementation reference model in conjunction with commercial tool builders, and developed a technique for analyzing software architectures for developmental qualities that has been used in dozens of evaluations.

David Blevins is the cofounder of the OpenEJB open source Enterprise JavaBeans container system and author of a forthcoming Addison-Wesley book on the Java 2 Enterprise Edition. He has also been involved in the development of other Java middleware technologies like the HJDBC API and Object Serialization for the Java platform. Blevins can be found speaking about Enterprise JavaBeans and Open EJB at conferences such as the Exolab Sessions, O'Reilly Conference on Enterprise Java, O'Reilly Open Source Convention, and JavaOne.

James Carey is currently the business content and component architect in IBM's WebSphere Business Components organization. He was previously the architect on the SanFrancisco team responsible for the Common Business Objects and domain specific frameworks. He is the coauthor of two books: *SanFrancisco Component Frameworks: An Introduction* and *SanFrancisco Design Patterns: Blueprints for Business Software* from Addison Wesley.

Brent Carlson is currently the Vice President of Technology for LogicLibrary, a component-based development consulting firm. Previously he served as lead architect in IBM's WebSphere Business Components organization. He was also the lead designer for IBM SanFrancisco's Warehouse Management and Order Management Core Business Processes and subsequently served as lead architect for that product. From that experience, he coauthored the book *SanFrancisco Design Patterns: Blueprints for Business Software* from Addison Wesley.

John Cheesman is Director of Enterprise Application Development for ComponentSource. He has extensive experience applying component-based development processes, tools, and standards within large corporations. John specializes in modeling, specification, and repositories, and was a key contributor to the development of the UML. He is a regular speaker at international conferences on component-based development.

Stephen Chow is a partner in the law firm of the Perkins, Smith, and Cohen. He is a member of the firm's e-Commerce & Communications, Corporate, Intellectual Property, International and Litigation Groups. Mr. Chow is a registered attorney with the United States Patent and Trademark Office. His forthcoming treatise, *Electronic Commerce and Communications*, to be published by Matthew Bender/Lexis Publishing, will uniquely analyze the intersection of commercial and intellectual property law in the New Economy.

Paul Clements is a senior member of the technical staff at the Software Engineering Institute (SEI. A graduate of the University of North Carolina and the University of Texas, he is a project leader in the SEI's Product Line Systems Program. His work includes collaborating with organizations that are launching product-line efforts. He is a co-creator of the Software Architecture Analysis Method (SAAM), which allows organizations to evaluate architectures for fitness of purpose. He is coauthor of *Software Architecture in Practice* published by Addison-Wesley-Longman and more than three dozen papers and articles about software engineering.

Bill Councill has advanced degrees in counseling and law; he has served as manager of software development, software testing, and systems and software process in various small businesses. He has published articles on the need for third-party certification and the licensure of software engineers to assure trusted components and the accountability of software component producers to their corporate boards and consumers.

Manoj Desai is an Associate Managing Engineer working in UL's Programmable Electronics / Software Services department. He focuses on the issues related to the software safety for Programmable Systems, specifically for the Information Technology and Telecommunications Equipment industry. He has 20 years experience in software development. Prior to joining UL, Manoj was with IBM Corporation, where he held a number of Technical and Management positions in Software Development, Test, and Assurance. Mr. Desai has presented and published papers at IEEE conferences on Software Testing and useability.

Tim Ewald is a Principal Scientist at DevelopMentor, where he spends his time working with component techologies. He is the author of *Transactional COM+: Building Scalable Applications* and a coauthor of *Effective COM*, both from Addison-Wesley.

Janet Flynt is the Program Manager for UL's Programmable Electronics activities in software certification, which includes the development of the ANSI/UL 1998 Standard for Safety-Related Software. Prior to joining UL, Ms. Flynt was employed with Research Triangle Institute where, under NASA and DoD funding, she developed approaches for achieving software safety and reliability. Ms. Flynt has also worked with the FDA 510(k) Guidance for Computer-Controlled Medical Devices and the FAA D0178b Guidance for Flight-Control Software. She has to her credit many papers, one of which is "Software Verification and Validation in the Next Decade," IEEE Software, May 1989. Ms. Flynt is a graduate of the University of North Carolina, receiving a B.S. in Mathematical Sciences in 1976, an M.S. in Operations Research and System Analysis in 1978, and a certificate in Technology Management in 1993.

Martin L. Griss is a Principal Laboratory Scientist at Hewlett-Packard Laboratories, Palo Alto, California, where since 1982 he has researched software engineering processes and systems, systematic software reuse, object-oriented development and component-based software engineering. He led HP efforts to standardize UML for the OMG. He is coauthor of the book *Software Reuse: Architecture, Process and Organization for Business Success* published by Addison-Wesley, which holistically addresses technology, people and process issues in a UML framework. He has over 30 years of experience in software development, education and research. He maintains a web site on reuse, CBSE and agents (www.hpl.hp.com/reuse).

George T. Heineman is an assistant professor of Computer Science at Worchester Polytechnic Institute. His research interests are in component-based systems, software engineering, and object-oriented design. Professor Heineman received a distinguished National Science Foundation CAREER award in 1997 to pursue his research on designing adaptable software components. He received his Ph.D. from Columbia University in 1996.

Brian Henderson-Sellers is Professor of Information Systems at the University of Technology, Sydney (UTS), Director of the Centre for Object Technology Applications and Research (COTAR) and a founder member of the OPEN Consortium. He is an internationally known methodologist in the field of Object Technology, and has authored many works on object-oriented metrics, metamodeling and methodology, including *OPEN Modeling with UML* published by Addison-Wesley.

Kelli Houston is a Senior Architecture Consultant at Rational Software. Her responsibilities include providing training, consulting and mentoring to customers on architectural representation and process, as well as facilitating the sharing of architectural experiences and artifacts within Rational. While at Rational, she has also served as the Product Manager for the Object Oriented Analysis and Design (OOAD) product family, and as a Software Engineering Specialist in the field organization.

Ivar Jacobson is the inventor of the OOSE method, and he is also the founder of Objectory AB in Sweden, which recently merged with Rational Software Corporation. Dr. Jacobson is the principal author of two influential and best-selling books *Object-Oriented Software Engineering – A Use Case Driven Approach* (Computer Language Productivity award winner in 1992) and *The Object Advantage – Business Process Reengineering with Object Technology*. He also authored the famous OOPSLA '87 paper entitled "Object-Oriented Development in an Industrial Environment," the first truly object-oriented method ever published.

Wojtek (Voytek) Kozaczynski is the director of Architectures and Application Frameworks at Rational Software. He works on tools and processes for development and application of reusable software assets. Previously, Wojtek was the Chief Architect at an ERP company, the Directory of the Software Engineering Laboratory at Andersen Consulting and an assistant professor at the University of Illinois. He has published over 20 journal articles and conference papers on database design, automatic code analysis, component-based development, software architectures and software reuse.

Steve Latchem has been within the IT industry for over 16 years, holding positions in large consultancy groups and IT Departments ranging from business analyst to object-oriented consultant, architect and project manager. Steve now specializes in helping organizations to analyze, model, and develop high-quality component-based solutions within multiple tier, distributed architectures, using his experience of multiple object technology projects over the last 9 years. Steve has been involved in the OMG since 1995, and has developed models for Financial Services components utilized within OMG Standards.

Andy Longshaw is a founding member of, and Principal Technologist at, Content Master. In this role he is responsible for the creation of various types of technical content such as training courses and whitepapers. Andy's areas of expertise include Java, XML and component systems. Throughout the past three years, Andy has given a series of conference sessions on Java, XML, middle-tier component architectures, and COM+.

Neil Maiden is Head of the Centre for Human-Computer Interface Design, a research department in City University's School of Informatics. He received a P.hD. in Computer Science from City University in 1992. His research interests include frameworks for requirements acquisition and negotiation, scenario-based systems development, component-based software engineering, ERP packages, requirements reuse, and more effective transfer of academic research results into software engineering practice.

Jason Mauldin is currently an Associate Project Engineer in the Programmable Electronics department at Underwriters Laboratories Inc. He has conducted numerous software safety investigations for a wide variety of product types. He is primarily focused in Industrial Control Systems and Household Appliances with a strong concentration in distributed control systems and multiprocessor design. He graduated from North Carolina State University in 1997 with a Bachelor's of Science degree in Computer Engineering. He can be contacted at Jason.R.Mauldin@us.ul.com

Barry McGibbon has worked in the IT industry for over 33 years, gaining a wide variety of experience ranging from programming through to holding very senior management positions with leading computing services providers. Barry has been a consultant since 1985 for significant enterprises in the UK, Europe, and the USA and has specialized in component-based development since 1995. He is author of *Managing Your Move to Object Technology: Guidelines & Strategies for a Smooth Transition* published by CUP/SIGS Books Inc. Barry is the current Technical Chairman for Europe's largest component and object technology conference and a series editor for Cambridge University Press.

Michael Meeks is an enthusiastic believer in Free software. He very much enjoys working for Ximian Inc where he gets paid to develop various free GNOME components, and the component infastructure.

Prior to this he worked for Quantel gaining expertise in real time Audio Visual editing and playback achieved with high performance focused hardware/software solutions. He holds a MEng in Electrical and Information Science from Cambridge.

Cornelius Ncube is currently an Assistant Professor at Zayed University, Dubai in the UAE and a visiting research fellow at the Centre for HCI Design at City University London where he obtained his Ph.D. in Computer Science. His current research interests include requirements engineering, selection processes and decision-making processes for leasing or renting COTS software and ASPs.

Davyd Norris is a Principal Consultant with Rational Software's Asia-Pacific Regional Services Organisation (RSO). With over 20 years of software development experience, he is based in Sydney and provides training, consulting and mentoring to corporate clients throughout Asia Pacific. Davyd is also a core member of the team working on Rational's Architecture Description Standard and the Reusable Asset Specification, the latter of which is being prepared for submission to the OMG.

Carlos O'Ryan is currently a graduate student in the University of California at Irvine Department of Computer Engineering; his advisor is Dr. Douglas Schmidt. He is a research assistant for the Distributed Object Computing Lab. He designed and implemented TAO's second generation real-time Event Service. He has also worked on TAO's IDL compiler, the pluggable protocol framework, the support for the CDR engine, Asynchronous Method Invocation, and memory management strategies in the ORB.

Jeffrey S. Poulin, Ph.D., works as a Systems Architect with Lockheed Martin Systems Integration in Owego, NY. He has led the technical activities on numerous large-scale programs for the United States Department of Defense, international postal services, and commercial customers. Dr. Poulin has over 70 publications on software measurement, software reuse, and domain-specific software architectures, including *Measuring Software Reuse* published by Addison-Wesley.

Donald J. Reifer is a leading figure in the field of software engineering and management with over 30 years of progressive experience in both industry and government. Recently, Mr. Reifer managed the DoD Software Initiatives Office; as part of this assignment, he also served as the Director of the DoD Software Reuse Initiative. While with the Aerospace Corporation, Mr. Reifer managed all of the software efforts related to the Space Transportation System (Space Shuttle). Currently, as President of RCI, Mr. Reifer supports executives in many Fortune 500 firms who are looking to develop investment strategies and improve their software capabilities and capacity. He is the author of *Practical Software Reuse* published by John Wiley & Sons.

Johannes Sametinger is an associate professor at the Johannes Kepler University in Linz, Austria. He currently holds a position at the University of Regensburg, Germany. His research interests include software engineering, software documentation, software maintenance, software reuse, object-oriented programming, component-based programming, and programming environments.

Douglas Schmidt is an Associate Professor in the Electrical and Computer Engineering department at the University of California, Irvine, USA. His research focuses on empirical analyses of object-oriented techniques that facilitate the development of high-performance and real-time distributed object computing middleware running over high-speed networks and embedded system interconnects. He is the lead author of *Pattern-Oriented Software Architecture, Volume 2: Patterns for Concurrent and Networked Objects* published by John Wiley & Sons.. He is currently serving as a Program Manager in the Information Technology Office (ITO) at DARPA, leading the USA research effort on distributed object computing middleware.

John R. Speed is a consulting engineer specializing in design and program management for public infrastructure and a frequent lecturer on engineering ethics and professional practice. He is the former executive director of the Texas Board of Professional Engineers, where he managed the state's regulation of the engineering profession. He holds a BS in civil engineering from Texas A&M University, an MA in political science with an emphasis in public management from Midwestern State university, and is a graduate of the Texas State Governor's Executive Development Program. He is a member of the National Society of Professional Engineers and the American Society of Civil Engineers.

Judith Stafford is a senior member of the technical staff at the Software Engineering Institute, Carnegie Mellon University. Dr. Stafford has worked for several years in the area of compositional reasoning and its application to software architectures with an emphasis on the use of software architecture as a foundation for early analysis of software systems. She currently co-leads the SEI's Predictable Assembly from Certifiable Components project.

Kevin Sullivan received his Ph.D. in Computer Science from the University of Washington in Seattle, Washington in 1994. He then joined the University of Virginia as Assistant Professor of Computer Science. He received a prestigious NSF Career Award in 1995, the first ACM Computer Science Professor of the Year Award from undergraduate students in 1998, and a University Teaching Fellowship in 1999. Sullivan is the author or coauthor of twenty-four peer-reviewed journal and conference papers and three book chapters.

Clemens Szyperski is a research Software Architect in the ComApps group in Microsoft Research. He is also an adjunct professor in the School of Computing Science, Queensland University of Technology. He is the author of the influential book *Component Software: Beyond Object-Oriented Programming* published by Addison-Wesley.

Will Tracz is a senior technical staff member for Lockheed Martin Systems Integration Owego. Currently, he is lead architect for several COTS and Reuse Repository projects as well as the Principal Investigator (PI) on an internal IR&D project focused on e-business. Dr. Tracz is also an ad hoc member of the Air Force Scientific Advisory Board COTS panel, chair of the Lockheed Martin Software Subcouncil Working Group on COTS Software and Reuse, as well as editor of ACM SIGSOFT Software Engineering Notes.

Mark Vigder is a Research Officer with the Institute for Information Technology, National Research Council of Canada where he has been working with clients on problems associated with software architecture, software maintenance, and integrating commercial off-the-shelf software applications. He has, over his twenty year career, worked in commercial, educational, research, and government organizations.

Nanbor Wang is currently a graduate student in the Distributed Object Computing Research Group, in the School of Engineering and Applied Science Washington University in St. Louis, Missouri.

Rainer Weinreich is an assistant professor at the Johannes Kepler University in Linz, Austria. His main research interests lie in the area of component-based and distributed software architectures. He is the architect of several frameworks for object-oriented, component-based, and distributed software systems and currently is leading a project for agent-based remote diagnosis and supervision of process automation systems.

Elaine Weyuker is a Technology Leader at AT&T Labs—Research in Florham Park, NJ, and is an AT&T Fellow. From 1977 to 1995 she was a professor of Computer Science at the Courant Institute of Mathematical Sciences of New York University. Her research interests are in software engineering, particularly software testing and reliability, and software metrics. She has published more than 100 refereed papers in journals and conference proceedings in those areas, and has been a frequent keynote speaker at conferences. She is also the coauthor of a book *Computability, Complexity, and Languages, 2nd Ed* published by Academic Press. Weyuker is a Fellow of the ACM, a senior member of the IEEE, and was recently elected to the Board of Directors of the Computing Research Association (CRA). She is a member of the editorial boards of ACM Transactions on Software Engineering and Methodology (TOSEM), the Empirical Software Engineering Journal, and the Journal of Systems and Software.

John Williams has over 25 years of IT and development experience. He is an internationally recognized expert on object and component technology. Each year he teaches on advanced technology subjects to audiences around the world. John has taught in Japan, England, Germany, Switzerland, Canada, and the United States. His book *What Every Manager Must Know To Succeed With Object Technology* is available from SIGS/Cambridge University Press. John has served as editor of Object Magazine and Component Strategies magazine. He currently serves as a contributing editor for Application Development Trends magazine, where he writes a monthly column on component strategies. John has led web development projects since 1994.

Alan Cameron Wills is a consultant in object and component design, working with a wide variety of clients in Europe and North America, and based in Manchester. Dr. Wills is technical director of TriReme International Ltd., which offers consultancy and training in component based and object oriented design, and on their use within a business. Dr. Wills has worked on methods and tools since 1982, and specializes in making frontline research practical and available for mainstream software engineering. Dr. Wills is coauthor of the book *Objects, Components, and Frameworks with UML: The Catalysis Approach*, published by Addison-Wesley.

Alexander L. Wolf is a faculty member in the Department of Computer Science, University of Colorado at Boulder. Previously he was at AT&T Bell Laboratories. Dr. Wolf received the Ph.D. degree in Computer Science from the University of Massachusetts at Amherst. Dr. Wolf's research interests are in the discovery of principles and development of technologies to support the engineering of large, complex software systems. He has published papers in the areas of software engineering environments and tools, software process, software architecture, configuration management, distributed systems, persistent object systems, networking, and security. His work in the area of software architecture has been focused on formal specification and analysis. Dr. Wolf is currently serving as Vice Chair of the ACM Special Interest Group in Software Engineering and is on the editorial board of the ACM Journal *Transactions on Software Engineering and Methodology*.

Index

Numerics

A

D

E

N

Q

R

S

T

U